Afro-Asian Culture Studies

FOURTH EDITION

Afro-Asian Culture Studies

FOURTH EDITION

Erwin M. Rosenfeld
Assistant Principal, Supervision of Social Studies,
Manhattanville Junior H. S., New York City

AND

Harriet Geller
Social Studies Dept., Manhattanville Junior H. S., New York City

ADVISORY BOARD

Phillip Lefton
Principal, Theodore Roosevelt High School, Bronx, New York

Theodore Strauss
Formerly Social Studies Dept., Phillip Livingston Junior H. S., Albany, New York

Barron's Educational Series, Inc.

bury, New York 11797

The authors would like to acknowledge and express their gratitude to the following people for the time and interest exerted in assisting them in locating suitable photographs for use in this text–Mr. John Roberts of "Africa Report"; Mr. Serec Wangpaichitr–Tourist Organization of Thailand; Mr. Vallery Dr. Uvarov of Intourist; Miss J. Akulian of the Arab Information Center; Miss Kathleen Seibert of Aramco; Mr. Chao-Ying Chang–Chinese Information Service; Mr. Tai Tsengi-Yi of Hsinhua News Agency; and Ms. Ralene Levy, Information Officer of the Consulate General Israel.

All inquiries should be addressed to:
Barron's Educational Series, Inc.
113 Crossways Park Drive
Woodbury, New York 11797

Library of Congress Catalog Card No. 78-23785

International Standard Book No. 0-8120-0993-2

Library of Congress Cataloging in Publication Data
Rosenfeld, Erwin M
  Afro-Asian culture studies.
  Bibliography: p.
  Includes index.
  1. Asia.   2. Africa.   I. Geller, Harriet,
joint author.   II. Title.
DS5.R64   1978   950   78-23785
ISBN 0-8120-0993-2

PRINTED IN THE UNITED STATES OF AMERICA

Table of Contents

Preface   ix

UNIT I

The Study of Man   1

Culture and Survival   1
Culture and Habitat   3
People of the World   4
Race and Culture   6
Cultural Diffusion   8
What It Is Like To Be Underdeveloped   9
Twentieth-Century Nationalism   14
Food: A Worldwide Problem   17
The Role of Women in the Modern World   22
Summary of Key Ideas   24
Exercises and Questions   26

UNIT II

The Union of Soviet Socialist Republics (USSR)   32

The Land and Topography   33
Climate   35
The People of the Soviet Union   38
Kievan Russia   41
Russia under the Mongols   44
Russia Is United by the Princes of Moscow   45
Peter the Great and the Westernization of Russia   46
Catherine Continues the Work of Peter   47
Alexander I and the Napoleonic Invasion of 1812   48
Russia in the 19th Century   50
The Peasantry—Serfdom and After   51
The Revolutionary Movement   52
The Russian Revolution of 1905   54
World War I and the Revolution of March 1917   56
Marx, Lenin, and the Revolution of November 1917   57
Russia under Stalin   59
The Soviet Economy   62
Standard of Living, Health and Welfare of the Soviet People   67
The Soviet Government   68
Cultural Life in the Soviet Union   70
Soviet Foreign Policy   77

U.S.-Soviet Relations in the 1970s 78

Soviet-American Relations: The Question of *Détente* 85

Summary of Key Ideas 87

Exercises and Questions 90

UNIT
III

The Middle East and North Africa 106

Introduction 107

Land and Climate 109

People of the Middle East and Their Way of Life 112

Islam—The Religion of the Middle East and North Africa 117

The Jews and Judaism 119

Early History of the Middle East 121

The Triumph of Islam-Moslem Civilization 622-1453 125

The Middle East in Decline 127

The Ottoman Empire 128

European Imperialism in the Middle East 129

The Middle East After World War II—Nationalism and the Question of Arab Unity 131

Oil Is King 133

Economic Development 139

The Arab-Israeli Conflict—The Israeli Side 142

The Arab-Israel Conflict—The Arab Side 144

The Problem of the Palestinians in the 1970s 145

The Middle East Between East and West 148

War, Oil, Politics—The Middle East Since 1973 150

The First Israeli-Egyptian Agreement 155

The PLO and More Talks 159

The Second Israeli-Egyptian Agreement 162

The Civil War in Lebanon 164

President Sadat's Visit to Israel 165

America's New Role in the Middle East 171

Summary of Key Ideas 177

Exercises and Questions 180

UNIT
IV

Africa — South of the Sahara 194

Geography and Isolation 195

Topography 197

The Climate 201

The People and Their Languages 203

African Families 207

African Tribalism 208

Religious Beliefs 210

African Arts 211

Early History 215

Kingdoms of West Africa 217

East Africa—Cities of the Coast 220

East Africa—Kingdoms of the Interior 222

Arabs, Islam and Africa 223

The Arrival of the Europeans 224

The Slave Trade 225

Africa Is Opened to the Western World: Explorers and Missionaries 227

European Imperialism in Africa 230

Nationalism and Independence 233

Africa Today—Problems of Independence 236

African Affairs in the Seventies 246

The Economy of Black Africa 251

Summary of Key Ideas 259

Exercises and Questions 261

UNIT
V

China

276

Topography of China 277

Climate 280

The People of China and Their Way of life 281

Life and Society in Traditional China 284

Social Classes: The Gentry and the Peasants 288

The Chinese Family 291

Language and Writing System 294

Ancient China 296

Empire China 298

Manchu China 301

The Chinese Revolution 303

The Chinese Communist Party and Its Leaders 309

Life and Society in Present-Day China 312

The Chinese Economy 317

The Economic Policy of China 321

China and Taiwan (Formosa) 326

China and the U.S. 327

The Sino-Soviet Dispute   331

Foreign Policy in the Seventies   333

Summary of Key Ideas   336

Exercises and Questions   339

UNIT
VI

The Subcontinent of India, Pakistan and Bangladesh   **353**

The Land   353

Climate   356

Peoples and Languages of India   357

Agriculture in India   358

The Village in Indian Life   360

The Hindu Religion   363

The Literature of Ancient India   366

Early History   369

The Guptas   371

The Muslims in India   372

The British in India   374

India after Independence   378

India Attempts to Modernize   380

India and World Politics   386

The Problem of Bangladesh   388

Summary of Key Ideas   391

Exercises and Questions   393

UNIT
VII

Southeast Asia   **402**

Introduction and Setting   403

Topography   404

Climate   407

Peoples and Languages   409

Village Life   412

Agriculture   414

Religion   415

Early History of Southeast Asia   418

The Empires of Southeast Asia   420

Westerners Come to Southeast Asia   421

Nationalism in Southeast Asia   423

World War II and Japanese Control   426

Independence and Its Results   427
The Economy of Southeast Asia   429
The Vietnam Conflict   434
Summary of Key Ideas   443
Exercises and Questions   445

UNIT
VIII   Japan   **454**

Land and Climate   455
The People and Their Language   458
Life in Japan   460
Religion   461
Japanese Arts   464
Early History   470
Japan Enters the Modern World   473
Japan After World War II   476
Japan's Economy   478
Japan's Place in the World Today   484
Summary of Key Ideas   491
Exercises and Questions   493

Final Review   501

Bibliography   506

Index   513

Preface

It is essential that, amid front-page reports of world unrest and rapid change, we develop a deeper awareness of events that are taking place in different parts of the world. To understand the complex world in which we live, it is necessary to develop insights into the thoughts and feelings of people whose way of life seems alien to our own. It is important for students to realize that people in different parts of the world have developed different cultures. Although man's needs are basically the same everywhere, differences in environment and history have played a determining role in establishing cultural differences. People of all nations, races, and religions have made contributions to world culture. A realization of this basic truth is crucial.

This book is intended to provide students with a much needed world view, to enable them to develop an understanding of peoples outside of their own culture, rather than to judge them in the light of Western civilization, as has too often been the case.

The new Social Studies Curriculum for the study of world geography stresses a regional approach. Accordingly, this book deals with 7 major areas: The Soviet Union, The Middle East and North Africa, Africa—South of the Sahara, China, The Subcontinent of India and Pakistan, Southeast Asia and Japan. In treating these areas, the authors have attempted to incorporate concepts drawn from various disciplines. An understanding of the history, geography, economy, political institutions and social and cultural life is basic to the study of man's development.

It is hoped that the book will encourage the development of critical analysis on the part of the students by the emphasis placed on concepts rather than a mere accumulation of facts. Materials have been incorporated that lend themselves to the methods of inquiry and discovery as well as to the development of social studies skills.

The authors have tried to avoid the ethnocentrism and bias prevalent in the study of non-Western areas by presenting materials and information gathered from non-Western sources and by presenting activities which will allow students to develop their own conclusions.

Each chapter contains a summary of key concepts, exercises for skills development and content review, and suggested student activities.

ACKNOWLEDGMENTS

The authors hereby express their sincere gratitude to the many social studies and area specialists who have read the manuscript, in whole or in part, and whose critical suggestions have played a decisive role in its development and final form. In particular, acknowledgment is accorded to Phillip Lefton and Theodore Strauss, of the Advisory Board, for their critical judgment in the pedagogical and social studies fields and in the areas of city and state 9th grade social studies syllabi. We thank Rabbi Harry Essrig (Los Angeles, California) and Professor Caesar E. Farah (U. of Minnesota) for the help given with the highly controversial unit on the Middle East and North Africa. To Professor Wing-tsit Chan (Chatham College) the authors are indebted for a critical reading and many constructive suggestions for the unit on China. Similarly, the units on the USSR and India have profited immensely from the criticisms of Frank Keetz (N.Y. State Council for the Social Studies).

The following sources are gratefully credited for permission to reprint material under their copyright: The Johns Hopkins University Press, Time-Life Books, McGraw-Hill Book Company and the National Industrial Conference Board. Full credit lines are given in this book on the pages where the material appears. All charts, graphs and tables in this book were prepared by the authors in accordance with data appearing in standard reference works.

UNIT I The Study of Man

Culture and Survival

Could you survive alone in the jungle? The desert? The Arctic? Most Americans are "civilized" and they know almost nothing of the ways of life of many "primitive" peoples. If you can answer more than half of the following questions correctly, you are good. Remember, however, that only one incorrect answer in a real situation might easily result in your death!

Directions: **True or False**

NOTE: An answer key appears at the end of the unit.

JUNGLE

1. The chances of being bitten by a poisonous snake in the jungle are about as remote as being struck by lightning.

2. While food is plentiful in the jungle, good water is difficult to obtain.

3. Tincture of iodine can be used to purify water in an emergency.

4. All jungle animals except a few travel toward water at dawn and dusk.

5. One should seldom, if ever, follow a direct compass line in the jungle.

6. Anything you see monkeys eat you can eat.

7. Man's worst enemy in the jungle is the mosquito.

DESERT

1. In the desert, on very hot days, it is very important for one to wear a woolen band around the stomach.

2. When walking in the desert it is desirable to wear two pairs of socks.

3. If one lies down to escape the force of a sandstorm, he should move around frequently.

4. Salt tablets should only be taken if there is water available.

5. Chewing gum increases thirst.

6. Because of the dry air, food spoilage is not a serious problem in the desert.

7. As long as you stay under cover, there is little danger of heatstroke.

ARCTIC

1. Very little snow falls in the Arctic during the winter.

2. Wearing loose clothing usually leads to frostbite.

3. A heavy beard is good protection against frostbite.

4. In the Arctic few if any clothes should be worn inside a sleeping bag.

5. The worst Arctic pest is the mosquito, but it is not a disease carrier.

6. Generally speaking, the Arctic coastline is friendlier than the interior.

7. Snow blindness can occur during a bright, overcast day as quickly as during bright, sunny weather.

Now that you have tried to answer the questions, you can see that it would not be easy for you to survive in a jungle, a desert or the frozen Arctic. People learn to live and make use of the things around them. You can live well in a city; but a person who has lived all his life in a desert will find the city strange and frightening, just as you and I would find the jungle or desert a frightening place.

Culture refers to the methods people use to live, or the way of life of a group of people at a particular time. There are many different cultures throughout the world. On the following pages we will discuss the various ways in which cultures are formed, and the reasons why they are different.

At this point, it is important to know that there are many differences and likenesses among peoples of the world. In studying other cultures, our main goal should be to explore the ways other groups of human beings have developed their cultures in response to problems of survival and in order to fulfill their dreams. We must try to look at them not through American eyes, but as they see themselves. We must not criticize them in the light of our history and culture, which is very young, but in the light of their own histories and cultures, which are much older than ours.

Culture and Habitat

To really understand people, you must know something about the *environment* in which they live. Environment is the setting in which man lives. Man is surrounded by people, objects and nature. These three things help decide the way in which man lives.

Habitat

From man's earliest history, people have adapted their way of life to the natural environment, the *habitat*. The habitat consists of such things as soil, land surface (topography), climate, plants and animals. These things are different throughout the world. For this reason man has had to learn to use them differently.

People in the warmer climates have ways of living which are different from those in colder climates. They build houses, wear clothing and eat foods that are different. Where soil is fertile and climate is favorable, men earn their living by farming. In places where the land is rocky and the soil poor, men have had to make their living in other ways.

As man's knowledge has grown larger, he has become better able to make the environment meet his needs. Earliest man was very dependent on his environment. He did not use the environment well. He lived in trees or caves and gathered food or hunted animals. When the food supply disappeared, he either died or moved to where the food was plentiful. When man learned to farm, make simple tools and build houses, he no longer needed to move about to get food. He began to make the habitat work for him.

Culture

The habitat is important, but there is another important part of the environment. This part is called the *culture*. The culture is the man-made part of the environment, and it must be learned. The culture includes all the changes that man has made in his habitat. As man has worked with the materials provided by the habitat, he has developed habits and customs of living. He has set up religions and governments. He has created music, art and language. He has set up rules of conduct. These rules of conduct are called *values*.

The culture of a people develops over a long period of time. Culture is affected by materials available in the habitat, as well as by whatever is brought in from the outside. The way in which ideas and materials are brought from one culture to another, and how they are used, is called *cultural diffusion*.

Culture, Habitat and Man

The material things that man has developed are things that can be touched. We can find them and study them. We can see how they differ from place to place (farms, factories, tools, food, clothing, shelter). The ideas that man has developed cannot be touched, but how these ideas affect the life of man can easily be seen.

Man has used his intelligence to create religion, government and education. The ideas behind them differ from one culture to another. However, the purpose for all cultures is the same, to set up an orderly way of life and to control how people act.

It is difficult to study the ideas of a culture. We can see church buildings, but may find it difficult to discover why the people believe in the religion or how deeply they believe. We can see written laws, but it may be difficult to judge how the government works and what effect it has on the people. We can see schools and books, and hear languages. However, it is hard to judge how valuable the education is and how many people are well-educated.

We must realize that to fully understand man's different ways of life, all aspects of the habitat and culture must be considered and studied.

People of the World

There are over three billion people living on the earth today. Because most of the land on earth is north of the equator, we should not be surprised to find that more than nine-tenths of the world's population lives north of the equator. This fact has been true throughout man's history.

ESTIMATES OF WORLD POPULATION BY REGIONS (1650-1975)
(Population in Millions)

Date	World	North America	South America	Africa	Europe	Asia	Oceania
1650	545	1	12	100	103	327	2
1750	728	1	11	95	144	475	2
1800	906	6	19	90	192	597	2
1850	1,171	26	33	95	274	741	2
1900	1,608	81	63	120	423	915	6
1950	2,406	166	162	199	594	1,272	13
1968	3,483	309	180	336	655	1,947	18
1973	3,807	330	204	387	655	2,211	20
1975	3,968	342	213	402	664	2,325	21

The Population Explosion

As you can see from the chart, more than half the world's people live in Asia, and a little more than one-sixth live in Europe. The rest are scattered over the other four regions. Note that there has been a steady increase in the growth rate of population throughout the world. It has been especially rapid during the past seventy years. This growth in the number of people is called the *population explosion*. The world population doubled from 2 billion in 1930 to 4 billion in 1976, and it will probably double again in the next 35 years.

Population Distribution

Within the area where people live they are not evenly distributed. There are areas of dense population, where many people live close together, and other areas of sparse population, where few people live. The areas of densest population are in Southeast Asia, India, Western Europe, Eastern China and the eastern part of the United States.

An accurate way of measuring the density of population of a region is to divide the number of people in the region by the number of square miles. Thus, if an area has one million square miles and ten million people, the population density would be ten people per square mile.

SIZE, POPULATION AND DENSITY OF THE WORLD'S LARGEST NATIONS AND REGIONS

Country	Size	Population (U.N. Estimate)		People Per Sq. Mi.	
		1968	1975	1968	1975
USSR	8,600,000 Sq. Mi.	238,000,000	254,000,000	28	29
CANADA	3,850,000 Sq. Mi.	21,000,000	23,000,000	5	6
CHINA	3,700,000 Sq. Mi.	730,000,000	853,000,000	197	231
USA	3,600,000 Sq. Mi.	200,000,000	214,000,000	57	59
BRAZIL	3,300,000 Sq. Mi.	88,000,000	107,000,000	27	33
INDIA	1,200,000 Sq. Mi.	534,000,000	600,000,000	437	473
		Other Areas			
JAPAN	143,000 Sq. Mi.	101,000,000	111,000,000	706	761
SOUTHEAST ASIA	1,692,000 Sq. Mi.	270,000,000	316,000,000	159	186
MIDDLE EAST	3,784,000 Sq. Mi.	261,000,000	293,000,000	69	77
AFRICA— SOUTH OF THE SAHARA	8,600,000 Sq. Mi.	254,000,000	292,000,000	30	34

(NOTE: the great increase of population in the 7 years that separate the two sets of figures. Scientists estimate that the earth's present population will double in the next 50 years or sooner.)

1970-1975 AVERAGE ANNUAL GROWTH RATES FOR WORLD REGIONS

Africa	2.6%	Latin America	2.7%	Oceania	2.0%
Asia	2.1%	Europe	0.6%	World	1.9%
North America	0.9%	USSR	1.0%		

How can you use this chart to estimate the future populations of these regions?

Some Parts of the World Are More Desirable Than Others

If you look around any large city, you will notice that people try to live in certain sections and avoid others. Just as people move to desirable areas of the city or a town, so do the peoples of the whole world tend to move to more desirable places and away from less desirable places.

What makes one part of the earth a desirable place to live and other parts less desirable? We can best answer this by taking actual examples. Few people live in Greenland because of the year-round cold climate. Few people live in the Sahara region of Africa because of the lack of rainfall. Thus, we see there are certain parts of the earth that are thinly populated because of extremes of temperature and rainfall.

The world areas with the largest populations, such as Eastern China, Japan, India, Europe, and the Eastern United States, have a generally temperate climate, enough rainfall, level land and fertile soil for raising food crops.

Climate is not the only reason people move from place to place. Many people came to the United States because land was cheap and they could own a farm of their own. Others came to escape the poverty of their land of birth, hoping to find new opportunities and a decent livelihood here. Land hunger has always been a strong reason for people to move from place to place.

Water is another attraction for people. People always move near rivers because most large rivers are bordered by level plains suitable for farming. In addition, rivers are sources of drinking water and a means of easy transportation.

In modern times, our industries and factories need tremendous amounts of raw materials. They need coal, iron, aluminum, copper, tin, oil. They also need cheap electric power obtained from moving water. Because of these needs, many people are attracted to towns and cities near important natural resources.

Thus, we see that for a variety of reasons people move from place to place. The places of their choice influence their customs and institutions and their occupations. We will continue in our study of people, and will look into the question of what the ideas of race and culture mean.

Race and Culture

Race

The term *race* is often used loosely and incorrectly. You hear people talk about the human race, the French race, the Jewish race and the yellow race. None of these terms is scientifically correct. All men belong to a single *species* (group) called *Homo sapiens* (meaning "man the wise"). Anthropologists divide *Homo sapiens* into groups according to physical characteristics (skin color, height, head form, hair color, eye color, shape of nose, hair form) . These groups are called *races,* and it is correct to use the term only in this way. Race has nothing to do with language, religion or the country in which people live. Nor is it correct to distinguish race by skin color alone. Not all members of any one race have the same skin color. For example, the skin color of the so-called white race ranges from pink to olive brown. Within any one race there is a great variety of individual types.

Some anthropologists classify the peoples of the world into three major races: the Caucasoid, the Mongoloid and the Negroid. The ending *oid* means the race is like the Caucasian (white), the Mongolian (yellow) or the Negro (black) . Over the long course of human history, race mixture has resulted in every imaginable intermediate type. It is important to note that racial characteristics are inherited.

Races of Mankind

	Caucasoid	Mongoloid	Negroid
SKIN COLOR	pale pink to olive brown	saffron to yellow-brown, some reddish-brown	brown to brown-black, some reddish-brown
STATURE	medium to tall	medium tall to medium short	very tall to very short
HEAD FORM	long and narrow to broad; medium high to very high	broad; medium high	long and narrow; medium high to low
HAIR COLOR	light blond to dark brown	brown to brown-black	brown-black
HAIR TEXTURE	fine to medium	coarse	coarse
HAIR FORM	straight to wavy	Straight	light curl to wavy or frizzly
EYE COLOR	blue to dark brown	brown to dark brown	brown to brown-black
NOSE	bridge usually high; form narrow to medium broad	bridge usually low to medium; form medium broad	bridge usually low; form medium-broad to very broad

Culture

Unlike race, *culture* is learned rather than inherited. Every group of people has a particular way of acting or behaving. Each individual learns the accepted ways of the group from the example of parents and from other children. He learns through the process of education. Although you are born into this or that race, you learn to live according to the ways of your culture.

A culture consists of traditional ideas and purposes, ways of communication, and material objects such as tools, buildings and machines. The following outline suggests the variety of things that combine to make up a culture.

a. Material Culture: Tools and skills, buildings, ways of making a living.
b. Social Institutions: Family, community, education, government, political parties.
c. Attitudes Toward the Unknown: Religion, magic, superstition.
d. Art: Graphic and plastic arts, folklore, music, drama, the dance.
e. Language and Writing: The means of communication.

Clearly, the different parts of a culture can be separated only for the purposes of study. Any attempt to understand the way a people lives must take into account how these different parts of a culture relate to each other. To take one example, religious beliefs sometimes have an important effect on the way people make a living, and on the things they eat and drink.

Cultural Diffusion

Our solid American citizen awakens in a bed built on a pattern which originated in the Near East, but which was modified in Northern Europe before it was transmitted to America. He throws back covers made from cotton first grown in India, or linen first made in the Near East, or silk, the use of which was discovered in China. All of these materials have been spun or woven by processes invented in the Near East. He slips into moccasins invented by the Indians of the eastern U.S., and goes to the bathroom, whose fixtures are a mixture of European and American inventions, both of recent date. He takes off his pajamas, a garment invented in India, and washes with soap invented by the ancient Gauls. He then shaves, a custom which seems to have been developed in ancient Egypt.

Returning to the bedroom, he removes his clothes from a chair of southern European type, and proceeds to dress. He puts on clothes whose form originally developed from the skin clothing of the nomads of the Asiatic steppes, puts on shoes made from skins tanned by a process invented in ancient Egypt, and cut to a pattern developed in Ancient Greece, and ties around his neck a bright-colored cloth which is a survival of the shoulder shawls worn by 17th-century Croatians of southern Europe. Before going out to breakfast he glances through the window, made of glass invented in Egypt, and if it is raining, puts on overshoes made of rubber first used by Central American Indians, and takes an umbrella invented in Southeast Asia. Upon his head he puts a hat made of felt, a material first used on the Asiatic steppes.

On his way to breakfast he buys a newspaper, and pays for it with coins of ancient Lydian invention. At the restaurant a whole new series of borrowed things face him. His plate is made of a form of pottery invented in China. His knife is of steel, an alloy first used in southern India, his fork is a medieval Italian invention, and his spoon comes from a Roman original. He begins breakfast with an orange from the eastern Mediterranean, a cantaloupe from Persia, or perhaps a piece of African watermelon. With this he has coffee, an African plant. After his fruit and first coffee he goes on to waffles, cakes made by a Scandinavian technique from wheat first raised in the Near East. As a side dish he may have eggs, first eaten in eastern Asia, or thin strips of the flesh of an animal first tamed in eastern Asia, which has been salted and smoked by a process developed in northern Europe.

When our friend has finished eating, he settles back to smoke, an American Indian habit, consuming a plant first developed in Brazil, in either a pipe developed by the Indians of Virginia, or a cigarette, derived from Mexico. If he is hardy enough, he might even smoke a cigar, brought to us from the Antilles by way of Spain. While smoking, he reads the news of the day, imprinted in characters invented in Germany. As he absorbs the information in the newspapers of the problems that exist in other countries he will, if he is a good conservative citizen, thank a Hebrew deity in an Indo-European language that he is 100% American.

This article by Ralph Linton clearly shows the origins of certain objects and activities with which Americans are familiar. He shows the origins to be outside of

SOURCE: This section is based on a selection from an article written in 1937 by Ralph Linton, the well-known anthropologist.

America. When culture traits or culture patterns are spread from one group of people to another and from one culture to another, this action is called *cultural diffusion.*

A culture pattern cannot move from place to place by itself. It must be carried by man. If the new pattern or object appeals to a group of people because it is useful and meets the needs of the group, cultural diffusion takes place. The new pattern is made part of the group's culture in a way that best serves the group.

Most of the cultural background and heritage of Colonial America was brought here from England, Spain and other European countries. Some items of America's culture, such as the potato, maize, types of cooking, and methods of warfare were contributed by the American Indian.

England and France diffused much of their culture from Italy. Italy, in turn, borrowed from the Greeks. It was once believed that Greece created her own culture. However, we now know that the Greeks borrowed much from Crete, and that Crete borrowed from Egypt. Egypt exchanged culture traits with the cultures of the Tigris-Euphrates Valley. The Tigris-Euphrates cultures exchanged traits with the Indus River civilizations. India, in turn, had interchanges with China. As you can see, there has been a vast amount of borrowing by one region from another.

Diffusion is not automatic when two groups come together. It is selective. If a particular trait fits in easily with a culture, it is quickly diffused. If it can be used or is needed, it will be adapted or changed slightly to fit the needs of a society. The Russians borrowed the Greek religion, but made it fit the existing culture of Russia.

An old Chinese saying reads, "I approach my older brother with respect, my father and mother with veneration (honor), my grandfather with awe (fear)." The long and continuous history of China is partly due to ancestor worship, with the importance placed on the past. The Chinese borrowed little from the outside and, what they did borrow, they made Chinese. Custom and tradition ruled in China. Cultural diffusion was resisted. Few new ideas entered. The Chinese civilization fell behind and began to crumble under the force of 20th-century progress.

It is important to note that societies and nations borrow from each other to better themselves. There is no single culture that has developed without diffusion, and has built a high form of civilization. We will note many examples of cultural diffusion in our study of the non-Western world.

What It Is Like to Be Underdeveloped

We Americans look about us at the underdeveloped areas of the world without having the slightest idea of the difficulties with which they are faced. We must try to understand what underdeveloped means to the two billion human beings who live with it.

It is not easy to make the mental jump. Let us try, however, by imagining how an American family, living in a housing development on a yearly income of 4,500 dollars, could be changed into a family of the underdeveloped world.

Our first step is to strip our American home of its furniture. Everything from the living quarters goes: beds, chairs, tables, television set, lamps. Leave a few old blankets, a kitchen table, a wooden chair. For clothing, each member of the family may keep his oldest suit or dress, plus a shirt or blouse. Permit a pair of shoes to the head of the family, but none for the wife.

In the kitchen the appliances have already been taken out, the water and electric power shut off. The box of matches may stay, as well as a small bag of flour and some sugar and salt. A few moldy potatoes, already in the garbage can, must be hastily rescued, for they will be much of tonight's meal. We will leave a handful of onions and a dish of dried beans. All the rest must go: the meat, fresh vegetables, canned goods, crackers.

The house itself, as well as the other houses of the development, must go. The family can move into a small shack. It may be crowded. Still, they are fortunate to have any shelter at all; an estimated 250,000 people in the Indian city of Calcutta live in the streets.

Communication must go next. No more newspapers, magazines, books. However, they will not be missed, since we are not able to read. Instead, in our community we will allow one radio—and that is generous.

Government services must go also. No more postman or fireman. There is a school, but it is three miles away and consists of two classrooms. It is not overcrowded, since only half of the children in the neighborhood go to school. There are, of course, no hospitals or doctors nearby. The nearest clinic is ten miles away. It can be reached by bicycle, if the family has one, which is unlikely. Or you can go by bus—not always inside, but there is usually room on the top.

Money? We will allow our family a cash treasure of ten dollars. This will help cover some of the costs of unexpected medical and family problems. Meanwhile, the head of the family must earn a living. As a peasant with three acres to farm, he may raise the equivalent of $100 to $300 worth of crops a year. If he is a tenant farmer, which is more than likely, a third of his crop will go to his landlord, and another 10% to the local money lender. But there will be enough to eat—or almost enough. The human body requires a daily input of at least 2300 calories to make up for the energy used by the body. If we do no better than the Indian peasant, we will average no more than 2000 to 2100 calories per day. Our bodies, like a machine that is not oiled enough, will run down.

And so we have brought our American family down to the very bottom of the human scale. When we are told that more than half the world's population "enjoys" a standard of living of "less than $100 a year," this is what that figure means.

The Road to Development

The description you have just read was adapted from Robert Heilbroner's book *The Great Ascent*. It gives you a vivid picture of what "underdevelopment" means to individual people. What does it mean to a country?

When we say that a country or a continent is "underdeveloped," we are comparing it to the United States, the U.S.S.R. and the countries of Western Europe. "Underdeveloped" suggests that if something were done about the situation, the country or continent would develop.

AVERAGE INCOME PER HEAD OF FAMILY (SELECTED COUNTRIES)

	1958	1966-1969	1972
UNITED STATES	$2,115	$3,815	$4,980
JAPAN	285	1,290	2,400
SOUTH AFRICA	315	675	730
TURKEY	180	315	430
GHANA	140	215	240
KENYA	70	105	210
LIBYA	110	1,195	1,850
MOROCCO	160	185	240
NIGERIA	45	80	90
RHODESIA	185	240	270
TANZANIA	50	70	90
TUNISIA	150	180	290
UAR (EGYPT)	110	166	390
BURMA	55	70	72
INDIA	65	75	90
INDONESIA	80	95	70
IRAN	145	250	490
PHILIPPINES	185	180	190
THAILAND	80	125	190
ISRAEL	610	1,300	2,010
KUWAIT	1,830	3,860	3,890
LEBANON	210	430	520
SAUDI ARABIA	125	290	440
IRAQ	160	250	280
SYRIA	155	205	290

The Role of Human Resources

A large supply of natural resources, such as water power and minerals (oil, coal, iron ore), does not guarantee development. A country's human resources are even more important than its natural resources. To turn rivers into electric power, there must be trained and educated people. They must build the dams and generators to produce and move the electricity. Crude oil lying under the ground is not valuable unless there are people who know how to get it out, refine it and use it. The education of an engineer, a scientist or a teacher cannot be accomplished overnight.

The Role of Capital

Development means not only improving the standard of living and education of the people. It also means the development of a sense of pride and satisfaction in oneself and one's country. The leaders of the "developing" nations are asking their people to work harder. The people are asked to raise more food than they themselves can use. The extra, or surplus, food can be exported for money. This money, or capital, can be used to build schools, factories and roads. The term *capital* can be used to describe goods, such as machinery and buildings, which are used directly in the production of other goods. Some forms of capital, such as a textile mill or a hydroelectric plant, immediately produce new goods, which create more capital. Other forms of capital, such as schools, hospitals and roads, are often called "social capital" because they, too, have a role to play in producing wealth, although not as immediate a role as capital goods (machinery, factories).

Outside Aid

Capital, then, can be raised from within a country only if the people do not use all that is produced. If the birth rate is high, and production of food does not keep up with the growth in population, there will be no surplus. No surplus means no capital for development. A "developing" nation must, therefore, get help from the outside.

Over a century ago Abraham Lincoln said that the United States could not exist half slave and half free. Today the world cannot exist one-quarter rich and three-quarters poor. The developed nations must be aware of the threat and the challenge this situation presents, and they must have a desire to help change the situation by supplying aid and advice.

The countries discussed in this book, with the exception of the Soviet Union and Japan, are developing nations. We are now ready to look at them and judge them in the light of their own history and experiences.

The Third World of Developing Nations

You may have heard people speak of the "Third World." You have probably wondered what is meant by this term. We have learned that there are political and economic differences among nations and peoples. These differences give us a basis for the term *the Third World*.

The world can be divided into three parts: The industrialized and developed nations of western Europe, Australia, the United States, and Canada make up the "First World." The Communist nations of eastern Europe and Asia make up the "Second World." The developing nations of Africa, South America and Asia are said to be the "Third World."

The Third World can be divided into two parts. One is made up of those nations which have natural resources such as oil, copper, gold. These resources can be used to get money for development. The second is made up of nations that are so poor that the hope of development is but a distant dream. This second group could someday become known as the "Fourth World."

First World	Second World
662 million people per capita income: $3,720	1.2 billion people per capita income: $1,049

Third World I	Third World II
903 million people per capita income: $784	942 million people per capita income: $149

A World Plan to Help the Third World

For a long period of time the appeals and requests of the Third World were ignored. At the 1964 U.N. Conference on Trade and Development, most of the Third World nations asked for changes in trade and production rules, higher prices for their resources, and more foreign aid. These requests would have put more of the world's wealth in the hands of the Third World. The Third World ideas were not followed.

Suddenly in 1973 the oil producing nations demanded and received large increases in the price of oil. In 1974, the Third World asked for the following program at the United Nations:

1. Prices for Third World goods should be raised immediately.
2. Third World nations should be given special lower tariffs on exported manufactured goods.
3. Developing nations could set their own terms and take over foreign companies, regardless of international law.
4. Debts of the poorer Third World nations should be canceled or greatly reduced.
5. Foreign aid to Third World nations should be greatly increased.
6. More technology and advisors should be given to Third World nations at bargain prices.

In 1975 at the U.N., the United States made a proposal which included the following ideas:

1. The International Monetary Fund (IMF) would lend up to $10 billion—at $2.5 billion per year—to aid development programs.
2. The poorest nations would not have to pay back these loans.
3. The United States would give Third World nations preferential tariffs for their goods beginning on January 1, 1976.
4. An international investment organization would be set up to attract new capital for industrial development.
5. An international institute would be set up to look for ways to improve energy development.
6. An international group would be set up to aid developing nations with research and to urge the exchange of technological information.

Following this proposal, the United Nations set forth a program which followed these suggestions. The U.N. Plan included the establishment of new international agencies for economic security, energy and technical exchange. In addition, the plan set up the means for food stockpiling, improved trade deals and more capital for lending purposes.

In March 1978, President Carter of the United States urged poor developing nations to join with the rich developing nations and rich industrial nations in a five-point program. The program would try to fight inflation, create jobs, and raise living standards.

The five-step program would:

1. Increase the flow of capital from developed to developing nations
2. Build a more open system of world trade
3. Moderate disruptive price changes in basic raw materials
4. ' Conserve energy and develop other energy sources
5. Strengthen the technology in developing nations

President Carter felt that "We need to share a responsibility for solving problems, not to divide the blame for ignoring them. Only by acting together can we expand trade and investments to create jobs, curb inflation and raise the standards of living of our peoples. The industrial nations share the same problems and cannot by themselves bring about world economic improvement."

Twentieth-Century Nationalism

Every morning the American flag is raised over the school. Soldiers and sailors salute the flag as it passes by in a parade. When we go to baseball, basketball or football games we sing our national anthem, "The Star-Spangled Banner." We do these things to show we are proud of our *nation* (country). We are also showing our respect and loyalty for the ideals upon which our nation is built. This feeling of pride, loyalty and respect to our nation is called *nationalism*.

What is a nation? A nation may be defined as a group of people united by *common* (same) history, common customs and a common language. Such a group of people is called a *nationality*. What makes a nation? A nation must have: (1) a definite area of land; (2) a government obeyed by all the people; (3) a people who have a feeling of nationality and nationalism; (4) a government that is fully independent and not forced to obey any outside group or nation.

The spirit of nationalism is found all over the world today. It is found in many places where a "nation" itself does not exist. In the last 10 years the spirit of nationalism has shown itself in Northern Ireland, where the Irish Republican Army (IRA) wishes to dispose of the British. In Canada the French-speaking Canadians of Quebec are discussing the establishment of a separate Quebec nation. In Africa the Somali nationalists in Kenya and Ethiopia wish to become independent. The Palestinian nationalists want a homeland in the Middle East. These are only a few examples of existing nationalist movements.

Hooded terrorist. A member of the Arab commando group who seized the Israeli Olympic team quarters at the Munich Olympic games, 1972. **Credit: Wide World Photos**

Nationalism and Terrorism

In an effort to achieve their goals, nationalists have used the *tactics* (methods) of terrorism. Terrorism is an old method, based on the fact that people can be influenced by fear. Terrorism is not new, but only recently have new means become available for a different type of worldwide terrorism.

Today terrorists obtain machine guns and make bombs that can then be used to threaten those in power. The terrorists aim to frighten and impress those in power so that they may grant the terrorists demands.

Today's terrorists are well aware of the power of the media. They plan their actions to impress the world with their power. They play to and for an audience. Their appearances and disappearances are carefully planned to gain maximum attention, thereby winning the sympathy of the world. Claims of ill-treatment, a seeming "desire for justice" and a variety of sophisticated propaganda methods combine to create a performance. In the interests of their "*sacred* (holy) nationalist cause," they use all possible means to create fear, thus forcing their opponents to yield to the threats.

Organization	Terrorist Activity (Example)	Purpose
Palestine Liberation Organization (PLO)	Massacre of 40 Israelis on bus near Tel Aviv—March 1978	To prevent talks for peace in Middle East
Popular Front for the Liberation of Palestine (PFLP)	Hijacking and destruction of 4 airline planes at one time—September 1971	To prevent the conclusion of peace treaties
Black September	Assassination of the prime minister of Jordan—1971 Munich massacre of members of Israeli Olympic Team—August 1972	Revenge for Israeli and Jordanian actions against terrorists
Irish Republican Army (IRA)	Repeated bombings of public places—latest, January 1978	To gain independence for Northern Ireland
Ulster Defense Association (UDA)	Attacks on Catholic leaders in Northern Ireland—latest, Early 1977	To keep power in hands of Protestants of N. Ireland
Sadarista National Liberation Movement	Kidnappings—latest in early 1977; limited terrorist attacks on government police stations—1978	To drive the dictator of Nicaragua out of office
Tupamaros (Uruguay)	Kidnappings of government officials and diplomats in early 1970s	To raise money and to get publicity—desire for democratic Uruguay
Italian Red Brigade	Kidnapped Aldo Moro, the head of the Italian Christian Democratic Party and former prime minister of Italy	To force Italian government to release Red Brigade leaders who are in jail
Baader-Meinhoff Gang (Germany)	Airline hijacking and murder of plane's pilot—October 1977	To force German government to release jailed leaders
United Red Army (Japan)	Massacre of 26 Christian pilgrims and tourists at Lod Airport, near Tel Aviv in Israel—1972	They feel they are "soldiers of revolution" and participate in all revolutionary groups and activities
Federation de Libération Québec	Bombings and kidnappings between 1965 and 1974 (FLQ stopped operations in 1975)	To set up an independent Quebec
Basque Separatists	The murder of Vizcaya's provincial governor and raids on the Guardia civil stations (police)—October 1977	Desire for Basque Independence from Spain
Croatian Separatists	Planting bomb at Laguardia Airport and hijacking or airliner	Desire for Croatian self-determination and independence (from Yugoslavia)
South Moluccan Nationalists (Indonesia)	Holding hostages and executing them in the Netherlands—March 1978	Desire for self-determination for South Molucca and freedom for Moluccan terrorists in jail
People's Revolutionary Army (ERP)—Argentina	Kidnappings of executives of large corporations (Exxon, Ford)	To raise money for a "more democratic Argentina"
Combined Terrorist Actions	Hijacking of Air France plane in Athens, Greece; took it to Uganda in Central Africa—Baader Meinhoff, PLO, & Carlos (South American)	To put pressure on Israel to release terrorists in Israeli and German jails

The reaction of the world to the terrorist acts is often varied. In the eyes of some countries, such actions are viewed as necessary to achieve freedom from oppression. At times, terrorists have traveled freely from country to country, with diplomatic *immunity* (freedom from punishment). They have been welcomed with honor to the United Nations. The media have made the terrorists famous by publicizing their actions on radio, on television and in newspapers.

As mentioned before, terrorism is not new. In 1914, a Bosnian nationalist hurled a bomb and killed the Archduke Ferdinand, the heir to the throne of Austria. This terrorist wanted Bosnian independence from Austria, but his action caused the beginning of World War I. Joseph Stalin robbed banks to help raise money to finance the Communist terrorism in Russia before the Revolution of 1917. The leader (Jomo Kenyatta) of the Mau Mau terrorist campaign in Kenya in 1952 fought against both blacks and whites and, until he died recently, was president of that country. Menachem Begin was the leader of the Irgun, which was a terrorist organization that fought the British and Arabs in Palestine before 1948. Today, Begin is prime minister of Israel. Algeria's Bouteflike was a member of the FLS (Front de Libération Nationale), which fought for Algeria's independence from France.

Terrorist acts have escalated. Whereas Kenyatta and Begin, as well as the Algerian nationalists, created terrorist acts only in their countries, the Palestine Liberation Organization (PLO) hijacked planes traveling all throughout the world. The Japanese Red Army terrorists attached Christian pilgrims in the Israeli Lod Airport. German terrorists hijacked a plane full of people in Athens, Greece, and took it to Entebbe, Uganda, in central Africa.

Food: A Worldwide Problem

In November 1974, more than one thousand delegates from 130 countries met in Rome for the United Nations World Food Conference. The conference lasted 10 days and dealt with the problems of food and hunger.

For the most part, hunger is unknown to typical Americans. Until recently, grain elevators in the rich farmlands were stuffed to bursting. The American government was paying farmers to let their lands lie *fallow* (unplanted). It was believed that the "Green Revolution" would take care of the rest of the world.

Suddenly, however, the prospect of mass starvation has become a real possibility. According to many estimates, at least 460 million people are threatened with starvation at present. Is it possible that the world is running out of food?

In Asia and Africa, nearly one-quarter of the 2.7 billion population *subsists* (lives) on a diet far below the thousand calories a day that are needed for anything more than just staying alive. In certain provinces of northern India, famished Indians have stripped the trees of all edible leaves. Newspapers carry stories of entire families who have committed suicide to avoid the agony of slow death by starvation. In northern Chad, a section of Central Africa that has experienced eight years of drought, a group of parents recently asked a United Nations relief official not to send drugs to treat a diphtheria epidemic which had broken out. They explained that it was better for their children to die than to suffer further from hunger or to grow up with their minds and bodies crippled by malnutrition.

What are the causes of this worldwide food crisis?

Weather Conditions

Over the last few years floods, drought and storms have destroyed crops in India, Africa, the Soviet Union, parts of China and the United States.

Since the end of World War II, the world has relied on the surplus grain reserves of the principal exporting countries—the United States, Canada, Australia and Argentina. But 1974 was a very bad year for American agriculture. An unusually wet spring prevented farmers from getting their tractors into the fields. When they finally did plant their corn and soybeans, heavy rains washed them out. It was necessary for some farmers to sow as many as three times. Then came a severe drought, withering crops in the middle of the growing season. And finally, in late September, an early frost destroyed much of the corn and soybeans that had survived the earlier disasters. The results were grain shortages and higher prices. Similar disasters hit major agricultural areas in the Soviet Union, China, and Canada. The severe drought in Central Africa is discussed on page 253.

Many scientists now believe that weather conditions all over the world are changing and that this could seriously damage food production in the future. It seems that the polar icecaps are now cooling. This situation creates droughts, early frosts, heavy rains and widespread flooding. It also accounts for the southern shift of the monsoon rains, which has left large sections of Asia dry during the rice-growing season.

The Energy Crisis

The energy crisis has had a disastrous effect on the world's food supply. Middle Eastern politics have brought about a reduction of oil production by members of the Organization of Petroleum Exporting Countries (OPEC). This created a severe shortage of fertilizer, which is based on petroleum. The Arabs, since 1973, have also increased the price of oil fivefold, thus putting the cost of fertilizer almost completely out of the reach of farmers in the underdeveloped countries. High oil prices have also driven up the cost of planting, harvesting and transporting grain all over the world.

Population Growth

World population continues to increase at the rate of 93 million people a year. Scientists estimate that if by the year 2000 food production has not increased sufficiently and births are not cut back, the situation will be catastrophic.

What are the steps that can be taken to *avert* (avoid) such a tragedy?

New Farmlands

At present only about 11% of the world's total land surface (about 3.5 billion acres) is under cultivation. *Agronomists* (specialists in crop production and soil management) believe that there are enormous areas of the globe—amounting to another 6.6 billion acres—that can be converted into farmland. These areas include remote jungles such as that of the Amazon River Basin and parts of West Africa that are at present infested with tsetse flies. The cost of converting this land, however, is enormous.

Increased Food Production

Scientists have always believed that modern technology could produce greater yields per acre. This would involve the use of new types of seeds, expanded irrigation systems and chemical fertilizers. In fact, during the 1960s, much of the world experienced a "Green Revolution." World production of wheat and rice increased tremendously, especially in Asia. The key to increased food production is cheap energy. It takes enormous amounts of oil to operate farm machinery, run irrigation pumps and produce fertilizer.

Population Control

All experts agree that unless the birth rate is greatly reduced throughout the world, even increased food production will not be able to subsidize all the people. Many experts believe that it is necessary to spend many more millions of dollars to spread the ideas of family planning.

New Food

Scientists continue to claim that they are capable of creating new types of food in their laboratories. So far, however, the high cost of producing these new foods, as well as the difficulty in making them appealing to human tastes, has prevented them from replacing our basic foods.

Eating Less

It takes seven pounds of grain to produce one pound of beef. Many food experts believe that if Americans would decrease the amount of meat they eat by 10%, enough grain would be released to feed 60 million people. It is also estimated that Americans waste 25% of the food they buy. However, suggestions that Americans eat more carefully and cut down on their meat intake run into much opposition.

Land Reform

In many parts of the world, especially in Asia and Latin America, vast areas of farmland are still in the hands of absentee landowners. The poor sharecroppers who work on this land have little desire to improve it and increase production. Those countries that have set up land reform programs, such as China, Mexico, Egypt and Taiwan, have shown great increases in food production.

International Cooperation

Most food experts believe that the only way to deal with the crisis is for all the countries of the world to join together and cooperate. One way is for the oil-rich Arab countries to provide loans on easy terms to the poorer countries. Another is to establish a grain reserve that would provide food to the hungry in emergencies. Still another proposal calls for the rich industrialized nations of the world and the underdeveloped nations to work out agreements whereby the latter would keep the prices of raw materials down while the industrial countries would provide them with skills and capital.

All the proposed solutions are in one way or another controversial; none will be fully accepted.

The Oceans' Resources

The oceans of the world have many riches. However, these riches will not be available forever. If used correctly, the oceans' resources can supply the world with more food and with new sources of energy.

The oceans provide for the people of the world in the following ways:
1. The world's catch of fish has tripled since the 1940s. With proper management, this harvest can again be doubled. However, overfishing or pollution in the wrong places can severely *diminish* (decrease) this vital food source.
2. Offshore oil wells now produce about 20% of the world's supply. They are expected to produce almost 50% by the late 1980s. Production in the North Sea has already greatly increased European supplies.
3. Small manganese stones lie scattered on the ocean floor. Other minerals that can be mined from the ocean bottom are cobalt, copper, lead and nickel.

OCEAN-MINING POSSIBILITIES

Mineral	Coastal Area Where Found	Use of Mineral
Magnetite	Australia, Japan, India, U.S. Pacific Coast	Source of iron (an iron ore)
Glauconite	U.S. Pacific Coast	Source of titanium — used in making steel and alloys
Rutile	Australia, U.S. Atlantic Coast	Source of iron and potassium
Zircon	Australia	Gemstone for jewelry
Tin	Malaysia, Indonesia, Thailand, Alaska, Great Britain	Canning, *plating* (coating) of metals alloys* of bronze and pewter
Silver	Alaska, U.S. Pacific Coast	Jewelry, coins, spoons, forks
Gold	Alaska, U.S. Pacific Coast	Coins, jewelry, plating of metals
Platinum	Alaska, U.S. Pacific Coast	Jewelry, catalyst† in chemical and oil industries
Diamond	Southwest Africa	Jewelry, cutting heads for industrial tools
Manganese	Atlantic Ocean, Pacific Ocean, Mediterranean Sea	Steel, glass, paints, medicine
Coal	Canada, United Kingdom, Japan	Making steel, heating, producing energy
Monazite	South India, Ceylon	Source of thorium—for atomic fission, electrolodes, optical glass
Sulfur	Gulf Coast of the U.S.	Matches, gunpowder, vulcanizing rubber, medicine

Alloys—Metals made by melting two or more metals together.
†*Catalyst*—An agent which brings about a change.

OFFSHORE OIL PRODUCTION (1975)

Country	Barrels Produced per Day
United States	910,000
Iran	480,000
Abu Dhabi	460,000
Nigeria	430,000
Dubai	250,000
Indonesia	245,000
USSR	230,000
Gabon	180,000
Egypt	165,000
Angola	140,000
Brunei	140,000
Malaysia	85,000

Past History   Like so many areas in the world today, the seas have become a battleground for nations. For centuries, the power to set up laws of the sea lay in the hands of a few powerful *maritime* (sea) nations. They believed in the idea of freedom of the seas. Hugo Grotius, a Dutchman, felt that the "ocean is common to all because it has no limits and it cannot become the possession of anyone." The sea, he said, "can be neither seized nor enclosed." He wrote this in 1609 and, for 350 years, freedom of the seas was the law of the sea.

The birth of many new nations since 1945 has strengthened the argument for changes in the these laws. Nations have also begun to drill offshore for oil and gas. The United States has said that all the resources found off the coast (continental shelf) of the United States belong to the United States. The United States has also said that the continental shelf is a part of the continental land mass. Other countries have done the same. Peru and Ecuador have prevented other countries from fishing in the waters off their coasts. Some countries have said that they have control and ownership of the sea as far as 200 miles off their coasts.

International Conferences   An international commission of the United Nations was set up to study the problem. As a result, two international conferences were held in Geneva in 1958 and 1960. There was a great deal of talk, but no agreements were reached. Since 1960 the situation has become worse. It is now of great importance that answers be found to some questions:

1. How can the resources of the seas and oceans be fairly distributed among the peoples and the nations of the world? (Some nations have long coastlines, while others are landlocked.)
2. How far offshore can a coastal nation extend its rule?
3. How far beyond this boundary can a nation claim economic control—for example, control of oil and fish resources?
4. Who owns the resources even farther out, in the high seas?
5. Should an international body be established to settle disputes involving the ocean and its resources?
6. How should such an international body be organized to represent various interests?

Third World Conference on the Sea   In 1974 and continuing into 1975, a Third World Conference on the Sea was held in Caracas, Venezuela, and then later in Geneva, Switzerland. Considering the vital questions listed above, the conference members divided into two groups. On one side were the 120 developing nations ranging in size from that of China (population 800 million) to that of the South Pacific island nation of Nauru (population 5500). These developing nations saw the chance to share in the oceans' wealth. To them the idea of "freedom of the seas" seemed to give an unfair advantage to the already developed nations.

On the other side was a group of 29 modern industrial nations, including the United States, the Soviet Union, the European nations, Canada, Australia and Japan. These countries felt that the development of the sea resources should not be *limited* (restricted).

Despite the larger number of nations that are considered developing, little was decided. The less-developed nations were not united; those that are *landlocked* (without coastlines) and self-locked (with small coastlines) did not like the idea of other nations dividing the richest parts of the oceans. Many coastal nations in Africa and South America were asking for a 200-mile *exclusive* (not allowing something else) economic zone (EEZ). They would offer the landlocked nations *access* (route use) to the sea and its food resources. However, they were not willing to share the mineral resources of the sea with their landlocked neighbors. Under these circumstances the landlocked nations would benefit from greater freedom of the seas, which would give them better opportunities to share the wealth.

Living resources (fish and whales) present a particular problem in international law. International fishery commissions have not been successful. Fish do not remain in one place. Many coastal states such as Iceland, Ecuador and Peru have set up 200-mile limits. These limits have created miniwars with other nations. Others try to protect their inshore resources while keeping the right to fish for salmon and tuna elsewhere.

The Fourth and Fifth World Conferences

The 4th and 5th Conferences on the Sea were held in New York City during 1976. For the first time, a complete deadlock developed over the issue of deep ocean mining. The majority of the less-developed countries wanted a powerful international organization to supervise this ocean mining. They hoped to control this organization because of their numbers. The industrial countries and the less-developed coastal countries wanted to set up such an organization with very limited powers. Because of this deadlock, little else was discussed or settled.

The outcome of future conferences is of great importance to all. The major powers know that their days of making *unilateral* (one-sided) decisions are over. They also know that if these conferences fail, it will affect international negotiations on food, energy, security and trade. These conferences have become a test to see if world problems can be worked out without using force.

If no world-wide agreements are reached, most nations will work out local agreements with each other on the oceans' use. This will create a confused situation of conflicting agreements. When there is such conflict, the seeds of war can be easily planted.

The Role of Women in the Modern World

Women make up over half of the world's population. In most areas of the world women are treated as second-class citizens. More than half of the world's 2 billion women live in the rural villages of poor countries. Although men are affected by the misery and hardships of poverty, almost everywhere women suffer more: infant mortality for girls is much higher than for boys; in cases of food shortages, girls get less to eat; when health care is available, boys are given it first. About 1 out of 3 of the world's adult women is illiterate.

Water in the desert. In the shelter of the trees, which have managed to thrive under oasis conditions, there are now water taps for village women. Credit: *United Press International.*

Israeli schoolgirls are given anti-Arab guerrilla training. All youngsters learn how to handle weapons and how to react to surprise attacks. *Credit: United Press International*

In many of the Third World countries, a woman has little choice in marriage. "Often," a United Nations report says, "she is passed on to her new master by her father even before puberty." In most countries women have an inferior position before the law and their rights are not as safe as those of men. Most women in the Third World have no voting or property rights.

In order to honor women and perhaps find ways to improve their position, the United Nations declared the year 1975 as International Women's Year. The U.N. set up a meeting in Mexico City to discuss the situation of women. Six thousand women (1500 delegates) from all over the world (133 nations) came to the meeting. The major goal of the conference was to set up a ten-year "World Plan of Action," emphasizing better health care, education, and a greater role in government for women.

Many views were presented as to how to gain this goal. It became clear that the things which most interested women in the United States and other industrialized Western countries (such as equal pay for equal work and day care centers) did not seem as important to the women of the Third World. Delegates from the poorer countries were in favor of gaining the economic and social reforms that would allow both women and men to escape from lives of hunger, ignorance, and poverty. As the conference continued it became clear that the gap between rich and poor nations must be bridged if equality between men and women is to mean more than shared misery. As one delegate stated, the world's women do not stand to benefit as much from economic or political revolutions as much as from "revolution in the heads of people. That's what the conference is about. It should be a massive consciousness-raising session." The conference helped to show the situation of women today.

ANSWERS to Culture and Survival Questions

JUNGLE		DESERT		ARCTIC	
1.	True	1.	True	1.	True
2.	True	2.	True	2.	True
3.	True	3.	True	3.	True
4.	True	4.	True	4.	True
5.	True	5.	True	5.	True
6.	False	6.	False	6.	True
7.	True	7.	False	7.	True

Summary of Key Ideas

The Study of Man

A. Culture is an important aspect of human life.

1. Different groups of human beings have developed different cultures to meet their needs and desires to survive.

2. Culture should be studied in the light of the environment in which individual groups of people live.

3. Habitat has a great effect on the development of culture.

4. Outside influences also greatly affect the development of culture.

5. Race is an anthropological term based on certain inherited physical characteristics. It has little to do with the ability to create and develop civilization and to contribute to human society.

B. People select a place to live because it meets their needs.

1. Climate and topography affect the selection of a place to live.

2. World population has shown a tremendous growth in the past 100 years.

3. A study of the "density of population" of an area gives us a clearer picture of population in that area than just a study of "total population."

C. Cultural diffusion has an important effect on the lives of people.

1. Man carries ideas with him when he moves from place to place.

2. Diffusion is not an automatic process. It is a selective process based on the needs of the group.

3. New ideas and customs are usually *adapted* to traditional customs and actions.

4. Cultures and societies borrow from each other to better themselves.

D. **Most of the areas of the world can be said to be underdeveloped.**

1. Underdevelopment is an economic idea which suggests that if something were done about the situation a country would develop.

2. A country can be called underdeveloped when it has not developed itself to the extent of the U.S., USSR and Western Europe.

3. Development depends on an adequate use of available natural resources.

4. Development means the improvement of the standard of living.

5. The development of a sense of pride and satisfaction in one's self and one's country is an important part of this problem.

E. **International cooperation can benefit developing nations.**

1. International cooperation between industrial nations and developing nations can help to expand trade, stop inflation and raise living standards for all.

2. International cooperation in developing the resources of the sea can provide more food and minerals for developing nations.

UNIT I
Exercises and Questions

Vocabulary

Directions: Match the words in Column *A* with the correct meaning in Column *B*.

Column A

1. Culture
2. Survival
3. Habitat
4. Environment
5. Values
6. Climate
7. Species
8. Race
9. Communication
10. Community
11. Anthropologists

Column B

(a) The weather of an area over a period of time.

(b) The setting in which man lives.

(c) Groups divided according to physical characteristics.

(d) People who study man.

(e) The rules of conduct of a group.

(f) The natural part of the environment.

(g) The man-made part of the environment.

(h) The act of talking; the exchange of ideas or opinions.

(i) The act of remaining alive.

(j) A group of plants or animals whose members are very nearly alike.

(k) A group of people living in the same place under the same rules.

Completion

Directions: Select from the following terms the one which best completes each sentence.

fallow	OPEC	agronomist	inferior	access
subsist	monsoon	illiterate	maritime	density

1. The measurement used to determine the number of people living in an area is called ....

2. An expert in the field of farming is called a(n) ....

3. Nations near the sea are called .... nations.

4. Farmland which is *not* planted is said to be .... land.

5. A person who cannot read or write is ....

6. To barely stay alive is to ....

7. A route or way of reaching a place is called a(n) .... route.

8. A person who is less able to do something is ....

9. An organization of oil-producing countries is ....

10. The winds of Asia are called ....

Multiple Choice

Directions: Select the letter of the correct answer.

1. The way of life of a group of people is called
   (a) diffusion (b) density (c) culture (d) attitudes

2. All of the following are part of the habitat *except*
   (a) soil (b) topography (c) climate (d) religion

3. An example of topography is
   (a) rain (b) mountains (c) government (d) factories

4. Which of the following statements is true about survival?
   (a) The ability to survive is born with a person.
   (b) People must learn to adapt themselves to a place to survive.
   (c) Survival has little or no relation to the culture of a group.
   (d) Civilized people learn to survive in all areas more quickly than "primitive" people.

5. To find the true accomplishments of a culture and a society we must
   (a) judge them by our accomplishments
   (b) judge them in the light of their own history and culture
   (c) look at their accomplishments in the twentieth century
   (d) none of these

6. In studying other cultures our main objective should be to
   (a) look at the riches gathered by those societies
   (b) learn how they have answered the question of survival
   (c) compare them to our culture
   (d) learn how to survive in other cultures.

7. Man is affected by his habitat in
   (a) the type of house he lives in
   (b) the type of clothing he wears
   (c) the kinds of foods he eats
   (d) all of these

8. The formation of a group's culture is affected by
   (a) the environment (b) cultural diffusion (c) both a & b (d) neither a nor b

9. Most of the world's people live
   (a) north of the equator   (b) near the equator   (c) south of the equator
   (d) in Southeast Asia

10. Using the World Population Chart (p. 4), find out which of the following statements is true:
    (a) The populations of Africa and South America have shown a steady rise every fifty years.
    (b) The population of Africa has increased at a greater percentage rate than that of Latin America.
    (c) The population of North America has shown the greatest percentage rate of gain.
    (d) The population of Asia has shown the greatest percentage rate of gain.

11. Density of population gives us an idea of
    (a) how many people live in a country
    (b) why people live in certain places
    (c) where large numbers of people live close together
    (d) why population has grown larger in the last hundred years

12. Using the chart on Size and Population Density (p. 5), select the statement which is *false*:
    (a) Japan has the largest density of the nations.
    (b) India has shown the greatest population rise between 1968 and 1975.
    (c) The Soviet Union is the largest nation in size and population.
    (d) The population density of China is about forty times greather than that of Canada.

13. Which of the following would *not* be an example of cultural diffusion?
    (a) The use of certain French words in English
    (b) The use of the Arabic (Hindu) number system in the United States
    (c) The belief in ancestor worship in China
    (d) The playing of baseball in Japan

14. Which of the following statements is *true* about cultural diffusion?
    (a) Diffusion occurs automatically when two cultures come together.
    (b) Adaptation is an important part of cultural diffusion.
    (c) Diffusion has had a great effect on the development of China.
    (d) Diffusion had almost no effect on the development of Greek culture.

15. A good example of an "underdeveloped" area is a country
    (a) that has resources which have not been put to use
    (b) that is controlled by another country
    (c) without any natural resources
    (d) that has a high standard of living

16. Which of the following countries would be considered underdeveloped?
    (a) Japan   (b) U.S.   (c) Russia   (d) India

17. Which of the following cities is correctly listed with a conference held there about a world problem?
(a) Rome—Law of the Sea   (b) Mexico City—Women's Rights   (c) Geneva—Cultural Diffusion   (d) Caracas—Food

18. The "Green Revolution" deals with
(a) industrial growth   (b) food production   (c) war in the Middle East   (d) war in Vietnam

19. Which of the following statements is *true*?
(a) Women in most areas have the choice of whom they marry.
(b) Women in most areas have property rights equal to men.
(c) Women in the U.S. have different goals than women of the Third World.
(d) More than one-half of the world's women are literate.

20. Hugo Grotius might be thought of as an expert on
(a) equal rights for women   (b) sharing the world's energy   (c) cultural diffusion   (d) freedom of the seas

21. Which of the following countries might be considered part of the "Third World"?
(a) Japan   (b) U.S.   (c) USSR   (d) India

Thought Questions

1. How does environment affect the lives of people?

2. How has man tried to use his environment to better his life?

3. Why is it difficult to study the ideas of a culture?

4. Why have people decided to settle in certain areas of the world instead of others?

5. What do you feel are the main differences between the concepts of race and culture?

6. How does the process of cultural diffusion take place?

7. "Habitat determines the culture of an area." Do you agree or disagree with this statement? Why?

8. "The different parts of a culture cannot be separated from each other." Do you agree or disagree? Why?

9. (a) If you were the leader of a newly independent nation, what problems of under-development would you face?
(b) How would you try to solve these problems?

10. Why is it important to study cultures in relation to their own environments?

11. What are the things that tell us a country is part of the "Third World"?

12. If you were the American representative in the U.N. what steps might you recommend to help nations of the "Third World"?

13. Compare the similarities and differences among the lives of women in various parts of the world.

14. If you were a reporter at the World Conference on Women, how would you describe what went on there?

15. The year 1975 was designated as International Women's Year. What is your opinion of this?

16. One of the delegates at the Mexico City Conference on Women said, "the world's women do not stand to benefit so much from economic and political revolutions as much as from revolution in the heads of people." Explain this statement.

17. (a) How have weather conditions affected the world food problem?
    (b) What are the other factors that have created growing food shortages?
    (c) If you were an agronomist, what suggestions might you make to solve the problem?

18. (a) How can we best use the ocean as a valuable resource?
    (b) What suggestion can you make to give all nations fair use of the ocean?

Chart Analysis

Directions: Using the chart on page 11 answer the following questions. Of the four choices choose only the correct answer.

1. Which of the following nations showed the greatest change in income per head of family between 1958 and 1969?
   (a) Israel   (b) Rhodesia   (c) Turkey   (d) Japan

2. Which of the following nations showed a decrease per head of family in income between 1958 and 1969?
   (a) Saudi Arabia   (b) India   (c) Philippines   (d) Turkey

3. Which of the following nations showed the greatest percentage of growth between 1958 and 1969?
   (a) U.S.   (b) Japan   (c) Israel   (d) Kuwait

4. This chart shows the growth of income per head of family for about a ten-year period. Another word for a *ten-year period* is
   (a) century   (b) era   (c) decade   (d) annual

5. A conclusion you might make from this chart is
   (a) Most of the countries of Asia are raising incomes faster than the countries of Africa.
   (b) Most countries will soon have enough income to start rapid industrialization.
   (c) There was a general trend during this period toward the raising of income.
   (d) Only industrial countries like the U.S. and Japan have shown any great growth of income during this period.

Puzzle

Directions: Place the words below in their proper place in the puzzle.

4 LETTERS	5 LETTERS	6 LETTERS	7 LETTERS	8 LETTERS
RACE	STUDY	VALVES	CULTURE	SURVIVAL
SOIL	GROUP	ACCESS	HABITAT	INFERIOR
	WORLD	SYSTEM	CLIMATE	MARITIME
		PEOPLE	MONSOON	RELIGION
		BELIEF	DENSITY	
			HISTORY	

9 LETTERS	10 LETTERS	11 LETTERS	13 LETTERS	14 LETTERS
COMMUNITY	AGRONOMIST	ENVIRONMENT	COMMUNICATION	ANTHROPOLOGIST
DIFFUSION	ILLITERATE			UNDERDEVELOPED
MOUNTAINS	GOVERNMENT			
	POPULATION			

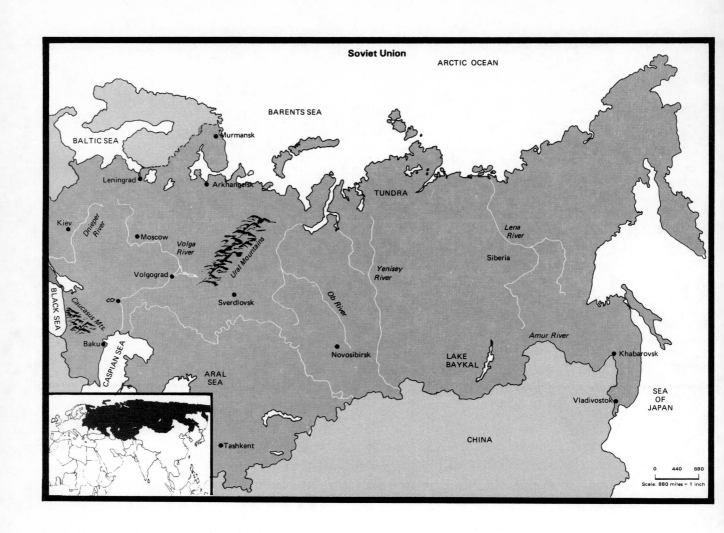

Soviet Union

ARCTIC OCEAN

BARENTS SEA

BALTIC SEA

Murmansk

Leningrad

Arkhangelsk

TUNDRA

Kiev

Dnieper River

Moscow

Volga River

Lena River

Volgograd

Ural Mountains

Siberia

BLACK SEA

Caucasus Mts

Yenisey River

Sverdlovsk

Ob River

Amur River

Baku

CASPIAN SEA

ARAL SEA

Novosibirsk

LAKE BAYKAL

Khabarovsk

Vladivostok

SEA OF JAPAN

Tashkent

CHINA

0   440   880

Scale: 880 miles = 1 inch

UNIT II Union of Soviet Socialist Republics (USSR)

The Land and Topography

Size and Location

The Soviet Union is the largest country in the world. It covers more than 8,500,000 square miles, or about 1/6 of the total land area of the earth. The Soviet Union is larger than the United States and Canada combined. The USSR is spread over two continents—Europe and Asia. It stretches from the Arctic Ocean in the north to the Black Sea and the mountains of Central Asia in the south; it extends from the Pacific Ocean in the east to the Baltic Sea in the west. Another way to look at Russia's huge size is to look at the following facts. There is a three-hour time difference between New York City on the Atlantic coast and Los Angeles on the Pacific. In Russia there is almost a 12-hour difference between Leningrad on the Baltic Sea and Vladivostok on the Pacific Ocean. When the sun is rising in Leningrad it has already set in Vladivostok.

Russia was not always a large country. During much of its early history it was a small country in Eastern Europe. It was completely surrounded by land owned by other countries and was hundreds of miles from the open sea. In the 16th century Russia began to expand until it reached its present size.

The Soviet Union is located far to the north of the equator. Its most southern point is 35° north latitude; the entire country is farther north than Los Angeles. Some of the most important cities are farther north than New York. New York City's latitude is 42° north, Moscow is 55° north latitude, and Leningrad is 60° north latitude.

Physical Features

1. Plain

Most of Russia is a great plain. This plain covers almost all of European Russia and extends eastward into Central Siberia. The plain makes transportation easy. At the same time since there are no natural barriers cold winds sweep southward and bring cold, harsh weather.

The plain has also made it easy for invaders from both east and west to march right in. Mongols from Asia, and Poles, Frenchmen and Germans from Europe have invaded Russia. These many invasions in the past may explain Russia's distrust of outsiders and its desire to have safe frontiers.

2. Mountains

In Asiatic Russia the land becomes more mountainous. The Ural Mountains divide the plain between the continents of Europe and Asia. However, the Urals are not very high and have many passes. They have never protected the country against Eastern invaders. The Caucasus Mountains form a barrier between the USSR, Turkey and Iran. The Pamir Mountains separate the Soviet Union from Afghanistan and Iran. In Southern Siberia are the Tien Shan Mountains and Altai Mountains which form a barrier in some places between the Soviet Union and the countries of Asia.

3. Coastline

The Soviet Union has a huge coastline—the longest in the world. However, only a small part is usable. Most of the waters are frozen a good part of the year or too shallow for use. The only Soviet port on the Arctic coast that is ice-free all year round is Murmansk. It is not of great use as a port, however, because of the great distance from Murmansk to other parts of the Soviet Union. The Pacific coast is also icebound much of the year. The port of Vladivostok requires icebreakers in the winter months to keep it open. Ports along the Baltic and Black Seas have their limitations for other reasons. The exits from the Baltic are controlled by the Scandinavian countries, while those from the Black Sea are controlled by Turkey. Thus, the Soviet Union could be bottled up in either of these two water approaches. These factors have affected the history of the country. Russian history can be explained in part by a continued search for ways to reach the sea or "windows to the world." Over the centuries, Russian expansion was over land and not over water. Only now, for the first time in history, the Russians are concentrating on becoming an important naval power.

4. Rivers

Throughout Russian history rivers have been very important to the development of the country. Most of Russia's rivers are wide and navigable and can be used for trading and transportation. The rivers have helped to unify this huge country. The centers of early Russian history were located on or near a river system—Kiev on the Dnieper, Moscow on the Upper Volga system. The rivers of western Russia flow from north to south. The Dnieper flows into the Black Sea, the Volga (the longest river) flows into the Caspian Sea, and the Don into the Sea of Azov. These rivers provided a route for Russians to trade with the lands to the south.

Three of the four rivers in Siberia—the Ob, the Yenisei and the Lena flow northward into the Arctic Ocean. They are of limited use for trade, but they possess tremendous potential for hydroelectric power. The fourth Siberian river, the Amur, flows generally in a northeast direction and forms a boundary between Siberia and Manchuria.

The Soviet Union has constructed and continues to construct canals to link up the major rivers and seas and to provide a continuous flow of river traffic throughout the country. These waterways provide an important transportation network for the Soviet Union. They connect major cities deep inside of Russia with coastal areas. For example, Moscow, many hundreds of miles from the sea, is connected to coastal areas by this vast system of rivers and canals and is sometimes called the "Port of Five Seas."

Climate

We have all seen pictures of Russia—the people are dressed in fur coats and high boots and there is snow all around. The reason for this is that Russian winters are long and severe. Temperatures of 30 or 40 degrees below zero are common. For months the land is covered with snow. Vast areas are permanently frozen below a depth of about one foot (this is known as permafrost.) Winter brings many hardships and much suffering to the Russian people. Spring is very short. Often when the ice begins to thaw, or melt, the surrounding area is flooded. Then comes summer—generally short and hot. Autumn does not last too long either. And soon it is winter again.

Most of Russia has this type of climate, which is known as continental. That is a climate with great extremes of temperature in summer and winter, short spring and fall seasons, and small amounts of rainfall. The only exceptions to this severe climate are to be found in the desert areas of Central Asia and in a few areas along the Black Sea and Transcaucasia.

There are several reasons why Russia has this kind of climate.

1. Latitude

Most of the country is in latitudes north of the United States. Moscow is farther north than Quebec. Leningrad is in the same latitude as Anchorage, Alaska. Even the "warm" section, the Black Sea area, is farther north than our Great Lakes.

2. Distance from oceans

From east to west the territory of the USSR stretches for a distance of about 6,000 miles. Most of the land is situated at great distances from the sea. Therefore, the Soviet Union is not greatly affected by the warm winds from the Atlantic and Pacific Oceans.

3. Mountain barriers

The warm tropical air currents from the Indian Ocean are prevented from penetrating into Russia by the high mountain barriers along Russia's southern borders.

4. Winds

Freezing Arctic winds blow across the land from early fall to late spring.

Many parts of Russia suffer from a shortage of rain. This is because winds from the oceans lose much of their moisture before they reach the interior of Russia. Only in the western part, near the Black and Baltic Seas, can farmers be sure of getting sufficient rainfall.

Because of its size, the Soviet Union has many climate or vegetation zones.

1. Tundra

In the far north along the Arctic shore is the tundra. Cold winds from the Arctic blow across it. The ground is frozen all year round except for a brief period in the summer when the ground thaws. There are no tall trees here. The vegetation consists of mosses, low grasses and small shrubs. The most common animal is the reindeer. The few people who live in this area make their living by fishing, hunting and herding reindeer.

2. Taiga

South of the tundra is the enormous taiga or forest zone. Taiga is the Russian word which means forest. This vast zone contains about ¼ of the world's supply of timber. Because of the cold climate, short growing season and poor soil much of the land is not good for farming. In the western (European) part of the zone the soil is better and the trees have been cut down to grow rye, barley and oats.

3. Steppe

Further south one comes to the steppe which means "plains" in Russian, but is also called the grasslands. Summers are warm and rainfall is from 10 to 20 inches a year. The fertile soil, especially the *chernozem* (black earth) of the Ukraine, is among the best in the world for farming. Vast fields of wheat and other crops are grown here. This is Russia's main agricultural area, its "breadbasket."

4. Desert

As one moves further south the rainfall decreases and one comes to the desert. The desert extends from the Caspian Sea eastward. It is hot and dry. Much of this land is barren. However, the Soviet Union has constructed many irrigation projects to provide water, so millions of acres of land have become good farmland. Cotton, tobacco, fruits and vegetables are grown.

5. Mediterranean

Along the shores of the Black Sea can be found a climate similar to that of southern California. Winters are short and mild with abundant rainfall; summers are hot and dry. Citrus fruits, grapes and olives are cultivated. This is also the great vacation spot of the USSR.

AVERAGE MAXIMUM-MINIMUM TEMPERATURES AND RAINFALL

City	Jan. Av. Max.	Jan. Av. Min.	July Av. Max.	July Av. Min.	Av. Yearly Rainfall
NEW YORK CITY	37	24	82	66	34.6 INCHES
KIEV	27	16	78	58	22.1 INCHES
MOSCOW	21	9	76	55	24.8 INCHES
ARKHANGELSK	9	2	64	51	24.1 INCHES
LENINGRAD	23	12	71	57	19.2 INCHES
SVERDLOVSK	6	−5	70	54	16.7 INCHES
IRKUTSK	3	−15	70	50	14.9 INCHES

Locate these cities on a map. What are the factors that might cause the differences in temperature and rainfall in each city?

A Georgian. (*Top*)

Kirghiz man. The Soviet Union is made up of many different groups of people. (*Bottom*)

Credit: *Soviet Mission to the United Nations*

The People
of the Soviet Union

There is an old peasant proverb which claims: "Russia is not a country, it is a world." According to the 1977 figures, the population of the Soviet Union is 257, 900,000 people. Many different *nationalities* (ethnic groups) make up the Soviet people.

The Slavs

About 75% of the people of the USSR belong to the group called Slavs. The three most important members of this group are: the *Great Russians,* the *Ukrainians* and the *Byelorussians* (sometimes called White Russians). The Great Russians are by far the most important people in the Soviet Union. They make up about 50% of the population of the country. Their language, Russian, is the official language of the nation. Most of the important jobs in the government are held by them. The languages of these three Slavic peoples are similar. All are written in the same alphabet—the *Cyrillic*—which is different from the alphabet used in the rest of Europe. In many other ways the cultures of these three ethnic groups resemble each other.

The Baltic Peoples

Along the southern shores of the Baltic Sea are the formerly independent states of *Estonia, Latvia* and *Lithuania.* These people had been conquered by the Russians centuries before. In 1919 they broke away and became independent, but in 1940 they were *reannexed* (taken over) by the Soviet Union. All three have a culture that is basically Western European. Their languages are written in the Latin alphabet. They are different from the Slavs in other ways. Most of the Slavs are of the Eastern Orthodox religion. The Estonians and Latvians are Lutheran (Protestant) while the Lithuanians are Catholic.

Peoples of Central Asia

In Central Asia there are the *Uzbeks, Turkmen, Kazakhs, Kirghiz* and *Tadzhiks.* Most of these people speak a Turkic language except for the Tadzhiks, whose religion and culture are Moslem. These people are mainly farmers and shepherds.

Peoples of the Caucasus

Armenians, Georgians and *Azerbaijanis* live in the land south of the Caucasus Mountains between the Black and Caspian Seas. These people are quite different

Beryozka dancers. Traditional Russian dances and costumes are still very popular in the USSR. (*Top*)

Great Russians. (*Bottom*)

Credit: *Soviet Mission to the United Nations*

from one another. The Azerbaijanis speak a Turkic language and are followers of Islam (Moslems). The Georgians and Armenians are Christians. The Georgian language and alphabet are different from the others found in the Soviet Union. This is true of the Armenian language and alphabet as well.

Jews

There are about 3 million Jews living in the Soviet Union. Unlike the other nationalities, however, they are not settled in one area, but are scattered over the entire country. Under the tsarist governments, Jews were often persecuted because of their religion. Today, although many Jews hold responsible positions in the Soviet Union, they are still not treated equally. Jews do not have the same opportunities to observe their culture as the other nationalities in the Soviet Union have. Jewish books are difficult to obtain. No schools exist where Jewish children can learn about their history, traditions or language. Many synagogues were closed by the Communists and Jews find it difficult to purchase religious articles such as prayer books and prayer shawls. Since the creation of a Jewish state in Israel in 1948, the Soviet government has suspected its Jewish citizens of being sympathetic to Israel. Many Jews would like to leave the Soviet Union and move to Israel, but the Soviet government makes it very difficult for them to leave the country. In 1970 a number of Jews were arrested and tried for supposedly trying to hijack a Soviet airplane and take it to Israel. Other Jews were rounded up and accused of taking part in the "plot." The accused were sentenced to several years imprisonment in Siberia.

In the summer of 1972 the Soviet government announced a special "education tax." All Jews who received an education in the Soviet Union, especially doctors, engineers, and scientists, would have to pay the government back for their education if they chose to *emigrate* from (leave) the Soviet Union. The whole world was shocked by this announcement since no country had ever done anything like it before. The tax was *exorbitant* (extremely high), amounting to anything between $10,000 and $64,000. It was obvious that almost no Soviet citizen could afford to pay this tax. Many Jews who had applied to move to Israel were fired from their jobs and found it very difficult to find other jobs. They complained that the police would break in and search their apartments and trouble them in many other ways. The Soviet press wrote many stories that were highly critical of Israel and Jews. Members of the United States government tried to persuade the Soviets to drop the tax. In the American Congress many senators refused to *ratify* (approve) the new trade agreement with the Soviet Union unless the USSR stopped charging Jews who wanted to leave the country. On several occasions in 1972 some Jews were allowed to leave without paying the tax. It was felt that this was done to please the Americans. In April 1973, the Soviet government announced that it would no longer apply the tax for Jews who wished to leave the country.

Nationality and Culture

How did so many different people come to live in one country? Over the centuries the Great Russians spread out, conquering the surrounding peoples, and forcing them into one great empire. Under the tsars, the Russian government made a systematic attempt to assimilate these people, that is, forcing them to adopt the Russian culture.

But these efforts failed. Today the Soviet government allows the various nationalities to use their own language, observe their own customs and religions, and enjoy their own music, dance, literature and costumes. In fact, the Soviet Union is made up of 15 republics, corresponding to the 15 major ethnic groups in the country. Within their own national republics, each group is allowed a degree of autonomy or self rule. In practice, however, the different nationalities have to learn Russian as a second language. Russian history and culture are taught in the schools of the various republics. And all the people of the Soviet Union, no matter what their nationality, find themselves under the close supervision and control of the Communist government in Moscow.

Kievan Russia

Early Russia

Russian history begins around the 7th century A.D. At that time a group of people known as the Slavs settled along the Dnieper River. Gradually they spread out along the other rivers of the great Russian plain. Many other peoples had lived on the territory of Russia before the Slavs arrived, but their empires had fallen and disappeared. Those that remained were conquered by the Slavs.

In the 9th century Russia was invaded by groups of Norsemen or Vikings from Scandinavia. According to legend these Norsemen were invited by the Slavs to come and rule them. Riurik, their leader, became the first Russian ruler in 862. These Norsemen were also called "Rus" and it is from them that Russia got its name.

At this time the capital of Russia was Kiev. These early years stand out as some of the brightest in Russian history. During this same period people in Western Europe were mainly farmers who never left their villages. Russia, on the other hand, had many wealthy cities and contact with other great civilizations. This was because the Dnieper River was an important trade route which the Russians used to trade with Constantinople and Asia. This trade brought Russia much wealth as well as many new ideas. There was some democracy in Russia at this time too. Each city had an assembly (veche) in which all free male citizens were able to vote on important decisions.

Greek Influence

Russian civilization was influenced by the Greeks in Constantinople. In 988 Prince Vladimir of Kiev decided to convert the Russian people to Christianity. He chose that form of Christianity practiced by the Greeks which was known as Eastern Orthodoxy. The first priests, prayer books and Bibles came to Russia from Constantinople. The Russian alphabet was adapted from the Greek. Russian churches, cathedrals and *icons* (religious paintings) were all modeled after the Greek.

Decline and Fall

Why did this civilization come to an end? There are several reasons but the most important is geography. Kiev is located in the steppe, an open plain where many nomadic peoples wandered. The nomads continually raided the Russian cities and robbed them of their wealth. The most dangerous of all the nomads were the Mongols. In 1237 the Mongols invaded Russia, destroying the most important Russian cities and killing thousands of people. For 200 years Russia remained under Mongol rule.

Russian (Cyrillic) Alphabet

CAPITAL LETTER	SMALL LETTER	EQUIVALENT LETTER OR SOUND IN ENGLISH	PRONOUNCED APPROXIMATELY AS IN
А	а	A	*f*ather
Б	б	B	*b*all
В	в	V	*v*ote
Г	г	G	*g*irl
Д	д	D	*d*ay
Е	е	YE	*ye*s
Ё	ё	Yo	*Y*ork
Ж	ж	ZH	plea*s*ure
З	з	Z	*z*one
И	и	ee	m*ee*t
Й	й	Y	bo*y*
К	к	K	*k*ind
Л	л	L	*l*arge
М	м	M	*m*ind
Н	н	N	*n*o
О	о	O	a*w*ful
П	п	P	*p*encil
Р	р	R	*r*ed
С	с	S	*s*peech
Т	т	T	*t*ime
У	у	OO	b*oo*k
Ф	ф	F	*f*ile
Х	х	H	(sound comes from the throat)
Ц	ц	ts	ca*ts*
Ч	ч	Ch	*ch*air
Ш	ш	Sh	*sh*ine
Щ	щ	Shch	Khru*shch*ev
Ы	ы	i	s*i*t
Ь	ь	soft sound	softens sound of a consonant
Э	э	E	m*e*n
Ю	ю	U	*u*nion
Я	я	Ya	*y*ard

St. Basil's Cathedral, Red Square, Moscow. This cathedral, which was built during the reign of Ivan the Terrible, is one of the most famous of Russia's churches. Today it is used as a museum. Credit: *Intourist*

Russia Under the Mongols

1237-1480

Many historians claim that the Mongol invasion retarded Russia's development by 200 years.

In the early part of the 13th century the Mongolian tribes in Central Asia were united under the leadership of Genghis Khan. Within a few years the Mongols were able to conquer all their neighbors, including Russia. Since there were no barriers in the steppe to bar their way, the Mongols were able to march right in.

Results of the Mongol Invasion

The Mongol invasion had many unfortunate results.

1. Thousands of Russians died. About 10% of the total population was enslaved.
2. The most important cities were burned to the ground. A Catholic missionary traveling through Russia in 1246 found countless bones and skulls lying by the wayside, while Kiev, once a city with a large population, contained only 200 houses.
3. The Mongols would not permit any democracy to exist in Russia. The assembly, where formerly Russians used to vote on their laws, was not allowed to meet any more.
4. The Russians did not communicate with the outside world. This was because unfriendly Germans, Poles and Swedes blocked contact between Russia and the West. The Mongols also discouraged this type of contact. At this time a great deal of progress was being made in Western Europe in science, math and art. However, the new knowledge and discoveries of this period, known as the Renaissance (c 1300-1600 A.D.), did not reach Russia.

Although the Mongols came to Russia as conquerors, in time the two cultures influenced each other. The Mongols gave up their nomadic ways, settled down among the Russians and even intermarried with them. Many Mongol words became part of the Russian language.

Mongol Rule

However, the Mongols were not really interested in ruling Russia. They did not even set up a real government in Russia. Their main interest was to collect taxes from the Russians and become rich. At first, they collected the taxes themselves, but later on they allowed the Russian princes to do it for them. In fact, the Russian princes were even allowed to rule their small regions, although the Mongols remained the real masters. At the beginning of the 14th century the Prince of Moscow received the title of Grand Prince from the Mongols. He was also given the right to collect taxes all over Russia. The princes of Moscow usually kept part of the money for themselves and as a result became the strongest princes in Russia. In 1380 the Prince of Moscow refused to turn over any of the tax money to the Mongols. In the battle that followed the Mongols were defeated. The people of Russia began to look at the princes of Moscow as the leaders of all of Russia. It took another 100 years for the Russians to finally free themselves from the Mongols.

Russia Is United by the Princes of Moscow

After more than 200 years under the Mongols, the Russians were finally able to overthrow their conquerors and become an independent nation once again. By the middle of the 16th century the Moscow princes had succeeded in uniting all the Russian lands under their rule and making Moscow the capital of the country. The Prince of Moscow became known as the *tsar,* or king of Russia. There are several reasons why this happened.

1. The Mongols themselves made this possible by allowing the Princes of Moscow to collect taxes for them. In this way they became the most powerful rulers in Russia.
2. The Russian church also helped the tsar to become all powerful. The Russian people were told by the church that the tsar was chosen by God and the people had to obey him as they would obey God. To disobey or question what the tsar said was considered a sin which was punished by *excommunication,* (being "put out" of the church.) Since the Russian people were very religious and believed in *salvation* (being saved and going to heaven) they were afraid to oppose the tsar.
3. Geography also helps to explain why Moscow became the capital. Moscow is located in the *taiga* (forest) region. The forest served to protect the people against enemy attacks. Moscow is also located where three rivers come together. This made it easy for the people in Moscow to trade and communicate with people in other parts of Russia.
4. Still another reason for the tsar's power was his use of force to get rid of all opposition. Anyone who opposed the tsar or questioned his policies was accused of *treason* (being disloyal to the government) and was tortured and *executed* (put to death). The cruelest tsar was *Ivan the Terrible.* He set up a special security police known as the *Oprichniki.* It was the duty of the police to spy on the people in order to discover who was disloyal. The victims included Ivan's own son, other members of his family, princes, nobles, priests, landowners, common people and even the executioners themselves.

The new Russian state, with Moscow as its capital, was very different from the old Russia of Kievan days. In Kievan Russia there had been some democracy, people were in some ways free to do as they pleased, and the power of the ruler was limited. In the new Russia the people were considered servants of the state and the power of the tsar was unlimited and absolute.

Peter the Great and the Westernization of Russia

1689-1725

Russia and the West

Since the fall of Kiev Russian leaders have been faced with the problem of catching up with the West. By the time Peter became tsar in 1689, Russia was far behind the rest of Europe in industry, science, education and power. Peter thought that if he could westernize Russia, that is, adopt the culture of Western Europe, he would make Russia strong.

First of all Peter decided to see Europe for himself. Together with a group of Russians, Peter spent several months in Holland, England and various German cities. In these countries he studied shipbuilding, navigation, artillery, architecture, engineering, fortification, printing and other subjects. He worked in shipbuilding yards and inspected factories. When he returned to Russia he brought with him hundreds of *technicians* (skilled workers).

Peter Brings Changes to Russia

On his first day back in Moscow, Peter was seen in public in European clothes, with a pair of scissors cutting off the beards of the nobles. Government orders were passed which said that all men and women except the clergy and peasants had to wear German and French styled clothes under threat of fines and cruel punishment.

Peter introduced the European calendar into Russia. The first newspapers appeared. Schools were set up and the first books were printed in arithmetic, geometry, geography, engineering and history.

To make Russia strong, it was also necessary to promote Russian industry. Russia's natural resources were explored, iron mines were opened and an important iron industry was developed. Factories were set up to manufacture military equipment.

The Wars of Peter the Great

To make Russia powerful, Peter thought it was necessary for Russia to control the Baltic Sea and the Black Sea. By controlling these two seas Russia could have access to the outside world. Since the Baltic Sea was controlled by Sweden and the Black Sea was controlled by Turkey, most of Peter's rule was spent fighting these two countries. After many years the Russians defeated the Swedes and received from Sweden territory on the shores of the Baltic Sea. Here Peter began to build a strong navy and a new capital, St. Petersburg, which gave Russia a door to Europe. Architects were brought from Europe and the new capital became a modern European city.

Peter's Policy Affects the Russian People

Peter's wars cost Russia a fortune. To pay for them, the government placed a tax on everything imaginable—mustaches, beards, hats, books, cucumbers, salt, and other things. Most important was the poll tax on all "male souls." This meant that every man had to pay the government a tax just for being alive. Since the *privileged* (rich) classes did not have to pay the poll tax, the poor peasants were left to pay for all the costs.

Peter's methods of bringing about reform were extremely cruel. The tsar did not hesitate to use force to change Russia. Those who suffered most were the poor. Beggars and criminals were rounded up and sent to work in factories where they had to remain permanently. In working on the gigantic public projects, such as the construction of the Baltic fleet and the new capital of St. Petersburg, thousands died from cold, hunger and disease. Russian soldiers, poorly dressed and poorly armed, often went to battle without supplies or pay and died by the thousands. Those who opposed Peter were tortured and executed.

Catherine Continues the Work of Peter

Catherine the Great, who ruled Russia from 1762 to 1796, was a remarkable woman in many ways. Like Peter she had two aims: to bring European culture to Russia and to make Russia powerful. Catherine showed great ability in running the Russian government, but many of her enlightened ideas about *reforming* (changing) Russia were never really put into practice.

Foreign Policy

Catherine's chief claim to fame was in the field of foreign policy. Under her rule the area of Russia increased by 200,000 square miles. Most of her reign, like Peter's, was spent in war against Turkey. Catherine was determined to destroy the Turkish Empire and acquire much of this territory for Russia. As a result of several important victories over the Turks, the Russians won the Crimea and other lands along the Black Sea. Here they built the important port of Odessa. The Russians also won the right of free navigation for their merchant fleet in the Black Sea. In the west, Catherine gained large areas of Poland by agreeing to divide up that country with Austria and Prussia, two European nations.

Influence of the West

Catherine was very much impressed with European culture, especially French culture, which she considered superior to that of Russia. Catherine herself spoke French and German in addition to Russian. Much of her time was spent corresponding with the greatest French writers of the day and exchanging ideas with them on various subjects. She read a great deal about European art, music, literature and political thought and spoke about introducing these ideas into Russia. The French language, French fashions and literature became very popular among Russia's upper classes. The rich invited French tutors to educate their children. Foreign artists and architects were brought to Russia; European authors were translated into Russian. Many valuable works of art were purchased abroad. Russian writers were also encouraged and books were printed. But for the most part, European culture was something reserved for the rich. The rest of the population was hardly affected. Some elementary and high schools were opened in the cities, but nothing was done about spreading education to the villages where most of the Russian people lived.

Catherine believed that Russia should have a constitution and legislative system based on European principles. A commission was appointed to discuss ways of reforming the Russian government, but nothing was accomplished. There were some changes made in local government. However, no real self-government was introduced.

Domestic Policy

New industries were promoted in various ways as well as trade with other countries. But Russia's finances were in a bad state, with budget deficits and debts acquired as a result of Catherine's lavish expenditures. By the end of her reign, Russia had not achieved any real economic advancement.

Catherine's reign has been called the Golden Age of the *nobility* (the upper classes who owned landed estates). Many laws were passed granting the nobility special privileges. They did not have to pay the poll tax. Their right to inherit property was protected. The landlords were given complete authority over their serfs (see section on serfdom).

At the same time, life for the majority of Russian people became worse. Laws were passed prohibiting the serfs from complaining against their landlords and preventing them from leaving their masters. Serfdom was extended to new territories. Catherine refused to consider *emancipating* (freeing) the serfs or even reforming the system to make their lives easier.

Peasants who worked for the state endured great hardships. They were forced to work in mines and factories under terrible conditions and low wages. The poll tax which they had to pay was increased. Their discontent made itself felt in the Peasant War of 1773-1774, when thousands of peasants, led by an ex-soldier named Pugachev, killed their landlords and destroyed their estates. It was only with difficulty that the Russian government succeeded in putting down this rebellion.

Alexander I and the Napoleonic Invasion of 1812

By 1801 when Alexander I became tsar, Russia was already one of the most powerful nations in Europe. During the years 1801-1815 Napoleon, who was the leader of France, tried to conquer the rest of Europe and bring it under his control. Russia and France were very suspicious of each other, and each was afraid the other would become too strong. For some time the two countries were allies in a war against England, but this alliance could not last.

Napoleon's Invasion

On June 24, 1812, Napoleon invaded Russia with a Grand Army of 575,000 men. Napoleon's army was the strongest army in Europe and the Russians were not prepared for war. The Russian tactics, therefore, were to retreat to Moscow, burning and destroying everything that could be of use to the enemy along the way. The Russian army then abandoned Moscow, and when Napoleon entered the city on September 14, he found it deserted.

Napoleon's soldiers began their retreat in October. By the time they left Russia in December all that was left of his Grand Army were 30,000 men. The Russian army now pursued Napoleon into Europe. In March 1814, Alexander entered Paris and Napoleon abdicated (gave up) his throne. Russian troops occupied Paris for three years.

How was Napoleon, one of the world's greatest conquerors, defeated? In the Soviet Union today the view is held that Napoleon was defeated by the courageous Russian people who fought bravely to drive back the enemy. In the West, however, it is believed that geography as well as hunger and disease among Napoleon's soldiers were responsible for his defeat. Alexander, himself, wrote in 1811 that if Napoleon starts a war, "We have vast spaces to which to retreat and we shall preserve a vast organized army . . . We shall leave it to our climate, to our winter to wage our war." As Napoleon went deeper and deeper into Russia, his army started running out of supplies. The food and ammunition were used up and the soldiers suffered from hunger, disease and the cold.

Effects of the Invasion

The war caused much suffering among the Russian people. The destruction brought about by the war as well as the high cost of the war made life much more difficult for the Russian people. Taxes were very high. Compared with the rest of Europe Russia was still backward. Russian courts were corrupt and the prisons crowded. Most of the people were enslaved by a system known as serfdom. Alexander made many promises to bring about changes and reform the Russian government, but nothing was done.

Young Russian officers and soldiers, returning home after several years in the West, suddenly realized the weakness, corruption and lack of freedom in their own country. Demands for change began to be heard more and more frequently. Poets and writers wrote about their longing for freedom. Groups were formed that demanded a constitution, freedom of the press and religion, the right to vote and other things. Some of them even spoke about the need for *revolution* (overthrowing the government) and *regicide* (killing the tsar). The government became more suspicious and watchful and did everything to crush the opposition. This only made the people more opposed to the government.

Russia in the 19th Century

The Security Police

Nicholas I, who became tsar in 1825, was aware of the discontent that existed in Russia. He also knew that he might not remain tsar for very long. Therefore, to prevent any possible revolution, he set up a new, all-powerful security police. The police "had to know what was going on among the people, what were their thoughts, what they talked about . . . it became necessary to penetrate into men's hearts and most secret thoughts." A huge network of secret agents was set up which included men and women from every class of society and even school children. The power of the police was unlimited. Throughout the 19th century thousands of people were arrested, sent to Siberia and some were even executed.

The government was especially suspicious of university students. After an unsuccessful attempt by a former student to murder Tsar Alexander II, the government ordered the police to keep a close watch on all students and prohibited all student activities. The government kept strict control over the curriculum that was taught in school. Subjects such as history and literature were not allowed because students might get revolutionary ideas from them. Teachers who in any way criticized the government were fired. Inspectors visited students at home and checked on them at all times. To make supervision easier students had to wear uniforms, even during their summer vacations.

Censorship

In 19th century Russia no writer could criticize the government. Censorship laws were passed. The purpose of censorship was to examine all books, newspapers, magazines, and pamphlets before they were published. Anything critical was not allowed to be printed. Many newspapers and magazines were prohibited from publishing. Editors and authors who dared to write anything against the government were arrested and sent to Siberia. Many of Russia's greatest writers were affected by these laws.

Bureaucracy

All those people who carried out the decisions of the government—the mayors, governors, judges, inspectors, school officials, and others—were known as the bureaucracy. Russia's 19th century bureaucracy was known for its corruption and inefficiency. Most of these officials hardly had any education and were incapable of making intelligent decisions. They were also corrupt and accepted bribes to get something done. The highest officials in the country were often friends or relatives of the tsar and in many cases they lacked the education or experience to do their job well. Decisions made by the tsar and his ministers were often not carried out for years. Money set aside for public projects such as schools, roads and hospitals found its way into the pockets of these officials. These people lived well, dressed in the most expensive clothes, ate and drank the best foods and wines, gave magnificent balls, and did not care that Russia was backward and its people were suffering.

The Peasantry— Serfdom and After

How Serfdom Began

Until 1861 Russia's *peasants* (small farmers or farm laborers) were enslaved by a system known as serfdom. Although not slaves in name, the serfs were often not better off than slaves in fact. Hundreds of years earlier the serfs had been independent farmers, but for various reasons their land had been taken over by powerful landlords. These landlords were princes, nobles, the church or even the Russian government itself. At first, the peasants were considered tenants and had to pay rent to their landlords. Sometimes they paid the landlords by giving them part of their crops, other times the tenants had to spend part of their time working on the land belonging to the landlord. Originally the tenants were free men who could leave the landlord at any time. Often, however, the peasants found themselves in difficult situations and had to borrow money from the landlords. Sometimes they were unable to pay it back. According to law, no peasant could leave his landlord until his debts were paid. Finally laws were passed which prohibited the peasants from leaving their landlords altogether. The peasant was now considered a serf, tied to the land and bound to his master. Since the system was hereditary, his children and grandchildren became serfs too.

Life Under Serfdom

The life of the Russian serf was very hard. The landlord had the right to sell his serfs, with or without their families, or just give them away. The landlord could force his serfs to become cooks, stableboys, tailors, bootmakers and carpenters. He could force a serf to join the army, he could beat him, send him to jail or deport him to Siberia. If a serf ran away and was found, the landlord himself decided the punishment. Under the law, serfs could not bring complaints against their landlords, nor were the landlords punished if they caused the death of their serfs.

The only way out for the serf was to flee. From the 16th to the 19th century thousands of serfs fled to the Urals, Siberia, Poland and the Caucasus. If the peasants were caught they would be severely punished. Peasant uprisings were frequent also. During the uprisings the peasants would murder their masters and set fire to their estates.

The Emancipation

By the beginning of the 19th century Russians began to talk about emancipation. It was not until 1861, however, that Alexander II, known as the Tsar-Liberator, emancipated the serfs. Alexander was only partly interested in the well-being of the serfs. He was more concerned with Russia's weaknesses and backward state, which he considered to be the result of serfdom. Alexander was also afraid of a peasant revolution. "It is better to abolish bondage (serfdom) from above than to wait for the time when it will begin to abolish itself spontaneously from below," he told the nobles.

Effects of the Emancipation

The serfs became free, but life was as hard as it had been before. According to the law, the peasants were supposed to be given an "adequate" amount of land. But the law did not state what was meant by "adequate", so that in many cases the peasant ended up with less land than before the emancipation. In addition, the peasants had to pay the landlords to acquire the land and the charges were usually very high. There were taxes to be paid to the government, including the poll tax. Debts piled up which the peasants found themselves unable to pay. The standard of living of the Russian peasantry was exceedingly low, with barely enough food remaining to feed one's family.

Throughout Russia in the late 19th and early 20th century, peasants began to revolt. The only solution seemed to be for the peasants to take over all the land belonging to the government and the nobility. The government took steps to help the peasants, such as, abolishing payments for the land and giving loans to the peasants. But the peasants wanted all the land to be given to them. The Communists, led by Lenin, were the only ones who understood this, and their promise to turn over all the land to the peasants contributed to their victory in 1917.

The Revolutionary Movement

The Revolutionaries

As the years passed more and more people came to believe that the only way to achieve a just and democratic society in Russia was to overthrow the government. The Russian revolutionaries of the 19th century were mainly young people, many of them in their twenties. They came from wealthy families and they were well educated. Yet they were willing to give up their comfortable lives and risk all kinds of hardships and even death in order to overthrow the tsar.

The Russian revolutionaries were greatly influenced by Western European ideas of democracy and equality. As a matter of fact, many of the revolutionaries spent a good part of their lives in exile in Europe in order to escape arrest by the Russian police. Here they printed newspapers and pamphlets describing the terrible conditions in Russia and demanding changes. The newspapers were smuggled into Russia. After some years, however, it became obvious that writing articles was not enough to overthrow the government. New ways had to be found.

The Populists

By the **1870s** most of the revolutionaries belonged to a group known as the *Populists*. These people believed that the peasants would be the ones to carry out the revolution. Their task, therefore, was to educate and organize the peasants for revolution. Thousands of Populists went to the villages, factories and schools to spread their ideas among the people. However, despite the hardships which they suffered, the peasants were not yet ready to rise up in revolt. They were too busy worrying about their harvest and trying to feed their families to think about revolution. In fact, most of the peasants were suspicious of the Populists and even helped the police round up and arrest the revolutionaries.

Land and Freedom

Most of the revolutionaries found themselves in jail. Those who escaped arrest realized that the people were not yet ready for revolution. Many then turned to political terror. They joined together in a secret society called *Land and Freedom* and made plans to assassinate the tsar and other important government officials. Bombs and ammunition were manufactured secretly and mines were placed in strategic locations. Many attempts were made on Tsar Alexander II's life and he was finally killed by a bomb in 1881. Hundreds of other government officials lost their lives.

The Failure of the Early Revolutionaries

But assassination did not bring the revolution any nearer. Alexander II was replaced by his son Alexander III, who was more undemocratic than some of the previous tsars. The secret police became even more powerful. Life in Russia became worse, not better.

Again the revolutionaries were mostly in jail or in exile. Bitterly disappointed with their failures, they began searching for a new plan that would bring success. Many of them turned to the ideas of Karl Marx, a great German thinker, as a possible answer. At the same time, the revolutionaries began to think that if they organized a party of dedicated, disciplined men, the party itself would overthrow the government.

The Russian Revolution of 1905

Causes of the Revolution

The years between 1890 and 1905 were very difficult ones for the Russian people. The famine of 1891-1892 and the crop failures of 1897, 1898 and 1901 caused great suffering among the peasants. The workers in the city were not much better off. Working conditions remained poor and wages were very low. In the 1890's workers all over Russia began going out on strikes. Student demonstrations became more frequent and most students became revolutionaries. Political assassinations continued to take the lives of many government officials.

To make matters even worse, in 1904 Russia went to war against Japan. Since the Russians were completely unprepared for this war, the Japanese were able to defeat them within a short time. The Russian people were shocked and humiliated. They felt that something must be very wrong with Russia if a small Asian country like Japan could beat them so easily.

Bloody Sunday

In January 1905 a strike broke out in St. Petersburg which rapidly spread to other parts of the country. On Sunday January 9, 1905, thousands of workers, carrying petitions and led by a priest, marched to the tsar's palace. Although the workers were orderly, government troops were ordered to fire on them and 130 were killed and several hundred were injured. This day became known as "Bloody Sunday" and for the next ten months there were riots and strikes all over Russia. By October, the situation had become so bad that banks, shops, schools, courts and government offices had to close down.

The Reforms of 1905

Tsar Nicholas II realized he would not remain tsar for very long unless he gave in to some of the demands of the people. Nicholas promised the Russian people their first constitution. There was to be freedom of assembly and freedom of the press. The tsar also agreed to set up a legislature (called a Duma) that was to approve laws proposed by the tsar.

Nicholas had been forced by events into making these promises. He was not at all sincere and within a few years all of the promises were broken. The freedoms which had been guaranteed were not carried out. Every time a Duma was elected whose members did not agree with the tsar, Nicholas simply closed the Duma and prevented it from meeting. Students and workers began to demonstrate again. Revolutionaries found themselves once more in jail or in Siberia.

Revolution did not break out at this time because the government did make attempts to improve the situation of the peasants. More land was given to the peasants

Lenin—father of the Communist Revolution. Statues and pictures of Lenin
are found throughout the Soviet Union. Credit: *Soviet Mission to the United Nations*

and better prices were paid to them for their crops. The payments which they had been required to pay for the land were ended. It would take another great blow for the peasants to rise up and revolt against the government.

World War I and the Revolution of March 1917

Russia in the World War

In 1914, Russia found itself involved in war on the side of Britain and France against Austria and Germany. For this war Russia was unprepared both militarily and economically. In the beginning most people supported the government's war effort. In a short time, however, discontent became widespread as the war added to the suffering of the Russian people. Everywhere there were food shortages; the price of food was four times as much as it had been before the war; wages declined. At the front there were shortages of ammunition, poor leadership, military retreats and great losses of men. The Russian government was completely incapable of dealing with the situation. In August 1915, Tsar Nicholas II decided that he would personally lead his army into battle. He left control of the government in the hands of his wife who was under the influence of Rasputin, a drunken, ignorant peasant. Everyone saw doom approaching. The peasants never understood the purpose of the war. There were mass surrenders to the enemy. Officers were afraid of being shot by their own men.

The March Revolution

In February 1917, disappointed housewives waiting in front of food shops in Petrograd (St. Petersburg) began to riot upon finding out that food was not available. In the following days more people joined the rioters and the violence increased. The tsar sent troops to fire on the people, but this time the troops went over to the side of the people. On March 2, Nicholas *abdicated*. The revolution had been carried out by the soldiers and people of the capital with the rest of the country accepting it.

The Provisional Government

For the first time in hundreds of years Russia was without a government. Therefore the Duma set up a Provisional (temporary) Government to maintain order and carry on the war. At the same time, soviets began to appear all over the country. In Russian, "soviet" means council. The soviets were councils made up of workers, soldiers and revolutionaries and had great power because the people supported the soviets more than the Provisional Government. The government was determined to continue the war. But the army wanted to go home and the people demanded peace. The Bolsheviks (Communists) who had great power in the soviets were also calling for an end to the war. As the months passed the Provisional Government lost the support of the Russian people.

Marx, Lenin and the Russian Revolution of November 1917

Life in 19th-Century Europe

In the 19th century Europe was in the midst of the Industrial Revolution. Most goods were no longer being made at home by hand, but were manufactured in factories by machines. People who owned factories and mines became very wealthy. The workers, on the other hand, were very poor because they received very low wages. In addition, the conditions under which they worked were very bad. Factories were dirty and not ventilated. Most workers worked twelve hours a day and some as many as eighteen hours a day.

If an accident occurred in the factory and the worker was injured or died he and his family would receive no compensation. Small children, often as young as six years of age, spent long hours working in the factory. Sometimes they slept on wooden benches or on the floor of the factory so as to be ready for work early in the morning. The workers and their families were crowded together in the poorest sections of the city.

Marxism—The Philosophy of Karl Marx

Karl Marx was a German thinker who looked around and saw all this misery. Marx believed that things could not go on as they were. In 1848 he wrote a small pamphlet called "Manifesto of the Communist Party" in which he outlined his ideas.

Marx believed that since the beginning of history people have always been divided into two classes. Sometimes they were called freeman and slave; sometimes lord and serf; but one was rich and the other poor. The two classes have always fought with each other and that is why Marx says that all history is the history of *class struggles*. The two classes of the 19th century Marx called *bourgeoisie* and *proletariat*. The bourgeoisie are the people who own the factories and the *capital*. They are the employers or the bosses. The proletariat are the workers. The bourgeoisie have become richer and richer until they finally are so powerful that they control the government. Their only interest is in making more money, and they use the proletariat for this purpose.

Masses of workers are crowded into factories; their work is monotonous. As soon as they receive their wages the landlord, the shopkeeper and the pawnbroker are after them for money. With the development of industry the proletariat increases in number, its strength grows and it feels that strength more. The workers form unions against the bourgeoisie. More and more collisions take place. The workers will rise up and overthrow the bourgeoisie. The victory of the proletariat is *inevitable* (has to happen).

Marx says that the interests of the Communists are the same as the interests of the workers. Their aim is to: organize the workers, overthrow the bourgeoisie, and take over the government by the workers.

The Communists are opposed to all private property. Once the working people are in power they will not allow private individuals to own farms, factories, mines, or banks. Everything will belong to all the workers together and will be run by the government. In time, a classless, stateless society will come into being in which people will be guided by the following principle: "From each according to his ability, to each according to his needs."

Differences Between Marx and Lenin

Nikolai Lenin is considered the father of the present Communist state in Russia. Born into a middle class family, Lenin at an early age became involved in revolutionary activity. His eldest brother was hanged for his part in the attempt to assassinate Tsar Alexander III, and the young Lenin was expelled from the university for his political activities. Later arrested and exiled to Siberia, Lenin emigrated to Europe where he remained until the eve of the Revolution.

Lenin was a faithful follower of Karl Marx, but, nevertheless, he made some important changes in Marx's ideas. Marx believed that revolution and the victory of the proletariat were inevitable. Lenin said that this was not necessarily true. If you want a communist revolution, said Lenin, you must have a group of organized, dedicated revolutionaries who would seize power (overthrow the government). Marx believed that in time the state (government) would "wither away" (disappear). Lenin and his followers made the Russian government more powerful than it had ever been.

Lenin and the November Revolution

Lenin was an excellent speaker and he was able to win people over to his side. The Provisional Government was having great difficulty because of its determination to continue the war and because it did nothing to help the peasants. Lenin's slogan "Peace, Land and Bread" won him the support of many. "Peace" appealed to the soldiers who were fed up with the war and wanted to go home. "Land" appealed to the peasants, and "Bread" won over most of the workers in the cities who were experiencing food shortages.

Most of the members of the Bolshevik (Communist) Party did not think that Russia was ready for a Communist revolution. But Lenin insisted that the Communists must seize power immediately. On November 7, 1917, armed groups of Bolsheviks occupied most of the government buildings and arrested the members of the Provisional Government. In less than 24 hours the Communists had succeeded in taking over the government.

Opposition Crushed

However, millions of people in Russia did not support the Communists. Soon after the revolution an election took place in which the Communists were defeated. But Lenin would not give up his power and sent his troops to prevent the elected representatives from meeting. Thousands of Russians fled the country. Many thousands more took up arms to fight. A bloody civil war broke out in 1918 and lasted for two years. Those who supported the Communists were known as Reds, while those who fought against them were known as Whites. At the same time England, France, Japan and the United States sent troops into Siberia to protect war supplies and to prevent the spread of Communist control to the Pacific Ocean.

The New Communist Government

The Communists were able to win for several reasons. First, the anti-Communist forces were divided among themselves and fought only half-heartedly. Second, Communist troops were organized, and led by the brilliant Leon Trotsky were able to defeat their enemies.

In order to keep the Communists in power, Lenin set up a new secret police. The *Cheka*, as it was called, was more efficient and more cruel than the tsar's secret police had ever been. Many people were executed by the police, including the tsar and his family. Once again newspapers and books were censored and opposition was prohibited.

The new Communist government called itself a dictatorship of the working class. By this they wanted people to believe that the workers were the rulers of the new society. In reality, it was a dictatorship of the small Communist Party headed by Lenin. The Communists made the official name of the country the Union of Soviet Socialist Republics and moved the capital to Moscow.

In 1924 Lenin died. He had succeeded in setting up a Communist government and setting Russia on the road to a Communist society.

Russia Under Stalin

Joseph Stalin

Joseph Stalin, the man who ruled the Soviet Union from 1924 until 1953, can be given credit for turning the USSR into the great power it is today. Stalin's real name was Joseph Djugashvilli, but he took the name Stalin which means "man of steel." Stalin was indeed a man of steel. He came from a poor family. (His father had been born a serf.) Stalin was not even Russian, but came from Georgia, a province ruled by Russia since the 19th century. As a young man, Stalin had been active in the revolutionary movement and had been arrested several times and sent to Siberia. Stalin was a very hard and cruel man. People were afraid of his violent temper, and Lenin before his death had warned that it would be dangerous for Stalin to have too much power. But Stalin was very clever and succeeded in gaining control of the government.

The Five-Year Plans

In 1928 Stalin began his program to end Russia's backwardness. He set up a Five-Year Plan which was aimed at turning the Soviet Union into a powerful industrial nation in ten years. The Plan had two parts: (1) to develop the industries of the USSR, and (2) to turn the land farmed by the peasants into great collective farms.

In order to industrialize the Soviet Union it was necessary to build factories, dams, power plants, railroads, and highways. Since the government did not have enough to pay the workers and the work was long and difficult, people were unwilling to work on the new projects. Forced labor was introduced and people were rounded up and made to work. Stalin said, "He who does not work does not eat." Workers who did not do their jobs properly were imprisoned and put to death.

To build up Russian industry, money was needed to buy machines abroad and also to pay engineers from other countries to teach the Russians how to use the machines. The only way Russia could get money for these purposes was by selling its crops abroad. But the Soviet Government did not have the money to pay the peasants for their crops and the peasants were unwilling to sell to the government. Therefore, in 1928, under Stalin's orders, the Soviet government took over all the land belonging to the peasants and forced them to work in huge farms that were run by the government. These were known as *collective farms*. The peasants had always wanted to own land and so they resisted. Stalin sent troops to force the peasants into the collectives. The peasants fought back, slaughtered their cows and horses and left their land untilled. The result was famine. It is believed that at least a million and a half people starved to death. Hundreds of thousands of others were sent to Siberia and many were executed.

The Purges

How was Stalin able to remain in power when the Russian people were suffering so much? One reason was that the Red Army remained loyal to him. Troops were well fed and soldiers received many promotions. Another reason was that Stalin's secret police, the NKVD, arrested and executed anyone who opposed Stalin. Between 1936 and 1938 Stalin carried out his purges. He ordered the execution of all those accused of being disloyal to him. Outstanding members of the Communist Party, army leaders, members of the government and industry were brought before the

Textile mill. Highly automated Soviet textile factory.
Note the limited number of workers. Credit: *Intourist*

public in great show trials. These men, who were accused of spying and treason, were forced by torture to confess to their crimes and were shot. In addition, many of the friends, relatives and co-workers of the accused were also eliminated.

Results of Stalin's Program

But perhaps the most important reason for Stalin's triumph was that he held out the hope of a better future to the Russian people. Stalin's industrialization cost Russia a vast amount in loss of personal freedom and human life. But his achievements were tremendous. Stalin declared that the USSR must accomplish in ten years what it had taken other nations a hundred years to do. Otherwise the Soviet Union would be crushed. In that decade (1928-1938) he pushed the Russian people forward into the modern age. Stalin created an industrial giant. He also carried out Marx's main goal; taking industry and agriculture away from private owners and having both owned and run by the government.

The Soviet Economy

Before the Revolution of 1917, Russia was a relatively weak agricultural nation. Today the Soviet Union is a powerful industrial nation, second only to the United States. The goals that Soviet leaders have set are: to increase Soviet military and economic strength so that the USSR can surpass the United States, and to improve the standard of living of the Soviet people.

With regard to mineral wealth, the Soviet Union is probably the richest country in the world. Some of the world's largest deposits of coal, iron, oil, copper, lead, and bauxite are found here. Diamonds, gold and other important minerals are mined. This wealth contributed greatly to industrialization.

INDUSTRIAL GROWTH IN THE SOVIET UNION

Item [Millions of Tons]	1913	1928	1950	1959	1969	1975
STEEL	4.2	4.3	27.3	59.9	100.3	141.1
IRON ORE	9.2	6.1	39.7	94.4	98.0	238.8
COAL	29.1	35.5	261.1	506.5	571.6	696.1
PETROLEUM	9.2	11.6	37.9	129.5	148.5	300.1
ELECTRIC POWER (billions kw. hrs.)	1.9	5.0	91.2	264.0	545.0	1015.0

What does the chart tell us about industrial growth in the Soviet Union since 1913?

Government Ownership

The Soviet economy is totally different from the American economy. The American economy is owned and run by private individuals. The Soviet economy is owned and run by the government. The Soviet Government owns all the natural resources of the country. It owns and operates the banks, mines, railroads, factories, farms, stores, housing, restaurants, newspapers, and communications. Legal private business is very limited in the USSR. A person may set himself up as a shoemaker, a repair man or a plumber and work at these trades alone, but he may not hire another person to work for him so that he can make a profit because that is illegal. A Soviet citizen may not buy goods and sell them at a profit.

Central Planning

The Soviet government decides what will be produced and in what quantity. There is a State Planning Commission (Gosplan) which is made up of a group of experts who receive information from all over the country. With this information it draws up a Five-Year Plan which determines in advance such matters as: how much shall be produced of different kinds of goods (how many dresses, shoes, machines, planes to produce), what factories shall be built and where, how many workers shall be employed in different factories, what prices shall be charged for different goods, what wages shall be paid. In the United States all these decisions are made by the individual owners and managers of the industry. Recently, however, there have been various attempts to reform the Soviet economy and managers of plants and factories are being given greater responsibility for deciding what types of goods to produce and how to produce them.

Capital Goods versus Consumer Goods

The aim of Soviet economic planning has always been to turn the USSR into a powerful industrialized nation. Therefore, Soviet planners have concentrated on goods that will make the country strong, such as dams, power plants, railroads, steel mills, factories, machinery, tanks, planes, hydrogen bombs. These are known as *capital goods*. Little emphasis has been placed on producing things that the people can enjoy such as clothing, housing, televisions, washing machines, and automobiles. These things are known as *consumer goods*. In the United States 70% of our production is consumer goods and 30% capital goods. In the Soviet Union it has been the opposite—30% consumer goods and 70% capital (heavy) goods.

However, now that the Soviet Union has achieved great power it is possible to pay greater attention to the consumer. Soviet leaders have been promising to improve both the quantity and quality of consumer goods and factories have been turning out more of these products in the last few years. But the USSR still has a very long way to go before it can come anywhere near the United States in the production of these articles.

Soviet Workers

Almost everyone in the Soviet Union works for the government. Workers are paid according to their skills, and the amount of work they do. A worker is given a quota, that is, a certain amount of work that has to be done. Those workers who do more than their quota receive rewards in the form of better housing, higher wages, and special vacations. Soviet workers have unions but they are not allowed to strike. This means that they have no choice but to accept the wages set by the government. In the late 1960s as part of the economic reforms, the word "profit" began to be heard more often than "quota." If the manager of a factory can increase his production and sell these goods he can make a profit which he will share with the workers. It is hoped that this will encourage the workers to work harder and produce more goods.

Collectivization of Agriculture

Soviet agriculture is organized into collective farms (kolkhoz) and state farms. A collective farm is made up of about 500 families who cultivate about 15,000 acres of land. The farm machinery and farm animals are owned collectively by all. The farmers divide the jobs among themselves on the basis of skills and abilities. Some do the planting, others are dairymen, and still others serve as mechanics and book-keepers. The government determines what crops should be raised, the amount to be produced, the amount that must be sold to the government, and the price for the crops. If the collective farm produces more than the quota, it is permitted to sell the remainder on the open market. Some of this income is set aside for new buildings, for purchasing farm machinery, and other expenses. The rest is divided among the farmers, on the basis of the work they do.

Each family on a collective farm is allowed to own a small garden in which it can plant whatever it wishes. The family can also own a cow, several pigs or sheep, and an unlimited number of chickens. Whatever he produces in his garden the farmer can sell for a profit.

The state farms are much larger than the collective farms. They are owned and operated by the government in much the same way as factories. Workers are paid a regular wage by the government.

Problems of Soviet Agriculture

Compared with industry, agricultural achievements have been poor, if not an outright failure. Agricultural production has fallen below the quotas set for it and there have often been food shortages. There are several reasons for these failings.

1. Much of the Soviet Union is not suitable for agriculture. In most of the country it is too cold or too dry for farming. Large areas have soil that is not suitable for raising good crops.
2. Soviet farming is not as efficient as it should be. There are shortages of tractors and other farm machinery, and insufficient quantities of fertilizer. Many peasants use old methods and do not want to modernize.
3. The collective farmer has very little desire to work hard and grow large amounts of crops because he does not own the land. He spends every moment he can

Subway in Baku. Subways in the Soviet Union are modern, clean and often beautiful.
The fare costs very little, making it easy for Soviet citizens to move around easily. (*Top*)

Health resort for workers in Yalta. The Soviet government has turned the tsarist palaces
in the Crimea into health resorts for Soviet citizens. (*Bottom*) Credit: *Intourist*

in his private garden because he can sell whatever he produces and keep the money. In fact, it is estimated that these small plots of land, which are less than 5% of the total cultivated area, produce 40% of the meat and milk, 60% of the potatoes, and 66% of the eggs in the whole country.

4. The Soviet government emphasizes industry over agriculture. Therefore, the government has not set aside enough money to develop agriculture fully.

The Soviet government has taken a number of steps to improve the situation. More chemicals and farm machinery are being produced. Scientific research is sponsored in order to find better farming methods. There are special programs to teach farmers the basics of scientific agriculture. Farmers have been guaranteed a minimum monthly wage, which has meant a large increase over what they had formerly earned. Soviet leaders hope that these measures will make it possible for the farmers to produce all the food needed by the Soviet people.

In 1975, the Soviet Union again experienced a bad harvest and resulting grain shortages. Thus the USSR found itself purchasing large amounts of grain from the United States, Canada and Australia. It was estimated by American experts that the Soviet harvest was at least 40 million tons below the Soviet target of 215.7 million tons. Part of the reason for the bad harvest was drought. But part of it was due to the inefficiency of the harvesting operation and the lack of enough mowers, combines, trucks and spare parts. An indication of the seriousness of the situation can be seen in the posters that are hung in many Moscow bakeries encouraging Soviet consumers to save bread: "Bread is our wealth. Save it." "Don't buy more bread than is necessary. Use stale bread for cooking." Feed is also in short supply. There has been some evidence that cattle was being butchered because of a lack of feed. To alleviate this situation, the Soviet Union in October 1975, concluded a five-year agreement with the United States to purchase between 6 and 8 million tons of American grain a year.

Soviet Economy in the Seventies

The most serious economic problem for most countries in the world is the energy crisis. The Soviet government has said that the Soviets have no such problem. In 1974, oil and natural gas production was increased through the use of the new Tyumen oil fields in Siberia. However, in late 1974 and into 1975 the Soviet government began to encourage the people to *conserve* (save) fuel. The official Communist newspaper *Pravda* (Truth) warned that every kilogram of fuel must be treated carefully.

Industrial development in the Soviet Union has been continuing through the early years of the 1970s according to plan. According to reports issued by the Soviet Economic Planning Council, industrial production and the productivity of the workers were at the highest in the history of the Soviet Union.

Standard of Living, Health and Welfare of the Soviet People

The Soviet Union has demonstrated its power to the world in recent years. It has exploded some of the most powerful bombs. Its sputnik, launched in 1957, was the first man-made satellite to orbit the earth. It has sent several rockets to the moon. Nevertheless, it has a standard of living that is lower than that of the United States, Canada, and many countries of Western Europe.

WORKTIME REQUIRED TO BUY SELECTED GOODS IN MOSCOW AND NEW YORK CITY (1966)

| | 1966 Worktime | | | |
| Commodity | New York City | | Moscow | |
	Hours	Minutes	Hours	Minutes
SUGAR (1 POUND)		3 M		47 M
TEA (1 OUNCE)		2 M		22 M
DRESS (RAYON)	5 H		49 H	
STOCKINGS (NYLON)		31 M	5 H	
BUTTER (1 POUND)		17 M		163 M
SOAP (1 BAR)		3 M		21 M
MEN'S SUIT (WOOLEN)	23 H	36 M	183 H	
EGGS (1 DOZEN)		14 M		108 M
MEN'S SHIRT (COTTON)	1 H	42 M	13 H	
WOMEN'S SHOES (LEATHER)	5 H	30 M	38 H	
MEN'S SHOES (LEATHER)	6 H	36 M	41 H	
MILK (1 QUART)		6 M		28 M
BREAD (1 POUND)		6 M		23 M
BEEF (1 POUND)		20 M		73 M
CIGARETTES (1 PACK)		8 M		20 M

Moscow worktime figures were computed on the basis of estimated average gross earning per hour of Moscow manufacturing workers and prices in state stores as reported in the Soviet press. New York City worktime figures were computed from Bureau of Labor Statistics survey of per hour earnings of production workers in manufacturing in New York City and retail prices.

Source: National Conference Board Inc. #1555

Consumer Goods Shortage

Life in the Soviet Union is not easy. Because of the housing shortage, many people have only one room for themselves and their families. Kitchens and bathrooms have to be shared with several other families on the floor. New apartment buildings are going up all over the country, but not fast enough. Rent is very low, however.

Most people have enough clothing to keep warm, but clothing is drab, poorly made and not stylish. Clothing is also much more expensive in the Soviet Union than in the United States. So many things which Americans take for granted—cars, refrigerators, television sets and many other items—are difficult to obtain.

AVAILABILITY OF CONSUMER GOODS AND SERVICES — USA AND USSR*

Consumer Goods	USA (population: 213 million)	USSR (population: 257 million)
Automobiles (per 100 persons)	31	5
Televisions (per 100 persons)	50	27
Doctors (per 10,000 persons)	16.7	31.5

*Data as of 1977.
Source: *USSR Facts and Figures Annual.*

In September 1971, the Soviet publication *Literaturnaya Gazeta* published statistics concerning automobile production and ownership in the Soviet Union. In Moscow, a city with a population of seven million people, total private car ownership was given as 110,000. In Leningrad, the second largest city with a population of four million, 82,000 people owned cars. Total private car ownership in the Soviet Union as a whole, with a population of 240 million was given as "more than 1.5 million."

Health Care and Pensions

And yet not many countries in the world provide for the health and welfare of their citizens the way the Soviet Union does. No Soviet citizen has to worry about paying hospital bills or supporting himself in old age.

Medical treatment for Soviet citizens is supplied by the government and is free to all. The Soviet Union spends large amounts of money on hospitals and clinics. Health resorts located near the Black Sea are available free of charge to all who need them. There are more doctors for every thousand people in the USSR than in any country in the world.

Men over 60 and women over 55 who have worked a certain number of years are eligible for old age pensions. The person receives approximately $40 to $50 a month and can live modestly after retirement.

Regardless of the difficulties, life in the Soviet Union is improving. More houses are being built, and more consumer goods are being produced. Soviet citizens are hopeful about the future.

The Soviet Government

On the surface the political system of the Soviet Union resembles that of the United States. Both countries have constitutions. Both have periodic elections. In the U.S. there is a congress made up of two houses. In the Soviet Union the legislature is called the Supreme Soviet and it also has two houses. In both countries there are supreme courts that interpret the law, judges who enforce the law, and police who keep order.

The Role of the Communist Party

But if we look underneath the surface we find the two countries quite different. The chief difference is that there is only one political party in the Soviet Union, the Communist Party, and this party completely controls the country and the people. How is the Party able to do this? The most important positions in the armed forces, police, courts, government, news media and educational institutions are held by Communists. Thus the government really does not run the country but the Party does, because top Communists hold key posts in the government as well as in the Party. This is shown on the chart on the next page. The Supreme Soviet, the law-making body of the USSR, is nothing more than a "rubber stamp." It meets only a few weeks each year and approves automatically what has already been decided by the Party. The top man in the Soviet Union is the Secretary of the Party, not the President who heads the government. All important decisions are made by the Party, such as: what is taught in school, what is said in the newspapers, on radio or TV, what kind of goods are manufactured, and what policy the USSR should follow in its relations with other nations. Even the army and secret police are controlled by the Party.

The Communist Party of the Soviet Union is quite small. Of a total population of almost 240 million people only about 12 million are members of the Communist Party. This is about 5% of the people. The Party is kept small deliberately, in order to be sure of a hard-working and completely dependable membership. The most able and ambitious people generally join the Party because one must belong to the party to rise to the top. A Party member must work hard and be disciplined. This means that he must support all decisions made by the top leaders without question. This is called "following the Party line."

Elections

The Soviet government has elections every four years in which all citizens over the age of 18 are allowed to vote. When the person reaches the voting place, he is handed a ballot on which there is only one candidate running for each office. The candidate is either a Communist or he has been selected or approved by the Communists. To cast his ballot the citizen simply has to put the ballot into a box that is out in the open. If he does not wish to vote for the official candidate he has to go to a secret polling booth and write in the name of another candidate. It is little wonder then that in all Soviet elections the Communist Party candidate receives over 99% of the votes.

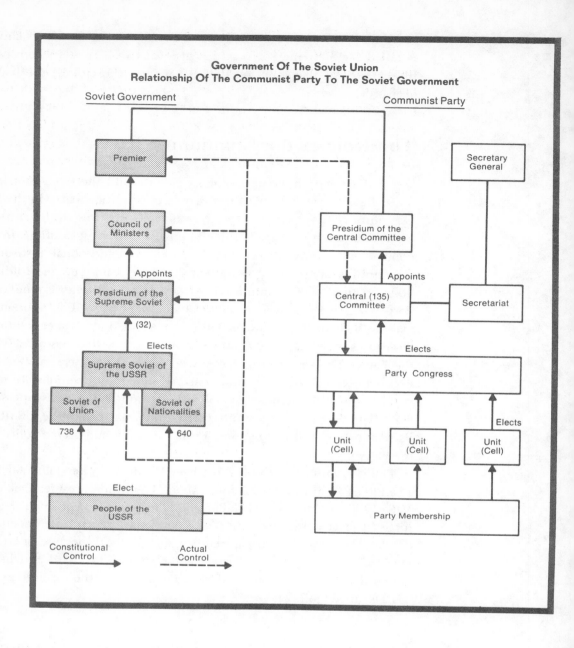

Government Of The Soviet Union
Relationship Of The Communist Party To The Soviet Government

Soviet Government

Communist Party

Premier

Council of Ministers

Appoints

Presidium of the Supreme Soviet

(32)

Elects

Supreme Soviet of the USSR

Soviet of Union

Soviet of Nationalities

738

640

Elect

People of the USSR

Secretary General

Presidium of the Central Committee

Appoints

Central (135) Committee

Secretariat

Elects

Party Congress

Elects

Unit (Cell)

Unit (Cell)

Unit (Cell)

Party Membership

Constitutional Control

Actual Control

Cultural Life in the Soviet Union

Education

The Soviet Union places great emphasis on education. When the Communists came to power most of the people in Russia were illiterate and very few had gone to the university. Today illiteracy has almost been wiped out and every year thousands of students graduate from universities.

Soviet leaders spend tremendous amounts of money on education. The aim of Soviet education is twofold: (1) to educate enough engineers, scientists, and technicians to make the country powerful and (2) to train people in Communism. Lenin once said, "Without education there is no knowledge, and without knowledge there is no Communism." Soviet schools try to make good Communists of students. All students must attend classes in the study of Communism. They are taught that Communism is the best system created by man. Textbooks and curricula are controlled by the Party. In all schools there are portraits and statues of Lenin and other Soviet leaders. Students are taught to be patriotic—to love their country and be loyal to it.

All Soviet children are required by law to go to school for eight years. For the most part, Soviet students work harder than American students. A Soviet child goes to school six days a week; his homework and examinations are more difficult than in the United States. Much time is devoted to the study of science and mathematics. After finishing eight years of school, a student may go on to a technical or vocational high school or take a special course preparing him for the university. Education in the USSR is free. In addition, university students who receive good grades are given financial support by the government. However, only the best students go on to college, since they are required to pass a difficult examination in order to be admitted.

Women are given the same educational opportunities as men. Seventy-five percent of all the doctors, 30% of the engineers and 50% of the economists are women.

Education continues after school hours. Practically all children belong to some organization of the Communist Party where recreation is combined with education. Children up to the age of 10 belong to a group known as the *Octobrists*. Between the ages of 10 and 15 a child belongs to the *Pioneers*. Clubs for Pioneers have sports stadiums, gardens, lakes, theaters, a planetarium. Here a child can play soccer, tennis, join the orchestra, learn ballet, engage in stamp collecting or photography. At the same time the young Pioneer is taught to be a good Communist. Upon becoming a member he must pledge "to love our Soviet motherland and to live and learn as the great Lenin told us and as the Communist Party teaches us." Between the ages of 15 and 27 young people belong to the *Komsomol* (Young Communist League).

Literature and the Arts

In the 19th century Russia produced some of the greatest writers of all time. Their novels, poems and plays are considered masterpieces of world literature. Again in the Soviet period the Russians have made important contributions to the world in the form of literature, music, ballet and films.

SELECTED RUSSIAN AND SOVIET AUTHORS

AUTHOR	BORN	DIED	SELECTED WORKS
Alexander Pushkin	1799	1837	Eugene Onegin, Boris Gudonov, The Captain's Daughter
Mikhail Lermontov	1814	1841	A Hero of Our Time
Nikolai Gogol	1809	1852	Dead Souls, Taras Bulba, The Inspector General, The Overcoat

(continued)

AUTHOR	BORN	DIED	SELECTED WORKS
Ivan Turgenev	1818	1883	Fathers and Sons, First Love, Smoke, On the Eve, The Diary of a Superfluous Man, The Hunting Sketches
Fyodor Dostoyevsky	1821	1881	The Brothers Karamazov, The Idiot, Crime and Punishment, The Possessed, Notes from the Underground
Leo Tolstoy	1828	1910	Resurrection, War and Peace, Anna Karenina, The Death of Ivan Ilych, The Cossacks, What is Art?, The Power of Darkness
Anton Chekov	1860	1904	The Cherry Orchard, The Sea Gull, Three Sisters, Uncle Vanya
Maxim Gorky	1868	1936	Mother, My Childhood, The Lower Depths, Among the People
Boris Pasternak	1890	1960	The Proud Beggar, Troubled Days, Dr. Zhivago
Mikhail Sholokhov	1905		The Fate of a Man, Virgin Soil Upturned, And Quiet Flows the Don
Alexander Solzhenitsyn	1918		One Day in the Life of Ivan Denisovich, The First Circle, Cancer Ward, August 1914
Yevgeny Yevtushenko	1933		Poems of Several Years, The Apple, Babi Yar

However, the arts like every other aspect of Soviet life are strictly controlled by the Communist Party. Soviet writers and artists are expected to use their talents to further the goals of Communism and to glorify the USSR. According to the Soviet government the purpose of art and literature is not to express the innermost feelings of the artist and writer as it is in Western society, but to show that life under Communism is beautiful. Since all the publishing houses are controlled by the Party, every book or article must be approved by the censors before it can be published. Some Soviet writers have discovered ways of avoiding government control. Their manuscripts have been taken out of the country and published abroad. Others do not have their works published at all, but type up several copies and circulate them among their friends, who in turn make other copies and distribute them.

In recent years three Soviet writers have received the Nobel Prize for literature. Boris Pasternak's *Dr. Zhivago* was rejected by Soviet publishers because it criticized certain aspects of the Russian Revolution. The book was published abroad in 1957 and the following year Pasternak was named as winner of the Nobel Prize. The Soviet government began a campaign against him in the press, criticizing him in the worst terms imaginable and prohibiting him from accepting the award. However, in 1965 when Mikhail Sholokhov won the Nobel Prize for his book *And Quiet Flows the*

Don, Soviet leaders were very pleased and boasted about the high quality of Soviet literature. In 1970 the Nobel Prize was awarded to Alexander Solzhenitsyn, the author of *One Day in the Life of Ivan Denisovich, The Cancer Ward,* and *The First Circle.* These books openly criticize various aspects of the Soviet system. At present, Mr. Solzhenitsyn is living in the West.

In 1965 Andrei Sinyavsky and Yuli Daniel, two Soviet writers, were accused of having their novels, which criticized the Soviet system, smuggled out of Russia and published abroad. They were tried, found guilty and sentenced to jail. When other writers protested their sentences, they, too, were found guilty and imprisoned.

However, writers whose works are acceptable to Soviet leaders are given many opportunities to carry on their writing. Two young poets, Yevgeny Yevtushenko and Andrei Vozhnesensky are very popular among the Soviet people. Both travel widely in the USSR and abroad and read their poetry to large audiences.

Soviet Attempts to Limit Dissent and Opposition

Russian governments have always been afraid of criticism by Russian writers (see pages 71-72). In 1974 another example of this fear and dislike of criticism occurred. Alexander Solzhenitsyn gave permission for the publication of his new work, *The Gulag Archipelago,* in the West. This book describes the Soviet forced-labor camp system. Following the publication of the book, Solzhenitsyn was arrested (in February 1974). Protests were made throughout the world. As a result of these protests Solzhenitsyn was freed, but he was forced to leave the Soviet Union. In addition, his Soviet citizenship was taken away.

Despite this and other attempts to prevent criticism, opposition among artists and writers continues. The Soviet government is greatly worried about underground (illegal) literature and pamphlets, called *samizdat.* Some painters and sculptors held an exhibition of their work despite government opposition. The exhibition was bulldozed into the ground and some of the pictures were ruined. Water-spraying trucks were used to drench onlookers and drive them away from the exhibition.

Reaction to Dissent—The Moscow Trials

The dissidents of the Soviet Union are a small group of intellectuals who write and speak out in favor of a more liberalized society, a society in which individuals have the freedom to express their views without fear of official punishment. Among these dissidents are also Jews who have applied for permission to emigrate but have been refused by the government. This group is known as "refuseniks." Some of the dissidents formed a group to publicize Soviet violations of the human rights provisions of the 1975 Helsinki agreement (see pages 84-85). The members of this group risk government harassment and even imprisonment in order to meet with Western newsmen and provide them with reports on Soviet human rights violations. The Soviet Government regards these people with great bitterness and anger since Western newsmen use their reports to publish stories that are read all over the world. The

Soviet government calls these actions "anti-Soviet agitation." This is considered a crime in the Soviet Union. People suspected of this "crime" lose their jobs and are carefully watched by the KGB (security police). Periodically, dissidents are put on trial and receive long prison sentences. In the spring and summer of 1978 there were several trials of dissidents that gained worldwide attention.

Yuri Orlov

In May 1978, Yuri Orlov, a physicist who organized a dissident group to expose Soviet violations of human rights, was sentenced to seven years in prison for the crime of "anti-Soviet agitation." A key charge against Mr. Orlov was that he provided reports on rights violations to foreign newsmen and to Western governments that had signed the 1975 Helsinki treaty. This severe punishment came despite appeals from the West and especially from the United States for more humane treatment of dissidents. It was meant as a warning to other dissidents that publicity and Western support are no protection for them.

Aleksandr Ginzburg

Aleksandr Ginzburg is a friend of Alexander Solzhenitsyn, the exiled Soviet writer. He was the manager of a fund to provide assistance to the families of political prisoners. Ginzburg had worked together with Orlov to expose Soviet violations of human rights. He was arrested and imprisoned in February 1977 and came to trial in July 1978. The key charge against him was "anti-Soviet agitation." During the year and a half he spent in prison, Ginzburg, who is 41, went completely gray. At his trial Ginzburg said he was innocent. He was sentenced to 8 years in a hard-labor camp. This prison term could be fatal to Ginzburg, who is suffering from tuberculosis developed during a previous prison sentence.

Anatoly Shcharansky

On the same day that Aleksandr Ginzburg went on trial, the trial of Anatoly Shcharansky opened in Moscow. This trial received more publicity in the West than has any other Soviet trial in years. Anatoly Shcharansky, age 30, is a Jewish dissident accused of treason. The maximum penalty for treason is death. Shcharansky, like Orlov and Ginzburg, was a member of a dissident group set up to publicize Soviet violations of human rights. Shcharansky was also the *liaison* (link) between Soviet dissidents and Western newsmen until his arrest in March 1977. In addition, he was the voice of the Jewish "refuseniks." Shcharansky himself had applied to emigrate to Israel in 1973, but the government refused to grant him permission to leave the country on the grounds that his job involved access to state secrets. Shcharansky's purpose was to let the world know what was happening to Soviet dissidents, and let the Soviet authorities know that his voice was being listened to abroad. Shcharansky was arrested and accused of working for the CIA. He was accused of having had regular contacts with foreign intelligence agents and of having passed them state secrets. Shcharansky denied this, called the charges absurd and said he was innocent. At his trial it was claimed that he had passed secrets to a reporter from the *Los Angeles Times*. Shcharansky had met with the reporter, who was writing an article on Jewish dissidents in the Soviet Union. But the only information passed to the reporter were the names and places of occupation of a group of refuseniks. Shcharansky was sentenced to 13 years in a prison labor camp.

The Shcharansky trial had more far-reaching implications than any other Soviet trial in years. From the beginning the United States was directly involved in the case. President Carter repeatedly denied that Shcharansky worked for the CIA. He also warned the Soviet Union many times that the trial would hurt Soviet-American relations. The Carter administration said that the trials violated the "fundamental principles of justice." To show his sympathies, Carter had Secretary of State Vance, Vice-president Mondale and the president's own wife and mother meet with Shcharansky's wife. Many people have seen the trial and its timing as a deliberate slap in President Carter's face. The Russians have always been very angry with Carter's outspoken support of Soviet dissidents. They have always resented his warnings that an agreement on a new arms-limitation treaty would be endangered by their treatment of the dissidents. The timing of the trials to coincide with the SALT talks in Geneva seemed intended to show that Carter cannot push the Soviet Union around. The trials also seemed to demonstrate what the Soviet Union means by *détente*—that the Russians accept the necessity of arms control and coexistence with the West, but have no intention of giving in to American demands for social change. The trials worsened relations between the United States and the Soviet Union to the point where many members of Congress demanded that the United States should not attend the SALT talks. The Carter administration did go ahead with the arms limitation talks in Geneva, but Carter canceled two trade deals with the Russians. One of these deals involved the sale of Univac computers to the USSR, something that the Russians greatly desired. The storm of international protests included even the Communist parties of France and Italy, which joined others in denouncing the brutal violation of human rights.

Another implication of the Shcharansky trial is the implied warning to Soviet Jews who choose to follow Shcharansky's example and apply to emigrate to Israel. The meaning of the trial for these people seems to be that if they are refused permission to emigrate and they protest this refusal, they will be considered traitors by the government and no amount of publicity or high-level American pleading can save them.

The trials also are a blow to the civil rights movement in the Soviet Union and to the people who want not to emigrate, but to stay and reform Soviet society. The trials carry the message to them that bringing pressure of the West against their country will not work.

Religion

Communists have always been opposed to religion. Marx considered religion the "opiate of the people" because it fooled people into believing that life on earth is not important compared to the afterlife. It was his belief that religion prevented people from struggling to obtain a decent life on earth. When the Communists came to power in Russia, they did everything possible to weaken the church. Church properties were *confiscated* (taken over by the government), church marriages were not recognized, and it was forbidden to teach religion to children under eighteen. Many churches and synagogues were closed. Bibles could not be sold legally.

Today after 50 years in power the Communists still discourage religion. Although the government officially allows freedom of religion to all its citizens, atheism—the belief that there is no God—is preached. Schools teach that religion is a superstition

Soviet classroom. The Soviets use the most modern methods and equipment in
education, as shown in this picture of Soviet students learning German.
Credit: *Soviet Mission to the United Nations*

that does not belong in a modern, scientific world. Nevertheless, religion has not died in Russia. Many people still attend church services, and although these are mainly old people, it is believed by some that interest among the young in religion is increasing.

Soviet Foreign Policy

The Comintern

In the early years after the Russian Revolution Soviet leaders believed that revolutions would soon break out in Western Europe. These, they believed, would be followed by revolutions all over the world. It was also felt that as long as the Soviet Union remained the only Communist country surrounded by unfriendly capitalist (non-Communist) states, the capitalists would do everything possible to overthrow the Communists in Russia and bring about a return of capitalism. Therefore, the Bolsheviks considered it necessary to promote revolutions in other countries. Lenin in 1921 organized the Comintern, or Communist International, a worldwide organization of Communist parties. It became the duty of all Communists in every country to stir up revolutions and to defend the Soviet Union. A Communist in France, China or the United States owed his loyalty to the Russian leaders and not to his own government.

Stalin's Foreign Policy

After several years, Soviet leaders realized they had been mistaken. Revolutions did *not* break out in the West. Therefore, Stalin gave up the idea of bringing about immediate revolution in the West and decided to concentrate on making the USSR powerful. To industrialize Russia, it was necessary to buy machinery in the West and get loans and experts from the West. Thus, the Soviet Union developed normal relations with the rest of the world. But neither Stalin nor the other Soviet leaders gave up their dreams of world revolution. Stalin until his dying day believed that the world was divided into two hostile camps—the Communist camp and the capitalist camp. War between the two, he believed, was inevitable. Communist parties throughout the world continued to work for revolution. In fact, when the Soviet Union was powerful enough following World War II, Communist governments were forcibly set up in all the countries of Eastern Europe that were occupied by the Soviet army. In 1950 the Soviet Union thought it could succeed in spreading Communism to South Korea. The Soviets, therefore, encouraged the North Koreans, who already had a Communist government, to invade South Korea and aided them with ammunition and war supplies.

Foreign Policy Since Stalin

Since the 1950s, however, Soviet foreign policy has again changed. With the development of nuclear weapons, responsible Soviet leaders have realized that war would mean the end of life on this planet. Stalin's idea that war between capitalism and socialism is inevitable has been given up. The Russians have struggled too much to achieve their present power to allow all this to be destroyed by an atomic war. Soviet leaders still look forward to the day when the world will be made up of only Communist states, and capitalism will cease to exist, but they agree that neither war nor violent revolution are the means by which to bring this about. Their present policy is called "peaceful co-existence."

Soviet leaders now believe that if they can *surpass* (get ahead of) the United States economically and raise the standard of living of the Soviet people, other nations, especially in Asia, Africa and Latin America will want to follow the Soviet model.

In recent years the Soviet Union has been trying to win friends among the developing nations by giving them great amounts of economic aid. Countries such as India, Egypt, Cuba and others have received millions of rubles worth of equipment for industry and military supplies. At the same time, where the risks are not too great, they will help Communist revolutionists in other countries to overthrow a pro-Western government. Thus the Soviet Union helped North Vietnam with ammunition and supplies. Yet the Russians took as few risks as possible in the Vietnamese struggle because they did not wish to become involved in war with the U.S.

However, the USSR does not hesitate to use force when it feels that its interests or security are threatened. In 1956 the Russians invaded Hungary to put down an uprising against the Communist government. Again in 1968, when Czechoslovakia tried to follow an independent policy and free itself from Soviet control, Russian troops were sent in and the Czechs were forced to submit to Moscow's control.

The Soviet Union considers Eastern Europe to be vital to its security. This is because in the past Russia was invaded many times from the west. Since there are no natural boundaries separating Russia from Eastern Europe, armies from Germany, Austria and other countries simply marched through Eastern Europe and attacked the Russians. The Soviet Union, therefore, believes that in order to protect itself against future invasions it must have governments in Eastern Europe that are completely loyal to Moscow.

U.S.–Soviet Relations in the 1970s

For the last few years the USSR has been trying to establish better relations with the U.S. The reason for this is that the Soviets would like to spend less money on military goods and concentrate more on improving the standard of living of their own people. Disarmament talks in which the two countries discussed ways of limiting the amount of nuclear weapons were started in 1969. A cultural exchange program,

Soviet Communist Party Chief Leonid Brezhnev. Soviet leaders, just as American leaders, enjoy the applause and approval of their people.
Credit: *Soviet Mission to the United Nations*

making it possible for artists, writers, and entertainers of each country to visit and perform in the other country, was established.

President Nixon Visits the Soviet Union

In May 1972 President Nixon visited the Soviet Union. For 8 days the American president met with Soviet leaders Brezhnev, Kosygin and Podgorny to discuss a variety of issues of importance to both nations.

For some weeks before it seemed that the visit might never take place. Americans were suffering heavy losses in Vietnam as the Vietnamese Communists attacked American forces with Soviet made weapons. Two weeks before the visit the United States mined the harbor of Haiphong, the main port of North Vietnam. This was done to prevent Soviet weapons and supplies from reaching their North Vietnamese allies. Tension between the Soviet Union and the United States was very great during those weeks in May 1972 and many people thought the visit might be cancelled. The fact that the visit did take place shows that both nations considered it to be of great importance to them.

Soviet leaders wanted to meet with President Nixon to discuss three very important issues: trade, arms limitation, and China. The Russians have been nervous about China ever since President Nixon's visit there in February 1972. They feel that in many ways China is a threat to them, and that any improvement in U.S.-Chinese relations would be at their expense. The Americans were anxious to meet with Soviet leaders also. Their feeling was that the more agreements the United States is able to make with the Russians, the greater the chances for world peace. The Americans also wanted to discuss trade and arms limitation with Soviet leaders.

After 8 days of meetings the Soviets and Americans reached several specific agreements.

1. **Health Research:**

It was agreed that both nations would exchange medical specialists and information.

2. **Environmental Protection:**

It was provided that the two countries would exchange specialists and ideas on everything from noise pollution to earthquake prediction.

3. **Science and Technology:**

The agreement will make it easier for Americans and Russians to share scientific information that until now was regarded as secret.

4. **Cooperation in Space:**

The two countries agreed to cooperate in almost every field of space exploration. It was also decided that by 1975 there would be a *rendezvous* (meeting) in space of the American satellite Apollo and the Soviet satellite Soyuz.

5. **Arms Limitation:**

For the last few years Soviet leaders have realized that the cost of manufacturing weapons, bombs, rockets, and missiles was extremely high and that much of this money could be used to improve living conditions in Russia. American leaders also came to feel that the "arms race" was simply too expensive. Since both nations were practically equal militarily, it was necessary to come to some kind of agreement. Negotiations began in November 1969, and were known as the SALT Talks (Strategic Arms Limitation Talks). After two and one half years of discussions the agreement was finally signed during the President's visit. The agreement consisted of:

a) A formal treaty limiting each country to two anti-ballistic missile systems
b) A five-year agreement limiting the number of *offensive* weapons to those in existence and under construction.

This agreement was regarded as a first step toward cutting back the dangerous and highly expensive arms race.

6. Trade:　　This was one of the most difficult issues discussed and no agreement was reached. One of the obstacles was that the Soviet Union had never repaid its Lend Lease debts to the United States from World War II. The Soviets offered to pay back $300 million while the United States wanted at least $1.1 billion. It was agreed, however, that there would be further talks on trade between Soviet and United States officials.

Despite these agreements, it was obvious from the talks that there were many issues on which the two countries did *not* agree. One such issue was the war in Vietnam, where the Soviet Union continued to arm the Vietnamese Communists and to train their pilots. The U.S. had hoped to be able to persuade the Soviet Union to reduce its aid to North Vietnam. Another area of conflict was the Middle East. The United States would not abandon Israel nor would the USSR lessen its support of Israel's Arab enemies—Egypt and Syria.

Obviously, competition between the United States and the Soviet Union will continue for many years to come, but it was hoped that the visit and the agreements would be an important step to insure world peace. As President Nixon said in a television speech to the Russian people "As great powers, we will sometimes be competitors, but we need never be enemies."

During the first week in May 1973, President Nixon's special advisor Henry Kissinger flew to Moscow for talks with Leonid Brezhnev. The main purpose of the trip was to discuss plans for Mr. Brezhnev's expected visit to the United States in June. This will be Mr. Brezhnev's first journey to the United States and the first by a top Soviet leader since Premier Aleksei Kosygin met with President Johnson at Glassboro, N.J. in 1967. The only other visit by a Soviet leader to the United States was when Premier Nikita Khrushchev was here as President Eisenhower's guest in 1959.

In June 1974, Richard Nixon, then president of the U.S., again visited Moscow. An agreement pledging U.S.—Soviet cooperation on artificial heat research and housing development was signed. The Soviets would make no concessions to the U.S. so little else was accomplished. It is believed the Soviets felt the Nixon government was very weak because of Watergate. In relation to the Watergate Affair the official Soviet reaction was *reserved* (calm) and *noncommittal* (taking no sides).

After Nixon resigned, a meeting between the new president, Gerald Ford, and the Soviet leader Brezhnev was set for November 1974. The two leaders met in Vladivostok in the Soviet Asia Maritime Province. The 2 men reached a *tentative* (not permanent) understanding to limit the number of *nuclear* (atomic) weapons to be produced until 1985. It seems that the Soviets were not interested in a nuclear arms race.

Soviet policy in the 1970s is influenced greatly by a desire to improve the economic life of the Soviet people. *Détente* (relaxation of tensions between nations) is the idea upon which the Soviets hope to gain this goal. In theory, *détente* means that the U.S. and the Soviet Union will work together to keep peace in the world. If this cannot be done then they will discuss other ways of preventing wars and/or trouble from spreading.

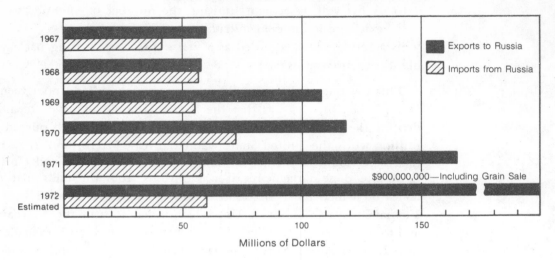

United States Trade With Russia 1967-1972

■ Exports to Russia

▨ Imports from Russia

$900,000,000—Including Grain Sale

Millions of Dollars

UNITED STATES EXPORTS TO THE SOVIET UNION

(millions of dollars)

EXPORTS	1972	1977
FOOD AND LIVESTOCK	$365	$876
HEAVY MACHINERY	62	374
RAW MATERIALS	71	181
MANUFACTURED GOODS	10	89
CHEMICALS	21	40

U.S.—Soviet Trade

Until recently trade between the United States and the Soviet Union was extremely limited. The United States had a list of hundreds of items that could *not* be sold to the Soviet Union because it was felt that these items would help make the Soviet Union stronger militarily. The USSR, for its part, did not show any great interest in trading with the Americans, except for buying wheat from us when it was really necessary, as in 1964.

Now, however, the situation has changed greatly. The Soviets have realized that economically they are behind the United States. In many areas of production, their methods are less efficient than ours. They now feel that in order to speed up their economic development and to produce more consumer goods to satisfy their people they could benefit greatly from American *capital* and *know-how*. The United States government is anxious for trade as well because it would like to open new markets for American businesses in the Soviet Union. In 1971 and 1972 the American government removed 2,000 items from the list of items that could not be exported to the Soviet Union. In 1972 alone 2,000 American businessmen travelled to the Soviet Union looking for markets.

Trade Agreement

In October 1972, a three-year trade agreement was worked out between the Soviet Union and the United States. It provided for:

1. Settlement of Russia's World War II Lend Lease debt to the United States. The Russians agreed to pay us back $722 million over the next 30 years.
2. The U.S. Export-Import Bank would give credits for the sale of goods to the Soviet Union. This means that when the Soviets buy goods in the United States they will not have to pay cash immediately.
3. The United States would get Congress to approve "most favored nation" status for the Russians. This means that goods imported from Russia would be subject to the lowest U.S. tariff rate.
4. Each nation would set up commercial offices in its capital to aid visiting businessmen. The Russians would build a large office-apartment trade center in Moscow for foreign businessmen.
5. Disputes which cannot be settled by both nations would be submitted to a third country for *arbitration.*

It was expected that this agreement would greatly increase trade between the two nations and would benefit both.

However, as of May 1973, this trade agreement had not yet been *ratified* (approved) by the American Congress. A number of United States senators, led by Senator Henry Jackson, Democrat of Washington, were trying to get Congress to refuse to grant special trading privileges to the Soviet Union until Jews in the Soviet Union were given the right to *emigrate.* (See section on "The People of the Soviet Union.") In early 1974 it seemed that the Soviets had agreed to an informal arrangement with Secretary of State Kissinger under which restriction of Jews who wished to leave the Soviet Union would be eased. The Soviet government later said its positions had been misinterpreted.

As a result, the trade bill which was passed in December 1974, had limitations on the granting of most favored nation treatment to the Soviet Union. In early 1975, the Soviets showed their unhappiness by refusing to sign any trade treaty with the U.S.

In the meantime, a number of deals have been negotiated between American firms and the Soviet Union. The Russians have signed an agreement to buy $40 million worth of tractors. In another $16 million deal an American company will build a synthetic fiber plant in the Soviet Union. Other possibilities are under discussion. One of these would be piping natural gas from fields in Siberia to Soviet ports where it would be liquefied and shipped to the United States. The Soviets would like to sell the United States oil, lumber, other raw materials and even some manufactured goods. It seems that the Soviet Union may be interested in buying $200 million worth of feed grains a year for the next 10 years.

The U.S.-Soviet Grain Deals

Normally, the Soviet Union is the world's largest grain producer, but in 1972 bad weather conditions reduced the Soviet grain harvest. The government decided to buy 28 million tons of grain abroad. In July it was announced that the Soviet Union and the United States had signed a three-year deal for the shipment of $750 million worth of American grain to the Soviet Union. Later, it was thought that grain sales to Russia might reach $1 billion in 1972 alone.

On October 20, 1975, the United States announced the conclusion of a five-year agreement with the Soviet Union under which the Russians would buy 6 to 8 million tons of American grain a year. The United States favored a long-term agreement of this kind because it is felt that unexpected Soviet purchases of grain during the last few years badly affected American consumer prices. It is said that massive sales of grain to the Soviet Union in 1972 contributed to the food inflation in the United States. The same thing was feared during the summer of 1975 when the USSR suffered one of its chronic droughts and again began making large purchases of American grain. Partly because of such fears American longshoremen imposed a boycott on grain shipments to the Soviet Union, and late in July the Department of Agriculture imposed a *moratorium* (an order to stop shipments) on further sales of grain to the USSR. By that time, however, the Russians had already purchased over 10 million tons of grain in the United States.

The moratorium on further sales that year was lifted with the conclusion of the five-year agreement. The Agriculture Department said that the agreement would have a stabilizing affect on the American economy. It would allow farmers to plan for full production and would bring the United States $1 billion a year in export earnings.

Soviet-American Linkup in Space

July 17, 1975, was a historic day. Astronauts of the United States and the Soviet Union joined their spaceships and shook hands. The American Apollo and Soviet Soyuz remained docked for two days. During that time the astronauts exchanged gifts, shared meals and conducted some scientific experiments. The event was symbolic of the desire by both nations to cooperate in the exploration of space. Many months of joint planning went into making this venture a success. Several years ago such an event would have been impossible, since the two nations were rivals in space as they were in most other affairs. Only the lessening of tension between the Soviet Union and the United States during the last few years was able to bring about this event.

The Helsinki Conference

The largest *summit* conference in European history took place in Helsinki, Finland, on July 30, 1975. This was the European Security Conference which was attended by the heads of almost all the European nations and the president of the United States. Its aim was to insure permanent peace in Europe. President Ford and Soviet Communist Party leader Leonid Brezhnev met privately as well and discussed means to

Пролетарии всех стран, соединяйтесь!

Коммунистическая партия Советского Союза

ПРАВДА

Газета основана
5 мая 1912 года
В. И. ЛЕНИНЫМ

Орган Центрального Комитета КПСС

№ 256 (21956) • Среда, 13 сентября 1978 года • Цена 3 коп.

В честь годовщины Конституции СССР

На предприятиях и стройках страны продолжается соревнование за достойную встречу 7 октября — первой годовщины со дня принятия новой Конституции СССР. Многие коллективы рапортуют о том, что выполняют повышенные обязательства, взятые в честь этого праздника. Ежедневно «Правда» публикует сообщения с мест о ходе ударной трудовой вахты.

Тон задают ударники

ХАРЬКОВ, 12. (Корр. «Правды» Н. Пахно). Досрочно, к Дню Конституции, завершат свои пятилетки — в честь годовщины новой Конституции СССР — в коллективе производственного объединения «Электротяжмаш» 75 процентов рабочих завода.

Более трехсот из них, в тех бригадах за участием трех лет пятилетки.

Победителем выступили инициаторами пересмотра прежних обязательств. Многие ударники коммунистического труда берут за то, чтобы к концу декабря выполнить по 3,5 годовых нормы и нечеткой пятилетки.

С таким почином выступили бригады слесарей-сборщиков И. Гайдуты, А. Зубова, И. Щербака.

С помощью кооперации

КРАСНОДАР, 12. (Корр. «Правды» И. Лунина). Хозяйства краснодарского треста «Плодопром» досрочно выполнили годовой план трех лет пятилетки по производству плодоовощной продукции. Страна получила на 1 миллиард 615 миллионов штук яиц и 75 тысяч тонн мяса больше.

В текущем году хозяйства выходят на рубежи, запланированные на конец 1980 года. Сейчас строится и реконструируется 30 бройлерных фабрик. Широкое применение нашла кооперация птицефабрик, инкубаторно-птицеводческих станций и птицесовхозов.

В результате производство куриного мяса достигнут в этом году семидесяти тысяч тонн, что значительно увеличивает мясные ресурсы края.

Верность слову

КАЗАНЬ, 12. (Корр. «Правды» А. Сабиров). Бригаду, возглавляемую ударником коммунистического труда государственным знаком качества Николаем Гриневым из Казанского управления производственно-технологической комплектации, образцы труда.

Передовой коллектив — инициатор соревнования в честь новой Конституции СССР.

Опережая сроки

ОМСК, 12. (Корр. «Правды» М. Сковородников). Социалистическое соревнование, развернувшееся к Дню Конституции СССР дало на заводе синтетического каучука — предприятии производящего продукцию на 75 тысяч рублей в год.

Без сомнения, цель будет достигнута.

ЗА ВЫСОКОЕ КАЧЕСТВО УБОРКИ

Уборка — самое напряженное время в деревне. Завершить ее организованно, взять урожай сполна — главная забота хлеборобов в эти дни. Отвечая на решения июльского (1978 года) Пленума ЦК КПСС, они широко поддержали инициативу ростовского союза «Гигант», приняли и настойчиво выполняют повышенные социалистические обязательства по продаже государству зерна, другой продукции.

«Стратегический лозунг партии — борьба за эффективность и качество» — должен стать боевым лозунгом всех тружеников сельского хозяйства, всех работников связанных с ним отраслей», — говорится в постановлении Пленума ЦК. И это соответствует чаяниям земледельцев, идущих нелегкую жатву: посевы, особенно в восточных районах, куда сместился центр, полеглые, увлажненные. Нужно собранно, организованно и дисциплина, отменное мастерство и крепкая взаимовыручка, чтобы преодолеть все барьеры на пути к урожаю.

Каждый день приносит вести о новых достижениях на осенней ниве. Сегодня «Правда» сообщает о большом успехе земледельцев Саратовской и Куйбышевской областей, с честью выполнивших обязательства по продаже колосовых. Саратовцы, одни из первых в стране более 4 миллионов тонн зерна. Подсчитав свои резервы, они решили довести его хлебозаготовкам до 4.750 тысяч тонн. На 300 тысяч тонн увеличивают продажу хлеба хозяйства Куйбышевской области. Наращивают темпы поставок зерна труженики Оренбуржья и Северного Казахстана. Значительная масса зерна труженики Оренбуржья — и твердых пшениц, которые обладают высокими достоинствами. Из хозяйств Украины, Молдавии, Средней Азии идет поток овощей и фруктов нового урожая.

Что помогает в соревновании уверенно взять намеченные рубежи, получать добротную продукцию? Прежде всего строгое соблюдение технологии уборки, правильная расстановка сил, умелый маневр техникой. Поучителен опыт земледельцев Целиноградской области, где в степи работают сотни уборочно-транспортных комплексов, а по маршрутам поля — ток — элеватор круглосуточно курсируют автопоезда. Партийные организации позаботились о том, чтобы повсеместно и дружно был осуществлен напряженный планы и графики уборки. Во многих районах при этом учитывают особенности погоды и биологии. В большинстве районов обеспечено оперативное и квалифицированное обслуживание агрегатов, что помогает использовать их с максимальной нагрузкой.

Решающий фактор в борьбе за отличное качество уборки — высокие темпы. Порой достаточно застрять лишь на один-два дня, и зерно теряет белок, а свекла — сахар. Однако не везде это учитывают. В Кемеровской, Свердловской областях, из-за неэффективного использования комбайнов, автомобилей в ряде хозяйств затягивают обмолот. Встречаются факты, когда зерно неоправданно долго держат без укрытия.

Партия поставила перед тружениками деревни конкретную и реальную задачу — дать стране не только больше сельскохозяйственной продукции, но и лучшего качества, в широком ассортименте. Каждый случай простоя машин, потерь или порчи урожая руководители хозяйств должны всесторонне разбирать, оперативно принимать меры к устранению недостатков, строго взыскивать с виновных за причиненный ущерб. Очень важно, чтобы все формы морального и материального поощрения прочнее увязывались с конечными результатами работы хлебороба.

Развивая социалистическое соревнование, партийные организации призваны постоянно воспитывать у людей хозяйское отношение к полю и его плодам, поощрять борьбу за высокую культуру земледелия, нацеливая каждую бригаду и звено на освоение прогрессивной технологии, лучшего опыта. Всеобщее признание нашел метод ипатовцев, позволяющий поднять производительность труда, с максимальной эффективностью использовать технику. Его признание с колхозника начало работы, передовой методе по-настоящему далеко не везде. Открыть подлинно широкую дорогу всему новому, прогрессивному — значит создать условия для своевременного завершения страды, сбора полноценного урожая.

Сейчас особенно велика роль районных партийных организаций. В их руках находятся важные рычаги воздействия на ход уборочных работ. Но встречаются факты иного рода. Вот, к примеру, из ряда районов Альшеевского, Башкирской АССР сообщают о случаях потерь зерна, часть его поступает на элеваторы некондиционной. Между тем сотрудники райсельуправлений больше заняты сбором всевозможных сведений, нежели помощью хозяйствам в организаторской работе. Партийные органы призваны поднимать ответственность этой службы за конечные дела на поле и в конечном счете — за урожай.

Осень всегда приносит земледельцу целый комплекс забот: одновременно с жатвой идут заготовка кормов, сев озимых, уборка пропашных культур. Успешно справляются с этим сложными задачами, обеспечивая надлежащее качество полевых работ, многие хозяйства Центрального Черноземья, республик Прибалтики. Творчески берутся за получение лучшей продукции свекловоды Украины. Здесь за получение высокого продукта свекловоды сахарного завода Зиньковского района Винницкой области, инициативы хозяйств недавно одобренные ЦК КПСС. Разработав детальный комплексный план заготовки, хранения и переработки корней, они стремятся выкопать их в лучшие сроки, не допуская потерь, сдать с каждого гектара по 50 центнеров белого сахара. С такой настойчивостью не выполнить все неотложные дела осенней поры.

Высокие результаты уборки — по качеству во многом зависят от партийной организации. Правильно поступают там, где коммунисты, возглавляя социалистическое соревнование земледельцев, учат их добрым приемам труда, без внимания ни единого случая потерь и брака в работе. Опираться на широкий актив, партийные комитеты и бюро призваны непрестанно заниматься различными заботами об урожае.

Труд хлебороба должен быть оценен по заслугам. Дело чести сельских тружеников за успешное проведение уборки, высокое качество работы, что позволит дать Родине больше продукции.

Во время вручения наград. Фото А. Пахомова.

ГЕРОИ НОВОГО МЕЖДУНАРОДНОГО ПОЛЕТА В КОСМОС

В Кремле вручены советские награды космонавтам СССР и ГДР

Генеральный секретарь ЦК КПСС, Председатель Президиума Верховного Совета СССР Л. И. Брежнев вручил 12 сентября в Кремле высокие летчику-космонавту В. Ф. Быковскому и гражданину ГДР космонавту-исследователю Зигмунду Йену.

При вручении наград выступил товарищ Л. И. Брежнев.

Выступление товарища Л. И. БРЕЖНЕВА

Уважаемые товарищи!

Мне доставляет большое удовольствие сердечно приветствовать в Кремле героев нового международного космического полета — Валеру Федоровича Быковского и Зигмунда Йена.

Поздравляю вас, дорогие друзья космонавты, с благополучным возвращением на Землю с успешным выполнением почетного и ответственного задания.

Хочу воспользоваться этим случаем, чтобы передать нашим партийным Коваленку и Иванченко, с которыми мы недавно расстались в космосе и которые мужественно продолжают свой нелегкий и ответственный полет.

Человек открыл путь в космос всего 17 лет тому назад. И многие думали тогда, что космические полеты еще долго будут испытанием физических воли и мужества людей, исключительной областью самых смелых, самых мужественных, самых подготовленных, если можно так сказать, особо выдающихся представителей человечества. За короткий срок было убедительно доказано огромное практическая ценность космонавтики.

И сегодня, когда вслед за гражданами Польши и Чехословакии гражданин Германской Демократической Республики побывал на орбите, трудящиеся всех социалистических стран воспринимают работу братских стран в космосе как общую победу мирового социализма.

Словом, можно сказать, что в космических делах социализм верен своим коренным принципам. И здесь он на первое место выдвигает братство, сотрудничество, взаимопомощь, интернационализм!

Товарищи, за успешное осуществление космического полета на орбитальном научно-исследовательском комплексе «Салют-6» — «Союз» и проявленные этом мужество и героизм летчик-космонавт СССР дважды Герой Советского Союза Валерий Федорович Быковский награждается орденом Ленина. Космонавту ГДР Зигмунду Йену присваивается звание Героя Советского Союза с вручением ордена Ленина и медали «Золотая Звезда».

Спасибо вам, дорогие товарищи, за образцовое выполнение вашей ответственной работы. От всей души желаю вам доброго здоровья, счастья, новых больших успехов.

Космические полеты международных экипажей в рамках программы «Интеркосмос» в немалой мере демонстрируют собой прогресс, достигнутый нашей социалистической содружеством в ведущих отраслях науки и техники. Они добиваются главной цели в деле благотворного влияния космических исследований. И можно с уверенностью сказать, что полезная отдача от освоения космического пространства в перспективе будет возрастать.

Получая награду, хочется от души заверить вас, что мы всю свою жизнь, все свои дела направим на то, чтобы укреплять нашу дружбу. Космонавту ГДР Зигмунду Йену я присказываюсь как Герою Советского Союза — вручением ордена Ленина и медали «Золотая Звезда».

Меня, сказал З. Йен, глубоко тронуло то, что я как гражданин Германской Демократической Республики принял участие в исследовании космического пространства в мирных целях. Этот космический полет является выражением крепкой дружбы, сотрудничества и понимания между нашими народами, партиями, армиями и государствами. Я рассматриваю эту награду одновременно как признание достижений социалистического отечества — Германской Демократической Республики и его народа.

Я Йен заверил, что и впредь буду отдавать все силы своей умение делу дальнейшего укрепления дружбы между Социалистической Германией и Коммунистической партией Советского Союза, между народами Германии и Советского Союза.

Космонавт ГДР в память об историческом полете вручил товарищу Л. И. Брежневу государственный герб Германской Демократической Республики, находившийся на борту космического комплекса «Салют-6» — «Союз».

Выступившие были встречены продолжительными аплодисментами.

При вручении наград были Политбюро ЦК КПСС, министр иностранных дел СССР А. А. Громыко, кандидат в члены Политбюро ЦК КПСС, секретарь ЦК КПСС К. У. Черненко, секретарь Президиум Верховного Совета СССР М. П. Георгадзе, помощник Генерального секретаря ЦК КПСС А. М. Александров-Агентов, заведующий Отделом международного ЦК КПСС В. М. Фалин, заместитель председателя Центра подготовки космонавтов имени Юрия Гагарина, дважды Герой Советского Союза генерал-майор авиации А. А. Леонов, а также посол ГДР в СССР Г. Отт.

(ТАСС).

Затем выступил З. Йен. Он выразил сердечную благодарность Центральному Комитету КПСС, Президиуму Верховного Совета СССР, лично Леониду Ильичу Брежневу за высокое доверие, оказанное советским правительству за оказанное доверие выполнить в третий раз этот космический полет на высокую нашу оценку нашей работы.

Я обращаюсь на борту станции «Салют-6» работали там коммунисты Советского Союза и коммунисты Германской Демократической Республики.

Сейчас, находясь на борту станции, за советским правительством я принят в ряды Коммунистической партии Советского Союза, где в это время, когда весь мир стал первым космонавтом.

Весом вклад хлеборобов

◆ САРАТОВ. Большую трудовую победу одержали хлеборобы Саратовской области: они засыпали в закрома Родины 4,1 миллиона тонн зерна, перевыполнив тем самым повышенные социалистические обязательства. На элеваторы доставлено еще 2 миллиона тонн зерна. Здесь уже дали стране более чем полтора миллиона тонн зерна.

Значительный караван хлеба пришел подлинно Энгельсского, Хвалынского, Новоузенского, Ершовского, Пугачевского и некоторых других районов.

Делом отвечая на решения июльского (1978 г.) Пленума ЦК КПСС, земледельцы области взяли новое обязательство — продать 1.600 тысяч тонн зерна колхозами.

Здесь, готовясь к уборочной, создали мощные отряды для перевозки зерна. На их оснащение пошло немало средств, решили до 4.750 тысяч тонн зерна.

◆ КУЙБЫШЕВ. Несколько дней назад в области встретили праздник урожая — в выполнение обязательства — продать 1.600 тысяч тонн зерна колхозами.

По пути в Эфиопию

11 сентября пролетом в Эфиопию на празднование 4-й годовщины эфиопской революционной партии в Москве находился Первый секретарь ЦК Коммунистической партии Кубы, Председатель Государственного совета и Совета Министров Республики Куба Фидель Кастро Рус. В состав государственной кубинской делегации, возглавляемой товарищем Кастро, входят член Политбюро ЦК Коммунистической партии Кубы, заместитель Председателя Государственного совета и Совета Министров Республики Куба Карлос Рафаэль Родригес и другие официальные лица.

Во время краткосрочной остановки в аэропорту между А. Н. Косыгиным и Фиделем Кастро состоялась теплая, дружеская беседа. (ТАСС).

Прием А. Н. Косыгиным А. Б. Ваджпаи

12 сентября Председатель Совета Министров СССР А. Н. Косыгин принял в Кремле находящегося с официальным дружественным визитом министра иностранных дел Республики Индии А. Б. Ваджпаи.

С обеих сторон было выражено удовлетворение развитием дружественных добрососедских отношений между обеими странами, укреплением их на прочной договорной основе.

БЕСЕДА В КРЕМЛЕ

12 сентября Председатель Совета Министров СССР А. Н. Косыгин принял в Кремле находящегося с официальным визитом вице-президента Иракской Республики Т. М. Маруфа.

В беседе, прошедшей в дружественной, сердечной обстановке, принял участие с советской стороны заместитель министра иностранных дел СССР В. Ф. Мальцев.

При обсуждении международных проблем особое внимание было уделено положению на Ближнем Востоке, где обстановка продолжает оставаться напряженной. Большую озабоченность обеих сторон, представляющих усилия Египта и Израиля по прямым участием США, направленным на сепаратное урегулирование за спиной арабских народов на Ближнем Востоке.

(ТАСС).

С ТЕЛЕТАЙПНОЙ ЛЕНТЫ

◆ ДНИ ТОЛСТОГО открылись в Париже в штаб-квартире ЮНЕСКО для чествования великого русского писателя.

◆ ЗА ИЗМЕНЕНИЕ СТАТУСА американских ядерных сил выступает президент Франции Валери Жискар д'Эстен. В интервью корреспонденту газеты «Дейли экспресс». Он подчеркнул, что необходима перестройка всей системы филиппино-американских отношений с США.

◆ ОКОНЧИЛИСЬ БЕЗРЕЗУЛЬТАТНО переговоры о муниципальных властей.

ТАСС — Рейтер.

limit nuclear arms, although no decision was reached. The most important part of the conference was a declaration that was signed by all the leaders. The declaration was 100 pages long, but great controversy was aroused over one phrase. This phrase stated that "the participating states regard as inviolable all one another's frontiers as well as the frontiers of all states in Europe." What this means is that the European leaders agree that boundary lines in Europe should not be changed. This has long been a Soviet goal. During the last days of World War II Soviet troops advanced as far west as the heartland of Germany. In all lands occupied by the Soviet army communist governments were set up. These governments exist to the present day. The Helsinki Declaration confirms that countries and borders should remain as they are. Therefore, countries like Lithuania, Latvia and Estonia, which were annexed by the Soviet Union during World War II, would remain under Soviet control with no hope of regaining their independence. President Ford was criticized by many for signing the declaration, but he claimed that it was aimed at lessening tension and improving East-West relations. Other parts of the declaration stated that the nations would refrain from intervening in the affairs of other participating states; that they would refrain from threats of force; that they would not be involved in activities directed toward the violent overthrowing of the government of another participating state. In the area of human rights it provided for the reunification of families, regular family visits across borders, marriages between citizens of different countries and promotion of travel. Many people voiced doubts as to whether the Soviet Union would fulfill its human rights commitments.

Soviet-American Relations: The Question of Détente

The word *détente* is defined by the dictionary as a lessening of tension and hostility between nations. A policy of *détente* with the Soviet Union has been followed by the recent presidents. It was mainly through the efforts of former Secretary of State Henry Kissinger that this policy was kept alive despite the ups and downs in Soviet-American relations. Yet the policy of *détente* is a *controversial* one. There are many people who are very critical of it. At the same time there are those who defend it with great force.

The possibility that the Soviet Union and the United States could work together has fascinated many people in both countries since the first cultural exchanges of the 1950s. Since then, thousands of Americans and many Soviet citizens have visited each other's countries. American and Soviet leaders have met from time to time and many agreements have been signed. The linkup in space during the summer of 1975 showed that both nations can use their military and industrial power for cooperation.

Yet many Americans still distrust Soviet motives. During the summer of 1975 Alexander Solzhenitsyn, the novelist, visited the United States and made many speeches in various cities during which he denounced the policy of *détente*. His American audiences responded with great applause. Solzhenitsyn called on Americans to understand the worldwide danger that Soviet power poses to their own freedom and security. He claimed that the purpose of the Soviet Union is "to destroy your society. You want to believe otherwise, so you cut down your armies, you cut down your research, but believe me, the Soviet Union is not cutting down on anything." He asserted that the American government was constantly being deceived about the Soviet Union's missiles and nuclear warheads. He called on the United States to put an end to its economic aid and trade policies with the Soviet Union. Many Americans agree with Mr. Solzhenitsyn. They expressed similar feelings when they criticized the strategic arms limitation accord between both countries. They expressed dissatisfaction with American grain sales to the Soviet Union. Perhaps the main reason that Americans react to *détente* without enthusiasm is that there were great expectations during the 1950s and 1960s that closer contact with the West would change Soviet society from within—make it more democratic. This has not happened.

Despite the policy of *détente,* genuine cooperation is still lacking on most of the important issues of war and peace. One example of this occurred when the Soviet Union failed to alert the United States that a Middle East war was about to break out in October 1973. At the same time, Mr. Kissinger did his best to keep the Soviet Union out of all the important negotiations involving the Middle East.

In January 1977, Jimmy Carter became president of the United States. Under Mr. Kissinger's control, all aspects of Soviet-American relations were considered as one. It soon became apparent that under President Carter the various aspects of Soviet-American relations would be considered and discussed separately. For example, as part of President Carter's fight for human rights throughout the world, the president attacked the Soviets for violating the Helsinki agreement on human rights. At the same time, he continued to carry on talks with the Soviets on the question of reduction of arms. The Soviet government reacted very sharply against President Carter's stand on human rights, but they continued discussing the question of disarmament.

Summary
of
Key Ideas

The Union of Soviet Socialist Republics
(The Bridge Between East and West)

A. **The geography and climate of the Soviet Union create both problems and opportunities.**

1. The vast size of the USSR provides a variety of climatic conditions.

2. Vast distances cause problems of transportation and communication.

3. River systems have played an important role in the development of the country.

4. Climatic factors make much of the land unsuitable for agriculture.

5. Most of the Soviet Union's coastline lies far from the centers of population and borders the frozen Arctic.

6. Much of European Russia is a plain. The land is open to invasion from east and west, but geographic factors have also helped to defeat invaders.

7. The great variety of natural resources serve as a basis for industrial development.

8. The location of Soviet cities is affected by geography as well as the needs of the nation.

9. There are great differences in housing materials, clothing, and customs in various parts of the Soviet Union. Geographic factors have greatly influenced this situation.

B. **The Russian past provides us with a key to understanding the Soviet Union today.**

1. Russia was not greatly influenced by the civilizations of Greece and Rome.

2. Russian cultural development was greatly influenced by the Byzantine culture of Constantinople, including the Orthodox religion.

3. Russian economic and political development was affected by invasions from east and west (e.g. Mongols, French, German).

4. Russia did not fully experience the revolutions in society and culture which took place in Western Europe from the 15th to the 18th centuries.

5. Ivan III began a system of serfdom that tied the Russian peasant to the land. After more than 300 years of serfdom Alexander II freed the serfs in 1863.

6. Efforts of Peter the Great and Catherine the Great in the 18th century and the defeat of Napoleon in 1815 contributed to the emergence of Russia as a world power.

7. Under the tsars and the Communists, Russia made outstanding contributions in science, art, literature, music and philosophy.

8. Rebellions, reform movements and attempts to repress them are a major theme of Russian history.

9. Russian literature is often related to contemporary events and reflects the underlying feelings of the people.

10. The roots of Communism are found in the works of Karl Marx, a West European.

11. The Communists took over Russia during World War I (1917) and turned Russia into a center for world revolution.

12. Stern measures used by Joseph Stalin to rule Russia had their roots in Russian history.

C. **Society and culture in the Soviet Union are, in some ways different from those in tsarist Russia.**

1. The social structure of Russia before the Revolution was like a pyramid. The tsar was at the top point of the pyramid. The nobility and high clergy were near the top of the pyramid, while merchants, workers and peasants were at the bottom.

2. In pre-revolutionary society, education and cultural enrichment were limited to a small part of the population.

3. The Soviet government and the Communist Party try to shape the values, thoughts and actions of the Soviet people by control of education, artistic expression and the mass media.

4. Many languages, religions and ethnic groups are represented in the Soviet Union. The government has encouraged the development of minority languages and cultures provided they conform to Communist ideas.

5. Anti-semitism was an official policy of old Russia. The Soviet government has made this policy illegal, but many of its actions can be interpreted as anti-semitic.

6. The social structure of the Soviet Union is not "classless." Social divisions are based on profession and party position.

7. Flexible social mobility has affected Soviet women as well as men. Some women have achieved high social and economic positions.

D. **Industrialization and economic progress in the Soviet Union occurred at a heavy price to the Soviet people.**

1. Russian economic growth was held back by the Mongol invasion.

2. The Russian economy until 1863 was based on a system of serfdom.

3. Modern Russian economic development began when the serfs were freed.

4. Today Marxism-Leninism provides a basic framework for the economic system.

5. State planning is the basis for the industrial and agricultural development of the Soviet Union.

6. Agriculture, organized in collective and state farms, produces a significant share of the nation's wealth.

7. Among weaknesses of the economy are low acreage production in agriculture and low quality in consumer goods.

8. The government provides housing, social insurance and medical care for all the people.

9. There has been a recent shift in production from placing the main emphasis on the production of capital goods to a greater emphasis on producing more consumer goods of higher quality.

10. Economic progress in the Soviet Union presents an alternative to capitalism for underdeveloped nations and a challenge to capitalist nations.

E. **The nature and structure of the Soviet government are based on Communist ideas and Russian history.**

1. The present government had its beginnings in the November Revolution of 1917, in which the Communists, led by Lenin, gained power.

2. In structure, according to the Constitution of 1936, there are many similarities between the governmental forms of the Soviet Union and the United States.

3. In practice, there are a great many differences in the objectives and functions of the governments of the two nations.

4. Only one party—the Communist Party—exists in the USSR. The Party controls the government and determines its policies.

5. The goal of the Communist leadership is world revolution—the establishment of Communism in all countries.

6. To achieve the goal of world leadership the USSR has set up programs of economic aid, propaganda, and military assistance to Communist and developing nations and trains revolutionaries for other countries.

7. A system of secret police and terror has been used by both the tsars and the Communists. Trials have been used to further the aim of keeping the Soviet people "in line."

8. Expression of opposition to the government is limited to mild forms of criticism. Censorship is an important weapon of the Soviet government.

UNIT II

Exercises and Questions

Vocabulary

Directions: Match the words in Column *A* with the correct meaning in Column *B*.

Column A

1. tsar
2. excommunication
3. treason
4. emancipate
5. serf
6. revolution
7. steppe
8. abdicate
9. soviet
10. bourgeoisie
11. proletariat
12. inevitable
13. westernize
14. purge
15. permafrost

Column B

(a) to free or liberate

(b) the working class

(c) Russian word for council

(d) stepped down; gave up the throne

(e) it is sure to happen

(f) to adopt the culture of Western Europe

(g) Russian word for king

(h) overthrowing the government

(i) capitalists; owners of factories and mines

(j) to get rid of opponents

(k) being disloyal to one's government

(l) ground that is frozen all year round

(m) peasant who cannot leave his landlord

(n) plain, grasslands

(o) being "put out" of the church

Who Am I?

Directions: Using the names listed below, name the person described in each of the sentences.

Riurik	Catherine the Great	Karl Marx
Prince Vladimir	Napoleon	V. I. Lenin
Genghis Khan	Alexander II	Stalin
Ivan the Terrible	Nicholas II	Boris Pasternak
Peter the Great	Rasputin	Yevgeny Yevtushenko

1. I was the French ruler who invaded Russia in 1812.

2. I turned the Soviet Union into a powerful industrial nation.

3. I was a German thinker. I developed the idea of class struggle.

4. I emancipated the Russian serfs.

5. I was the leader of the Norsemen who invaded Russia in the 9th century.

6. I was harshly criticized by the Soviet government for my novel *Dr. Zhivago*.

7. I was the ruler who converted the Russian people to Christianity.

8. I united the Mongol tribes into a powerful army.

9. I was the leader of the Communist revolution of November 1917.

10. I am a very popular poet in the Soviet Union today.

11. I spent several months in Europe studying shipbuilding and fortification. I tried to westernize Russia.

12. I was the last Russian tsar. I abdicated in 1917.

13. I thought European culture was superior to Russian culture. Under my rule French art, music and literature became very popular in Russia.

14. I was a drunken, ignorant peasant and priest. During World War I, I practically ruled Russia.

15. I was the first tsar to rule Russia by force and terror. My security police executed anyone who opposed me.

Completion

Directions: Select from the following terms the one which best completes each sentence.

Pravda	conserve	Komsomol	tentative	emigrate
samizdat	know-how	dissent	*détente*	ratify

1. Another word for approving a law or treaty is ....·

2. Something that is temporary is also ....·

3. People leaving a country to live in another country are said to........................·

4. The name of a Russian newspaper which means "Truth" is........................·

5. The name of the Russian Young Communist League is ....·

6. The act of disagreeing with an idea or an action is called........................·

7. Another word meaning "to save" is ....

8. The policy of Russian-American cooperation is called ....

9. The ability to set up an advanced industrial complex is called ....

10. The underground Russian press is called ....

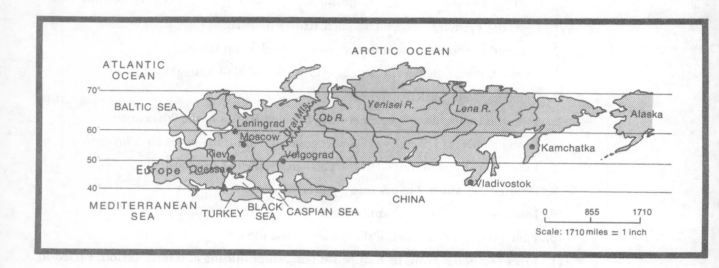

Map Exercise

Directions: Look at the map above. Select the best answer for the following questions.

1. The distance from Leningrad to Vladivostok is about
   (a) 3000 miles   (b) 4500 miles   (c) 6000 miles   (d) 7500 miles

2. Most of the Soviet Union is located
   (a) north of the Arctic Circle   (b) close to the equator   (c) between 40° and 70° north latitude   (d) between 40° and 70° south latitude

3. Which of the following is most like a lake?
   (a) Black Sea   (b) Baltic Sea   (c) Sea of Japan   (d) Caspian Sea

4. Most of the rivers of Siberia flow
   (a) north   (b) south   (c) east   (d) west

5. Kamchatka can best be described as
   (a) an island   (b) a sea   (c) a strait   (d) a peninsula

6. If you go from Moscow to Vladivostok you are traveling
   (a) north   (b) south   (c) east   (d) west

7. A tundra would most likely be found near
   (a) the Chinese border   (b) the Arctic Ocean   (c) Central Asia
   (d) the European border

8. One reason that Moscow became the capital of Russia is that it is
   (a) far from large population centers
   (b) located in the center of Russia's river systems
   (c) far from Russia's European borders
   (d) located in the warmest part of the country

9. Leningrad is located on the
   (a) Black Sea (b) Baltic Sea (c) Caspian Sea (d) Sea of Japan

10. Moscow is about 600 miles from
    (a) Vladivostok (b) Leningrad (c) Kiev (d) Volgograd

True or False?

Directions: Tell whether the following statements are true or false. Correct the false statements.

1. Russia got its name from the *Slavs*.

2. The letters USSR stand for *United Soviet Socialist Republics*.

3. The *Great Russians* make up about 50% of the population of the USSR.

4. The *European* part of Russia is known as Siberia.

5. Lenin set up a secret police known as the *Cheka*.

6. Cars, TV sets, and clothing are known as *capital goods*.

7. Each farmer on a *state farm* can own a small garden and a few animals.

8. In the Civil War of 1918 those who supported the Communists were known as *Reds*.

9. The amount of work that has to be done by a worker is known as his *quota*.

10. Stalin believed that war between the Soviet Union and the *Communist* countries was inevitable.

Graph Analysis

Directions: Look at the graph on page 94. Tell whether the following statements are true or false. Correct the false statements.

1. The Soviet Union is closest to the United States in the production of *steel*.

2. Soviet production of *consumer goods* is closer to the United States than its production of *resources*.

3. The U.S. production of electricity is *twice* that of the Soviet Union.

4. *Consumer goods* are used in the production of *natural resources*.

5. This graph is an example of a *line graph*.

6. This graph would be important to people interested in information about the production of *consumer goods*.

The Soviet Union And The United States
A Comparison Of Resources And Consumer Goods

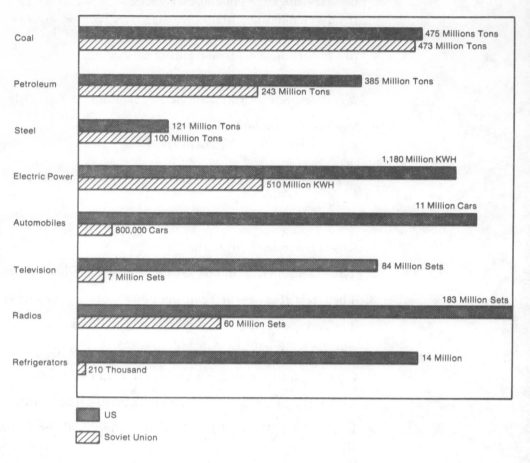

Chart Analysis

Directions: Turn to the table on page 67. Tell whether the following statements are *true* or *false* or the *information is not given* (ING) on the table. Base your answers only on the information from this table.

1. The numbers *1H 42M* next to men's shirts stands for *one hour and forty-two minutes*.

2. It takes a Russian worker three minutes work to earn enough money to buy a lb. of sugar.

3. A woman living in New York City works about 5½ hours to earn enough money to buy a pair of shoes.

4. In Moscow a person has to work about 10 times as many hours as a person in New York City to be able to buy a dress.

5. In Moscow it is necessary to work about 18 hours to buy a man's suit.

6. Many people living in Moscow own television sets.

7. The figures for the work time in New York City were gathered from statistics of the Bureau of Labor and the National Conference Board.

8. The items listed in this table are called capital goods.

9. Automobiles are more expensive in Moscow than in New York City.

10. From information given in the table we can conclude that in 1966 food and clothing were more expensive in Moscow than in New York City.

Multiple Choice

Directions: Select the letter of the correct answer.

1. Most of the land of the Soviet Union is
   (a) plateau (b) plain (c) mountainous (d) desert

2. Most of the Soviet Union's coastline is
   (a) very good because it is the longest in the world
   (b) very good for trade because it is straight
   (c) not very useful for trade because it stays frozen part of the year
   (d) not very useful because there are not too many good ports

3. Which of the following does not belong with the others?
   (a) Don (b) Volga (c) Caucasus (d) Dnieper

4. Siberia's three main rivers—the Ob, Lena and Yenisei—are
   (a) not good for transportation because they flow north to the Arctic
   (b) not good for transportation because they have many rapids
   (c) very good for transportation because they are long and wide
   (d) very good for transportation because they flow from south to north

5. The climate of most of the Soviet Union is known as
   (a) tropical (b) continental (c) temperate (d) humid

6. All are factors affecting the climate of the Soviet Union *except* which of the following?
   (a) Arctic winds blow across the land.
   (b) Most of the Soviet Union is far from the Atlantic and Pacific Ocean.
   (c) Most of the USSR is located far away from the equator.
   (d) Monsoons bring heavy rainfall.

7. Not many people live in the tundra because
   (a) the ground is frozen almost all year round
   (b) farming is almost impossible
   (c) cold winds from the Arctic blow across it
   (d) all of the above

8. The great forests of the Soviet Union are found in the
   (a) tundra (b) taiga (c) steppe (d) desert

9. The Soviet Union's main agricultural area is found in the
   (a) tundra (b) taiga (c) steppe (d) desert

10. Much of the land of the Soviet Union is not suitable for agriculture because
    (a) it is either too cold or there is not enough rainfall
    (b) it is too hot and there is too much rainfall
    (c) most of the country is very mountainous
    (d) there is almost no fertile soil in the USSR

11. The people of the Soviet Union
    (a) speak many different languages
    (b) follow many different religions
    (c) practice many different customs
    (d) all of the above

12. Which of the following made the others possible?
    (a) The Russians borrowed many ideas from the Greeks.
    (b) Many cities arose in Russia.
    (c) The Russians traded with Constantinople.
    (d) Russian cities became wealthy.

13. Which of the following happened *first*?
    (a) The princes of Moscow united Russia.
    (b) The Slavs settled along the Dnieper River.
    (c) The Mongols conquered Russia.
    (d) Russia was invaded by Norsemen from Scandinavia.

14. An icon is a
    (a) religious painting   (b) church   (c) prayer book   (d) museum

15. The Mongols were able to invade Russia easily because
    (a) there were no barriers in the steppe to stop them
    (b) the Russians had an excellent army
    (c) many Russians welcomed the Mongols
    (d) the Mongols had the help of other nations

16. The Mongols helped the prince of Moscow to become the most powerful prince in Russia because they
    (a) appointed him tsar
    (b) built up his army
    (c) allowed him to collect taxes for them
    (d) enlarged his territory

17. One of the reasons that Moscow became the capital after the Mongols were driven out was that it was located
    (a) in the mountains
    (b) in the taiga
    (c) in the steppe
    (d) near the sea

18. The security police of Ivan the Terrible were known as
    (a) NKVD   (b) Cheka   (c) Oprichniki   (d) Komsomol

19. Peter the Great wanted to westernize Russia because
    (a) he wanted to make Russia strong
    (b) Russia was far behind the rest of Europe in science and industry
    (c) the European countries were more powerful than Russia
    (d) all of these reasons

20. Russia went to war against Turkey many times to gain control of the
    (a) Baltic Sea   (b) Black Sea   (c) Sea of Japan   (d) Caspian Sea

21. The poll tax was
    (a) charged by the Mongols
    (b) was a tax on the rich
    (c) was paid by everyone equally
    (d) was a tax on all "male souls" and was mainly paid by the poor

22. Peter the Great and Catherine were alike in all of the following ways *except*
    they both
    (a) admired European culture
    (b) spent many years at war with Turkey
    (c) increased the size of Russia by conquering Poland
    (d) showed very little concern for the suffering of the poor

23. In the years following Napoleon's invasion many people began to demand change
    because
    (a) Russia was corrupt and backward
    (b) the war had caused much destruction and suffering among the Russian people
    (c) the tsar did nothing to reform the government
    (d) all of these reasons

24. The purpose of the security police was
    (a) to spy on the people in order to prevent a revolution
    (b) to protect the serfs from their masters
    (c) to defend Russia from foreign invaders
    (d) all of these

25. Most of the officials in the Russian bureaucracy were
    (a) corrupt and ignorant
    (b) very educated
    (c) skilled and able to do their jobs well
    (d) very honest

26. Which of the following was an example of censorship in Russia?
    (a) The security police were able to search a person's home.
    (b) The tsar ruled without a constitution.
    (c) Every newspaper, book and magazine had to be examined before it could be
        published.
    (d) Many people were sent to Siberia.

27. Alexander II decided to emancipate the serfs because
    (a) he was afraid of a peasant revolution
    (b) he believed that Russia's weakness was due to serfdom

    (c)   he believed that Russia was backward because of serfdom

    (d)   all of these reasons

28.   The Russian peasant's life was not much better after the emancipation for all of the following reasons *except*

    (a)   he did not get enough land

    (b)   the cost of the land was very high

    (c)   the law did not allow the peasant to leave his landlord

    (d)   the peasant had many taxes to pay

29.   The Russian revolutionaries of the 19th century were mainly

    (a)   factory workers in the cities

    (b)   serfs and poor peasants

    (c)   educated young people from wealthy families

    (d)   foreign spies

30.   The Revolution of 1905 was in part caused by Russia's defeat in a war with

    (a) England   (b) Japan   (c) Germany   (d) France

31.   "Bloody Sunday" was the day in 1905 when

    (a)   the tsar was killed

    (b)   Russian soldiers were killed by the Turks

    (c)   130 demonstrators were killed by government troops

    (d)   women and children died of starvation

32.   Nicholas II reacted to the events of 1905 by

    (a)   giving up his throne

    (b)   executing millions of people

    (c)   promising the people a constitution

    (d)   asking other nations to help him

33.   The Duma set up in 1905 was a

    (a) court   (b) legislature   (c) cabinet   (d) security police

34.   The Russian people were unhappy with the Provisional Government because the Government

    (a)   wanted to continue the war against Germany

    (b)   wanted to make peace with Germany

    (c)   tried to bring back the tsar

    (d)   was made up of many Communists

35.   Which of the following events happened *last*?

    (a)   emancipation of the serfs

    (b)   Napoleon's invasion of Russia

    (c)   abdication of Tsar Nicholas II

    (d)   World War I

36.   Marx's idea of *class struggle* is that

    (a)   since the beginning of history the rich and the poor have always fought with each other

    (b)   the factory owners are only interested in making more money

(c) the bourgeoisie use the proletariat to become rich

(d) all of the above

37. Marx believed that the revolution would be carried out by the

(a) farmers   (b) factory workers   (c) government   (d) students

38. Marx believed that revolution was inevitable for all of the following reasons *except* which?

(a) The workers are very unhappy with their lives.

(b) The farmers are unhappy with serfdom.

(c) The proletariat is growing in strength.

(d) The proletariat will rise up and overthrow the bourgeoisie.

39. Which of the following statements is *not* true?

(a) Lenin's slogan "Peace, Land and Bread" won many people over to his side.

(b) Lenin believed that the Communists had to carry out their revolution in November 1917.

(c) Lenin believed that Russia had to continue the war against Germany until Germany was defeated.

(d) Lenin and the Communists carried out the revolution in less than 24 hours.

40. Which of the following caused the other three to happen?

(a) The peasants slaughtered their cows and horses.

(b) The peasants left their land untilled.

(c) Stalin forced the peasants to join collective farms.

(d) Many people starved to death and others were executed.

41. Which of the following is *not* true?

(a) Stalin turned the Soviet Union into a powerful nation.

(b) Stalin forgave many people who opposed him.

(c) Stalin had his opponents executed.

(d) Stalin said, "He who does not work does not eat."

42. Which of the following statements is *not* true about the Soviet economy?

(a) Many private businesses exist in the Soviet Union.

(b) The Soviet Union concentrates on building factories, machines and tanks rather than producing TV sets and cars.

(c) All the natural resources are owned by the government.

(d) Workers are paid according to their skills and the amount of work they do.

43. Which of the following are *not* considered *capital goods*?

(a) dams   (b) washing machines   (c) tractors   (d) combustion engines

44. The State Planning Commission

(a) runs all the schools of the Soviet Union

(b) tries to win other countries over to Communism

(c) decides what kinds of goods will be produced

(d) is in charge of training young soldiers

45. On a collective farm all of the following are true *except* which?

(a) The machinery and animals are owned collectively by all the farmers.

(b) The farmers sell whatever they want to sell and keep the profits.

(c) The farmers divide the jobs among themselves on the basis of skill.

(d) Most of the crops are sold to the government at prices set by the government.

46. Food shortages in the Soviet Union are caused by all of the following *except* which?

(a) Much of the USSR is either too cold or too dry for farming.

(b) Heavy rains destroy many crops.

(c) There are shortages of farm machinery and fertilizer.

(d) Farmers often don't work as hard as they should because they don't own the land.

47. The Soviet Government provides for the security of its people by

(a) old age pensions and free medical care

(b) high wages for workers and farmers

(c) charging low prices for food and clothing

(d) providing low cost vacations abroad

48. The Supreme Soviet is called a "rubber stamp." This means that it

(a) is concerned mainly with the rubber industry

(b) automatically approves everything the Communist Party decides

(c) is the most important branch of the Soviet government and makes all the decisions

(d) is the highest court in the land

49. The Communist Party of the Soviet Union

(a) requires every adult citizen to be a member

(b) is one of many parties in the Soviet Union

(c) is very small, with only 5% of the people being members

(d) is outlawed by the Soviet government

50. Between the ages of 15 and 27 young Soviet people may belong to the

(a) Komsomol (b) Octoberists (c) Comintern (d) NKVD

51. Which of the following does not belong with the others?

(a) Boris Pasternak (b) Mikhail Sholohov (c) Alexander Solzhenitsyn (d) Alexander Pushkin

52. Which of the following statements about religion in the Soviet Union is *not* true?

(a) Many churches and synagogues have been closed.

(b) Schools teach that religion is superstition.

(c) Only religious people can get good jobs.

(d) Many people still go to church.

53. Many countries are suspicious of the Soviet Union because the USSR has

(a) always tried to help small countries

(b) always hoped to make other countries Communist

(c) built Germany into a powerful nation

(d) used atomic weapons against other nations

54. Soviet leaders have given up the idea that war between capitalism and Communism is inevitable because

(a) an atomic war would destroy the whole world

(b) the Soviet people have struggled too much to build up their country to allow it all to be destroyed

(c) they believe that they can spread Communism by means other than war

(d) all of the above reasons

55. To prevent these countries from becoming anti-Communist and to maintain Soviet control over them, Soviet troops were sent into

(a) Hungary and Yugoslavia

(b) Hungary and Italy

(c) Czechoslovakia and Hungary

(d) Czechoslovakia and Austria

Thought Questions

1. Geography has had a great effect on Russian history. Give examples from each of the following periods to prove this statement.

(a) Kievan Russia

(b) the Mongol invasion

(c) the rise of Moscow

(d) the reign of Peter the Great

(e) the Napoleonic invasion

2. Russian history provides us with many examples of cultural diffusion. What evidence can be found to support this statement from the following periods?

(a) Kievan Russia

(b) the reign of Peter the Great

(c) the reign of Catherine the Great

(d) the Communist Revolution of 1917

3. It has been said that the Mongol invasion retarded Russia's development by about 200 years. Do you agree or disagree with this statement? Why?

4. How did the Russian church help to bring the people under the complete power of the government?

5. How did Peter the Great go about westernizing Russia?

6. How were the Russian people affected by Peter's efforts to change Russia?

7. Why did Napoleon fail in his attempt to conquer Russia?

8. Freedom of the press did not exist in 19th century Russia. Freedom of the press does not exist in the Soviet Union today. Explain.

9. There could be no personal freedom in Russia as long as an all-powerful security police existed. Explain.

10. How did serfdom develop in Russia?

11. Why did many Russian people become revolutionaries during the 19th century?

12. What were some of the methods used by the revolutionaries to bring about revolution? Why were they unsuccessful?

13. How did World War I help to bring on the revolution of 1917?

14. If you were a worker in 19th-century Europe how might you have felt about Marxism? As a worker in America today why might your opinion be different?

15. Lenin was a faithful follower of Marx. Nevertheless, he changed some of Marx's basic ideas. Explain.

16. Lenin and the Communists lacked the support of the majority of the Russian people. What evidence is there to support this statement?

17. Why is it possible to compare the policies of Stalin with those of Peter the Great and Ivan the Terrible?

18. How did the Five-Year Plans change the Soviet Union from a backward country into an industrial giant?

19. How does the Soviet government control the entire economy of the USSR?

20. If you were living in the Soviet Union what problems would you have to face with regard to   (a) clothing   (b) housing   (c) food?

21. How does the Communist Party control the Soviet Union?

22. What are some of the advantages of the Soviet educational system? What are some of its disadvantages?

23. What are some of the problems faced by writers in the Soviet Union?

24. How is the Soviet Union trying to win over other countries to Communism today?

25. How does the government of the Soviet Union deal with dissent and opposition?

26. If you were writing a book on the Soviet-American *détente,* what examples might you give of this policy?

27. How has the question of the Jews affected Soviet-American relations?

ACTIVITY

PRETEND THAT YOU ARE ONE OF THE FOLLOWING. WRITE A LETTER TO A FRIEND DESCRIBING YOUR LIFE AND WHAT YOU ARE EXPERIENCING.

1. A Russian at the time of the Mongol invasion.

2. A Mongol in the army that has invaded Russia.

3. A Russian at the time of Napoleon's invasion.

4. A soldier in Napoleon's army.

5. A Russian serf.

6. A Russian landlord owning many serfs.

7. A Russian revolutionary.

8. A Russian worker or peasant during World War I.

9. A Russian student during the 19th century.

10. A worker in Europe during the Industrial Revolution.

11. A Soviet peasant during the Stalin period.

12. A writer in the Soviet Union today.

In Moscow, Russian girls present bouquets of flowers for their new teachers. They salute as the national anthem is played. *(Top) Credit: United Press International*

Soviet shoppers jam the counters of a department store, as more consumer goods become available. *(Bottom) Credit: United Press International*

Puzzle

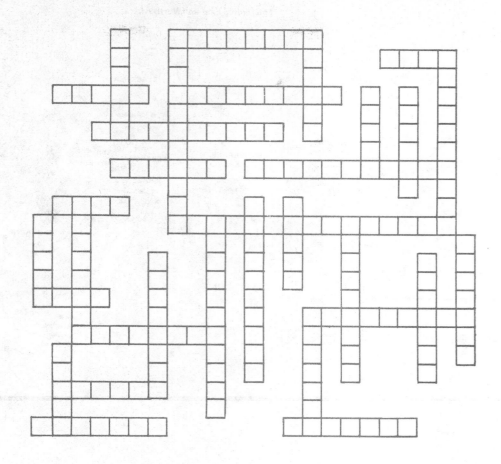

Directions: Place the words below in their proper place in the puzzle.

4 LETTERS	5 LETTERS	6 LETTERS	7 LETTERS	8 LETTERS
TSAR	PURGE	STEPPE	TREASON	CONSERVE
SERF	CHEKA	SOVIET	KNOW-HOW	EMIGRATE
ICON	SLAVS	RATIFY	DISSENT	BACKWARD
	GRAPH	DESERT	DETENTE	SECURITY
	QUOTA	ARCTIC	CAPITAL	

9 LETTERS	10 LETTERS	11 LETTERS	15 LETTERS
TENTATIVE	EMANCIPATE	BOURGEOISIE	EXCOMMUNICATION
RESOURCES	REVOLUTION	PROLETARIAT	
COMMUNIST	WESTERNIZE	CONTINENTAL	

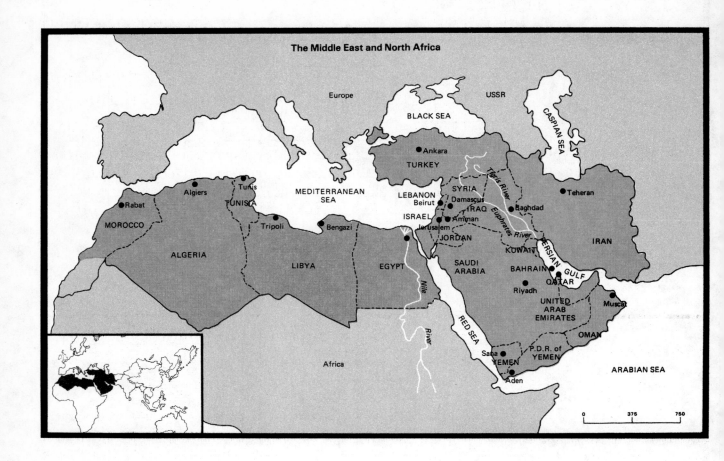

The Middle East and North Africa

UNIT III The Middle East and North Africa

Introduction

The term "Middle East" is rather vague. The phrase was coined to describe a geographic area and to distinguish this area from other lands that are referred to as the "Far East." But the terms "middle" and "far" only have meaning if looked at from the point of view of the Western world. The people of the area do not like to be considered on the basis of how near they are to Europe.

Nevertheless, the term "Middle East" refers to the area which connects three great continents—Europe, Asia, and Africa. Along the Mediterranean coast are the nations of North Africa—Morocco, Algeria, Tunisia, Libya and the United Arab Republic (Egypt). To the east of Africa is the Arabian Peninsula, on which are located the nations of Saudi Arabia, Yemen Arab Republic, People's Democratic Republic of Yemen, Oman, the United Arab Emirates, Bahrein, Qatar, and Kuwait. North of the Arabian Peninsula are Jordan, Israel, Lebanon, and Syria. North of Syria is Turkey; further east are Iraq and Iran.

These lands can be studied as one region because they are similar in several ways.

1. The climate of this region is generally hot and dry—in fact most of the land is desert.
2. Most of the people speak the Arabic language.
3. Over 90% of the people in the Middle East are Moslems, that is, they follow the religion known as Islam.
4. The people of the area share a related history and have similar problems today.

It is important to know about the Middle East for many reasons.

1. The Middle East is very rich in oil. It is believed that two-thirds of the world's total oil reserves lie in the Middle East. Oil is vital to industry throughout the world.

Oasis in Saudi Arabia. This moist and fertile oasis is found on one of the driest places on earth. (*Top*)
Credit: *Arabian American Oil Company*

The famous pyramids of Giza are considered one of the seven wonders of the ancient world. They were built about 5,000 years ago as tombs for the kings of Egypt. (*Bottom*)
Credit: *Arab Information Center*

2. The Middle East has always been of great importance because it is located at the crossroads of three continents. Trade between Asia, Africa and Europe has had to pass through the Middle East, and its waterways have been used as trade routes since the beginning of civilization. The Mediterranean Sea is one of the busiest trading routes in the world. The Suez Canal, which connects the Mediterranean Sea to the Red Sea and the Indian Ocean, is also found here. The Canal shortens the distance between Western Europe and India, Southeast Asia, and China by thousands of miles. The countries of Western Europe and the United States send their products to Asia and Africa through the Canal. In turn, rubber, oil, tin and other products from Africa and Asia are shipped through the Canal to the countries of the West.

3. Some of the earliest civilizations developed in the Middle East. (Egypt, Babylonia, Persia)

4. Three of the world's great religions—Judaism, Christianity, and Islam—began in this part of the world. Many places in Israel, Jordan and Saudi Arabia are thought of as holy by Christians, Moslems, and Jews.

5. The Soviet Union has always been interested in the Middle East. The countries of the Middle East lie south of the Soviet Union. The Soviets would like to control the rich oil fields of this region. The USSR would also like to control the important waterways of the Middle East. The United States is not very happy about the growing Soviet power in this area.

6. Finally, the Jewish state of Israel stands in the middle of the Arab countries of the area. Israel is a democracy in a part of the world where most people have very little voice in their own government. Since this country was formed in 1948, the Arab nations have wanted to destroy it. Four wars have been fought—in 1948, 1956, 1967, and 1973. All have been won by Israel, but a lasting peace has not been achieved. The United States and the Soviet Union have reason to fear that continued trouble in the area could lead to a world war.

Land and Climate

An Area of Deserts

North Africa and the Middle East is a region of deserts. There are mountains and plateaus as well, but the desert most affects the life of the people. The largest desert on earth, the Sahara, is located in northern Africa and covers the southern portions of Morocco, Algeria, and Libya. In addition, desert lands extend eastward to the Red Sea. Beyond the Red Sea there is desert again. The Arabian Peninsula contains one of the largest true deserts in the world—the Rub àl Khali (roob' al Kah'lee), which is known as the "Empty Quarter." (A true desert has no vegetation at all.) There are no settlements in the Empty Quarter and few people have ever crossed it. This region is a continuation of the Sahara and part of a desert chain that extends through large parts of Southwest Asia some 5000 miles from the Atlantic to the Indian Ocean.

Rainfall Is Scarce

The Middle East is probably the driest place on earth. The major economic problem that people living here have to face can be summarized in one word: *water*. Although some areas may have a lot of rainfall, the rain is concentrated so that it falls over a short period of time, leaving the ground dry through most of the year. During the rainy period, the water flows into seasonal streams called *wadis*. This water runs off rapidly, carrying with it most of the topsoil. As a result the land is left in worse condition that if it had not rained at all. It is along the Mediterranean coast and some of the other coasts, as well as in the mountains that rain falls most heavily during the rainy season. The rainy season comes in the winter and spring. Summers are hot and dry with no rainfall at all. Farther away from the coast there is less rainfall. Where there are tall mountains along the coast, these mountains block the rain from moving into the interior regions. This is true of Arabia, where in some regions of the interior, the amount of rainfall cannot even be measured. Because of the lack of rainfall much of the Middle East is totally *uninhabitable* (people cannot live there). Only about 15% of all the land is suitable for agriculture.

Mountains

Parts of the Middle East and North Africa are hilly or mountainous. The highest mountains are found in Northern Turkey and Iran. In northwest Africa are the Atlas Mountains of Morocco and Algeria, which lie between the desert and the Mediterranean Sea. The Atlas extend well into the interior and form a high plateau several hundred miles wide. Plateaus make up most of the land in Turkey and Iran.

The mountains are very important to the people living in the area. It is in the mountains that most of the rain falls (in addition to the rainfall along the coasts). Water trapped by the mountain peaks travels for hundreds of miles underground. In some places it comes to the top of the earth in springs. In others it is reached by digging wells at the base of the mountains.

Rivers

Because of the water from the mountains there are two great river systems—the Tigris-Euphrates Rivers in Iraq and the Nile in Egypt. The Tigris River and the Euphrates flow south from the mountains of Turkey. The two rivers flow almost parallel or next to each other as they wind through Iraq. They finally join together and empty into the Persian Gulf. At the point where the two rivers almost meet, the ancient city of Baghdad is located. For thousands of years the people living along these two rivers have used the rivers to irrigate their land.

The Nile is the longest river in the world. It begins south of Egypt in the highlands of East Africa. The Nile is joined by other streams that rise in Ethiopia. The great river flows northward through Egypt until it reaches the Mediterranean Sea over 4000 miles from its *source* (beginning). The river brings both water and rich soils to the people of the Nile Valley. Without the Nile few people could live in Egypt. Beyond the waters of the Nile is the desert—approximately 96% of the total land of Egypt.

Bedouin shepherd. Sheep herding is an important Bedouin occupation throughout the Middle East.
Credit: *Israel Government Tourist Office*

Climate and Agriculture

The best land for farming, therefore, is found in the river valleys and along the seacoasts. The land along the Mediterranean Sea has a pleasant climate. This is known as a Mediterranean climate and is similar to that of California. The summers are long, hot and dry; winters are mild and moist. Olives, fruits and grapes are grown on the hillsides along the coastal areas. In addition, the waters and banks of the many seas of the Middle East have long provided food for man. Fishing and sailing are possible on the Black, Caspian, Mediterranean, Red and Arabian Seas and on the Persian Gulf. All the countries of the Middle East have at least some access to the sea.

The People of the Middle East and Their Way of Life

There are three very different ways of life in the Middle East. The farmer, the nomad herder and the city dweller almost seem to live in separate worlds. Yet, each is dependent on the others for the fulfillment of basic needs.

Nomads of the Desert

The nomads who inhabit the deserts of the Middle East make up about 5% of the people of the area. They are known as *bedouins* and they live in tribes. Their time is spent moving through the desert in search of water and grass for their herds of sheep, goats and camels.

Because he is always on the move, the nomad has few goods besides his cooking pots, his loose flowing clothes, his rugs and his blankets. He lives in a tent and sleeps and eats on rugs. The men and boys live in one half of the tent and the women and girls live in the other half.

The animals provide the nomad with most of his needs. Goat's milk and cheese are his main foods. He rarely eats meat. His blankets, his tent and most of his clothes are woven from the hair of goats and camels. Leather from the hides of the animals is used to make baskets and sandals.

Whatever his animals do not supply, the nomad buys when he reaches an *oasis*. (An oasis is a place in the desert where there is water and vegetation. The water comes from underground streams.) In this way the nomads are dependent on the farms and cities that lie beyond the desert. Part of the nomad's diet consists of flour, dates and fruits that come from the farms and groves. From the towns and cities he obtains his utensils, cloth, coffee, tea and sugar. The bedouins in turn provide the farmers and city people with animals and animal products.

Duties and responsibilities among the bedouins have always been divided according to sex. It is the man's duty to fight and look after the camels, while the woman takes care of the other animals, the household and the children, and sees to it that the family has enough water.

The bedouins are very proud individuals who believe in equality and do not like to be ruled by other people. Nevertheless, the family, clan and tribe are considered to be more important than the individual. (A group of related families make up a clan and a number of clans together form a tribe.)

For the bedouin the tribe carries out the same functions that the government does in our society. The tribal leader, or *sheik*, meets together with a council of elders to make all the important decisions for the whole tribe. They make treaties with other tribes, fix wanderings in the desert, educate the children to be loyal members of the tribe, and punish those who have committed crimes.

Since humans are so helpless in the desert, there is complete dependence of man upon other men. Generosity is an important quality found among bedouins. A guest is treated as well as or better than one's own family. No bedouin may refuse another man protection from an enemy. He must admit the pursued man to his tent and offer him food and a place to sleep for three days, even though he is a stranger. The enemy cannot attack the person during the time that he is being sheltered in someone's tent.

In the past, the herders of the desert were the rulers of the Middle East. They crossed and recrossed borders as they pleased. They were able to attack the village farmers and force them to give up a large part of their crops because they could move swiftly on their horses and camels. The bedouins policed the desert and protected the caravans that crossed it. Today as a result of changes in transportation and communication the bedouins have come under the control of the governments in the cities. As a result, their whole way of life has changed. Thousands have left the desert to take jobs in the oil industry—especially in Iraq and Saudi Arabia. Others have become soldiers. Large numbers have settled down on the oases and in the cities. Many of the tribal chiefs are now rich landowners. Those living on land where oil has been discovered have adopted a way of life that is totally different from that of their fellow bedouins in the desert.

The Village Farmers

In the Middle East more than 75% of the people are farmers, or *fellahin* as they are known in Arabic. Wherever there is enough water to grow crops there is certain to be a farming village. Basically the farming villages of the Middle East show great similarities.

Most of the farmers own small plots of land—often too small to support their families. In some cases, however, the farmers do not own their land but rent land from the rich landlords who live in the cities (absentee landlords). These farmers are known as tenants, and the rent they pay to the landlord is very high. There are also farmers who work as sharecroppers on the land belonging to the landlord. They use the tools, seeds, animals and water that belong to the landlord, and in return they must turn over two-thirds to four-fifths of the crops to the landlord. In the past this situation existed all over the Middle East. Today it has been almost entirely abolished in Egypt, Syria and Iraq, but it continues to exist in the other countries.

The majority of farms are not modernized. Nearly all of the peasants work with simple tools—the hoe, the wooden plow, the hand sickle and the threshing board.

Their houses, which are made of sun-dried mud, are concentrated in the center of the village. Fields surround each village. The best land is divided into small plots and then divided up among the villagers. The poorer land is used for pasturing animals. Usually the land is rotated so that a farmer who works a poor strip of land, or one far from the village, can look forward to having a better strip of land in a succeeding year. A problem arises from this custom, however. Farmers have little desire or need to give long term care to the land or improve it, since the land will not always be theirs.

The farmer of the Middle East lives out his life in poverty. Because the amount of land he owns is so small and the tools he uses are primitive, his production is very low. As a result his income is low, debts pile up and he often has to borrow from the money lenders whose interest rates are extremely high—often 100%. The fellahin also have many children, another factor which contributes to their poverty. Until recently the villages where the farmers live had no electricity, no running water and no paved roads. Disease was widespread and there were few medical facilities. The village peasant was isolated from the cities and unaffected by what was happening in the rest of the world.

Now the Arab village is awakening and undergoing changes. Newspapers and radios are helping villagers to become aware of the world outside. Village youth are going to the cities to study. Welfare centers are being built to improve the health of the villagers. Some of the governments are passing land reform laws taking land away from the rich landlords and distributing it to the poor peasants. Even though some progress has been made, much remains to be done to improve the lives of the fellahin.

The only country in the Middle East where farming does not follow the pattern described above is Israel. In Israel there are no rich landlords and very few private landowners. Most of the land is organized into large collective farms called *kibbutzim*. All the farmers together own the land, the tools, the animals and the farm buildings. The work is divided up among the kibbutzniks (members of the collective farm), and after the crops have been sold, the profits are divided up among them as well. Israeli farmers use the most advanced methods and equipment.

Cities of the Middle East—The City Dweller

In the Middle East today as elsewhere, it is the city that dominates the rest of the country. All power is concentrated in the city—political, economic, social and cultural. This is where decisions are made and styles set that affect the entire nation. From the cities come the trained and educated people to lead the country.

There are several large cities in the Middle East.

CITY	POPULATION	CITY	POPULATION
Cairo	5,715,000	Algiers	1,200,000
Teheran	4,002,000	Beirut	938,940
Alexandria	2,259,000	Damascus	923,253
Baghdad	2,760,000	Aleppo	639,428
Istanbul	3,135,354	Tunis	647,640
Ankara	1,553,897	Izmir	819,276
		Tel Aviv	1,156,800

(estimated—1977)

The Middle East-Urban Population

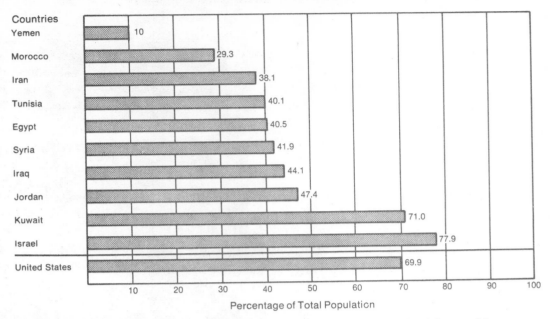

Percentage of Total Population

What conclusions can we reach from the information given in this graph?

In the cities of the Middle East the old and new exist side by side—the old Arab town alongside the modern city of the 20th century. The old Arab town was built with two things in mind—religion and protection. For the sake of security the town was built on a hill or near a river or sea. Religion required that the mosque be built in the center of the city. The mosque is the main gathering place for all purposes.

Not far from the mosque, the bazaar or marketplace is located. Here are the booths with all kinds of wares for sale, which provide a living for skilled craftsmen and merchants. Working chiefly with their hands, Middle East craftsmen manage to turn out products of remarkable quality and beauty. Moroccan leather and Persian rugs are world famous. Gold and silversmiths, workers in metal, and jewelers produce objects that are equally fine. Fathers and mothers pass their skills on to their children. Craftsmen work at home or in a workshop with five or six other people. Frequently all the workshops making the same product will be on the same street. Often the shops are located behind the booths in the marketplace. The bazaar is a fascinating place. In addition to the craftsmen, villagers from the countryside sell their goods. No item has a fixed price. The price is haggled over by the merchant and the customer. The customer tries to get the merchant to lower his price, while the merchant tries to keep it as high as he can. This is part of the enjoyment of making a sale.

Farther away from the center of town are the residential districts. These are divided into different quarters (sections). People living in each quarter usually share the same occupation, religion, nationality and customs.

This was the Arab town of old. It still stands today just as it was in former times with its mosque, its bazaar and its narrow winding streets. But alongside of it modern cities

The Dome of the Rock in Jerusalem is holy to Moslems because according to tradition
Mohammed ascended to heaven from this spot. It is holy to Jews as well because
the Dome marks the site of Solomon's Temple and it is believed to be where Abraham
prepared Isaac for sacrifice. (*Top*)
Credit: *Israel Government Tourist Office*

At prayer—Moslems kneel and pray beneath the graceful arches of the Great
Mosque at Mecca, Saudi Arabia. It is toward Mecca, Islam's holiest city, that
Moslems throughout the world turn five times each day and pray. (*Bottom*)
Credit: *Arabian America Oil Company*

have arisen. The new sections of the city are built in the European style. Broad avenues contain modern residential and commercial buildings, fine shops, hotels, theaters, and restaurants. People wear Western clothes and motion picture theaters show American, British and French films. Radios, newspapers and television keep people in touch with the rest of the world.

The old Arab town was made up mainly of two groups of people—the merchants and craftsmen. In the city of today one finds, in addition to these two groups, bankers, industrialists, landowners, engineers, doctors, lawyers, writers, army officers, office workers, factory workers, porters, and messengers.

The cities of the Middle East today have almost all the problems of modern cities anywhere—slums, housing shortage, traffic congestion. But worst of all is the problem of poverty. Middle Eastern cities have not yet developed into major industrial centers. There are some factories, such as spinning and weaving, cement plants, flour mills, fertilizer factories and soap factories. But there are not enough factories to provide jobs for the thousands of people who leave the countryside each year and come to the cities. Since there are far more people than there are jobs many people find themselves without work and those who do work earn very little money.

Islam—The Religion of the Middle East and North Africa

In the Middle East and North Africa most of the people are Moslems, that is, people who are believers in the religion known as *Islam*. Islam is more than a religion, however. It is a way of life, affecting almost every aspect of a person's life.

Mohammed — Founder of Islam

The Moslem religion was founded by Mohammed* in the 7th century. Mohammed was an Arab merchant who lived in the city of Mecca in Arabia. The people of Mecca worshipped many different gods, but Mohammed, who had frequent contacts with Christians and Jews, came to believe in only one God. Mohammed tried to spread his ideas to the people of Mecca, but they wouldn't accept them. In the year 622, Mohammed was driven from Mecca and fled to Medina. Moslems call this flight the *Hegira,* and that year is considered to be the year one of the Moslem calendar. In Medina the people accepted Mohammed as their leader. Here Mohammed built the first mosque and continued to preach his religion. From here the religion spread to the rest of Arabia and, within a century after Mohammed's death, to distant parts of the world. Mohammed was recognized as the Prophet, or messenger of God.

Mohammed called his religion Islam. Islam means "submission to God," that is, living according to God's will. After Mohammed's death, all his teachings were collected and put together in one book called the *Koran.* This book is holy to Moslems, because they believe that the words in it were spoken to Mohammed by God. Every aspect of life is regulated by the teachings in the Koran. The Koran is the most important book used in Moslem schools.

*Also spelled *Muhammad*

The Western Wall of the Temple (Wailing Wall) is one of the most sacred Jewish sites in the Holy Land.
Credit: *Israel Government Tourist Office*

Orthodox Jew blowing the traditional ram's horn.
Credit: *Israel Government Tourist Office*

Mohammed's Teachings — The Ideas of Islam

Mohammed taught that there was only one God, Allah. In this Mohammed was influenced by the monotheism of the Jews and the Old Testament. God rewards men who act according to his laws and punishes those who disobey them. There are angels who intercede for men. Moslems are taught to believe in the prophets of Allah, of whom Mohammed is considered the most important. The Koran speaks of the Day of Judgment when Allah will reward all men with either everlasting bliss or punishment.

Mohammed set up the rules that all Moslems had to follow and which are still followed today.

1. Moslems must repeat every day in Arabic, "There is no God but Allah, and Mohammed is his prophet."
2. A Moslem must pray five times a day. When praying, the person must turn towards Mecca, the holy city.
3. Moslems are required to give charity to the needy.
4. Moslems are supposed to *fast* (go without food or drink) from sunrise to sunset during the holy month of Ramadan.
5. It is the duty of every Moslem to try to make a trip to Mecca at least once during his lifetime. This religious trip is called a *pilgrimage*. Each year, thousands of Moslems from different parts of the world travel to Mecca to fulfill this duty.

Each Moslem city has at least one *mosque*, or temple of worship. Every morning the Moslem is awakened by a call to prayer from the mosque. Every adult male must attend the Friday noon service. There are no statues or *images* (pictures of people or animals) in the mosque.

The Islamic religion had an elevating effect on its followers. Islam emphasized kindness and forgiveness, respect for parents, protection of the weak and charity towards the poor. Mohammed taught that all men who followed Islam were brothers. "Know ye that every Moslem is a brother to every other Moslem, and that ye are now one brotherhood." All Moslems were considered equal before the law.

Moslems believe that theirs is the only true religion. They honor Moses and Christ as prophets of the one God. Jews and Christians are called "People of the Book" and are given a special place in the Islamic religion.

The religious beliefs that Moslems share have brought Moslems all over the world closer together. These beliefs have been carried over into the modern world and into their present forms of government.

The Jews and Judaism

The Ancient Hebrews

About 1400 B.C. a group of people called *Hebrews* moved into the land that is now called Israel. This land, which was formerly known as Canaan or Palestine, is a small fertile region located between the Arabian Desert and the Mediterranean Sea. These people were shepherds, and it is believed that they came from Mesopotamia (Iraq) in search of water and new land. After reaching Palestine they settled down, became farmers, set up a government, and began to develop as a nation. Under King David and

King Solomon ancient Israel reached its greatest glory. Trade was carried on with distant lands, wealth poured into Israel, and Solomon built a magnificent temple in Jerusalem. But the Hebrew nation lasted only a short time before it was destroyed by outside enemies. The Hebrews, or *Jews* as they were later called, were scattered over the entire world. However, during the few hundred years that the Hebrews lived in Palestine they developed ideas which influenced other civilizations, especially our own. The ideas about God and man, which the Hebrews put into the Bible, live on today not only in the religion of the Jews, but in Christianity and Islam as well.

The Hebrews and God

The Hebrews were the first people to believe in one God. Other nations before and after the Hebrews continued to believe in many gods which were connected with the forces of nature—sun, moon, rain, trees. In the beginning the Hebrew religion also involved the worship of many gods, but gradually the idea of one God developed. The Hebrews called their God, Yahweh (YHWH), and believed that he created man and the entire universe. The belief in one God is known as *monotheism*.

The Hebrews believed that their God demanded strict obedience. God made his demands known in the Ten Commandments which he gave to Moses on Mount Sinai. Yahweh was a jealous God, and his first commandment was, "Thou shalt have no other God before me."

But the Hebrew God was also a loving father who looked upon men as his children whom he protected. The Hebrews believed that God had made a *covenant*, or agreement, with them. God promised that if the Hebrews obeyed his commandments he would be on their side and protect them. The Bible tells many stories which show how God protected his people. According to one story, God asked Abraham to sacrifice his only son, Isaac. As Abraham laid Isaac on the altar and took the knife to slay him, an angel appeared telling him not to touch his son, "for now I know that you fear God." God then promised that Abraham's descendants would multiply and be victorious over their enemies. Thereafter, the Egyptians who pursued the escaping Hebrews were drowned in the Red Sea; David defeated Goliath; and the Hebrews were able to conquer Canaan and create a Hebrew state.

The Ideas of Justice and Righteousness

The God of the Hebrews demanded worship, but not worship alone. God was much more interested in man's *ethical* (moral) behavior. God was just and demanded justice of his people; he was righteous and he demanded righteousness of his people. After the Hebrews settled down and gained wealth and power, many people began to worship other gods. Then the prophets (Elijah, Jeremiah, Amos, Isaiah) came on the scene to keep the faith in Yahweh alive by condemning the worship of other gods and by saying "The Lord is one." But the prophets were also concerned with man's relation with his fellow man. The prophets claimed that God was not interested in sacrifice and offerings but in justice and right living. The prophets spoke out against the oppression of the poor by the rich and the powerful. They criticized the kings for living in luxury while the people suffered. The prophets said that God would punish those people who had strayed from the path of righteousness. And when the ancient Hebrew state in Palestine was destroyed by powerful neighbors, the prophets explained this by saying that God was punishing the Hebrews for their wicked ways. Thus, for the first time in history religion was combined with ethics and morality. The other people of the ancient world believed that by offering sacrifices they could make their gods happy. These gods could bring rain and make the sun shine, but they were not concerned with the affairs of men. It was the Hebrews who believed that man was responsible for his fellow men and that God demanded righteousness of his people. It is because of these ideas that the Hebrew (Jewish) religion has had such a powerful influence on the rest of the world.

The Dignity of Man

Not only was the Hebrew idea of God different from that of other people, but their idea of man differed as well. Other nations of the ancient world thought of man as a lowly creature, who was nothing more than a slave of the gods. The Hebrews developed the idea of the *dignity* of man. In the psalms they wrote,

"What is man, that thou shouldst think of him,
And the son of man that thou shouldst care for him?
Yet thou hast made him but little lower than God,
And dost crown him with glory and honor!"

The Bible and the Talmud

Originally the Old Testament (Bible) contained all the teachings and laws that Jews were expected to follow. As the years passed, new situations and living conditions arose for which no provision was made in the Bible. *Rabbis*, or religious teachers, interpreted the laws and made new decisions to fit the new situations. After several hundred years all these decisions were put together in volumes called the *Talmud*. The observance of these laws is what kept the Jews together for almost 2000 years even though they were scattered all over the world.

Early History of the Middle East

River Valley Civilizations

The first great civilizations in the world developed along the banks of rivers. Historians believe that there have been four cradles of civilization and that two of these have been in the Middle East. (The other two developed in India and China.) One of these was in Egypt, in the Nile Valley. The other was in Mesopotamia (known as Iraq today) between the Tigris and Euphrates Rivers. From the Nile Valley and Mesopotamia civilization spread northward and westward, eventually reaching Europe and America.

From the beginning, conditions in the Nile Valley and Mesopotamia favored agriculture. The great rivers annually overflowed their banks, depositing a rich layer of soil. This fertile, well-watered soil produced abundant harvests. These in turn made possible a large increase in population. Cities and villages arose.

It was in these river valleys that man first worked out rules for living together in communities. The earliest rules dealt with irrigation. In order for a farmer to get water from the river to his fields, there had to be a system of dams and canals. The cooperation of whole villages and often whole districts was required to build and defend these canals. Leaders were needed to supervise the building, and laws were needed to ensure that every farmer repaired his own ditches and used only his fair share of water. Thus, the need for water helped create the need for government.

So fertile was the soil of the Nile Valley and Mesopotamia that a farmer could produce more than enough food for himself and his family. The surplus he could sell. As a result trade and commerce developed and with it came the exchange of ideas and inventions between people of different regions. Since there was enough food available, some men could turn their attention to develop art and skills. Potters learned to shape clay into beautiful vases; weavers learned to make fabrics; carpenters learned to build furniture; and architects and stonemasons learned to construct elaborate buildings.

Cities and towns grew. These were places where farmers could sell their crops, where craftsmen could live and practice their skills, and where rulers could establish their centers of government. In the cities where men lived close together ideas developed and spread.

Let us examine the various nations that developed in the Middle East and see what contributions they have made to mankind.

The Ancient Egyptians

The history of ancient Egypt dates back to 5000 B.C. or even earlier. At that time the Egyptians were already using copper tools. Great advances in agriculture had been made through the introduction of the plow and the use of irrigation systems. During the next few thousand years Egyptian civilization reached a very high level.

Although most Egyptians were farmers, many industries existed. Copper mining, stone quarrying, cabinet making, tanning, metal working, glass blowing and weaving were some of the most important occupations. Egyptian craftsmen produced wares that were exceptionally beautiful. Since these products were in great demand, seagoing ships carried them to distant lands.

Progress was made in the art of government. The villages were united to form one nation with all power in the hands of the *pharaoh*, or ruler, who maintained order throughout the kingdom. Religion was very important to the ancient Egyptians, whose main concern was with the immortality of the soul. They believed that by mummifying, or preserving the corpse, the soul would have eternal life. Later they developed the idea that everlasting life was a reward for those who were good while alive.

One of the most important Egyptian contributions to civilization was the development of the art of writing. The Egyptians did not develop a real alphabet. Their system of writing was known as *hieroglyphics*. Picture-like signs represented objects and later ideas. Still later these signs were used to represent the sounds of words and then the sounds of syllables. Ink was made, and writing was done on roles of papyrus which were stored in earthen jars. This made it possible to accumulate knowledge and pass it on to future generations.

It is also believed that the first calendar in the world was developed in Egypt, perhaps as early as 4241 B.C. This calendar consisted of 12 months with 30 days each. At the end of the year 5 days were added on.

Architecture was highly advanced in ancient Egypt. Because of their concern with life after death, the Pharaohs concentrated on building huge tombs to preserve their bodies. These pyramids still stand today, 4,000 years after they were constructed. The pyramids, as well as the magnificent temples that were built, are proof that the Egyptians were skilled engineers who knew the principles of architecture and mathematics. Sculpture and painting were also developed and were used for decoration of the palaces and pyramids.

The Egyptians were the first people to develop the science of mathematics. Exact measurements were needed to build pyramids. Since the Nile frequently overflowed its banks and erased field boundaries, precise land measurements were necessary. To meet these needs the Egyptians learned to add and subtract. They also could multiply and divide by two and three. They knew the basic principles of geometry and algebra.

During the three thousand years that the Egyptians were developing their civilization, equally important advances were being made by other people living in Mesopotamia between the Tigris and Euphrates Rivers and along the Mediterranean Sea. However, since there were no natural barriers to protect them, this area was the scene of constant warfare and the rise and fall of numerous nations.

The Peoples of Mesopotamia

Sumerians   By 3500 B.C. the Sumerians already had an advanced civilization in the fertile land lying between the Tigris and Euphrates Rivers. Here, as in Egypt, the mild climate and good soil produced abundant harvests. The need for irrigation led to the growth of government. Flourishing cities arose where craftsmen produced textiles, metal products and other goods. The Sumerians are given credit for being the first people to use wheeled vehicles. They also made important progress in mathematics. They developed a number system based on 60, which today is the basis for dividing a circle into 360° and an hour into 60 minutes. Geometric formulas were devised to compute the area of a triangle. The Sumarians also developed a system of writing known as *cuneiform.* There were 350 signs representing complete words or syllables. Writing was done on soft clay tablets. Many other people of the Middle East borrowed this system of writing and used it until the introduction of the alphabet centuries later. The Sumerians were practical business people and were probably the first to use contracts in business. Sumerian literature included stories of the creation and the flood, which are similar to the later Hebrew stories found in the Bible.

Babylonians   The Sumerians were conquered by a group of people whose capital was Babylon, and who came to be known as Babylonians. The Babylonians are famous for the law code of Hammurabi, their greatest ruler. This law code provided that "If a man destroy the eye of another man, they shall destroy his eye. If a builder builds a house for a man and does not make its construction firm, and the house which he has built collapses and causes the death of the owner of the house, that builder shall be put to death." Even though the punishments were harsh, the code was an attempt to provide some form of justice.

The dhow has been used by Arabs for centuries to carry goods to and from Asia and Africa.
Credit: *Arab Information Center*

Hittites

The Hittites reached the height of their power around 1500 B.C. in the area that is today Turkey and Syria. They were among the earliest people to use iron, and it was through them that the metal came to be used throughout the Middle East.

Lydians
Phoenicians

The Lydians were the first people to use coined money in the 9th century B.C.

The Phoenicians who lived in cities along the Mediterranean were the greatest traders, navigators and colonizers of their day. They were skilled manufacturers, and their purple dye, textiles, metal goods and glassware were famous throughout the Mediterranean world. Their most important contribution was the alphabet which they developed, consisting of 22 consonant signs arranged in definite order. Their first two symbols were called aleph and beth, and it is from these that the word alphabet comes.

Hebrews
Chaldeans

The major contribution of the Hebrews was in religion, which was discussed earlier.

In the 7th century B.C. Mesopotamia came under the control of the Chaldeans. These people were important because of the progress which they made in astronomy. Through systematic observation of the heavens, the Chaldeans were able to identify many stars and planets and even predict eclipses.

Persians

By 500 B.C. all the lands of the Middle East had been conquered by the Persians, the people who now live in the area we know as Iran. In fact, the Persian empire was so large that it extended up to the frontiers of India in the east and included parts of Greece in the west. In this vast empire many different people mingled together and exchanged ideas and inventions. The Persians ran their empire very efficiently. Roads were built connecting distant lands. It may be said that the Persians developed the first pony express. Every fourteen miles there was a post station where fresh horses could be obtained by the king's messengers. The Persians treated the conquered peoples humanely, granting equal rights to all and respecting the gods of all. Their religion, *Zoroastrianism*, taught that there was a continuous struggle in the world between two great forces—righteousness and evil, and that righteousness would *prevail* (triumph).

Decline of the Middle East Kingdoms

As we have seen, the ancient Middle East made tremendous contributions to the civilization of mankind. However, after several thousand years of advance, progress seemed to level off and come to a standstill. By the 5th century B.C. the center of civilization had shifted west along the Mediterranean Sea to Greece. For the next thousand years most of the advances in Western civilization came from the Greeks and the Romans. However, many of the ideas and discoveries of the ancient Middle East were borrowed by the Greeks and then developed still further.

The Triumph of Islam— Moslem Civilization 622-1453

The Spread of Islam

Until the 7th century A.D. the people of Arabia had never played a large part in the development of the Middle East. Living in an area that was mainly desert, most of their time was spent looking after their flocks and wandering in search of water. In the sixth century the Arabs had not yet reached the high level of civilization that the Hebrews, Egyptians and other people of the Middle East had reached centuries earlier. However, in the 7th century, inspired by the teachings of Mohammed, the Arabs suddenly came to life.

In their search for converts to the new religion and economic gains, the Arabs swept over Persia, Mesopotamia, Palestine, Egypt and North Africa. They conquered one settlement after another. In the west, Arab armies conquered Spain. They swept across south and central France until they were finally stopped at Tours, in the famous battle of 732 A.D. Although stopped in the west, the Arabs continued their successses in the east, extending their power into Central Asia and later into India and Southeast Asia. Within a century after Mohammed's death, the Arab empire extended from the Atlantic Ocean in the west to India in the east.

How were the Arabs able to conquer and rule so vast an empire? First the Arabs were magnificent warriors. Mohammed had taught that any Arab dying in battle while fighting to spread Islam was assured entry into heaven. This made the Arabs fearless in battle. Their life in the desert gave the Arabs a toughness which easily defeated all who stood in their way. Second, after the poverty of desert life, the possibility of gaining rich and fertile lands only encouraged the Arabs to fight harder. Third, many people found it easy to become Moslems because Islam did not discriminate against people on account of their race. Finally, the Moslems were very tolerant rulers and allowed the Christians, Jews and other people to continu their way of life and follow their own religion.

Contributions of the Arabs

For the next 500 years Moslem civilization far surpassed that of Europe. Historians have used the words "magnificent," "splendid" and "brilliant" to describe the civilization of the Moslems during this time. No other people contributed so much to learning during this period as did the scholars and scientists of the Moslem world. The luxury and wealth that existed in the Moslem lands was unknown in Europe.

The book *Arabian Nights* gives a good description of the splendor of Baghdad, which was the capital of the Moslem world from 750 to 1258. Around the bazaars were merchants who brought fabulous carpets from Persia; silks from China; steel from Damascus; cotton from Egypt; leather from Morocco; spices and dyes from India, ivory, gold and slaves from Africa; honey, wax and white slaves from Russia. Industry and commerce prospered.

The cultural contributions of the Moslems were tremendous. This was partly due to the generosity of the *caliphs* (the men who ruled the Islamic empire) who welcomed artists, writers, scholars and scientists to their courts and encouraged them in their work. The Moslems had an ability to recognize what was best in other cultures, adopt it, add to it and then pass it on to other people. The Moslems were especially influenced by the philosophy and science of ancient Greece and India. Most of the outstanding Greek writers were translated into Arabic. This learning was improved upon and later transmitted by the Moslems to Western Europe.

The Moslems made important advances in medicine. Various diseases were diagnosed and described, including measles and smallpox; all the medical knowledge of the day was collected and published in several huge encyclopedias; the first drug stores and schools of pharmacy were set up; druggists and doctors had to pass an examination; hospitals were built throughout the empire. Physics and chemistry also progressed under the Moslems. To advance the study of astronomy, they developed good astronomical instruments and built observatories. Most of their knowledge of mathematics came from the Hindus in India. This knowledge included the numbers we use today, but since it was the Arabs who introduced these numbers to Western Europe, they are commonly referred to as Arabic numbers. The Arabs made great progress in algebra, which is itself an Arabic word. Because of their trade with distant lands as well as their pilgrimages to Mecca, the Moslems became the most important geographers of the time. A great deal of geographical knowledge was collected, and maps were printed.

The Moslems made important contributions to literature as well. Arabs have always had the special gift of storytelling and poetry. The Arabic language itself is suited to colorful tales about life in the desert or palace. Hundreds of poets created poems of great beauty. The one most known in the West was the Persian poet Omar Khayyám. The *Arabian Nights* is a collection of tales that is quite popular all over the world. Many histories were written during this period. Arab historians specialized in biographies of Mohammed and other important Moslem leaders, accounts of the spread of Islam and world histories.

In art the two fields in which the Moslems excelled were architecture and the decorative arts. Beautiful mosques were built with spacious interiors, large domes, great pillars and arches to provide Moslems with a dignified place in which to pray. Besides the mosques, the Moslems built large palaces, of which the most famous is the Alhambra in Granada, Spain. Beautiful patterns from flowers and geometric figures were used to decorate the interior of mosques and palaces. Skilled craftsmen produced rugs, pottery, tiles and metalwork of original and delicate designs.

The Middle East in Decline

Between the years 700 to 1200 A.D. the Moslems had the most advanced civilization in the world. Then something went wrong. Moslem civilization stopped advancing. By 1600 the civilization of Europe began to develop more rapidly and surpass that of the Moslems. There are a number of reasons which help to explain this decline.

1. Political disunity

By the middle of the 10th century it was evident that there was no real unity in the Moslem lands. Although most of the countries recognized the caliph in Baghdad as their ruler, local leaders did pretty much as they wished. Different religious groups arose, each claiming to be the true followers of Islam. These groups plotted against and fought with each other. Arabs, Persians and Turks rivaled one another for important positions and for leadership. Therefore, in the face of a common enemy the Moslem lands could not really put up any resistance.

2. The Crusades

From 1097 to 1291 the Christians in Europe tried to reconquer the Holy Land from the Moslems. The coastal cities of Palestine, parts of Syria and Turkey were captured by the Christians. During this period Moslem rulers made alliances with Europeans against other Moslems. Finally the famous ruler of Egypt, Salah-al-Din (Saladin) was able to unite enough territory and in 1187 to defeat the Christians, who were driven from Jerusalem. During the 200 years of warfare there was considerable destruction in the Middle East.

**3. European
   expansion**

**4. Nomadic
   attacks**

**5. Sea route
   to India**

In general, as the Christians in Europe grew stronger they began to expand at the expense of Islam. Areas such as Spain, which had been part of the Moslem world, were gradually taken over by the Europeans.

Periodically, over a period of several hundred years various group of nomads invaded the Middle East and North Africa and caused tremendous destruction from which the area never recovered. In the middle of the 11th century nomadic Arabs invaded North Africa destroying the land and the irrigation systems. This was never repaired and as a result farming seriously declined.

During the 13th century far greater destruction was caused by the Mongols. The Mongols were nomadic horsemen who came from the steppes of Central Asia. Sweeping down on the Middle East, the Mongols conquered Persia, Iraq, and Syria. Baghdad, the capital of the Islamic world, fell in 1258. Hundreds of thousands of people died, cities vanished, and governments fell. Never before had the Middle East suffered such a shock from invaders. Great disorder followed the invasion. Trade routes became dangerous and trade broke down. Industry declined. Iraq, which had been the center of the whole Moslem world, was ruined. The final blows by the Mongols came in 1380 under the leadership of Timur Leng (Tamerlane). The Mongols captured Baghdad, Damascus, Aleppo, Ankara and other cities. Schools, mosques, libraries, and palaces were destroyed. The Mongols left pyramids of human heads behind them in each city.

The discovery in 1497 of an all-water route between Europe and India contributed to the decline of the Middle East. Formerly Middle Eastern cities profited from the overland trade between Asia and Europe. With goods moving by sea, these cities lost their main source of income.

The Ottoman Empire

The Rise of the Ottomans

During the same period that the Arab world was declining in power and importance, a new people in the Middle East were beginning to make their strength felt. They were the Turks, who had originally come from Central Asia and over the centuries settled in the country that is today known as Turkey. At the beginning of the 14th century they created a small, powerful state in Turkey. For the next few centuries Turkish history consisted of a series of wars to capture territory and extend their empire. By the 16th century southeastern Europe, North Africa and most of the Middle East had been conquered by the Turks. These Turks were known as Ottoman Turks, and, therefore, the territory under their control was known as the Ottoman Empire.

During the 16th century Ottoman civilization reached its peak. The Turks were great soldiers and good administrators and ruled their vast empire quite efficiently. Under their greatest ruler, Suleiman the Magnificent, who ruled from 1521-1566, the Ottomans built a strong navy and became the strongest naval power in the Mediterranean. The Turks of this period were also master builders and poets as well. Many beautiful mosques and palaces were built, and there were important achievements in literature, especially in the field of poetry, essay writing and history.

Government in the Ottoman Empire

Although the Turks were Moslems, there were a number of other religious and *ethnic* (national) groups in the Ottoman Empire. The Turks allowed each group to keep its own religion, laws, language and customs. Each group had its own courts, which tried all cases except those involving public security and crime. These groups were required to pay taxes to the Ottoman government, but in other respects they enjoyed a good deal of freedom.

The *sultan* was the ruler of the empire and the head of Islam. He had absolute authority over all matters. The second most powerful man in the empire was the grand vizier who was the Sultan's chief deputy. To rule such a vast empire many qualified men were needed. Every five years representatives of the Sultan travelled through the European provinces selecting the healthiest and most intelligent Christian boys between the ages of 12 and 20. They were converted to Islam, taught Turkish and assigned to military units. The best of these boys were brought to the royal palace and trained to govern the empire. Others were recruited for the army. Education, religious matters and law were exclusively in the hands of Moslem *mullahs* (wise men).

Decline of the Ottomans

During the 17th century the Ottoman Empire began to decline. By the 18th century the Ottomans were already losing territory to the more powerful Europeans. There were many reasons for this decline. In the early years the Empire had been ruled by capable sultans. After Suleiman the Magnificent, however, the sultans became more interested in the luxuries and pleasures of life than in ruling the empire. In the beginning also, government officials were appointed on the basis of merit—those most qualified to do the job. Later, important positions were given to favorites who were often not fitted for the job. Bribery was used to obtain many jobs, and the government became very corrupt. As the sultans grew weaker and the officials less capable, the problems of ruling a vast empire increased. At this time the Europeans were making great progress in science and industry. The Turks looked down upon the Europeans as inferiors and would not learn new ideas from them. Trade between Europe and Asia was almost completely in the hands of the Europeans. Thus an important source of wealth was gone. As the Ottoman Empire grew weaker, Russia and Austria tried to capture some of its territories and these wars further weakened the Empire. Gradually the Turks lost control over many of their territories.

European Imperialism in the Middle East

European Interest in the Middle East

During the 19th century the Ottoman Empire became known as "the sick man of Europe." The Empire was falling apart and the Europeans stood by waiting to take their share of it when the opportunity arose. The Europeans were expanding just when the Ottoman Empire had reached its lowest point. They wanted to rule over the less developed countries because they would gain markets for the goods that their factories produced. They would have areas where they could invest their money with the promise of high profits. The Europeans at first tried to avoid sending armies to conquer and rule the people directly. They found it easier to create puppet rulers to protect European interests. When the local ruler could not control the people, the Europeans sent armies in to protect their citizens and their investments. The presence of the armies led to anti-European uprisings by the people of the area. The threat of more uprisings forced the Europeans to keep their armies there even longer.

The Europeans Gain Control

The period of European penetration into the Middle East began with Napoleon's invasion of Egypt in 1798. Napoleon defeated the Egyptians who were still part of the Ottoman Empire. A few weeks later an English fleet arrived and defeated the French forces. This incident was important for two reasons. First, it demonstrated that European military power was superior to that of the Middle East. Second, the British became the protector of the Ottoman Empire and gained a very important voice in the affairs of the Middle East.

Throughout the 19th century, Russia fought many wars against Turkey in the hope of gaining territory belonging to the Turks. It was only because of Britain's coming to the aid of Turkey, that the Russians were prevented from breaking up the Empire.

Nevertheless, the British and French began to take over parts of the Empire themselves. France gained Algeria in 1830 and Tunisia in 1881. In 1882 the British took over Egypt. In 1912, France and Spain set up protectorates in Morocco. Italy held Libya from 1911 until World War II. The Arab countries of the Middle East came under the control of the British and French after World War I.

In 1856 the ruler of Egypt granted permission to Ferdinand de Lesseps, a French engineer, to dig a canal connecting the Mediterranean with the Gulf of Suez. The Suez Canal, which was opened in 1869, shortened the sea voyage between Europe and Asia by thousands of miles. Although built by the French, the Canal soon became Britain's most important waterway for trading with India. In 1875, when the ruler of Egypt was in need of cash, he sold his shares in the Canal Company to the British. In this way the British came to own a major share in the Canal, and their future policy in Egypt was determined by the need to protect this investment.

In 1881 rioting broke out in Egypt, and the Egyptian government called on the British for help. The British landed troops and promised to withdraw them from Egypt as soon as order was restored. British armed forces did not leave the country until 1956! Egypt never really became a colony, because the occupation was considered to be temporary. Until World War I, Egypt continued to be an Ottoman province, but real power was in the hands of the British.

World War I and the Middle East

World War I brought about the collapse of the Ottoman Empire. The Empire found itself fighting on the side of Germany against England, France and Russia. The British encouraged the Arabs to revolt against the Ottomans. In return, the British promised independence and the establishment of an Arab state for the Arab lands east of Suez. But these promises were very vague, and no boundaries were specified. In addition, Britain and France had already secretly agreed to divide up the territory between themselves. The Arabs revolted against the Turks in 1916 and fought hard, expecting to be rewarded at the end of the war. Their leader, Sharif Hussein, dreamed of an Arab state that would stretch from Iraq to the Mediterranean Sea and would include the Arabian Peninsula.

At the end of the war the League of Nations turned over Syria and Lebanon to the French as mandates. Iraq, Palestine and Transjordan became British mandates. This meant that these countries were to be ruled by the British and French until they were considered ready for independence. The Arabs were very bitter over what they regarded as betrayal by the Europeans.

Nationalism in the Middle East

After the war nationalism gained great strength. In Egypt there were frequent riots and demonstrations as people demanded "Egypt for the Egyptians." British rule had brought many improvements to Egypt. A modern tax system was set up; Egypt's finances were administered efficiently; irrigation works were built, including a dam at Aswan; slavery and forced labor were banned; improvements were made in medical care and sanitation. But the British did nothing to improve education. Egyptians were given no voice in their own government. Nor were factories built. The standard of living of the Egyptian people remained very low. At the end of the war Egyptian nationalists demanded immediate independence. In 1922, Britain declared that Egypt was independent, but certain matters relating to Egypt's foreign affairs were left for the British to decide. In 1936 a treaty was signed giving Egypt greater self-government. But the British reserved the right to intervene, if the Canal was threatened. British troops did not leave Egypt until 1956.

Saudi Arabia's independence was recognized in 1927. Iraq was declared independent in 1922, but the British mandate did not end until 1932. Even then British troops continued to occupy important places in Iraq, and major decisions continued to be made by the British. In Syria and Lebanon the French held absolute power until the end of World War II. Control over the foreign affairs, education, justice and economy of these two countries was in French hands.

It wasn't until after World War II that the Middle East achieved real independence.

The Middle East After World War II—Nationalism and the Question of Arab Unity

Independence After World War II

In 1939 war broke out in Europe. The countries and the peoples of the Middle East watched the events in Europe with great interest. Their leaders saw in the war an opportunity to gain their freedom. In the years that followed the end of the war, the nations of the Middle East and North Africa gained their independence.

Common Heritage and Traditions

Despite many problems all the countries of the area have some important things in common—the Moslem religion and the accomplishments of Islamic civilization. Of all the countries in this wide area, only Turkey turned its back on this heritage and tried to use modern and Western ideas to solve its problems. The leaders of the other nations followed an idea that would combine both the Islamic heritage and modern ideas. They did this because they knew how firmly most of the people believed in Islam.

One key idea of Islam was that there is *one* unified Islamic state. This idea is often called *Pan-Islamism*—that is the goal of creating a state under a single ruler for all Moslems. This is not realistic, for Moslems are scattered over a wide area of the world from Morocco to the Philippines. In addition, because of the environment in which they live, the religious practices and customs are very different among the various groups that follow Islam.

Pan-Arabism was another idea that gained importance. This idea involved the establishment of a single country for all Arabic-speaking people. The non-Arabic countries of Turkey and Iran would be left out, but this country might someday include all of Arabia, Iraq, the eastern shore of the Mediterranean and all of North Africa. *Pan Arabism*, as this idea is called, became important after 1945.

The first organization of Arab countries was the Arab League, formed in 1945 and still in existence today. From the beginning it was clear that forming a single Arab state would be difficult because the Arab countries disagreed with each other on a number of things. They could not agree on which country should be the leader of this state. Egypt was most powerful, but the other nations were not willing to accept its leadership.

Political Instability

Another very serious problem preventing unity is political instability. Each country in the Arab world has faced revolution and attempts to change the government by force. Syria has had many governments changed by force, few, if any by free elections. King Faisal of Iraq was murdered, and his cousin King Hussein of Jordan faces continued opposition and attempts to remove him from his throne. The government of Lebanon is divided between Moslems and Christians and cannot act strongly in times of crisis.

Most recently, a revolution in Iran, led by the forces of Ayatollah Ruhollah Khomeini, overthrew the government of the Shah, Mohammed Riza Pahlevi. Ayatollah Khomeini is now struggling to establish a new government in which Islam will play a major role. His prime minister, Mehdi Bazargan, is meeting opposition from Marxist forces, however, and the eventual nature of this government remains uncertain.

Egypt has had less instability than some of the other countries. In 1952 the army led by Gamal Abdel Nasser forced the King of Egypt out and set up a republic. Nasser tried to improve the lives of the Egyptian people, but because of his dream of a Pan-Arab state led by Egypt, his reforms fell far short of his goals. To achieve this dream, Nasser needed military power and, in the search for this power, he forced the Egyptians to spend money for guns—rather than for improvements in the lives of the people.

Israel and Arab Unity

In 1948 the State of Israel was created. This will be discussed at greater length later. Israel as a non-Arab, non-Islamic state has become a uniting force among Arabs. However, this unity does not go very far. Most Arabs are united in their opposition to Israel, but they agree on very little else.

The dream of creating a united Moslem or a united Arab state is not close to achievement, but the idea is still powerful and Arab leaders continue to fight for the establishment of this state and the honor of being its leader.

Oil Is King

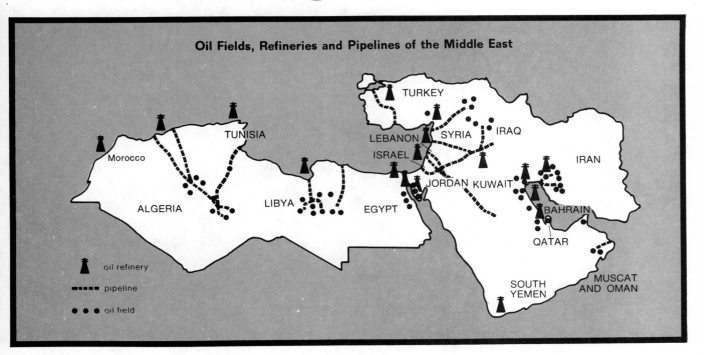

Oil Fields, Refineries and Pipelines of the Middle East

The major natural resource of the Middle East is oil. The Middle East is the world's leading producer of oil. Most of this oil is found in Saudi Arabia, Kuwait, Iran, Iraq, Libya, the United Arab Emirates and Qatar. Saudi Arabia alone is the world's largest exporter of oil–shipping six million barrels a day. In addition, the Middle East has the largest oil reserves in the world. These oil reserves are for future use. Saudi Arabia is considered to have the largest proven oil reserves, estimated at 145 billion barrels.

OIL IN THE MIDDLE EAST

Country	Oil Production Barrels a Day (in millions)	Proven Reserves (in billions of barrels)	Population (in millions)	Oil Revenues (in billions)
Saudi Arabia	6	145	8.2	2.3
Kuwait	3.3	66	.8	1.1
Iran	5	55.5	30.2	2.1
Iraq	1.4	36	10.4	.9
Libya	2.2	25	2	1.6
United Arab Emerates	1	18.9	.4	.4
Qatar	.4	6	.1	.2

An Arabian American Oil Company (Aramco) drilling rig in Saudi Arabia. Note that drilling takes place in the heart of one of the world's great deserts.
Credit: *Arabian American Oil Company*

Foreigners Develop Oil Resources

Oil was first discovered in Iran in 1908. In 1927, the Kirkuk oil fields of Iraq began to produce, and in 1935 oil fields in the Arabian Peninsula were developed. The real growth in oil production, however, came about after World War II.

The oil fields of the Middle East were developed by European and American companies and *not* by the countries of the Middle East. This was because the Middle Eastern countries did not have the money, the trained personnel, or the equipment to carry out their own oil operations. They, therefore, granted *concessions* (special privileges) to American and European (mainly English, French and Dutch) companies. In Saudi Arabia, the major concession was obtained in 1932 by the Arabian American Oil Company (ARAMCO). In Kuwait vast fields were drilled by the Kuwait Oil Company, which was owned by British Petroleum and Gulf Oil. In Iraq, development since 1927 was in the hands of British Petroleum, Royal Dutch Shell, Compagnie Française de Petroles, Mobil and Exxon. The same companies operated the oil wells of Iran, Qatar and the United Arab Emirates.

The companies were responsible for surveying, drilling and finally transporting the oil by means of pipelines to seaports along the Mediterranean, from where it was shipped abroad, mainly to Europe. As a result, the foreign companies had almost complete control of the oil. The companies decided how much oil to produce, where to sell it and how much to charge. And, of course, most of the profits went to the companies. The government of the country in which the oil was located received a fixed *royalty* (payment), usually 12.5% of the sale price and a tax.

In the 1960s disputes developed between the companies and the governments of the oil producing countries. By 1969 these governments were engaged in a major struggle with the oil companies to get a larger share of the profits and to gain greater control over the oil companies. In 1970 Libya demanded an increase in prices and tax rates. To force the companies to give in, Libya cut its oil production by 800,000 barrels a day. The companies fought the increases for seven months until finally Occidental Petroleum, an American company, accepted Libya's terms. The other companies, including Shell, Texaco, and Standard of California followed suit. Within a few months the other oil producing nations were demanding increases in payments and getting them from the companies. In June 1972, Iraq *nationalized* (the government took over) the big Kirkuk fields. Other countries nationalized oil fields as well.

Since 1971 the oil producing countries have gained control of their oil resources. They are in a position to dictate prices and terms to the companies and to the countries that must import this oil.

Oil Brings Wealth

The oil producing countries are now accumulating vast fortunes. This is mainly the result of having forced oil prices to double since 1970. Kuwait, a tiny country of only 800,000 people, received more than $1 billion in oil revenues in 1972. The United Arab Emirates, the oil-rich state on the Persian Gulf, received almost half a billion dollars. Saudi Arabia's income in 1972 was over $2 billion. In addition to the oil producing countries, other nations in the Middle East receive a substantial income from oil. Pipelines from Saudi Arabia and Iraq pass through Syria, Lebanon and Jordan. These countries are paid a fair amount of money for the movement of oil through their territories. Oil tankers, which moved through the Suez Canal until it was closed in 1967, paid tolls to Egypt amounting to about $60,000,000 annually.

Until recently, much of this money was wasted on luxuries by the rulers of the oil producing nations. Former King Saud of Saudi Arabia spent millions of dollars building royal palaces and providing the members of his family with air-conditioned cadillacs. The former ruler of the United Arab Emirates (formerly Abu Dhabi) kept all of the oil royalties for his personal use. Even today, the sheik of that nation keeps about $70 million for himself.

Oil Brings Progress

Much of the progress and modernization in the Middle East originally centered around the oil company. When an oil company entered an area in the Middle East changes followed rapidly. Nomadic herdsmen, drawn by attractive wages, left their flocks to work for the oil company. Complete new towns were built for workers in the oil fields. Instead of tents, workers found themselves living in concrete homes. Many received wages for the first time and bought goods they could never have afforded before. Companies like ARAMCO established schools for workers and their children. Specialized technical training has been provided for the workers as well as free medical care. The companies played a major role in building railroads and highways, clearing ports, constructing hospitals and housing developments. Since most of the oil produced in the Middle East is also refined there, oil refineries were built in Saudi Arabia, Kuwait, Iran, Turkey, Israel, Lebanon and the countries of North Africa. These refineries provide thousands of people with jobs.

In recent years, with so much oil money flowing in, the governments of the oil producing countries have been spending a greater part of this money on local development projects. Kuwait is a good example. This tiny country has one of the highest per capita incomes in the world. The government provides for the health and welfare of its people almost from the moment they are born. Great sums of money are spent by the government on education. Kuwait City, located in the middle of the desert, has been converted into a modern city with broad avenues, steel and glass buildings and thousands of automobiles. For the last ten years the government of Saudi Arabia has been providing scholarships for study abroad. Thousands of people who have benefited from these scholarships are now working in the government and in business. In 1964 the Petroleum College opened in Saudi Arabia. Hundreds of young people are trained as engineers here. Tuition, board and study materials are free, and Saudi Arabian students receive a monthly *stipend* of $80. The College has installed an advanced computer and trained systems analysts and programmers to run it.

Oil and Politics

Not only is oil important to the economies of the Middle Eastern countries, but it is also an important factor in international politics. Western Europe depends on the Middle East for most of its oil. France and Italy are especially dependent on Middle Eastern and North African oil. "When a million Bedouins in Libya have the power, by denying their oil, to paralyze the economy of a modern European nation of 50 million people such as Italy, that is a ridiculous situation, but that is where we are," a

European oil company official commented. This situation obviously influences the policy of France and Italy in cultivating relations with Iraq and Libya and selling them arms. As for the United States, the supply of oil from the Middle East has not been very important until now. However, it is believed that by 1980 the United States will depend on imports for 40% of its oil. The Arab states of the Middle East are therefore in the position to use oil as a "weapon" by limiting or halting supplies. All the Middle Eastern oil countries, until recently with the exception of Iran, are more or less at odds with the United States policy of support for Israel. With so many countries dependent on them for oil, their power to make their views felt will be even greater in the future.

The Organization of Petroleum Exporting Countries— OPEC

Since 1973 the Organization of Petroleum Exporting Countries, or OPEC as it is known for short, is frequently in the news. This organization has become a powerful force in world politics and economics. OPEC is made up of the major oil producing countries in the world, including nations in the Middle East, Africa, and South America. The organization was formed in the early 1960s. The purpose was to give the oil producing nations an opportunity to coordinate their policies. If these nations worked together it was believed that they could get the best deal for their oil.

In June 1967, just after Egypt, Syria, and Jordan were defeated by Israel in the Six-Day War, the Arab nations imposed an oil embargo against the United States, Israel, and its allies in Western Europe. They hoped that this would pressure Israel into withdrawing from the Arab areas it had captured in the war. But Algeria and Tunisia continued to sell oil to West Germany and the oil companies increased their production in Venezuela and Africa. The United States, which was supposed to be the chief target, was producing 80% of the oil it used at the time. Realizing the embargo was a failure, Saudi Arabia and Kuwait gave it up at the end of June. The Arabs realized that oil could be an effective political weapon only if *all* the producers, including such non-Arab nations as Iran, Venezuela, Nigeria, and Indonesia acted together. OPEC suddenly took on a new importance.

The next big opportunity came during the Arab-Israeli war of 1973. Two days after the outbreak of the war the Arab oil producers ordered a 25% cutback in production and a total embargo against the United States and Holland. This created a critical shortage of oil in the world. As the countries competed for the oil that was available, OPEC raised the price of oil from $2.50 a barrel to $10 a barrel. The cutback in production as well as the embargo lasted several months. The price increase, however, remained unchanged. Western Europe and Japan were badly hit and oil rationing went into effect. Many difficulties were experienced in the United States as well.

The countries that have been most seriously affected by the increase in oil prices are the underdeveloped nations of the Third World. Most of the countries in Asia and Africa have to import almost all of their oil. Their cash reserves are extremely limited. Industrial development projects are not moving forward as rapidly as was planned. Food production has slowed down as well. The Arab oil producers had promised to set up a special fund using their surplus *petrodollars* (money received for oil) to aid the developing countries, but not much has been done. Many African nations are now voicing their resentment. Until 1973 most of the Africans enjoyed a very good relationship with Israel. Then during the Arab-Israeli war they broke relations with Israel, hoping to win the favor of the Arabs and oil benefits as well. But they have received very little in return and now they are angry.

Since 1973 the oil ministers of OPEC have been meeting periodically to discuss oil matters. In 1974, when it seemed likely that another Arab-Israeli war might break out, OPEC again discussed the possibility of another oil embargo against the United States. Many in the United States considered the idea of sending troops to the Middle East to take over the oil wells should this happen. Secretary of State Kissinger stated that, "I'm not saying there's no circumstance where we would not use force, especially where there's some actual strangulation of the industralized world." Later Kissinger added, "I do not foresee this happening." The oil ministers also meet from time to time to consider oil prices. One group of members led by Iraq, Libya, and Algeria favors raising the price of oil. Another led by Saudi Arabia actually wanted to lower the price of oil or at least maintain it at the same level. At the last OPEC meeting held in September 1975 it was decided to raise the price of oil by 10%. This represented a compromise between the two groups.

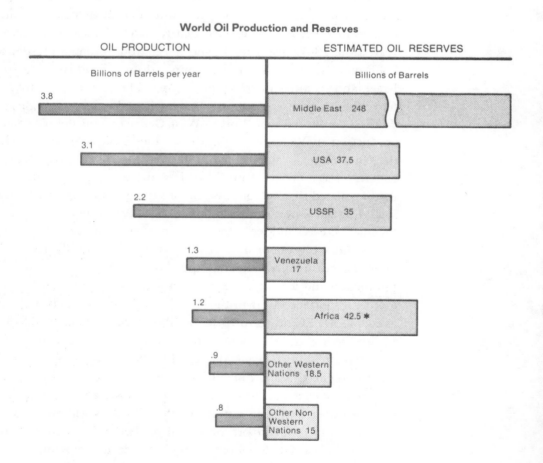

World Oil Production and Reserves

OIL PRODUCTION   ESTIMATED OIL RESERVES

Billions of Barrels per year   Billions of Barrels

3.8   Middle East   248

3.1   USA   37.5

2.2   USSR   35

1.3   Venezuela 17

1.2   Africa 42.5 *

.9   Other Western Nations 18.5

.8   Other Non Western Nations 15

The situation of the last few years has forced the industrialized countries to search for new sources of energy. The United States has turned to the Alaska pipeline as one possible answer. This project, which had long been delayed, was suddenly speeded along by President Nixon. The two million barrels a day which the Alaska pipeline will carry to American markets will almost equal the amount of oil imported from Arab nations. British Petroleum and other companies speeded up their development of fields under the North Sea. It is expected that oil from the North Sea will make Britain and the Scandinavian countries almost completely independent of Arab oil by 1980. If this situation develops, the future of OPEC remains uncertain.

Economic Development

Problems Facing the Middle East

Poverty is everywhere in the Middle East. Capital and technical know-how have been scarce and, except in Israel, the existing natural resources, until recently were either badly used or totally neglected.

The European powers went into the area for the sake of markets and raw materials for their own use and not to improve the lives of the people of the area. As a result, only small groups of the people of the Middle East improved their living conditions. The countries of the region face the problem of erasing the huge gap between a small well-off minority and a large poverty stricken majority.

The problem of soaring population further worsens the situation. Egypt, as well as the other nations, is engaged in a race to increase economic productivity to at least the same rate as the population. Shortage of usable land and of water for irrigation continues to block greater food production. Even if the great river development projects for the region are carried out, there still will not be enough land. Since 8 of 10 people in the area live on the land, it will be difficult to raise their low standard of living. Disease, primitive agricultural methods, poor water use, crop diseases and pests and the distribution of land with the few owning the largest share have continued the cycle of poverty in the area.

State Planning: A Possible Solution

Practically all countries of the region have established planning organizations and set up 3-year, 5-year, 7-year or 10-year development programs. The planning organizations gather economic and social information, develop plans and prepare budgets to improve economic conditions. These plans usually cover the entire country. Each country must set up its plans to meet its specific needs and to make use of the resources available. In almost all cases the planners hope to reduce rural overpopulation by developing new industries. Workers will be needed and will leave rural areas. However, certain problems stand in the way of rapid modernization.

Capital

Large amounts of *capital* (money) are needed to build industry. Most of the countries do not have the money and must borrow from the large nations. These large nations can affect the direction of development and greatly affect economic, social and political policy. In this way the independence of the nations of the area is restricted.

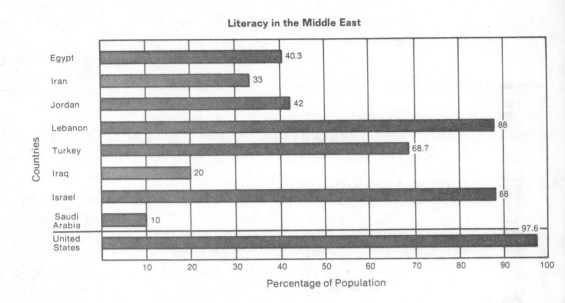

Literacy in the Middle East

Education

Engineers, factory managers, technicians and skilled workers must be found or trained to run the new plants and mills. Every country of the Middle East has found it necessary to provide basic education and professional training. The job of ending illiteracy is difficult. Despite attempts at reform many children still are receiving no education. In the future these children will join the ranks of the illiterate.

Social and Political Instability

Another problem is to coordinate industrial and agriculture development, so that urban and rural populations progress together. The major block to this development is the social and political instability of the area.

Industrialization Causes Problems

Industrialization tends to speed up the growth rate of cities. It does this without being able to build enough houses or sanitary facilities to meet the needs of the new city dwellers. In addition, not enough food is produced to meet the needs of this non-agricultural population. At present the rate of population growth is barely met by the growth in food production. There is little, if any, left for export. Some Arab countries, especially Egypt, have to import food to meet their needs.

In order to keep up with the rise in population, better use of existing farm land must be achieved. It is also of great importance to create more land for farming by modern technology.

An elementary school in Libya. Education is becoming increasingly important
in the Middle East.
Credit: *Arab Information Center*

The Problem of Peace

A key factor in the improvement of the economic situation is the necessity of achieving some kind of peace between the Arab countries and Israel. The energies now devoted to war and preparation for war must be released to meet the challenge of making all the countries of the Middle East and North Africa better places for people to live.

The Arab-Israeli Conflict: The Israeli Side

The Jewish Dream: A Homeland in Israel

The roots of the Jewish people in the Middle East are very ancient. When Moses led the Hebrews out of slavery in Egypt to find the "promised land," their history as a nation began. In 70 A.D. the Hebrew state came to an end when the Romans destroyed Jerusalem. Many Jews left Palestine and settled in other parts of the Middle East, North Africa and Europe. But the Jews regarded Palestine as their true homeland and prayed that they would one day return to their ancient land.

Those Jews who settled in Europe found life very difficult. In most countries restrictions were placed upon them. They were forbidden to own land, hold political office or enter most professions. In addition, they were forced to pay heavy taxes and even wear special garments to identify them as Jews. At times feeling against them reached such a pitch that they were tortured and massacred. This happened particularly in Russia where the Jews were ordered to live in ghettos in a specific region and could not move to the large cities. Periodically, there were pogroms in which hundreds of homes were looted and burned and many people were put to death.

Many Jews came to believe that the only solution was to have a land of their own. During the 1880s some Jews left Russia to settle in Palestine, which was then part of the Ottoman Empire. In the 1890s Theodore Herzl, an Austrian Jew, wrote a pamphlet called *The Jewish State*. This was the beginning of the *Zionist* movement. Zion is the name of one of the hills in Jerusalem and it became the symbol for the land of Israel. A Zionist is a person who wishes to have a Jewish homeland in Israel. Zionist organizations were set up in many countries and money was raised. Small groups of pioneers began to settle in Palestine, where they were determined to create a new way of life. Land was purchased from the Turks, land that in many cases consisted of desert and rocks. The pioneers cleared the fields, drained the swamps, built irrigation projects and planted crops. As more people came, cities began to grow up.

The British and Palestine

During World War I, the British Foreign Secretary Lord Balfour issued a document which has become known as the Balfour Declaration. This document stated that Britain would "view with favor the establishment in Palestine of a national home for the Jewish people. . . ." At the same time, however, the British made promises to Arab leaders about the future of the Arab provinces of the Ottoman Empire. At the end of the war, with the defeat of the Ottoman Empire, Palestine became a British mandate.

This meant that Britain was to rule Palestine until it was ready for independence. The British were also supposed to help the Jews settle in Palestine.

The Arabs Protest

As Jewish immigration increased, the Arabs living in Palestine began to fear that they would soon be outnumbered. Arab nationalism grew stronger, and the Arabs demanded an end to Jewish immigration and the creation of an independent Arab state in Palestine. Many times the Arabs expressed their resentment through violence, attacking Jewish settlements and killing the people.

World War II

In the 1930s Hitler's persecution of the Jews speeded up the rate of Jewish immigration into Palestine. But just at the outbreak of World War II, in response to Arab protests, a British "White Paper" limited this immigration. Hundreds of thousands of Jews who might otherwise have made their way to Palestine, died in Nazi concentration camps. At the end of the war it became known that the Nazis had killed six million Jews. Jewish leaders around the world began to demand the immediate establishment of a Jewish state in Palestine. The Jews felt that only by having their own country could they avoid such catastrophes in the future.

A Jewish State Is Set Up

The British recognized that they could not find a solution that would be acceptable to both Jews and Arabs. Therefore, they turned the matter over to the recently created United Nations. In November 1947 the U.N. voted to have Palestine divided into a Jewish state and an Arab state. In May 1948 the new state of Israel declared its independence. As the British withdrew their troops, Arab armies from six neighboring Arab states came to the aid of the Palestine Arabs. Although outnumbered by about 50 to 1 and with inferior military equipment, the new state of Israel proved to be more than a match for the Arabs. The Arabs failed in their effort to "drive the Jews into the sea." As a result of the war, three-quarters of a million Arabs fled to nearby countries.

Israel Protects Its Independence

In 1956 Israel and Egypt fought a brief war in the Suez Canal area. The war was in part caused by continued guerrilla attacks from Egypt against Israeli settlements. Israel invaded the Sinai Peninsula and the Gaza Strip where, it said, the guerrillas were based. The United Nations stepped in and stopped the fighting and then set up a U.N. Emergency Force (UNEF) to patrol the frontier between Israel and Egypt. Although the UNEF did have some success in preventing border incidents between Israel and Egypt, trouble continued along Israel's borders with Syria and Jordan.

In May 1967, Egypt demanded that the UNEF leave its territory and began to send troops and tanks into the Sinai Peninsula to threaten Israel. Egypt also closed the Strait of Tiran, preventing ships from reaching Israel through the Gulf of Aqaba.

This led to the third war between Israel and the Arabs, fought in June 1967. In six days of fighting Israel destroyed the Arab armies on the Egyptian front, the Syrian front, and the Jordanian front. Israel occupied the Sinai Peninsula and the Gaza Strip, which had been Egyptian territory, the West Bank of the Jordan River, which had been part of Jordan and the Golan Heights of Syria. The Israelis also captured vast amounts of Russian equipment and supplies.

Since 1967 the situation has remained serious. The Arab lands captured during the 1967 war are still occupied by Israel. The Israeli position at present is as follows: 1. Israel agrees to return most of the captured territories if the Arabs will meet them face to face to discuss the terms of a peace treaty. 2. The Arabs must recognize the right of Israel to exist. 3. Certain areas Israel refuses to return to the Arabs. The key one is Jerusalem, because of its great historical importance to the Jews. 4. On the issue of the Palestine refugees (those Arabs who left Palestine during the war of 1948) Israel is willing to help pay for their resettlement in the Arab lands, but it will not allow most of them to return to Israel. The Israelis claim that most of the Arab refugees were persuaded to leave by their own leaders. Over the years these people have been indoctrinated by Arab propaganda and are filled with hatred of Israel. To permit them to return would seriously endanger Israel's security. They have been replaced by a similar number of Jews expelled from Arab lands, such as Egypt, Morocco and Syria.

After the 1967 war there were frequent attacks along all of Israel's borders. Arab guerrillas entered Israeli territory, planted mines and killed Israeli soldiers. Israeli troops then attacked Arab patrols.

In August 1970, a ceasefire between Israel and Egypt came into effect. For three years all was quiet along the Suez Canal which separated the armies of the two countries. At the same time, U.N. Ambassador Gunnar Jarring held talks with both nations in the hope of working out a more permanent agreement. His mission failed, however, and the talks were ended on February 1971.

The Arab-Israeli Conflict: The Arab Side

The Arabs look at Palestine in a very different way than do the Israelis. As far as most Arabs are concerned, the state of Israel does not exist. The area that is now Israel they call Palestine. For centuries Arabs lived in Palestine, and therefore they claim that Palestine should be an Arab state. Most Arabs feel that the establishment of the Jewish state of Israel in Palestine was a great injustice. During the war of 1948 about 725,000 Arabs left Palestine and fled to the neighboring Arab countries. The Palestinian refugees, as they are called, claim that they were driven from their homes by the Israelis. Most of the refugees and their children hope to return. Many of them dream of setting up a Palestinian Arab state in which they will be able to live according to their traditions and culture.

The Palestinians and all Arabs look on the Jews of Israel as imperialists. They do not see Israel as a tiny, struggling nation. Rather they regard Israel as an international giant with strong friends. They fear Israel and its close ties with Western nations. The Arabs say that the Israelis are foreigners—people who came to the Middle East from Europe and do not belong in an area that is mainly Arab.

Arab nationalists feel their dreams cannot come true as long as a non-Arab state exists in the heart of the Middle East. They feel their cause is just, and many have never given up the hope of destroying the state of Israel and setting up an Arab state in its place. The Arabs regard their defeats by the Israelis in three wars (1948, 1956 and 1967) as humiliating disasters. There are some Arabs who are willing to face death in order to destroy Israel. Among these are the Palestinian guerrillas. In recent years they have tried many tactics. Israeli offices in foreign countries have been bombed. Bombs have been placed in supermarkets, bus stations and theaters in Israel. Several planes flying to or from Israel have been hijacked. Mines have been planted in border areas. While these tactics have resulted in many deaths and considerable destruction, they have not succeeded in weakening or destroying Israel.

At present there are differing attitudes among the Arabs as to what their policy toward Israel should be. There are those who say that no peace settlement is possible with Israel. They say that the Arab states should continue fighting until they are successful in setting up an Arab state in Palestine. Some of the Arab governments, such as Egypt and Jordan, claim that they are willing to come to a peaceful agreement with Israel. However, they demand that Israel withdraw from all the occupied Arab lands first. Another Arab demand is that Israel take back most of the Arab refugees who left Palestine in 1948.

Arabs and Israelis continue to build up their defenses. Several of the Arab states, especially Egypt and Syria, have obtained the most advanced planes, tanks, missiles and radar equipment from the Soviet Union. Egyptian ground and air forces have been trained by Soviet officers. Israel has received jet planes from the United States. This type of situation is very dangerous, because a small incident could easily explode into a major war.

The Problem of the Palestinians in the 1970s

Thirty years after the creation of the state of Israel, the Palestinian Arabs not only are at war with Israel but are in conflict with the Arab governments and among themselves. Many of the Palestinians feel that the Arab governments have let them down. The Palestinians have been demanding that the Arab countries join forces for a military showdown with Israel. But the Arab governments are not willing to risk another defeat in a war with Israel at present. Some of the Arab countries have said they are willing to reach a settlement with Israel, but the Palestinians reject this idea.

The Palestinians would like to use the Arab countries as a base for attacks against Israel. For a long time they had bases in Jordan, the Arab country having the longest border with Israel. From here they periodically attacked Israel. However, in 1970 and 1971 King Hussein of Jordan decided to crack down on the guerrillas. As a result of a bitter war between the Jordanian army and the Palestinian guerrillas, the guerrillas were expelled from their bases in Jordan.

The Palestinian guerrillas next decided to use Lebanon as their base. Refugee camps located along the border with Israel were heavily armed, and from here attacks into Israel were frequently launched. But these attacks resulted in Israeli *reprisals*. The Israeli army bombed border areas in Lebanon causing substantial destruction. The guerrillas were becoming a headache to the government of Lebanon, just as they had been to Jordan earlier. In May 1973 violent fighting broke out between the Palestinian guerrillas and the Lebanese army and several hundred people were killed. The government of Lebanon seemed determined to place stricter controls on armed guerrilla activities on her territory. Syria has also sharply limited guerrilla raids into Israel since suffering heavy damage from Israeli bombing in January 1973. As a result of these actions by the governments of Jordan, Lebanon and Syria, the Palestinians feel betrayed by their "Arab brothers."

The Palestinian struggle also suffers from the lack of a unified political leadership enjoying broad support. All the major guerrilla groups are represented in the Palestine Liberation Organization. The chairman of the organization, Yasir Arafat, lacks many qualities that a good leader should have. His military skills are not outstanding, he is not a strong public speaker, and he does not have the personality to attract people. There are great differences and rivalry among the guerrillas themselves, and this does not help their cause.

It is estimated that there are about three million Palestinians. About half of these are *refugees*. The new generation of refugees are angrier than their parents, because they grew up in the bitterness of the refugee camps. They have a stubborn belief that one day they will return to their homes and lands because their cause is just. But because they have suffered only setbacks, many claim they have become desperate. In their desperation a large number have turned to terrorism.

Palestinian Nationalism is a movement with two objectives:

1. to achieve the return of the Arab Palestinian to his lost lands.
2. to alter the political situation which has excluded him or given him only a small role in forming plans concerning his future.

The organized Palestinian guerrilla movement began in 1965 under the P.L.O. The Palestine Liberation Organization was created by the Arab heads of state. It stands for total opposition to the existence of the State of Israel. P.L.O. calls for "a democratic and secular Palestinian state where the rights of all religious communities would be respected." Israelis and the world's Jews read that to mean (at best) Arab toleration of a Jewish minority in a sea of Arabs. The doors would be closed both to Jewish self-government and to future Jewish refugees from persecution elsewhere.

In 1974 it looked as if the Palestine Liberation Organization (PLO) had finally become a force to be reckoned with. At an Arab summit conference in Rabat, Morocco, Arab leaders officially proclaimed the PLO as the sole representative of the Palestinian people. The future of all Palestinians regardless of which country they were living in would be decided by the PLO. They stated that if the West Bank, which is now occupied by Israel, is ever returned to Arab control, it would be a Palestinian state run by the PLO. Two months later in December 1974, Yasir Arafat, head of the PLO, was invited to address the United Nations. It seemed that the PLO had received new respectability and recognition.

Since the Six Day War of 1967 Arab guerrilla groups have intensified their campaign of terror with raids, bombings, plane hijackings and assassinations. And Israel has responded with violent reprisals.

Below is a partial list of Arab terrorist actions and Israeli reprisals.

1968	Sept.	Arabs bomb Tel Aviv bus station.
	Oct.	Israeli soldiers blow up suspected terrorist's house after a grenade wounded 48 people in Hebron.
	Nov.	Dynamiting of a Jerusalem market results in 12 deaths.
	Dec.	Lebanese planes destroyed in Beirut by Israeli paratroopers in retaliation for an attack on an Israeil airliner.
1969	Feb.	Four Arab terrorists machine-gun Israeli (El Al) plane in Zurich, Switzerland.
		Terrorist bombing of Jerusalem supermarket causes 2 deaths.
	March	Cafeteria at Jerusalem's Hebrew University bombed.
	Aug.	Arab hijackers order TWA jet to Damascus, bomb the cockpit and hold 2 Israelis hostage.
	Nov.	Arabs bomb El Al office in Athens. A child is killed.
1970	Feb.	Israeli air strike into Egyptian territory kills 70.
	March	Bomb explodes aboard Swissair plane bound for Israel causing plane to crash.
	May	Arab bazookas attack Israeli school bus near the Lebanese border, killing 8 children and wounding 20.
1971	May	Israeli Consul-General kidnapped and slain in Istanbul.
1972	Feb.	Israelis destroy several Lebanese villages in a reprisal raid.
	May	Terrorists hijack Sabena airliner on the way to Israel.
	July	Three Japanese guerrillas, supporting the Palestinian cause open fire with their machine guns at Israel's airport, killing 28.
	Sept.	Arab terrorists kidnap and kill 11 Israeli athletes at the Olympics in Munich, Germany.
	Nov.	Letter bombs are mailed to Israeli embassies in many countries as well as Jewish firms.
1973	Feb.	Israeli jets shoot down Libyan airliner that had wandered off course over the Sinai Peninsula. 106 people die.
	April	Arab terrorists bomb the residence of Israel's ambassador in Cyprus.
		Israeli commandos assassinate three guerrilla leaders in Beirut.
		Arabs burn U.S. oil tanks in Lebanon.
		Arabs murder Italian clerk at El Al office in Rome.
	July	Palestinians attack El Al office in Athens; release hostages after negotiations with police.
	August	2 Palestinians machine-gun passengers in lounge of Athens airport; 4 dead, 55 wounded.

Sept.	3 Jewish immigrants from Russia taken hostage by 2 Palestinians aboard train bound for Vienna; hostages released after Austrian government promised to close transit camp for Russian emigrants en route to Israel.
Dec.	5 Arabs attack Pan-American and Lufthansa planes at Rome airport; 32 passengers killed; Pan Am plane badly damaged and Lufthansa plane hijacked with 13 hostages.

1974	April	3 Arab terrorists kill 18 men, women, and children in Israeli town of Qiryat Shemona.
	May	3 Arab terrorists kill 20 teenage students, a four-year-old boy and his parents, 2 Arab-Israeli women, and one Israeli soldier at the Israeli village of Ma'alot.
	June	3 Arab terrorists murder 3 women at farm settlement of Shamir; 4 Israelis killed in raid on Nahariya by Arab terrorists.
	Nov.	3 Palestianian terrorists machine-gun their way into apartment building in Israeli town of Beit She-an; 4 dead, 23 wounded.
1975	Jan.	2 Arab terrorists attempt to machine-gun El Al jet; 20 people wounded.
	March	8 Arab terrorists shoot their way into Savoy Hotel in Tel Aviv and take hostages. In the shoot-out 3 Israeli soldiers and 8 civilians killed.
	July	Bomb explodes in Zion Square in Jerusalem, killing 13 and wounding 63.
1976	June	Arab and other terrorists hijack an Air France plane carrying a majority of Israeli and Jewish passengers and fly it to Uganda. They threaten to blow up the plane and kill the passengers unless their demands are met. On July 4, 1976, Israeli commandos in a daring raid free the captives and fly them to safety.
1977	Dec.	Explosion in Netanya—2 killed, 2 wounded.
1978	Jan.	Explosion in Jaffa—2 killed.
	Feb.	Explosion in a Jerusalem bus—2 killed, 46 wounded.
	March	Arab terrorists hijack bus outside Tel Aviv—34 Israelis, 1 American killed.
	June	Bomb explodes on Jerusalem bus—6 killed, 19 injured. Explosion in Jerusalem market—2 killed, 35 wounded.
	August	Explosion in Jerusalem's Carmel Market—2 killed, 50 wounded.

The Israeli government has responded to many of these acts of terrorism by bombing Palestinian camps in southern Lebanon.

The Middle East Between East and West

Events in the Middle East are greatly affected by the relations among the big powers. The leaders of the Middle Eastern nations have taken advantage of East-West rivalries and have played one side against the other for their own benefit.

The Roots of Soviet-American Rivalry

Until 1945, the Middle East and North Africa were controlled by France and Great Britain. During World War II France was greatly weakened, and by 1945 French influence in the area had declined considerably. After the war Britain faced many problems at home and began slowly to pull out of the Middle East. The Soviet Union and the United States both stepped in to fill this vacuum. The Soviet Union saw this as an opportunity to gain greater influence in the area and perhaps even to spread Communism. The United States moved in to limit Soviet advances.

Soon after the war the Soviet Union supported a guerrilla movement in Greece, which almost succeeded in setting up a Communist government there. In Turkey, they asked for military bases, territory and guaranteed passage for Soviet warships from the Black Sea to the Mediterranean. If the USSR had succeeded in these demands, they would have obtained a position of great importance in the Middle East. But the United States came to the aid of these two countries with the Truman Doctrine of 1947. The doctrine provided for economic and military aid to countries threatened by Communism. The aid strengthened both Greece and Turkey, and they successfully resisted the Russians. Turkey has since been a strong supporter of the West and has received billions of dollars of economic and military assistance from the United States. Turkey became a member of NATO in 1952, and the United States has built military bases there.

Soviet Influence Grows

In their relations with the Arab countries, the Soviet Union has been far more successful than the United States. Until World War II the Soviet Union had practically no direct contact with the Arab world. After the war the Soviets saw the possibility of replacing the West and becoming the most important power in the Middle East. The Soviet Union hopes to be able to limit the West's use of the oil resources of the Middle East. The USSR would also like to be in control of the important waterways of the Middle East.

Although the Soviet Union has not established control over any Middle Eastern nation, the USSR has made great gains in the area. Through large scale economic and military USSR has made great gains in the area. Through large scale economic and military aid to Arab countries, the Soviet Union has made many friends in the Middle East. Billions of dollars worth of planes, tanks, missiles, machinery, and technical aid have been given to Egypt and Syria since 1955 and to Iraq since 1958. In 1958 the Soviet Union agreed to provide the money, equipment and engineers to build the high dam at Aswan in Egypt. In diplomacy, the Soviet Union has consistently backed the Arabs in their conflict with Israel. Before, during and since the June War of 1967, the USSR has supported all the demands made by the Arabs.

Hundreds of young Arabs have gone to study science and technology in the Soviet Union. Hundreds of Soviet engineers, pilots, and army officers have come to Egypt and Syria to train the Arabs. Soviet dancers, singers and actors have frequent performances in the Arab countries as a sign of the friendship that exists between the USSR and the Arabs.

Although Soviet-Egyptian relations have deteriorated in recent years, a Marxist government is now in power in the People's Democratic Republic Yemen. In addition, the governments of Syria, Iraq, Libya, and Algeria are considered leftist. The Soviets are watching carefully the development of the new government in Iran as well.

The United States: Between the Arabs and Israel

American policy has not succeeded to a great extent because it is not always clear what the policy of the United States is in the Middle East. The problem is that the interests of the U.S. are in conflict. We are trying to be friendly to both the Arabs and Israel. On the one hand, the United States has pledged not to allow Israel to be destroyed by the Arabs. On the other hand, the U.S. would like the friendship of the Arabs because of the enormous oil resources which they control. Also many Americans feel that if we can establish better relations with the Arabs, perhaps we can prevent the USSR from becoming even more powerful in the area.

Relations with the Arab nations began to worsen after the United States recognized Israel as a nation in 1948. The Arabs feel that the United States is only interested in Israel and does not care about them. Each time that the United States has sold planes and tanks to Israel to balance the weapons received by the Arabs from the Soviet Union, the Arabs complained bitterly. The Arabs claim that the United States is arming Israel with weapons that will be used against them.

When the United States sent arms and planes to Jordan and Saudi Arabia so that they would not turn to the Soviet Union, the Israelis were very unhappy.

The U.S. in turn is suspicious of Egypt, Syria, Iraq, and Algeria because of their dependence on the Soviet Union for arms. The American government feels that Egypt has gone out of its way many times to embarrass the United States.

The hostility between Israel and the Arabs and the rivalry between the Soviet Union and the United States in the Middle East have created much instability in the area. There is continued unrest and mutual distrust, and the possibility of war is always present. Both the Soviet Union and the United States now seem to be looking for ways of finding a peaceful solution to the conflict.

War, Oil, Politics— The Middle East Since 1973

The Yom Kippur War

On October 6, 1973, Egyptian troops crossed the Suez Canal and attacked Israeli troops stationed in the Sinai Peninsula. At the same time, Syria attacked Israeli positions in the Golan Heights. In this way the fourth Arab-Israeli war began. This war has come to be known as the Yom Kippur War because the Arab attack

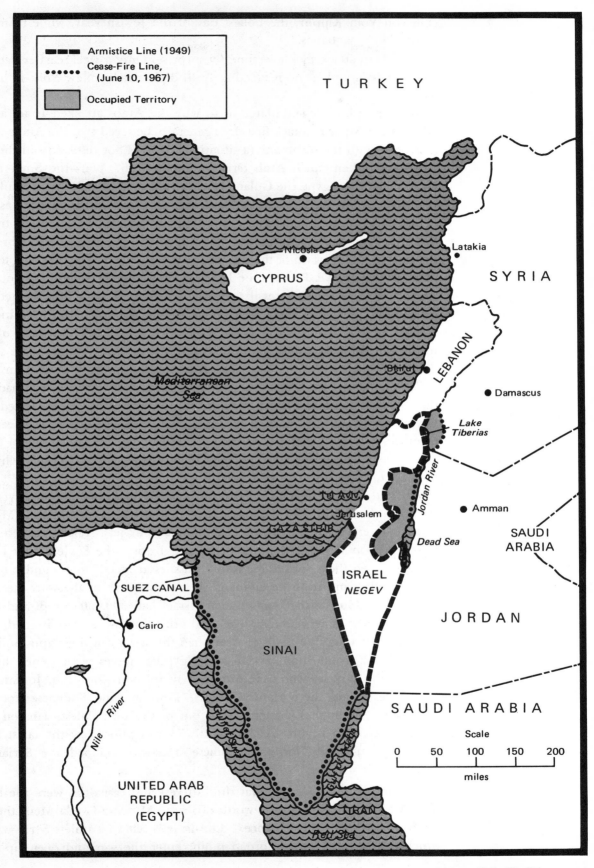

Legend

- ━ ━ ━ Armistice Line (1949)
- • • • • Cease-Fire Line, (June 10, 1967)
- ▨ Occupied Territory

TURKEY

Latakia

Nicosia

CYPRUS

SYRIA

Mediterranean Sea

Beirut

LEBANON

Damascus

Lake Tiberias

Jordan River

Tel Aviv

Jerusalem

Amman

GAZA STRIP

Dead Sea

SAUDI ARABIA

ISRAEL

NEGEV

SUEZ CANAL

JORDAN

Cairo

SINAI

SAUDI ARABIA

Nile River

Scale

0   50   100   150   200

miles

UNITED ARAB REPUBLIC (EGYPT)

IRAN

Red Sea

came on Yom Kippur, the holiest day of the Jewish year, while many Israelis were praying in synagogues.

The Arab attack took everyone by surprise. Only a week earlier Secretary of State Henry Kissinger had been meeting Arab diplomats in New York in a peace-making effort.

Many people have speculated as to why the Arabs attacked Israel and why Israel allowed the Arabs to attack first. It is generally believed that the Arabs were becoming frustrated with the *stalemate* (a situation which is not resolved) in the Middle East. Israel had taken much Arab territory in the 1967 War—the Sinai Peninsula and Gaza Strip from Egypt, the Golan Heights from Syria and the West Bank from Jordan. It seems that the Arab goal was to get back as much of this territory as possible. It is believed that Israeli intelligence saw signs of Syrian and Egyptian troop buildups, but either misread or disregarded these signals. Just before the war broke out, when the Israelis were certain of the approaching Arab attack, they decided to let the Arabs make the first move. Perhaps the Israelis feared that they could not count on the full support of the United States if they attacked first. Perhaps they wanted the world to see that it was Egypt and Syria who started the war. (In 1967, fearing an Egyptian attack, the Israelis attacked first and won a decisive victory. But most of the countries in the world then claimed that Israel was the *aggressor*.) Israel's late start benefitted the Arabs greatly and their armies scored some impressive early gains.

For the Arabs, much had changed since 1967. The Soviet Union had poured more than $3 billion worth of planes, tanks, missiles and other sophisticated weapons into Egypt and Syria. Thousands of Soviet advisors and technicians had been sent to both countries to teach the Arabs how to use the equipment. The crossing of the Suez Canal is believed to have been planned by the Russians years ago. Israel, which has one of the best air forces in the world, used it very effectively in 1967. In 1973, however, the sophisticated missile systems of the Arabs largely reduced the effectiveness of Israel's air force. Soviet-built SAM-2 missiles hit high-flying Israeli jets. SAM-3 and SAM-6 missiles intercepted low-altitude Israeli Phantom jets. The Syrians also had a new terror weapon which had never been used before—the Soviet built FROG 7. The Syrians aimed these ground-to-ground missiles at Israeli towns and kibbutzim in the north, killing and injuring civilians. At the outbreak of the war, the Egyptians and Syrians had 450,000 men under arms; Israel had 300,000. Egypt and Syria had 900 combat planes; Israel had 500. The Arabs this time were a disciplined, well-led fighting force. In 1967 thousands of Arabs had thrown down their guns and run; in 1973 they fought. In addition, Syrian and Egyptian forces were joined by troops from other Arab countries who were quickly sent to their side. Iraq, Jordan and Morocco sent forces to aid the Syrians. Kuwaiti, Tunisian, and Sudanese troops joined the Egyptians. Although Lebanon stayed out of the war, Palestinians on the Lebanese border fired into Israeli villages. North Korean pilots flew the latest Soviet jets for the Egyptians, and North Vietnamese instructors helped the Syrians with their surface-to-air missiles.

Fighting in the 1973 war was the bitterest and casualties were the heaviest of all four Arab-Israeli wars. In the words of Prime Minister Golda Meir, the Israelis were "defending their very existence." The Israelis felt that unless Syria was finished off quickly King Hussein of Jordan might enter the war and open up a third front.

During the first two days of fighting, the Syrians outnumbered the Israelis 10 to 1. During the early hours, the Israeli Air Force suffered heavy losses to the Soviet SAM-6 missiles. These were the latest and best missiles the Soviets had, better than anything the Americans had faced in Vietnam. By the sixth day of fighting, Syrian troops were repelled and pushed off the Golan Heights. Israeli troops then moved in the direction of Damascus, the Syrian capital, and came within 20 miles of it. Syria lost 50% of its tanks and 30% of its jets in the first week of fighting. In retaliation against Syrian use of FROG missiles, Israeli jets bombed targets in Damascus. This was the first time an Arab capital had been bombed in a Middle Eastern war. The counter-offensive against the Egyptians came on the fourth day of fighting. Again the Israelis suffered early losses. Within days, however, the Israelis were able to stop the Egyptian offensive and keep the Egyptians from advancing further into the Sinai. By the third week the tide of war had changed. Led by General Sharon, Israeli tank forces crashed through a weak spot in the Egyptian line in the Sinai and swept across the Suez Canal. Israeli tanks destroyed many of Egypt's ground-to-air missile installations. This enabled the Israeli Air Force to operate more freely and Israeli pilots then demonstrated their superiority. When the Egyptians tried to stop this operation, they suffered heavy losses. The Israelis continued building up their forces on the other side of the Suez Canal until they completely surrounded 20,000 Egyptian soldiers. These men found themselves without food, ammunition or water.

On October 16, the day after the Israeli force crossed the Suez Canal, Soviet Premier Alexei Kosygin arrived in Cairo. Premier Kosygin returned to Moscow on October 19 convinced that the Egyptian forces faced disaster and urgently requested a cease-fire. Soviet leaders then invited Secretary of State Kissinger to Moscow and he arrived on October 20. Kissinger immediately agreed to the Soviet demand for a cease-fire between Israel and Egypt. President Sadat called for a cease-fire as did many member nations at the United Nations. Just as Israel was completing the encirclement of the Egyptian Army's III Corps, a cease-fire was pushed through the United Nations on October 22. Israel was pressured into accepting the cease-fire even though it was close to winning the war. It is interesting to note that during the early days of the war while the Arabs were winning, no one called for a cease-fire. It was only when the Israeli army was on the point of a decisive victory that demands for a cease-fire began to be heard from all sides.

Big Power Politics

Almost as soon as the fighting began, the Soviet Union started a massive round-the-clock air and sea lift to Egypt and Syria. The Soviet Union sent its Arab friends hundreds of tanks, anti-tank missiles, and very accurate surface-to-air missiles. This rearming continued throughout the war and for many months afterwards. In addition, Soviet diplomats in the Middle East tried to encourage countries like Lebanon, Algeria and Jordan to join in the fighting. This infuriated the Americans who felt that Soviet actions were a direct violation of U.S.-Soviet agreements not to stir up the Middle East.

In response to the Soviet airlift, American cargo planes were soon carrying 1,000 tons of war matériel to Israel each day—roughly the same amount that the Soviets were sending to the Arabs. The U.S. supplied Israel with Skyhawk missiles, Phantom jets, bombs, anti-radar missiles, and air-to-air missiles. The United States faced a serious problem in rearming Israel. American cargo planes carrying war supplies were not able to fly the entire distance between the United States and war supplies were not able to fly the entire distance between the United States and Israel without stopping somewhere in Europe to refuel. All of America's European allies, such as Britain, Spain, and Germany, refused to allow these planes to land on their territory. Portugal was the only nation that allowed American planes to refuel at the United States air base in the Azores (a group of Portuguese islands in the Atlantic). The reason our friends in Europe refused to allow refueling on their territory was that they were afraid the Arabs would accuse them of helping Israel and place an *embargo* on oil shipments to them.

Most of the nations of the world turned away from Israel. The countries of Western Europe and Japan, depending heavily on oil from the Middle East, were afraid that the Arabs would cut off their oil supplies. Nations in Africa, like Dahomey and Upper Volta, broke diplomatic relations with Israel. These nations, realizing how wealthy and powerful the Arabs had become lately, hoped to win favor with the Arabs. In general, except for American support, Israel found itself alone in the world and in the United Nations.

The Oil Weapon

As soon as the war broke out, King Faisal of Saudi Arabia threatened the United States with an oil boycott if the United States supplied Israel with new war matériel. The leader of Kuwait openly admitted that "we will use oil as a means of putting pressure on countries that take a side with Israel." Within days, at a meeting in Kuwait of the Organization of Arab Petroleum Exporting Countries, it was agreed that the Arab nations would cut their oil production. It was further stated that "supporters of the Arab cause" would continue to get the same amount of oil as before. Saudi Arabia, the largest oil producer, a few days later cut off all its oil shipments to the United States and Holland.

The oil embargo against the United States and Holland, as well as the cutback in oil production, lasted many months. In the end, the Arab oil cutback came to about 30%. The United States, which is least dependent on oil from the Middle East, suffered least. However, there were gasoline shortages for many months and in many parts of the country gasoline was rationed. Also, the price of oil for heating homes increased greatly. Americans were told to form car pools, lower their thermostats at home and find other ways of *conserving* energy. But in Europe and Japan a real state of emergency developed. Japan depends on the Middle East and North Africa for 85% of its oil; Western Europe for 50%. As countries desperately competed for the oil that was available, the price rose from $2.50 a barrel to $10 a barrel. All over Europe the rationing of oil went into effect. Japan faced the "worst threat to its economy and way of life since World War II." The Arabs, taking advantage of the situation, demanded that Japan break off diplomatic relations with Israel. The Japanese finally admitted that they might have to shift their foreign policy closer to the Arabs to avoid economic catastrophe.

With the cease-fire of October 22, 1973, the war came to an end. Neither side won. For the Israelis a long period of doubt and questioning began. How did their intelligence fail them? Why did they not know in advance that the Arabs were preparing to attack? Why were they not better prepared? For the Arabs the war had the opposite effect. Arab self-respect had been badly shattered in the war of 1967 when they suffered a humiliating defeat. But in 1973 all the myths that were built up since 1967—that the Arabs are not fighters, that the Israelis are supermen—were destroyed. The war of 1973 helped overcome Arab feelings of inferiority and restored their pride and self-respect.

The First Israeli-Egyptian Agreement

The problems of peace proved to be as complicated as the problems of war. In November, Israel and Egypt agreed to an immediate exchange of their prisoners of war, but talks between Israeli and Egyptian generals concerning the separation of their forces in the Sinai Desert broke down. Syria, who was holding 100 Israeli POWs, even refused to discuss an exchange. In December, representatives of Israel, various Arab nations, the United States and the Soviet Union met in Geneva, Switzerland, to discuss a peace solution, but this conference broke up after one day. Into this state of affairs stepped Henry Kissinger, who from late 1973 had tried unceasingly to work out agreements between the two sides. Whatever agreements were worked out in the Middle East were largely due to him.

In January 1974, Kissinger succeeded in working out a disengagement agreement between Israel and Egypt. *Disengagement* means a separation of forces. After the 1967 War, the line separating Israeli and Egyptian troops had been the Suez Canal. During the 1973 war, however, Egyptian troops crossed over to the Israeli side of the Canal and later Israeli troops crossed over to the Egyptian side. After days of traveling back and forth between Israel and Egypt (*shuttle diplomacy*), Kissinger worked out a separation agreement which both sides accepted. Israel agreed to withdraw its troops from the eastern and western banks of the Suez Canal for a distance of several miles. Troops from the United Nations Emergency Force (UNEF) would separate the two armies. Strict limits were set on the numbers and deployment of tanks, missiles, artillery and other heavy weapons each side would be allowed to have along the new UN *buffer zone*.

The agreement was a set of compromises. Many important things were left out. Israel's demand that Egypt issue a statement of *nonbelligerence* (a promise not to go to war) was left out because the Egyptians refused to accept it. The Egyptian demand for a timetable for total Israeli withdrawal from all Arab territory occupied in the 1967 War was also left out because Israel refused to accept it. An indication of the hatred and bitterness between Arabs and Israelis was seen in the tremendous

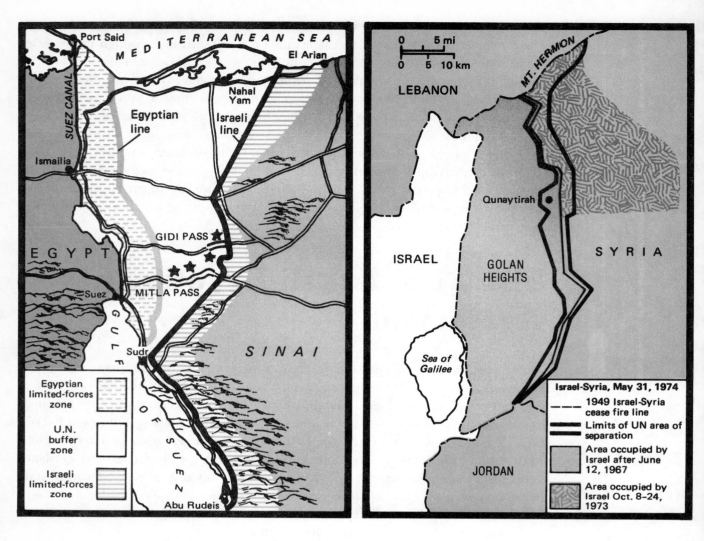

criticism that Egyptian President Sadat faced from other Arab leaders who accused him of "selling out" to Israel. Israeli Prime Minister Golda Meir also faced great opposition in Israel from people who accused her of "surrendering" to the Arabs. But the agreement was viewed by many as a first step toward future agreements. President Sadat said, "Let us hope that the road we have paved is for a lasting peace in the Middle East."

The United States also benefited from the agreement. Since Kissinger was able to keep the Russians out of the picture, American *prestige* in the Middle East rose greatly while Soviet prestige declined. In fact, the Soviet Union felt left out and resented Kissinger's "one-man diplomacy." They felt that American influence was growing at Soviet expense.

Agreement with Syria

One of the many unsolved problems was the border between Israel and Syria. Since the 1967 war the Israelis have controlled the Golan Heights which extend about 12-15 miles inside Syrian territory. During the 1973 war, Israel pushed her lines 10 miles further into Syrian territory. Syria, of course, demanded the return of all her territory, but Israel offered only to discuss the return of territory captured in the 1973 war. Since 1967, Israel has insisted on holding on to the Golan Heights. This is because these mountains overlook Israeli settlements in the north, and the Syrians, who kept artillery up there, had earlier been able to shoot directly into Israeli villages.

In February 1974, one month after he worked out an agreement between Egypt and Israel, Henry Kissinger flew to the Middle East again, this time to start negotiations between Syria and Israel. In May he returned to the Middle East and for 28 days flew back and forth between Damascus and Jerusalem, finally producing an agreement. The agreement was signed in July by Israel and Syrian representatives who met in Geneva, Switzerland. This meeting was in itself historic because it was the first time that these two bitter enemies met face to face other than on the battlefield.

It was agreed that Syria would get back 300 sq. mi. of territory that it lost in 1973 in addition to the city of Quneitra in the Golan Heights, which it lost in 1967. A 1,200-man U.N. force would police the ceasefire. The agreements also provided for the repatriation (sending home) of the last of the prisoners of war and for the return of the dead. The signing of the agreements ended the artillery duel between Syrian and Israeli troops that had taken many lives since the end of the October war. Kissinger assured the Syrians that he didn't regard the disengagement line as a permanent boundary, but as a first step toward a just and lasting peace. He assured the Israelis of continued American economic and military support.

Each side benefited from the agreement. For Israel it meant a return of the prisoners of war and quiet on its northern border. For Syria there was a new feeling of self-respect and pride in regaining lost territory. Syria, still a backward nation spending 70% of its budget on defense, hoped that peace would bring foreign investment and economic development. Again for the United States, there was increased prestige in the Arab world as well as a decline in Soviet influence.

President Nixon Visits the Middle East

Taking advantage of America's new popularity in the Arab world and trying to overcome criticism concerning Watergate at home, President Nixon decided to visit the Middle East. In June 1974, President and Mrs. Nixon, Secretary of State Kissinger and numerous advisors flew to the Middle East for a nine-day trip. They visited Cairo, Jidda, Damascus, Jerusalem and Amman. No American president ever received a more impressive welcome outside his own country. In Cairo it was estimated that two million people filled the streets for the president's arrival screaming "Nixon-welcome." All the suspicion and hostility toward America which existed since the founding of Israel in 1948 seemed gone. Nixon tried to present himself as a "peace president" and as a symbol of the new, close relationship between the United States and the Arab world. In Egypt, Nixon promised President Sadat a nuclear power plant for peaceful uses. (This caused an outcry in both Washington and Israel.) He promised that the Americans would help clear and modernize the Suez Canal and offer other economic aid. In Syria, President Nixon and President Assad announced that both nations would resume diplomatic relations. (Syria had broken off diplomatic relations with the United States during the 1967 Middle Eastern

The Golden Mosque in Iraq. Note the contrast between the old and new. *Credit: Rapho/Photo Researchers*

war.) President Nixon also urged Syria, Jordan and Saudi Arabia to accept United States aid, technical help and private investments in return for friendship and oil. Israel viewed the President's trip with deep anxiety. Although Nixon also promised Israel a nuclear reactor for peaceful uses and long-term military and economic aid, the Israelis were very uneasy. The Israelis were upset by U.S. hints that they would have to return much of the Arab territory they now held and by Mr. Nixon's unwillingness to sign a strong declaration opposing Arab terrorism. The promise of a nuclear reactor for Egypt also upset them. Israel felt that as American relations with the Arabs improved, the United States would turn away from Israel and Israel would be left alone in a hostile world.

The PLO

During the next few months there was no progress toward further agreements. If anything, there was a great increase in tension and talk of war. The chances for peace seemed further to decline when Arab leaders met for a summit conference in Rabat, Morocco, in October 1974. They met to decide once and for all who should speak for the Palestinian people. The Palestine Liberation Organization (PLO) claimed that it alone could speak for all Palestinians. King Hussein of Jordan, however, had always claimed that he should have the authority to speak for the Palestinians living in Jordan and in the Israeli-occupied West Bank. Since the Israelis had stated many times that they would never negotiate with terrorist organizations (the PLO), Kissinger said that the only hope for the Arabs to recover the West Bank would be for King Hussein to speak for the Palestinians. President Sadat had promised Kissenger that he would support King Hussein. However, when the Arabs met at Rabat they all supported the PLO and gave them the responsibility of "liberating" the Israel-occupied West Bank. This was a great blow to King Hussein who claimed the West Bank as part of his kingdom, it was an insult to Kissinger, and it was a further sign to Israelis that the Arabs did not genuinely want peace. There was tough talk at Rabat about preparing for a new war and for months afterwards both Israelis and Arabs spoke about the possibility of a new war. Many believed that it would come in a few months. Syria, as a matter of fact, between October 1973 and November 1974, had received $2 billion worth of war matériel from the Soviet Union. This included the Soviet Union's newest tank, the T-62 and their most advanced ground-to-air missiles—the SAM-6 and SAM-7—and swift and powerful MIG-23 jet fighters.

While tension remained high during the fall of 1974, the United Nations by a vote of 105 to 4 invited the PLO to participate in the U.N. debate on Palestine. This was the first time that any organization other than an official government was permitted to address the General Assembly of the U.N. To Israel this came as a great shock. The Israelis wondered how people they regard as terrorists responsible for the murder of Israeli athletes at the Munich Olympics and innocent schoolchildren in the town of Maalot could be invited to speak at the U.N. Yasir Arafat, the PLO leader, addressed the General Assembly in November with a gun strapped to his hip. At no time did he promise to give up terrorism. On the contrary, he made it clear that he would continue to work to dismantle (take apart) Israel and replace it with a Palestinian nation. Arafat appealed to the American people and the world to support "right and justice" for the Palestinians. He received a standing ovation from the General Assembly.

Soviet-Egyptian Rift

In January 1975, it was announced that Soviet Communist Party Leader Leonid Brezhnev was cancelling his long-planned visit to Egypt. This came as a great surprise because the Soviet Union had long been Egypt's main supporter and arms supplier. However, it became known that relations between the two nations had been deteriorating (getting worse) for almost a year. The Soviet Union, on the one hand, seemed more and more suspicious that Egypt was moving away from its ties to the USSR and coming closer to the West. The Egyptian press was full of anti-Soviet articles. Egypt, on the other hand, was very unhappy that the Soviet Union was not moving faster to replace the weapons Egypt lost in the 1973 war. President Sadat may also have decided that Egypt would gain more from the peace efforts of Kissinger than from massive new supplies of Soviet weapons. Soviet Foreign Minister Andrei Gromyko visited Cairo in February but his trip was a failure. When Sadat pressed him for more Soviet weapons he only agreed to a limited amount of military aid. The Soviet Union, he said, would only agree to resume large shipments of armaments to Egypt if Sadat would allow the return of Soviet advisers whom he expelled in 1972.

In February, Sadat visited Paris. The French government agreed to sell Egypt $1 billion worth of Mirage jets, electronics, missiles and other arms. This deal opened up the possibility of ending Egypt's dependence on Soviet weapons. So Sadat, with the backing of King Faisal of Saudi Arabia, worked out a plan for Egypt to switch to French and British military equipment over the next five years. Faisal, anxious to remove all traces of communism from the Middle East, agreed to help foot the bill. Despite Sadat's complaints that he hadn't been receiving Soviet tanks and planes since April 1974, nevertheless, he acquired considerable amounts of Soviet equipment from his Arab allies, and early in February 1975 there were indications that Egypt was again receiving advanced Soviet arms when a Soviet ship arrived bearing six MIG-23 jet fighter bombers.

Attempts at a Second Israeli-Egyptian Agreement

Talk of war between Israel and the Arabs continued throughout the winter of 1974-1975. The Israelis claimed that Egypt was rearming for another war. It seemed that except for air power Egypt was as strong as she had been just before the October 1973 war. Israel, however, had moved ahead considerably in military strength due to $2 billion worth of sophisticated arms it received from the United States.

Nevertheless, in January 1975 both the Egyptians and Israelis indicated to the Americans that they were interested in a second agreement in the Sinai. Any agreement would involve another Israeli pullback in the Sinai. The American government was putting great pressure on Israel to give up territory in the Sinai, otherwise it could not continue to count on American support and military aid.

Both sides remained far apart. President Sadat insisted that Israel would have to withdraw from areas in the Sinai, including the *strategic* (militarily important) Mitla and Gidi passes. Israel would also have to return the Abu Rudeis oil fields to Egypt. Many in Israel were unwilling to give up the oil fields or the Sinai passes until there was a final and guaranteed peace settlement in the Middle East. They asked "What is Egypt willing to give up in return?" The Abu Rudeis oil fields supplied Israel with 80,000 barrels of oil a day—more than half of its needs. The Israeli government told Kissinger that they would not give up the Sinai passes or the oil fields without a public non-agression pledge from Egypt. This meant that Egypt would have had to promise not to go to war against Israel. The Egyptians said that if they did this they would be accused of betrayal by the other Arabs. For several months Kissinger talked to both sides. But the talks failed and there was no agreement. Neither side was willing to back down from its demands. Sadat, fearful of being accused by Arab militants of making a separate peace with Israel, refused to sign a non-belligerency pledge. Israel said that without the pledge it could not give up the strategic passes or oil fields.

The immediate result of the failure of Kissinger's talks was an increased state of tension in the Middle East. Egypt stated that the only way open was to return to the peace conference at Geneva, a step favored by the Russians and the PLO, but not by the United States or Israel. Israel opposed going back to a conference at Geneva because it knew it would be outnumbered by all the Arab states and there would be the sure problem of admitting the Palestinians. The United States was opposed to Geneva because it would be a ready-made opportunity for the Soviet Union to extend its influence in the Middle East.

Following the breakdown in Kissinger's negotiations between Israel and Egypt, the United States announced that it was "reassessing" (reviewing) its Middle Eastern policy. Since the United States had always been Israel's chief supporter it was felt that the reassessment was directed against Israel. In fact, President Ford and Secretary of State Kissinger hinted strongly that they held Israel responsible for the breakdown in peace talks because Israel was not flexible enough. Thus began a chill in relations between the United States and Israel. Kissinger made it clear that Israel had to come up with new concessions. In fact, many people felt that the Ford administration was "twisting Israel's arm" to make concessions.

Murder of King Faisal

Instability seems to be a permanent condition in the Middle East. Within a few weeks after Kissinger's peace mission failed there was more shocking news from the area. King Faisal of Saudi Arabia had been murdered by his mentally deranged nephew. The king was peacefully succeeded by his brother Khalid ibn Abdel Aziz but his death ushered in a period of uncertainty. Faisal, as the leader of the country with the world's largest known oil reserves, was a leading figure in Arab politics. The money received by oil exporting countries for their oil is known as *petrodollars* and Saudi Arabia has been accumulating surplus petrodollars at the rate of $20 billion a year. With this money Faisal was able to write enormous checks for other Arab leaders like Sadat of Egypt, Hussein of Jordan and Arafat, leader of the Palestinians. This enabled him to influence the policy of those Arab leaders.

Faisal, a conservative with a strong distrust of communism, is given credit for helping Egypt turn away from the Russians. His strong backing helped Sadat put his faith in Secretary of State Kissinger's peace missions despite the opposition of other Arab leaders. Even though Faisal was responsible for using the ultimate Arab weapon—the oil embargo—against the United States, he had tried since 1973 to influence the other oil producing states not to raise their oil prices. With Faisal gone, many questions remained unanswered.

The Suez Canal is Reopened

On June 5, 1975, President Sadat of Egypt officially reopened the Suez Canal. The day was chosen to mark the anniversary of the War of 1967. Since that war the Canal had been closed to shipping, depriving Egypt of two billion dollars of vital revenue (money). The Canal is not expected to be as important as it once was to world trade because almost all the oil tankers that have been built since the canal was closed in 1967 are far too large to use the waterway. These supermarkets will continue to take the longer route around the Cape of Good Hope. But it is expected that the canal will be used heavily by freighters. Egypt's depressed economy badly needs the revenue that the canal will provide. It is also expected that towns along the canal which have been "ghost towns" since 1967 will revive. There was great jubilation all over Egypt when the opening was celebrated. However, other Arabs, such as Syria and the PLO, were openly hostile to the Egyptian move. Their feeling is that if Egypt builds up the Canal area Egypt will be less likely to go to war against Israel in the future for fear that this area will be destroyed again (see also the map of Africa on page 194).

The Second Israeli-Egyptian Agreement

Talks between Israel and Egypt had broken down in March, but by April Israel was submitting new proposals to the United States aimed at reaching an agreement with Egypt. Negotiations continued through the spring and were speeded up during the summer, with Kissinger again taking a leading role. Kissinger continued to urge Israel "to take risks for peace." The Israelis seemed to feel that the United States was forcing the Israelis to make concessions so that American prestige in the Arab world would be increased.

After shuttling back and forth between Israel and Egypt, Henry Kissinger finally worked out an agreement that was acceptable to both sides. On September 1, 1975, both Israel and Egypt initialed the agreement. It provided for further Israeli withdrawal from occupied territory in the Sinai Desert. Israel was to return the strategic Mitla and Gidi passes to Egypt as well as the Abu Rudeis oil fields. The

Egyptians and Israelis pledged that the conflict in the Middle East should be resolved not be military force but by peaceful means. Both pledged not to threaten or to use force against each other for as long as the agreement remained in effect. A key part of the agreement called for the setting up of early warning systems in the Sinai Desert to be operated by American civilians. This meant that the latest electronic equipment would be used to warn each side if the other was planning a surprise attack. It would be up to the Americans who operate the equipment to provide the warning.

The agreement is in no way considered to be a peace accord. It is simply another step along the road to a peaceful settlement of disputes. In the agreement it is stated that both countries see it as a "significant step toward a just and lasting peace." President Ford, in praising the accord, said that "it reduces the risk of war in the Middle East."

The Egyptians hope to benefit from the agreement in several ways. First they are getting back the oil wells as well as territory that is of military importance. The additional territory will protect the Suez Canal, and the Egyptians hope that this will encourage world shippers to return to the canal. The Egyptians also hope that a peaceful climate will bring to Egypt foreign investors who will instill new life into the economy. President Sadat also thinks that by involving the Americans in the Middle East he will gradually draw the United States away from its role as Israel's chief supporter. Mr. Sadat would like to see the United States more "even-handed" in its Middle Eastern policy. Then, he believes, the United States will put more pressure on Israel to withdraw still further from Arab territory.

The Israeli view of the pact was expressed by the following: "it was the best we could get under the circumstances." There had been great hostility on the part of many Israelis to Mr. Kissinger and his negotiations. During his visits to Israel there were street demonstrations and rioting. Many Israelis felt that Kissinger was forcing them into giving up positions that were vital to their security and that they were getting nothing in return from Egypt. An important Israeli air base in the Sinai, which had given Israel control of the air, is now exposed to Egyptian attack. The withdrawal from the two passes leaves Israel without a natural line of defense in the central Sinai. There are few natural obstacles to block any advance of Egyptian forces.

After the pact was concluded it became known that the United States made a number of secret promises to both Egypt and Israel. Some of these promises are slowly becoming known to the American public. It seem that Secretary of State Kissinger had promised Israel some of the most advanced weapons the United States has. There are reports also that he promised the Egyptians American weapons too. The American Congress had to approve that part of the agreement that calls for the stationing of American technicians in the Sinai. Many Congressmen were opposed to this. Others insisted that they would not approve the agreement until they found out what secret promises Kissinger made to Israel and Egypt. They were afraid that the United States might become involved in another situation similar to Vietnam.

The situation in the Middle East remains extremely complicated. Far more difficult issues remain—the question of a homeland for the Palestinians, the question of Israeli withdrawal from the West Bank and the Golan Heights. The most complicating factor is that many Arab governments today still refuse to accept the fact that Israel exists and they are still determined to destroy it. This can be seen from the anger and the hostile criticism that Sadat received from other Arabs after he signed the pact with Israel. Arab countries such as Libya and Iraq as well as the PLO have called Sadat a "traitor" to the Arab cause. It can also be seen in the attempt made by the Arab nations to have Israel expelled from the United Nations. After having failed in this attempt, the Arabs were successful in getting the General Assembly of the United Nations to pass a resolution equating Zionism with racism.

The Civil War in Lebanon

Another trouble spot in the Middle East is Lebanon where a civil war began raging in the middle of 1975. In many ways, Lebanon is a unique country in the Middle East. This is because it is made up of many different religious and ethnic groups. The main religious groupings are Christians, Moslems and Druzes. Within the Christian group there are many different sects, the Maronite Christians being the largest. The Moslems are divided between the Sunnite and Shiite sects. For this reason, when Lebanon received its independence from France in 1943, a government structure was set up that was to maintain a balance between the different religious groups. The president of Lebanon has traditionally been a Maronite Christian; the job of premier is reserved for a Sunnite Moslem and the president of the legislature is a Shiite Moslem. However, many key posts in the government and administration were reserved for Christians.

Since independence, Lebanon has worked toward achieving the following goals: furthering democracy, developing the economy, maintaining a livable arrangement between Christians and Moslems, and sustaining good relations with the other Arab nations as well as with the West.

For many years, Lebanon prospered under these conditions. It became one of the most economically developed countries in the Middle East. It became the commercial and financial center of the Arab Middle East. Unlike the other Arab countries, it has a large thriving middle class and about 75% of its population is literate.

But there were many problems as well. Since 1948 when the state of Israel was established, about 150,000 Palestinian refugees moved to Lebanon. Many of these Palestinians became guerillas and organized attacks against Israel. The Israeli government retaliated and caused heavy destruction in Lebanon. For many years the Phalange party, the main party of the Lebanese Christians, was violently opposed to the PLO's use of Lebanese soil to attack Israel. The Christians wanted to drive the Palestinians out of the country or to force the government to bring them under stricter control. In April 1975, fighting broke out in Lebanon between right-wing Christian Phalangists and left-wing Lebanese Moslems aided by the Palestinians. Other groups became involved in the fighting until it turned into open warfare between Christians and Moslems. The issues also became more complicated. The Moslems saw this as an opportunity to change the structure of the government. They felt that the Moslem population had increased greatly over the years until they now outnumbered the Christians. They also felt that the Christians had far too much influence in the government. The Moslems decided that they would fight until they were successful in achieving a dominant position in the government.

A typical Israeli newspaper, *Maariv*. Credit: *Israel Communications, Inc.*

President Anwar Sadat prays at El Aqsa Mosque in Jerusalem. Credit: *Consulate General of Israel*

In 1975 armed bands of Christians and Moslems began roaming the streets attacking each other, as well as innocent civilians. By 1976 this turned into a full-scale civil war. Thousands of people died. Business in Lebanon came to a standstill. Many of the foreign businesses closed their doors and left Lebanon. During the many months of fighting many cease-fires were set up and temporary truces established, but each time these broke down after a few days or a few weeks.

Other countries became involved. For many months Syria supplied the PLO and Moslems with Soviet-made weapons. However, in April 1976, Syria suddenly changed its position. The Christian situation in Lebanon had become desperate. The Moslem-Palestinian coalition was on the point of winning. Syria decided it was not in its interest to have a radical nationalistic government in Lebanon run by Moslem Palestinians. At the end of May, therefore, Syrian troops entered Lebanon and came to the aid of the Christians. In June, representatives of all the Arab nations met to discuss the problem. They decided to send a peace-keeping force to Lebanon made up of representatives from the various Arab nations. Syrian troops made up the main part of this force. The civil war officially ended in 1976, but periodically fighting still erupts between Christians and Moslems. In July 1978, the Syrians suddenly attacked Christian villages in Lebanon. It was only the threat that Israel would come to the aid of the Christians that stopped the Syrians. (Israel has been supplying the Christians in Lebanon with weapons and medical care.) Again in August Syrian forces attacked the Christians. By September and October Syrian bombardment of Christian villages and the Christian sections of Beirut had become so intense that it seemed that Syria was determined to wipe out the Christans in Lebanon. In October, another cease-fire came into effect and the fighting slowed down. Most people, however, do not believe that the cease-fire will last. The situation remains tense and Syrian troops are still in Lebanon.

President Sadat's Visit to Israel

On November 19, 1977, an event took place in the Middle East that stunned most of the world. On that day President Anwar el-Sadat of Egypt arrived in Israel on what he called "a sacred mission," to speak directly to the people of Israel about peace. This was the first visit ever of an Arab leader to the Jewish state. Egypt had been the bitter enemy of Israel in four Arab-Israeli wars. These wars had cost thousands of lives on both sides. Therefore, when President Sadat was greeted at the airport by Prime Minister Begin of Israel, as well as by hundreds of Israeli dignitaries, and when the Israeli army band played the national anthems of both countries while Egyptian flags flew throughout Israel, most people believed that this dramatic voyage had raised new hopes for peace in the Middle East.

In the months preceding Sadat's visit, the United States tried to get Israel and the Arabs to come together in the city of Geneva to discuss a peace settlement. Israel was unwilling to attend this kind of conference because it was afraid of facing a unified front made up of the United States, the Soviet Union and the Arab countries, all of which would put pressure on Israel to make concessions. There were months and months of discussions, but no real movement toward peace. It is believed that Sadat could no longer endure this long period of waiting—a period of no-war, no-peace. The Egyptian economy was in a very bad state with debts of $13 billion. Egypt depended on subsidies (grants of money) amounting to $5.4 billion from the United States, Saudi Arabia and other Arab oil states merely to keep going. In January 1977, food riots in Cairo and Alexandria had left 79 people dead. The violence ended only when President Sadat agreed to roll back price increases on wheat, oil and other products. The Egyptian economy could improve only when peace returned to the Middle East. Egypt could then spend less money on weapons and use this money to improve the lives of the people. With the coming of peace, investors from industrialized nations would be eager to invest large sums of money in Egypt to build up its economy. Therefore, Sadat decided that a dramatic move, such as a visit to Israel, would get the peace process moving. President Carter, who served as postman in transmitting the messages between Egypt and Israel, said that he hoped the trip would clear the way for "a just and lasting peace."

But President Sadat was taking a big risk. Success of his mission could mean the end of twenty-nine years of a state of war. Failure could mean another war, the loss of his position as leader of the moderate Arabs, and even the loss of his life. Reaction to his trip by many of the other Arab countries was violent. Threats to assassinate him came from many quarters. Libya and Iraq called Sadat a traitor to the Arab cause. Libya also broke diplomatic relations with Egypt and demanded that Egypt be expelled from the Arab League. Syria declared a day of mourning and lowered its flags to half-mast. Syrian radio urged the Egyptian army to "overthrow Sadat and drown him in the Nile." (Before leaving for Israel, Sadat flew to Syria to confer with President Assad and get his approval but Assad refused.) The PLO violently condemned Sadat's trip, stating that "he has sold his soul, Egypt, and the Arab struggle to the Zionist-American devil." Egyptian embassies in Athens, Beirut, Damascus and Tripoli were attacked by Arabs, and in Tripoli Libyans burned the embassy to the ground. Sadat faced opposition even in his own government. Foreign Minister Fahmy resigned when the trip was announced. But for the most part, the Egyptian people stood behind Sadat and, most important of all, he had the backing of the military. Three moderate Arab states, Tunisia, Morocco and the Sudan, approved of the trip.

Arab opposition to Sadat's trip was based on the following reasons: (1) fear that Sadat might abandon the Arab cause and make a separate peace agreement with Israel; (2) fear that Sadat, by setting foot in Israel, was granting de facto recognition to (recognizing the existence of) a state that Arab radicals refuse to accept; (3) that Sadat, by addressing the Knesset (Israel's Parliament) was acknowledging Israel's right to consider Jerusalem as its capital. Sadat insisted that his purpose was not to make a separate peace with Israel, which would only isolate Egypt from the rest of the Arab world. Even Prime Minister Begin said he would not use the visit to divide the Arabs.

After prayers at the Al Aqsa Mosque, a visit to the Church of the Holy Sepulcher, and a trip to Yad Vashem, Israel's memorial to the six million Jews who died in World War II, Sadat addressed the Israeli Parliament (Knesset). Sadat told the Israelis that he accepted the existence of Israel and that "we welcome you to live among us in security and safety." This statement in itself was momentous, since for twenty-nine years the Arabs had refused to admit that Israel existed, and even today many Arabs refuse to recognize this fact. Sadat made a strong plea for peace, but neither he nor Mr. Begin in a speech following Sadat's offered any compromise on the major problems dividing the Arabs and Israelis. Sadat said that he did not come to Israel to make a separate peace agreement between Egypt and Israel but to deliver a message that the Arabs insisted on "peace with justice." A lasting peace in the Middle East, he said, depended on Israeli withdrawal from all the occupied Arab lands, including East Jerusalem and recognition of the rights of the Palestinians. Although Sadat did not mention the PLO by name, he did call for the establishment of a Palestinian state. Sadat also called for an "open city" of Jerusalem. Sadat said "there is a need for hard and drastic decisions. I already took one in my decision to come here, and I shall be looking forward to similar decisions from Premier Begin." But while the tone of Sadat's and Begin's speeches was friendly, it was obvious that the differences separating the two countries were enormous.

Further Contacts—The Meeting in Ismailia

When Sadat returned to Egypt he addressed the Egyptian Parliament and spoke of the results of his trip to Israel. Sadat claimed that his trip had already broken down the "psychological barriers" separating the two countries. Now it was time for all the parties concerned to come to a meeting in Cairo, where they could prepare for a peace conference to be held in Geneva that would end the Arab-Israeli conflict "not in years, but in months." Sadat invited the United States, the Soviet Union, Jordan, Syria, Lebanon and Israel. Israel and the United States immediately accepted the invitation, but the Soviet Union, Syria and the other Arab states rejected it. At the same time, Colonel Qaddafi of Libya invited Syria, Algeria, South Yemen, Iraq and the PLO to a meeting in Tripoli to protest the actions of Sadat and to take steps against him. In December, Israeli and Egyptian representatives met in Cairo with American observers present. Following several weeks of talks, Sadat invited Prime Minister Begin to come to Egypt.

On December 25, 1977, the second meeting between President Sadat and Prime Minister Begin took place, this time in the Egyptian city of Ismailia. The Israelis were very warmly received in Egypt, but the meeting did not produce any major breakthrough or any quick peace, as had been spoken about earlier. Begin offered to return to Egypt almost all of the Sinai Peninsula that was still occupied by Israel. Sadat refused to accept a separate agreement on the Sinai but demanded full Israeli withdrawal from all occupied Arab territories. Sadat insisted on the need for a Palestinian state; Begin would only agree to self-rule for the Palestinian Arabs living on the West Bank. Sadat was determined to show that he would accept only an overall settlement of the Arab-Israeli conflict, and not a separate agreement between Egypt and Israel. The two leaders pledged to continue their efforts for peace and created two standing committees to continue the Egyptian-Israeli discussions. A Political Committee to be headed by the foreign ministers of both countries would meet in Jerusalem and a Military Committee headed by the defense ministers of both would meet in Cairo. The two committees would start meeting in January. While both sides remained hopeful, Israeli Foreign Minister Moshe Dayan admitted after the meeting that a "wide gap" still separated the two countries.

Issues Dividing Egypt and Israel

Many meetings were held between Egyptian and Israeli officials between November 1977 and January 1978 to try to work out a solution to the problems that divided them.

ISRAEL BEFORE 1967 WAR

The shaded area shows the boundaries of Israel that existed between 1949 and 1967. At its narrowest point near the city of Netanya Israel is only 9 miles wide.

When these direct discussions broke down in January, contacts between the two countries continued, with the United States as an intermediary. Prime Minister Begin came to the United States in March and May of 1978 for meetings with President Carter. President Carter met with President Sadat in Egypt in January and again in the United States in February. American Secretary of State Cyrus Vance and special American representative to the Middle East Alfred Atherton made many trips to Egypt and Israel to transmit proposals from one side to the other. In July, Israeli Defense Minister Ezer Weizman visited Egypt to talk to Sadat. But both sides remained deadlocked with no movement toward a peaceful settlement. The issues that divide them are deep and crucial.

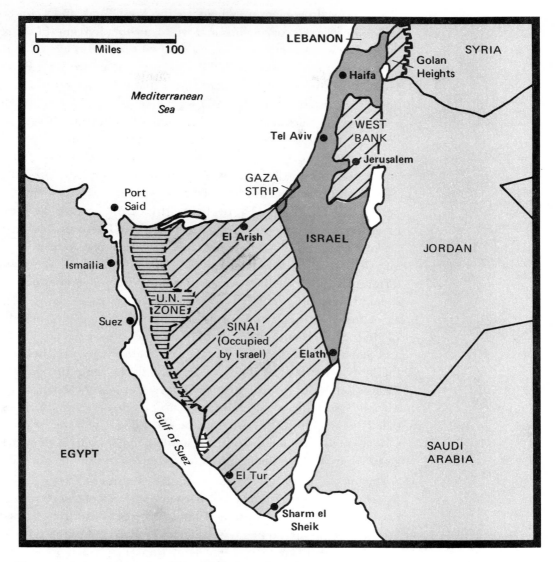

The occupied territories: The West Bank, Gaza Strip, Sinai Peninsula and Golan Heights.

A close look at the map of Israel before 1967 indicates why Israel is reluctant to give back the West Bank and Gaza Strip. These areas give Israel what is known as defensible borders.

The Occupied Territories

During the 1967 war the Israeli Army captured vast areas of Arab lands. These are: the Golan Heights, captured from Syria; the West Bank of the Jordan River, taken from Jordan; and the Gaza Strip and Sinai Peninsula, taken from Egypt. In November 1967, the United Nations Security Council passed a resolutioncalling for the establishment of peace and security in the Middle East. This resolution, known as Resolution 242, says among other things that Israel should withdraw from Arab territories captured in the June 1967 War. The resolution does *not* say that Israel should withdraw from *all* the captured territories. The resolution was deliberately left vague. In the years following the 1967 war, Israeli leaders said they were willing to discuss the return of *some* of these territories if there were a peace settlement.

The crucial problem now involves the West Bank and Gaza Strip. Sadat insists that Israel must make concessions and withdraw totally from these areas. He further insists that a Palestinian state must be established there. But a look at any map of the Middle East shows why Israel is unwilling to return the entire West Bank and Gaza Strip. The Israeli government has repeatedly said that it cannot return to the insecure boundary lines that existed before the 1967 war. A return to pre-1967 borders would leave Israel about twelve miles wide at its narrowest parts, and in danger of being cut in two by enemies from the West Bank. These boundary lines made it very difficult for Israel to defend its territory against enemy attacks. Israel insists it must have defensible borders, and defensible borders means holding on to part or all of the captured Arab territory. There is a great controversy in Israel now over this issue. There are many Israelis who believe that Israel should agree to withdraw from parts of the West Bank and Gaza Strip in order to get talks going again with Egypt. These people, including the opposition Labor Party, feel that a major chance for peace may vanish if Israel does not agree to give up some of this territory. But Prime Minister Begin and other Israelis feel differently. They say they cannot rely on Egyptian promises of peace when there are still so many Arabs insisting that Israel should be destroyed. Israel, they say, must hold on to all of the West Bank and Gaza Strip for its own security. In addition, Prime Minister Begin believes that the West Bank, which he calls by the ancient Hebrew name of Judea and Samaria, and the Gaza Strip were historically part of the land of Israel, are part of the biblical heritage of the Jews, and should not be returned to the Arabs. Since U.N. Resolution 242 calls for Israel to withdraw from the Arab lands occupied in the 1967 war without specifying which those lands are, Begin says that 242 does not necessarily mean that Israel has to withdraw from the West Bank or Gaza Strip. There can be no peace settlement as long as Egypt insists that Israel must return *all* of the West Bank and Gaza and Prime Minister Begin insists that Israel won't return any of it.

During the winter and spring of 1978, President Carter put increasing pressure on Israel to make a decision on the permanent status of the occupied Arab territories. The debate over this issue continued for many weeks within the Israeli government. Prime Minister Begin threatened to resign rather than commit his government to giving up the West Bank and Gaza Strip. Finally in June, the Israeli government issued a statement saying it would put off deciding on the permanent status of the West Bank and Gaza Strip for five years. The statement, which was vaguely worded, said Israel would negotiate "the nature of future relationships" after an interim period of five years, during which time the Palestinians living there would have limited self-rule. The wording of the statement indicates a willingness on the part of the Israeli government to reconsider the form of government for the West Bank and Gaza Strip after five years.

A Palestinian State   The question of the Palestinians and a Palestinian state is very complicated and a deeply emotional one as well. President Sadat insists that the Palestinians cannot be ignored because they are "the core and the crux of the problem." President Sadat says that an independent Palestinian state must be created, most likely on the West Bank and Gaza Strip, to solve the Palestinian problem. At times Sadat uses the word *self-determination* for the Palestinians, but since this means the right of a people to determine their own form of government, the Palestinians would surely decide on an independent state.

Prime Minister Begin is totally opposed to an independent Palestinian state on Israel's borders, as are most Israelis. Begin says that the self-determination for the Palestinians urged by Sadat amounts to the same thing as a Palestinian state. Such a state, he says, would be taken over by the PLO, who would turn it into a Soviet base directed against Israel. This could lead to Israel's destruction. Begin instead proposes "self-rule" or "autonomy" for the Palestinian Arabs living in the West Bank and Gaza Strip. In December 1977, Begin proposed a plan to grant civil autonomy or self-rule to the 1,100,000 Palestinian Arabs living in the West Bank and Gaza. Under this plan, local Arab councils would be elected by the Arabs and these councils would carry out all government functions, except police and military control. Israel would end its military government there but would still retain military and police control over the areas. After five years this plan would be reviewed. This proposal by Begin for self-rule was rejected by Egypt.

Israeli Settlements in the Occupied Territories

After occupying the West Bank, Gaza Strip, Golan Heights, and Sinai Peninsula during the 1967 war, Israel began to set up military outposts to defend itself against attacks. In time, as Israel began to think more seriously of keeping at least part of these territories, the government encouraged Israeli people to settle around some of these outposts and to establish new civilian settlements in the occupied territories. Thousands of Israelis left their homes and jobs and moved to the Sinai, West Bank and Golan Heights. There they built new homes, factories, roads and schools, and set up farming communities. Much money and effort went into building these settlements and now the people living there, as well as the Israeli government, are unwilling to give them up. During the negotiations between Begin and Sadat, Israel claimed that these settlements in the northeastern part of the Sinai should remain under Israeli control even after all of the Sinai is returned to Egypt. Sadat refused to hear of this. In February, the Begin government decided to expand the Jewish settlements in the Sinai and to establish three new ones on the West Bank. This decision caused much tension between Israel and the United States, Israel and Egypt, and within Israel itself. Public opinion in Israel is divided over this issue. There are people who, like Defense Minister Ezer Weizman, believe that there should be a freeze on all new settlements—that Israel should not establish any more. Then there are others who, like Agriculture Minister Ariel Sharon, favor establishing as many new settlements as possible in the occupied lands.

America's New Role in the Middle East

The Deterioration of U.S.–Israeli Relations

From the time of its creation as a state in 1948 until the present, Israel has always looked upon the United States as its chief friend and protector. The United States always provided Israel with the latest weapons and supported Israel in the United Nations when decisions were taken against it. But in 1973 the entire picture in the Middle East began to change. The Arab oil embargo in 1973, followed by a rapid rise in world oil prices, made Americans realize how dependent they were on the good will of the Arabs. As America (as well as Western Europe and Japan) continued to import more oil, the Arab oil states grew in wealth and power. Wealthy Arabs with millions of *petrodollars* (paid for Arabs petroleum) began to look for places to invest their money. The 1970s saw Arabs buying American hotel chains, banks and real estate and donating large sums of money to American universities. And the threat of another oil embargo or rise in oil prices was ever present. As a result of this situation, many people within the American government and others with business interests in the Middle East began to demand a more "even-handed policy" on the part of the United States. What these people say is that the United States should be impartial and not support Israel at the expense of the Arabs. In reality this "even-handed policy" often turns out to be a pro-Arab policy. American public opinion has also shifted. A public opinion poll revealed that between October 1977 and April 1978 American support for Israel declined from 54% to 43%. The question that people were asked was whether the United States should pay more attention to the Arabs even if it means antagonizing Israel, or if the United States should give its strongest support to Israel even if it means risking an oil boycott. Sadat's visit to Israel made a deep impression on the American people. Americans began to see him, and by extension the Arabs, as the true seekers of peace, while Israel seemed to the Americans to be *intransigent* (refusing to compromise). In the same public opinion poll, most Americans thought that neither Israel nor Egypt had made enough concessions toward peace. Yet more than half approved of the way Sadat had handled relations with Israel, while only one-third backed the actions of Prime Minister Begin.

During his election campaign, President Carter repeated over and over that the United States must stand firm in its support for Israel. However, after the election, Carter's position seemed to undergo a big change. Fear of another oil embargo, the desire for Arab friendship, and the wish to replace Soviet influence in the Middle East by American influence combined to bring about a real strain in relations with Israel. Acting on the advice of people like Zbigniew Brzezinski, the National Security Adviser, the Carter administration is trying to pressure Israel into making concessions. In addition to this general background there are a number of specific issues that are causing tension between Israel and the Carter administration.

The Occupied Territories

The Carter administration insists that peace can be achieved only if Israel makes concessions. (There is very little mention that Egypt or the other Arabs should make concessions.) President Carter says that Israel should return to its pre-1967 borders with "minor modifications" in exchange for peace with its Arab neighbors. The United States says that according to Resolution 242 Israel is obligated to at least a partial withdrawal from all the areas occupied in the 1967 war, including the West Bank and Gaza Strip. As we have seen, the position of the Israeli government on this issue is very different. The attitude of the government in Israel is "why should we leave the fate of our country to the judgment of Washington?" The statement by the Israeli Cabinet in June 1978 that it would put off deciding on the permanent status of the occupied territories for five years was criticized by the United States. The Carter administration said that this statement fell short of U.S. hopes and did not go far enough to persuade President Sadat to resume negotiations. The United States had wanted Israel to say that Israeli control over the occupied territories would end after five years, and that during the interim five-year period the eventual solution for these areas would be worked out. The United States also had wanted Israel to affirm that Resolution 242 applied to the West Bank and Gaza as areas from which Israeli forces would have to withdraw substantially.

السادات : لن نقبل فرض الشروط

الرئيس يعلن : نحن نتحدث بلغة واحدة .. وإسرائيل تتحدث بلغتين .. الاحتفاظ بالأرض وفرض الشروط
المبادرة في أيدينا .. وسنظل أسياد مصائرنا ولا بد لإسرائيل أن تتفهم الحقائق

رئيس مجلس الإدارة ورئيس التحرير
موسى صبري
مدير التحرير
احمد زين

مؤسسة أخبار اليوم بشارع الصحافة بالقاهرة

الأخبار

أسسها مصطفى أمين وعلي أمين سنة 1952

AL-AKHBAR, 27 MARCH 1978

الاثنين 18 ربيع الآخر 1398 ـ 27 مارس (آذار) 1978 ـ 18 برمهات 1694 • العدد 8043 • السنة السادسة والعشرون

الخارجية الأمريكية : لا بد من سياسة جديدة لإسرائيل .. أو رئيس حكومة جديدة حتى يتم السلام

الرئيس لوفد الجامعات الأمريكية :
90% من مشكلة السلام تتركز في حل القضية الفلسطينية

قال الرئيس أنور السادات أننا نستطيع الوصول الى السلام في أيام اذا انتهت اسرائيل الظروف والحقائق التي ظهرت في المنطقة بعد زيارة القدس ...

وكالة اليونايتد برس تقول :
هبوط التأييد الأمريكي سيؤدي الى نهاية بيجين

واشنطن ـ ب.ا.ب :
اعلن مسئولون في وزارة الخارجية الأمريكية ان العلاج الوحيد للصدع الخطير في العلاقات الأمريكية الاسرائيلية الآن هو : اما سياسة جديدة او رئيس حكومة جديدة في اسرائيل ...

ممدوح سالم رئيس الوزراء يلقى كلمة في مؤتمر الثقافة والاعلام وبجانبه عبد المنعم الصاوى وزير الثقافة والاعلام (القراءة ص 6) (الصورة : إبراهيم مسلم)

المعارضة في اسرائيل تبحث سحب الثقة من بيجين
اعتبار صيغة أسوان أساسا للسلام

رسالة للسادات من كارتر
يحملها السفير اشرف غربال الذي يجتمع بالسفير قبل سفره

واشنطن ـ ا.ا.ف :

الرئيس يستقبل قائد البحرية الامريكية

اشتباكات متفرقة بين الفلسطينيين والاسرائيليين
القوات السويدية حوصرت بين الطرفين

بيروت ـ النبأ ـ وكالات الانباء :

ماذا فعلنا .. وماذا فعلوا ؟
يقرر : احمد زين (ص 6)

متحدث اسرائيلي يعلن : اسرائيل تتخذ خطوات لاستئناف المباحثات مع مصر

الساندوز جافيتش يعلن : خلافات حادة بين امريكا واسرائيل

اطلاق سراح البارون امبان
باريس ـ وكالات الأنباء :

دمشق تشجع بدخول الساعات للفلسطينيين لبنان وتقول : لا !

صحيفة دافار الاسرائيلية : استقدام لبنان قريبا
القدس ـ وكالات الأنباء :

وايزمان يزور القاهرة
تل أبيب ـ ا.ا.ف :

اجتماع وزراء الخارجية العرب يبدأ اليوم في الجامعة العربية

سكرتير الاتحاد الحر يعلن : 80 مليون عامل في العالم يؤيدون مبادرة السادات للسلام
كتب احمد زمان :

قتل زوج شقيقته وتعهد بالثأر !!

An Arabic newspaper. Credit: Permanent Mission of the Arab Republic of Egypt to the United Nations

An Egyptian woman carries an empty oil drum past billboards advertising the latest movies. *Credit: United Press International*

Israeli Settlements   The question of Israeli settlements in the occupied areas has caused great strain between Washington and Israel. President Carter was very upset when Israel decided to establish new settlements on the West Bank of the Jordan in January 1978. Carter calls these new settlements "illegal settlements" and Secretary of State Vance says they "should not exist." Carter claims that Prime Minister Begin had promised him that Israel would not establish any more settlements on the West Bank except for a limited number of military bases.

A Palestinian State   The position of the Carter administration on the issues of the Palestinians, a Palestinian state, and the PLO seems to *vacillate* (sway back and forth) and this leaves Israel with deep feelings of insecurity. In October 1977, the United States and the Soviet Union issued a joint declaration on the Middle East. The declaration said that a peace conference should be convened in Geneva as soon as possible. But more important, the declaration spoke about ensuring "the legitimate rights of the Palestinian people." Until this point, the United States had always spoken of Palestinian "interests" and not "rights." In international language the difference in the meaning of one word can be crucial. Since all the Arab governments insist that self-determination is one of the rights of the Palestinians, Israel felt that the Carter administration had taken the first step toward accepting the idea of self-determination without explicitly saying so. Prime Minister Begin has repeatedly said, "To us, self-determination means a Palestinian state, and we are not going to agree to any such mortal danger to Israel." This declaration was also frightening to Israel because the Soviet Union was again becoming involved in the Middle East. For several years after the 1973 war, the United States did everything it could to keep the Soviet Union out of all important discussions on the Middle East. Since Soviet policy has been to support the Arabs against Israel, Israel was very unhappy about the possibility of the Soviet Union being included in any future decisions. Israel felt that the Carter administration was sacrificing Israel in order to improve American relations with the Soviet Union.

In January 1978, President Carter visited Egypt. In a public statement Carter said, "There must be a resolution of the Palestinian problem in all its aspects. The solution of the problem must be the legitimate rights of the Palestinian people and enable the Palestinians to participate in the determination of their own future." Although he did not call for a Palestinian state, many thought that Carter came close to calling for self-determination for the Palestinians. In recent months, however, there have been indications from the Carter administration that it does not prefer an independent Palestinian state but favors instead a Palestinian homeland linked to Jordan.

Periodically the PLO repeats what it has always said: that it will not recognize Israel and that its goal is the destruction of the Jewish state. The United States has repeatedly said that it will not have any dealings with the PLO as long as this goal remains unchanged. In December 1977, President Carter said that the PLO had forfeited the right to speak for the Palestinian Arabs at any peace talks because of its intransigent hostility to Israel's existence.

However, despite these public statements, Israel fears that the United States is not only leaning toward accepting a Palestinian state but is willing to accept the PLO as well.

American Plane Sale   In February 1978, the Carter administration made public a proposal to sell fighter jets to Saudi Arabia, Egypt and Israel in a package deal. In the past the United States has sold limited amounts of arms to Jordan, Egypt and Saudi Arabia. But what President

Carter was now proposing to do was to sell 60 F-15s to Saudi Arabia and 15 to Israel. The F-15 is the most advanced military plane that the United States has. There was an immediate outcry in Israel that the United States was moving away from its traditional support of Israel and was endangering Israel's security. There was tremendous opposition in the United States as well. In Congress there were very strong feelings against supplying Saudi Arabia with these fighter planes. But President Carter and his associates put enormous pressure on Congress, and after weeks of bitter debate the Senate approved the plane sale in May.

There are a number of reasons why President Carter chose to sell America's most advanced planes to Saudi Arabia. Saudi Arabia has claimed that it needs these planes for defense against Iraq and South Yemen. Both of these countries have received Soviet military aid, as has Ethiopia, which is across the Red Sea from Saudi Arabia. The United States is now more and more dependent on Saudi Arabian oil. Over the last five years Saudi Arabia has resisted the efforts of other oil-producing nations in OPEC to raise oil prices even higher. This dependence on oil makes America vulnerable to Saudi pressures. Saudi Arabia is the most powerful country in the Middle East because of its oil wealth and because of its position as guardian of Islam. Since Saudi Arabia provides large sums of money to other Arab countries as well as the PLO, Saudi Arabia is in a position to influence their policies. It is believed that without Saudi support, Sadat would never have gone to Israel. The United States uses the term *moderate* to describe Saudi Arabia and Egypt. Moderate means less extreme, less violent, unwilling to make extreme changes. The PLO, Libya and Iraq are known as "radicals." They seek the destruction of Israel, and welcome Soviet aid. The United States believes that supporting "moderates" like Saudi Arabia and Sadat is in the interests of peace. Saudi Arabia is very religious and very conservative and therefore very fearful of Communism. American and Saudi interests are identical with regard to keeping the Soviet Union out of the Middle East.

The decision to sell war planes to Saudi Arabia and Egypt marks a "political watershed" in America's relations with the Middle East. Many people see it as a change in the special relationship that the United States and Israel had for thirty years. It indicates a formal decision to treat the Arabs as friends. Israel will be affected by this decision in many ways. Militarily, the effect on Israel will be great. Until now Israel was the only country in the Middle East to receive advanced American weapons. Israeli air power was responsible for its victories in the wars of 1967 and 1973. That advantage is now reduced by the sale of American fighter planes to Saudi Arabia and Egypt. In addition, Saudi Arabia is receiving advanced missiles from the United States and Egypt is getting Mirage fighter planes from France. Syria, Iraq and Libya are receiving sophisticated equipment from the Soviet Union, including planes, tanks and missiles. This combination of events greatly weakens Israel's position.

PLO Terrorism and Israeli Retaliation

In March 1978, Palestinian guerrillas hijacked an Israeli bus outside Tel Aviv. It was the worst terrorist attack inside Israel in years, and when it was over thirty-four Israelis, one American woman and the nine terrorists were dead. A few hours later, PLO representatives in Lebanon took credit for this brutal massacre of innocent civilians. President Sadat was the only Arab leader to denounce it, calling it a "sad and tragic event." Saudi Arabia, in a radio broadcast, first praised the PLO's massacre, but then quickly retracted the statement, fearing Congress would block the sale of the F-15 fighter planes.

A month earlier, Yasir Arafat, leader of the PLO, had written to President Carter and had hinted that the PLO would resort to new acts of violence if the PLO were excluded from the Middle East peace process. It was widely believed that the attack on the Israeli bus was to torpedo the peace negotiations between Israel and Egypt and to show that the PLO cannot be left out.

A week later Israel retaliated, sending its armed forces into southern Lebanon. Israeli troops moved about nine miles into Lebanon, attacking Palestinian villages, while Israeli fighter planes bombed Palestinian guerrilla bases. The purpose of the Israeli invasion was to drive the Palestinian guerrillas from the border areas, which they used to attack Israel. Prime Minister Begin's explanation was that the Israeli troops were sent into Lebanon "to cut off the evil arm of the guerrillas." In addition, Israel had recently become aware of a force of several hundred Syrian-oriented Palestinian guerrillas called Al Siaqa moving into position just across the border from Israel with large stores of Soviet-made artillery pieces and mortars.

Hundreds of people were killed and tens of thousands fled north after their villages were destroyed. Syria, which has 30,000 troops in Lebanon, did nothing to stop the Israeli invasion. (After a PLO rocket attack on Israel in November 1977, President Assad of Syria warned the PLO not to provoke Israel because if they did Syria would not help them.) The United Nations met to discuss the situation and passed a resolution calling for Israel to withdraw and for the establishment of a U.N. peacekeeping force. Soon after, Israeli forces began their withdrawal from Lebanon, which was completed by the middle of June. At the end, the Israelis turned over the major posts to the Lebanese Christian militia units rather than to the U.N. peacekeeping force. This was in line with the long-standing Israeli policy of helping the Lebanese Christians in their bitter conflict with the Moslems and Palestinians.

The Camp David Summit Conference

In an effort to get Egyptian-Israeli peace talks moving again President Carter invited Israeli Prime Minister Begin and Egyptian President Sadat to meet with him in the United States. The meeting of the three leaders began on September 5 at Camp David and lasted until September 17. Despite many pessimistic reports that nothing would come out of the meeting, on September 17 a historic announcement was made to the world. Begin and Sadat had at last reached an agreement, and on this day the agreement was signed at the White House and televised throughout the world. According to the agreement Israel is to return the Sinai Desert to Egypt and remove the Jewish settlements there. Both sides agreed that the fate of the Palestinians living on the West Bank and Gaza Strip would be decided with five years. Both sides agreed to begin peace talks within a few weeks that would lead to an Egyptian-Israeli peace treaty by the end of the year.

There was violent opposition to the Camp David accords in the Arab world. President Assad of Syria led a campaign to persuade the other Arab rulers not to back the Camp David agreement. Assad met with King Hussein of Jordan and Sinai Arabian rulers. Then leaders of Syria, Algeria, South Yemen, Libya and the PLO met together and agreed to break relations with Egypt and seek closer political and military ties with the

Soviet Union. At the same time President Carter sent Secretary of State Vance to the Middle East to try to win Arab backing for the accords. His trip was not a success.

Two weeks later the Israeli Parliament voted to ratify the Camp David accords. The agreements were approved by an overwhelming majority. The Parliament called the vote the most momentous occasion in the history of Israel. Begin and Sadat both stated that there were now no obstacles toward reaching a peace treaty by the end of the year. This peace treaty would end the 30-year war between Israel and Egypt. In October, Israeli and Egyptian representatives came to Washington to begin negotiations for a peace treaty. Just when the negotiations seemed to be coming to a standstill, President Carter intervened and the negotiations were concluded.

President Sadat's arrival in Israel. **Credit:** *Consulate General of Israel*

Negotiations between Israeli and Egyptian officials continued for several weeks and then broke down. Each side blamed the other for the failure. It had been hoped that a peace treaty between Israel and Egypt would be concluded by December 1978. This did not happen. In February 1979 President Carter again intervened and invited both sides to come to Washington to continue their negotiations.

In March, 1979 the historic treaty between Israel and Egypt was signed in Washington. This treaty officially ended the state of war that had existed between the two nations for thirty years.

EGYPT AND ISRAEL SIGN FORMAL TREATY, ENDING A STATE OF WAR AFTER 30 YEARS: SADAT AND BEGIN PRAISE CARTER'S ROLE

President Anwar el-Sadat, President Jimmy Carter, and Prime Minister Menachem Begin join hands after signing the pact. **Credit: United Press International**

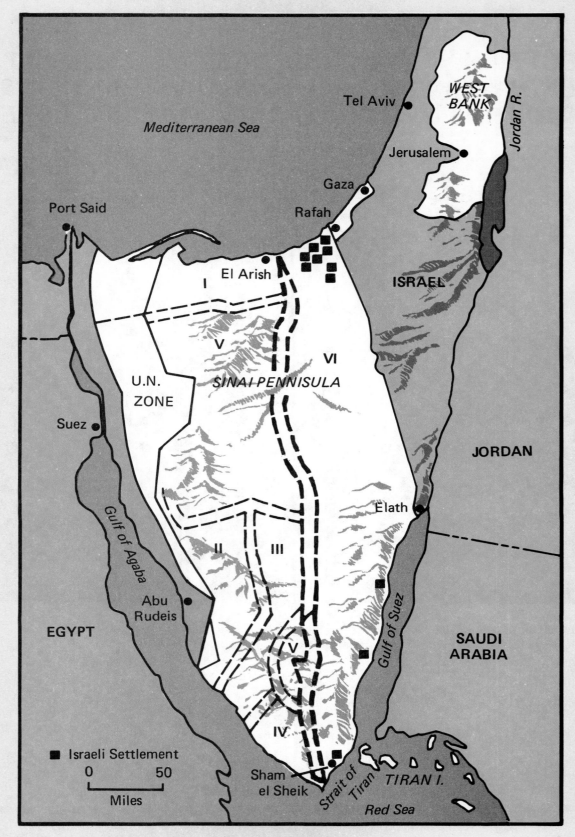

Mediterranean Sea

WEST BANK

Tel Aviv

Jordan R.

Jerusalem

Gaza

Port Said

Rafah

ISRAEL

El Arish

I

V

VI

U.N. ZONE

SINAI PENNISULA

Suez

JORDAN

Gulf of Agaba

Elath

II

III

EGYPT

Abu Rudeis

SAUDI ARABIA

V

Gulf of Suez

IV

■ Israeli Settlement

0   50

Miles

Sham el Sheik

Strait of Tiran

TIRAN I.

Red Sea

The Egyptian-Israeli Treaty and the 6 steps of withdrawal

1 In 2 months   4 In 7 months
2 In 3 months   5 In 9 months
3 In 5 months   6 In 3 years

The treaty provides for the gradual withdrawal of Israel from positions in the Sinai. The map above shows the phases of that withdrawal. The treaty also provides for future talks on Palestinian self-rule for the West Bank and Gaza Strip.

Summary of Key Ideas

The Middle East and North Africa

A. **The location of the Middle East has made the region important in world affairs.**

   1. Its location at the crossroads of three continents, and the existence of the Suez Canal make the Middle East a strategic area.

   2. This region forms a land bridge that connects Europe, Asia, and Africa. Historically, it has been a crossroads for traders going from Europe to India, and from Asia to North Africa.

B. **Geography has played an important role in the development of the Middle East.**

   1. Deserts are a major feature of the topography of the Middle East.

   2. Scarcity of water is a major problem.

   3. Climatic and soil factors would be favorable to agriculture if adequate and cheap water resources could be found.

   4. Large populations are concentrated in flood plains and deltas of the major rivers (Nile, Tigris-Euphrates).

C. **Cultural factors have served both to unite and separate the peoples of the Middle East.**

   1. Most of the people of the Middle East belong to the ethnic group known as Arabs (exceptions: Israelis, Turks, Persians).

   2. The people of the Middle East can be divided into three groups: e.g., farmers, nomadic herdsmen (Bedouins) and city dwellers.

   3. Islam is the major influence in the area. It influences the values, thoughts and actions of most of the people.

   4. Nationalism has influenced developments in the Middle East and has tended to divide the Arabs.

   5. Pan-Arabism is a political movement with the aim of uniting all Arabs, but such forces as lack of interest, local tribal loyalties, and rivalry among national leaders have prevented its success.

D. **The history of the Middle East has been marked by great accomplishment, then steady decline and foreign domination.**

   1. The Middle East contains the longest span of recorded history.

2. Discoveries and inventions made in the Middle East have helped shape cultures throughout the world.

3. Various ethnic and racial groups contributed to the cultural development of the area.

4. The river valleys of the Nile and the Tigris-Euphrates were cradles of early civilization.

5. Three great world religions were born in the area (Judaism, Christianity and Islam).

6. The Arabs have made significant contributions to world civilization in the field of religion, science, art, literature and mathematics.

7. Arab empires ruled the Middle East and North Africa for centuries.

8. From the 15th century to the middle of the 20th century, Arab areas remained under the control of non-Arab rulers. Progress remained at a standstill.

9. World War I and World War II led to a growth of nationalism and finally to independence.

E. **The economy of the area is based on farming and oil.**

1. Most of the people of the Middle East are farmers and herdsmen. Many of them do not own the land they work on.

2. Farming methods are unscientific, outdated and primitive.

3. The Middle East is a region of economic underdevelopment, low standards of living and low levels of production.

4. Oil is king. The Middle East has vast known oil reserves.

5. Until recently oil sales were not used to better the lives of the people.

6. Strong desires for complete freedom from foreign influence conflict with dependence on Western technology in operating the oil fields.

7. The United States and the Soviet Union are engaged in rivalry to control the rich oil resources.

8. Arab socialism is the economic idea followed by the developing nations in the Middle East.

9. Most governments regulate industrial development and supervise many aspects of economic life.

10. The Middle East faces all the economic problems of developing nations.

F. **Conflict between Israel and the Arab nations adds to the problems of the area.**

1. Israel is an island of Judaism in a sea of Islam.

2. Israel bases its claim to Middle Eastern land on historical and Biblical grounds.

3. Israel has been an independent state since 1948.

4. Israeli society and economy differ from those of the other countries of the Middle East in religion, language, science, farming, government and methods of development.

5. Most Arab nations are still pledged to the defeat of Israel.

6. Wars were fought in 1948, 1956 and 1967. Israel emerged victorious, and now occupies territory of Jordan, Egypt and Syria.

7. Arab refugees who left Israel in 1948, and their children, present a difficult problem to the solution of the Arab-Israeli conflict.

8. The United States has tried to play a role in the settlement of conflicts in the Middle East. The Soviet Union has followed a policy of close support and aid for the Arabs.

9. President Sadat's 1977 visit to Israel has increased pressure on Israel to make concessions in order to get peace negotiations moving.

10. The most difficult peace issues include the security of Israel, Palestinian nationalism, and the future of the occupied territories.

A collection of Arabic stamps.

UNIT III

Exercises and Questions

Vocabulary

Directions: Match the words in Column *A* with the correct meaning in Column *B*.

Column A	Column B
1. caliphs	(a) Mohammed's flight from Mecca to Medina.
2. Islam	(b) Turkish ruler.
3. Moslem	(c) holy book of the Moslems.
4. Hegira	(d) submission to God.
5. mosque	(e) follower of Islam.
6. Koran	(f) belief in one God.
7. Allah	(g) Arabic for God.
8. pilgrimage	(h) place of worship.
9. monotheism	(i) religious journey.
10. sultan	(i) rulers of the Islamic empire.
11. wadis	(k) seasonal streams found in deserts.
12. oasis	(l) a part of the desert where water and vegetation can be found.

Column A	Column B
1. bedouins	(a) collective farm in Israel.
2. sheik	(b) marketplace.
3. fellahin	(c) ancient Egyptian ruler.
4. bazaar	(d) desert nomads.
5. rabbi	(e) idea of a single state for all Moslems.
6. Talmud	(f) book containing Jewish teachings.
7. kibbutz	(g) Arab peasants.

8. Zionism

9. pharaoh

10. Pan-Islamism

(h) Jewish religious teacher.

(i) tribal leader.

(j) belief in a Jewish state in Israel.

THE MIDDLE EAST: POPULATION, DENSITY AND INCOME

Country	Area (thousands of square miles)	Population (millions of people)	Density of Population (people per sq. mi.)	Income Per Person In Dollars (per capita)
United States	3,615	203.2	56	3,910
Egypt	386	32.5	84	156
Iraq	173	9.5	55	255
Israel	8	3.0	375	1,470
Jordan	37	2.3	62	225
Kuwait	6	0.7	117	3,335
Lebanon	4	2.8	700	465
Saudi Arabia	870	7.8	8	310
Syria	72	6.1	84	215

Chart Interpretation

Directions: Select the statement which best answers the question or completes the sentence. Use only the information given in the chart and graphs.

1. The number 386 next to Egypt in the *area* column stands for
   (a) 386 square miles
   (b) 3,860 square miles
   (c) 38,600 square miles
   (d) 386,000 square miles

2. The number 9.5 next to Iraq in the *population* column stands for
   (a) 95 people
   (b) 950,000 people
   (c) 9,500,000 people
   (d) 95,000,000 people

3. The Middle Eastern country with the largest area is
   (a) Saudi Arabia
   (b) Egypt
   (c) Iraq
   (d) Kuwait

4. The Middle Eastern country with the smallest population is
   (a) Saudi Arabia
   (b) Lebanon
   (c) Israel
   (d) Kuwait

5. The Middle Eastern country whose per capita income is closest to that of the United States is
   (a) Saudi Arabia
   (b) Israel
   (c) Jordan
   (d) Kuwait

6. The column which tells us about standard of living is
   (a) Income Per Person
   (b) Population
   (c) Area
   (d) Density

7. The population of Lebanon is closest to that of
   (a) Jordan
   (b) Kuwait
   (c) Iraq
   (d) Saudi Arabia

8. The density of population of Israel is greater than all of the following *except*
   (a) Lebanon
   (b) Kuwait
   (c) Iraq
   (d) Jordan

9. This chart would be of great value to
   (a) an anthropolgist
   (b) an historian
   (c) a psychologist
   (d) an economist

10. Which of the following statements is true according to the information given in this table?
   (a) Most of the people in the Middle East live in Lebanon.
   (b) Iraq has a larger per capita income than Saudi Arabia.
   (c) Much of Saudi Arabia has a a low density of population.
   (d) The population of Kuwait is about is about three times that of Jordan.

Multiple Choice

Directions: Select the letter of the correct answer.

1. The lands of the Middle East can be studied as one region because they are similar in all of the following ways *except* which?
   (a) They all have the same kind of climate.
   (b) Most of the people are Moslems.
   (c) They are all ruled by the same government.
   (d) They have similar problems.

2. Much of the world's trade passes through the Middle East because
   (a) the people of the Middle East are among the world's best traders.
   (b) the Middle East connects three continents.
   (c) the best harbors are found in the Middle East.
   (d) all of these.

3. The Suez Canal connects the
   (a) Atlantic Ocean with the Pacific Ocean.
   (b) Atlantic Ocean with the Black Sea.
   (c) Mediterranean Sea with the Red Sea.
   (d) Mediterranean Sea with the Black Sea.

4. Most of the land of the Middle East is
   (a) jungle   (b) steppe   (c) desert   (d) savanna

5. Only about 15% of the land of the Middle East is suitable for farming. 85% is unsuitable because
   (a) it is too dry.
   (b) it is too hilly.
   (c) there are too many factories.
   (d) none of these.

6. The longest river in the world is the
   (a) Tigris   (b) Euphrates   (c) Nile   (d) Congo

7. The best land for farming is found in
   (a) the mountains
   (b) the river valleys
   (c) Turkey
   (d) all of these

8. Which of the following is true of the nomads of the desert?
   (a) They are always moving in search of water.
   (b) Their animals supply them with most of their needs.
   (c) Guests are treated well by the nomads.
   (d) All of these.

9. All of the following are true about farmers in the Middle East *except*
   (a) Farmers make up 75% of the population of the area.
   (b) Most of the farmers use tractors and other machinery.
   (c) Most farmers own small plots of land.
   (d) Many farmers rent land from rich landlords.

10. Farming in Israel is very different from farming in the rest of the Middle East because
    (a) there are no rich landlords in Israel.
    (b) all the farmers together own the land, tools and animals.
    (c) Israeli farmers use modern methods.
    (d) all of these.

11. Cities of the Middle East are very interesting because
    (a) there are no slums or poor people.
    (b) old Arab towns exist alongside modern cities.
    (c) most of the people are factory workers.
    (d) all of these.

12. All of the following are true of the marketplace *except* which?
    (a) Every item has a fixed price.
    (b) Beautiful jewelry, rugs and leather goods can be found.
    (c) Workshops are often located behind the booths in the market.
    (d) Craftsmen pass their skills on to their children.

13. Craftsmen earn a living by
    (a) making goods by hand.
    (b) using modern machinery.
    (c) selling goods to the farmers.
    (d) importing goods from other countries.

14. All of the following are true about Islam *except* which?
    (a) Mohammed was the founder of the religion.
    (b) Mohammed was influenced by the teachings of the Jews.
    (c) Mohammed believed that there is only one God.
    (d) Mohammed's ideas were very popular among the people of Mecca.

15. A good Moslem does all of the following *except*
    (a) believes that Mohammed was God's prophet.
    (b) goes to church on Sunday.

(c) reads the Koran.

(d) fasts during the month of Ramadan.

16. The Hebrews made their greatest contribution to the world in
    (a) architecture   (b) government   (c) religion   (d) science

17. The Prophets were very important in ancient Israel because
    (a) they condemned the worship of other gods.
    (b) they said that God demanded righteousness from his people.
    (c) they criticized the rich and powerful people who were unjust.
    (d) all of these.

18. The main reason that civilization first developed in the Nile Valley and Mesopotamia was that
    (a) there were excellent harbors for trade.
    (b) the soil was fertile for farming.
    (c) many industries developed.
    (d) cities provided many jobs.

19. In the river valleys the need for water led to
    (a) wars among the different people.
    (b) crop failures.
    (c) growth of government.
    (d) none of these.

20. Hieroglyphics and cuneiform were
    (a) ancient systems of writing.
    (b) ancient Babylonian art.
    (c) warfare methods practiced by the Sumerians.
    (d) forms of architecture.

21. The Egyptian pharaohs built huge pyramids because
    (a) they wanted to show that they were good architects.
    (b) they wanted to preserve their bodies for the life after death.
    (c) they wanted to provide jobs for thousands of people.
    (d) all of these.

22. Probably the earliest people to use iron were the
    (a) Lydians.   (b) Hittites.   (c) Phoenicians.   (d) Hebrews.

23. The Moslems made great contributions to the world in
    (a) medicine.   (b) mathematics.   (c) literature.   (d) all of these.

24. All of the following are true of Moslem culture *except* which?
    (a) The Moslems were influenced by the learning of ancient Greece and India.
    (b) The writings of Greek philosophers were translated into Arabic and later passed on to Europe.
    (c) The numbers which we use today were first developed by the Arabs.
    (d) Knowledge of mathematics came to the Arabs from India, but the Arabs added to this and passed it on.

25. Omar Khayyám was famous as
    (a) a Persian poet.
    (b) an Arab scientist.
    (c) an Egyptian general.
    (d) a Moslem priest.

26. The Crusaders were
    (a) Arabs who became Christians.
    (b) European Christians who tried to reconquer the Holy Land.
    (c) Moslems who visited Europe.
    (d) Christian soldiers who defended Europe against Arab attacks.

27. The nomads who invaded the Middle East in the 13th and 14th centuries and caused much destruction were
    (a) Crusaders. (b) Persians. (c) Mongols. (d) Indians.

28. All of the following statements about the Ottoman Empire are true *except* which?
    (a) The Turks were good soldiers and conquered vast territories.
    (b) The Turks forced all the people in their empire to become Moslems.
    (c) Important contributions were made by the Turks in literature and architecture.
    (d) The most intelligent Christian boys were converted, assigned to military units and trained to rule.

29. The Ottoman Empire declined when
    (a) the rulers became more interested in pleasure than ruling.
    (b) Europe began to make great progress in science and industry.
    (c) Russia fought many wars against Turkey to capture territory.
    (d) all of these.

30. A famous Ottoman ruler was
    (a) Ferdinand de Lesseps.
    (b) Suleiman the Magnificent.
    (c) Mohammed.
    (d) Salah-al-Din.

31. The engineer who built the Suez Canal was a (an)
    (a) Turk. (b) Frenchman. (c) Egyptian. (d) Englishman.

32. The Suez Canal was important because it made it easier for
    (a) Russia to trade with the Mediterranean countries.
    (b) European nations to trade with Asia.
    (c) the United States to trade with Latin America.
    (d) the United States to trade with Europe.

33. Until the end of World War II the most important decisions affecting the Middle East were made by the
    (a) Russians and Americans.
    (b) Egyptians and Syrians.
    (c) British and French.
    (d) Germans and Italians.

34. A mandate is related to which of these areas?
    (a) Egypt   (b) Palestine   (c) Morocco   (d) Saudi Arabia

35. A serious problem that many of the countries of the Middle East have faced since World War II has been which of the following?
    (a) European nations have tried to take over the Middle East again.
    (b) The United States has tried to turn these countries into colonies.
    (c) Many governments have been changed by force.
    (d) Arabs have united to form one Arab state.

36. Approximately how much of the world's oil reserves is the Middle East believed to contain?
    (a) 30%   (b) 50%   (c) 66%   (d) 85%

37. The oil fields of the Middle East have been developed by European and American oil companies for all of the following reasons *except* which?
    (a) Nations of the Middle East do not have enough money.
    (b) Nations of the Middle East do not have the necessary equipment.
    (c) Nations of the Middle East do not have enough engineers.
    (d) Nations of the Middle East are not very interested in their oil reserves.

38. Which of the following is the cause of the other three?
    (a) Desert nomads work for wages.
    (b) New towns are built.
    (c) An oil company begins to drill for oil.
    (d) Many people receive technical training.

39. A very important reason why the nations of the Middle East find it difficult to improve the living conditions of their people is that
    (a) the population continues to grow faster than the rate of food production.
    (b) these nations have no important source of income.
    (c) Russia has been charging the countries of the Middle East high interest rates on loans.
    (d) heavy rainfall has destroyed many crops.

40. The Balfour Declaration stated that
    (a) the British intended to take over Palestine for themselves.
    (b) the British Government favored a national home for the Jews in Palestine.
    (c) Palestine should be an Arab state.
    (d) the British and French would rule Palestine together.

41. Which of the following was *not* a result of the first Arab-Israeli War?
    (a) An Arab state was set up in Palestine.
    (b) Israel defended its independence.
    (c) Thousands of Arabs left their homes in Palestine.
    (d) Israel proved its military strength.

42. Which of the following was true of the 1956 Arab-Israeli War?
    (a) The Arabs captured the Suez Canal.
    (b) The UN set up a force to try and keep peace.
    (c) Israel was defeated.
    (d) Egypt was able to blockade the Gulf of Aqaba.

43. Since the Six Day War of 1967
    (a) the Arabs have gained control of Palestine.
    (b) peace and recognition of Israel have been achieved.
    (c) Israel and the Arabs have been unable to reach a settlement.
    (d) Arab refugees have been resettled in Israel.

44. The Truman Doctrine was important because
    (a) it promised American aid to countries threatened by Communism.
    (b) it helped Greece and Turkey resist Russian demands.
    (c) it won friends for the United States.
    (d) all of these.

45. The Soviet interests in the Middle East are all of the following *except*
    (a) to limit the West's use of the important oil resources of the Middle East.
    (b) to make sure that Israel remains strong.
    (c) to win friends among the Arabs.
    (d) to control the important waterways of the Middle East.

46. The United States policy in the Middle East has been
    (a) to win the friendship of the Arabs only.
    (b) to win the friendship of Israel only.
    (c) to be friendly with both Israel and the Arabs.
    (d) to stay neutral and not take sides.

47. Which of the following statements is *not* true about the 1973 Middle East war?
    (a) Syria and Egypt launched an attack against Israel.
    (b) The United States provided Israel with vast shipments of arms.
    (c) The Soviet Union remained neutral during the conflict.
    (d) The cease-fire went into effect as Israel was about to win a decisive victory.

48. Which of the following statements is true?
    (a) The Arabs used oil as a weapon during the 1973 war and later.
    (b) Western Europe and Japan were hard hit when the Arabs cut back their oil production.
    (c) The Arabs announced a total oil embargo against the United States and Holland.
    (d) All of these.

49. The best known American in the Middle East today is
    (a) Richard Nixon.
    (b) Henry Kissinger.
    (c) Gerald Ford.
    (d) Nelson Rockefeller

50. Which statement is *not* true about the Palestinians?
    (a) The Palestinians want to return to Israel, which they call Palestine, because they consider it their homeland.
    (b) The Palestinians are ready to make peace with Israel at any time.
    (c) Many Palestinians are involved in acts of terrorism.
    (d) The Palestinians often find themselves in conflict with other Arabs.

Thought Questions

1. Why is it very important for us to know about the Middle East today?

2. Why is water a problem to the people of the Middle East?

3. How do the lives of the desert nomad, village farmer and city dweller differ from each other?

4. What are some of the things a Moslem believes?

5. Why has the Jewish religion had a great influence on other religions and civilizations?

6. Why did civilization develop in the Nile Valley and Mesopotamia?

7. How were the Arabs able to spread Islam to many different parts of the world?

8. Why have historians used such words as "brilliant" and "magnificent" to describe Moslem civilization from 700 to 1200 A.D.?

9. Why did the civilization of the Moslems decline after 1200?

10. Why did the Arabs feel that Britain and France had betrayed them after World War I?

11. (a) What are some of the ways in which the Arabs hoped to unify the lands of the Middle East following World War II?
    (b) Why have these hopes not been realized?

12. Why has oil been called "king" in the Middle East?

13. What are the problems Middle Eastern nations face in trying to erase poverty and build up their industries?

14. If you were the leader of one of these nations, how would you try to solve these problems?

15. Why have many Jewish people always hoped to return to Palestine and to set up a Jewish state?

16. Why are the Arabs opposed to a Jewish state in Palestine?

17. Why has the Soviet Union been successful in winning much influence in the Middle East?

18. Why does the United States face many problems in its relations with the countries of the Middle East?

Chart Interpretation

Directions: Answer the following questions by indicating whether the statement is *True* or *False* or *Information Not Given*. Base all answers on information given in the chart.

1. All the nations of the Middle East increased their imports from the United States between 1968 and 1969.

2. Israel is the leading trading partner of the U.S. in the Middle East.

3. Oil is the leading trade product between the U.S. and the Middle East.

4. The greatest increase in exports between 1968 and 1969 was made by Iran.

5. In conclusion we can say trade increased between the U.S. and the countries of the Middle East between 1968 and 1969.

UNITED STATES TRADE WITH THE MIDDLE EAST AND NORTH AFRICA (Selected Areas)

Country	Exports*		Imports*	
	1976	1977	1976	1977
Algeria	487	527	2,344	3,228
Egypt	810	983	111	188
Iran	2,776	2,731	1,631	3,032
Iraq	382	211	123	420
Israel	1,409	1,446	437	590
Saudi Arabia	2,774	3,575	5,847	7,012

*Values in Millions of Dollars

SOURCE: Bureau of Statistics, International Monetary Fund, *Direction of Trade*, May 1978.

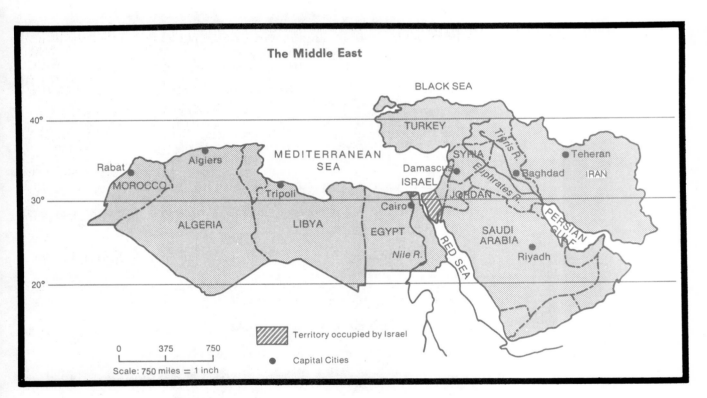

The Middle East

Territory occupied by Israel

● Capital Cities

0   375   750
Scale: 750 miles = 1 inch

Map Exercise

Directions: Tell whether the following statements are *True* or *False*. Correct the false statements.

1. The distance from Algiers to Cairo is about *1600 miles*.

2. Most of the Middle East is located *south* of the equator.

3. *Baghdad* is located on the Nile River.

4. Territory occupied by Israel is located near *Algeria and Morocco.*

5. Rabat is located on the *east* coast of North Africa.

6. *Turkey* is probably the largest country of the Middle East.

7. The Tigris and Euphrates rivers flow south into the *Red Sea.*

8. The capital of Syria is *Damascus.*

9. Libya is located to the west of *Algeria.*

10. Turkey can be described as an *island.*

Completion

Directions: Complete the following sentences by selecting the correct word or phrases below

OPEC	disengagement	terrorism
petrodollars	oil embargo	non-belligerence
shuttle diplomacy	Golan Heights	Suez Canal
Sinai Desert	**PLO**	West Bank

1. The agreement to separate Israeli and Arab troops is known as.....................

2. The money accumulated by the oil rich countries is known as ....

3. The weapon used by the Arabs against the United States during the 1973 war is ....

4. The trading route that was once very important to world commerce is.................

5. The organization that represents most Palestinians is.....................

6. Former Jordanian territory that is presently occupied by Israel is ....

7. The term that refers to Mr. Kissinger's traveling back and forth between Israel and the Arab countries is ....

8. Israel would like a promise from the Arabs not to use force. This is known as ....

9. The organization that represents the oil producing countries is.....................

10. Syrian territory that is held by Israel is called ....

11. Methods used by many Palestinians against Israel are termed ....

12. Vast territory that had been taken by Israel from Egypt during the 1967 war is...................

Israelis march for solidarity, marking an International Workers Festival. *(Top) Credit: United Press International*

Arabs astride their donkeys pass through one of the narrow thoroughfares of the Old City of Jerusalem. *(Bottom) Credit: United Press International*

Exercises and Questions   191

The Ayatollah Ruhollah Khomeini. *Credit: United Press International*

Puzzle

Directions: Place the words below in their proper place in the puzzle.

3 LETTERS	5 LETTERS	6 LETTERS	7 LETTERS	8 LETTERS
ISM	LACKS	DEMAND	MANDATE	CONFLICT
IST	UNITY	PREFIX	PIONEER	CREATION
		REGION	REFUGEE	INCIDENT
		STRAIT	TACTICS	OCCUPIED
		SUFFIX		PROPOSAL

9 LETTERS	10 LETTERS	11 LETTERS	13 LETTERS
GUERRILLA	IRRIGATION	AGRICULTURE	INDOCTRINATED
INJUSTICE	PROPAGANDA	IMMIGRATION	
PREVENTED	RESTRICTED	IMPERIALIST	
		NATIONALISM	

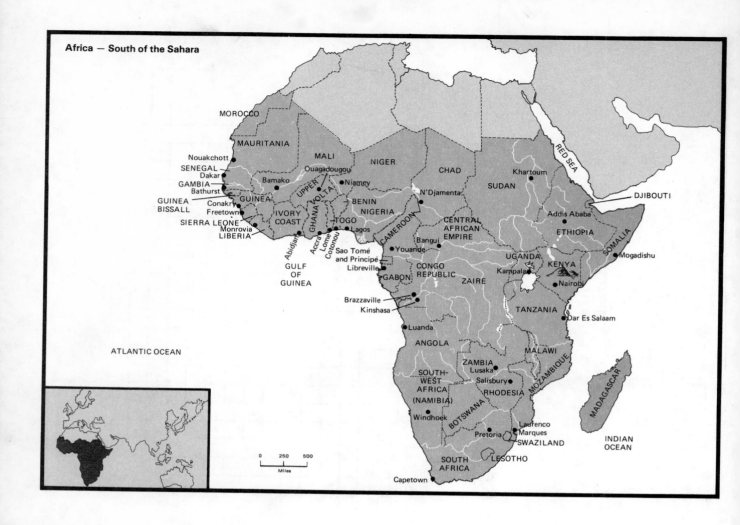

Africa — South of the Sahara

MOROCCO

MAURITANIA

Nouakchott
SENEGAL
Dakar
GAMBIA
Bathurst
GUINEA
BISSALL
Conakry
Freetown
SIERRA LEONE
Monrovia
LIBERIA

MALI

Bamako

UPPER
VOLTA

Ouagadougou

Niamey

NIGER

IVORY
COAST

GHANA

TOGO

BENIN

NIGERIA

Accra
Lome
Cotonou

Lagos

Abidjan

GULF
OF
GUINEA

Sao Tomé
and Principé
Libreville

CHAD

N'Djamenta

CAMEROON

Bangui

CENTRAL
AFRICAN
EMPIRE

Youande

GABON

CONGO
REPUBLIC

ZAIRE

Brazzaville
Kinshasa

Luanda

ANGOLA

ATLANTIC OCEAN

SOUTH-
WEST
AFRICA
(NAMIBIA)

Windhoek

BOTSWANA

ZAMBIA
Lusaka

Salisbury

RHODESIA

MALAWI

MOZAMBIQUE

Pretoria

Laurenco
Marques
SWAZILAND

LESOTHO

SOUTH
AFRICA

Capetown

SUDAN

Khartoum

RED SEA

DJIBOUTI

Addis Ababa

ETHIOPIA

SOMALIA

Mogadishu

UGANDA

Kampala

KENYA

Nairobi

TANZANIA

Dar Es Salaam

MADAGASCAR

INDIAN
OCEAN

0   250   500

Miles

UNIT IV Africa— South of the Sahara

Geography and Isolation

Isolation

Africa has been called the "Dark Continent," a land of mystery and the unknown. To describe what Europeans knew of Africa, we can look at a poem written over 250 years ago:

> So geographers, in Afric maps,
> With savage pictures fill their gaps,
> And o'er uninhabitable downs,*
> Place elephants for want of towns.
>
> *Jonathan Swift*

Little was known of Africa south of the Sahara because, for most of its long history, it was isolated to a great extent from the rest of the world. Geography is largely responsible for this. Perhaps the main cause of Sub-Saharan Africa's isolation is the Sahara Desert.

The Sahara Desert

The Sahara is the world's largest desert. It covers an area greater than that of the United States. It extends from the Red Sea in the east to the Atlantic Ocean in the west. The desert is more rocky than sandy. It has been an *obstacle* (block) to travel between North Africa and Central Africa. It has also limited the exchange of ideas between the heartland of Africa and the Mediterranean coastlands.

---

*grassy, rolling uplands

Mt. Kilimanjaro, in northern Tanzania, rises 19,565 feet above sea level. Its peak
is snow covered all year round.
Credit: *Public Relations Department—Tanzania*

The Sahara was not always as dry as it is today. During the last part of the Ice Age (7,500 years ago), people and the animals they hunted lived comfortably in the area. As the ice melted, the climate of Africa changed. The Sahara became drier and warmer, and the people who lived there were forced to move to the south. The region began to dry out about six thousand years ago. This was at about the same time that civilization was beginning to develop in Egypt and Southwest Asia. The Sahara seems to have reached its present desert condition about four thousand years ago. It is quite possible that if the Sahara had remained well watered and fertile, Sub-Saharan Africa might have been one of the world's most economically developed areas.

Other Factors

Other factors have helped to cause Africa's isolation. Sub-Saharan Africa has an almost unbroken and regular coastline. Because of this, there are few natural harbors for ships to anchor in, for trade and exploration. It is also difficult for ships to sail northward along the west coast, because the winds and ocean currents are always from the northeast.

As if these disadvantages were not enough, Africa has a very narrow coastal plain. Not far from the sea, dense jungles in the west and an *escarpment* (sharp, steep cliffs), in the east appear. Where they drop down from the inland plateau on their way to the sea, Africa's rivers have falls and rapids. These rapids were another obstacle to opening Africa to the world.

Topography

Size

Africa is a huge continent. From east to west, at its widest point, the distance is almost the same as that between Moscow and New York (4,000 miles). The north-south distance is almost the same as the distance between northern Alaska and the Panama Canal (5,000 miles).

The Plateau Topography

About ninety percent of Sub-Saharan Africa is five hundred feet or higher. In the eastern half of the area a plateau rises 5,000 to 6,000 feet. The plateau does not level off gradually to the sea. It drops off sharply (escarpment). As a person travels westward, however, the plateau drops more slowly to sea level.

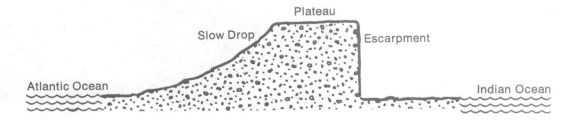

Rivers

The plateau is not completely flat. It is broken by mountains and rivers. In West

Bishop Abel T. Muzorewa, president of one of the two rival wings of the African National Council of Zimbabwe (Rhodesia). *Credit: United Press International*

Africa we find the Zaire (Congo) and Niger Rivers; in East Africa, the Zambezi River; in South Africa, the Limpopo River. The Nile River, with its two major branches, has its sources in Central Africa (Blue Nile—Lake Tana; White Nile—Lake Victoria). The history of Africa, in many ways, is the story of the rise, growth and fall of civilizations along the river systems. It is also the story of the attempts of outsiders to climb the plateau and control it.

Mountains

On the eastern coast there is a string of mountains that extend from South Africa northward to Ethiopia. In this range the main mountains are Mt. Kilimanjaro, Mt. Kenya and the Ruwenzori Mountains. These mountains are located almost on the equator, yet they are covered with snow and ice. Most Europeans live in the highland areas near the mountains because it is cooler.

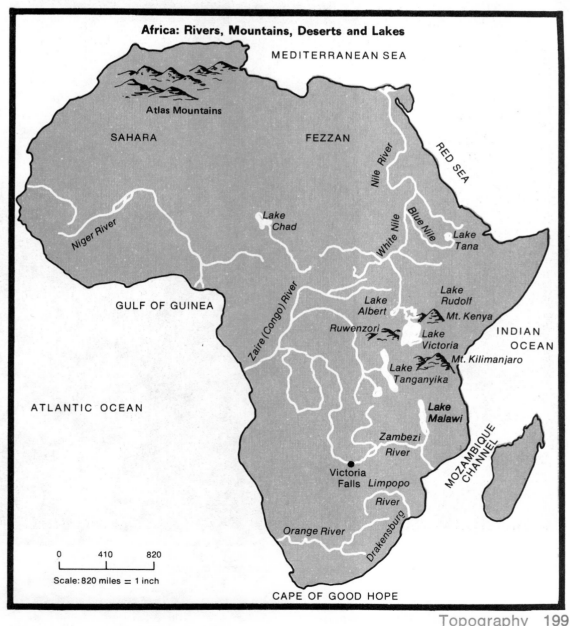

Africa: Rivers, Mountains, Deserts and Lakes

Animals such as this giraffe are found on the savannas of East Africa.
Credit: *Public Relations Dept., Tanzania*

The Rift Valley and the Lakes

Some huge lakes have been formed in the deep valleys of these African highlands. Along a line running from the Red Sea to South Africa, the plateau is split by a huge *rift* (canyon). Parts of this narrow but deep canyon have filled with water, and are today some of the world's largest and deepest lakes.

The widest section in this rift is the Red Sea, which separates Arabia from Africa. The rift then runs southward toward Lake Tana, in Ethiopia, and into the lake country of Central Africa. Lake Victoria, Lake Tanganyika and Lake Malawi are among the world's ten largest bodies of fresh water.

The Rain Forest

Many people imagine that Africa is a jungle or rain forest continent. Actually, there is less true tropical rain forest in Africa than in either Asia or South America. In addition, the African forest is not uninhabited. Many sections of the African "jungle" are thickly populated by farmers, who cut down the trees for farmland.

Savanna

The area around the tropical rain forests is open woodland or savanna. In some places, the savanna country is mainly grass with only a few large trees. In other places it looks more like a park, with high grass in place of the usual forest underbrush.

Deserts

Africa has three large desert regions—the Sahara in the north and the Kalahari and the Namib in southern Africa. Other sizable deserts are found in Somalia, Ethiopia and northeastern Kenya.

The Sahara Desert has often been thought of as a great wasteland and barrier. This idea is not completely true. People, although few in number, have lived in the desert throughout history. Caravans have crossed the desert for thousands of years. In the same way, the other African deserts have provided a place for man to live. The Somali people raise sheep and goats on the "Horn," as the northeastern desert is often called. For long periods of time men have hunted and gathered food in the Kalahari.

Within the African deserts there is a great variety of topography. We can find rocky, waterless wasteland and mountains and plateaus with some vegetation. Also, constantly shifting sand dunes can be found. During the day the desert is hot. At night temperatures can fall below freezing.

The Climate

Factors Affecting Climate

It is important to remember that the equator runs through the middle of Africa. *Latitude*, therefore, helps to explain much about the climate of Sub-Saharan Africa.

The area extends from about 20°N to 35°S latitude. Thus, we can always remember the climate of Africa south of the Sahara with the following statement: "Africa is warm, but some places are warmer than others."

Another factor that determines climate is *altitude*. The Kenya highlands, for example, lie on both sides of the equator. Yet temperatures are far lower than in the lowlands, and the air is less humid. Europeans preferred this cooler climate, since it was more like the climate in their homelands.

The cold *winds* in the highlands and the warm winds that blow from the northeast have an effect on the climate. These winds tend to *modify* (change) climate in unexpected ways. The cold winds on the equatorial plateau serve to further cool the land. The warm, dry winds from the Arabian Peninsula serve to make the lowlands in part of East Africa warmer and drier.

The cold *ocean current* (Benguela), flowing north toward the equator on the southwest side of Africa, cools and dries the climate of the coastal zones and for miles inland. In the east, warm ocean currents flow south from the equator and bring warm, humid air, which moves far inland.

Rainfall

A great problem faced by Africans is the lack of water. The amount of rainfall and where it falls vary greatly. About sixty percent of the continent does not receive enough rain to support a farming population. An important fact to remember is that the rainfall has a seasonal character. Almost everywhere, apart from the lowlands near the equator, there are wet and dry seasons, not the summer, autumn, winter and spring we have in America.

Climate Zones

Near the equator is a large *tropical rain forest*. The climate is always hot, rainy and unhealthy. (The rain forest is full of mosquitoes, which carry malaria and yellow fever.) North and south of the tropical rain forest are the grassland *savannas*. Here summer is the rainy season, and winters are dry and dusty. It is always hot. North and south of the savannas are the *steppe* and *deserts*. Here it is usually hot and dry. Altitude is the main cause of difference in temperature. The *steppe* (veld) gets between ten and twenty inches of rain. It rarely, if ever, rains on the desert, where it is hot during the day and cold at night.

In southwestern Africa, near Capetown, we find still another climate region. Since Capetown's latitude is 35°S, the climate is sunny and *temperate* (mild). The summers are almost rainless. Whatever rain there is falls during the winter months. This climate is very similar to the lands that border the Mediterranean Sea and Crimean Russia. This type of climate is called *Mediterranean*.

On the southeastern coast is an area of *humid-subtropical climate*. This area is also about 35 degrees from the equator. The climate is much like that of Florida. The summers are hot and the winters are mild. Rain falls throughout the year, with a slightly greater amount falling in the summer.

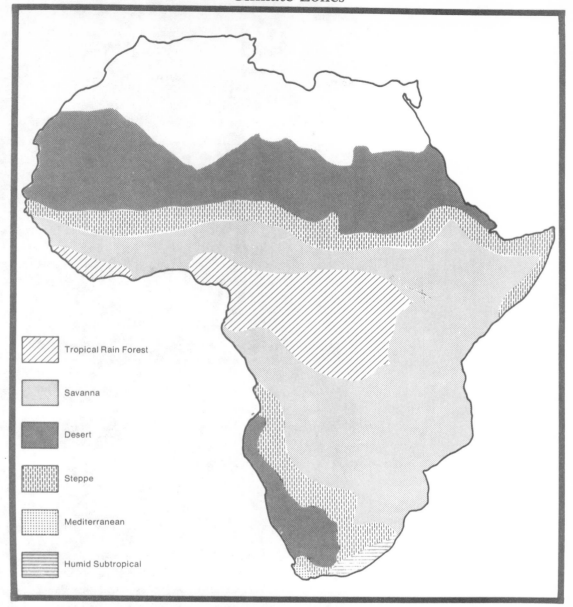

Tropical Rain Forest

Savanna

Desert

Steppe

Mediterranean

Humid Subtropical

The People and Their Languages

Africa is a continent of about 390 million people. (About 310 million people live in Sub-Saharan Africa.) Although people speak of "Black Africa," there are perhaps a greater number of different peoples living in Africa than on any other continent. The African people differ from each other physically as well as culturally. There is no such thing as a typical African or an African way of life. This is because over thousands of years Africans intermarried with people of different races and cultures. Also, because of geography, Africans were often separated from other Africans and therefore developed separately. The common factor is that nearly all the people of Sub-Saharan Africa are Negroid. This means that they contain in varying degrees physical characteristics associated with the Negroid race.

Tanzanian warriors with their brightly decorated shields. Decorating shields is a skilled art. (*Top*)
Credit: *Public Relations Department, Tanzania*

A young Xhosa girl of South Africa.
Credit: *Africa Report* (*Bottom*)

Above: Ivan the Terrible had St. Basil Cathedral built after a victory over the Tartans (courtesy DuMont Buchverlag). *Right-hand column, from top to bottom:* After a long hard winter it is a pleasant sight to see colorful flowers (courtesy DuMont Buchverlag); Children in the U.S.S.R. still learn traditional folk dances (courtesy DuMont Buchverlag); A visit to Red Square as a wedding celebration (courtesy DuMont Buchverlag); Rehearsal for the 1980 Olympics — University students take part in festive games (courtesy DuMont Buchverlag).

above: African scene (courtesy of N. Myers, Alpha); *left:* Primitive African[?] Nigeria ca. 1550 (courtesy of The Metropolitan Museum of Art, The Micha[?] C. Rockefeller Memorial Collection of Primitive Art). *Facing page, above le[ft]* Lid of canopic jar of Egyptian King Semenkh-Ka-Re, 18th Dynasty (courtes[y] of The Metropolitan Museum of Art, The Theodore M. Davis Collectio[n] Bequest of Theodore M. Davis, 1915); *above right:* Gold statuette of th[e] Egyptian god Amun from the Great Temple of Amun at Karnak (courtesy [of] The Metropolitan Museum of Art, the Carnarvon Collection; gift of Edward [S.] Harkness, 1926); *below:* Scene from the Valley of the Kings, Egypt (courte[sy] of D. Edwards, FPG).

above: Basilica of Gethsemane and Mt. of Olives, Jordan, Jerusalem (courtesy of D. Edwards/FPG); *left:* 18th Dynasty Egyptian musicians from the tomb of Zeser-Ka-Ra-Sonbe (courtesy of The Metropolitan Museum of Art).

op: Benaras Ghat Benaras (courtesy Tourist Office of Government of India); *bottom:* Floating market (courtesy of Tourist Organization of Thailand).

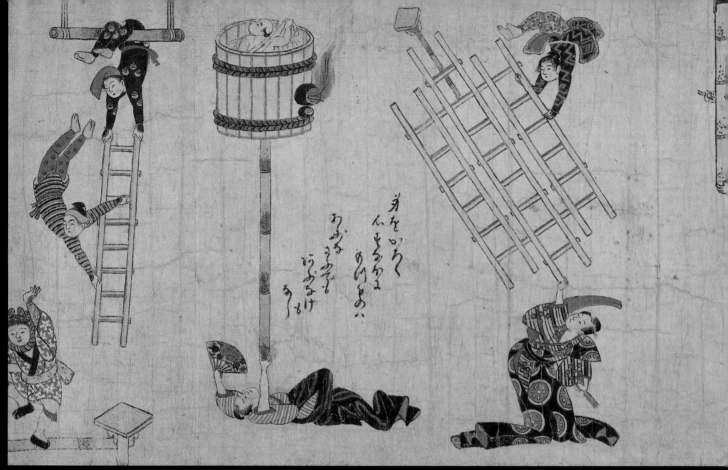

above: 19th cen. acrobats, Ukiyo-e school of Japanese art (courtesy of The Metropolitan Museum of Art, gift of Mrs. Henry A. Bernheim, 1945); *right:* Japanese suit of armor, ca. 1550 (courtesy of The Metropolitan Museum of Art, Rogers Fund, 1904); *far right:* Porcelain bottle, 18th cen. Japan (courtesy of The Metropolitan Museum of Art, gift of Charles Stewart Smith, 1893).

Differences Among Africans

Many people have the false idea that all Africans look alike. This is not so. There are short Africans like the Pygmies, who are a little over four feet in height. There are also tall Africans like the Watusis, who are between six and seven feet tall. Skin color among the African people ranges from almost black to dark brown, grey brown, tan, to the very light skin tone associated with the people of the Mediterranean area. Hair varies from dark and curly to hair that is light in color and straight. Most Africans have dark eyes, but there are people with blue eyes and blue-grey eyes as well. Along the east coast of Africa there are people who have the slanted eyes that are usually associated with Asia.

Africans also differ from each other culturally. There are differences in language, religion, customs, ways of earning a living, house types, dress, methods of farming and others.

There are also many other peoples who have made Africa their home. These peoples are:

1. **Europeans**

There are over 5 million people of European origin living in Sub-Saharan Africa. They live mainly in the Republic of South Africa, Rhodesia and Kenya.

2. **Arabs**

Hundreds of years ago people from Arabia settled along the coast of East Africa. In recent years many Arabs from Syria and Lebanon settled in West Africa. It is estimated that there are about one million Arabs in Africa south of the Sahara.

3. **Asians**

Hundreds of thousands of Indians and Pakistanis live in the cities of southern and eastern Africa. They are the shopkeepers, traders and factory workers of South and East Africa. Most have kept to their own customs and refused to become citizens of the new African nations in which they live. For this reason the African governments have been putting pressure on them to give up their foreign citizenship or leave the country. Many have chosen to leave.

Languages

There are many languages spoken in Africa. It is estimated that there are about 800 languages, however, the actual number may be even greater. These languages can be divided into four major language groups.

1. **Niger-Congo family**

The largest of the language groups and the one that covers the largest geographical area is the Niger-Congo family. This group is divided into seven subfamilies. One of these subfamilies is the well known Bantu. Bantu languages cover most of Central and South Africa. These languages are closely related to one another.

2. **Sudanic**

The languages spoken in the western Sudan and the area of the middle Niger River belong to the Sudanic family.

3. **Afro-Asian group**

This group includes ancient Egyptian, Cushitic, and the languages spoken in Somalia and around Lake Chad. The most important language in this group is Hausa.

4. **Click languages**

Are spoken by the Hottentots and Bushmen.

Development of educational facilities is one of Africa's most pressing needs. Here children are studying the Koran at an outdoor school in Lagos, Nigeria. (*Top*)
Credit: *UNESCO—United Nations*

Children grind millet from sunrise to sunset after harvest. Millet is a relatively good source of protein. (*Bottom*)
Credit: *UNICEF*

With so many different languages, it is difficult for Africans to communicate with each other. In Nigeria there are 250 languages. An African leaving his own village may not be able to speak to people living in the next village. Therefore, European languages are used by many Africans to communicate with each other. The two most important European languages which have become the official languages of many countries are English and French. Two African languages are used in the same way. Swahili is spoken by several million people living in East Africa. Hausa is spoken in northern Nigeria and in other parts of West Africa.

African Families

There is an African proverb which says,"A man or woman without kin is as good as dead." This indicates how important the family is to an African. Family life is important in all societies. The family satisfies the most basic human needs—the need for companionship, for food, for reproduction and for teaching and training the young. But Africans are far more closely tied to their families than are Americans or people in Western countries. In a number of ways African family life is different from that of American families.

Marriage and the Family

In America when a young couple marries,they move into a home of their own. In Africa the wife goes to live with her husband's family. In our country young people choose the husband or wife whom they wish to marry. In Africa the marriage is usually arranged by the parents. This means that the parents may actually pick the mate for their son or daughter to marry. More often, however, a young man meets a girl whom he likes. He then reports this fact to his father and must get his approval. His father and several other members of the family then arrange to visit the girl's parents to get their approval and to discuss the marriage. Part of the discussion involves the payment of what is known as "bride price" or "bridewealth." The young man has to make some kind of payment to the girl's father before he is allowed to marry her. This payment is usually in the form of cattle or sheep or another type of currency. This does not mean that the man is buying his wife. The bride price is a symbol that the union of the two people is legitimate. It is also a form of compensation for the father of the bride who is not only losing a daughter but a worker as well.

An African man may have several wives at the same time providing he is able to support them. This is known as polygyny. Actually, although polygyny is found throughout Africa, it has been estimated that not more than 10% of African men have more than one wife. There are several reasons for polygyny. By having more than one wife a man can be certain of having many children. In this way his name and spirit, as well as that of the whole family, will live on. Also the more wives a man has, the more workers he will have to help him in the fields. African women do not object to sharing their husband. While jealousy often does exist, in most cases the co-wives learn to get along and to work together quite well. The children of several wives live together as sisters and brothers. Often when a child cannot get what he wants from his own mother he will turn to one of his father's other wives.

The Extended Family

Most African families are known as extended families. An extended family consists of several generations living together in the same household or group of houses. This includes the oldest male, his wives, their unmarried daughters, the married sons and their wives and children.

The extended family provides for the social security of its members. There is no need for old age homes or orphanages in Africa because the family takes care of its orphans, widows and old people. In many cases when a man dies his widow marries her husband's brother. Loneliness is not a problem in Africa. In case of illness the family can be relied on for support. When crops fail, what little there is will be shared. When money is needed to pay for a child's education, relatives will often assist the parents. When relatives request help, it is considered an obligation to provide it. People do not undertake these duties out of the goodness of their hearts—they know that they will be able to demand help from their kin when they need it.

Family Life in the Cities

The family system described here is found in the traditional villages of Africa. In the cities, however, family life is similar to that found in large cities all over the world. Living in apartments makes it difficult for a man to have more than one wife. The city family (nuclear family) consists of the father, mother and children, rather than the extended family. Young people have greater opportunities to choose their own mates. But people who have moved to the cities still maintain close ties with those relatives remaining in the village.

African Tribalism

A tribe may be defined as a group of people who share the same customs and language, and who believe they have descended from a common ancestor. The people also have a special feeling of belonging together. Many anthropologists today prefer to use the term "nation" "ethnic group" or "people" in place of "tribe."

It has been estimated that there may be from 600 to 1000 different tribal groups in Africa. Some tribes are quite small and consist of only a few thousand members. Other tribes are very large and have as many as several million people. Some of the most important African tribes are the Ashanti, Fanti, Kikuyu, Ibo, Masai, Watusi, Zulu, Yoruba, and Hausa.

We in America, as well as people in Western countries, generally believe that the individual is most important. We believe that the individual has a right to do what he alone wants to do, providing that no one is hurt. In other cultures the individual is less important than the group. This has always been true of Russia and China, and it is true of Africa as well. According to the African view of life, a person can only achieve happiness by being part of a group. From birth to death the African is always part of a group. First there is the extended family living together in one household or group of houses. Then there is the clan, a group of related families. And finally there is the tribe, made up of many related clans.

The Individual and the Tribe

Beginning at a very young age a child learns to become a good member of his tribe. From his parents the child learns the laws and customs of the tribe. Tribal customs cover all the important aspects of life from birth to death. As a result a person knows what he is supposed to do on all occasions and how to do it. He is taught the penalties that result from not following the customs of the tribe. Each member is supposed to make a contribution to the tribe by doing his share of the work and obeying its customs.

At the same time the tribe provides its members with security. A person who belongs to a tribe feels that he is not alone. In bad times he can turn to the other members of the tribe and feel confident that they will help him. For this reason an African feels great pride in belonging to a tribe and believes that the customs of his own tribe are the best. This pride is shown by a *tribal mark*, which is usually a cut made on the face in a particular pattern. Although this custom is going out of style, many of today's African leaders still have the tribal marks from their childhood.

A person does not automatically become a member of a tribe. When a boy or girl reaches puberty, he or she has to go through a complicated ceremony known as *initiation* to be admitted into the tribe. As part of the ceremony, the boy must show that he has reached manhood by proving that he is brave and skilled. The girl must also prove that she has reached womanhood.

Each tribe has its own chief to whom the members of the tribe owe complete loyalty. Decisions for the tribe are made by the chief assisted by a Council of Elders. These people are selected from the different families of the tribe. The tribe provides the law and order needed by any organized group of people. There has been very little crime and almost no juvenile delinquency in African tribes. To kill or steal from another member of the tribe is considered shameful and is severely punished. The worst kind of punishment a person fears is to be thrown out of the tribe.

Tribalism in Modern Africa

To many Africans today, the tribe is more important than the nation in which he lives. The African will think of himself as a Yoruba or an Ibo rather than a Nigerian. This is because the nations that exist in Africa now did not exist before the coming of the Europeans. When the Europeans took over Africa and divided it up among themselves, they drew many boundaries separating their territories from each other. The present nations of Africa came into existence with those boundary lines. As a result many tribes were split up and found themselves in different countries. In other cases many different tribes were grouped together in the same nation.

There are many problems resulting from this situation. Where many tribes find themselves in the same country there is a problem in communication. In Nigeria 250 different languages are spoken. People in one village often do not understand people living in the next village. No tribe wants another tribe to dominate the government of the country. In elections people often support those candidates from their own tribe rather than voting for the person best suited for the job.

An example of how tribal feeling can affect events in an African nation is the selection of a name for the nation. Until November, 1971, the former Belgian Congo, which became independent in 1960 was known as the Democratic Republic of the Congo. The present government felt this name paid too much honor to the Bakongo tribe which lives along the lower part of the river. Most of the people of the country are not from the Bakongo. In November, 1971, the name of the country was changed to *Zaire* to please the non-Bakongo peoples. Zaire was the old name of the great river (Congo) before the Europeans came. Zaire is also the new name that was given to the Congo River.

Today the influence of the tribes and the tribal chiefs is slowly decreasing. As education is spread, more roads are built and more people move away from the tribal lands to the cities, loyalty to the tribe is gradually being replaced by loyalty to the nation.

Religious Beliefs

While many Africans today are Christians or Moslems, most people still believe in the traditional religions. They continue to cling to the old beliefs and rituals. Tribal religion is an inseparable part of tribal culture. Although religious practices vary from tribe to tribe, there are certain beliefs that almost all the African religions have in common.

Gods and Spirits

Nearly all the African religions believe in a Supreme Being or God who created the earth and all mankind. God then withdrew and left the affairs of the world to man. God is *remote* (far away) and not often prayed to. Only in case of major crises do people seek God's help. This is usually when the entire tribe (not the individual) is threatened by drought, epidemic, or some other catastrophe.

Between God and man are the lesser gods and ancestor spirits. These gods are believed to live in rivers, caves, mountains and trees. Africans do not worship rivers and mountains. They worship the spiritual forces that these things represent. These spirits are of great importance in man's daily life and are always close to him. Since Africans live close to nature, if the rains fail or the crops are flooded or eaten by pests, people may be threatened by starvation. Therefore, it is best to keep the gods on your side.

It is believed that the ancestral spirits watch over the fortunes of their descendants. These spirits can punish the living if they are forgotten and not honored. Therefore, on all important occasions—such as births, deaths, initiation ceremonies, weddings, planting and harvesting—prayers and offerings are made to the departed ancestors. Even on lesser occasions, for example, the building of a new house or the judging of a person accused of wrongdoing, the spirits of the ancestors are appealed to for guidance and are offered beer or some other offering. In their prayers, Africans ask for health for themselves and their families, for the welfare of the tribe as a whole, and for the fertility of their fields. Africans do not worship their ancestors; they communicate with them. We have learned how important the family is to African people. This includes both the living and the dead members of the family. Therefore, Africans consider it only right to involve the spirits of the dead ancestors in the affairs of the living.

The Medicine Man

When misfortune strikes, Africans turn to a *diviner,* or medicine man, to discover the cause of the misfortune. The diviner is believed to have special powers which enable him to find out the cause as well as the cure for whatever has happened. The African may know the scientific cause for the calamity, for instance, that malaria is caused by a mosquito bite. But this does not explain why that particular person was bitten. When tragedy occurs, people usually ask the question "why me?" The diviner tries to find out why a certain misfortune has befallen a particular person or group. Often the reason is the anger of an ancestor whose spirit has been neglected and is therefore punishing the descendent. Through the use of many techniques, such as throwing animal bones or palm nuts on the ground to form certain patterns, the diviner tries to find out which spirit has been offended and what must be done to satisfy it. Sometimes an offering of beer to the ancestral spirit is enough. In most cases, however, it is necessary to sacrifice an animal, such as a chicken, goat or sheep. The blood of the animal or its insides are then smeared on the person and then the animal is eaten. Sacrificing an animal which is the symbol of life to one's ancestors, is believed to be a means of communicating with them. Many Africans believe that in case of illness medical treatment alone is not enough. This may cure the symptoms but not the basic cause of the disease. Thus, although Africans may go to a clinic for treatment, at the same time they will follow the ritual that has been described. For this reason the diviner has great influence in most African tribes.

In many cases magic and religion go hand in hand, and sometimes it is not easy to separate the two. Magic may be used to protect the individual against illness or misfortune; to guarantee success in agriculture, hunting and even love; and sometimes even to bring harm to another person. This last type of magic can bring severe punishment to the person who practices it. In general, the purpose of magic is to give people confidence in difficult situations. Many people carry a charm with them to protect them from danger.

While many aspects of African religions may seem strange to us, it must be remembered that our religious practices may very well seem strange to them. If we are able to understand why people believe and do certain things, these beliefs will make much more sense to us.

African Arts

African Art Was Unknown in the West

The great qualities of African art and music were not appreciated, recognized or understood by people of the West until fairly recently. There are many reasons for this. African art and music were quite different from what Westerners were used to

Bangwa—female figure.
Credit: *Africa Report*

Ogoni mask.
Credit: *Africa Report*

seeing and hearing. Our knowledge of African culture was very limited. Westerners did not realize that the art works were part of the religious and cultural life of the Africans. The music seemed to be without rhythm, and the sculpture seemed almost childish. These art objects did not fit into the ideas of what Westerners considered "art."

Only in the last fifty years have artists begun to recognize that the African forms and creations are related to their own experiences and efforts.

It should also be kept in mind that our knowledge of African art, sculpture and music is still limited. We do not have many objects that date back to much earlier than the nineteenth century. Recently, discoveries have been made that give us information about earlier times. Although early artists used stone, bronze and terra cotta, the favorite material used was wood. Unfortunately, the moist climate and hungry insects have destroyed all but the most recent wood carvings.

Early African Art — The Bushmen

The first artists were among the earliest inhabitants of Africa. Bushmen artists left a record of striking rock paintings and engravings in limestone. These paintings tell us much about the Bushmen's nomadic life, which was based on hunting and food gathering. The drawings of buffaloes, rhinos and lions in reds, browns and ochers, are realistic and lifelike. This rock art was probably begun about eight thousand years ago.

Nok Culture

Some 2,500 years ago, where the Niger and Benue Rivers join in northern Nigeria, lived a highly skilled people. They made pottery, figurines and life-sized heads from *terra cotta* (baked clay). By means of trade, these art objects moved throughout West Africa. Archaeologists refer to the culture as the *Nok culture* because it was in the town of Nok in Nigeria in 1931 that some tin miners first found these terra cotta pieces.

Ife Art

Not far from Nok is the holy city of *Ife*. A number of sculptured heads were found here. They date from the thirteenth century. The heads of Ife were made of bronze. The method used to make them was called the "lost wax" process. This was a difficult and complicated method which only highly skilled artists could use. This method is still used today.

The "lost wax" method consists of modeling the piece in wax, covering it with clay, then baking it. After the wax has melted and run out, being "lost" through holes at the bottom of the clay, the holes are then stopped up and liquid bronze poured in.

The faces of the pieces seem almost alive. The lines found on many of the faces are smiliar to marks still found on the people of Nigeria. These skin patterns are called "scarifications." Such scars often showed the rank of the person and the tribe into which he was born.

Benin Art

The bronzes of the Benin also show the great skill of the West African. Their pieces are so beautifully made that art experts today often compare them to the finest works by Western artists. The Benin artists also made sculptures in ivory, a material reserved for the king. The ivory elephant tusks were carved and hollowed out to serve as cups for water, combs, serving spoons and ceremonial knives, as well as for pendants and small statues or figurines.

Characteristics of African Sculpture

Wood sculpture is a favorite activity of many African tribes. There are different styles. Each group, tribe or section has its own favorite form of expression. However, most African sculptures show certain common characteristics:

1. The sculptor tried to make the piece as beautiful as he could. This did not mean that the statue necessarily had to resemble the ancestor, god or spirit. Too great naturalism was not considered proper.

2. Much of the sculpture is abstract. The sculpture simplified the most important features of the figure, and then exaggerated these features for emphasis.

   (a) The increase of population (fertility) was the most important concept of life. The symbols of fertility used by the sculptor were the reproductive organs and the breasts, and he often exaggerated them to show their importance.

   (b) Artists also showed the navel as large and sticking out, as a symbol of continuity of life.

   (c) The head was made oversized. It was carved with great care, as it was the seat of intellect and the origin of power.

   (d) Artists preferred to show still poses, instead of poses showing movement.

   (e) Artists also preferred front views of figures, rather than profiles and side views.

3. Few portraits were carved or painted because Africans felt it was undesirable and lacked humility to make things too realistic. Some figures, like the wood statues of the kings from Benin and Ife, were carved. They were usually *idealized* (godlike).

4. The different tribes also carved statues to be used as *fetishes*. A fetish is an object thought to have magical powers. It can be protective or threatening.

5. Figures of animals were also carved or cast in bronze to express certain admirable qualities. For instance, speed was often characterized by the antelope, and strength was symbolized by the crocodile. The lizard signified life, the tortoise old age, the snake swift movement or death. Birds were often thought of as intermediaries between the earth and heaven.

Masks

Tribal masks are probably the most familiar kind of African art. Their use goes back to very early times. For example, some of the figures on the prehistoric rock paintings are wearing elaborate masks.

Masks were worn mainly in religious ceremonial dances related to the growing of crops, celebrations of births, deaths and important tribal and secret society ceremonies.

Masks were based on human or animal forms, or a mixture of both.

Many masks were thought to be *sacred* (holy), and were kept locked up when not in use. Women were not permitted to wear them and, in many cases, not even to see them. Some masks were deliberately terrifying so as to frighten women away from secret ceremonies. Colors were often used as symbols. To some tribes black meant "the earth," and stood for strength and vitality. White meant the supernatural.

Types of Masks

1. The most basic type is the face mask. Often a stick was placed across the back of the mask and the man wearing the mask held it in place by holding onto the stick with his teeth. A costume of some sort was usually attached around the edge of the mask, although few of the costumes remain today.

2. Ivory was used by some tribes in the making of miniature masks. These were often given to young boys to show their future rank in the tribe or society. They were prized and worn by each boy under his clothing until he finally passed the initiation rituals. Then he proudly wore them on his belt or arm, where they could be seen.

3. Another type of mask is the helmet, which may partially or completely cover the head.

4. The last type of mask sits on the top of the head. The face would normally be covered by a costume.

African Art and the West

At the beginning of the twentieth century, African carvings appeared in Paris, France, and influenced the work of a number of European artists. Pablo Picasso, for example, began to experiment in what is now called his "African phase," and produced *Woman in Yellow, Young Woman of Avignon* and *Head*, to name just a few. Amedeo Modigliani carved *Head of a Woman* and painted many canvases which show that he was influenced by African art.

The artistic work of the people of Africa is now recognized as being the artistic equal of anything produced by any other civilization of man.

Early History

Birthplace of Mankind

Most scientists now believe that Africa was the birthplace of mankind. In 1959 Dr. Leakey, an anthropologist, discovered the fossilized bones of a skull in northern Tanzania. This, he claimed, was the "oldest example of man on earth," born over 600,000 years ago. It is now thought that this creature lived as far back as 1,850,000 years ago. What this creature looked like, what color his skin was and how much hair he had is impossible to know. But Dr. Leakey called this creature a man because it was found together with chipped pebble tools. The ability to make tools is one of the things that distinguishes man from the apes. In February, 1971, bones were found in Kenya dating back about 5 million years. On the basis of all this evidence it is believed that mankind began in Africa and from there gradually wandered to other parts of the world.

Until about six or seven thousand years ago, the Sahara Desert was not the dry area that it is today. Cave paintings found in the Sahara are evidence that people and animals lived there. These people earned a living by hunting, gathering and fishing. Then dryness set in and the area became desert. The people who had lived there either moved north or south. The people who moved north intermingled with the peoples of the Mediterranean area. This accounts for the physical and cultural similarities between Europeans and Africans. Those who moved south intermarried with the people living between the desert and the rain forest. They became the ancestors of the African people. Gradually they spread out over the entire continent. The Bushmen who had inhabited most of South and Central Africa were pushed to the southwest by these Negroid people.

Beginnings of Agriculture

The first Africans hunted, gathered and fished for food. A great step forward in civilization was the introduction of agriculture. Once people started farming, they had to settle down and live in one place, villages grew, and governments were set up. Farming was probably first practiced in Egypt around 4000 B.C. or earlier. But the Egyptian crops of wheat and barley were not suited to the conditions of tropical Africa. A few hundred years before the birth of Christ, people from Indonesia settled on the island of Madagascar. They brought with them crops that grew in the tropical climates of Southeast Asia, such as yams, bananas, and plantains. These crops were quickly adopted by African farmers. The African people also learned to domesticate animals and the use of cattle spread to the interior. Farming and herding became the basis of African life.

Introduction of Iron

Another great advance came when the African people learned how to take iron from the ground and to turn it into tools and weapons. This happened about 2000 years ago along the Nile River. From there the use of iron spread to the west. With iron tools it was possible to hunt and farm better. Iron weapons made it easier for people to defend themselves. In this way it was possible to build strong communities and governments.

Early Trade

Trade was very important to the people of Africa. Trade between different tribes was common. In some places there were market days set aside and metal bars were used as money. Trade was carried on with Egypt. Africa supplied gold, precious stones, ivory, slaves, ostrich feathers, hides and animals to Rome. It is believed that the Romans introduced the camel, which has been called the "ship of the desert," to Africa. Trade brought wealth, new ideas and the growth of cities. Very important also was the trade between East Africa and Asia that was carried on across the Indian Ocean. We have already mentioned that Africans learned how to raise yams, bananas and other crops from the people of Southeast Asia. Trade existed with China. Chinese porcelain as well as ancient Chinese coins have been found along the east coast of

Africa. Chinese paintings from the 5th century show giraffes, and giraffes are not native to any area but Africa. African ivory, gold, slaves and iron ore were important items in the trade with India, China and other Asian countries. Wealthy trading cities grew up along Africa's east coast.

Early African Kingdoms

The names of several important early civilizations stand out. One was the Nok culture in northern Nigeria, dating from about 800 B.C. to 200 B.C. Excellent pottery, fine sculpture and metal tools have been found here. Another important civilization was at Kush, along the banks of the Nile to the south of Egypt. In the 8th century B.C. the Kushites became so powerful that they invaded Egypt and ruled that country for almost a hundred years. The capital of Kush, Meroë, became an important iron producing area. From here the use of iron probably spread to the rest of Africa. Remains of buildings as well as a system of writing have been found at Meroë. The kingdom of Axum in the country that is today known as Ethiopia was also very important. This kingdom became wealthy by trading with India, Egypt and perhaps even China. About the 4th century after Christ the rulers of Axum were converted to Christianity.

Kingdoms of West Africa

We have very few written records of African history. Most of what we know about Africa's past are stories handed down from generation to generation. For a long time many people thought that if a people had no written records they had no history. However, history exists wherever man exists. It is only now that we are beginning to discover Africa's rich past.

Although tribalism has been important from earliest times, Africa has a long history of organized political states. Much of West Africa was the setting for a series of great African empires. The three most powerful ones were the kingdoms of Ghana, Mali, and Songhai. Each of these grew rich because it was able to control the important cross-Sahara trade in salt from North Africa in exchange for gold from tropical Africa. This trade resulted in the exchange of ideas, the growth of cities and the accumulation of wealth. Arab visitors to the West African kingdoms were amazed at the order and prosperity in those lands. A 14th century Arab writer wrote that, "The Negroes are seldom unjust. . . . There is complete security in their country. Neither traveller nor inhabitant in it has any fear from robbers or men of violence."

These kingdoms had the following features in common: they were headed by kings who were looked on as *divine* (appointed by God); these rulers had great power; they appointed many officials to carry out their orders throughout the kingdoms; the king and government were supported by taxes collected throughout the kingdom; trade was usually controlled by the king; women of the royal family had much power; the strength of these kingdoms was based on the use of iron; most of the people were farmers; many earned a living by herding; there were many cities and huge armies.

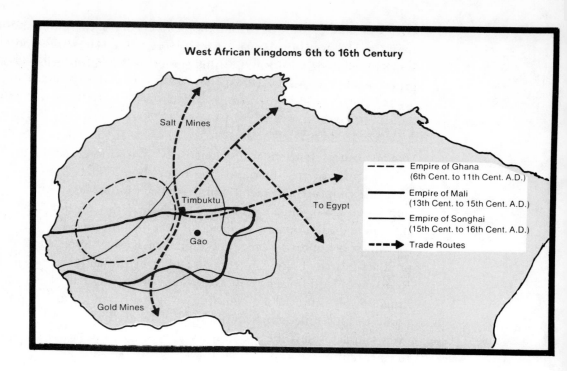

West African Kingdoms 6th to 16th Century

Salt Mines

Timbuktu

Gao

To Egypt

Gold Mines

- - - - Empire of Ghana
(6th Cent. to 11th Cent. A.D.)
—— Empire of Mali
(13th Cent. to 15th Cent. A.D.)
—— Empire of Songhai
(15th Cent. to 16th Cent. A.D.)
- - -► Trade Routes

Ghana

Possibly the earliest kingdom in West Africa was Ghana, founded in the 3rd or 4th century, A.D. Archeologists have uncovered examples of a fine civilization. Such iron products as nails, farming tools, knives, scissors, and lances have been dug up. The windows of the king's home were made of glass, a product that had not come into use in Europe at that time.

The kingdom's name comes from the title of its king, the Ghana, or ruler. The boundaries of present day Ghana do not in any way correspond to the old empire of Ghana, which stretched from the Atlantic Ocean to the Niger River.

Ghana reached the peak of its power in the 9th and 10th centuries. Ghana's ambassadors were welcomed in European courts. The power of Ghana was based on two things. The kingdom lay between the salt mines of the north and the gold mines of the south. The Africans needed the salt for their bodies, and gold was in great demand in Europe. By controlling this trade Ghana became very rich. The people of Ghana were able to expand their territory and conquer their neighbors because they had learned to make iron weapons while their enemies still used wood. Iron was good for tools as well. The use of iron tools helped Ghana to produce more food—another way in which they were stronger than their neighbors.

People living in Ghana were able to obtain many products. From North Africa came wheat, raisins and dried fruits; from Spain and Morocco came clothing; and from the countries south of Ghana came cattle, sheep and honey. African craftsmen produced fine leather. Ghana's goldsmiths, coppersmiths and ironsmiths contributed their handiwork in jewelry, utensils, tools and weapons.

The government took advantage of this trade and made it a major source of income. All traders had to pay a tax. The tax money was used to pay for the court, army and government. The king had a splendid palace decorated with fine sculptures and paintings. Law and order was maintained with the help of a large army.

In the 11th century Ghana was attacked by armies from Morocco. In the beginning the army of Ghana was able to fight back and defeat the invaders. But the attacks broke down the gold-salt trade. Agriculture was also damaged and never recovered. Thus Ghana's economy weakened. Many people moved on in search of a better home. At the end of the 11th century Ghana was conquered by the North Africans. Although it became independent again later, it continued to decline. By the end of the 13th century, Ghana no longer existed as a country.

Mali

The empire of Mali was even larger than Ghana. In the 13th century a prince and warrior named Sundiata destroyed what was left of Ghana and united his own people under his rule in the empire of Mali. Sundiata encouraged people to become farmers and before long Mali became one of the richest farming regions in West Africa.

The most famous ruler of Mali was Mansa Musa who came to the throne in 1312. During the 25 years of his rule Mali's prestige increased greatly. Musa was an excellent "public relations man" and made sure that the splendor of Mali became known far and wide. A 14th century Arab wrote that of all the Moslem rulers of West Africa, Mansa Musa was "the most powerful, the richest, the most fortunate, the most feared by his enemies, and the most able to do good to those around him."

There are many reasons why Musa earned this description. The strength of Mali was based on the income which the government obtained by placing a tax on trade. Musa encouraged this trade by opening up new routes and exchanging a wider variety of goods. He saw to it that travel over the caravan routes was safe. The greatest income came from the gold-salt trade. But Mali also profited from the trade in copper.

Mali was also prosperous because the people raised sufficient quantities of food. The chief food crops were sorghum, rice, yams, beans, and onions. Poultry, cattle, sheep and goats were raised for their meat, eggs, milk and skins.

Mali's government was efficient and maintained law and order throughout the kingdom. Legal cases were examined by Mansa Musa himself. Mali also had a large standing army.

The most outstanding event of Mansa Musa's reign was his famous pilgrimage to Mecca. What stands out is the style in which he travelled. There were 12,000 slaves dressed in silks and brocades. Five hundred of these preceded Mansa Musa. Each carried a staff of gold weighing six pounds. Behind him were 80 camels, each carrying 300 pounds of gold dust. In Cairo and the holy city of Mecca, Mansa Musa distributed gifts of gold. This made a tremendous impression on the people of Africa, Asia and Europe.

When Mansa Musa came back from his journey he brought with him a famous Arab architect who designed a great mosque at Gao and a mosque and palace for Mansa Musa at Timbuctu. Moslem scholars and traders began to come to Timbuctu, and in later years this town became an important center of learning.

After Mansa Musa died in 1332, the empire began to decline. Invaders from the south burned down Timbuctu. The Songhai city of Gao was not happy about being ruled by Mali, and soon after its people refused to pay taxes and rebelled. At the same time people from the Sahara attacked the northern towns of Mali. Another important reason for Mali's decline was that the farmers of the countryside lived a very different life from the city people. Jealousy and suspicion divided these two groups and created instability. In time of crisis the empire fell apart.

Songhai

The empire of Songhai centered around the commercial city of Gao near the Niger River. Songhai's beginnings seem to go back to the 7th century, but its expansion into a great empire came during the 15th century. This was because of its great leader Sunni Ali. Ali was a powerful warrior who drove out all the foreign invaders and created a unified country under his rule. He also set up an efficient government with many officials to rule his vast empire.

The most important king of Songhai was Askia Mohammed. Askia's pilgrimage to Mecca rivalled that of Mansa Musa in magnificence. Askia fought many battles and conquered much territory. He was determined to make the whole empire one big Moslem community. Moslem judges were appointed to all the districts of the empire, and justice was administered according to Moslem principles.

During Askia's reign, the city of Timbuctu became famous as a center of learning in Africa. Medical operations were performed here that were not attempted in Europe until 200 years later. A historian who wrote at the time said, "At Timbuctu sit numerous doctors, judges and clerks, all are appointed by and receive good salaries from the king. More profit is made from the book trade than from any other line of business." The large cities, fine buildings and well-administered government were proof of the advanced civilization of Songhai.

Askia was overthrown by his own sons. Following this event, there was a struggle between many people who tried to take over the throne. Trouble lasted for several years and greatly weakened Songhai. At the end of the 16th century an army from Morocco was able to invade Songhai and capture its important cities. Normal trade was disrupted and a great empire came to an end.

East Africa—Cities of the Coast

In the 14th century a Moslem travelling down the long coast of East Africa passed through many important trading cities and some small towns. He described the peace and prosperity which he saw along the way. The famous city of Kilwa impressed him the most. He wrote "Kilwa is one of the most beautiful and well-constructed towns in the world." In Kilwa could be found many palaces, mosques and large houses.

More than 2,000 years ago small trading villages grew up along the east coast of Africa. The Arabs called this area Zanj. The settlements were market places for the goods traded between East Africa and other countries along the Indian Ocean, especially Arabia. About 1,200 years ago many people from Arabia moved to the islands along the east coast of Africa. They brought the Moslem religion with them and inter-married with the Africans. Between the years 1000 and 1500 the Arabs had the greatest influence on the settlements of East Africa. The Arabs controlled most of the East African trade, which increased. Things made in China began to reach Kilwa, and East African ivory was sent to China. Trading was also carried on with India, the countries of the Persian Gulf and Arabia.

Then the African people of the interior began to offer gold for the things they needed from other countries, the most important of which was cotton for clothing. The cities of the coast took the gold and sold it to other countries. Gold from Mozambique and Rhodesia had begun to leave the seaports of East Africa in the 10th century. A few hundred years later the traders of Kilwa had charge of this gold trade. They became very rich and made all traders from other countries pay heavy taxes. Kilwa grew and became a large and powerful city.

There were many other big trading cities. Some could even be called city-states because they controlled large areas. Some of these were Sofala, Pemba, Mogadishu, and Mozambique.

These cities began to decline in the 16th century. Portuguese sea captains attacked and robbed city after city. The Indian Ocean trade was taken over by the Portuguese, depriving East Africa of its greatest source of wealth. The cities on the southeastern coast of Africa, especially Kilwa, never really recovered from these attacks.

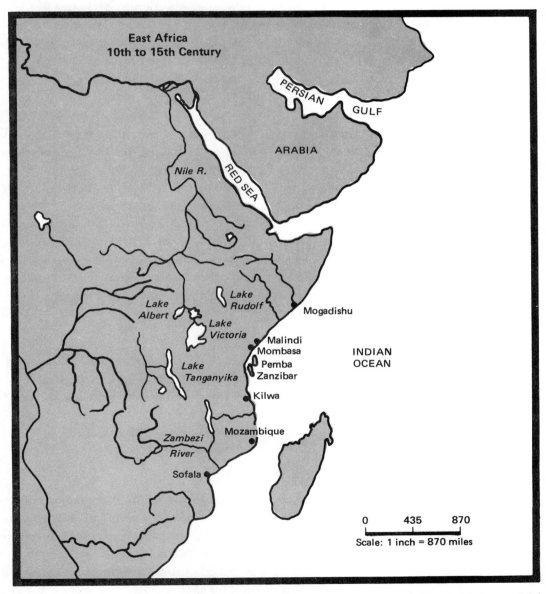

East Africa – Kingdoms of the Interior

In the country that is now known as Rhodesia great stone ruins have been found. The largest of these, Great Zimbabwe, had walls that were 30 feet high and 20 feet thick. These walls were built without any kind of cement. It is believed that the stone ruins may have been forts, burial places, a temple and royal palaces. About five hundred years ago an advanced civilization existed here. Historians think that this civilization was based on mining, trade and stone building. From objects that have been excavated here it seems certain that Zimbabwe was an important center of trade.

Sometime between the years 1000 and 1200 A.D., new groups of people came to Rhodesia. They were Bantus who had come from the north looking for new lands on which to live. The people who were already living in the area knew how to mine for gold and other metals and also exported these metals. The new arrivals, however, changed the way these people lived. They set up a system of government in which all power and wealth were held by a few people at the top and the rest of the people, who were poorer and weaker, had to obey them.

Monomotapa Empire

After a few hundred years, some of the ruling men of the southern part of Rhodesia set out to conquer other people and lands. The conquerors were known as Rozwi. In 1440 the Rozwi king Mutota began a war of conquest and within ten years he had gained control of most of the gold mines between the Zambezi and Limpopo Rivers and of the trade routes to the East African coast. This king and his son Matope, who followed him built the empire known as Monomotapa. This name comes from the title given to Matope by one of the conquered people—Mwene Mtapa, which means "lord of the conquered lands." They brought all of southern Rhodesia and Mozambique under their rule. In the empire of Monomotapa the chief sources of income came from farming, cattle-raising, and gold, copper, iron and ivory.

Changamire Empire

About 1485 war broke out between the king of Monomotapa and one of his biggest chiefs, Changa. The king lost, and the leaders who came after Changa set up an empire of their own with their capital at Great Zimbabwe. This empire was known as Changamire and it prospered for about three hundred years. The strong stone walls of Zimbabwe were constructed by the Changamire.

The Effect of Outside Forces

Thus there were two empires in the interior of East Africa—that of Monomotapa in the northern part of Rhodesia, and that of the Changamire in the southern part and in Mozambique. The Monomotapa suffered much at the hands of the Portuguese. The Portuguese came up the Zambesi River in small bands. Armed with guns called muskets, the Portuguese gained control by siding with some of the Monomotapa rulers against the others. In 1628 fighting broke out between the Monomotapa and the

Portuguese. The Portuguese won, and after that, the Monomotapas were practically puppets of the Portuguese and their empire disappeared.

The empire of the Changamires with the capital at Great Zimbabwe was never really threatened by the Portuguese. They continued to live in peace and to progress. The people earned a living by raising animals, mining for metals and trading with the cities of the coast. Peace lasted until 1830 when Ngoni Bantus from South Africa entered the cities and stone palaces, robbed and ruined them, and took some of the land for themselves. Less than one hundred years later Europeans took over the whole country.

Arabs, Islam and Africa

In the 7th century A.D. a new religion was born in the Arabian Peninsula, the religion known as Islam. In the centuries that followed, Arab traders and conquerors spread their religion to millions of people in different parts of the world. Africa was no exception and today Islam is one of the most important cultural influences in Africa.

Islam Spread to Africa in Various Ways

1. Conquest

In the 8th century the Arabs conquered North Africa and converted most of the people to Islam.

2. Trade

During the 7th century many Arabs settled in the port cities of eastern Africa and on the islands off the east African coast. From here they controlled the trade between Africa and the Far East. Iron ore, ivory, slaves and gold from Africa were exchanged for cotton cloth from India and porcelain from China. This trade brought great prosperity to the cities along the east African coast. Arab control of this trade lasted until the Portuguese took over 800 years later.

In West Africa Islam was spread by the Arabs who controlled the trans-Sahara trade. They brought salt from the Mediterranean and exchanged it for the gold of Sub-Saharan Africa.

3. Intermarriage

The Arabs who settled along the east coast married African women and spread their culture. As a result, the east coast of Africa is mainly Islamic.

4. Political control

When the ruler of an African kingdom converted to Islam the entire country officially became Moslem. This was true of Mali, Songhai and the Hausa kingdoms.

There were many reasons why the Africans were able to adopt Islam as their religion. Islam makes no distinction between people on the basis of color. All Moslems are considered brothers, whether black or white. Islam did not interfere with many African customs. It was possible for Africans to be Moslems and still continue to worship the forces of nature. Islam permitted the marrying of four women at the same time, and Africans had often followed the custom of marrying more than one woman. Other Islamic ideas such as divine kingship, the absolute power of the ruler and the importance of the family and the community corresponded to African ideas and customs. African rulers found that by converting to Islam they could maintain good trade relations with the Arabs, whose trade was so important to Africa.

The Arab Role in Africa

In the 15th and 16th centuries cities in West Africa such as Gao and Timbuctu became important centers of learning for Moslems. Scholars came from foreign lands to study in these places.

The Africans who converted to the Moslem religion took over other aspects of Islamic culture as well. They learned how to write Arabic and this provided them with a means of keeping records and developing a literature. It also led to the growth of a class of educated men who could help run a stable government. Eventually a new language arose, Swahili, which was a mixture of Arabic and Bantu languages. Swahili today is one of the most important languages in Africa.

The Arabs were also important because of the descriptions that they published about African life. Much of our knowledge about Africa before the arrival of the Europeans comes from Arab geographers and travellers such as Leo Africanus.

In one way, however, the Arab role in Africa was destructive. The Arabs are generally considered to have been the originators of the African slave trade. Arab traders reached into Central Africa, carrying away masses of slaves, which were then sold to India, China and other places in the East. When the Europeans came to Africa they continued and enlarged a practice that had been begun by the Arabs.

Today there are between 50 and 60 million Moslems in Africa and it is believed that in the future even more Africans will convert to Islam. The Islamic religion as well as the Arabic language, provides a link between Sub-Saharan Africa and the Mediterranean area.

The Arrival of the Europeans

Africa south of the Sahara was almost completely unknown to the people of Europe until the late 1400s. In the 15th century Europeans wanted to find an all water route to the East Indies and Asia for the purpose of obtaining silks, spices, and precious stones. They realized that by sailing around Africa they could reach the Indies. In addition, the Europeans believed that somewhere in Africa there was a Christian kingdom of Prester John. They were anxious to find this kingdom and also to obtain the gold and ivory for which Africa was famous.

Portugal Becomes Interested in Africa

The Portuguese were the first to set out. They sailed along the west coast of Africa each time going farther and farther south. They traded with the African tribes along the coast and returned to Europe with shiploads of gold and ivory. In 1487 Bartholomew Diaz reached the Cape of Good Hope at the southern tip of Africa. Finally in 1498 Vasco da Gama rounded the tip of the continent, turned north, sailed up the east coast and on to India.

Portugal's main interest in Africa at this time was trade. For this purpose the Portuguese established trading posts along the eastern and western coasts of Africa.

At this time the relationship between Africans and Europeans was one of mutual respect. In 1487 the Portuguese landed at the mouth of the Zaire (Congo) River

A young Masai warrior. Today this proud and fierce tribe of western Kenya is being forced through drought and politics to come to terms with 20th-century life. *Credit: United Press International*

President Carter laughs with Nigerian ruler Lt. Gen. Olusegun Obasanjo. The African ruler dislays his native robe. *Credit: United Press International*

bringing rich presents for King Nzinga, the Congo ruler. King Nzinga was so impressed that he asked King John of Portugal to send him missionaries and builders to instruct the people of the Congo in the new European techniques. King John responded by sending three ships of priests, skilled workers, tools and religious objects. King Nzinga, the royal family and most of the nobility became Christians. Between 1506 and 1512 the Congo ruler Affonso I (son of Nzinga) tried to convert his whole nation to European ways. The Portuguese were asked to send more teachers, priests and technicians and young Congolese were sent to Portugal for an education. But efforts to convert the Congo people to European ways failed mainly because of Portuguese greed and their involvement in the slave trade.

Portugal Gains Control of the East African Trade

Following Vasco da Gama's voyage Portugal controlled the trade between East Africa and Asia. Portuguese ships carried slaves and ivory from Africa to India where they were exchanged for spices, cloth and glassware. The ships then sailed back to East Africa for repairs and for gold and then returned to Portugal. When some of the African cities along the coast, such as Kilwa and Mombasa, tried to resist Portuguese control, they were defeated and burned. Portugal's control of this trade greatly affected the kingdoms of East Africa. The wealth which trade had formerly brought to Africa's east coast now went to Portugal. As a result the civilizations along the east coast of Africa gradually declined.

By the middle of the 16th century other European nations became interested in the profitable African trade and began to challenge Portugal. The English, French, Dutch and others came to the West African coast for gold and ivory. In the 17th century Portugal's control over the East African trade declined as other Europeans and Arabs began to take over this trade. At the same time the trade in gold and ivory was becoming less important to the Europeans and being replaced by another type of "gold."

The Slave Trade

Slavery Before the Arrival of the Europeans

From the beginning of history slavery in one form or another existed in many parts of the world. Slavery had existed in Africa hundreds of years before the arrival of the Europeans. Enemies captured in battle, criminals and debtors were often forced into slavery. But this type of slavery existed only on a small scale and was not necessarily hereditary. It was also different from the type of slavery which developed later because Africans did not regard slavery as the total ownership of another human being. The slave trade had existed long before the arrival of the Europeans as well. Long before the Africans were carried to the New World, they were being captured by Arabs and sold in the markets of the East—in India, Indonesia, Egypt, Turkey and Persia.

In 1441 a Portuguese ship returned to Lisbon, bringing back among other things 12 men, women and children from Africa. These were the first African slaves to be sold in Europe. But there was not much need for slaves in Europe and so the slave trade was not very important to the Europeans in the beginning.

The Need for Slaves in the New World

It was not until the European planters in the West Indies discovered that they could make fortunes by growing sugar with the labor of African slaves that the trade in human beings assumed massive proportions. By the mid 1500s the slave trade had grown tremendously. As the European demand for sugar and tobacco grew, the need for slaves in the New World grew as well. The profits of the slave trade for the Europeans were enormous. These profits and the labor of millions of African slaves in part made possible the industrialization of Europe and the development of America.

How the Slave Trade Operated

Slave trading posts were set up on the west coast of Africa by the Europeans. The Europeans did not go into the interior to get the slaves. The slaves were captured by Arab slave traders and by stronger African tribes who raided the villages of other tribes. Africans living in the coastal villages were given guns by the Portuguese and were encouraged to attack the tribes living in the interior. The slaves were then brought to the coast.

After buying the slaves the Europeans kept them in stockades—sometimes for weeks —until the slave ships arrived. On the ship the slaves were packed in so tightly that there was barely room to lie down. The more slaves jammed into a ship the larger the profit. Many died of beatings, disease, and lack of food and water.

Results of the Slave Trade

1. The slave trade had tremendous affects on Africa. The population of the area was greatly reduced. About 15 million of the healthiest and most intelligent young men and women of Africa were removed from the continent. Thus Africa was deprived of future leaders at a time when they were most needed.

2. A second result was the increase in tribal warfare. Crops were burned and entire villages destroyed during the slave raids. Millions of Africans died in these wars and on the way to the coast during the three centuries of the slave trade. Insecurity and fear were created. The slave trade broke down respect for tribal laws and customs.

3. Another result of the slave trade was that the trans-Sahara trade was destroyed. The Sub-Saharan peoples stopped raising crops and producing goods which they had formerly traded. Contact with the people of North Africa ended. As a result, the Sub-Saharan kingdoms, whose wealth and power had been based on this trade, declined.

4. The coastal states became rich and strong from the profits of the slave trade. European products such as iron, guns, gunpowder, rum and brandy, cloth, brass, and other goods came to be regarded by the coastal people as necessities. These products could only be purchased in exchange for slaves. So the people of the coastal states undertook to enslave their neighbors. Some states, such as Ashanti and Dahomey, became powerful and wealthy. When the slave trade was finally ended, these kingdoms lost their most important source of wealth, and economic problems grew.

5. We can conclude that the slave trade was a major factor in holding back the progress of Africa for centuries.

Between the 16th and the 19th centuries Europe's main interest in Africa was obtaining slaves. There was very little communication between Europeans and Africans, and no exchange of culture and knowledge. No missionaries or teachers visited Africa during this time. The Europeans rarely went inland. Thus during 300 years of contact with the Europeans, the Africans had no opportunity to learn European techniques so that they could modernize their way of life.

The Slave Trade Comes to an End

A strong anti-slave movement sprang up in Great Britain and other countries by the end of the 18th century. In 1772 the British abolished slavery in England, and in 1807 it became illegal for British subjects to take part in the slave trade. British pressure forced Spain and Portugal to officially end their participation in the slave trade in the early 1800s. The United States abolished the slave trade in 1808. For more than 50 years the British navy hunted down slave ships in the Atlantic Ocean. But as long as there was a demand for slaves on American plantations, slave boats tried to get past the British patrols. Only after the defeat of the South in the American Civil War in 1865 and the abolition of slavery in Cuba and Brazil in the 1880s, did the slave trade finally come to an end in the West. However, even today the United Nations estimates that some 30,000 blacks are still kidnapped each year to be sold as slaves in the Middle East, mainly in the villages of Saudi Arabia.

Africa Is Opened to the Western World: Explorers and Missionaries

European Explorers

Until the 19th century the only contact Europeans had with Africa was limited to the coastal areas. This situation changed during the 19th century. The anti-slavery movement had made Europeans curious about the land and people of Africa. European explorers came to Africa and explored the interior of the continent. Missionaries followed and soon businessmen came. By 1880 most of the interior of Africa was known to the Europeans.

1. **James Bruce**   was the first major European explorer of Africa. In 1770 he sailed up the Nile River and discovered Lake Tana in Ethiopia, the source of the Blue Nile.

2. **Mungo Park**   was the first European to explore the Niger River in 1796.

3. **René Callié**   a Frenchmen, was the first European explorer to enter Timbuctu and return alive. This took place in 1828. The account of his expedition stimulated great interest in the exploration of Africa.

4. **Johann Rebmann**   a German missionary, saw Mount Kilimanjaro in 1848. This is the great snow-covered mountain located on the equator. Rebmann kept a careful record of his journey through East Africa.

| 5. David Livingstone | was the one who did more than anyone else in opening up Africa to the Europeans. Livingstone first came to Africa as a doctor and missionary in 1840. Until his death in 1873, Livingstone attempted to do the following: |

a) explore and map the area
b) expose the evils of the slave trade
c) cure the sick
d) translate the Bible into several African languages

In 1849 Livingstone reached Lake Ngami in what is now Botswana in Southern Africa. He surveyed the area and put his observations into writing. This account aroused great interest in Europe. Following this, Livingstone explored the Zambezi River. In his search for the source of the river, Livingstone travelled across Africa to the west coast and then turned east again. In 1855 Livingstone saw the world's greatest waterfall, which he named Victoria Falls, in honor of Britain's queen. By 1868 Livingstone had stopped corresponding with the outside world. In 1869 a New York newspaper sent one of its reporters, Henry Stanley, to find the missing Livingstone. Stanley found Livingstone two years later near Lake Tanganyika. Together they explored the northern shore of Lake Tanganyika and other parts of East Africa.

| 6. Richard Burton and John Speke | were two Englishmen who were determined to find the source of the Nile River. They were the first Europeans to visit Somaliland. In 1858 they reached Lake Tanganyika, never before visited by Europeans. Some time later Speke discovered Lake Victoria, which he claimed was the source of the Nile. |

| 7. Sir Samuel Baker | discovered a great body of water in 1864, which he named Lake Albert. This is the source of the White Nile. The river which comes out of Lake Victoria is known as the Victoria Nile. It flows into Lake Albert and when it comes out it is known as the White Nile. |

| 8. Henry Stanley | remained in Africa after Livingstone's death and continued exploring on his own. Stanley was the first European to explore the Zaire (Congo) River. |

Accomplishments of the Explorers

In this way the four great African rivers were explored. The explorers wrote books and drew maps, making it easier for others to follow. But new land and rivers were not all that the explorers of Africa found. Mungo Park found a highly developed civilization in the Sudan. Speke found African kingdoms on the banks of Lake Victoria. The explorers are important not only for their discoveries but also for the picture of the African peoples and their cultures that they provided Europe with. By reporting these things to the people in Europe the explorers aroused interest in Africa and paved the way for the coming of more Europeans to the continent.

The Missionaries

The missionaries followed the explorers into the interior of Africa. The missionaries came to Africa to spread the Christian religion and to wipe out the slave raids which were still being carried on. The missionaries built schools, hospitals and churches. They also worked out systems of writing for many of the African languages.

While the missionaries did a great deal to help the African people they also hurt them in other ways. Many of the reports sent back to Europe by the missionaries were filled with bias and errors. In order to justify their own attempts to spread the Christian religion, the missionaries looked down upon many African customs as "savage" and "primitive." Many of the myths about Africa originated with the missionaries.

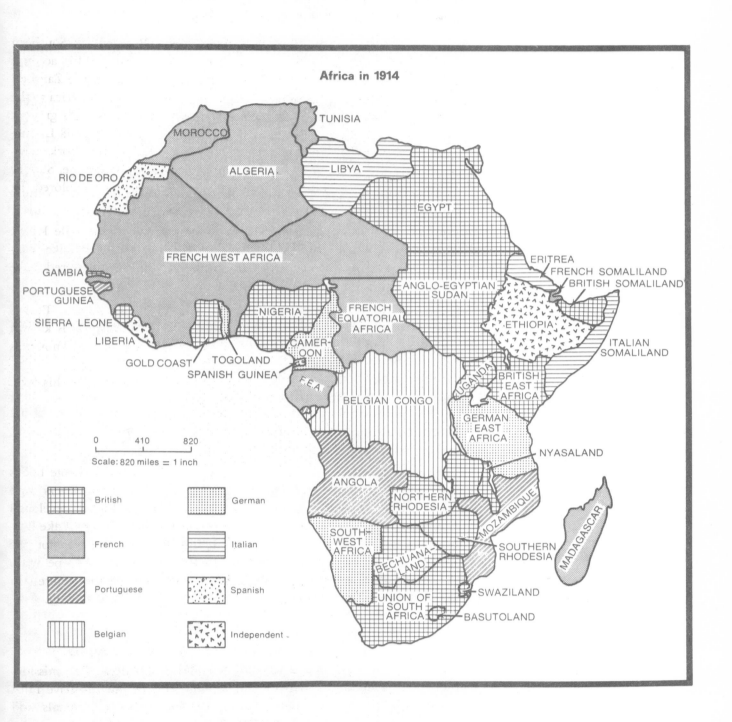

Africa in 1914

TUNISIA
MOROCCO
RIO DE ORO
ALGERIA
LIBYA
EGYPT
FRENCH WEST AFRICA
GAMBIA
PORTUGUESE GUINEA
SIERRA LEONE
LIBERIA
NIGERIA
ERITREA
FRENCH SOMALILAND
BRITISH SOMALILAND
ANGLO-EGYPTIAN SUDAN
FRENCH EQUATORIAL AFRICA
ETHIOPIA
ITALIAN SOMALILAND
CAMEROON
GOLD COAST
TOGOLAND
SPANISH GUINEA
F.E.A.
UGANDA
BRITISH EAST AFRICA
BELGIAN CONGO
GERMAN EAST AFRICA
NYASALAND
ANGOLA
NORTHERN RHODESIA
MOZAMBIQUE
MADAGASCAR
SOUTH-WEST AFRICA
BECHUANA-LAND
SOUTHERN RHODESIA
SWAZILAND
UNION OF SOUTH AFRICA
BASUTOLAND

0   410   820
Scale: 820 miles = 1 inch

British
French
Portuguese
Belgian
German
Italian
Spanish
Independent

European Imperialism in Africa

By 1875 European possessions in Africa consisted of some forts and trading posts along the coast and a few tiny colonies. Between 1880 and 1910, however, Africa was divided up among the Europeans. For the next 50 years decisions affecting Africa and its people were made not in Africa, but in London, Paris, Lisbon and other European capitals.

France acquired a huge empire in North and West Africa. Algeria, Tunisia, Morocco, Ivory Coast, Dahomey, Mali and other areas in West Africa came under French rule. Britain's colonies were scattered throughout the continent. Although the French controlled the most territory, Britain ruled the greatest number of people. Gambia, Sierra Leone, Gold Coast, Nigeria, South Africa, Rhodesia, Uganda, Kenya, Egypt, the Sudan and others were taken over by Britain. Belgium acquired the Congo, an area 35 times as large as Belgium. Portugal annexed the interior areas of Angola and Mozambique. Italy took over Eritrea, a large part of Somaliland and Libya. Southwest Africa, Tanganyika, Togoland and Cameroon were ruled by Germany until Germany's defeat in World War I. By 1914 there were two independent countries left in Africa—Liberia and Ethiopia. And even Ethiopia was taken over by Italy in 1935. (Italy controlled Ethiopia until 1942 when the British drove the Italians out.)

Reasons For Imperialism

There are several reasons why the European nations competed with each other to gain colonies in Africa. They all wanted to gain power and prestige. The more territory that they were able to control in Africa the more powerful and important they thought they could become. Africa was tremendously rich in natural resources, which could be brought to Europe and turned into manufactured goods. Europeans also needed markets for their manufactured goods. These goods could be sold in Africa for large profits. Often a European nation would take over territory in Africa simply to prevent another European country from taking it.

How Imperialism Spread

European rule came to Africa in many different ways. Sometimes a European trading company made agreements with African chiefs permitting the company to trade and keep order in the area. The traders then put pressure on their government in Europe to take over in order to protect them. In a few cases tribal chiefs voluntarily asked for the protection of one European nation in order to avoid being taken over by another European nation. Sometimes the Africans even asked for European protection against other African tribes.

Treaties were signed by the African chiefs in which they gave the European company or government the right to keep order (govern) and to take over the land and resources in their area. Thousands of treaties were signed by African rulers giving away most of their rights to the Europeans, but the Africans never really understood these treaties and did not realize what they were giving away.

How Imperialism Changed Africa

European rule brought about great changes in Africa.

1. When the Europeans divided up Africa, they made deals with each other over who was to get what. Boundary lines were drawn that had nothing to do with the needs of the African people. Many tribes were divided and found themselves under the rule of two or three different foreign nations. Other tribes who had nothing in common with each other were grouped together in the same territory. Some of the problems that the new African nations are having today are the result of this situation.

2. The Europeans did not want to spend large sums of money governing their African colonies. Therefore, the Africans were forced to pay taxes for the cost of ruling the colony.

3. The Europeans were interested in exploiting Africa's natural resources. Using various methods, the Europeans forced the Africans to work for them in the mines and on the plantations and farms that the Europeans now owned. In the Belgian Congo the system was the cruelest of all. Forced labor was introduced and those Africans who did not produce the required amount of rubber were brutally beaten. Rubber from the Congo came to be called "red rubber," because of the thousands of Africans who died tapping it and bringing it to the coast.

4. In places, such as, Rhodesia and Kenya, where large numbers of Europeans settled, the best farming land was reserved for the Europeans.

5. European conquest did not bring about the immediate destruction of traditional African governments. The Europeans did not have enough manpower to rule the Africans directly. Also, they wanted to avoid the costs of setting up new governments, so in many cases they allowed the tribal chiefs to keep some of their power. The British, especially, did this. However, the Europeans were the real masters and told the Africans what they could do and what they could not do. This is known as "indirect rule." The French, on the other hand, removed local rulers and governed through the Africans they appointed or through French officials.

6. Nevertheless, Africa's traditional political system was completely changed. The chiefs lost the power and respect which they formerly had. Once the Africans realized that the chiefs no longer had the final say, they did not feel it necessary to obey them. In the past it was believed that the chiefs had been given their power by the tribal god. Thus the African's religious beliefs required that he support the tribal chief. However, under European rule many Africans converted to Christianity and they no longer believed that their chiefs were appointed by God. Many Africans who went to work in the cities and gained some wealth did not accept the authority of the chiefs when they returned to the villages. In some cases wealthy people were actually more important than the chief.

7. The Europeans provided some Western education for the Africans. This was because the Europeans needed people with at least some training to fill the minor government jobs and also to work as semi-skilled workers and clerks for the trading companies. Britain also believed that the colonies would one day become independent and so some attempt was made to train Africans for leadership. This group of Western-educated Africans rejected the tribal chiefs' powers, but at the same time they demanded a greater voice in the rule of their countries. These were the first "nationalists," the people who led the struggle for independence from the Europeans.

President Mobutu of Zaire (center), conferring with his troops. *(Top) Credit: United Press International*

Lt. Col. Mengistu Heile Mariam, of Ethiopa. *(Bottom) Credit: United Press International*

8.　In order to reach Africa's resources more easily, the Europeans improved both transportation and communication. They also built hospitals and improved sanitation among the Africans.

Nationalism and Independence

Nationalism may be defined as the strong devotion to one's nation which puts the nation above all other things. World War II (1939-1945) was a turning point in the development of African nationalism. Before the war, only a small number of educated Africans were nationalists. Their main demand was that Africans have a greater voice in the running of their governments, which were controlled by the Europeans. By the end of the war, nationalism had spread to the masses. Now they demanded complete independence from the Europeans.

The first African nationalists were those people who had received a Western education. They left their tribes and went to the cities to study in the schools set up by the Europeans. Many of them later went on to Europe and America to complete their university education. Kwame Nkrumah, who later became the President of Ghana, spent many years working and studying in New York. Jomo Kenyatta, who led Kenya to independence and until he died recently was its president, studied in London. Others went to Paris. In Europe and America they saw that people had liberty and rights which had been unknown to them—freedom of speech, press and assembly; the right to vote and hold office; and trial by jury. The Africans felt that they, too, were entitled to the same rights as Englishmen and Frenchmen.

Dissatisfaction with European Rule

Nevertheless, when these Africans returned to Africa they found that despite their university education there was little they could do. They could only get the lowest paying jobs as clerks in European companies or minor officials in the government. The best jobs with the highest pay as well as all the highest positions in the government, were reserved for the Europeans. The Africans felt humiliated that the Europeans would not accept them as equals. The Europeans looked down on the Africans as primitive and regarded Western civilization as superior. This they believed was due to their own racial superiority. In those parts of Africa where many Europeans had settled there was strict segregation in housing, education and social life. Africans had the lowest standard of living while the Europeans lived in greater comfort. Africans had very little to say about how their government should be run, because all the final decisions were made by the Europeans. Under these circumstances it is little wonder that African nationalists began to demand a better life for their people and finally complete independence.

World War II and the Growth of Nationalism

Why did World War II strengthen African nationalism to such a great extent? During the war years many Africans left their villages to work for high wartime wages in the cities. Others spent years in the army fighting alongside the Europeans. For the first time they were free from their tribal rulers. In the cities they learned new skills and were exposed to new ideas. Some for the first time began to read newspapers and to listen to the radio. They became aware of what was going on in the world and in Africa. Some joined clubs and labor unions that were led by educated nationalists. Many Africans got important positions in the governments, and thus acquired some of the necessary experience and training to lead their people later. In the cities they met other Africans with different languages and cultures. They realized that they shared many of the same interests and problems. Gradually the loyalty they had felt to their chief and tribe was weakened and replaced by a new loyalty to the ideal of a modern, independent African state.

The war left many problems such as inflation and unemployment. The Europeans were unable to do anything about these problems because they had serious post war problems at home too. So the Africans showed their discontent in boycotts, strikes and riots.

After the war a number of countries in Asia such as India, Pakistan, Burma and others obtained their independence from the Europeans. The success of the Asians in gaining independence encouraged the Africans to demand the same thing for themselves. The ideas of peaceful resistance and non-cooperation practiced by India's nationalist leader Mohandas K. Gandhi made a deep impression on the Africans.

The United Nations was established near the end of the war. The preamble to its Charter spoke of "faith in the fundamental human rights, in the dignity and worth of the human person, in the equal rights of men and women and nations large and small. . . ." The Africans understood this to mean that they had the same rights as anyone else. The U.N. Charter also called upon all U.N. members "to develop self-government, to take due account of the political hopes of the people and to assist them in the progressive development of their free political institutions. . . ."

The young educated Africans now became the spokesmen for their people. They organized the discontented masses and led them in making demands on the European governments. They rejected the old promises made by the Europeans that in time they would have greater participation in their governments. They demanded immediate and complete independence. Workers in the cities and even many in the villages supported the new leaders in their demands for independence.

Independence Comes to Africa

Faced with this pressure, the European governments had to give in. In 1957 Ghana gained its freedom from Britain. It became the first black nation in Sub-Saharan Africa to win its independence from the Europeans. During the next 12 years 35 other nations became independent. France had hoped to make its African colonies part of a Greater France with the Africans having the same rights as Frenchmen. But in 1958 French President de Gaulle gave the French colonies a choice. They were to vote whether they wanted complete independence and separation from France, or self government in their own territory with France in charge of foreign affairs, defense and finance. Guinea, led by Sekou Touré, voted for complete independence. In 1960 the other 11 French colonies requested and were granted complete independence.

Most of the countries in Africa gained their independence without bloodshed or violence. But in the highlands of East Africa where many Europeans had settled independence was achieved only after a long period of struggle and violence. The settlers put pressure on the European government not to place the government in the hands of the African majority. In Kenya members of the Kikuyu tribe formed an organization known as the Mau Mau, which turned to terrorism toward Africans and Europeans in the hope of driving out the Europeans. Rebellion broke out in 1952. There was considerable bloodshed and many more Africans died than Europeans. In 1963 Kenya finally became independent.

Portugal was the last European country to give up its colonies in Africa. In 1974, the government of Portugal was overthrown and new rulers came to power. They set about making many changes in Portugal's policies. One of the most important changes was the decision to grant independence to Mozambique and Angola. In 1975, these two African nations became independent.

The role of these new African nations in world affairs is an important one. Representatives from the forty countries have a great deal of influence in the United Nations. Countries of both the East and the West have been offering military and economic assistance to the African states in the hopes of gaining their support.

INDEPENDENCE COMES TO AFRICA*

Country	Year of Independence	From
SOUTH AFRICA	1931	BRITAIN
SUDAN	1956	BRITAIN & EGYPT
GHANA	1957	BRITAIN
GUINEA	1958	FRANCE
CAMEROON	1960	FRANCE
CENTRAL AFRICA EMPIRE	1960	FRANCE
CHAD	1960	FRANCE
CONGO (PEOPLE'S REPUBLIC OF)	1960	FRANCE
THE CONGO (DEMOCRATIC REPUBLIC OF—ZAIRE)	1960	BELGIUM
DAHOMEY (BENIN)	1960	FRANCE
GABON	1960	FRANCE
IVORY COAST	1960	FRANCE
MALAGASY REPUBLIC (MADAGASCAR)	1960	FRANCE
MALI	1960	FRANCE
MAURITANIA	1960	FRANCE
NIGER	1960	FRANCE
NIGERIA	1960	BRITAIN
SENEGAL	1960	BRITAIN
SOMALIA	1960	ITALY & BRITAIN
TOGO	1960	FRANCE
UPPER VOLTA	1960	FRANCE
SIERRA LEONE	1961	BRITAIN
BURUNDI	1962	BELGIUM
RWANDA	1962	BELGIUM
UGANDA	1962	BRITAIN
KENYA	1963	BRITAIN
MALAWI	1964	BRITAIN
TANZANIA**	1964	BRITAIN
ZAMBIA	1964	BRITAIN
GAMBIA	1965	BRITAIN
RHODESIA	1965	BRITAIN
BOTSWANA	1966	BRITAIN
LESOTHO	1966	BRITAIN
EQUATORIAL GUINEA	1968	SPAIN
SWAZILAND	1968	BRITAIN
GUINEA-BISSAU	1974	PORTUGAL
MOZAMBIQUE	1975	PORTUGAL
ANGOLA	1975	PORTUGAL
CAPE VERDE ISLANDS	1975	PORTUGAL
COMORO ISLANDS	1975	FRANCE
SÃO TOMÉ E PRINCIPÉ	1975	PORTUGAL
DJIBOUTI	1977	FRANCE

*Liberia and Ethiopia already independent.
**Tanzania was formed by the union of Tanganyika and Zanzibar. Tanganyika gained independence in 1961 and Zanzibar in 1963.

Africa Today— Problems of Independence

Tribalism and Nation Building

The modern nation requires each person to consider himself first and foremost a citizen of that nation. But the nations of Africa are relatively new creations. For centuries Africans considered themselves to be members of a particular village, clan or tribe. To transfer one's loyalty from the village or the tribe to the nation requires education and a change in a person's thinking. It cannot be done overnight. Almost all the African nations face the problem of uniting people who differ greatly from each other in language, culture, religion and levels of economic development. For the new nations to survive, the Africans must learn to think of themselves as Nigerians rather than Yorubas, as Ghanaians rather than Ashanti. Most of the African nations are made up of many different tribal groups. In many of these nations there is rivalry among the various tribes, and each is afraid of being dominated by the others.

Civil War in Nigeria

Nigeria offers a good example of this situation. It has been estimated that there may be as many as 150 different ethnic groups in Nigeria. The most important of these are the Hausa, Fulani, Ibo and Yoruba. Some of the smaller tribes have resented the fact that they are dominated by the larger ones. And among the larger tribes there is rivalry over who will have the most important positions in the country. Over the years many Ibos left their area in the eastern region of Nigeria and went to live in the north, the area that is mainly inhabited by the Hausa and Fulani. The Ibos were disliked by the Hausa and Fulani because their education and skills gave them the best jobs in government and business.

In 1966 there was an army rebellion. General Ironsi, an Ibo, proclaimed military rule and made plans for a stronger central government. The Hausa, fearing Ibo domination, overthrew the government several months later. The new leader, General Gowon, tried to limit Ibo power in the central government. At the same time there was a masacre of Ibos living in the north. The Ibos then attempted to *secede* (separate) from Nigeria in 1967, proclaiming their region as the independent republic of Biafra. A bitter civil war followed which lasted into 1970. Most of the African nations supported the government of Nigeria against Biafra. Their feeling was that if Biafra were allowed to secede then other tribes all over Africa would try to break away and set up their own states. Biafra and the Ibos were defeated and Nigeria became united once again.

Tribal Conflict in Rwanda and Burundi

Another example of tribal conflict in Africa is the situation that exists in the two small East African nations of Rwanda and Burundi.

In Burundi, the Hutu tribe forms the majority of the population. But the Tutsis, who are a minority, control the government. In 1972, the Tutsi-controlled government conducted nationwide massacres that resulted in the death of 50,000 to 100,000 Hutus. Many thousands of Hutu officials, civil servants, soldiers, teachers, students and others who might hold leadership positions were among those put to death. All were accused of treason and of plotting to exterminate the Tutsis. More than 150,000 Hutus have left Burundi and moved to neighboring countries. Thousands of them have gone to Rwanda, where Hutus control the government.

In Rwanda, Hutus are said to have killed more than 1,000 Tutsis between December, 1972 and March, 1973. Tutsis have been fleeing their homes and more than 25,000 have come to Burundi in 1973. Between 1959 and 1962, 100,000 Tutsis left Rwanda when the Hutus took control of the government. It is believed that 20,000 Tutsis lost their lives at that time.

The Hutus, a Bantu people, came to this region many centuries ago from the southwest. They settled down and became farmers. About a thousand years ago the Tutsis began drifting into the area from the north. The Tutsis are a Hamitic people —tall and slender, with sharp features like the people of Ethiopia and Somalia. The Tutsis were cattle raisers. The Tutsis established the practice known as "ubuhake"— an agreement whereby they provided the Hutus with cattle in exchange for the Hutus' services. This resulted in a feudal system under the Tutsis that lasted until modern times. When the Germans ruled the area and later the Belgians, both of these countries maintained Tutsi supremacy. The Tutsis believed that they were superior, and they treated the Hutus as inferiors.

Both the Hutus and Tutsis are intensely nationalistic. Each group greatly fears and distrusts the other. If they are to live together in peace they will have to overcome these fears and suspicions. Each will have to give up its dreams of dominating the other.

The Problem of Separate Development (Apartheid)

Population

In the southernmost part of the continent of Africa is the Republic of South Africa. It is the homeland of over 21 million people. Africans (Bantus) make up about 69% of the population (14.7 million); Europeans 19% (3.8 million); Coloreds (mixed European or Asian, Hottentot and Bantu) 9% (2 million people); and Asians 3% (.6 million people). The whites of South Africa are made up of two groups of people —the Afrikaners, who are descendants of the original Dutch settlers and the English descendants of the original British settlers.

"A Unique Situation"

Of all the independent countries in Sub-Saharan Africa, only two, the Republic of South Africa and Rhodesia, are ruled by white minorities. South Africa's rulers believe that their nation is unique in the world and that their problems can only be solved in a unique way. Since 1948 the government of the Republic has followed a policy of separate development, or "apartheid" as it is sometimes called in other nations.

The Nationalist Party Program

In the years before 1948 governments containing Afrikaners and the English ruled the Republic. Social and economic separation between the whites and the Bantus, Asians and Coloreds had existed for a long time. In 1948, the Nationalists, an all Afrikaner party, won the election. Their policy as stated by their leader Dr. Daniel F. Malin emphasized social and political "separateness" of the races. (The other political parties favored a policy of racial integration.)

The Nationalists felt that they had won the election mainly on the issue of "separateness" (apartheid). Therefore, they soon began passing laws to put their program into effect. The Group Areas Act of 1949, provided for segregated residential (housing) areas for each race. In 1950 a population register classified the entire adult population according to race. Laws were passed forbiding mixed marriages. Other laws reserved skilled jobs for whites. Separation of facilities for whites and non-whites was put into law. (This was similar in many ways to the separate facilities that existed in the United States in the years before 1960.) It should be noted that the Nationalists put into law customs and traditions that had existed for over fifty years. The Nationalists did not introduce segregation into South Africa because segregation had existed long before they took over. But the Nationalists did make separation of the races the official policy of the government.

The Bantu Authorities Act

In 1951 the Bantu Authorities Act was passed. The Act set up a blueprint for the development of the Bantu (African) peoples. The Nationalists felt that Africans should develop within their own tribal groups under tribal laws and traditions instead of trying to achieve equal political rights with whites. When the Africans became capable of self-rule, they would rule themselves. The areas set aside for blacks would become "Bantustans" or semi-independent Bantu states. In 1956 the Transkei Territorial Authority was set up and in 1961 the Transkei was given self government. The Transkei is located on the east coast of the Republic of South Africa and contains the largest single Bantu population group in the republic.

Education

In the field of education the Nationalists passed laws which would further separate the races. The Bantu Education Act of 1953 made the local Bantu communities responsible for the education of Africans. The Extension of University Education Act of 1959 forbids all non-Europeans to attend the English-speaking universities. This law also provides for the creation of separate "university-colleges," not only for each of the four racial groups, but even for each of the three main African language groups.

General Law Amendment Acts

Various laws have been passed by the Nationalists which forbid practically any form of opposition, by peaceful means or otherwise. The General Law Amendment Act of 1962 further extends the government's powers. It provides for a minimum sentence of five years of prison and a maximum sentence of death for sabotage. Sabotage includes any attempt to promote disturbance, to disrupt any industry, to hamper the maintenance of law and order, and to promote hostility between the different sections of the population. Illegal possession of explosives or illegal entry into any building is considered sufficient evidence of an intention to carry out acts of sabotage. The law also extends the governments's powers to ban newspapers, organizations, and gatherings, and to imprison any person for any length of time without due process of law. The General Law Amendment Act of 1963 allows repeated detentions of persons for ninety days at a time for questioning; refusal to allow anybody, including legal counsel, to see the detained persons; indefinite imprisonment without trial; and the death penalty for receiving training in the use of violence outside South Africa.

The Homelands Program

The creation of the homelands program is a basic part of the Republic of South Africa's long-range plan of survival for South Africa's whites. This policy calls for dividing the country's 18.6 million blacks and 4.3 million whites into ten states. Nine will be for the blacks and one for the whites. The white state will hold 87% of the land, which will include all 17 existing major cities.

Eventually all black South Africans will be given citizenship in one of the tribal homelands. Seventy percent of the population of South Africa will be packed into 13% of the land. Only one of the planned homelands will be established with a single piece of land. The others are broken into two or more parts surrounded by white South Africa.

Under the homelands program, when a black person's homeland becomes independent, he automatically becomes a citizen of that "nation," and loses South African citizenship. Black workers who are needed to run South Africa's mines and industries will be permitted to continue on their jobs. Without them, South Africa's economy would collapse. However, the wives and children of all those workers must "return" to live in the homelands most of them have never known. This policy will cause much additional hardship for black families in South Africa.

Two of South Africa's nine homelands have become independent. In October 1976, *Transkei* became independent. It was a united area located on the Indian Ocean. It is fortunate to have a deep-water port, which will help its trade. The people of the Transkai depend mainly on agriculture and livestock to earn a living. Cattle, sheep, goats and horses are raised. The first prime minister of the homeland was Kaiser Daliwonga Matanzima, who was the tribal chief before he became prime minister (*kaiser* is the Afrikaner word for king). Among the first acts of the Transkai government was the official acceptance of the idea of multiracial schools. (However, at present there are very few whites who are permanent residents of the Republic.)

In December 1977, the second of the homelands became independent within the Republic of South Africa. The new republic is called *Bophuthatswana*. It consists of seven patches of territory scattered in northeast South Africa. It is completely *landlocked* with no coastline. The area is rich in platinum, asbestos, chromium, and manganese. Little of the land is good for agriculture.

As in the case of the Transkai, the nations of the world have not given recognition to the Bophuthatswana Republic. However, Lucas Mangope, the first president of the Republic, feels it is a good start to freedom. He said, "We cannot take the humiliations of the South African system any longer. We would rather face the difficulties of ruling a *fragmented* (broken up) territory and the *wrath* (anger) of the outside world. It is the price we are prepared to pay for being masters of our own destiny."

Criticism of the Policy of Separate Development

The policy of "separate development" (apartheid) has come under strong attack by most of the countries of the world. They feel that apartheid means not only separate, but also *unequal* development. They say that the establishment of Bantustans is no different from the old system whereby the government appointed and controlled the tribal chiefs. Critics feel that the education laws set up racial segregation at all levels of education. They say that the aim of the Education Act of 1953 was to "keep a Bantu child a Bantu child." Manual labor is stressed to prepare the Bantu for an inferior role in South African society. Instruction in Bantu languages is emphasized at the expense of European languages.

Attempts at Change

African attempts to bring about changes in this policy have not been successful. The African National Congress (ANC) under Chief Albert Luthuli and the Pan African Congress (PAC) formed by Robert Sobukwe have planned campaigns of *passive resistance* (nonviolent). In 1960 they both began a drive against the laws requiring Africans to carry a pass. Africans regard it as the most hated part of the apartheid system. On March 21, 1960, a large group of unarmed demonstrators were fired on by a few policemen and 69 Bantus were killed. It is estimated that as a result of the demonstration and the events following it 18,000 people were arrested. The government claimed that both the ANC and the PAC were closely connected with Communists and desired to overthrow the government. As a result all the leaders of both organizations were arrested and the two parties were declared illegal.

The Seventies   In the seventies the situation has not changed to any great degree. The Nationalists are still in power. They point to the advances made in the Transkei and 5 other Bantustans with internal self-government: the 25% growth in wages for black workers and the greater percentage rise of black wages over white wages in the period September, 1970, to February, 1973; the advanced social and health services; the educational programs which exist and the *multinational* (different races and ethnic groups) games which have gone on for the last two years. Most of the nations of Africa and many in the rest of the world feel that blacks still lack political equality and freedom. In September, 1977, the black leader Steven Biko died after a hunger strike while in police detention. This was just one more incident that brought world attention to the plight of South African blacks.

Rhodesia and the Problem of Black Majority Rule

South Africa and Rhodesia are the two African nations where white-controlled governments oppose and block majority rule. In 1965 the white ruling group of the then British colony of Southern Rhodesia declared the independence of Rhodesia. In 1976 they established the Republic of Rhodesia. The purpose of their sudden action was to prevent an orderly transfer of power from the British to the black Africans who comprise 96% of the seven million people of Rhodesia. That kind of orderly change to black majority rule has been achieved in the other former British African colonies, like Nigeria. In Rhodesia, the government, the army and the police are entirely in the hands of the white minority. All the industries and most of the good land is controlled by the whites.

Rhodesia's black majority has demanded equal voting and economic rights since the early 1960s. Until recently, the whites have refused any move which could lead to control of their country by the black majority. There is much pressure on the minority government of Prime Minister Ian Smith to change. Most of the countries of the world have refused to recognize (exchange ambassadors with) the Republic of Rhodesia. Many nations have refused to trade with Rhodesia. The United Nations imposed economic sanctions (penalties), including a *boycott* of (a refusal to buy) Rhodesian chrome. Chrome exports earn money to buy Rhodesia's imports.

Unlike Namibia, where black Africans are united behind one nationalist group (SWAPO), Rhodesia's blacks are represented by various organizations and leaders.

These form two rival groups which have not cooperated with each other. Bishop Abel Muzorewa is president of the United African National Council. He and the Reverend Ndabaningi Sithole are the leaders of the more moderate groups. They seek cooperation between the races and have avoided acts of violence. Joshua Nkomo leads the National Democratic Party (NDP). Nkomo was an early leader in the demand for immediate black majority rule. Robert Mugabe heads the Zimbabwe African National Union (ZANU). (*Zimbabwe* is the ancient name of Rhodesia, and will become the name of the black majority-ruled nation.) Nkomo and Mugabe represent the more *militant* (strongly active, warring) groups. They believe in using any method, including terrorism and guerrilla warfare to obtain their goals.

Following the independence of neighboring Mozambique from Portugal in 1975, Nkomo and Mugabe set up guerrilla bases there for raids into Rhodesia. Those raids have killed many black and white Rhodesians. In an effort to destroy the guerrillas, Rhodesian troops have carried out other raids deep into Mozambique. The situation became more and more dangerous, with the possibility of war in Africa. The United States and Great Britain tried to bring about discussions among the opposing groups. They also presented Prime Minister Smith with a peace plan in 1976. The major elements include:

1. Surrender of power by the Rhodesian white government, and protection for its members;
2. An *interim* (in between) government under British supervision, backed by an international peacekeeping force under United Nations control;
3. Disbanding the Rhodesian army (though not the police), and replacing it with a new African army based on the liberation forces;
4. Free and impartial elections based on universal adult suffrage;
5. Provision of a Zimbabwe Development Fund of at least one billion dollars to spur economic development. The United States and Great Britain would be major contributors to the fund.

In November 1977, Prime Minister Ian Smith announced that he was prepared to accept majority rule for Rhodesia immediately. However, Smith refused to meet with any of the black nationalist leaders who were outside Rhodesia. (Nkomo and Mugabe were in Mozambique leading the guerrilla operations; they refused to return to Rhodesia.) A conference was set up in December that included Smith, Muzorewa, Sithole and Jeremiah Chirau, leader of a small group called the Zimbabwe People's Organization (ZPO). The major problem was if and how to give minority whites any veto power in a black controlled government.

In March 1978, an agreement was reached. The *accord* (agreement) gives majority rule, but not full majority power to the blacks. The whites are guaranteed 28 seats in Rhodesia's 100-seat parliament for 10 years. Under the new constitution, these 28 votes could block any constitutional change. In addition, many economic guarantees were given to the whites. These included payment for *expropriated* (taken away by force) property. All agreed these economic guarantees were necessary to keep the whites from leaving.

Nkomo and Mugabe objected to the agreement. They especially opposed the economic guarantees and the length of time for the white parliamentary veto. Bishop Muzorewa, who would probably be the leader of the new government, has said that the compromise was not entirely satisfactory, but it was a very important step forward. He felt that cooperation was necessary and that black majority rule was guaranteed for the first time.

The days of Rhodesia's white government are numbered. There is increasing white emigration. The boycott of trade causes economic difficulties and further damages morale. Black guerrillas have been trained in Angola, Botswana, Mozambique, Tanzania and Zambia. (See map on p. 250.) The transition to black majority rule in Zimbabwe will soon come. It will also bring another problem into focus. The Rhodesian nationalist movement has been divided since 1961 among leaders with strong differences in personality and ideas. Both African and Western leaders are trying to obtain cooperation and compromises among those rivals. Only a stable agreement and a peaceful changeover will enable Zimbabwe's first black government to end that country's diplomatic and economic isolation, and ensure its survival.

Politics in Sub-Saharan Africa

In most of the countries of Africa only one political party is allowed. Very few African nations have opposition parties or free elections as we know them in the West. Therefore, many Americans have claimed that the new African nations are undemocratic. This is not necessarily true and many Africans give good reasons for the existence of one-party systems.

Many Africans believe that the greatest need at present is for unity. The people need the firm leadership of one party or one man for the time being to hold the nation together and set it on the road to economic development. In some countries, the opposition parties are seen as a danger to the nation, representing groups wishing to break up the nation into smaller units. Some of the African nations owe their existence to the abilities of individual leaders, such as Sekou Touré in Guinea and Jomo Kenyatta in Kenya. There is a strong feeling among many that opposition to such men and their policies is the same as disloyalty to the nation. In addition, democratic elections as we know them in the West are difficult when the majority of the population is illiterate, and not used to voting for leaders and representatives.

In recent years, the governments of many African nations have been overthrown by the army which has substituted military government in place of the civilian government. Military leaders rule in the Congo (Zaire), Dahomey, Togo, Upper Volta, Nigeria, Sierra Leone, Ghana, Burundi and others. In many cases army leaders have claimed that they felt compelled to take over because the government was not successful in solving the nation's problems. They have promised to return power to the civilian leaders when the nation is ready. Nevertheless, armies will probably continue to play an important role in African politics for years to come.

Uganda in Turmoil

General Amin Seizes Power

In January, 1971, General Idi Amin seized power in Uganda and overthrew President Milton Obote. At that time many Ugandans regarded Amin as a savior. Uganda, which had been independent since 1962, had many problems which President Amin promised to solve. At first he released many political prisoners and broke up the secret police. He promised the people elections and political freedom. But in a short time he forgot these promises and began a reign of terror. The army was *purged* (people the General did not approve of were removed or killed), and President Amin filled it with people from his own tribe. Since then the army has become feared and hated throughout Uganda. Soldiers roam free and commit atrocities at the expense of innocent people. Prisoners have been tortured, mutilated and executed.

The Asians

Among those suffering the most have been Uganda's 80,000 Asian residents. Centuries ago their ancestors came to East Africa from India and settled in the countries that are now Kenya, Uganda and Tanzania. In 1962 these three nations became independent from Britain. The Asians were given the choice of accepting British citizenship or becoming citizens of the countries in which they were living. Most of the Asians chose to be British citizens while they continued to live in East Africa.

Expulsion of the Asians

Almost all the business and commerce of Uganda was in the hands of the Asians. In August 1972, President Amin announced that he was giving the Asians until November 8 to leave the country. Those who were not out by that date would be rounded up and sent to special camps. While this order was only supposed to apply to those Asians who were not citizens of Uganda, many Asians who had Ugandan citizenship were also forced to leave. President Amin declared that "we are not racists," but he blamed the Asians for retarding the economy of the country. The government declared that the Asians who were leaving Uganda would not be allowed to sell their property to other Asians remaining behind. They would have to sell to Africans (who could buy the property at rock bottom prices) or abandon their property entirely. Each expelled family could take out of the country only the equivalent of $140. What actually happened was that the government seized most of the Asians' property. Soldiers went on a house by house search for Asians. Many were manhandled and robbed by the soldiers; some were shot. About 50,000 Asians did leave before the November 8 deadline, most of them going to Britain, and some to Canada, India, the United States and other countries.

Effects on the Economy

Many of Uganda's blacks were probably pleased with the *expulsion* (throwing out) of the Asians, since they no doubt wanted to take over their wealth. But it seems likely that, for a while at least, the country as a whole will suffer. Many schools which were staffed mainly by Asian teachers have closed. In Kampala, the capital city, 80% of the shops closed and many Africans were left jobless as a result. Uganda is on the edge of bankruptcy. The skills of the Asians were essential to the economy of the country and at the moment there is no one to replace them. In fact, the economy of Uganda has been going downhill ever since General Amin came to power. There is a shortage of hard cash in the country because approximately one-third of the budget is spent on the army. Countries such as Libya and Saudi Arabia have promised financial aid to Uganda, but this is not enough.

Attempt to Overthrow General Amin

In September 1972, an attempt was made to overthrow the government of General Amin. Ugandan soldiers, who had fled to Tanzania after the ouster of President Obote, invaded Uganda from Tanzania. But the invasion was poorly planned and in less than 24 hours most of the invaders were killed. It was mainly after the invasion that Amin's reign of terror began. Many foreigners were arrested. The army turned on the Baganda, Uganda's largest tribe, and killed thousands. The Chief Justice, the head of the University, the president of the National Students Union and many other prominent people were arrested.

World opinion turned against Amin when he was accused of helping Arab terrorists who hijacked an Air France jetliner in June 1976. The terrorists landed at Entebbe airport in Uganda, where they held Israeli and Jewish passengers hostage.

The Current Situation

The fighting seems to be nearing an end, but many questions have still not been answered. How long will big power involvement continue in the Horn? The situation in the Ogaden affects the situation in Eritrea. Will the Ethiopians demand Soviet and Cuban help in defeating the Eritrean rebels? It will not be easy for the Russians and Cubans to refuse and still retain their influence in Ethiopia.

If they do give help to the Ethiopians against the Eritreans, they create problems for themselves. The Eritreans consider themselves Marxist-Leninists, as do the Russians and Cubans. The Eritreans are supported by Syria, Iraq and South Yemen. These three nations are among the few Arab states still friendly to the Russians.

The situation is complicated and very unclear. However, one thing is clear; for the immediate future, the Moslems of Somalia and Eritrea will continue to hate the non-Moslem Ethiopians and the Ethiopians will continue to hate the Somalis and Eritreans. Peace will not be a fact until this hatred can be changed.

The Horn of Africa

The Horn of Africa is located in the northeast corner of the continent and is bounded by the Red Sea on the north and east. The Red Sea is an important waterway, especially for the transportation of oil from the Middle East to the rest of the world. Ethiopia, Somalia and Djibouti are the three nations located in the Horn of Africa. Ethiopia is the largest. Ethiopia had been ruled since 1916 by Haile Selassie but in 1974 the army revolted.

Ethiopia is a poor country. For about ten years before the revolt, the people showed their unhappiness with strikes and demonstrations. They wanted a fairer division of the land, higher wages and, most important, a greater say in the ruling of the country. In 1974, the opposition to the Emperor gained enough strength to force the beginning of a change. For the first time the army joined the protest. In September 1974, Haile Selassie was forced to leave office and was put in jail; Ethiopia was no longer a kingdom. (However, to date there has been no official announcement declaring Ethiopia a republic.)

The army now rules Ethiopia and has begun to make many socialist *reforms* (changes). Land has been taken over by the government and given to peasant associations. These associations were to decide how the land should be used, but little has been done yet to divide the land. In addition, the army has done little to increase civil rights or to raise wages. The reason for this slowness in reform is that the army is faced with other very serious problems.

The Problem of Eritrea

Eritrea is located in the northeastern part of Ethiopia along the Red Sea. A former Italian colony, Eritrea was given to Ethiopia at the close of World War II. It is important because it provides Ethiopia with a coastline. Before 1945, Ethiopia was a landlocked country. The people of Eritrea are mainly Moslems and they are not related ethnically to the Ethiopians. Since 1945, opposition to the Ethiopian rule has existed and fighting has continued for over thirty years. In the past few years, the rebels have been aided by

Moslems in Djibouti and Somalia. The rebels want independence but would probably settle for *autonomous* (self) rule for the area.

The Border Dispute with Somalia

A far more serious problem is the Ethiopian border dispute with Somalia. This dispute, involving an area called *Ogaden*, has existed since 1960 when Somalia became independent. The Ogaden is located next to Somalia in eastern Ethiopia. Between 1960 and 1977, there was much discussion about the territory. Most of the people who live in the Ogaden region are Moslems and are ethnically Somalis. They wish to be independent or be able to join the Ogaden to Somalia. In June 1977, the dispute broke out into open war. The fighting was between the Ethiopian army and the West Somalia Liberation Front (WSLF). The WSLF is a guerrilla organization founded in 1974, and supported and armed by Somalia. The Somali government position is that the Ogaden should be given self-determination.

The Soviet Union is deeply involved in the dispute. The Soviets have supplied arms and economic aid to Somalia since 1968. In return, the Soviets were given the right to use the important port of Berbera. However, in 1976, the Soviets began to send military and economic aid to Ethiopia. (The United States had supplied aid to Haile Selassie's government.) Russian and Cuban military advisors came into Ethiopia to train the army. In the dispute between Ethiopia and the WSLF, the Soviets supported the Ethiopians.

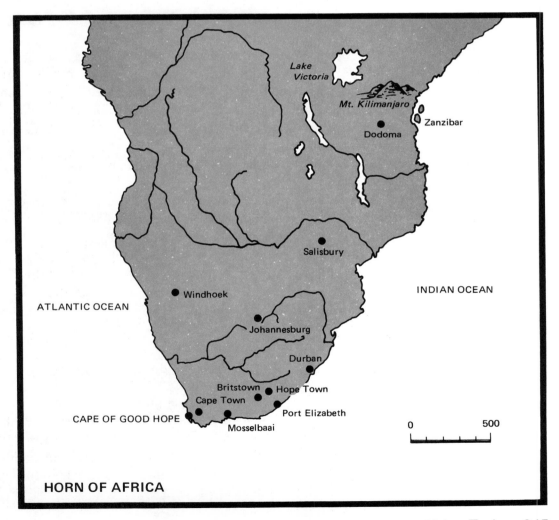

HORN OF AFRICA

This angered Somalia and, in November 1977, the Somalis broke their treaty of friendship with the Soviets and told the Soviets to leave Somalia. The Soviets were also not to be allowed the use of Berbera.

In the early fighting in the Ogaden, the WSLF won many victories, aided by about 10,000 Somali soldiers. They occupied almost all of the Ogaden. In February 1978, the tide began to turn. With the help of 11,000 Cuban and 1,000 Russian troops, the Ethiopians drove the WSLF back. In March, the Somalis said they were pulling out their soldiers. At the same time, they refused to give up their claims to the Ogaden.

African Affairs in the Seventies

The years 1974 and 1975 were full of important events in Africa. Portugal's 400-year-old empire in Africa collapsed. Guinea-Bissau became the forty-fourth independent nation in September, 1974. Mozambique and Angola received their independence in 1975.

The drought continued to affect millions in Africa. When the rains did come they caused floods. These floods made it more difficult to bring in food and medical supplies. The shortage of food was worsened by lower harvests in a large part of Africa and the using up of world food reserves.

The world energy crisis, causing higher oil prices, seriously hurt the economies of all the countries of sub-Saharan Africa except for the four oil producers (Nigeria, Angola, Gabon, and Zaire). The region's economic performance continued downward. Agriculture, the most important activity in the area, declined by about 10%. Manufacturing increased by less than 2%, far less than the 8% target set by most countries. Mineral production and exports, however, continued to rise. By the end of 1974, about 10% of the world's petroleum production came from Africa (including North Africa).

The coming of independence to Mozambique under a government led by *Frelimo* (Mozambique Liberation Front) has caused Rhodesia and the Republic of South Africa to look to their positions and policies. Rhodesia, a white-ruled republic, had depended in the past largely on Mozambique for its easiest route to the sea (see map of Southern Africa). It may become difficult to bring in needed goods and export Rhodesia's produce. Also the anti-white guerilla movement could hope for Frelimo's support once it took power. Rhodesia's long border with Mozambique could prove to be of great danger to the Rhodesians.

For South Africa, the effect is less serious but still important. Workers from Mozambique — 100,000 of them — worked South Africa's gold mines. In addition, South Africa was counting on the output of Mozambique's Cabora Bassau hydro-electric project for cheap energy (the project was to begin operating in late 1975). Faced with this situation, the South African government, led by Prime Minister B. J. Vorster, tried to improve relations with black African governments. Vorster persuaded the Rhodesian leader Ian Smith to release all political prisoners and to hold a constitutional conference sometime in 1975. In return, the Africans agreed to stop guerilla activities.

In relation to Namibia (Southwest Africa), which South Africa has said it owns, the South African government has changed its policy slightly. Mr. Vorster has said that his government would take "a more flexible policy" toward the future independence of that area.

The Rise of Soviet-Cuban Influence in Africa

Africa has always been a continent where foreign powers have competed with each other to gain influence. In the 1970s the country making the greatest effort to expand its influence throughout Africa has been the Soviet Union. In this effort the Soviet Union is assisted by Cuba. To a lesser degree other Communist countries, mainly in Eastern Europe, have sent special units to Africa to serve Soviet foreign policy interests. These countries are East Germany, Czechoslovakia, Hungary, Poland and Bulgaria. In 1978 there were over 40,000 Cuban troops in Africa—20,000 in Angola, 17,000 in Ethiopia and about 4,000 scattered in places like Mozambique, the Congo, Equatorial Guinea, Guinea-Bissau, Libya and Tanzania.

In the past Africa was never given top priority in Soviet foreign policy plans. In the 1970s, however, the Soviet Union has become increasingly interested in Africa. There are several reasons for this new interest. Africa is an excellent location for Soviet air and naval bases. These bases can help the Soviet Union extend its control to the Indian and Atlantic Oceans. The Soviet Union and China are engaged in a worldwide competition to win underdeveloped countries to their own form of Communism. The Soviet Union would like the African nations to follow the direction of Moscow rather than Peking. Africa, with its wealth of natural resources, is very important to Western Europe, which lacks many of these resources. This situation makes Africa valuable to the Soviet Union as well. Since the Soviet Union does not have a history of colonialism in Africa as Western nations do, it is in a position to support African liberation movements such as the one in Angola. The United States, because of its close ties to the former colonial rulers and because of its association with South Africa, is not looked on with favor by African revolutionaries. While the Soviet Union is supplying economic and military aid to a number of African countries and revolutionary movements, there are several areas where the Soviet Union is making an all out effort.

Angola Angola, which for nearly 500 years was a Portuguese colony, received its independence in November 1975. More than a year before Angola became independent, fighting broke out among three Angolan liberation groups, each of which hoped to lead Angola once the Portuguese were out. Following independence, the fighting increased and soon the country was involved in a civil war. Many foreign nations became involved in the struggle, aiding one side or another. The three Angolan liberation groups were: (1) MPLA, headed by a Marxist, Dr. Agostinho Neto; (2) FNLA, led by the Black Nationalist leader, Holden Roberts, and backed by his brother-in-law President Mobutu Sese Seko of Zaire; (3) UNITA, under the leadership of Jonas Savimbi and supported by the majority of Angola's 500,000 white people. Immediately following independence these three rival liberation movements set up two separate republics in Angola, each with its own capital and own government. Agostinho Neto, head of the MPLA, announced the creation of the People's Republic of Angola. The FNLA and UNITA joined together to form the Democratic People's Republic of Angola.

Because of Angola's vast oil and mineral wealth, a number of foreign countries became involved in the struggle. The greatest outside support was given to the MPLA by the Soviet Union and Cuba. The Soviet Union supplied the MPLA with tanks, planes, huge supplies of arms and military personnel. In fact, the Soviet Union exported more military equipment to Angola than to any other area in recent years with the exception of the Middle East. By February 1976, when the civil war ended, there were 10,000 Cubans in Angola fighting on the side of the MPLA. Fighting on the side of the MPLA were also some Algerians, North Vietnamese and refugees from Zaire who were enemies of President Mobutu. The FNLA was supported mainly by the United States, France and Zaire. UNITA had the support of Portugal, China, South African business interests and white Angolans. Fighting alongside the FNLA-UNITA forces were *mercenaries* (soldiers serving for pay in a foreign army) from Zaire, Portugal, Rhodesia, Mozambique and South Africa. Many of these mercenaries were recruited, trained and paid by the CIA. Millions of dollars in aid and military equipment from the United States was sent to the FNLA-UNITA forces through Zaire in an attempt to keep this fact secret from the American public.

In February 1976, the seven-month-old civil war came to an end. The MPLA had won. Dr. Agostinho Neto is now the leader of Angola. There are a number of reasons why the MPLA was able to defeat its opponents. One reason is the weakness and corruption of the opposition. The FNLA lacked good leadership at any level. Its leader, Holden Roberts, was widely regarded as corrupt and inefficient. The FNLA ignored the suffering and widespread starvation brought on by the civil war. The union of the FNLA and UNITA was a military necessity, but the two groups had strong tribal hatred for each other. The FNLA was made up almost totally of the Bakongo tribe. UNITA was made up almost totally of the Ovimbundu tribe. In 1961, when the guerrilla war for independence began in northern Angola, the Bakongo savagely murdered and mutilated hundreds of the Ovimbundu tribe. This was never forgotten or forgiven. And so during the civil war, despite their union, soldiers of the FNLA and UNITA often fought each other. There was no joint field command and no soldier of one group took orders from an officer of the other group. On the other hand, the MPLA had good organization. In the final months of the war, more and more African nations recognized the MPLA as the government of Angola. This was because the black African nations considered the FNLA to be a puppet of the United States and were opposed to the support given to it by South Africa.

In December 1975, the United States Senate voted to cut off funds for military aid to Angola. In February, the House of Representatives voted the same way. Many people in Congress were fearful that American involvement in Angola might be the first step toward another Vietnam situation. Many were opposed to the secret nature of the involvement. Many also felt that Angola was not crucial to United States interests. At the same time, a massive Soviet airlift of arms helped the MPLA win victory after victory on the battlefield. Soviet-Cuban support was the single most important factor that led to the MPLA's triumph.

Ethiopia   See the section on the Horn of Africa, page 244.

Zaire   In 1960 the Congo (now known as Zaire) gained its independence from Belgium. Almost immediately, there was bloodshed and rebellion. (Moïse Tshombe led a rebellion against the central government of the Congo. The goal of this rebellion was the secession of Katanga Province from the Congo.) Katanga province (now known as Shaba) in southeastern Zaire is very rich in copper and other minerals. Katanga is the homeland of more than 1,500,000 people of the Lunda tribe. There are other Lunda tribesmen in northwestern Zambia and in eastern Angola. Tshombe's followers wanted to preserve their mineral wealth from their enemies—the government and the Bakongo tribes. The rebellion was crushed, but Tshombe's followers fled to Angola after President Mobutu came to power in 1965. In Angola, the Katangese, as these refugees are known, have considerable autonomy in their region in the northeast. The Katangese helped Agostinho Neto and the MPLA come to power in Angola, and Neto allows them to use Angolan territory to prepare for invasions of Zaire. The Katangese are now led by Nathaniel Mbumba, who founded the Congolese National Liberation Front (FNLC) in 1968.

In May 1978, Katangan rebels based in Angola invaded the copper mining province of Shaba (Katanga) in southern Zaire. The rebels brutally massacred several thousand blacks and whites living there. A force of 1,900 French and Belgian paratroopers, assisted by United States jets, prevented the invasion from succeeding. French and Belgian troops forced the Katangan invaders to retreat back to Angola. They also rescued more than 2,500 Europeans trapped in Shaba and airlifted them to Europe. The goal of the invaders was to disrupt Zaire's economy and bring about the downfall of President Mobutu Sese Seko. The copper mines in Shaba province are the main source of Zaire's wealth. One-half the world's annual supply of cobalt comes from this region as well as large quantities of zinc. The European exodus could mean economic disaster for Zaire which does not have enough competent technicians and managers to run the copper mines. There is no hope for Zaire's economy unless the mines can be protected against new attacks. (In 1977 the French helped Mobutu beat back a similar invasion of Shaba by the same rebel forces from Angola.) There is no reason to believe that the rebels will not return. Belgium has over $1 billion invested in Zaire and 100,000 citizens living there. France also has sizable investments in Zaire. Therefore, both countries have said that they will keep some of their troops there to guard the remaining European technicians who are needed to keep the mines working. At the same time they agreed to organize and train a special Zairian force to guard the country against attack.

The question of Soviet-Cuban involvement in the invasion is complicated and as yet unclear. Immediately following the invasion Zaire charged that Cubans were involved in the fighting on the side of the rebels. The Carter administration sharply criticized the Soviet Union and Cuba. Several days later, however, Premier Fidel Castro of Cuba told the American representative in Cuba that his country had no part in the invasion of Zaire. At another time Castro told a group of visiting Americans that Cuba had been aware of "rumors" of the impending invasion and had tried unsuccessfully to persuade President Neto of Angola to prevent it. The fact remains that over the years, Cubans and Angolans had armed and trained the Katangese. Cuba still has 20,000 troops in Angola. There are 4,000 Cubans troops stationed along the Angolan border, the area from which the Katangans launched their invasion. President Carter, in a news conference on June 13, 1978, charged that Castro could have done much more to prevent the Katangan invasion of Zaire. Cuban troops could have blocked the invasion themselves or Castro could have notified the Organization of African Unity in advance had he genuinely wished to stop the invasion.

The United States government has no desire to get involved in the fighting in Zaire or anywhere else in Africa. But President Carter did promise Zaire several million dollars in military supplies and the International Monetary Fund has promised $1 billion in economic assistance. Zaire, however, will continue to have problems unless serious efforts are made to reform its economy. There is widespread popular discontent and Mobutu, whose regime is considered inept and corrupt, is blamed for this.

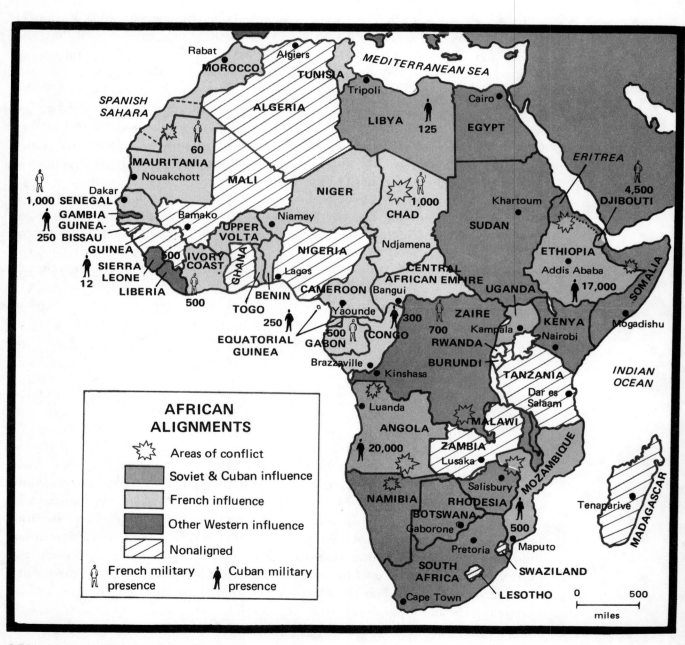

AFRICAN ALIGNMENTS

Areas of conflict

Soviet & Cuban influence

French influence

Other Western influence

Nonaligned

French military presence

Cuban military presence

The Economy of Black Africa

Agriculture

Agriculture is the life blood of the African economy. Well over 70% of Africans depend on agriculture for a living. The African is mainly a *subsistence* farmer. He, himself, produces most of what he needs. He grows enough foodstuffs for himself and for his family, and rarely sells or trades any part of his harvest.

However, the situation is changing. Today, African leaders are trying to increase the production of *cash crops*. These crops are not used at home, but are sold to cities or to other countries. Most African states depend upon the export of agricultural goods to help pay for the development of industry and a modern economy.

The many climates of Africa allow a great variety of farm products to be raised. Because the grasslands of the savannas make good pastures, cattle raising is important. Cattle provide the African with milk, meat and hides. In the highlands of Tanzania and Kenya sheep and goats are raised. These animals are well suited to the hilly lands and low rainfall.

Corn is an important crop of South Africa. Wheat, peanuts, rice, beans and peas are also raised. The Mediterranean climate area of South Africa is small, but it is important to agriculture. It is about two hundred miles long and forty miles wide. Peaches, plums, grapes and citrus fruits are raised. These fruits ripen during Europe's winter season, when prices are highest. Because of this, they make a valuable export to Western Europe. Cereals, such as wheat, oats and barley, are also raised.

The world depends on Africa for many important products. About 60% of the world's *cacao* is raised there. Nearly every chocolate candy bar eaten in the world has an African coating. *Palm oil* and vegetable oils, used in making soap and salad oil, and *sisal*, used for making rope and sacking, are also produced in Africa in large amounts. In addition, Africa produces large quantities of tea, coffee, cotton, tobacco, peanuts and natural rubber. These crops are raised for export.

Because there is often not enough land to support everyone in the village, many Africans go to work on farms or plantations which grow the crops that the rest of the world wants to buy. These export crops are important to countries without mineral wealth. For example, peanuts make up over 90% of Gambia's total exports; cocoa makes up 70% of Ghana's sales, while coffee and cotton together are about 87% of Uganda's exports.

Problems of African Agriculture

The new African nations face many problems in improving agricultural production. First, most of Africa's soil is poor. Most African soil is *tropical laterite*. This type of earth, usually reddish in color, is damaged by heavy rains. The rains *leach* the soil, that is, they wash away the minerals in the soil. As a result, most African lands are not very fertile. Even when modern agricultural methods are used, crop yields per acre are low. The best agricultural areas are found in the higher plateau regions. These areas have rich, volcanic soils. The river valleys are also fertile.

Second, there is the problem of not enough or irregular water supply. The seasonal character of rainfall does not allow the African to make full use of the land. The

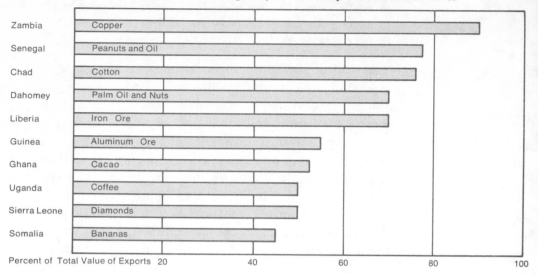

Monoculture – ("Single Export" Economy) in Sub-Saharan Africa

Zambia	Copper	
Senegal	Peanuts and Oil	
Chad	Cotton	
Dahomey	Palm Oil and Nuts	
Liberia	Iron Ore	
Guinea	Aluminum Ore	
Ghana	Cacao	
Uganda	Coffee	
Sierra Leone	Diamonds	
Somalia	Bananas	

Percent of Total Value of Exports   20   40   60   80   100

Many African nations depend on one mineral or crop for export to earn money. If the price of that product drops a few cents, these nations will have economic problems. Why?

great fear of the African farmer is that rain may not fall. When this happens, the earth dries and crops will not grow. The result is famine. On the other hand, if too much rain falls, it may wash away the newly planted seeds and cause floods. Africa has a great need for both large and small dams, and irrigation facilities, to control and store the water.

The tsetse fly still remains a discouraging problem in Africa. The tsetse fly carries sleeping sickness to humans, cattle and horses. The existence of the tsetse fly has closed some areas of Africa to human settlement. The form of the disease called "nagara," which cattle and horses suffer from, is also a serious problem. Much land that could be used for raising cattle cannot be developed, since animals cannot survive because of the tsetse fly.

Africans must be trained to use new equipment and new methods. Africans are not necessarily slow to learn or to change their ways. They have to be shown that new methods are better than the old. Africans have often been criticized for their custom of burning grassland in the dry season. We know now that the ashes produce minerals and are a good substitute for expensive fertilizers. African crop farmers in many areas still clear the bush by hand, and then burn the trees they have cut down to provide ash seed beds for their crops. This method, called "slash and burn," also fertilizes the soil.

In the same way, "bush following," the traditional method of farming an area of land for a few years, then moving on to a new stretch and allowing the old plot to lie *fallow* (unused), is a way of allowing the soil to regain its fertility. When land is plentiful, "bush following" is as good a way as most to use land properly. It is now a problem because, as the population increases, land becomes less available, and people have to settle down on one plot of land.

The landowning system also creates some problems. The land in many African societies is often owned by a group of people, not by one person. An individual can use what he needs, but he cannot sell the land. It always remains the property of the group. A farmer is, therefore, discouraged from using new methods or spending money to develop the land, because the land he uses is not his own. He is not sure that he or his children will receive the benefits from improvement.

Marketing the products raised is the final problem. Poorly developed road and railway systems are part of the difficulty. In addition, storage facilities are lacking. Besides this, distribution of food from farmer to consumer is poorly organized.

In summary, there is little reason to feel that Africa's agricultural problems cannot be solved. But to solve them, there must be great efforts made in agricultural research, development of dams, irrigation and transportation systems, farmer education, and marketing procedures. Agricultural development is more than likely the key to African progress.

The Sahel Drought — A Major Disaster and Tragedy

The *Sahel* (from an Arabic word meaning shore) is a large area in West Africa. The Sahel stretches from the Atlantic Ocean on the west through Mauritania, Mali, Upper Volta, Niger, and Chad to the center of the continent. Parts of Senegal, Ghana, Cameroon, Niger, the Central African Empire, and Ethiopia can also be considered part of the Sahel because of similar geography, ecology, and climate. The Sahel is the boundary between the Sahara Desert and the fertile land and forests that stretch down to the West African coast.

The people of the North Sahel are nomads. They raise camels and cattle. In the south there are thousands of villages which depend on the raising of subsistence crops such as millet, maize, and sorghum.

For the past six years this area has been having a severe drought. Millions of people of the Sahel are starving. The cause of the problem goes back many years. In the 1960s rains were plentiful. New wells were built. The cattle population grew. In addition, a great population explosion took place.

However, after 1965, weather conditions in the Sahel began to change. It is believed that the polar ice caps are cooling. This is affecting weather conditions all over the world. Monsoon winds and rains have shifted southward. This has brought about droughts in many parts of the world, including Africa. In some areas, the Sahara is spreading its sands southward at the rate of thirty miles a year.

In 1968, bad weather with very little rainfall gave the first warnings of trouble. Few people and cattle died but around the wells lay vast areas of dead land, without grass or trees. Cattle and goats would never again find grass here. The governments of the Sahel countries did not take the warning. They did little to protect their people or prevent the coming disaster.

Between 1969 and 1972 almost no rain fell. The large cattle herds had eaten what little desert grasses there were. The herds moved south to the Niger and Senegal Rivers, but they found the river beds dry. Millions of cattle died — Mauritania's herd loss was 70%, Mali's 55%, Niger's 80%, and Chad's 70%. But the real problem was that nearly 3 million people were faced with starvation and death from disease and hunger.

Diseases multiplied the effects of the drought. In villages of northern Niger, half the school children died from measles. In Mauritania, influenza and chicken pox were the killers. In Chad, diphtheria was widespread.

What were other results of the drought? Food production in each of the Sahel countries was down. Local food crops — yams and rice — have dropped. So has production of export crops — cocoa and coffee. These reductions affect the economy of each country.

In Niger, the civilian government was overthrown by army leaders. In Ethiopia, the drought brought about great unrest and unhappiness, leading to Emperor Haile Selassie's downfall.

There will never be exact figures as to how many died — estimates are between fifty and one hundred thousand. However, of long-term importance is the effect of malnutrition on the lives of the children who survived.

Finally, in late 1974, the rains came. These rains broke, at least for the time being, the drought that had lasted for six years.

What lessons have been learned? Research in climate has shown that the Sahel will be a desert in the near future and not suitable for human life within the next 20 years. Studies also show that long-term attempts to irrigate (water) and restock the Sahel will fail. In other words, the culture and future of the proud but poor nomads is dead.

But the most important lesson learned by the Third World is that rural development must never overstrain the local ecological balance — human and animal population, resources and climate. Is there a lesson for Americans in this disaster?

Natural Resources

Minerals and hydroelectric power are the muscles of industry. Fortunately, Africa has great sources of both. Africa has about 40% of the world's water power resources. This is more than any other continent. However, less hydroelectric power has been developed in Africa than in any other continent except Australia. The reasons for this are: first, most of the waterfalls are far from the cities; second, Africa's industries are so few that there is little demand for electric power. As more factories are built, more power will be needed.

Almost half of the world's gold is mined in Africa, mainly in the Republic of South Africa. The mining and processing of gold gives jobs to four out of five of the hired workers of the Republic. Diamonds of high quality, also mined in the Republic, are used to make jewelry. The Katanga area of Zaire (the Congo) produces much of the world's supply of industrial diamonds. These low quality diamonds are used in factories for cutting and grinding, because diamonds are the hardest mineral known.

Large deposits of uranium are found in Zaire (the Congo) and the Republic of South Africa. Uranium is used in the making of atomic energy. Uranium is also mined in Rhodesia, Zambia, Malawi, Tanzania and Southwest Africa.

More copper is mined in Africa than anywhere else in the world except for the United States. Cobalt, used in the manufacture of steel, is mined in Zambia. Ghana has large deposits of manganese, gold, diamonds and bauxite (used in making alumi-

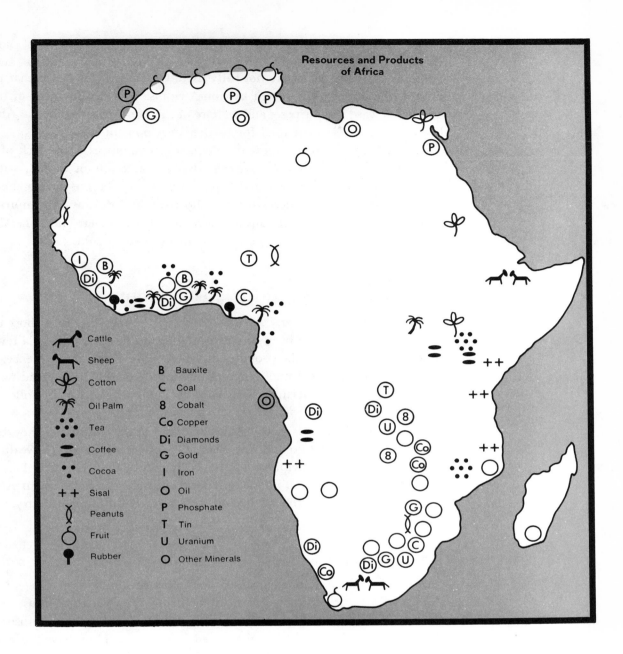

Resources and Products of Africa

Cattle	B	Bauxite
Sheep	C	Coal
Cotton	8	Cobalt
Oil Palm	Co	Copper
Tea	Di	Diamonds
Coffee	G	Gold
Cocoa	I	Iron
Sisal	O	Oil
Peanuts	P	Phosphate
Fruit	T	Tin
Rubber	U	Uranium
	O	Other Minerals

num). The small nation of Guinea has the world's largest supply of bauxite. Nigeria has rich supplies of tin. Iron ore deposits are found in Guinea, Liberia and Sierra Leone. Zinc, radium, chromite, asbestos and manganese are found in Katanga and Zambia.

Great forests still cover about one-third of Sub-Saharan Africa. From certain trees come the raw materials for many waxes and medicines. In the rain forests are valuable hardwood trees (mahogany, ebony). African forests can supply the world with by-products of wood, including cellulose, plastics and industrial alcohol.

However, fuels used to supply power are scarce. There is little coal, except in the Republic of South Africa. There is almost no oil in the region, except for the offshore wells near Nigeria. We have already noted that the water power resources have not been used to a great extent.

Poor Use of Resources

Most of Africa's riches are not fully used. One reason for this is that until recently most of the mines were owned by non-Africans. The development of the mines was directed toward the purposes and welfare of the non-Africans, not the Africans. Profits left Africa and were not used for further development.

A second reason for the slow development of resources is the lack of capital. The production of hydroelectric power needs large amounts of capital, with little hope for profit during the early years. Power is necessary for the development of Africa's minerals. Money is also necessary to build roads and railways, to improve transportation and communication. Roads are needed to get to where the minerals are located, and to get the minerals to where they can be used or sold.

The Desire for Industrial Development

Take a walk through any African city. Visit its markets. In a short time you will learn that Africans have been bitten by a "bug." The "bug" causes a fever of activity. The fever started with the promises of a better life after independence. It has grown with Africans' increased knowledge of the outside world. It is spreading rapidly. The Africans want to modernize. The road to modernization must follow the path of industrialization.

Almost all of Africa's new nations want to build industry. They believe industrialization to be the golden key that will unlock the door to wealth and power. Factories, as we know them, have never been seen by most Africans. Large steel plants, airplane factories, automobile factories and shipyards do not exist in Africa. In some African states we find the beginning steps toward building industry.

Why Industry Has Not Developed

Africa has not developed industry for many reasons.

First of all, for industry and manufacturing to grow, there must be people who want to buy and can pay for what is made. Most Africans are subsistence farmers. They produce much of what they need themselves. They have little or no money to buy manufactured goods.

Second, to build industry there is a great need for capital. Money must be saved by the people to invest, or to be given to the government in the form of taxes. When a new nation starts with very little in the form of capital, development is slow and difficult. The average yearly income in Africa, south of the Sahara, is often not higher than two hundred dollars per person and, in some countries, is as low as fifty dollars. With this as the fact, little money can be saved or taxed to make industry grow.

Climate also has held back industrial development. The high temperature and humidity are harmful to both man and machines. Workers find it difficult to work in the heat, and machines rust and break down more quickly. In drier climates sand and dust get into machinery and cause breakdowns.

Industrial development needs skilled workers. Most Africans have not had the opportunity to go to school and learn the skills necessary to aid industrial development.

Country	% Literacy	Persons Per Teacher
CAMEROON	7	360
ETHIOPIA	5	2,000
GHANA	25	151
KENYA	30	287
MADAGASCAR	35	601
MALAWI	5-10	420
MALI	5	1,017
NIGERIA	30-35	531
RHODESIA	24	190
SOUTH AFRICA	45	219
TANZANIA	5-10	729
UGANDA	25	430
ZAIRE	30	274
UNITED STATES	98	85

Without a good system of transportation and communication there can be little industrial and economic development. Africa's present road and rail systems are clearly not good enough for modern industry. In all of Sub-Saharan Africa there are less than 40,000 miles of railroad track, and a third of this is found in the Republic of South Africa. Sub-Saharan Africa has about one mile of track for every 350 square miles of territory. Most of the rail lines are old and in poor condition. They were built in colonial times to meet military, not economic needs. There are almost no rail connections between African countries. Africa also lacks good harbors because of its regular coastline, and much money is needed to build artificial ports. Little money is left for improving inland water and land routes.

Finally economic development can only happen when there is peace and stability in the African states. Yet, as we have seen, tribal rivalries and tensions exist in many nations. Rival political leaders are fighting for power. This situation does not lend itself to outside investment necessary for development. Nor does it allow for continuous planning and policy for development.

African Industrial Accomplishments

As yet, there are few large factories in Africa which can produce heavy machines, cars, tractors or locomotives in great quantities. However, there is an increasing number of light industries which make goods for the consumer.

In many cities and towns there are factories which make soap, canned vegetables and fruits, and cloth. There are also some meat packing plants, furniture factories, sugar refineries and flour mills. All these products are used chiefly as consumer goods.

Africans have also developed industries to process and refine the raw materials of their countries. Mills and factories have been built to press the oils from the oil palm fruit, the cottonseed and the peanut. Latex from the rubber trees is made into sheets of crépe rubber. Logs are cut into lumber, and some of the wood is used in making furniture. Ores such as copper and chromite are processed at smelters close to the mines.

Africans for centuries have been skilled craftsmen. By hand they have made tools, household goods, and other items. These handicraft skills are still being used today. Skilled Nigerians make high quality Morocco leather goods. In Ghana gold thread is woven into cotton goods to make them more attractive. Woven blankets, beautiful rugs, and wood and ivory carvings are other handicrafts of the people. Often these skills are handed down for generations from family to family.

Development of African Trade

Trade has always been important in the development of any nation. Since 1945 African export trade has increased almost 700 percent. The story of imports from other countries is very much the same. The chart below will show you the amount of trade carried on by selected countries.

AFRICAN INTERNATIONAL TRADE IN 1976 (Selected Countries)

Country	Exports (in millions of dollars)	Imports (in millions of dollars)	Trade Balance (in millions of dollars)	Leading Trading Partners Exports	Imports
Cameroon	549	629	− 80	France 27%	France 46%
Ethiopia	375	342	+ 33	U.S. 20%	Saudi Arabia 15%
Ghana	881	937	− 56	Great Brit. 15%	U.S. 16%
Kenya	891	870	+ 21	West. Germ. 13%	Great Brit. 19%
Madagascar	202	315	− 113	France 34%	France 36%
Malawi	98	124	− 26	Great Brit. 42%	South Africa 29%
Mali	190	78	+ 112	France 27%	France 24%
Nigeria	10,771	8,213	+2,558	U.S. 29%	Great Brit. 23%
Rhodesia	14	89	− 75	Zambia 25%	Great Brit. 30%
South Africa	7,874	6,769	+1,105	Great Brit. 25%	U.S. 22%
Tanzania	644	536	+ 108	West Germ. 14%	Great Brit. 12%
Uganda	153	368	− 215	U.S. 33%	Kenya 50%
Zaire	841	1,391	− 550	Belgium-Luxembourg 38%	U.S. 18%

SOURCES: *Encyclopaedia Britannica*; Bureau of Statistics, International Monetary Fund.

UNITED STATES TRADE WITH SUB-SAHARAN AFRICA
(values in millions of dollars)

	Exports 1976	Exports 1977	Imports 1976	Imports 1977
GHANA	133	146	162	224
IVORY COAST	64	89	263	332
KENYA	43	77	66	98
LIBERIA	92.4	100	105.3	114.9
NIGERIA	770	958	5,251	6,440
SOUTH AFRICA	1,458.1	1,121.5	526.8	948.7
TANZANIA	36	39	52	82
UGANDA	6.3	7.4	120.3	227
ZAIRE	99	114	200	180

SOURCE: Bureau of Statistics, International Monetary Fund, *Direction of Trade.*

The success of African development plans depends a great deal on foreign aid. Loans or gifts from other nations and from international organizations must continue to flow into Africa, or development cannot progress. The United States gave about two hundred million dollars in aid to Africa in 1967. France and Great Britain are also large givers of aid. Aid from the Soviet Union is small, but it is increasing.

Foreign aid is a help, but it cannot solve the many economic and developmental problems facing Africa. The Africans must face and solve the problems in their own way and over a long period.

Summary of Key Ideas

Africa - South of the Sahara

A. **Size and diversity of geographic features have greatly affected Africa's past and present.**

   1. Deserts have to some degree isolated Sub-Saharan Africa from the outside world.

   2. The narrow coastal plain, jungles and a steep escarpment have prevented greater contacts between Africa and the world.

   3. The rivers serve as centers of development and population, but, by their nature, have not been useful for transportation and communication.

   4. The Great Rift Valley has divided Africa from itself.

   5. Africa's vast size has led to the development of varied cultures and civilizations.

   6. The regular coastline has retarded the development of harbors, trade and a sea-faring tradition, thus furthering isolation.

   7. There are at least five distinct climatic regions: tropical rain forest, savanna, steppe, desert, and Mediterranean.

B. **African cultures and societies are varied and complex.**

   1. People of many races, religions, languages and cultures live in Africa.

   2. Tribal society is central to the social structure, political organization and economic activity of Africa.

   3. Tribal structure is based on family and kinship relationships.

   4. Tribal societies have played an important role in Africa's history.

   5. African art is rich and varied in terms of form, style and technique.

   6. The transition from tribal to modern, industrial society is changing African traditions and institutions rapidly. Great problems have also resulted.

C. **The history of Sub-Saharan Africa has been a long and continuous process.**

   1. European and American awareness of African history is filled with myths, such as their "backwardness."

   2. There is some archaeological evidence that earliest man made his home in Africa.

   3. Much of the story of Africa and its heritage has been transmitted orally.

   4. Ancient Egyptian civilization influenced, and was influenced by, the rest of Africa (religion, government, economy, technology, language).

   5. Ancient empires flourished in Africa (Kush, Axum).

6. Outside influences have had great effects on African culture and society (Islam, as a religion and way of life; the impact of Western imperialism on African culture and development).

7. Empires such as Ghana, Mali, Songhai, Zimbabwe flourished in Africa.

8. The European slave trade reduced the population of the continent and weakened the economic, cultural and political institutions. It greatly speeded up the decline of African kingdoms.

9. The scramble for African colonies by the Europeans in the 19th and 20th centuries led to a partition of Africa among these Europeans.

10. Nationalism in Africa resulted from Western influences, and led to the development of independence movements.

11. World War I and World War II speeded up the movement toward independence.

12. There are now forty independent nations in Africa with more in view.

D. **Economic development is the key to the future of Africa.**

1. Agriculture is the most important economic activity in Africa. Mining is the most important industry.

2. Few areas in Africa possess good soils.

3. Agriculture is divided between subsistence and plantation (cash-crop) farming.

4. Natural resources are varied and in excellent supply. Only coal and oil are lacking in great quantities.

5. Resources have not been developed to their greatest potential.

E. **Sub-Saharan Africa faces all of the problems that developing nations have.**

1. African expectations are rising from a life of mere survival to expectations of a modern life of abundance.

2. Modern political patterns of Africa reflect colonial rule by Europeans. Political divisions were made with little understanding of or regard for local conditions, customs and traditions.

3. Tribalism and nationalism have caused conflicts in many African states (e.g., Nigeria, Ghana, Sudan, Ethiopia).

4. Political life in many African nations is controlled by one political party.

5. The lack of political stability is a grave problem for African nations.

F. **African nations play a vital role in world affairs.**

1. The forty-four nations of Africa have great influence in the United Nations.

2. Countries of East and West try to gain the support of African states by giving economic and military assistance.

3. Apartheid has become an international issue resulting from the subjugation of a majority, black African group by a minority, white African group in South Africa.

UNIT IV

Exercises and Questions

Vocabulary

Directions: Match the words in Column *A* with the correct meaning in Column *B*.

Column A

1. fetish
2. tribe
3. terra cotta
4. missionary
5. polygyny
6. clan

7. imperialism

8. nationalism

9. anthropologist
10. literacy
11. secede

Column B

(a) the ability to read.

(b) a person who tries to spread his religion.

(c) a group of related families.

(d) when a strong nation takes over a weaker nation.

(e) a person who studies man's past.

(f) a group of people who share the same customs and language and believe they have descended from a common ancestor.

(g) an object thought to have magical powers.

(h) having several wives at the same time.

(i) baked clay used to make art objects.

(j) love of country above all else.

(k) to leave or break away; separate.

Column A

1. escarpment
2. isolation
3. plateau
4. latitude
5. topography
6. altitude
7. canyon

Column B

(a) area that is near the equator.

(b) used in making rope.

(c) measures distance from sea level.

(d) sharp, steep cliffs.

(e) description of the earth's surface.

(f) deep cuts in the earth's surface.

(g) where the river begins.

8. sisal

9. tropical

10. source

11. reserves

(h) cut off, separated from other people.

(i) fairly flat land high above sea level.

(j) measures distance from the equator.

(k) land set aside for Africans in South Africa.

Who Am I?

Directions: Select the name of the correct person.

Mansa Musa
Henry Stanley
David Livingstone
Jomo Kenyatta
Sekou Touré

Vasco da Gama
Dr. Leakey
King Nzinga
Mungo Park
Kwame Nkrumah

1. I was a European missionary and explorer. I hoped to end the slave trade. ....

2. I was famous for reaching India by sailing around Africa. ....

3. I am an African nationalist. I am president of Kenya today. ....

4. I explored the Niger River. ....

5. I found the oldest human bones in Africa. ....

6. I was famous for my pilgrimage to Mecca. I impressed everyone with my wealth in gold. ....

7. I was the newspaper reporter who found Livingstone. ....

8. I ruled the Congo nation at the end of the 15th century. I admired the culture of Portugal. ....

9. I was an African nationalist. I became the first president of Ghana. ....

10. I led my nation to independence from the French. I am the president of Guinea today. ....

Sources of Information

Directions: Which of the below sources would be the best place to find information about the following.

DICTIONARY   ATLAS   INDEX   TABLE OF CONTENTS   ENCYCLOPEDIA

1. The distance from Capetown, South Africa, to Nairobi, Kenya.

2. A chapter in your Social Studies book dealing with the Land and People of Africa, South of the Sahara.

3. The meaning of the word *culture*.

4. A detailed account of the life of Jomo Kenyatta.

5. The pages in your Social Studies book discussing David Livingstone.

6. The pronunciation of the word *escarpment*.

7. The capital of Zaire.

8. The different units that are covered in your Social Studies textbook.

9. Pictures of the different peoples who live in Africa.

10. How many pages in your book deal with the minerals of Africa.

Pictogram Exercise

Directions: Study the pictogram entitled "A Kikuyu Homestead." Tell whether you agree or disagree with the following statements. Give reasons for your answers.

1. The Kikuyu are farmers and herders.

2. Water for the crops comes from irrigation ditches.

3. Kikuyus have little to do with other tribes.

4. Kikuyu men and women have different jobs to do.

5. Kikuyu women move to their husbands' families' homestead after marriage.

6. The Kikuyu are religious people.

7. The Kikuyu live in buildings made of brick.

8. The main crop of the Kikuyu is wheat.

9. The Kikuyu use all of their fields for raising crops.

10. The land belonging to the Kikuyu is mainly rocky and desert.

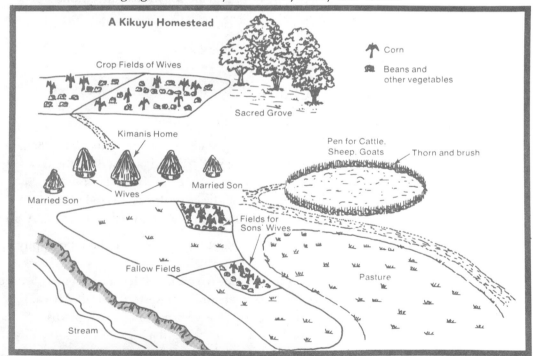

Credit: New York State Education Dept. publication *Teaching About Africa*.
1970. Bureau of Secondary Curriculum Development

True or False?

Directions: Tell whether the following statements are true or false. Correct the false statements.

1. All of Africa is hot and humid.

2. Most of Africa is jungle.

3. The Sahara Desert is larger than the United States.

4. In most of Africa when a young couple marries they move into an apartment of their own.

5. Africans are usually very proud of their tribal mark.

6. A member of a tribe obeys the decisions of the elders whether he likes them or not.

7. African art shows the human body the way it actually is.

8. Most African sculpture was made of marble.

9. Africa was never civilized before the Europeans came.

10. Africans traded their gold in exchange for salt.

11. European traders raided African villages to obtain slaves.

12. Africa continued to progress despite the slave trade.

13. Africa was known as the Dark Continent because most Africans belong to the Negroid race.

14. The purpose of the Mau Mau rebellion was to drive the British out of Kenya.

15. Africa depends on foreign aid for industrialization.

16. Most African farmers can be called subsistence farmers.

17. Cacao is used in the making of soap.

Multiple Choice

Directions: Select the letter of the correct answer.

1. Which of the following statements is true about the Sahara Desert?
   (a) The Sahara is the world's second largest desert.
   (b) Most of the Sahara is a sandy, dry wasteland.
   (c) The Sahara was not always as dry as it is today.
   (d) The Sahara extends from the Atlantic Ocean to the Arabian Sea.

2. Which of the following does *not* describe the topography of Sub-Saharan Africa?
   (a) Most of Sub-Saharan Africa is 500 feet or lower in elevation.
   (b) There is a large plateau in the eastern part of Africa.
   (c) Sub-Saharan Africa has very narrow coastal plains.
   (d) The coastline of Africa is regular.

3. Which of the rivers of Africa has its source in Lake Victoria?
   (a) Niger   (b) Nile   (c) Zambesi   (d) Congo (Zaire)

4. The Rift of Africa is a

   (a) large lake   (b) deep canyon   (c) deep sea   (d) plateau

5. Traveling is often difficult on Africa's rivers because
   (a) most of the rivers flow inland
   (b) most of the rivers are frozen part of the year
   (c) many rivers have rapids and falls
   (d) there is a lack of boats

6. Most of the Europeans settled in the highland areas of East and
   South Africa because
   (a) the climate is cooler
   (b) the people were friendlier
   (c) trading opportunities were greater
   (d) the land was unsettled

7. The Benguela current
   (a) brings plenty of rain to West Africa
   (b) warms the coast of East Africa
   (c) affects the climate of North Africa
   (d) cools and dries the land on the southwest side of Africa

8. Which of the following statements is true about rainfall in Africa?
   (a) About 60% of Africa does not receive enough rainfall to support
       a farming population.
   (b) Rainfall in most of Africa is seasonal.
   (c) It rarely rains in the desert.
   (d) All of the above.

9. West Africa has been called "The White Man's Grave" because
   (a) many wars were fought here in which white men were killed
   (b) Africans living here attacked all foreigners
   (c) the rain forest is hot, rainy, and unhealthy
   (d) none of these

10. All of the following are true about the African people *except* which statement?
    (a) There are great physical differences among the Africans.
    (b) Africans are different from each other in culture.
    (c) Most Africans look alike.
    (d) Africans have intermarried with people of different races.

11. Most of the people living in Sub-Saharan Africa belong to the
    (a) Caucasoid race
    (b) Negroid race
    (c) Mongoloid race
    (d) none of these

12. Swahili is
    (a) the main language spoken in West Africa
    (b) the main language spoken in East Africa
    (c) the language spoken mainly by Pygmies
    (d) all of these

13. Which of the following is true about language in Africa?
    (a) There are hundreds of different languages spoken in Africa.
    (b) Often Africans living the same country find it difficult to communicate with one another.
    (c) English and French are often used by Africans to speak to each other.
    (d) All of these.

14. An "extended family" consists of
    (a) several generations living together
    (b) the father, mother and their children
    (c) the bride, groom and their in-laws
    (d) all the people of the tribe

15. African men may have several wives because
    (a) they want to have many children
    (b) they want the family name to live on
    (c) they will have more workers to help them in the fields
    (d) all of these

16. All of the following are true of the "bride price" *except* which statement?
    (a) It is usually in the form of cattle or sheep.
    (b) It is a symbol that the marriage is legitimate.
    (c) It is proof that African men buy their wives.
    (d) It compensates the father of the bride for losing a worker.

17. Which of the following statements is *not* true about African tribes?
    (a) The African can count on his tribe to protect him and help him.
    (b) The tribe is considered to be more important than the individual.
    (c) All African tribes are about the same in size.
    (d) Disobeying the customs and laws of the tribe results in serious punishment.

18. As more people move to the cities the importance of the tribe is expected to
    (a) increase   (b) decrease   (c) remain the same   (d) disappear

19. Many of the new African nations are having difficulty uniting their people because
    (a) many people are more loyal to their tribes than they are to the nation
    (b) there are many disloyal Europeans
    (c) most African nations are still ruled by the Europeans
    (d) all of these

20. All of the following are African tribes *except*
    (a) Ashanti   (b) Kalahari   (c) Kikuyu   (d) Yoruba

21. Which of the following is true of African religions?
    (a) Africans do not believe in a Supreme Being or God.
    (b) Africans worship rivers, trees and mountains.
    (c) Africans worship their dead ancestors.
    (d) Africans believe that the spirits of their ancestors can protect or harm them.

22. The diviner (witch doctor) is important in most African societies because
    (a) he is responsible for maintaining law and order in the tribe
    (b) it is believed that he can find the cause and cure for many misfortunes
    (c) he is in charge of educating the young to be loyal members of the tribe
    (d) all of these

23. All of the following are true of African art *except* which statement?
    (a) Exaggeration of the head and reproductive organs was common.
    (b) Poses showing movement were preferred by the artists.
    (c) Much of the sculpture was what we would call abstract.
    (d) Africans painted few portraits.

24. Which of the following are correctly paired together?
    (a) Ife—Rock paintings
    (b) Benin—Bronze heads
    (c) Nok—Lost wax process
    (d) Bushmen—Terra cotta figurines

25. Anthropologists believe that man originated in Africa because
    (a) Africa probably had the best climate for farming
    (b) there are many African folk tales which talk about the beginning of the human race
    (c) the oldest known human bones have been found in Africa
    (d) all of these

26. Cave paintings found in the Sahara Desert are evidence that
    (a) thousands of years ago the Sahara was not a desert
    (b) people and animals once lived in the Sahara
    (c) the Sahara was very different from what it is today
    (d) all of these

27. The very first people earned a living by
    (a) farming and hunting
    (b) mining and trading
    (c) hunting and gathering
    (d) herding and weaving

28. Pictures of giraffes found in China and dating from the 5th century are evidence that
    (a) China had many giraffes at that time
    (b) the Chinese were good artists
    (c) trade existed between China and Africa
    (d) none of these

29. Trade was very important in early African history because
    (a) the Africans learned how to grow crops such as yams and bananas from the people of Southeast Asia
    (b) trade brought wealth and new ideas to Africa
    (c) important trading cities grew up
    (d) all of these

30. All of the following are true about the kingdoms of West Africa *except* which statement?
    (a) Glass was used in Ghana before it was used in Europe.
    (b) The kingdoms became wealthy from the gold-salt trade.
    (c) The governments were poorly run—there was injustice and insecurity.
    (d) The kingdoms grew powerful because they used iron weapons and tools.

31. Timbuctu was famous as
    (a) an important center of learning
    (b) the scene of a famous battle
    (c) the headquarters of the slave trade
    (d) a legendary city

32. The earliest kingdom in West Africa was
    (a) Songhai   (b) Ghana   (c) Mali   (d) Ethiopia

33. Islam spread to Africa in all of the following ways *except*
    (a) The Arabs conquered South Africa and forced the people to convert.
    (b) Arabs married African women and spread their culture.
    (c) Arabs spread their religion by controlling much of Africa's trade.
    (d) The rulers of Mali and Songhai became Moslems and converted many of their subjects.

34. Which of the following is *not* true about the Arab role in Africa?
    (a) The Arabs probably began the African slave trade.
    (b) Arab geographers left many records providing much information about African life.
    (c) The Arabic language and Bantu language were combined to form a new language—Swahili.
    (d) The Arab influence on Africa was not great.

35. The Europeans became interested in Africa in the 15th century because they
    (a) wanted to settle in Africa
    (b) were interested in African culture
    (c) were looking for a new route to the Indies
    (d) were looking for markets for their manufactured goods

36. The first European nation to set up trading posts along the coast of Africa was
    (a) Spain   (b) England   (c) Portugal   (d) France

37. The trading cities of East Africa declined during the 16th century because
    (a) they fought many wars against each other
    (b) their trade and wealth were taken over by Portugal
    (c) bad weather conditions resulted in poor crops
    (d) all of these

38. Which of the following statements is *not* true?
    (a) Slavery never existed in Africa before the arrival of the Europeans.
    (b) Long before the Europeans came African slaves were being sold in India and other places of the East.
    (c) Africans raided the villages of other African tribes to capture slaves for the Europeans.
    (d) On a slave ship the slaves were packed in so tightly they barely had room to move.

39. The slave trade became very important to the Europeans because
    (a) they needed slaves to work on the plantations in Europe
    (b) they needed slaves to work in the factories of Europe
    (c) fortunes could be made by using slaves on the sugar plantations of the West Indies
    (d) all of these

40. The slave trade was finally ended when
    (a) the Africans threatened to declare war on the Europeans
    (b) slavery was abolished in the United States, Brazil and Cuba
    (c) the United Nations demanded an end to the slave trade
    (d) the Europeans realized they were doing the wrong thing

41. The explorers of Africa were important because
    (a) they explored the four great African rivers
    (b) they wrote books and drew maps of the places they explored
    (c) they provided the Europeans with much information about Africa and its people
    (d) all of the above reasons

42. Europeans became interested in Africa after 1880 because they
    (a) were looking for a new route to the Indies
    (b) needed slaves and ivory
    (c) wanted raw materials and markets
    (d) wanted to help the Africans

43. By 1914, most of Africa was controlled by
    (a) Spain and Portugal
    (b) Britain and France
    (c) the United States and the Soviet Union
    (d) Germany and Holland

44. Which of the following statements is *not* true?
   (a) By 1914 there were only two independent countries in Sub-Saharan Africa.
   (b) African rulers signed treaties with the Europeans which they did not understand.
   (c) African rulers sometimes asked the Europeans to come in and protect them.
   (d) Belgium was the only European country without colonies in Africa.

45. Under the Europeans the tribal chiefs lost much of their power because
   (a) Africans realized that the chiefs no longer made all the decisions and so they did not feel that they had to obey them
   (b) Africans who became Christians didn't believe that the chiefs were appointed by God
   (c) wealthy people became more important than the chiefs
   (d) all of these

46. The first African nationalists were
   (a) the people who had received a Western education
   (b) the tribal chiefs
   (c) the farmers and herders
   (d) none of these

47. Which of the following statements is *not* true?
   (a) Nationalism spread greatly among the African people after World War II.
   (b) By 1969 most of the countries in Africa were independent.
   (c) The Europeans fought long and bitter wars to hold on to their African colonies.
   (d) Most of Africa became free without bloodshed or violence.

48. An important cash crop of Sub-Saharan Africa is
   (a) corn   (b) wheat   (c) cacao   (d) barley

49. The tsetse fly carries the disease known as
   (a) malaria   (b) sleeping sickness   (c) small pox   (d) yellow fever

50. All of the following are true about African agriculture *except*
   (a) Most Africans use the most modern farming methods and machinery.
   (b) Much of Africa's soil is very poor.
   (c) Too much or too little rainfall is a problem in much of Africa.
   (d) Africans practice "slash and burn" methods to fertilize the soil.

51. Less hydroelectric power has been developed in Africa because
   (a) there are few water power resources in Africa
   (b) there has been little demand for electric power in the past

(c) African industries use other sources of power

(d) the water is used to irrigate the soil

52. Which of the following groups of minerals are found in *great* quantities in Sub-Saharan Africa?

(a) uranium, coal, gold

(b) diamonds, copper, silver

(c) oil, cobalt, iron ore

(d) diamonds, uranium, copper

53. Which of the following minerals is used in making aluminum?

(a) diamonds   (b) bauxite   (c) cobalt   (d) uranium

54. Africa has a scarcity of

(a) fuels   (b) water power   (c) minerals   (d) lumber

55. A subsistence farmer is one who

(a) produces a crop for sale

(b) produces only cereal crops

(c) produces mainly for his own needs

(d) produces what he is told to produce

56. Which of the following statements is true about literacy in Africa?

(a) Literacy is no longer a problem in Africa.

(b) Nigeria has the highest literacy of African countries.

(c) Cameroon has the lowest literacy rate in Africa.

(d) No African country has more than half its people literate.

57. The type of industry one would most likely find in Africa is

(a) steel factories

(b) airplane factories

(c) food packing plants

(d) missile plants

Thought Questions

1. How did geography isolate Africa from the rest of the world?

2. (a) What are the factors that cause the different climates of Africa?

   (b) What effect does climate have on the people of Africa?

3. "If you have seen one African you have seen them all." Do you agree or disagree with this statement? Give reasons for your answer.

4. How does the African family differ from the American family?

5. How does the African family take care of its members?

6. How is an African's whole way of life influenced by his belonging to a tribe?

7. Why have the accomplishments of Africa in art and music not been appreciated or recognized until recently?

8. Why can we say that masks served a vital function in African life?

9. Why can it be said today that Africa's accomplishments in art are the equal of that produced by any other civilization?

10. A careful study of African history shows that Africa was never completely isolated from the rest of the world, but merely less accessible. Give evidence to prove or disprove this statement.

11. Cultural diffusion has been as important to Africa as it has been to other parts of the world. What evidence of cultural diffusion do we have from African history?

12. What are some of the things anthropologists use to study man's ancient past?

13. Why can we say that the kingdoms of West Africa reached a high level of civilization?

14. Why was it not difficult for Africans to become Moslems?

15. How did the slave trade affect Africa?

16. How did the missionaries affect developments in Africa, South of the Sahara?

17. How did European nations gain control of African areas?

18. Why did the European nations divide up Africa among themselves?

19. How did European imperalism affect Africa?

20. Why did Africa's nationalists want independence from the Europeans?

21. Why did World War II greatly strengthen African nationalism?

22. Why is agriculture "the lifeblood" of the African economy?

23. (a) What problems are faced by African farmers?
    (b) If you were an African leader, what solutions might you suggest?

24. Why have Africans not made the best use of their large supply of natural resources?

25. (a) What problems do Africans face in trying to develop their industries?
    (b) What solutions might be suggested to solve these problems?

26. As a reporter, describe the changes that have taken place in Africa during the past 5 years.

27. (a) Why can we call the Sahel Drought a major disaster?
    (b) How did the drought in Sahel come about?

28. How is the South African *Homelands* program similar to the United States' creation of Indian reservations in the 1800s? How is it different? (Clues: forcible removal, citizenship)

Rhodesia's Joshua Nkomo, leader of the African National Council. *Credit: United Press International*

Lt. Gen. Olusegun Obasanjo, president of Nigeria. (*Top*)   **Credit: United Nations/Y. Nagata**

Masai tribesmen tending cattle in Kenya. Their herds of longhorns once provided for all their needs; now a continuing drought has turned their lands into dustbowls. (*Bottom*)   **Credit: United Press International**

Puzzle

Directions: Place the words below in their proper place in the puzzle.

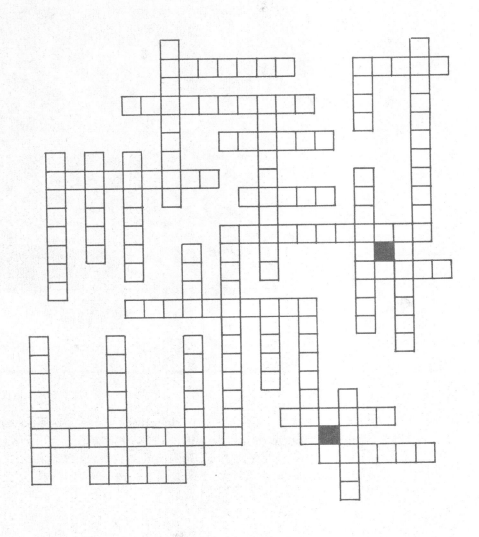

4 LETTERS
CLAN
GOLD

5 LETTERS
CACAO
IVORY
SLAVE
TRADE
TRIBE

6 LETTERS
EMPIRE
FETISH
JUNGLE
KIKUYU
SOURCE

7 LETTERS
MARKETS
PLATEAU
SWAHILI
URANIUM

8 LETTERS
DIAMONDS
EXTENDED
LITERACY
TROPICAL

9 LETTERS
APARTHEID
ISOLATION
SCULPTURE

10 LETTERS
BRIDE PRICE
TERRA COTTA
TOPOGRAPHY

11 LETTERS
AGRICULTURE
IMPERIALISM
NATIONALISM

12 LETTERS
INDEPENDENCE

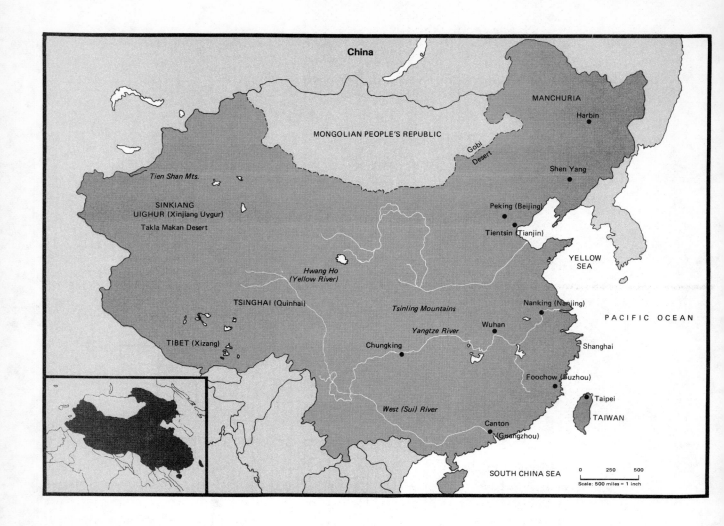

China

MANCHURIA

MONGOLIAN PEOPLE'S REPUBLIC

Harbin

Gobi Desert

Shen Yang

Tien Shan Mts.

SINKIANG UIGHUR (Xinjiang Uygur)

Takla Makan Desert

Peking (Beijing)

Tientsin (Tianjin)

YELLOW SEA

Hwang Ho (Yellow River)

TSINGHAI (Quinhai)

Tsinling Mountains

Nanking (Nanjing)

PACIFIC OCEAN

Yangtze River

Wuhan

TIBET (Xizang)

Chungking

Shanghai

Foochow (Buzhou)

West (Sui) River

Taipei

Canton (Guangzhou)

TAIWAN

SOUTH CHINA SEA

0   250   500

Scale: 500 miles = 1 inch

Note: Early in 1979 it was decided to use a different system of transcribing Chinese characters to English. This new system, Pinyin style, spells the names of cities, rivers, and other geographical references slightly different. Note that we have shown both old and new spellings on this map.

UNIT
V China

Topography of China

Geography and Isolation

China, like most other regions, has been influenced by geography. Probably the most important of these geographic factors has been *isolation* (separation). Chinese civilization began and grew in the easternmost part of Asia. It is an area far from other centers of civilization. High mountains and wide deserts isolated this area from other parts of Asia. These natural and protective barriers allowed the Chinese to develop their culture without constant interruption from outside. China also enjoyed conditions favorable for the development of a great culture. Wide plains, fertile soil, great rivers and coastal harbors were used to support a high level of civilization. Geography also explains why Chinese civilization turned out to be *unique* (one of a kind). It developed with only minor contacts with other major cultures and, therefore, only minor instances of cultural diffusion occurred. Where cultural diffusion did take place Chinese culture was diffused into Vietnam, Korea and Japan.

The Chinese call their country *Chung-kuo* 中國 , which means the "Middle Kingdom." To the Chinese, their country is the center of the universe. The name China came from the Ch'in Dynasty (royal family), which created the Chinese Empire more than 2,000 years ago.

Rivers

China is a huge country. It is the third largest in the world (after the Soviet Union and Canada). China was not always as large as it is today. About 3,500 years ago China was located in a small area on the banks of the Yellow River (Huang-ho, in

A natural gas worker at a Takang oilfield. Chinese women play an important role in industrial development. *Credit: Wide World Photos*

Chinese). The Yellow River flows three thousand miles across the North China Plain. Tracing the river's course in reverse, about 400 miles inland you discover the river turns sharply north. About two hundred miles closer to the source (beginning) it turns west again, and then south to Tsinghai (now Quinhai). Geographers call the shape that the Huang-ho forms the great "Horseshoe Bend" of the river.

Here, at the southern, open end of the Horseshoe Bend, Chinese civilization was born. This area was chosen because of its rich, *loess* soil (loess is the German word for wind deposits). The topsoil is renewed every year by rich, new soil brought by winds. In the Horseshoe Bend the loess is sometimes four hundred feet thick. With so much free topsoil delivered every year, it is no wonder the Chinese have been farmers for forty centuries. It was here, in the rich loess highlands of the Horseshoe Bend, that the Chinese built their first capital, An-yang.

The heartland of China has always been located in the eastern section, often called China Proper. The three great rivers (Yellow, Yangtze and West (Sui)) have shaped China's history and life. They are the arteries of China Proper.

The Yellow River takes its name from the color of its waters. The <u>silt</u> (small pieces of earth) from the loess soil muddies the water. Though the Yellow River is not very useful for navigation, its water is important for millions of farmers.

The most important river of China is the Yangtze. The Yangtze is the fifth largest river in the world. The Yangtze is navigable for almost a thousand miles inland from the mouth. For centuries the Chinese have used this river for travel and transportation. Many of China's most important cities are on the Yangtze (Shanghai, Nanking, Hankow, Chungking). The annual (yearly) flooding of the Yangtze brings rich soil to the farmland of the river valley.

Located in the far south, the West (Sui) River flows through rough lands for almost seventeen hundred miles. Canton, an old and famous seaport, lies near the mouth of the river. Since the lower part of the river is navigable, the river serves as a major transportation route.

Coastline

The coastline of China is long and irregular. Along this coast there are many good harbors, such as Darien, Tsingtao, Tientsin, Shanghai, Foochow and Canton (in order from north to south). The irregular coastline also serves as a highway for coastal trade from city to city.

Mountains

Mountains are another feature of China's topography. In the southwest are the Himalayas, which separate China from India. The cold plateau of Tibet lies in these mountains. North of Tibet is Sinkiang, mountainous and difficult to live in. East of Sinkiang is the dry plateau of Inner Mongolia. In the western part of this area is the Gobi Desert. These dry, mountainous lands in which few people live make up about a third of China's land area.

Most of South China is made up of low hills. Between these highlands are fertile river valleys and flat plains. It is in these plains that most of China's people live. In the far north of China is the Manchurian Plain. This plain is almost completely surrounded by mountains.

In the next few years, you will see different spellings of the Chinese cities, rivers, mountains, and provinces. This is because the Western world has shifted its system of spelling out the Chinese characters. The new system being used is the Pinyin style.

Climate

The climate of China can be discussed by comparing its differences in North China and South China. The Tsinling Mountains and the West (Sui) River divide the country.

North China

Summer on the North China Plain is warm and, at times, hot. During the winter fierce northern winds whip across the area, and snowfalls are common. For protection against the cold, the people wear heavy, quilted clothes. North China has little rainfall. The farmers in this part of China have irrigated their lands since ancient times. When the water supply fails, famine results.

South China

The south is very different from the north. Mountains and dense forests cover much of the south. (The north is practically treeless.) This area is warm during most of the year, and the southernmost parts are hot. Winters are much milder than in the north and, in some parts of the south, snow has never fallen. The Tsinling Mountains block the cold northern winds from blowing into the south. Because of the high temperatures and the many forests, the people of South China build wooden houses that can be easily ventilated. (In the north, houses are made of mud or mud-brick.)

The Monsoons

During the summer season, from June through September, drenching rains are brought by the monsoons (moist winds that blow from the Pacific Ocean) and by typhoons. Some areas have so much rain that rivers overflow and flood the land. Again, the Tsinling Mountains play an important role. They act as a barrier between the monsoon winds from the south and the loess winds of the north. The mountains divide the dry wheatlands of the north from the wet rice lands of the south. Rainfall ranges from ten to twenty-five inches in the north to between forty and ninety inches in the south. While northerners can count on a growing season of only five to eight months, crops are grown the year round in most of South China.

The West

As you move west in China, the land becomes drier and drier. Roughly half the land is steppe and the other half desert. It becomes drier for two reasons. First, the mountains block the rainfall carried by winds blowing from the ocean. Second, western China is far from the ocean, in the middle of the vast land area of Asia. The winters here are bitter cold and the summers very hot.

The People of China and Their Way of Life

It is difficult to describe the Chinese people. In the past, so little was known of China that legends and myths grew about its people. It would be difficult to find two people who would agree on "Who are the Chinese?"

Physical Characteristics

The Chinese people belong to the Mongoloid race. Anthropologists say that people of this race have yellowish or light brown skin, straight and coarse black hair, and almond-shaped eyes. (A skin fold in the inner corner of the eye makes it look slanted or almond shaped.) But all Chinese do not look alike. For one thing, skin coloring varies. In the north the Chinese skin coloring is light, while in the south it is much darker. In some parts of China less than half the people have the almond-shaped eyes. The northern Chinese are described as tall and slow moving, while the southern Chinese are thought of as small and active. But hundreds of thousands of exceptions exist.

The great majority of Chinese call themselves "Han people." However, about thirty-five million Chinese are not Han people. Among this group are Kazakhs and Uighurs of Sinkiang, Tibetans, Li people of the south and Penglung people of Southwest China.

Character of the Chinese People

The Chinese people believe that they have the longest history, and the most civilized culture of any people in the world. As a result, they are a self-confident people, proud of their heritage.

The Chinese people believe that if a government becomes too harsh and it cannot keep peace and order, it is right to rebel and set up a new government. They have become masters of the ways of secret societies and secret activity. Chinese history is full of stories of groups overthrowing emperors and setting up new ones.

The Chinese are considered to be skillful and hard working. Chinese workers helped build the transcontinental railroad across the United States in the nineteenth century. The Chinese have a reputation for patience, but they will fight for their rights.

The Chinese have established businesses in all major areas of modern life. They have become bankers, plantation owners, mine operators, merchants, money lenders, and leaders in other types of businesses in Singapore, Hong Kong, Rio de Janeiro, San Francisco and New York.

Above all, the Chinese people have a sense of history. They call history a "mirror," in which they can see the past, the present and the future. No Chinese sees himself apart from other men. He is an important part of the history, tradition, language and culture of China. Thus, the Chinese people attach great importance to historical writing. No other people have so long and continuous a record of the past as the Chinese.

The Chinese people have had the ability to wait, not to be impatient or in a hurry. Peoples of the West, especially Americans, find great difficulty in understanding this about the Chinese. An old Chinese proverb says, "If a solution to a problem is not found now or in our lifetime, it will be found in the lifetime of my son or grandson." This is a sense of time that comes from 50 centuries of history. It makes it more difficult to talk to the Chinese about quick solutions to problems which are very important to us today.

The Chinese Way of Life

What is the Chinese way of life? For centuries the Chinese people accepted nature as it was. Unlike Westerners, the Chinese people had no interest in changing nature by science to meet their needs and wishes. The secrets of the universe and discovering what controlled the universe did not interest them. Their aim in life was to live in peace with nature, out of respect and fear. Chinese art often shows tiny man overshadowed by the great peaks and other natural features. The Chinese believe man is a small part of a great universal machine.

Most Chinese live in villages, and often spend their entire lives in their local district. Since they were tied to the land only a very small number would leave home to work, to trade or to serve in the government. The need to take care of the parents as well as respect for ancestors also kept the Chinese at home.

Like any other culture, the Chinese culture did change over a long period of time. But the changes in the twentieth century have probably been greater than all the changes in the centuries before.

Acupuncture

Acupuncture is the ancient Chinese medical practice of stimulating certain nerve points with needles. Developed thousands of years ago, acupuncture is used through-

The earliest printed text in the world, dated May 11, 869 A.D., this is part of the Diamond Sutra, a prayer to Buddha. *(Top)* **Credit: British Museum**

Bronze ritual vessel from the Chou Dynasty, 11-10th century B.C. *(Bottom)*

out China as a means of *anesthesia* and as a treatment for illnesses such as appendicitis, asthma, migraine headaches and even deafness.

There are 500 to 800 nerve points in the body that are used in acupuncture. Inserting needles at these specific nerve points, acupuncturists have done things that have amazed Western observers.

Western doctors and other visitors to China have witnessed major operations where needles were used as the only anesthetic, while the patient remained fully conscious. In one such operation which was performed in the City of Hankow, a tumor was removed from the throat of a woman. The woman remained fully conscious during the operation and never twitched. Minutes after the operation was over, she sat up and ate sections of an orange. Then she rose from the operating table, thanked the doctors and walked out. The doctors explained to the American observers that 30 minutes before the operation two needles had been inserted into the nerve points of each wrist, numbing the tumor area. Throughout the operation, the acupuncturists kept twisting the needles. The moment the operation was over they removed them.

Americans have also seen open-heart surgery performed in China in the same manner. In heart surgery, in addition to the needles inserted in the wrists, a needle was placed in each forearm. The chest was opened, a rib removed and the heart exposed. The woman patient remained fully conscious, and while the surgeon cupped her heart in his hand, she drank orange juice through a straw and smiled at the observers.

Chinese doctors admit that they cannot explain acupuncture scientifically, that they do not know *why* it works, but they know that it *does* work. They claim to have cured many cases of deafness in children in this way.

In America there is a great debate over acupuncture at present. Many Americans have become interested in this practice in the last few years and would like to see it accepted by American doctors. Many Americans have gone to China and to Taiwan to learn how acupuncture works. But others remain skeptical. Whether or not acupuncture will become an accepted medical practice in the United States in the future remains to be seen.

Life and Society in Traditional China

Chinese Philosophy: Confucianism and Taoism

The philosophies of Confucianism and Taoism originated between the 5th and 3rd centuries B.C. This was a troubled period for China. There was civil war and great unrest. It was also a time in which the old ideas and values seemed to have lost their importance, and new ones had not yet taken their place. The people of China had two basic needs: to end the bloody wars between the states and to set up a new social order.

During this difficult time the philosophies of Confucianism and Taoism were developed. Confucianism and Taoism are considered philosophies and not religions because they were not concerned with God or life after death. They were mainly concerned with ways of improving society and achieving a better life on earth.

From the 5th century to the 2nd century B.C. these two philosophies as well as a number of others competed with each other. About 100 B.C. Confucianism was adopted by the government as the official philosophy. For the next two thousand years, that is, until the 20th century, Chinese life and society were almost completely modeled after the ideas of Confucius.

Confucianism

Confucius is the Latinized name of Kung Fu-tzu. Confucius was born in 551 B.C. and died in 479 B.C. The philosophy that is known as Confucianism comes mainly from the speeches and writings of Confucius. Disciples (followers) of Confucius, such as Mencius, made important contributions to Confucianism as well. The ideas of Confucianism are found in nine works: the "Four Books" and the "Five Classics."

Confucianism is an ethical system rather than a religion. (Ethics deals with the rights and wrongs of human conduct.) Confucius was mainly concerned with how human beings behaved toward each other. He paid little attention to such matters as sin, salvation and the soul. He developed a system of government, society and justice which we call Confucianism.

Confucius believed that people, because of their nature, desire to live in the company of other people, that is, in society. Only unnatural and abnormal people live outside of society. It is only in society that men reach their fullest development.

The Idea of Jen

One of the most important ideas of Confucianism is expressed in the word "jen." Jen is that human quality which leads people to live in society. The Chinese character jen combines the symbol for *man* and the symbol for *two*. This combination conveys the idea of a relationship between people. No word in English expresses the full meaning of jen. Perhaps the word *sympathy* can give us an idea of what jen is. The idea of sympathy expresses such a close relationship that whatever affects one person affects the other. Sympathy involves a sharing of interests and feelings; an understanding that arises from a common nature.

Jen also involves the desire to help others. You look into yourself for the answers to the problems of others. Self-understanding leads to an understanding of the hopes and fears of others. It also means "Do not do to others what you do not wish yourself."

The Five Basic Relationships

Confucius wanted jen to be expressed in right action. He therefore set up five principal relationships in which people might be involved. According to Confucius, each person had a specific place in society and certain duties to fulfill. Confucius hoped that if people knew what was expected of them in their relations with other people, they would behave correctly. These relationships were: 1. ruler and subject; 2. father and son; 3. elder brother and younger brother; 4. husband and wife; and 5. friend and friend. All, except the last, involve the authority of one person over another.

Power and the right to rule belong to superiors over subordinates; that is, to older people over younger people, to men over women. Each person has to give obedience and respect to his "superior"; the subject to his ruler, the wife to her husband, the son to his parents, and the younger brother to the older brother. The "superior," however, owes loving responsibility to the inferior.

The Family and the State

Confucius placed great importance on the family. Family life was seen as a kind of training ground for life in society. It is at home in the family that the child learns to deal with problems that he will face later in the world. The family is responsible for educating the child to be a good member of society. Confucius emphasized the importance of education, the aim of which is to turn people into good family men and good subjects of the emperor.

The state was regarded as an extension of the family in many ways. The emperor and his officials were referred to as the parents of the people. Subjects owed the same loyalty to their rulers that they owed to the senior members of their family.

However, the emperor had duties to fulfill as well. Confucius believed that for society to be well ordered and for people to live in peace and prosper, it was necessary to have a good government and a virtuous ruler. It was the duty of the emperor and his officials to set a good example for the people. The good example of the ruler would transform the people and make them better. Confucius believed that only the wisest and most humane men should rule. He further believed that if the emperor was not morally perfect, heaven would cause the world to suffer.

The emperor also had to maintain the proper relationship between himself and heaven. Heaven was regarded as the governing authority of the universe and the final judge of right and wrong. It was the duty of the emperor to carry out ceremonies and sacrifices throughout the year. When the emperor did his duty and the officials and common people did theirs, there was harmony in the world. If, on the other hand, the emperor or people failed to carry out their duties, the consequences were national disasters such as floods, droughts, and famine.

For two thousand years Confucianism was the official philosophy of the state. The only way in which a person could achieve an important position in the government or society was by having a good knowledge of Confucianism. To become a government official it was necessary to pass a difficult civil service examination. It took years of studying the ideas of Confucianism to prepare for this examination. This had two unfortunate results. First of all, since the majority of Chinese peasants lived in great poverty, they were unable to spend years studying Confucian philosophy. As a result very few of them ever became part of the ruling group. Only the rich could afford the luxury of years of study, and they became the "scholar-officials" who ruled China. Secondly, since it was Confucianism that kept the leaders in power, these men were opposed to any changes. The Confucianists believed that they were the only civilized community in the world and they looked down on the beliefs and cultures of other people. This attitude made the Chinese unwilling to change their way of life when they were first exposed to Western culture. This unwillingness to adopt Western ideas and techniques in the late 19th and early 20th centuries proved to be disastrous for the Chinese.

Confucius himself was not very interested in the ideas of a God, an after-life, heaven and other things that we associate with religion. However, when Confucianism became the official philosophy of China, religious functions were incorporated into it. Confucius, together with his ancestors and famous followers, became objects of worship. Confucian temples were built all over China and sacrifices and rituals were performed.

Taoism

The philosophy of Taoism takes its name from the Chinese word *Tao* meaning "The Way." The three principal teachers of this philosophy were Lao Tzu, Tang Chu, and Chuang Tzu. According to tradition, Lao Tzu (meaning "Old Master") was the founder of Taoism, but modern scholars have questioned his very existence.

The philosophy of Taoism stated that man should live naturally. Man is happiest when he lives according to his own nature. However, society does not permit man to live naturally. Society forces human beings to live according to the rules of man which are not natural. This results in suffering and problems. To escape from this unhappiness, man must free himself from all the rules that are forced upon him by society. He must find the Tao, or "Way" of the universe.

It is very difficult to say what Tao is. The early Taoists (followers of Taoism) never defined it because they believed that language could not give its exact meaning. "Those who know the Tao do not speak of it; those who speak of it do not know it." The Tao is the unseen power beneath all the life and movement in nature. The Tao is present everywhere in all things. It has no beginning or end. The Tao is the force that gives life and a particular nature to all things. It is the nature of a fish that it cannot live out of water. It is the nature of man that he must breathe air. It is because of Tao that this is so. To act contrary to the Tao or nature; for example, to deprive a fish of water or a man of air, can only be harmful.

The Taoists spoke of a golden age in the past when people lived naturally. They wore the clothes they had woven and ate the food they had grown. All the creatures of sky and earth lived together in peace and harmony. People were not restrained by rules or codes of behavior. They lived and acted spontaneously (freely). But as civilization advanced, this situation changed. People stopped acting naturally. The Taoists believed that society corrupted men and separated them from their true nature. To live in society and obey its rules of behavior is contrary to man's nature and harmful. Men can be truly happy only when they are able to express themselves freely.

Since the Tao exists in everything, the Taoist feels that he possesses all things. He does not fear or desire anything. Because of his union with the Tao everything is part of him and he is part of everything. As a result of man's corruption by society, people fight one another, feel frustrated and live in fear of death. The Taoist has no fear of death. He knows that he is at one with the eternal Tao. To him, death is merely a change of form and has no significance. Being at one with the Tao makes one in complete control of all the things of the universe. The Taoist, therefore, feels that he is the master of the world.

In later years, Taoism came to be associated with spirits to whom the Chinese peasant would turn in times of need. Taoists were called upon to select lucky days for weddings and funerals, to choose sites for housing, and to do other things of this nature.

Taoism had a great influence on the Chinese people and their culture. This can be seen in Chinese literature and painting. Because of its view of nature and the universe, Taoism has fascinated scholars for more than two thousand years.

Social Classes: The Gentry and the Peasants

The Gentry

The gentry and the peasants were the two main classes of traditional Chinese society.

The gentry were at the top of Chinese society. They were the land-owners who possessed vast landed estates. They were also the officials who administered the government of China. The gentry were a leisure class. They looked down upon any kind of physical work. Because of their wealth and comfort they had time to engage in social activities and political affairs. They devoted much time to cultural activities such as poetry, painting, writing, and the art of *calligraphy* or brush-writing.

Economic Characteristics of the Gentry

The gentry received most of their income from the land which they owned. However, they did not cultivate this land themselves, but rented it out to tenants from whom they collected rent. The gentry did not live on their land either. They lived mainly in the towns. This was because the towns were the political and cultural centers. In the towns they could lead a leisurely life. The rents collected from their tenants were usually quite high. With this money they were able to buy such luxuries as paintings, musical instruments, jewelry, clothing of fine silk and different art objects. The towns provided them with amusements and entertainment such as teahouses, restaurants, and theaters.

Those gentry families who stayed in the countryside and lived solely off their land soon became quite poor. In each generation the family property was divided among all the sons, and after a few generations, instead of one large landowning family there were many small landowners.

By moving to the towns the gentry found other sources of income besides the land. Gentry families often added to their incomes by opening shops, usually pawn shops and rice shops. Since the Chinese people frequently lived through periods of economic crisis and needed ready cash, the pawnshops served as banks and lending agencies. The gentry kept the interest rates high. The rice shops also brought the gentry high profits. They would buy the rice immediately after the harvest when it was cheap and store it until it was in short supply. Then they sold it at a high price or loaned it out at a high interest.

Social Characteristics of the Gentry

The gentry lived in large families that sometimes included four or five generations. The head of the family ruled over the family almost in the same manner as the emperor ruled over the state. He had complete authority in all matters and no one questioned anything he did. There was a specific code of behavior which the members of the family followed in their relationships with each other. Much time and care was spent training the younger members of the family in the proper behavior.

Large families gave the gentry power. This power was used by the gentry to maintain its position at the top of Chinese society. In fact, marriage was a way of increasing the power of gentry families. Marriages were arranged to establish alliances among important families. All the family property and wealth was preserved as a unit. The individual members strove to maintain the power and important position of the whole family. However, since there were so many people living together, there was often jealousy and arguing among the family members. While the head of the family was alive he was able to keep the entire family together as one unit. After his death, however, the wives of the sons often influenced their husbands to have the property divided, and the large family was broken up into smaller, independent groups.

Political Characteristics of the Gentry

The Chinese people have always placed great emphasis on education. Scholars and educated men had the highest place in Chinese society. Teachers were held in such high esteem that they were considered to be one of the five objects worthy of worship, the others being heaven, earth, the emperor, and parents. One of the basic ideas of Chinese culture was that only educated people should have government positions.

To become a government official in China it was necessary to pass a difficult civil service examination. Years of studying were required to pass this examination. The gentry were the people who had the money and leisure to devote to education. Therefore, they became the *scholar-officials* who administered the government of China.

As government officials the gentry were able to protect their own interests. They had the land and wealth that the emperor might desire. By filling all the government posts with their own people they were able to check the power of the emperor.

The gentry carried out many important political functions. Their services were needed by both the government and the peasants. The gentry assisted the officials of the central government in dealing with local matters. They helped the government collect taxes, construct public works, and preserve the peace. When the peasants felt that their taxes were too high or that the government required too many soldiers from their district, they turned to the gentry for help in getting the government to moderate its demands. In cases of land quarrels and feuds, the gentry acted as arbiters. Thus it can be said that the gentry carried on an informal countryside government. This kept the central government from interfering too much in local matters.

The gentry maintained their important position well into the 20th century. In modern times they became lawyers, doctors, engineers, and professors. Many found employment in industry, commerce and banking. However, when the Communists came to power in 1949, one of their first steps was to break up the power of the gentry and take away their wealth.

The Peasants

The majority of Chinese people were peasants. They made up between 80–90% of the population of China. The life of the peasants was very different from the life of the gentry.

One of the basic differences between peasants and gentry was that the peasants earned a living doing physical work. Their income came mainly from cultivating the land. Some peasants were the owners of their small piece of land. Other peasants were tenants who cultivated the land for others. And some were farm laborers who received a salary for farming the land. But in all cases the peasants worked very hard. Most of their time was spent working in order to produce enough food to feed their families. The peasants also found it necessary to add to their incomes by means of different types of handicrafts. At night and during the slack season the whole family would weave, embroider, work with silk, make baskets and other goods. These products they would then sell in the nearby towns. Most often the additional money was used to buy the necessities of life and not luxuries.

The peasants rarely left their villages. The constant need to work kept the peasants close to home. On occasion the peasant did go into town, but this was only to buy the few things he could not produce at home or to sell the surplus crops of handicrafts he had made at home. The peasants had no time or money for the entertainment or luxuries of the towns. The teahouses, theaters, and restaurants were beyond their reach.

The peasant's life was one of hard work. Only rarely did he enjoy any form of entertainment. Sometimes, storytellers who roamed from village to village arrived and spent a few days reciting various kinds of tales. On special occasions, theatrical companies came to the villages. The peasants tried to make their festivals, especially New Year, as happy as they could. Weddings were another time for celebrating.

The peasants generally lived in small families. Their tiny pieces of land could not support many people. To preserve this small piece of land intact, they often permitted only one son to inherit the property. (The gentry usually allowed all the sons to inherit the property equally.) The peasants offered sacrifices to their ancestors when they could, at least once or twice a year. In choosing a wife the peasant placed the greatest importance on obtaining a strong helpmate. Earning a living was so important that the family was regarded as a working group. What was looked for in a wife was a strong back, sturdy legs and firm hands. It was not important for the woman to be pretty, she had to be healthy and strong.

Chinese peasants were independent individuals. They relied on their own labor and physical strength. They solved their problems by themselves and with the help of their sons. When problems arose that they could not handle alone, the peasant turned for help to the gentry or the village elders, but not to the government.

The peasants regarded the government with deep suspicion. They associated it with such evil things as taking their scarce food for taxes, taking their strength for public works, taking their sons for the army, and often also taking their land away. In general, the peasants felt that the less they had to do with the government the better.

Life for the Chinese peasants was difficult in every way. The peasants worked from sunrise to sunset and yet most of their life was lived in poverty. Malnutrition

Chinese men view wall posters describing the opening of diplomatic relations between the U.S. and China. *Credit: United Press International*

精打細算「炒地皮」 「經濟頭腦」虧老本

國中老師想發財偷雞不着蝕把米

獻身國民教育四十五年

默默耕耘造福三義學童

徐春木退休捐金幫助清寒學生

呂佳蓮花蓮輪上出生

受優待終身免費乘船

義犬救主喪命棍下

兇手被捕移送法辦

張壽南脫險決「厚葬」忠狗

打死討債人被起訴

高木金「三代同堂」

水餃風波

教師暑期開店賣水餃教育界看法不同

勞力換取報酬無損人格有何不可

作育英才必須心無旁鶩不宜鼓勵

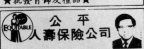

and disease were common. During periods of drought, famine, or floods the peasants suffered more than any other group. Yet despite their hardships and suffering, the peasants were *conservative* by nature. They were content to live out their lives in their accustomed way, rather than try to change the political system. Throughout Chinese history, when life became unbearable for them, the peasants rose up and helped overthrow the government. But they were mainly interested in throwing out the unjust rulers, not in changing the political system. Once the rulers had been changed and the injustices remedied, the peasants returned to their traditional way of life.

It was the hope of all classes in China, especially the peasant class, to become members of the gentry class. Throughout Chinese history, peasants did move up into the gentry class. One way in which peasants could move into the gentry class was through education and government service. Bright peasant boys were often helped by relatives to get an education. If they passed the examination and became government officials, this immediately placed them and their families in the gentry class. Peasants who became wealthy educated their sons, set them up in government careers, and thereby entered the gentry class. Sometimes a gentry family might lose its wealth and descend into the peasant class. Thus a certain degree of mobility (movement) between classes existed in China.

The Chinese Family

The Importance of the Family in China

The Chinese people have always considered the family to be the most important part of society. The individual person in many ways was considered to be less important than the family. In fact, the family was regarded as so important that even the state was seen as an extension of the family.

The individual thought of himself as a member of a family, and others saw him in the same way. If the individual was successful, the prestige of the family was increased. If the individual was a failure, that brought shame upon the whole family. The family was held responsible for the acts of its individual members.

Confucianism emphasized the importance of the family. It was in the family that the individual learned his role in Chinese society. Of the five basic social relationships necessary to the right functioning of Chinese society, three were family relationships—the relationships between father and son, elder brother and younger brother, and husband and wife.

Family Size

In traditional China three types of families existed: the small, the middle-way, and the large family. The small family usually consisted of the parents and their unmarried children. The middle-way family was made up of the parents, all their unmarried children, and one married son with his wife and children. The large family included the parents, both married and unmarried children, and all the wives and children of the married children. Sometimes other close relatives, such as grandparents, uncles, aunts, cousins and nephews, might live in this family. The head of the family was usually the father, but sometimes it might be the elder brother. He supervised the common property and watched over the moral life of its members.

From the time of the T'ang Dynasty until very recently the large family was praised and encouraged as the ideal family. However, only certain wealthy families were able to achieve this goal. The majority of the Chinese people lived in small and middle-way families. These families numbered on the average from five to seven members. There are several reasons why most Chinese were not able to achieve the ideal of a large family. Malnutrition, disease, and famine were very common in China. Many children died at a young age and many mothers died at childbirth. The small amount of land that the poor people possessed was not enough to support a large family.

In present-day China the small family, consisting of the parents and their children, is typical.

Family Relationships

Until recently the parents had almost complete authority over their children. Chinese fathers were regarded by their sons with a great deal of fear. Since untrained and undisciplined sons gave the community a bad impression of the father, Chinese fathers were very strict in training their sons. Relationships between fathers and daughters were usually warmer and closer. The relationship between the mother and her children was generally one of love and affection. She was often the one who protected the children, especially the sons, from the anger of their father. When the grandfather headed the family, he often protected his grandchildren from the father and mother. Children would run to their grandparents to escape from their father's punishment. Often, children received more love from their grandparents, uncles, and aunts than from their own fathers.

Social Training

Parents were supposed to train their children to fulfill their proper role in Chinese society. For each generation, for each age, for each sex there was an accepted form of behavior which had to be learned. From the age of four to sixteen children were taught their future duties. The boys of gentry families were sent to schools or to private tutors. The boys of peasant families were taught field work at an early age. All boys were taught the ancestral rituals. Both peasant and gentry girls had to learn the household duties of sewing, cooking, washing, and cleaning. Peasant girls, in addition, learned to help in the fields.

Marriage

Marriage was very important in China because only through marriage could the family line be continued. Arranging marriages was the responsibility of the parents.

The bride and groom had little to say about the choice of their mate or the marriage arrangements. In fact, they rarely saw each other before the wedding. There was no question of love in arranging a marriage in China. Of great importance in choosing a mate was the social and financial position of the family. This was carefully checked out before the marriage contract was signed.

A middle-man always negotiated the marriage. He or she did the talking and bargaining and carried the messages back and forth. One of the most important questions to be settled was the size of the dowry to be paid by the family of the bridegroom to the family of the bride. The girl's family used part of the dowry money to buy the bridal outfit. If there were unmarried sons in the family, part of the money was used to obtain wives for them.

On the day of the wedding, the bride was taken to the home of her bridegroom. Here the bride faced a completely new environment. Usually she had not seen any of the family members before, including her husband. The most difficult adjustment was to her mother-in-law. The mother-in-law was responsible for training and disciplining her daughter-in-law. The husband and wife were not supposed to show affection in public. The young bride spent most of her time in the company of her mother-in-law. There are many stories in Chinese literature of mothers-in-law whose cruelty drove their daughters-in-law to flee from their homes and even to commit suicide. The son could not interfere with his mother's treatment of his wife, because both he and his wife were subordinate to his mother.

Old Age

Old age and childhood were thought of as the happiest times in life. The Chinese looked forward to old age and growing old was pleasant. Age was respected. It was a time of leisure and little responsibility. Children had to do everything to provide for the comfort and happiness of their parents. Children were required to support their parents in their old age. Another duty was to carry out the ceremonial rites after their death.

Women also achieved respect and importance as they grew older. As the years passed the one-time timid bride became a mother-in-law and head of her own household. Once she had sons and daughters-in-law of her own, all owed her respect, obedience, and support.

The Family in China Today

In China today people are taught to think in terms of loyalty to the state first and the family second. While families are still held responsible for teaching the young their roles in society, there are now other places where the young person can learn this. Nurseries, schools, clubs, factory committees, and party groups serve the function that the family did in the past. Young people in China today are no longer dominated by their elders as they were in the past. In fact, young people are placed in many positions of authority. The role of women is totally different from what it used to be. All these changes have taken place under the Communists. However, in places with large Chinese populations such as Taiwan, Hong Kong, and Southeast Asia, many Chinese people still retain the old customs and traditional family patterns.

The Clan

A clan is a group of people who trace their ancestry back to a common ancestor. Descent is traced back to the father's ancestor. Some clans have thousands of members. Included in the clan are all those people having the same surname who can trace their descent back to the common ancestor who first settled in the area.

Since the Chinese people place such value on the family, the dead ancestors and the descendants of these ancestors are important to them as well. The Chinese keep genealogies—charts and written histories tracing the clan's descent from the common ancestor and showing the relationship between the members.

Every clan usually had a center where the ancestral hall was built and where most of the ancestral graves were located. Each ancestor had a tablet, a rectangular piece of wood on which was written the name, title, date of birth and death of the ancestor. Once or twice a year the clan met to honor their common ancestors. Westerners have called this ancestor worship, but the Chinese did *not* worship their ancestors. They had memorial services for them to show their respect and reverence. The Chinese believed their ancestors continued to live as spirits. These spirits had the power to help their descendants if they were given the proper rites. If they were neglected, however, the descendants would suffer misfortune. One reason that the Chinese considered it so important to have sons was that they would have descendants to carry out the proper rites to their spirits after their death.

Clan leaders met periodically to discuss clan matters. Special funds were set aside to take care of orphans, widows, and the sick. In times of crises, such as floods, famine, war, the clan helped its members. Funds were also used to help educate the promising children of the poorer members. Civil and criminal cases affecting clan members were judged by the clan instead of the government. For serious offenses the punishment was expulsion (being thrown out) from the clan.

Language and Writing System

Language

How a person speaks or expresses himself is one way of telling us something about that person. Studying some of the characteristics of the Chinese language may add to our understanding of the Chinese people and their culture.

Chinese belongs to the Sinitic or Sino–Tibetan language family (Tibetan, Burmese, Siamese, Chinese). Most Chinese speak *Kuo-yu* (meaning national language), also known as Mandarin Chinese. This language and its dialects are spoken in the northern and western parts of China. Throughout the southern part of China many other dialects are in common use. Educated people in the south usually learn the national language, in addition to the dialects of their area.

All words in *Kuo-yu,* as well as in all Chinese dialects, are made up of single syllables. For this reason the language is called monosyllabic. For example, *chop suey* means "mixed small pieces"; *chow mein* means "fried noodles"; *kow tow* means "bow the head"; *typhoon* means "big wind"; *ting hao* means "very good"; *tsai chien* means "see you again." The city *Shanghai* is a combination of *shang* meaning "above" and *hai,* meaning "sea." The name *Mao Tse-tung,* like most Chinese names is made up of three parts. The family name, which comes first, is *Mao.* (As a family name Mao was a place in ancient China.) *Tse-tung,* the given name consists of two parts meaning "east marsh," the same as the first and middle names in America. Our 37th president's name would be "Nixon Richard-Milhous."

The Chinese language uses many homonyms, or words that are pronounced alike but have different meanings, like *to, too* and *two* in English. Communication between speakers would be difficult without a way of making clear the differences in meaning of words pronounced the same way. Context, or the position of the word in a sentence and its use, is one way of making meanings clear. But still another method is the use of tone.

The national language generally uses four tones. In learning a new word in Chinese, it is necessary to know both its sound and its tone. A word pronounced with a rising tone may mean something different from another word with the same sound, but said in a falling tone. The tones give you the feeling that Chinese is sung, and not merely spoken.

Contact with the West has added many words to the Chinese language. The Chinese express their ideas by putting two or more syllables (words) together like *ting hao* (very good). Today, with new and strange terms having to do with science, technology and ideas, the Chinese have borrowed and pronounced foreign words as much like the originals as possible. Sometimes new combinations have been made like *fei chi* ("flying machine"—airplane); *huo ch'e* ("fire wagon"—train); *yuan tzu tan* ("primary unit egg"—atom bomb).

The Chinese Writing System

The Chinese began developing their writing system more than 3,500 years ago. Chinese writing began with the drawing of rough, but recognizable pictures of things. Even today it is possible to guess the meaning of some of the ancient Chinese pictographs (pictures used for writing). The Chinese have developed a means of expressing ideas in writing. The symbol for an idea is generally formed by combining pictographs to suggest it.

日　＋　月　＝　明　　女　＋　子　＝　好

| JIH (sun) | + | YUEH (moon) | = | MING (bright) | NU (woman) | + | TZU (child) | = | HAO (good) |

Other characters in Chinese writing are composed of a "meaning" symbol and a "sound" symbol. The meaning symbol gives a clue to the meaning, and the sound symbol suggests the pronunciation. Most of the characters in present-day Chinese writing are of this kind.

Chinese writing includes more than 50 thousand characters. A great many of these are rarely used, but a knowledge of a thousand to fifteen hundred characters is necessary for even elementary reading and writing. This need to memorize so many written characters resulted in widespread illiteracy among the Chinese people. However, in an effort to do something about the problem of illiteracy in China, the Communists are trying to simplify the language.

The writing system has served to unify the Chinese. The same written characters were used throughout China, even though the dialects may have been different.

Some words written in Chinese:

Numbers (HI) :

一	二	三	四	五	六	七	八	九	十
1	2	3	4	5	6	7	8	9	10

子	女	筆	食	行	朋	友	光	人
boy	girl	pen	eat	walk	friend	(PONG-U)	light	man

It has always been difficult to translate the sounds of Chinese into the words formed from the Roman alphabet. Recently, a general agreement was made to use a different system—Pinyin—to reproduce these sounds. This means that you will begin to see different spellings of some Chinese names: *Teng Hsiao-ping* will be Deng Xiaoping, Mao Tse-tung as *Mao Zedong*, and so forth.

Ancient China

China shares with several parts of Asia and Africa the honor of being one of the oldest areas where man decided to live. Archaeologists have discovered a great deal of information. They have found important clues in the story of man's advance toward civilized life.

Early Civilization

Chinese civilization began about four thousand years ago in a river valley in northern China. The first people were wandering hunters and fishermen. After they learned to farm (sometime before 1800 B.C.), they did not need to roam around in search of food. They settled down, built homes and farmed. Even more important, they developed cities and government, religion and writing, coined money and made a calendar. These early Chinese learned how to raise cattle, horses and sheep. They learned to make pottery from clay and to shape it on a wheel. They made jewelry from shells, played music on whistles, and learned how to make silk. The Chinese mined copper and tin, and mixed the two metals together to make bronze. The tools and weapons made of bronze were better shaped and sharper than stone tools, which had been used before. Since bronze was used a great deal, this period of human history is called the Bronze Age.

The Shang Dynasty

According to legend, the Hsia was China's first ruling family (dynasty). Archaeologists have never discovered its location, nor have they found any objects that they can prove were made by its people. The first dynasty for which archaeologists have found actual evidence is that of the Shang (C. 1766 B.C.-1122 B.C.). In 1929 these archaeologists discovered the remains of a Bronze Age city near the present day city of Anyang, just north of the Huang-ho. This city was one of the capitals of the Shang Kingdom. The Shang kings seem to have been very wealthy, for they built large palaces. The people of the Shang were mainly farmers, but some were highly skilled craftsmen who made beautiful jewelry and other articles out of bronze. Shang bronzes are considered the finest the world has ever seen. The people of the Shang left behind the oldest form of Chinese writing yet found. It was mainly carved on cattle bones and on tortoise shells ("dragon bones").

The Chou Dynasty

The Shang Dynasty was replaced by the Chou (1122 B.C.-221 B.C.). Few of the Chou kings were strong rulers. As a result, China was divided into small states. The rulers of these states spent a great deal of time fighting each other. At last, one lord was able to destroy all the others. The victor became the first Chinese emperor in 221 B.C.

Art in the Chou Dynasty

The artists of the Chou Dynasty continued to work in bronze. They made bronze bells, mirrors, and cups. On their bronzes they carved birds and animals, dragons and other symbols. Other cultures and nations have never made better bronzes than these ancient Chinese.

Many of the Chou buildings had curved roofs which overhung the walls. Roofs were made with tiles of various colors, mostly blue and green. The tiles of the royal palace were of yellow. Yellow was the royal color. The Chinese liked bright colors and used them a great deal. The wooden beams and pillars of buildings were carved and brightened with gold, lacquer and inlays of different kinds.

The Chous also followed the Shangs in work in jade. Jade is a hard stone which is found in many colors. Green is the most common color. Chou artists made rings, bracelets and buckles of jade. Other things of jade were made for use in temples. The government used jade for seals, medals and badges of high office.

The Hundred Schools

The scholars of Chou times are called the "Hundred Schools." The Chou Dynasty is known as a time when freedom of thought existed, because of the ideas that scholars of the Hundred Schools discussed and argued with each other.

It was during the Chou Dynasty that the first sections of the Great Wall of China were built. The wall was built to protect China against the people of the north, who raided Chinese land. Later emperors added to the wall until it reached the length of two thousand miles.

Because of the accomplishments of the Chou Dynasty, the Chinese feel it is one of the greatest periods in their long history.

Empire China

The Ch'in Dynasty

The Chou period was a time of fighting among small states. One state, called Ch'in, defeated all the others. The ruler of this state took the name Shih Huang-ti (The First Emperor), and made China an Empire (a great country ruled by an emperor). We get the name China from Ch'in.

Shih Huang-ti did many things to unify China. He insisted that all businessmen use the same coins and the same system of weights and measures. He also ordered that the same writing system be used by all. He angered the people by forcing them to read books that only agreed with his ideas. All books which did not agree with his ideas were burned. Several hundred scholars who disagreed with the Emperor were said to have been buried alive. Some books were saved by burying them under ground and by hiding them in walls. Chinese scholars memorized others.

The Chinese believed that a family (dynasty) ruled as long as it held the "Mandate of Heaven," that is, the right to rule. The people felt they had the right to say whether or not the ruler had the Mandate. When the Emperor did not see to it that there was water for irrigation, that canal barges could transport rice, that rivers did not flood and that roads were safe for traveling, the people suffered. When the people suffered, they were sure that Heaven had taken away its protection of the Emperor, so they rebelled. When the rebellion was successful, the Mandate of Heaven was given to the leader of the rebellion. He became the emperor of a new dynasty.

The Chinese revolted against the Ch'ins because they felt the Mandate had been taken away. The revolt was led by a peasant who organized the farmers into a strong army. This dynasty, which was called the Han, lasted for over four hundred years, until 220 A.D. (The Ch'in had lasted only fifteen years.)

During the over 2,100 years of Empire China, there were only nine important dynasties and twenty-three minor ones. The nine important ones cover eighteen hundred years, whereas the weaker dynasties cover only three hundred years. For most of China's history it was blessed with stable government.

The Great Wall of China—A Chinese architectural wonder. Note the mountainous topography found throughout North China.
Credit: *Hsinhua News Agency*

The Han Dynasty

The Han emperors did a great deal during their rule. They set up a system of government under which China was ruled for two thousand years. They made the ideas of Confucius the law of the land. They extended China's land to the west and south. Under the Han, the Chinese invented paper and porcelain. They also developed a rich trade with the far-off Roman Empire. China's first and greatest historian, Ssu-ma Ch'ien, lived in the Han. The Han rule was so great that many Chinese today call themselves "Sons of Han."

The Time of Troubles

The four hundred years after the fall of the Han Dynasty was a time of great troubles. During this time China broke up into several independent states. Life became difficult for the Chinese people, and many turned to a new religion, Buddhism, for hope. They found hope and gained peace of mind in Buddhism. China became a stronghold of Buddhism after it grew weak in India, the country where it originated.

There were many wars between the independent states. The commanders and soldier heroes of the wars became great heroes to the Chinese. Their acts of bravery were told over and over again in homes and tea houses. After hundreds of years, these stories were written down in *The Romance of the Three Kingdoms,* one of China's greatest novels.

The T'ang Dynasty

After a time, the Empire was again united by the Sui Dynasty. The Sui Dynasty ruled only for 30 years. In 618 A.D. a dynasty as powerful as the Han was set up. The T'ang Dynasty ruled for the next 300 years. This period is one of the greatest times in Chinese history. This greatness was caused in part by the expansion of China to the west and south. Their influence *extended* (stretched) westward into Central Asia and southward into Southeast Asia and beyond.

The T'angs excelled in many ways. It is in art and poetry that they are most remembered. Their appreciation of beauty was the center of their artistic skill. Little remains of the paintings of the T'ang Chinese. We know from copies and reports of those who saw T'ang paintings that they painted much and they painted well. They painted scenes from nature. They drew horses, flowers, and birds in fine, exact detail. But they especially liked to paint landscapes.

The Chinese did not often paint pictures of people. Sometimes people were put into landscapes. In those paintings people were very small and *insignificant* (of little importance) in the middle of the greatness and marvelous work of nature.

Chinese paintings were not framed. They were painted on scrolls that could be hung or rolled up and stored.

The Chinese have created a vast literature. They wrote essays, fiction and beautiful poetry. They wrote much history, mainly about their own past.

Among the great poets of the T'ang period were Li T'ai-po, Tu Fu, and Po Chü-i. It is during this period that one of China's most famous tales of love and tragedy began—the drama of the great king Hsuan Tsung and the beautiful Yang Kuei-fei.

Under the T'angs trade and commerce grew. Gunpowder and the techniques of printing from wood blocks were invented in T'ang China. One of the oldest printed books we have comes from this time. It is a Buddhist text printed in 868 A.D.

The Sung Dynasty

The Sung Dynasty, which followed soon after the T'ang, made contributions in art and scholarship. Sung landscape paintings are now national treasures. The Sungs also developed the use of paper money in trade and commerce. During the Sung period Mongols invaded from the north and slowly took power away from the Sungs.

The Yuan and Ming Dynasties

The Mongols were nomads who herded sheep. They were excellent horsemen. In 1280 A.D. the Mongol leader, Kublai Khan, became China's ruler. The Yuan Dynasty, or Mongol Dynasty, lasted for about ninety years. Marco Polo visited China during this Dynasty. He wrote a book about his experiences in China. This book sparked the interest of European traders in China.

The Mongols lost the Mandate of Heaven to the son of a poor worker. The new Dynasty was called Ming, and was the last Chinese Dynasty. It lasted about three hundred years. It is most famous for its great trade with other nations and for its fine porcelain. A Ming vase has become a symbol of beauty and refinement. The Mings were great architects, and made Peking, their capital, one of the most beautiful cities in the world. They also set up many schools and libraries for the education of the people.

The Mings, in their turn, were overthrown by invaders from the north, the Manchus.

Manchu China

In the seventeenth century peasants began to rebel against the Mings. In 1644 the rebels entered Peking, and the Mings fled southward. The Ming commander of the Great Wall defenses united his forces with nomads from the Manchurian plains, the Manchus.

The Chinese have a saying, "Never call in a tiger to chase out a dog." By allowing the Manchus into China, the Chinese commander had not followed these wise words. The Manchus, once allowed in, refused to leave. The Manchus took over the Empire and set up a new Dynasty, the Ch'ing.

The Manchus, or Ch'ings, were few in number, but ruled China for almost three centuries. They respected and encouraged the development of Chinese culture. They permitted the Chinese to take part in ruling the government. The Manchus rarely interfered in village affairs. The villagers themselves handled most of the problems of government.

During the Manchu Dynasty the population of China grew. The Manchus provided good government, kept law and order, and operated public works well (irrigation canals, roads, bridges). They introduced new crops, such as kaoliang (a cereal), potatoes, corn and peanuts, and more land was used for farming. These efforts increased the food supply. But, as usable farm land became scarce and population grew, and the government began to neglect law and order and public works, peasant rebellions began to break out.

The Manchus had succeeded in extending the power of the Chinese Empire throughout East, Central and Southeast Asia. The Manchus increased trade with the West. Europeans, however, found it difficult to carry on trade with China, since the Chinese put many restrictions on trade. European merchants could only trade in the city of Canton on the mouth of the West River in South China.

Chinese silks and porcelain found good markets in Europe. The Chinese also exported brocades (silk textile), sugar, ginger and tea. The Chinese, however, were not interested in European goods. Western textiles were too expensive and not as good in quality. To trade with China, Europeans had to ship large amounts of silver to buy Chinese goods.

The Opium Problem

However, the situation changed quickly. In the 1700s the Chinese began to smoke opium. Opium is a narcotic drug that is made from the seed pod of certain kinds of poppy plants. The Chinese had grown the opium poppy for use in making medicines. In the eighteenth century increasing numbers of people became slaves to the drug. By the early 1800s the "foreign mud," as opium came to be known in China, had become a curse. The British and Dutch made use of this curse. They bought opium in India and sold it to the Chinese. Soon silver was flowing out of China instead of into it, to pay for the opium.

The Chinese tried to halt the trade by law. These laws were not enforced. The British wanted to trade freely in China, but were refused this right. When the Chinese government *confiscated* (took without payment) and destroyed British stores of opium at Canton in 1839, the British sent warships and troops to China. The Opium War was won by the British and five treaty ports were opened to trade. In addition, all trade and commerce policy was to be decided in treaties between China and the Western governments.

The power and prestige of the Manchus was badly damaged. Within a short time, the first of a series of rebellions broke out in China. These rebellions weakened China and led to the collapse of the Manchu Dynasty.

The Chinese Revolution
THE FALL OF THE MANCHUS

Problems Facing the Manchus

As China entered the nineteenth century, the glory of the Manchu Empire seemed to be as great as ever. However, powerful forces were being set in motion which were to shatter the old order.

Population Growth

As we have seen in the last section, China's population had grown without an equal increase in agricultural production. In 1700 the population of China was about 150 million. By 1800 it had passed the 400 million mark. However, land used for farming was about eight million *ching* (a *ching* is about fifteen acres) in 1701, but was not more than ten million *ching* in 1850. Such a situation had never happened before in Chinese history.

Peasant Revolts

At the same time, the Manchus were faced with the same type of opposition that dynasties had faced many times before in Chinese history. The peasants were unhappy and did not trust the Manchus as rulers. The result was the feeling that the Mandate of Heaven had been removed from the hands of the Manchus. A series of peasant revolts broke out in northern and western China. From 1850 to 1865 the worst of these revolts, the Taiping Rebellion, almost succeeded in toppling the Ch'ing Dynasty. Many peasants joined the rebellion because its leaders promised land, equality and brotherhood. The Manchus were not successful in defeating the rebels. They asked the Europeans for men and money. With this help, and after much fighting, the Manchus crushed the Taipings.

European Imperialism

This brings us to the second powerful force that tore apart the Manchu Empire. This force can be called Western imperialism. Imperialism takes place when a strong country uses a weaker, less developed country to its own advantage. Sometimes the weaker nation is made a colony after military conquest.

China's troubles in the nineteenth century made it easier for European imperialism to succeed. The settlement of the Opium War in 1842 was the first of a long series of "unequal treaties." For years China was forced to give Western nations special privileges in China.

Japanese Imperialism

The Japanese also decided to take advantage of China's weakness. Japan's victory in the first Sino (China) -Japanese War was a disaster for China and the Manchus. The great weaknesses of China were obvious, and encouraged the Western powers and Japan to press for even more rights and privileges in China.

In the late nineteenth century, the Chinese Empire was ruled by a boy whose aunt controlled the government. She allowed some reforms to be made. However, her main interest was to keep the Manchu Dynasty and her own power intact. She used the Chinese resentment of the West to try to get rid of the Westerners and the Japanese. In 1900 a group called the Boxers attacked the foreigners, but were defeated.

By the opening of the twentieth century, it seemed that China was to be divided by the Western powers and Japan. The United States wished to protect its own trading interests and possibilities. These might be lost if China came under foreign control. The United States had asked other nations to stop looking for special privileges in China and to respect her independence. The American government proposed equality and an "open door" for China's trade and privileges. However, no one seemed to pay attention to this plea.

Weak from rebellions and wars, the Manchus were doomed. They could not fight the West, they could not keep order, and they could not reform China. Therefore, they had to be overthrown, for they had obviously lost the Mandate of Heaven.

The Nationalist Revolution

A revolution happens when important changes are brought about in the form of the government, the economy or the society of a country. Revolutions can be peaceful or violent. The causes for a revolution take many decades to develop, but the revolution itself usually occurs in a short period of time. This was true in the American and Russian Revolutions.

The years of preparation for revolution in China took many decades. However, the revolution itself has lasted for over fifty years, and still seems to be going on. It is interesting to note that in the past, when the Chinese revolted against their rulers, the revolutions also lasted for long periods of time and went through many stages.

The Ideas of Dr. Sun Yat-sen

The Chinese Revolution started when a bomb exploded in the city of Wuchang, in Central China, on October 10, 1911. A republic was set up in Nanking, with Sun Yat-sen as its first President. Dr. Sun is known as the Father of the Chinese Revolution. He was a thinker and a planner. He was trusted by the people, and he had trust in the people's ability to run the government. For years he spread the idea that the Chinese people should have a government "of the people, by the people and for the people." He spoke all over China, and wrote about his ideas, which he called *Three Principles of the People;* in Chinese, San Min Chu-I (Sahn min jooee).

The three principles were *nationalism, democracy,* and *socialism.* Nationalism meant love and sacrifice for China; democracy meant government of the people; and socialism meant economic equality, for all the Chinese people would share in the wealth of China equally.

These ideas were difficult to put into practice. Dr. Sun mistakenly gave the Presidency to Yuan Shih-kai, who betrayed the ideas of San Min Chu-I, and drove Sun out of the country. Yuan was not powerful enough to rule the whole country. Generals and leaders of bands of soldiers became independent rulers in their own provinces. They were given unlimited power and were known as warlords. These greedy men cared little for China, and fought each other for power. China became badly divided, and civil war broke out. The central government broke down.

Dr. Sun then formed the Kuomintang (KMT), the Nationalist Party. The Party was set up to work for the unity of the country under the Three Principles. The KMT received important help from Soviet Russia. The Russians sent an advisor to aid Sun. He helped to organize the KMT and make it into a powerful revolutionary party. The Russians also helped the Nationalists set up a military academy at Whampoa, near Canton. Here, officers devoted to the ideals of the Chinese Revolution were trained for a new revolutionary army.

Dr. Sun died before his ideas were fulfilled. His spirit and dream lived on. He soon became the symbol of the Chinese Nationalist Revolution and of the Communist National Revolution.

Chiang Kai-shek Follows Dr. Sun

Dr. Sun's death caused problems. Who was to be the new leader? Chiang Kai-shek was one possiblity and Mao Tse-tung was another. Chiang was president of the military academy at Whampoa and an important leader of the KMT. Mao was a Communist. The Chinese Communist Party (CCP) had been set up in 1921. It had joined the KMT in 1923. The KMT leaders hoped that by uniting to destroy the power of the warlords, they could avoid a battle between Chiang and Mao.

Chiang Kai-shek Rules China

Chiang led the new KMT army, and united most of China. He then turned on the Communists. The main Communist centers in Hankow and Shanghai were attacked, and the Communist leaders, except for Mao, were slaughtered. When Peking was conquered by Chiang, the second revolution had occurred, and the Second Republic was set up. Chiang renamed Peking, *Peiping*, which means "northern peace." He also moved the capital to Nanking in the Yangtze Valley because of its central location. Chiang made himself leader with unlimited powers. (When the Communists came to power in 1949 they returned the traditional name of *Peking*, meaning "northern capital," and made the city their capital.)

Chiang faced a number of problems. The warlords still controlled a large part of China. The Communists, although greatly weakened, still blocked national unity. Finally, the Japanese continued to cause problems for the Chinese.

Japan Invades China

The Japanese invasion of 1931 was a deadly blow to Chiang's government. Japan took Manchuria and made it an industrial and military base. Chiang's difficulties with Japan gave the Chinese Communists a chance to recover their strength.

In 1934 the Communists, led by Mao, fled to Yenan, in Shensi Province near the Yellow River (Huang-ho). This retreat is known as the Long March. The Long March covered over 5000 miles. Of 130 thousand men who started out, only 25 thousand survived. In the caves of this northwest province, the Communists were safe from Chiang's army. They were also closer to the Russian border. The Russians sent some aid to the Chinese Communists, but not very much. Here, the Communists formed a peasant army, and trained it in guerrilla warfare.

At this point in 1937, the Japanese again invaded China. The Japanese quickly gained control of the eastern coastal areas. Hundreds of thousands of Chinese fled westward. Chiang and the other members of the government fled to Chungking, in southwest China near the Yangtze River, where a new capital was set up. Chiang would have been happy to continue fighting the Communists. However, soldiers on both sides refused to fight their brothers while the Japanese took over China. Chiang and the Communists agreed to join forces to fight the Japanese. Mao's soldiers were successful in using guerrilla tactics against the Japanese.

During the eight years of war, Chiang's Nationalists were severely battered. Not only was the country exhausted, but the morale of the people was low. Help from the United States allowed Chiang to survive the war, but not to solve the many economic and social problems.

After the Japanese were defeated in 1945, the Nationalists of Chiang and the Communists of Mao were ready to continue their battle and fight to the finish. The stage was now set for the Third Revolution.

Civil War and the Success of the Communist Revolution

During the Second World War the Chinese Communists cooperated with the Nationalist (Kuomintang) armies of Chiang Kai-shek. They wanted to free China from the Japanese. When the Japanese surrendered in 1945, the Communists were not yet strong enough to take over all of China. They agreed to work together with the Nationalists to rebuild China. Yet, as we have already learned, both the Communists and the Nationalists were eager to fight each other to the end.

The United States was very anxious to bring peace to China. In December, 1945, President Truman sent General George Marshall to China. The purpose of this visit was to try to set up a lasting peace. Unfortunately, Marshall was not successful. At this point, the United States decided to help the Nationalists. Between 1945 and 1948 the U.S. poured more than two billion dollars worth of arms into China. This was in addition to the one and one-half billion dollars loaned to the Chinese during the war.

Full scale civil war between the Nationalists and the Communists broke out in 1947. In 1949 the Communists won a smashing victory over the Nationalists. They set up a Communist government in Peking to rule all of mainland China. They have been in power ever since.

Reasons for the Communist Victory

Why did the Communists win? In 1945 Communist forces numbered only about one million men, while the Nationalists had over three million men. The money which the U.S. sent to China went to the Nationalists. How could they lose? There are many reasons for the Communist victory:

1. The Nationalist government of Chiang Kai-shek failed to use its power well. Many officials in his government were *corrupt*. They were more interested in becoming rich than in doing anything for the Chinese people. The Chinese people were poor and tired of war. All they wanted was a little land to farm and a chance to live in peace. Chiang did not pay any attention to what the people wanted. As a result, the people were unhappy and did not have confidence in the government of Chiang. The people of China did not want a dictator.

2. The Communists lived for many years under very difficult conditions. Many of the Communists had been slaughtered by Chiang. For years they lived in caves in Yenan, where they could be protected from attacks. During this time, they built up their strength and *discipline* so they could be ready for the final battles when they came. They became tough and fearless, and ready to die for what they believed in.

3. The Communists had many good generals. In 1948 the Communists won one battle after another. Nanking, Hankow, Shanghai, Canton and Chungking fell into their hands. In many places thousands of Nationalist soldiers surrendered without firing a shot, or deserted to the Communists.

4. Another important reason that the Communists were successful was their policy toward the Chinese peasants. In October, 1947, the Communists called on the Chinese people to get rid of the Chiang government and build a new China. At the same time, they carried out a land *reform* which Chiang had promised for many years, but had never done. In the land reform, the Communists took land away from the rich landlords and gave it to the poor peasants. It was for this reason that the peasants supported the Communists. (It is interesting to note that many peasants in South Vietnam also support the Communists. The Viet Cong, too, has promised land reform, while the government in Saigon, supported by the U.S., has not been able to gain the support of the peasant.)

5. In addition, the Communists received aid from the Soviet Union. At the end of the war in 1945, the Russians turned over large amounts of captured Japanese arms to the Communists. The Russians also helped the Communists take over Manchuria. Manchuria, with its industry and natural resources, became a base for the Communists of Mao Tse-tung.

In 1949 Chiang Kai-shek fled from China to the island of Formosa (Taiwan). With .complete control of the mainland, the Communists set up the People's Republic of China, with Mao as its leader.

Former Chairman Mao Tse-tung
Credit: *Hsinhua News Agency*

Former Premier Chou En-lai
Credit: *Hsinhua News Agency*

The Chinese Communist Party and Its Leaders

In China today, as in the Soviet Union, real power lies in the hands of the Communist Party, and not in the government. In China the Communists, who control all the power, are men of the older generation. Until his recent death, Mao Tse-tung was at the very top, with a small group of men who set up the Communist Party and led the Revolution. These men were all over seventy years of age. Under them are men who run the government ministries and the Party, and hold key posts in the army and the police. These men are in their fifties. Following the unrest and difficulties of the late 1960s, younger members of the party were put into some positions of importance. Their influence and ideas will most likely lead to changes in policy and methods in the future.

Until his death, the most important man in China was Mao Tse-tung, former chairman of the CCP. All *policies* were decided by Mao and his associates. Once a decision was reached, everyone was expected to obey and carry out the decision. There was very little criticism or debate. The government in China can not be considered democratic by Western standards.

In China, as in Russia, there is only one political party, the Communist Party. The Party controls the government. The most important people in the Party are also in the government. Members of the Party have special privileges and great influence. The Party Manual says that a member must be willing to sacrifice even his life "without the slightest hesitation, with a feeling of happiness" for what the Party tells him to do.

The Communist leaders of China want to make loyal Communists out of the young people. To do this, they have set up an organization called the Young Communist League. Young people between the ages of fourteen and twenty-five belong to it. Here they study the ideas of Communism, do Party work, and become *disciplined*. Children between the ages of nine and fifteen can join a Communist organization called the Pioneers. Both the Young Communist League and the Pioneers are copies of *similar* groups set up by the Communists in the Soviet Union.

Periodically, the Communists have tried to arouse the people. Huge military parades and demonstrations are held, in which hundreds of thousands of people get together to cheer and listen to speeches, and wave flags and banners. In this way, the Communists arouse enthusiasm for their policies and win over the people. The Chinese people are constantly being told that they must be brave, and that they must make sacrifices and obey. Artists and writers, as well as television, radio and newspapers, are being used by the Communists to sell their ideas and programs to the people. As in the Soviet Union, artistic efforts must be in accord with the standards set by the government and the Party. A People's Militia (an army of citizens) keeps a check on the people to make sure that they do not disobey or disagree with the Party.

China's Vice-Chairman Teng Hsiao-ping (Deng Xiaoping). *Credit: United Press International*

The Cultural Revolution

For years Mao's leadership position was not challenged. Mao did not find it necessary to discipline any members of his loyal band. But, in the early 1960s, cracks appeared in the solid front of the Party. Many Party chiefs began to question Mao's domestic and foreign policy. During the next few years the cracks widened. In mid-1966 the split occurred, and Mao and his enemies fought an open battle for power.

Lin Piao, an army leader, threw his support behind Mao. The Red Guards were also called on for their support. This national organization of teenagers and young adults was fanatically devoted to Mao. Taking their cues from him, the Red Guard began a "Proletarian Cultural Revolution." Their goal was to keep the "purity" of Mao's ideas. The Red Guard attacked Mao's rivals and critics. Thousands of people were killed. Destruction was great. By their activities and demonstrations, China was plunged into chaos. Armed bands of workers and farmers began to fight the Red Guard. Civil war seemed to be tearing the Chinese apart. Finally, after great damage was done to industry and farmland, Mao disciplined the Red Guard and order was restored. The leader of the opposition, Liu Shao-ch'i, was driven from power, and Lin Piao became a most important member of the government.

After Mao, Who?

For many years the big question in China was: Who would succeed Mao Tse-tung? Chairman Mao was a very old man. He led China since he and the Communists took control of China in 1949. The number 2 man in China used to be Chou En-lai, Mao's associate for forty years, but Chou died on January 8, 1976. A short time later, in September 1976, Mao died at the age of 82.

Twice before it seemed that Mao had chosen a successor, but in each case Mao removed him later. The first one was Liu Shao-ch'i. In the early 1960s, Liu was a very powerful figure. It seems, however, that as Liu's power grew he became more and more critical of Mao's policies. Feeling threatened by his rival, Mao decided to remove him. In 1966, with the help of the army and its leader Lin Piao, Liu Shao-ch'i was *purged* (removed). As part of the Cultural Revolution, the entire Communist Party and government organization were shaken up and everyone associated with Liu was eliminated.

Following this shake-up, Mao built Lin Piao up as his successor. Lin was named Defense Minister, and everyone regarded him as the number 2 man. But it seems that by 1970, Lin and Mao were having serious differences. It is believed that they had very different ideas over military strategy, the economy, and relations with the Soviet Union. Then, as a great surprise to everyone, Lin's name was not mentioned in the newspapers or over the radio. For more than a year, no one outside China knew what had become of him. Finally, early in 1973, Mao made the facts known. According to mao, Lin had plotted to assassinate him and seize power in 1971. When this scheme became known, Lin tried to escape and died in a plane crash in Mongolia. Following the plot, the government, party, army, navy, and air force leadership was purged again. Hundreds of officials connected with Lin Piao were removed.

Following these events, it was feared that the old revolutionaries would continue to refuse to transfer power to younger men.

When Mao died, a collective leadership was set up under the direction of Hua Kuo-feng. By early 1977, it seemed that Hua had become the sole leader of the People's Republic. The other leaders, including Mao's wife, Chiang Ch'ing, were either in jail or had dropped out of sight.

In mid-1977, China announced the formation of a new 26-member Communist Party Politburo. Party Chairman Hua Kuo-feng and Deputy Chairmen Yen Chien-ying and Teng Hsiao-ping will share the power. Then early in 1979, Deputy Teng Hsiao-ping came to the United States with his wife to meet with President Carter and to tour U.S. factories.

Life and Society in Present-Day China

Before the Communist Revolution, life for the great majority of Chinese people was very bleak. Famine was frequent, death from starvation common and disease widespread. Everywhere there was thievery, graft and corruption. The poor lived a life of utter poverty and were exploited by the rich. Peasants and workers were regarded with contempt by the educated and the well-to-do. Today, the poverty and misery of the past have been eliminated. Americans who have visited China in the last few years report that the change has been remarkable. Litter and beggars no longer fill the streets. There is no prostitution, no drug addiction, and no alcoholism. Opium smoking has been wiped out. There is no pollution, no slums, and no robbers. The rich are gone from the scene. Gone, too, is the total poverty in which the great majority of the people lived.

The goal of the Chinese Communists has been to reshape Chinese society and to create "a new Chinese man." In this goal they have largely succeeded. The working people in China today have a sense of purpose and a feeling of self-confidence and dignity. They know that they are helping to build their country into a powerful nation and they are proud. When they are told by their leaders to "work harder" they know that everything they do will benefit themselves and not some rich landlord as was the case in the past. Visitors to China report that the Chinese people give the appearance of health and well-being. The people have the security of having food, paid-work and old age pensions. In the past, providing enough food for China's people was always a problem. *Drought* meant that thousands would die of starvation.

Now, new dams and reservoirs have brought drought, floods, and famine under control. Hunger is no longer a problem.

One of the key ideas of Mao Tse-tung's philosophy is "Serve the People." Everywhere one goes in China there are posters and signs with this slogan. The Chinese people seem to believe this. It is believed that they *do* work harder to serve the people and not to get more money. "The people" are the workers, peasants and soldiers. Those who come from the landlord, rich peasant or merchant class are not considered "the people." They are not accepted members of society until they can prove that they have adopted the ideas of Mao Tse-tung and given up their old ideas.

The Peasants

Before the Revolution, the peasants were looked down upon and despised. Now they are proud of themselves and their work and are regarded with respect. The peasants used to live in mud and straw huts together with their chickens and pigs, but these have been replaced by brick houses and separate chicken coops and pig sties. The older peasants remember the days before the Revolution. Then they had many debts and were exploited by the landlords. When the Communists came to power they took the land away from the landlords and gave it to the peasants. Large numbers of landlords were executed. In 1958 the land was organized into vast communes.

What is it like being a peasant in China today? The peasant rises at dawn. Before breakfast he spends about two hours plowing his fields. After his wife cleans up she joins him in the fields. The peasant works until sundown, taking time out for breakfast and lunch. If there is time before supper he will work on his private plot of land. The vegetables he grows there provide his family with additional food and extra cash. The average pay of a peasant is about 30 yuan per month (about $12). But his rent is only about 1 yuan, and his basic foods such as rice, noodles and bread are given to him as his share of the production of the commune. Medical care is free. For entertainment, there are traveling companies of actors and musicians who visit the communes. TV sets have not yet come to the countryside, but many peasants do have radios. While a peasant's life may not be very exciting, the old days of hardship are over.

The Workers

Life in the cities is brighter than in the countryside. Wages for factory workers are higher than on the farms. The majority of factory workers earn about $25 a month, and this money goes a long way. Rent might amount to 80 cents a month for a two-room apartment and medical insurance $3 a year. Millions of workers are able to buy radios and watches which are still considered to be luxuries, and most have small savings accounts. For entertainment there are movies, theaters, and athletic events. Sports such as table tennis and hockey are very popular. The magnificent palaces, temples and gardens of China's emperors are now open to the public.

The worker rises at 6:30. He usually lives a short distance from the factory and rides his bicycle to work. The workday begins at 7:30 with a study session on Maoist thought. Actual working time is usually from 8:30 a.m. to 12 p.m. and then from l p.m. to 4:30 p.m. Often there are study sessions after working hours. Working conditions are adequate, although there usually is no air-conditioning in the summer or heating in the winter. In case of accident, the worker receives compensation. Workers work six days a week.

Single workers usually share an apartment with a factory friend. For married workers, there are government built apartment houses with gardens and nurseries.

The Soldiers

At one time, soldiers were the lowest class in society. Today it is considered an honor and a privilege to be a soldier in the People's Liberation Army. To join the three-million-man, all-volunteer army, one must pass a stiff medical and political examination. Aside from the necessary drill, the soldiers' time is spent in peacetime duties. Soldiers engage in farm work, run post offices, factories and communes. Much time is spent in political study sessions. The normal period of service in the army is three years, but this can be extended. It is easy to find a job after leaving the army. The ex-soldier becomes a member of the local militia and must return to service if called.

Maoism

The thoughts and ideas of 800 million Chinese people are strictly controlled by the Communist Party. The Chinese people are taught that Marxism (Communism) is the only truth. Maoism (the ideas of Mao Tse-tung) is the only acceptable form of Communism. For the people in China today Mao Tse-tung is almost a god. Portraits and statues of Mao are everywhere. "Quotations from Chairman Mao," that famous little red book with Mao's sayings, is in every pocket. For some people it is the only book they have ever owned or read. In every school, neighborhood, office, commune and factory there are study groups of Marxism-Leninism and Mao Tse-tung's thoughts.

The main ideas of Maoism can be summarized as follows: 1—service to the people, 2 — increased production, 3—self-reliance, 4—revolutionary consciousness. The people are taught to believe that if the thoughts of Mao are studied and applied correctly there is a solution to everything — from improving crops to curing the deaf. Workers who work six days a week very often spend the seventh day attending lectures and study sessions of Mao's thoughts.

Nearly all the books printed in China today deal with Marxism-Leninism or Maoism. Listening to the radio one hears patriotic songs, news and thoughts of Chairman Mao. Only a few plays are considered acceptable enough to be performed in the theater. These plays, as well as all films, and all forms of art are used to spread the ideas of Mao and Communism.

As a result, the Chinese people are not very well informed about what is really going on in the world. They know very little about what is happening outside their jobs or neighborhoods. They also know very little about Chinese history before 1949.

What is most important to the Chinese leaders today is that the people remain dedicated to the Communist Revolution. Periodically, people in the government and professionals are sent to the countryside for several months to do manual work and to be "re-educated" in the ideas of Mao Tse-tung.

Women in China Today

An old Chinese proverb states "A wife married is like a pony bought; I'll ride her and whip her as I like." This proverb shows how low a woman's position in China was. There are a number of examples in Chinese history of women becoming empresses and ruling with great power, but women were never considered to be equal to men. The ancient Chinese custom of footbinding was supposed to keep a woman's feet small and beautiful. At the same time it made it very difficult for a woman to walk, thereby keeping her at home and dependent on her husband. (Footbinding was not practiced among the poor where women had to work in the fields alongside their husbands.) When there was famine girls were often sold by their parents who regarded them as just another mouth to feed. These girls were usually used as slaves by the families who bought them. Children as young as six were often *betrothed* (promised in mariage). If the girl's parents experienced bad times, she would be sent to work in the house of her future husband. Young brides were very frequently mistreated by their mothers-in-law. Chinese literature is full of stories of women throwing themselves down wells or hanging themselves. When a woman's husband died, it was considered unacceptable for her to remarry.

Today all this has been changed. Women are now regarded as equal to men. They work and fight side by side with their men. In 1950 — a year after they came to power — the Communists passed a new marriage law. This law made husbands and wives equal in the marriage relationship, outlawed dowries and forced marriages, forbade mistreatment of children and infanticide, permitted divorce for women, and gave women property rights. All over China women's study groups were set up to discuss the new law and inform women of their rights. This law has completely changed women's lives.

Women today feel proud of the useful role they have in building China. The newspapers and radio constantly criticize women who stay at home and do nothing but gossip and take care of household chores. The government encourages women to do productive work outside the home for pay, just as men do. Women receive equal pay for equal work. Today they drive heavy trucks and bulldozers and fly planes in the air force. Half of the doctors in China are women.

Both men and women wear clothes which don't require ironing or dry cleaning, and in general, clothes and hair styles for women are very plain. Occasionally, women wear flowered blouses and skirts and hair ribbons. In most cases, women don't curl their hair; they either wear it short or in braids, and they don't wear make-up.

Young people today choose their own marriage partners. (In the past this was done by their parents.) The government discourages early marriages. This makes it possible for a woman to get all the education she can. Also if a woman has a chance to work for several years before she is married, she will be more independent of her husband. Divorce is discourged. The court will first try to help the couple work out their problems. Only after many failures to settle things, does the court agree to grant a divorce. Chinese women seem less anxious to get a divorce than American women. Even if a woman cannot get along with her husband, she has her work, her outside activities and her friends.

Chinese women, as well as men, consider their work to be a very important part of their lives. Often women and men will leave their families for weeks or months if their jobs require them to go to the countryside, the army or another part of the country. Neither the women nor the men seem to mind leaving their families, because they say that their work keeps them happy. This practice, which is now quite common in China, shows how independent women have become. Formerly, a woman's place was in the home.

In the past Chinese women had many babies. Today the people are told that the ideal couple should only have two children. At study groups, at local clinics and at their places of work, people can learn about family planning. Birth control is encouraged and abortions are very easy to have. After giving birth, a woman worker gets 50 to 60 days off with full pay. If a woman has to stay away from her job longer, she is paid for the days she is out. To make it possible for the woman to return to work as quickly as possible, children can be left in special child care centers. Between the ages of 6 weeks and 18 months, a child is looked after in a "feeding station" in the same place where the woman works. The mother is given time during the day to feed and hold her baby. From 18 months to 3½ years, children are left in nurseries. (If there is a grandmother at home, children are left with her.) At the age of 3½ the child enters kindergarten and stays there until he is old enough to start school. Sometimes, children are left in the centers overnight if their parents work the night shift or have meetings in the evening.

Women in China have not reached complete equality yet. The great majority of leaders in the government, the Communist Party, the army and industry are still men. But more and more leadership positions are being taken over by women. Chinese women have come a long way.

Education

Education plays a very important role in any Communist nation. As in the Soviet Union, education has two main goals in China—one is practical: to educate enough people to be engineers, technicians, and skilled workers in order to build up China; the other is political: to remake society by instilling the ideas of Communism in every child and adult. The Chinese have discovered that education is much more effective than using force to change the Chinese way of life.

In 1949 when the Communists took control of China only about 10 to 20% of the people could read and write. The new government began a campaign to improve this situation. Schools were built. The difficult Chinese writing system was made simple. As a result of these changes, more than 80% of the Chinese children now attend school. A larger percentage of the Chinese people are now able to read than in any other time in Chinese history. But education in China is not limited to children. Programs in adult education are carried out after working hours. Here again, the goals are to wipe out illiteracy and to teach the values of Communism.

Teaching people to be loyal Communists begins as early as nursery school, where such plays as "The Little Truck Driver Goes to Peking to See Chairman Mao" are presented. In kindergarten, children climbing over chairs and crawling through hoops are told that this represents the hardships of Mao's Long March. A typical elementary school math problem asks: "If 473 students out of 500 volunteered to go to the countryside to do farm work, what percentage volunteered?"

The basic Chinese curriculum includes math, geography, art, literature, politics, the Chinese language, and foreign languages—with English becoming the most common foreign language. Yet in these subjects too, politics is brought into the curriculum. Examples of some of the earliest English sentences learned are: "We have boundless love of Chairman Mao" and "My brother is in the People's Liberation Army." Every school child and adult spends hours memorizing the writings of Mao Tse-tung.

While most learning is still carried out by means of reciting and memorizing, the Chinese have brought about some very big changes in education. They are trying to *eliminate* (do away with) grades and competition. Exams are used to let the student find out what he doesn't know and to tell the professor where he has failed as a teacher. Group criticism is a very important part of education in China now. At the end of a term, students break up into small groups and review everything—teachers, curriculum and fellow students. They debate what was right and what was wrong and try to correct problems before starting a new year. It is believed that children learn best by doing, and often Chinese students construct the very things they are learning about. In some places students construct the school buildings themselves. Every high school graduate must spend time "serving the people" — by working in a factory or a commune or by joining the army for as long as three years. The person who succeeds is the one who volunteers for the most difficult assignments.

Thus the Chinese people are taught that capitalism is evil, that Communism is superior, and that work is dignified. In addition, all the newspapers, motion pictures, ballet, opera, radio, paintings are used as part of the process of educating the people.

In 1966 during the Cultural Revolution the universities were closed. They reopened in 1969 and 1970. It was felt that university students were losing contact with the masses and developing a feeling of superiority. Since 1970 universities have only been accepting students from the masses — workers, peasants and soldiers. The emphasis in all course work is on Communism. Many courses are purely vocational. The Chinese are told continually that they are building a great nation and that they must use all their talents in achieving this goal. All actions taken by the government are followed by widespread educational campaigns in the belief that the Chinese people must have the information so they can actively assist in making the government's program successful.

The Chinese Economy

Agriculture

Shen-nung was a great king of ancient China. His name meant "divine farmer" and "holy laborer." The Chinese believe it was he who taught men to raise crops. They also believe he invented farm tools for them to use.

The story of Shen-nung is a myth. But we know that about the time he was supposed to have lived—4700 years ago—farmers were raising grain in the Yellow River Valley. The Chinese have been planting and harvesting for perhaps 5000 years. No wonder they are good at it. By patient work they can make each acre give a surprising amount of food. Farming is the way of living for at least 80% of the Chinese people.

For centuries China has been one of the world's greatest producers of food. Because of the uncertainty of the water supply in North China, the principal crop of the North has been wheat. The annual wheat crop of China is the third largest in the world, after the Soviet Union and the United States. Other important crops are also raised, including barley, millet and sorghum, all cereal grains. Many Chinese of the North have never eaten rice. From the cereal grains the Chinese make such food as noodles, porridges (cooked cereal), dumplings and pancakes. In Southern Manchuria the main crops are kaoliang, a kind of cereal grain, wheat and soy beans.

AGRICULTURAL PRODUCTION OF CHINA (Estimated)
(in millions)

	1972	1973	1974	1975	1976
RICE (metric tons)	102	107	113	114	114
CORN (metric tons)	29	30	31	33	34
WHEAT (metric tons)	35	35	37	31	43
BARLEY (metric tons)	19	20	20	21	21
POTATOES (metric tons)	32	32	35	40	41
SOYBEANS (metric tons)	12	12	11.8	12	12
SUGAR (metric tons)	3.5	3.5	3.5	3	4
TEA (metric tons)	203	205	290	300	320
TIMBER (cubic meters)	176	178	188	188	190
FISH (metric tons)	6.9	7	7	6.8	6.8
CATTLE	63	63	63	63	64
SHEEP	72	72	73	73	74
PIGS	235	235	239	238	233
GOATS	59	59	58	60	61
HORSES	7	7	7	7	7

SOURCES: *Encyclopaedia Britannica;* Food and Agriculture Organization *Production Yearbook;* United Nations *Statistical Yearbook.*

South China is rice country. Rice *paddies* (fields) are part of every farm found in the south. The farmers flood the paddies many times during the year, and then transplant young rice plants, which have been grown from seeds in nursery beds. South China has a long growing season because of its warm weather. Often, the farmers can grow two or three crops a year.

Central China is tea and silk country. China's finest teas grow here, for the hilly country south of the Yangtze River is well suited for raising the tea bush. Conditions are also favorable for the growth of the white mulberry. This tree has leaves which are used as food for silkworms. Thus, China's world-famed silks are produced in this area.

A few crops important to the Chinese diet and economy are grown nearly everywhere in China. Enough cotton is raised to meet China's needs. Flax and jute are also raised. China is a major producer of soy beans, sweet potatoes, peanuts and oil-bearing seeds. The Chinese farmer also raises green vegetables, apples, oranges and watermelons.

The small amount of protein in the Chinese diet comes mainly from fish, pork or chicken. People living near the seacoast eat fish. But, even though China is one of

Tea culture. Picking tea, Szechuan Province—central China, north of the Yangtse River. (*Top*)

Tientsin electronic instruments plant. Tientsin is a center of high precision electronic production. (*Bottom*)

Credit: *Hsinhua News Agency*

the world's major fishing nations, there is not enough fish to meet the demand of the Chinese people. Every once in a while, Chinese enjoy a piece of pork or chicken. Pigs and fowl are much easier to raise than cattle.

Despite the tremendous amount of food raised in China, the people have often felt the pain of hunger. Even today, the Communists face the great problem of feeding the Chinese people adequately.

Natural Resources and Industry

Coal is China's most abundant natural resource. Most of the coal fields are found in Manchuria. China also has large deposits of iron ore in Manchuria, Wuhan (the cities of Hankow, Hanyang, and Wuchang) in Central China and Sinkiang. Because of the iron and coal deposits, the Chinese have been able to develop a growing steel industry. The leading steel producer is the Manchurian city of Anshan, which turns out about half the nation's steel. Most of Anshan's mills were built by the Japanese. They have been enlarged and modernized with Russian help since 1945. Other important steel centers are Mukden, also in Manchuria, and Wuhan, on the Yangtze River.

China has good supplies of tungsten, antimony and tin. Tungsten is used in making steel and the filaments in light bulbs. Tin is also used in making steel, and in food containers. Antimony is used in printing. There is sufficient copper to meet China's needs.

The Chinese have a large textile industry. Cotton, silk, flax and jute produced in China supply the industry with raw materials.

China has more raw materials for industry than any other nation in Asia. However, the Chinese do not have the capital to develop the potential water power of their rivers. While China has large deposits of oil in Sinkiang, it is difficult to bring the oil to where it can be used because of a lack of railroads and roads.

No one knows how much oil there is in China. There are no *reliable* (proven) statistics. The lowest *estimate* (guess on limited facts) made of Chinese oil *reserves* (oil in the ground) is about 20 billion barrels. This estimate was made in 1977. If this guess is proved to be true, it would put China in ninth place in world oil reserves. The CIA estimates that China has 39 billion barrels below dry land and about that much in offshore reserves. If this estimate is proved true China would be close to the two leading producers—Saudi Arabia and the Soviet Union.

China's production of oil has multiplied by six times since 1965. The main operating field is the Ta Ching fields in Manchuria. China does not export much oil at present. Much of China's oil is used for its own industry. Some is exported to Japan, Vietnam and North Korea. Agreements have been made with the Japanese to increase the amount of oil exported for the next ten years. China must use her oil to pay for the industrial equipment it buys from the Japanese. By 1990 the Chinese are expected to increase production of oil another 700%.

Other nations of Southeast Asia are interested in buying Chinese oil (Thailand, the Philippines, Hong Kong). There is evidence that the Chinese will use their oil to buy friendship and cooperation, and China seems to be willing to sell her oil at a lower price than it can be bought anywhere in the world. Before his death Chou En-lai was quoted as saying, "This is a friendship price."

China's problems in industrial development are great. The transportation system is inadequate. There is a shortage of capital (money) necessary for industrial development. Skilled manpower is in very short supply.

To solve some of these problems, the government decided on several Five Year Plans, which will now be discussed.

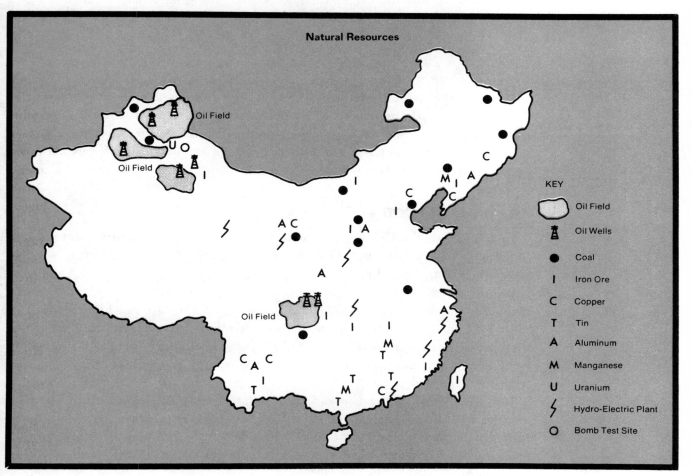

Natural Resources

KEY

Oil Field
Oil Wells
Coal
Iron Ore
Copper
Tin
Aluminum
Manganese
Uranium
Hydro-Electric Plant
Bomb Test Site

The Economic Policy of China

Nationalization

An early slogan of the Chinese Communists was "Twenty Years *Compressed* Into One Day." This slogan expressed the determination of the people to make their country a modern nation in as short a time as possible. When the Communists took control of China in 1949, the economy was in bad shape as a result of the great destruction during World War II and the Civil War that followed. Mao Tse-tung was determined to build up the country as quickly as possible, and to set China on the road to Communism. The first thing the government did was to take all the land owned by wealthy landlords and divide it among the peasants. All businesses, banks, factories and industries were also taken over by the government. Many people who resisted were executed.

State Planning

The second step taken by the government was to plan the entire economy. China's first Five-Year Plan was announced in 1953. This established an ambitious set of production goals which workers and peasants were to reach. The general aim of the Plan was to industrialize China as fast as possible, using the Soviet Union as a model and guide. Emphasis was placed on electric power, chemicals, and steel production. Heavy industry was stressed, at the expense of consumer goods.

Soviet Aid

During these years China received vast support from the Soviet Union in its attempt to industrialize. About thirty thousand Soviet technicians built 291 industrial projects in China. This was done at great expense to the Russians. However, China was expected to pay Russia by sending large amounts of food, raw materials, and manufactured goods to Russia.

Collectivization of Agriculture

In 1949 when the Chinese Communists defeated the Nationalists, most Chinese did not own their own land. One of the promises the Communists made was that each farmer would own his own land.

Within a short time the Communists took the land away from the landlords and divided it among the farmers. Each farmer was given two acres as his very own.

In 1953 the Government of the People's Republic told the village farmers that their two acres were too small for useful farming. The farmers were told they would be able to grow more if they put their fields together and farmed them as if they were one large farm.

Just as the Russians had done earlier, the Chinese *collectivized* agriculture. All land soon became the property of the state. Most of what was produced on the land was taken by the government. The peasants were allowed to own a house, a few animals, and a small garden plot where they grew vegetables for their families.

Results

Mao's efforts brought *moderate* results. *(See graph on p. 323)* New industries were started, but production was not as great as the Communists had hoped. In agriculture the results were even more disappointing. In North China grain production increased only slightly. In the South, where the most efficient unit for rice production is the family and the small, flooded paddy, collective farming actually lowered production. Food continued to be exported to the Soviet Union at the expense of the Chinese people.

By the late 1960s use of chemical fertilizer had increased agricultural production. But in the early 1970s mules and water buffaloes still provided much of the power. The goal today is to achieve mechanization: that is, for machines to replace the bent human figures pushing their water buffaloes.

The Great Leap Forward

In the late 1950s Mao decided to further speed up economic progress. This program was known as the "Great Leap Forward." Everyone was to work harder to increase industrial and agricultural production. Factories were to be kept busy around the clock. To increase farm production and to have greater control over the peasants, the Communists set up People's Communes. A commune was much larger than a collective farm. The average commune was made up of five thousand families.

The peasants at first greatly resisted the whole idea of the communes. The long hours, the barracks system and the starvation diet were not to their liking. In 1959 the Communist government admitted that their goals had been too high. The "Great Leap Forward," was given up in part. It was decided that economic progress would have to come more slowly. Today communes are the rule all over China.

Industrial and Grain Production 1957-1965

Industrial Production (Index: 1965 = 100 units)

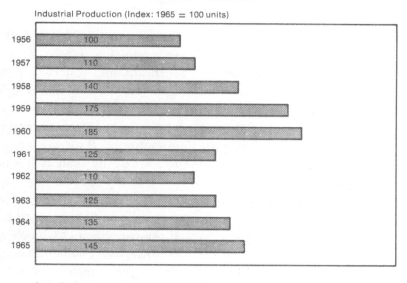

Grain Production (Millions of Metric Tons)

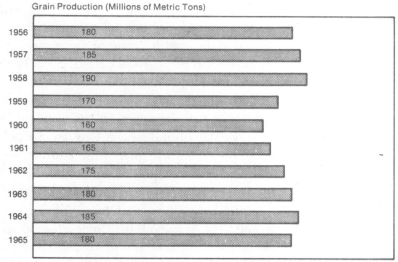

These graphs show ups and downs in two important parts of China's economy after the start of China's Second Five-Year Plan (1957). Note that the drop in grain production started before the drop in industrial production.

And so it has been. The Chinese economy has been improving, but only slowly, and with some setbacks. Droughts, floods, typhoons have caused food shortages and, in some cases, even famine. Political disturbances have slowed production.

Nevertheless, despite these setbacks, the Chinese People's Republic has accomplished a miracle. From a weak, backward, divided country, China has become a strong, unified, modern nation. The country's tremendous potential for scientific and technical development has been evidenced by its production of atomic weapons in the 1960s. It is both feared and respected by the whole world. China today is trying to set an example for the underdeveloped countries of Africa, Southeast Asia, and Latin America who wish to enter the modern world as modern, industrial nations.

Economic Developments in the Seventies

In 1974, the Chinese government said that it had become *self-sufficient* (able to take care of itself) in food production. However, facts show that the Chinese must still import wheat, corn, soybeans, and cotton.

Industrial development to serve the needs of agriculture has continued. New factories to produce farm machinery, fertilizers, and pesticides are being built. Another major area of development has been in the improvement of China's transportation system. Road construction continues. Railroads are constantly improved. Jet transports, helicopters, and trucks are being bought from Japan and the West. (Is there a connection between these two areas of development?)

China is playing an increasing role in the world energy crisis. Some oil experts see China as becoming one of the world's biggest oil producing and exporting nations by the end of the 1970s. At present, much of China's oil is used for her own industry but almost 10% is exported to Japan, Thailand, and the Philippines.

What are the effects of this development of oil resources? Until 1972, China exported more than it imported and therefore had trade surpluses. The money gained from the trade surpluses was used for economic development. But in 1973 and 1974 China imported more than it exported. This meant that the Chinese had to give up gold—which is badly needed—to pay for imports. Economic development had to slow down. With an increase in oil production there again will be a surplus, and more money will be available for economic development.

Another effect of this development has been the decision by the Japanese not to go ahead full speed with aid to the Russians in developing the Siberian oil fields. The Japanese now are selling oil-drilling equipment to the Chinese. They also want to help the Chinese to develop the oil north of the Yellow Sea between China and Korea. This area is very close to Japan and could become a cheap source of oil for the Japanese. In 1978 China and Japan signed a long-term trade agreement. The Japanese would get Chinese oil; the Chinese would receive help from Japanese experts in modernizing their industry and upgrading their economy.

If this oil development continues, the U.S. may also become a large customer of the Chinese.

Chairman Mao Tse-tung greeting former President Nixon in Peking. A new era in Chinese-American relations begins. (February, 1972)
Credit: *Hsinhua News Agency*

China and Taiwan (Formosa)

"Two Chinas"

A hundred miles off the coast of Southeast China lies the island of Taiwan. Portuguese sailors first saw Taiwan in the 1580s, on their way to Japan. They sailed by, but they noted on their maps, "Ilha Formosa," which means "Isle of Beauty." Europeans and Americans still call the island Formosa. To the Chinese and Asians, however, it is know as Taiwan, which means "Terrace Bay."

Taiwan was a part of the Chinese Empire from the early years of the Manchu Dynasty. After the war with Japan in 1895, Taiwan was given to the Japanese. Fifty years later, the island was returned to China.

In 1947, a group of Nationalist Chinese arrived from the mainland. Two years later, after the Nationalists were defeated by the Communists, 600 thousand Nationalist troops, led by Chiang Kai-shek, came to Taiwan. They brought with them the money that was left in the national treasury. They also brought several thousand packing cases filled with paintings and other kinds of art. About another million and a half Chinese came with the troops.

Although violently opposed to each other's government, the leaders of the Nationalists and the Communists agree on one point: There are not "Two Chinas," there is only one government of China. Mao believes that the government in Peking is the legal government of China, while the Nationalists believe that the government in Taipei (capital of Taiwan) is the legal government.

The "Two Chinas": Problems

The existence of the Nationalist government on Taiwan greatly irritates the Chinese Communists. Mao cannot consider his victory complete as long as the Nationalists hold Taiwan. Mao may have intended to send his army against the island as soon as his grip on the mainland was firm. However, the Communists became involved in war with the U.S. in Korea, and his plans had to be put off.

The U.S. announced at that time that its Seventh Fleet would patrol the Taiwan Straits, which separates Taiwan from the mainland. To Mao, this American move meant that Taiwan had been placed beyond the striking power of his army. To Chiang, it meant that he could count on time to build up his strength for an attack on the mainland.

The U.S. had given Chiang a great deal of military and economic aid. In addition, the U.S. signed a treaty of defense with Chiang. These moves by the U.S. showed Mao that the U.S. would resist an invasion of Taiwan. The U.S. made it clear to Chiang that he would receive no American support if he tried to recover the mainland by force.

For Mao, the Taiwan issue is more than a matter of politics. It is an issue of national pride. The Chinese Communists feel that the continued existence of

The Nationalist government is a humiliation for China, and to be blocked by the U.S. was a great insult to the Chinese people. With the passing of years, the U.S. became the main target of Chinese propaganda. The U.S. was called an imperialist power. The Communists also blamed the U.S. for the war in Vietnam. The slogan "liberate Taiwan from the foreign imperialists" is a battle cry which is used to unite the Chinese people behind the Communists.

The existence of "two Chinas" presented a problem to the United Nations. The problem was: who should represent China in the United Nations? Until October 1971, the Nationalists held membership and Communists did not. One solution which had been offered called for membership for both Chinese governments in the U.N. However, neither the Communists nor the Nationalists agreed to sit with the other.

Year after year, the Soviet Union and India tried to get membership in the U.N. for Mao's government. These attempts had been blocked by the United States. Over the years, however, more and more nations came to believe that the People's Republic of China should be represented in the U.N.

Then in October 1971 the inevitable took place. The U.S. removed its objection to seating The People's Republic in the U.N. The American delegation fought for the seating of both Chinese governments. When the vote was taken on the evening of Monday, October 25, the Communist Chinese were admitted to the U.N. and the Nationalist Chinese were *expelled* (thrown out) from the organization.

A new era in world affairs was dawning.

China and the U.S.

For many, many years China and the U.S. were close friends. During World War II both nations fought together on the same side against the Japanese. The U.S. sent China several billion dollars in aid. Then, in 1950, the two nations became bitter enemies. It was only necessary to open a newspaper to see how each side accused the other of the greatest crimes. How did all this come about, and how long will it continue?

Years of Bad Feeling

In 1949 the Chinese Communists came into power. In 1950 the Korean War broke out. American troops fought on the side of the South Koreans, while the Chinese sent hundreds of thousands of troops to support the North Korean Communists.

From then until 1971 the U.S. had little to do officially with The People's Republic of China. We had no diplomatic relations with China. That means that we did not recognize the Communists as the legal government of China. For twenty-two years the

U.S. had kept The People's Republic out of the U.N. In addition, the American government had greatly restricted American businessmen from trading with China.

In 1950 the Communists began a carefully planned "hate America campaign." In daily broadcasts, in posters, newspapers and street demonstrations the Chinese leaders told their people that the U.S. was their enemy. The Chinese were told that the U.S. was the number one enemy of mankind and that an attack by the U.S. was likely.

Reasons for Bad Feelings

Why did the Communist leaders of China attack our government so? One reason is that the U.S. supported the Nationalist government on the island of Taiwan. The Nationalists and the Communists fought each other for control of China for many years.

Mao Tse-tung often said that he was ready to come to terms with the U.S. if the U.S. would agree to the following: 1) stop supporting the Nationalist government, 2) remove the Seventh Fleet, 3) remove its troops from Asia, and 4) give up its defense treaties with Asian nations. In other words, the Chinese Communists would like the U.S. to get out of Asia and leave Asia to the Asians. The U.S. is not prepared to do this.

People's Republic and were trading with her. The people who favored a change in policy felt that if we offered friendship to the Communists we could hope that in the years to come the Chinese would become more friendly and more peaceful.

The opponents of a change in policy felt that the Communists were warlike and would always remain warlike. They said that China was overcrowded and poor, and so the Communist leaders would always try to conquer new lands for their people. They said that the Communists sent troops to Korea, Tibet and India, and that the Chinese Communists were encouraging the North Vietnamese to attack South Vietnam, Laos and Cambodia. Therefore, the U.S. must be prepared to stop the Chinese Communists, by force, if necessary. For a long time the debate continued. Sooner or later an American President would have to decide whether or not to change our policy toward China.

Signs of Change

However, early in 1971, in a surprise move, the Communists invited the American Ping Pong team which was in Japan to visit China. The Americans accepted and for the first time since 1949 Americans officially visited the Chinese mainland. The American team members were met with great friendliness and brotherhood. American newspapermen were allowed to accompany the team into China. Chou En-lai, the Chinese Premier, greeted the team in friendly terms and said that he would like to visit the U.S. Then on July 15, 1971, President Nixon announced that he would go to China before May 1972, on invitation of the Chinese.

Nixon also recommended that The People's Republic of China be admitted to the United Nations, provided that Nationalist China also be allowed to remain in the U.N. This was a historic change in American policy, since it was mainly due to American actions that China had been kept out of the United Nations for more than 20 years.

In late 1971 the United States began to allow Americans to visit China and to resume trade relations.

President Nixon's Visit to China

For seven historic days in February 1972 (February 20 to February 26), the whole world's attention was focused on one event — President Nixon's trip to China. Almost from the beginning it seemed evident that the Chinese went out of their way to make the visit a big success. The Chinese greeted the American president with warmth and friendliness and President Nixon responded in kind. Although there were no large crowds waving enthusiastically at the airport, nearly all of China's senior leaders, except Mao Tse-tung were there. The People's Liberation Army's guard of honor was present and the Stars and Stripes were raised at the airport. A few hours after his arrival, Chairman Mao called to invite the President to his home. The two leaders met for an hour and shortly afterwards the Chinese released photographs of the two smiling leaders.

For seven days the President and his aides held meetings with Chou En-lai and other Chinese officials. The Americans went sightseeing; they were wined and dined and taken to the theater. Among the historic sites the Americans visited were the Great Wall, the Imperial Palace, and the Ming Tombs — the famous burial place of 13 Ming Dynasty emperors. Many of the 87 newsmen who accompanied the President visited factories, schools and other places of interest.

The Chinese showed in many ways that they were interested in better relations between the two countries. At the first banquet at the Great Hall of the People held in honor of Mr. Nixon the Chinese band played "The Star-Spangled Banner," "America the Beautiful" and "Home on the Range." Chairman Mao told his guests that "the gates to friendly contact have finally been opened." President Nixon was cordial as well. At the first banquet he quoted Mao's poetry. In his toast he proposed that China and the United States "start a Long March together." After visiting the Great Wall, President Nixon said that he hoped that "walls will not divide peoples of the world, that people regardless of differences in philosophy and background will have an opportunity to communicate with each other and know each other." When the presidential party saw the revolutionary ballet "The Red Detachment of Women" the President praised the "excellent theatre and excellent dancing and music and really superb acting."

The visit received unprecedented coverage in the Chinese press. The most important newspaper, Peking's *People's Daily,* featured continuous front page articles and numerous photographs. (The pictures, showing Mr. Nixon, Chairman Mao Tse-tung and Chou En-lai smiling, contrasted with the grim faces of Chou and Soviet Premier Aleksei Kosygin during their 1969 talks at Peking airport.) Radio broadcasts carried news of the trip all over China. No other foreign leader in recent years has received such coverage in China.

What did President Nixon's journey accomplish? President Nixon repeatedly warned that "no miracles should be expected." Perhaps the greatest miracle was the fact that the leaders of two nations, which for 22 years showed only outright hostility toward each other, met in an atmosphere of cordiality and friendliness. The trip achieved the goal of breaking a silence that had lasted more than two decades. Neither side had any illusions. Both realized that wide differences exist between the two countries and many obstacles stand in the way of closer relations. But the leaders of both nations seemed to indicate that despite the differences in beliefs there are common interests. President Nixon expressed this when he said that "while we cannot close the gulf between us, we can try to bridge it so that we may be able to talk across it." It is an advantage to both nations to see an expansion in trade. Reassurance of China's peaceful intentions made it easier for the United States to get out of Vietnam. If China were assured that the United States would reduce its military forces in Asia, China could then pay more attention to its problems at home as well as its problems with the Soviet Union.

At the end of the visit there was a *communiqué* (an official statement summarizing the results of the meetings). In it, both nations agreed to make it easier for Americans and Chinese to have contacts with each other. The two countries agreed to expand trade and to make relations between the two nations more normal. The two sides would stay in contact and America would send a senior U.S. representative to Peking from time to time for meetings. The communiqué indicated that the question of Taiwan was the major obstacle to normal relations between the United States and China. President Nixon agreed that the Taiwan issue would have to be settled by the Chinese people themselves. The United States would reduce its forces and military installations on Taiwan as tension in the area declines. But President Nixon would not agree to what the Chinese wanted most — to cut all ties with the Nationalist government in Taiwan.

At a banquet held the last night before President Nixon left China, Premier Chou En-lai promised that he would work to improve relations between both nations.

Within the first year after that historic meeting, some 2,000 Americans and many Chinese crossed the Pacific to talk business and exchange ideas. American firms agreed to build earth-satellite stations in China, to sell Boeing 707 airliners, and to train pilots and maintenance men. Corn and wheat sales to China worth over forty million dollars were arranged.

In February 1973, Henry Kissinger, President Nixon's special assistant who had been to China the year before to arrange the President's trip, visited Peking for special meetings with Chinese officials. During these meetings it was agreed that the United States would establish a mission in Peking and a Chinese mission would be set up in Washington. This is a first step toward full diplomatic recognition after 23 years of tense relations and distrust. These missions would make it possible for both countries to have contact with each other on a regular basis. Talks are already in progress to make it easier for scientists, doctors, reporters, businessmen, athletic teams, and cultural groups from China and the United States to visit each other's countries.

In January, 1979, the United States and China announced that they would establish diplomatic relations. For the first time in thirty years the two countries would exchange ambassadors. Several weeks after this historic announcement, Teng Hsaio-ping, the senior Deputy Prime Minister of China, visited the United States. Teng is the most powerful man in China today, and his visit was very important. It was a symbol of the improved relations that now exist between both countries. However, China's recent invasion of Vietnam has led to increasing uneasiness about this new alliance. Because setting up diplomatic relations with China also means breaking off relations with Taiwan, some people are especially apprehensive about China's use of force against Vietnam and feel that it could also be used against Taiwan.

The Sino-Soviet Dispute

Almost every day we open the newspapers and read some of the insults and *accusations* that the Soviet Union and China are hurling at each other. This seems to puzzle us. We know that both countries are Communist. Therefore, shouldn't they also be friends?

Changes in Sino-Soviet Relations

At one time, the Chinese Communists and the Soviet Communists were close friends. The Russians provided the Chinese Communists with large amounts of arms, which helped them to take over the country. After the Communists took control of the Chinese government in 1949, the Russians poured millions of rubles into China to help build up its industries. Thousands of Russian scientists and engineers were sent to China. The Russians gave the Chinese information on how to develop atomic power. The leaders of the two countries said that the friendship between the two nations would last forever.

Then suddenly, in the late 1950s, relations between the USSR and China began to cool. At first they tried to keep their quarrel a secret, but gradually it came out into the open. Russian scientists and engineers began to leave China. Aid to China was sharply cut, and the Russians demanded that China repay them for previous aid. By the early 1960s Chinese newspapers were calling the Soviet leaders traitors and cowards. What brought about the change? What are some of the causes behind the quarrel between these two Communist giants?

Causes of the Sino-Soviet Dispute

1. Rivalry for Leadership

In Russia the Communists came into power in 1917. In China the Communists took over in 1949. For years the Soviet leaders felt they were more experienced and, therefore, Communists all over the world should follow them. The Chinese didn't like this, because they felt they had as much experience as the Russians. Both countries would like to be the leaders of world Communism. Each nation is trying to win over Communists from other countries to its side.

2. Economic Position

For almost fifty years Soviet leaders have worked hard to build up modern industries, cities, highways and railroads. Now that the Soviet Union has achieved all this, its citizens would like to settle down and enjoy the comforts of a good life. China, on the other hand, is still developing, which means that its industries have not yet been built up, and its people have a low *standard of living*. This makes the two countries look at things differently.

3. Attitude Toward War

Communists always believed that there could be no lasting peace in the world until all countries had a Communist form of government. As long as there were *capitalist* nations, they might try to attack the Communists. Therefore, it was the duty of Communists everywhere to wage war against capitalists and bring about their downfall. Now, however, with the existence of atomic weapons, such wars might destroy the world. The Russians are not willing to risk this. They would not like to see everything that they have worked for for over fifty years destroyed. Thus, the Russians now believe in *peaceful coexistence*, that is, living peacefully with other countries. The Chinese have much less, and so they have been more willing to take risks. The Chinese still believe that all capitalist governments should be overthrown, even if that means war. Therefore, they call the Russians cowards and traitors. (In the **1970s** the Chinese have tried to improve relations with Western nations in order to achieve their goals by peaceful means.)

4. Territorial Disputes

The Russian-Chinese border extends over 6,500 miles. The Chinese have charged that Russia holds over 700 thousand square miles of land that once belonged to China. (This area is about the size of all of Arizona, New Mexico, Texas, Louisiana, Mississippi, Alabama and Florida combined.) This land is rich in undeveloped resources, and is sparsely populated. China's land is overcrowded. The Russians fear that China might one day try to take back this land for its surplus population.

Sino-Soviet Relations Today

Although Russian leaders are not very happy with the way things stand between the Soviet Union and China they have done very little to improve the situation. On the issue of how to make world revolution, Soviet Russia and Communist China have continued to be wide apart. To the Russians, the Chinese are reckless in an age of atomic weapons. Soviet caution leads the Chinese to say that Russia is not really interested in world revolution.

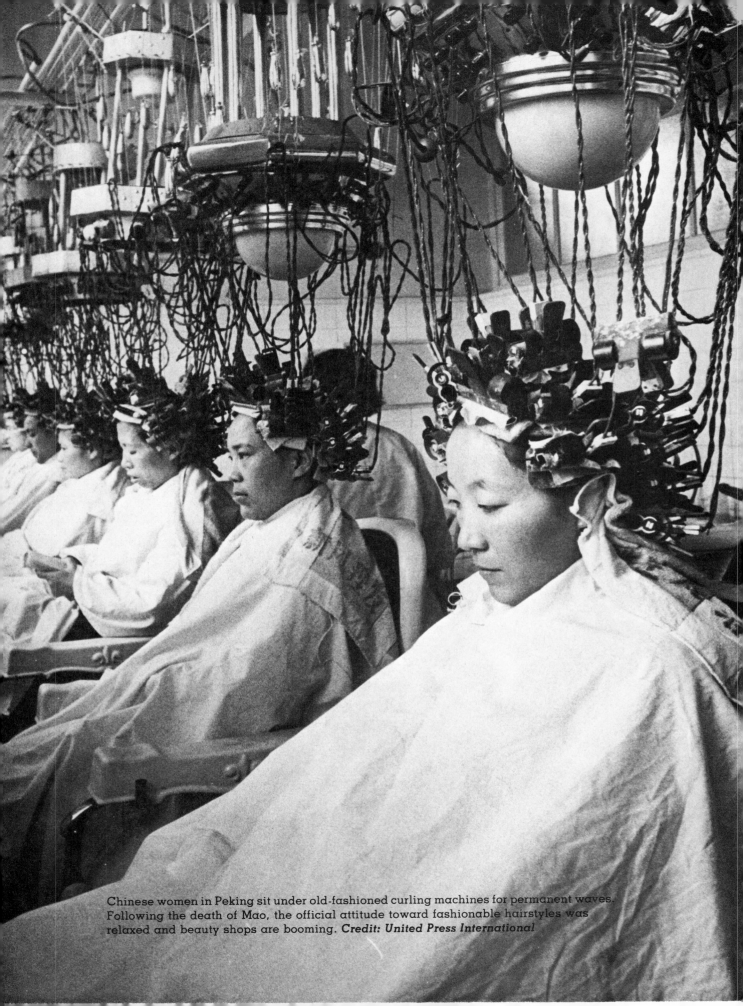

Chinese women in Peking sit under old-fashioned curling machines for permanent waves. Following the death of Mao, the official attitude toward fashionable hairstyles was relaxed and beauty shops are booming. *Credit: United Press International*

A young woman in Shanghai wears shorts instead of the usual baggy pants. *Credit: United Press International*

This difference has worked to China's advantage in the struggle to win friends among the new nations of the world. They would like to achieve what the Chinese have achieved, and have little to lose by "foolish recklessness." In addition, they look to the Chinese as non-white "brothers" and anti-imperialists.

The Sino-Soviet border dispute has worsened. In March 1969, fierce battles between Russian and Chinese soldiers broke out along the border between the two countries. The first battles were along the Ussuri River. Later, the action shifted to the thinly populated area where China's Sinkiang Province meets the Kazakh SSR. Each side said that the other attacked first, and invaded territory that belonged to the other. Hundreds of dead and wounded soldiers on both sides show the seriousness of the fighting.

The most recent example of the conflict between China and the Soviet Union was China's recent invasion of Vietnam. The Chinese attacked their neighbor to the south in retaliation against Vietnam's frequent border intrusions and against Vietnam's recent invasion of Cambodia. China claimed that it had no intention of pursuing the Vietnamese into the central portion of their country, preferring to capture and hold border towns. The Soviets strongly protested this attack against their Vietnamese ally and began supplying the Vietnamese with arms. The conflict remains to be resolved, but appears to be a test of strength between China and the Soviet Union.

Foreign Policy Statements

The main points of Chinese foreign policy remain: (1) opposition to U.S. and Russian domination in world affairs; (2) *détente* with the U.S. and Western Europe as a balance against the threat of a Soviet attack on China; (3) close friendship with Third World nations against the "socialist imperialism" of the Soviet Union and the "capitalist imperialism" of the U.S.

To carry out these policies and to improve relations, discussions have gone on beween the U.S. and the People's Republic. Trade and business agreements have been worked out with the Japanese and the countries of Western Europe. The Chinese have given support and backing for many Third World groups (such as the Palestine Liberation Organization, the Pathet Lao, the Viet Cong, the Khmer Rouge, and the African guerrillas in Rhodesia and South Africa). Relations with the Soviets still remain poor. Movements of troops by both sides on their common border are constantly reported. Conferences involving the two sides have made little progress.

A Policy of Friendly Cooperation

The principles behind the foreign policy of the People's Republic of China are the defense of its national independence, sovereign freedom, rights and territorial integrity; supporting a lasting internal peace and friendly cooperation among the people of all countries; and opposition to the imperialist policy of aggression and war. (Chou En-lai)

Friendship with the Socialist Countries, Neutral Countries, and Colonial People

Our country's principles in dealing with international affairs should be as follows: (1) to continue to consolidate and strengthen our unbreakable friendship with the Soviet Union and the People's Democracies; (2) to establish and develop friendly relations with the Asian, African, and other nations which support peace and are against imperialism. (Chou En-lai, 1954-1955)

For the Sake of Peace, America Must Leave Asia

The United States must completely get out of the southern part of Vietnam; it must get out of all Asia! Only in this way can the peace of Indochina and Asia be effectively safeguarded. (*People's Daily*, July 20, 1960)

China Not to Blame for Bad Chinese-American Relations

Quite a number of countries have voiced concern over the relations between China and the United States hoping, out of good intentions, to promote an improvement in the relations between the two countries. The Chinese people do wish to be friendly with the American people. However, we are not to blame for the long failure to improve relations between the U.S. and China. It is the U.S. government which is using the international disputes between China and the U.S. as a lever to create tension in the Far East, is obstructing improvement in Sino (Chinese)-American relations. . . . The United States not only refuses to recognize the People's Republic of China, but it is also hampering other nations from establishing friendly relations with China. It continues to block the return to China of its rightful place in the United Nations. It continues to apply a trade embargo against China, and is further stepping up its efforts to prevent other nations from developing trade on the basis of mutual benefit with China. What is most serious is that the U.S. not only refuses to negotiate seriously on the question of Taiwan, but it is strengthening its military control over it. This is a deliberate attempt to aggravate the tension in the Taiwan area. Moreover, the U.S. also attempts, through the Sino-American talks, to induce China to recognize the present state of U.S. occupation of Taiwan, thus to create a situation of two Chinas. (Chou En-lai, March 5, 1957)

China Needs Peace

Peace is in the best interests of this country. The 650 million freed Chinese people have worked hard to change the poor, bleak background of their own country. We need an environment of lasting international peace. Therefore, the Chinese Government and people have all along pursued a peaceful foreign policy, and upheld the principles of peaceful co-existence between countries of different social systems. (*People's Daily*, August 28, 1960)

Peace Through Struggle

In the final analysis, the securing of world peace mainly rests on the struggles undertaken by the peoples of the world. The present world situation is more favorable than ever to the struggle in defense of world peace. The countries in the socialist camp are growing stronger. The national and democratic movements in Asia and Africa and Latin America are developing vigorously. From South Korea to Turkey, from Cuba to Algeria, anti-imperialist revolutionary storms are breaking out continuously. (Teng-Hsiao-ping, May 20, 1960).

These are official statements of the Chinese government and its leaders over a period of time. Which statements seem to be still true of Chinese policy today? Do you see any changes?

Quotations from Mao Tse-tung

Mao's quotations have been read by millions of Chinese, in the so-called *Little Red Book*. The *Little Red Book* is also the handbook for revolutionaries and guerrilla movements throughout the world. Below is a selection of Mao's ideas from the book:

On Power:	"Political power grows out of the barrel of a gun."
On Victory:	"Just because we have won a victory, we must never relax our *vigilance* (watchfulness) against the mad plots for revenge by the imperialists and their running dogs."
On Revolution:	"A revolution is not a dinner party, or painting a picture; it cannot be leisurely, gentle, kind, courteous, and restrained. A revolution is an insurrection by which one class overthrows another."
On Ignorance:	"It is to the advantage of *despots* (rulers with unlimited power) to keep people ignorant; it is to our advantage to make them intelligent. We must lead all of them gradually from ignorance."
On Youth:	"The world is yours as well as ours. China's future belongs to you. You young people, full of vigor and vitality, are in the bloom of life. Our hope is placed in you."
On Women:	"Enable every woman who can work to take her place on the labor front, under the principle of equal pay for equal work. Genuine equality between the sexes can only be realized in the process of changing society as a whole."
On Guerrilla Warfare:	"The enemy advances, we retreat The enemy camps, we *harass* (bother) The enemy tires, we attack The enemy retreats, we pursue."

Summary
of
Key Ideas

China

A. **Geographic and physical features have influenced Chinese history and culture.**

1. China is one of the largest countries in area and population.

2. Pressure of population has made the supplying of food a major and continual problem.

3. Geographic differences have resulted in different ways of living in North and South China.

4. Ancient civilizations in China grew in the great river valleys.

5. Geographic barriers isolated China from the West in the past.

6. Geographic factors prevented the full development of China's natural resources.

7. The monsoon plays a vital role in the life of the Chinese people.

8. The river systems play a life and death role in the lives of the Chinese people.

B. **Chinese civilization has had a great influence on the different peoples throughout the world.**

1. Chinese civilization is one of the oldest in the world.

2. The importance of Chinese customs and traditions prevented change when the Europeans made their influence felt.

3. Chinese history and culture has followed a continuous and unbroken road.

4. The rise and fall of dynasties has occurred over and over in Chinese history.

5. Chinese fear and hatred of outsiders and the Chinese belief in the superiority of Chinese ways has influenced China's cultural history and foreign relations.

6. The Chinese have accepted and developed parts of many cultural and religious systems. (Buddhism, animism, Confucianism)

7. Confucianism was the model for the value system of the Chinese culture.

8. Chinese contributions in art, architecture, ceramics, literature, religion, theatre and music have influenced civilization in Asia and in the rest of the world.

C. **Western ideas, values and customs have affected traditional Chinese life and the course of Chinese history.**

1. In the 19th century, the great increase in population put great pressure on Chinese resources.

2. Traditional Chinese society and values were changed by contact with the West, Western interference in Chinese life, civil war and a long war against Japan.

3. The idea of "The Mandate from Heaven" greatly influenced the course of Chinese history.

4. Revolutions in 1911 and 1912 overthrew the traditional monarchy and plunged China into a long series of civil wars.

5. After the Communists won the military victory of 1949, a vast program was begun to reshape Chinese political, economic and social institutions along Communist lines.

6. The Chinese people speak many different dialects; the written language can only be read by the well-educated. The Communists are trying to simplify the language.

7. All media of communication are used to make people think in terms of the Communist idea.

8. Artistic effort must conform to the rigid standards set by the Communist Party and the government.

D. **The victory of Communism in China presents challenges to Asian nations as well as to the Soviet Union and the non-Communist world powers.**

1. The military victory of the Communists in 1949 was due to many factors.

2. The structures of the government and the Party are modeled after those of the Soviet Union.

3. Two governments, Nationalist (Taiwan) and People's Republic (Mainland) claim legal rule over all of China.

4. The People's Republic of China was recently admitted to membership in the U.N., and the Nationalists were expelled.

5. The People's Republic of China is active in Asia and Africa in support of revolutionary activities for the establishment of Communism.

6. Troubles between the Soviet Union and China have historic roots. Today they are rivals for leadership of the world Communist movement.

7. The foreign relations of the Chinese are based on strong anti-western, anti-American and anti-imperialistic ideas.

8. President Nixon's recent visit to China marked the beginning of a new era in Chinese-American relations.

E. **China appears to have the human and industrial resources** for becoming a great power.

1. The Communists introduced a system of government ownership and control of the land and the means of production.

2. Industrialization has been promoted in a series of Five Year Plans.

3. Rapid industrialization (Great Leap Forward Program) was not successful.

4. Agricultural production still remains a major problem.

5. Chinese scientific and technical potential is great, as shown by the production of atomic weapons.

6. Personal income and the production of consumer goods remain at low levels.

New students at a Chinese middle school put up wall posters to usher in the new term.
Credit: Wide World Photos

UNIT V

Exercises and Questions

Vocabulary

Directions: Match the words in Column *A* with the correct meaning in Column *B*.

Column A

1. loess
2. traditional
3. unique
4. dynasty
5. opium
6. rebellion
7. imperialism
8. communes
9. kaoliang
10. mandate
11. revolution

Column B

(a) one of a kind.

(b) important change in government, economy or society.

(c) a narcotic drug.

(d) large farming or factory units set up by the Communists.

(e) the control of a weak country by a strong one.

(f) order or command.

(g) wind deposits of soil.

(h) a cereal grain raised in China.

(i) open resistance to authority or government.

(j) a group of rulers from one family.

(k) customs that have been handed down from generation to generation.

Directions: Using the words below complete the following sentences:

| Chung kuo | Chou Dynasty | Sung Dynasty | Boxers | Kuomintang |
| Shang Dynasty | Taoism | Taipings | San Min Chu-I | The Long March |

1. .... was the first Chinese Dynasty for which archeologists have found evidence.

2. .... was the Dynasty famous for its literature and philosophers.

3. .... are the group who rebelled against the Manchus.

4. .... means The Middle Kingdom and is what the Chinese call their land.

5. .... is a view of man and the universe in which man must find "the way."

6. .... occurred when Mao Tse-tung fled to Yenan with his Communists to escape the Nationalists.

7. .... was the Dynasty which made great contributions in art and civilization.

8. .... was the party formed by Sun Yat-sen to work for the unity of China.

9. .... were the three principles of Dr. Sun Yat-sen.

10. .... were a group of Chinese who tried to drive out the Westerners from Manchu China.

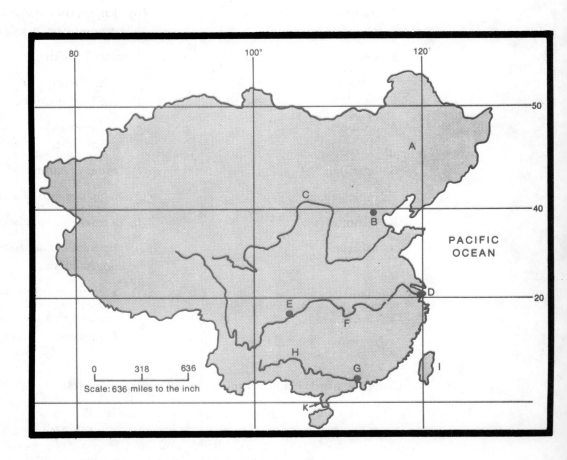

Map Exercise

Directions: **Select** the number of the correct answer.

1. An *island* is shown by the letter: (1) C   (2) F   (3) K   (4) I

2. A *peninsula* is shown by the letter: (1) C   (2) F   (3) K   (4) I

3. The distance from B to G is about   (1) 250 miles   (2) 500 miles   (3) 1000 miles   (4) 1500 miles

4. The place located closest to 120° east longitude and 30° north latitude is   (1) A   (2) B   (3) D   (4) K

5. Which of the following statements is true?
   (1) The climate of A is probably warmer than that of G.
   (2) The climate of I is probably warm and rainy.
   (3) As you move from D to E the climate will become cooler.
   (4) The climate of B and D will be exactly the same.

6. As you travel from B to G you are going   (1) North   (2) South   (3) East   (4) West

7. The rivers shown on this map all flow in a   (1) northern direction   (2) southern direction   (3) eastern direction   (4) western direction

8. This is a map of China. Which river is indicated by the letter C?
   (1) Hwang Ho   (2) Yangtze   (3) Hsi   (4) Yalu

9. The Yangtze River is indicated by the letter
   (1) C   (2) F   (3) H   (4) K

10. You would most likely find the delta of the Hsi (West) River in
    (1) North China   (2) Central China   (3) South China   (4) West China

CHINA'S FOREIGN TRADE

Import Source	Export Destination	Main Exports
JAPAN 21%	HONG KONG 25%	TEXTILES
W. GERMANY 8%	JAPAN 13%	CLOTHING
UNITED KINGDOM 5%	UNITED KINGDOM 5%	METAL ORES
		TEA
		RICE
		COAL

Chart Analysis

Directions: Answer the following questions by indicating that the statement is *True* or *False* or that the *Information Is Not Given*. Base all answers on information given in the chart.

1. China's leading trading partner is probably Japan.

2. China sends much of her goods out of the country through Hong Kong.

3. More than 90% of the goods China buys is bought from Asian countries.

4. China has no trade with the U.S. and the Soviet Union.

5. In conclusion we might say that China mainly sells light industrial products and raw materials.

Multiple Choice

Directions: Find the letter of the correct answer.

1. China's rivers have
   (a) greatly influenced the lives of the people
   (b) not influenced the lives of the people
   (c) only recently influenced the lives of the people
   (d) slightly influenced the lives of the people

2. Which of the following statements is *true* about Chinese geography?
   (a) The mountains of China are along the east coast
   (b) The rivers of China are navigable for only a short distance
   (c) Geography has in part isolated China from the world
   (d) Geography has had little to do with China's unique development

3. The most densely populated areas of China are found
   (a) near industrial cities   (b) in the river valleys
   (c) in the western mountains   (d) on the southern plateau

4. The irregular coastline of China is important because
   (a) it prevents the development of trade
   (b) it allows the cold winds from the north to destroy crops
   (c) it aids the development of trade and harbors
   (d) it prevents communication between North and South China

5. The best way to discuss the climate of China is to
   (a) compare the differences between North and South China
   (b) study the entire country because there are few variations
   (c) study only the southern area because most of the Chinese live there
   (d) compare the differences between China and Southeast Asia

6. Which of the following would have the greatest effect on the lives of the Chinese people?
   (a) the mountains   (b) the monsoons   (c) the North Wind   (d) the desert

7. As a person travels west in China he is most likely to find
   (a) densely populated cities   (b) large agricultural areas
   (c) mountains and desert country   (d) dry loess plains

8. Which of the following statements is *true* about the Chinese people?
   (a) All Chinese have the same physical characteristics
   (b) The great majority of the Chinese people are not "Han people"
   (c) Anthropologists have proved the Chinese are not a Mongoloid people
   (d) It is difficult to decide on a single set of characteristics for the Chinese

9. The Chinese people believe in all of the following things *except*
    (a) the importance of history
    (b) the need to live in peace with nature
    (c) the right of rebellion
    (d) the importance of the individual over the family

10. Which of the following statements is *true* about Chinese culture?
    (a) The Chinese way of life remained unchanged until modern times
    (b) The Chinese family plays only a small role in Chinese life
    (c) Chinese art shows the great part man plays in the universe
    (d) Great changes in culture have taken place in the 20th Century

11. Confucianism is a
    (a) philosophy   (b) religion   (c) form of writing   (d) style of architecture

12. Confucius was *not* interested in
    (a) how people acted   (b) how the government was run   (c) heaven and hell
    (d) family relationships

13. Which of the following is *not* one of the Five Basic Relationships of Confucius?
    (a) father and son   (b) husband and wife   (c) mother and daughter
    (d) friend and friend

14. Confucius believed that the emperor should be
    (a) rich and powerful   (b) wise and humane   (c) friendly and sociable
    (d) strong and cruel

15. Which of the following statements is true about Confucianism?
    (a) Salvation of the soul is a very important part of Confucianism.
    (b) According to Confucianism there is only one God.
    (c) Confucianism was mainly concerned with life after death.
    (d) Confucianism was mainly concerned with achieving a better life on earth.

16. Which of the following is *not* an idea of Taoism?
    (a) People are happiest when they live according to the rules of society.
    (b) Tao is the unseen power that controls all life and movement in the universe.
    (c) People must find out what Tao is and live according to it.
    (d) Society causes unhappiness and problems for people.

17. The gentry made money from all of the following *except*
    (a) large landed estates   (b) rice shops   (c) pawn shops   (d) hard work

18. The gentry lived
    (a) in villages   (b) on their land   (c) in the towns   (d) along the coast

19. In arranging marriages for their sons, it was important to the gentry that the
    (a) bride be beautiful
    (b) bride be educated
    (c) bride be capable of hard work
    (d) bride's family have wealth and social position

20. The gentry became the scholar-officials of China because
    (a) the Chinese believed that only educated people should run the government
    (b) years of studying were necessary to pass a difficult civil service examination

(c) the gentry had the money and leisure to devote to education

(d) all of these

21. Which of the following is *not* true about the peasants of China?

    (a) The peasants earned a living doing hard physical work.

    (b) The peasants lived mainly in small families.

    (c) The peasants enjoyed many forms of entertainment and luxuries.

    (d) The peasants looked for wives who were capable of doing hard work.

22. Life for Chinese peasants was difficult because

    (a) they lived in great poverty

    (b) disease and hunger were common

    (c) they suffered from droughts, famine and floods

    (d) all of these

23. Which of the following is *not* true about family life in China?

    (a) The family was considered to be more important than the individual.

    (b) If a person did something wrong he brought shame on the whole family.

    (c) Young people became independent only after marriage.

    (d) The oldest male was the most important person in the family.

24. Which of the following *is* true about family life in China?

    (a) Chinese fathers were very strict with their sons.

    (b) Daughters were often sold as slaves.

    (c) Parents had to train children to behave properly in society.

    (d) All of these

25. Which statement is true concerning Chinese marriage customs?

    (a) Young men and women married on the basis of love.

    (b) Mothers helped pick husbands for their daughters.

    (c) Often the bride and groom did not see each other before the wedding.

    (d) The bride's family had to pay a dowry to the family of the groom.

26. In China, old age was

    (a) something to look forward to   (b) considered to be a terrible time

    (c) not respected   (d) not considered to be important

27. The Chinese language

    (a) is similar to European languages in the use of vowel sounds

    (b) uses tone and sound to make meanings of words clear

    (c) has changed very little despite contact with the West

    (d) has not influenced other parts of the world to any extent

28. The Chinese writing system

    (a) has served to unify the Chinese   (b) has only a few characters to learn

    (c) is similar to our writing system   (d) all of these

29. The earliest people of North China

    (a) developed little culture and lived in a primitive way

    (b) developed cities and an agricultural civilization

    (c) used only the simplest tools and weapons made of stone

    (d) left few records so we know little of the culture

30. Which of the following is *not* an idea of Confucius ?
    - (a) He felt man should live by his senses and reject knowledge
    - (b) He felt that people had a place in society and duties to fulfill
    - (c) He felt obedience to one's parents was important
    - (d) He felt that the family was the foundation of Chinese society

31. Which of the following is *not* an accomplishment of the Han
    - (a) The Han made the ideas of Confucius the law of the land
    - (b) The Han Chinese destroyed the power of the Mongols
    - (c) The Han Chinese invented paper and porcelain
    - (d) The Han Chinese developed trade with the Roman Empire

32. (a) Yuan Dynasty   (b) Sung Dynasty   (c) Ming Dynasty
    In which order did the above dynasties rule China ?
    - (a) abc   (b) bca   (c) bac   (d) cab

33. The Manchus were able to rule China for all of the following reasons *except* which?
    - (a) They outnumbered the Chinese in men and arms
    - (b) They respected and encouraged the development of Chinese culture
    - (c) They allowed the Chinese people to take part in the government
    - (d) They rarely interfered in village life

34. Invaders of China until the 19th century usually
    - (a) adopted Chinese culture   (b) destroyed Chinese culture
    - (c) paid little attention to Chinese culture   (d) changed Chinese culture

35. The Chinese sold which of the following groups of products to Europeans
    - (a) brocades, opium, tea   (b) silk, opium, porcelain
    - (c) porcelain, silk, tea   (d) silver, porcelain, tea

36. The Opium War was fought because the
    - (a) Chinese were not allowed to sell their opium in India
    - (b) Chinese wished to stop the British opium trade in China
    - (c) British and Chinese could not agree on how to split the profits
    - (d) British wanted to make China a colony

37. The Manchus were faced with the problem of
    - (a) overpopulation   (b) peasant revolts
    - (c) European imperialism   (d) all of these

38. Which of the following events was the result of the other three?
    - (a) The Opium War breaks out
    - (b) The Chinese begin to smoke opium
    - (c) Rebellions break out against Manchu rule
    - (d) The British try to sell opium to the Chinese

39. Which of the following nations did not take territory from the Chinese?
    - (a) United States   (b) Japan   (c) Great Britain   (d) Russia

40. Which of the following events happened *after* the other three?
    - (a) The Taiping Rebellion   (b) The Boxer Rebellion
    - (c) The Sino-Japanese War   (d) The Chinese Revolution

41. Which of the following was *not* an idea of Dr. Sun Yat-sen?
    (a) government of the people (b) economic equality
    (c) sacrifice for China (d) cultural revolution

42. Chiang Kai-shek:
    (a) was successful in his attempt to unite China
    (b) joined with the Communists to unite China after Dr. Sun's death
    (c) joined with the Communists to fight the Japanese
    (d) joined with the war lords to defeat the Communists

43. The Communists were successful for all of the following reasons *except*
    (a) Russian troops were used to fight against the Nationalists
    (b) The Nationalists were corrupt and were not supported by the people
    (c) The Communists were given large amounts of captured Japanese arms
    (d) The Communist army was better disciplined and had better generals

44. Which of the following events occurred *before* the other three?
    (a) The Long March takes place
    (b) Chiang Kai-shek flees to Formosa
    (c) The Cultural Revolution takes place
    (d) The Japanese surrender at the end of World War II

45. Which of the following statements is *not* true about the Chinese government?
    (a) There are many political parties in China today.
    (b) Real power is in the hands of the Communists.
    (c) Important decisions are made by a small group of people.
    (d) Young people are not in positions of power.

46. The purpose of the Young Communist League and the People's Militia is to
    (a) give people an opportunity in making important decisions
    (b) train people to participate in the government
    (c) promote the ideas of the Communist Party and check on the people
    (d) train people to exercise freedom of speech and press

47. The Cultural Revolution involved a (n)
    (a) attempt to bring back capitalism
    (b) struggle for power between Mao Tse-tung and his opponents
    (c) great change in the way of life of the Chinese people
    (d) attempt to remove the communists from power

48. The question who will replace Mao Tse-tung is of great interest because
    (a) Mao is a very old man
    (b) people are concerned as to what policies Mao's successor will follow
    (c) people wonder whether there will be important changes in China
    (d) all of these

49. Which statement is true about life in China since the Communist Revolution?
    (a) Life is not very different from the way it was before the Communist takeover.
    (b) The Chinese people feel that the government is not doing anything for them.
    (c) The Communists have wiped out opium smoking, prostitution and poverty.
    (d) The Communists have failed in their goal to create "a new Chinese man."

50. Peasants in China today
    (a) are still exploited by the rich gentry
    (b) have less land than the large landowners
    (c) are living better than ever before
    (d) still suffer from famine and widespread hunger

51. Workers and soldiers in China today
    (a) are the lowest classes in Chinese society
    (b) are oppressed by their bosses and officers
    (c) have no time for leisure and recreation
    (d) have to spend time studying Maoism

52. The ideas of Mao Tse-tung are presented to the Chinese people
    (a) in school   (b) in the newspapers and on the radio
    (c) in movies and the theater   (d) all of these

53. Women in China today
    (a) are considered inferior to men
    (b) often leave their families for months in order to work
    (c) cannot get a divorce
    (d) still practice the custom of footbinding

54. In China today it is believed that
    (a) a woman's place is in the home
    (b) men have more to contribute to building up China than women
    (c) a woman's family is more important than her job
    (d) men and women should get equal pay for equal work

55. Which of the following statements is *not* true about education in China today?
    (a) An important goal in Chinese education is to promote the ideas of Communism.
    (b) The Chinese have largely succeeded in wiping out illiteracy.
    (c) Confucianism and Communism are the two most important philosophies taught in Chinese schools.
    (d) Most learning is still carried out by means of reciting and memorizing.

56. The main crop of North China is wheat because
    (a) the people do not know how to raise rice
    (b) there is too much rain for rice growing
    (c) there is not enough water for rice growing
    (d) the people like to eat wheat products

57. A major problem of China is the lack of enough food to feed the people. This is true because
    (a) little food is raised
    (b) poor soil covers most of China
    (c) China has a very large population
    (d) most food is destroyed by insects

Which of the Following Does Not Belong in Each Group?

Directions: Indicate which of the following does not belong in each group

1. Problems of Industrialization: lack of sufficient capital, inadequate transportation, lack of iron and coal, oversupply of trained manpower

2. Chinese Communist leaders: Mao Tse-tung, Chiang Kai-shek, Chou En-lai, Lin Piao

3. Rivers of China: Yangtze, Mekong, Yellow, Si (West)

4. Actions of the Communists: Long March, Cultural Revolution, Great Leap Forward, Retreat to Formosa

5. Harbors of China: Chungking, Shanghai, Tientsin, Canton

Thought Questions

1. How has geography affected the development of Chinese civilization?

2. If you were a sociologist how would you describe the major characteristics of the Chinese people?

3. How do the Chinese feel about the part each man plays in the cycle of life?

4. "Confucianism was not a democratic philosophy." Give reasons to prove or disprove this statement.

5. Compare Confucianism and Taoism
   (a) show how the two philosophies were similar
   (b) show how the two were different

6. Compare the peasants and gentry in traditional China in each of the following ways:
   (a) where they lived
   (b) the type of life each group led
   (c) the economic position of each
   (d) the family structure

7. How was the traditional Chinese family different from the typical American family?

8. "The Chinese language and writing system have served both to unify and separate the Chinese people." Explain this statement.

9. How did each of the following periods contribute to Chinese and world civilization?
   (a) Bronze Age   (b) Chou Period   (c) Han Period   (d) Manchu Period
   (e) Nationalist Period

10. How is the idea of the "Mandate from Heaven" similar to the ideas of the Declaration of Independence?

11. What were the factors that led to the fall of the Manchus?

12. What were the main ideas of Dr. Sun Yat-sen?

13. (a) What problems did Chiang Kai-shek face when he became leader of China?
    (b) How did he try to solve these problems?

14. How did the war with Japan 1931-1945 affect China?

15. Why were the Chinese Communists able to gain control of China after 1945?

16. How did the Chinese Communists try to solve the problems of China?

17. Write a newspaper editorial describing your feelings about the Chinese Communist Party and the organization of the Chinese government?

18. How has life improved for the majority of Chinese people since the Communist Revolution?

19. How is the position of women in China today different from what it was in the past?

20. (a) Explain the slogan "Twenty Years Compressed into One Day"
    (b) Describe the program which was called "The Great Leap Forward"
    (c) How did this program affect China?

21. (a) What is the Chinese feeling about relations between the U.S. and China?
    (b) Explain why you agree or disagree with their position?

22. Why has Taiwan become a serious problem for the U.S. and China?

23. Describe the causes and effects of the Sino-Soviet dispute

24. What economic changes have occurred in China in the past 5 years?

Bronze figure of a flying horse standing by one leg on a swallow, excavated in 1969 at Wu-wei, Kansu.

Height 34.5 cm, length 45 cm
Eastern Han dynasty : 2nd century AD

Shanghai, China. *Credit: United Press International*

Puzzle

Directions: Place the words below in their proper place in the puzzle.

4 LETTERS	5 LETTERS	6 LETTERS	7 LETTERS	8 LETTERS
RICE	CLASS	GENTRY	DYNASTY	COMMUNES
SILK	LOESS	REFORM	MANDATE	CULTURAL
	OPIUM	SOURCE	PEASANT	DIFFUSED
		UNIQUE	TYPHOON	MONSOONS

9 LETTERS	10 LETTERS	11 LETTERS	12 LETTERS	13 LETTERS
DEMOCRACY	COMMUNISTS	ACUPUNCTURE	NATIONALISTS	RELATIONSHIPS
ISOLATION	PHILOSOPHY	TRADITIONAL		
PORCELAIN	PICTOGRAPH			
REBELLION				
SOCIALISM				

14 LETTERS
OVERPOPULATION

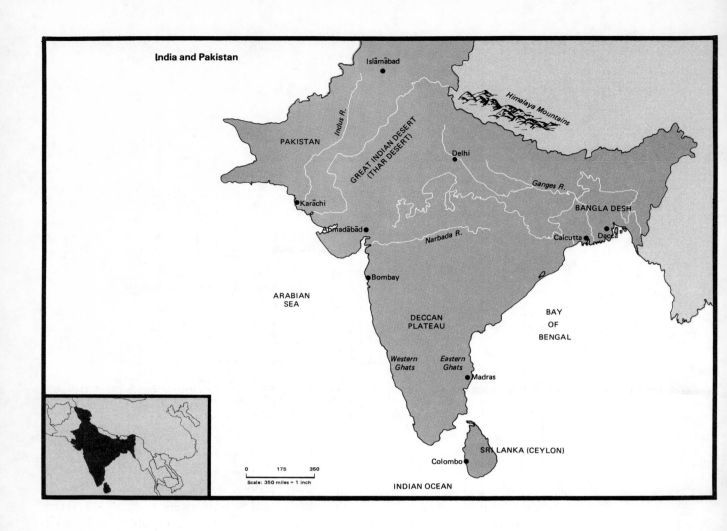

India and Pakistan

PAKISTAN

Islāmābad

Indus R.

GREAT INDIAN DESERT
(THAR DESERT)

Himalaya Mountains

Delhi

Ganges R.

Karāchi

BANGLA DESH

Ahmadābād

Narbada R.

Calcutta

Dacca

Bombay

ARABIAN
SEA

DECCAN
PLATEAU

BAY
OF
BENGAL

Western
Ghats

Eastern
Ghats

Madras

0   175   350

Scale: 350 miles = 1 inch

SRI LANKA (CEYLON)

Colombo

INDIAN OCEAN

UNIT VI

The Subcontinent of India, Pakistan and Bangladesh

The Land

India is the home of one of the world's great civilizations. It covers a vast area. It is the seventh largest country in the world. Because of its large size, and because it is separated from the rest of Asia by mountains, India is often called a subcontinent.

Historic India includes both India and Pakistan. The Indian peninsula juts southward from the Asian continent into the Indian Ocean. On the east is the Bay of Bengal and, on the west, the Arabian Sea. At the southern tip of the peninsula is the island of Sri Lanka (Ceylon), separated from India by a shallow strait. The subcontinent is bounded on the north by the towering mountains of the Himalayas in the northeast, and the great ranges known as the Karakorum and the Hindu Kush to the northwest. In these mountains are some of the highest peaks in the world. Mt. Everest in the Himalayas is the highest peak known to man.

The high wall of mountains is very hard to cross. However, there are a few places where long passes cut through these mountains. Here, through the Khyber Pass and other passes of the Hindu Kush, great *migrations* (movements) of peoples, and invasions of armies pushed down into the lush river valleys of northern India.

The Thar Desert is found in the northwestern part of the subcontinent, just south of the Indus River. It is almost impossible to cross this dry wasteland. The Thar has successfully prevented the march of invading armies, customs and ideas from moving from the northwest into the great insides of India.

The Rivers of the Subcontinent

What made Northern India so desirable to invaders was its fertile land, watered by two great river systems. The Indus River, which flows down from the northern mountains, is one of the most important in the subcontinent. India takes its name from this great waterway. With its four *tributary* (branching) rivers, the Indus forms a large fertile plain in Pakistan. This region has long been known as the Punjab, which means "five rivers" in Hindustani.

The second great river is the Ganges. It rises in the Himalayas and flows for hundreds of miles across northeastern India. The Ganges plain is the most densely populated part of the entire subcontinent. Many of India's major cities are located there. New Delhi, the capital, and Calcutta, the leading seaport, are found on the plain.

Another great river, the Brahmaputra, flows across Bangladesh (Northeast India). This long river has its source in Tibet and empties into the Bay of Bengal. Near its mouth, it joins the Ganges. The large delta area of the two rivers is densely populated.

The Deccan Plateau

The central part of India is known as the Deccan Plateau. Deccan means south. In this area there are many flat-topped hills and high rolling plains. The plateau is divided by deeply cut river valleys. Many of these valleys are very wide. On each side of the Deccan are low mountains called Ghats. The word *Ghats* means steps or a steep place. These mountains isolated the Deccan from other parts of India for hundreds of years. Today the airplane and railroads connect the Deccan and other parts of India. Many of India's minerals are mined in the Deccan. The population here is the least dense of any part of India.

The Coastal Plain

Between the uplands and the sea is a narrow coastal plain. This coastal plain borders much of the eastern or Carnatic coast and the western or Malabar coast. The plain is broken in places by hills which come all the way to the water. In many places these hills end as cliffs.

Nature has given the Indian subcontinent a long coastline, but unfortunately it is a very long, regular (straight) one. As a result there are few good harbors. Except for one or two river mouths there are almost no indentations that can give ocean-going ships shelter from a storm.

The coastal plains are very fertile. They are heavily populated. The rich land has been used for centuries for raising rice. The countries which wished to trade with India set up trading posts on these narrow coastal strips. Many of India's largest cities are located there. Calcutta, India's second largest city, is the center of trade on the east coast. Bombay is the most important trading center on the west coast. Madras, the fifth largest city, has become the most important port of South India.

The South

South India is a separate world in India. It is a land of mountains, forests, and jungles. Most of the coastal areas have rich farm land. The inland parts of South

The Ganges Plain is flat and fertile. It is the center of the production of rice, sugar cane and cotton. Irrigation makes it possible to grow two crops a year. (*Top*)
Credit: *Information Service of India*

Typical bazaar. Bazaars are important social and business events in Indian life. (*Bottom*)
Credit: *Government of India Tourist Office*

India have never been good places for people to live. Most of the people live on the narrow coastal plains. These plains have always been very crowded places. Because of the crowding and the nearness to the sea, South India's people have often left India for other places to trade and to live. The people of South India have settled in Sri Lanka (Ceylon), Malaysia, Singapore, the islands of the South Pacific, and East and South Africa.

Climate

A Wide Range of Climates

The Indian Subcontinent stretches from the latitude of 8° north to 37° north. Although this is a wide range of latitude, temperature does not vary very much throughout the country. In the northern mountains we find snow and, two thousand miles to the south, at the tip of the peninsula, we find palm trees and beaches of golden sand near a tropical rain forest.

Seasons

In most of India, the year may be divided into three different seasons. One is hot, another is cool, and the third is rainy. The cool season, from October to February, is winter. The winds blow from the north, making the climate cool. The very cold winds from Central Asia do not reach India because they are blocked by the Himalayas. Along the coasts the temperature is higher because those lands are heated by warm ocean currents.

During the hot and dry season, from March through June, the land is brown and dusty, the muddy waters of the Ganges are low, and the irrigation ditches are empty. The temperature in many parts of India often rises above 100° F, making it difficult to work very hard. It is slightly cooler in the upland areas and along the coast.

From July to September is the rainy season. India's rainfall is controlled by the seasonal winds called monsoons. The southwest monsoon, beginning in late June, blows across thousands of miles of ocean, and is soaked with moisture when it reaches India. It rains when the monsoon is forced to rise over the Ghats and other highlands. The southwest monsoon brings about ninety percent of all the rain that falls. It lessens from September until the beginning of January. Then the northeast monsoon takes over and blows from the land toward the sea. Since it can pick up very little moisture, except as it blows over the Bay of Bengal, it brings very little rain.

Climate and Its Effect Upon History

Topography and climate have had a great effect on the course of Indian history. Tropical and subtropical conditions in the south provided the rice, cotton, sugar, pepper, cinnamon and other spices that make the south a natural market place. But the same conditions weakened the people. In the north, the more moderate climate and rich soil made for good crops and a hardy people, more ready for warfare and empire building. Thus it was that northern ideas spread to the south and Hinduism, the main binding force of modern India, was brought south by its northern followers.

The south was rich enough to attract northern invaders, and weak enough to be conquered. The rough terrain could not keep northerners out. However, once they had gained control of the area, northerners found it difficult to hold onto, because they could not supply armies or maintain proper communication with the south.

Peoples and Languages of India

India Is a Land of Many Peoples

The population of India is more than 500 million, about two-and-a-half times larger than the population of the United States. Since India is about one-third the size of the United States, it is a crowded land, especially in the cities.

There are many groups of people in India. They have a common culture, but they are different in many ways. No one description can be used to fit all Indians. In the north and central regions the men and women are quite tall and well built. They have light skins and black or brown hair. Their hair may be either straight or wavy. They have dark or light brown eyes. In the northeast and south many Indians are short and slight in build. Skin colors range from heavy tan to dark brown or black. Their eyes are usually dark. In the hill country of central India and in the far north one can find still other types of people. In the Himalayan border region of India there are people who strongly resemble the Chinese or Japanese.

India Is a Land of Many Languages

Racial diversity is matched by the variety of languages. The national language of India is Hindi, but also recognized are thirteen regional languages. More than a hundred dialects are spoken. Some of the languages belong to the Indo-European language family. This means that they are related to Western languages like English and French. They are quite different from all other languages spoken in Asia. The language spoken in Southern India belongs to still another group, the Dravidian language family. This, too, is unknown in other parts of Asia.

Historically, the difference in languages has raised important political problems. It has contributed to the *fragmentation* (breaking up) of India into hundreds of small states. For modern India, it has hindered the building of a truly national state. Officials in Delhi have difficulty in making their wishes known to members of the National Assembly and to governors in the provinces. Attempts to standardize the nation's schools have been hindered by the unwillingness of the various regions to accept a common language.

Principal Languages of India and Pakistan

People Speaking (in millions)	Language
170	Hindi
90	Bengali
58	Urdu
55	Telugu
42	Tamil
40	Marathi
38	Punjabi
30	Kannada
30	Gugerati
20	Malayalam
20	Oriya
15	Rajasthani
10	Assamese
8	Kashmiri

Language Diffusion—East to West

Many words from the various local languages of India, especially Hindi, have been borrowed by the English. Some of these borrowed words have become a part of the English language and are in daily use. Here are some examples:

Brahmin: a wealthy person of the highest classes

bungalow: a small cottage—*bungalow* is a Bengali word

calico: a type of cloth developed in India

chintz: another type of cloth developed in India

coolie: a laborer who works at odd jobs for low pay

curry: a highly spiced dish of rice

divan: a couch—usually found in a palace

khaki: another type of cloth developed in India

loot: stolen goods

madras: another type of cloth developed in India

mogul: a rich or important person

pajamas: loose-fitting clothes

pariah: a poor person, not welcome in society

punch: a drink (originally had 5 ingredients—from *panch,* Hindi word for "five")

pundit: a teacher or scholar

shawl: a scarf worn over the shoulders

thug: a gangster or a cutthroat.

Agriculture in India

Climate Affects India's Agriculture

Most people of India live today as they lived for hundreds of years, chiefly as farmers. Most of the farmers live on the North India plain and on the coastal lowlands

The crops that are to be raised are largely determined by the climate. The northeastern part of India near Calcutta, and most of the southwestern coastal region receive very heavy rainfall. Even during the dry season a great deal of moisture remains in the soil. Some of the lowland areas near the east coast receive less rain, but streams, wells and man-made ponds provide water for farming. In these well-watered areas rice is the most important crop. It is grown in flooded fields called paddies.

In the warm, wet lowlands that border the western coast, farmers raise coconuts, pepper, ginger and other tropical crops. Large amounts of jute are raised in the eastern part of India. This plant provides fibers for making burlap bags. Toward the middle of the North India Plain, where there is less moisture, farmers often grow corn and sugar cane.

The western part of the North India Plain receives little rainfall. However, here the great Ganges River and other rivers provide water for farming. Thousands of miles of canals have been dug to carry water to the fields. Wheat, barley, flax, sugar cane and cotton are raised in the irrigated fields.

The hilly plateau region has less rainfall, and irrigation is not possible. Here wells and ponds are being dug, and millet and sorghum are grown. Large quantities of peanuts are also grown.

Products

India is the world's leading producer of tea. Large numbers of modern tea plantations were set up by the British. Tea is India's most important export. Much of it is raised in the northeast (Assam), and the south peninsula of India.

India has about 40 million sheep and 175 million cattle. The Hindus believe it is wrong to kill these animals. However, cattle are used to provide milk, and to do farm work.

India Cannot Feed All Its People

India is a major producer of a number of farm products, but it also has many people to feed, and many of the over 500 million people do not have as much food as they need. There are several reasons why this is so. Millions of farmers have so little land that they cannot raise the food that they and their families need. The crop yield per acre in India is among the lowest in the world. Farmers are too poor to invest in fertilizers, improved seed and insecticide. Farming methods are the same as were used centuries ago. Land holdings are very small, averaging about five acres. Many Indian farmers have so little to eat that they do not have the energy to work hard. They do not raise as much food as they need, and they do not have the money to buy more.

The Indian government is working hard to overcome these problems. More land has been put into use through the expansion of irrigation. Food production has been increased yearly, and now food production in India has nearly doubled since 1947. Laws have been passed to protect farmers against high rents. In addition, the government has sent workers to teach the farmers better ways of farming. The United States has also sent agricultural machinery, seeds and farm experts to help Indian farmers increase the amount of food they are able to raise.

AGRICULTURAL PRODUCTION IN INDIA, 1972–1976 (Estimated)

Commodity	1976	1975	1974	1973	1972	
WHEAT	28,3	25,8	22,0	24,9	26,4	
RICE	70,5	70,5	60,0	67,5	57,9	
BARLEY	3,1	2,9	2,3	2,3	2,5	
CORN	6,5	5,5	5,0	6,5	6,2	thousands
POTATOES	7,4	6,1	4,6	5,0	4,8	of
CASSAVA	. . .	6,3	6,3	6,3	5,9	metric tons
BANANAS	3,4	. . .	3,2	2,9	3,1	
PEANUTS	5,7	6,6	5,2	6,0	3,9	
SUGAR (raw)	4,6	5,3	4,3	4,3	3,3	
JUTE	1,2	0.8	1,0	1,2	0.8	
CATTLE	180.6	180.3	179.9	179.4	176.9	
SHEEP	40.0	40.0	40.0	40.2	43.3	
BUFFALOES	61.5	. . . .	60.0	55.0	55.0	millions
GOATS	70.4	. . . .	69.0	69.0	69.0	
POULTRY	142.0	. . . .	118.4	117.7	118.0	

SOURCES: *Encyclopaedia Britannica;* United Nations *Statistical Yearbook.*

In 1974 India had a devastating agricultural year. Severe drought led to predictions of widespread famine. By the end of 1974, there were reports of famine and hunger in many parts of India; hunger among the Indians was a result not only of lack of food but of lack of money. In some parts of India, rice was available but doubled in price. The government was forced to take strong action against hoarding. Some rain fell late in 1974, and with food aid from the United States and the Soviet Union a major disaster was avoided.

The 1975–76 grain production total and that of 1976–77 showed a tremendous increase. This has allowed India to build up a reserve for 1978. Drought conditions still exist in South India and there are still many areas where there is not enough food to feed all the people. However the threat of famine has disappeared at least for the immediate future.

The Village in Indian Life

The village is the heart of Indian life. This has been true throughout the history of India, and today four out of five Indians live in villages. Most of India's 550 thousand villages are small, with an average of one hundred families each. The typical village consists of a small group of huts and cottages. If it has a street at all, it is usually rutted and narrow, no better than a cowpath. Yet, for most Indians, their village neighbors are the only people they ever know because many live out their lives without traveling more than a few miles from their home village.

The well is an important part of village life. Most villages depend on the well for all or part of their water supply. Getting the water from the well is woman's work. The women of the village go to the well every day as many American women go to the supermarket every day. It is a good time to trade news and gossip and to show off new saris and bracelets.

The village is usually ruled by a council of older men. The *panchayat* or "Council of Five" is the most common type of village council found in India. The members of the *panchayat* are usually elected by the villagers. However, in many cases the richest villagers and members of the highest caste are elected. The *panchayats* became very important in history because of the failure of India to unite under a single

A pair of snake charmers. Snake charming is a favorite form of entertainment in India.
Credit: *Information Service of India*

national government. They are still important today. Over 90% of village-India is ruled by them. In general they are responsible for agricultural production, local industry, maintaining village streets, ponds, and sanitation. In addition some village councils decide local taxes and make decisions about elementary school education.

Indian Food

India is a country with millions of different groups of peoples and religions. One group eats pork but not beef, another beef but not pork. A third group is completely vegetarian. The religious beliefs of the group of people determine which foods may be eaten and which may not be eaten. However throughout all of India one ingredient is found in the food—curry.

Curry is a mixture of spices. In India the housewife buys individual spices. She grinds and blends them together to her own recipe. No two curries are alike. Curry dishes vary from village to village, from city to city, and from family to family in any village or city.

Ghee, a form of clarified skimmed butter, is used instead of oils and fats in cooking. Yoghurt also is important in cooking. The main food eaten by Indians is a boiled rice (Chawal) prepared with herbs and spices and Chapattis which is Indian bread.

Housing in the Indian Village

The climate of an area and the building materials available influence the kinds of houses built by the villagers. Trees were uprooted centuries ago to make room for farming. With little wood, the farmers build houses of sun-dried brick. Often, in times of flood and heavy rain, the houses "melt" away.

In northeastern India and in the south, where wood is available, construction is very different from that of the North Indian Plain. The houses here are built of wood and various kinds of reeds. Houses built in this manner are fairly livable during most of the year. At least they are well ventilated, an important thing to think of in that hot, humid climate. But the houses are not waterproof. They get damp and uncomfortable during the rainy season, and they are often destroyed by floods.

Houses in the Indian villages do have certain things in common. They usually have few rooms, three at most. The floor of the hut is the bare earth. There is little or no furniture. The family takes its meals sitting on the floor. The bed is a mat or blanket. The family's possessions are stored around the room, suspended from pegs or hung from the rafters. Most Indians live in one room. The second or third room often houses the family's water buffalo or cow.

Problems of Village India

1. **Poverty**

Village India presents a picture of continuing struggle and poverty. Farms are small. The average size for an Indian farm is five acres, but many farmers must be satisfied with an acre or two. Those villagers who do not farm are carpenters, blacksmiths, potters, weavers, or barbers. They earn a living by trading their services to the farmers for grain. The average yearly income of most village farmers is less than your father earns in a week, and many Indians are hopelessly in debt. Often the debts are inherited from parents, and tradition demands that they be paid.

2. Diet

The diet of the villager consists mainly of rice in the south and wheat in the north. Little meat is eaten because the Hindu religion feels that it is sinful to eat beef, and Muslims do not eat ham, bacon, or any form of pork for the same reason. Most Indian villagers go to sleep much of the time without having eaten as much as they would have liked. Most will die before they reach the age of forty-five and many will suffer from disease during their lives.

3. Young Population

Because of the relatively short life span of the Indian villager, most of the people in the village are young. About half of them are under fourteen years of age. In all India, three out of four persons are under fourteen years of age. Only one out of ten is more than fifty-five. Look at the chart below and you will realize just how young India's population is.

Age	U.S.	India
55 and over	19%	10%
35-54 years	24%	15%
15-34 years	26%	25%
under 14	31%	50%

4. Illiteracy and Isolation

Most of the villagers are illiterate, that is, they are not able to read or write. And because of poverty and poor transportation, millions of villagers have never had an opportunity to leave their birthplaces. Roads between villages have been little more than dirt paths. Today villages have more contacts with the outside world. New roads are being built, and primary schools have been set up in most villages. Also, most villages have at least one radio to keep people informed about events.

Many villagers are getting jobs in the cities, as India becomes more industrialized. They seldom return, but news of city life gets back to the families they leave behind. Despite these new contacts, however, the villager is hardly part of the modern world today.

In spite of all the hardship and lack of possessions, many Indian villagers feel that life in the village suits them. They know little about other ways of living, and they prefer what they know.

The Hindu Religion

"Hinduism is much more than a religion; it is a total way of life, including the customs, beliefs, practices, institutions of the people in all parts of the subcontinent (India), developed in all periods of human settlement there. . . . Hinduism is not a single religion, but many religions *tolerating* one another in the shifting framework of *caste*."[1]

Hinduism's Main Ideas

Three main ideas are important in understanding the religion of the Hindus, and the defense of the *caste* system. The first of these ideas is *reincarnation*. According to this belief, each person and all living things have a soul. When the living thing dies, its soul moves into another human being or animal. In other words, when death comes, the soul is reborn in a newly created life.

[1] W. Norman Brown, from S. Fersh, *India and South Asia* (New York: Macmillan, Inc.), p. 35.

A frieze from the temple at Konarak in Orissa that is a fine example of temple.
sculpture. The figures portray the pleasures of life.
Credit: *Government of India Tourist Office*

The second idea is *Karma*. Karma teaches that every action brings about certain results. If a person behaves badly, the results will be bad. If one behaves well, the results will be good. There is no escaping the results of one's actions. If a person or an animal does what he is supposed to do, his soul will be rewarded in the next rebirth by being reincarnated into a higher ranking human or animal.

Thus, if an Untouchable does his job well and does not complain, he may be born into a higher caste. Some day, if he continues to behave well, he may reach the highest caste and become a Brahmin.

The third idea is *Dharma*. Dharma is a set of rules which must be followed by each living being if he wishes to work his way up the ladder of reincarnation. Each person's Dharma is different.

The Caste System

The caste system began in India more than three thousand years ago. The Aryans, who conquered India, took for themselves the kind of work which they thought was desirable. They became the religious leaders, the rulers, the traders, and the land-owner farmers. The other people were forced to become servants for the Aryans, or do kinds of work which were necessary but took more labor, or were considered less respectable. This included the work of the barber, carpenter, tailor, potter or street cleaner (sweeper).

Lowest of all the jobs were those of sweeping the streets, handling dead people and animals, and tending pigs which fed on village garbage. No one even liked to come near people who did these jobs which other villagers considered to be unclean. There was probably a belief that disease was carried from person to person, and that it was better to stay away from anyone touched by dead or dirty things.

The caste system divides the Indian population into *hereditary* social groups. There are five general orders of castes. The three higher orders, or groups of castes, are Brahmin (priests), Kashatriya (soldiers), and Vaishya (merchants). The fourth order is Shudra (laborer). The members of the fifth group of castes, ranked lowest of all, are referred to as Untouchables or Outcasts. To many Hindus, Untouchables rate so low as to be considered outside or beneath the caste system itself. They must live apart from the rest of the village, and cannot use the village wells.

A major idea of the caste system is that people are born unequal in both opportunity and ability. Thus, while Untouchables have few privileges, less is expected from them than from a Brahmin.

An Indian belonged to a caste from birth. His life, marriage and work were governed by specific caste rules. The son of a laborer became a laborer. The son of a teacher became a teacher. And, of course, the son of a king usually became a ruler at the death of his father. Girls were regarded as inferior to boys. They were married into families which did the same work as their fathers and brothers did. In this way, a small kingdom or a village was almost certain, year after year, to have all of the kinds of work it needed.

Therefore, the purpose of the caste system was to develop a plan by which the villagers could live and work together. Its main goal was to produce enough food and to provide enough labor so that each family might have what it needed.

Each caste has its own Dharma. This is carefully taught to the young by the elders.

Within the caste Dharma, each person begins to understand his own personal Dharma as well.

Perhaps you can see how Hinduism and the caste system are related. The caste into which a person is born has been determined by the way he has acted his Dharma in a previous life. If you are an Untouchable, you have no one to blame but yourself, according to the law of Karma. Instead of complaining, you had better do a good job. If you don't, you will sink to the level of an animal that crawls.

If a person behaves well through an unknown number of reincarnations, his soul will reach *Moksha*, the final resting place. To enter Moksha is desired because the soul will be free of all the pain which life brings. The soul will be able to rest from its long, sad travels on earth.

The Literature of Ancient India

India has a tradition of learning which stretches far back into the past. Much of its culture and writing grew out of Hindu teaching and practices. Many of the stories and traditions were passed on from generation to generation by the village story teller. Usually an elderly person served as the storyteller. By hearing the stories over and over again and by seeing them staged at holiday festivals, Indians remained close to their great traditions.

It was many centuries later that the great literature of the early Indians was written down to be enjoyed not only by the village Indian but also by all the peoples of the world.

The Vedas

We know something about the customs, institutions and religious practices of the Aryans from four collections of sacred writings called *Vedas*. The Vedas are very ancient. They are the earliest collection of writing in India (1500 to 800 B.C.). The Vedas are a collection of hymns, sacred prayers and chants that are still recited at weddings and funerals today. The Vedas tell of nature worship. (There were gods of the sun, the wind and the rain.)

The most famous Veda was the *Rig-Veda*, written about 800 B.C. This is the oldest known religious document in the world. (*Rig* means hymn and *Veda* means knowledge.) There are 110 Hymns of Knowledge. One of these, called the Hymn of Creation, is in many ways similiar to the Creation story told in the Old Testament of the Bible. There is also a belief shown in a universal spirit or Creator.

The three other Vedas should be mentioned. The *Sama Veda* is a collection of hymns; the *Yajur Veda* is a manual used by priests in the performance of their religious duties; the *Atharva Veda* is a book containing many magical spells.

The Vedas were passed by word of mouth from one generation to the next for many centuries before being written down. In the Vedas may be found the roots of Hindu beliefs and ideas.

Folk dancers from Himachal Pradesh.
Credit: *Government of India Tourist Office*

The Upanishads

The Upanishads, a collection of rituals and ceremonies written about 2500 years ago, is a valuable source of information about Hinduism. It is written in both prose and verse. The writers discuss the origins of the universe. They also talk of the meaning and importance of the soul. The prayers contain messages on religious thoughts and present a way of life for the Indian people. ("Truth conquers ever, falsehood never")

The Mahabharata

The Mahabharata is the longest poem in the world. It is about 200,000 lines long (100,000 couplets). *Maha* means great and *Bharat* is the legendary name of India during the ancient Vedic Age.

The Mahabharata tells the story of a war between two Indian families. The war was fought so savagely that few survived its end. Within the poem is a section that has become famous throughout the entire world, the *Bhagavad-Gita* or *Gita* (The Song of God).

The *Gita* tells the story of Arjuna, the perfect warrior. Arjuna was unhappy because in the army opposing him were many of his friends and relatives. He did not want to kill them but he didn't want to lose the fight either. He turned for advise to one of his soldiers. The soldier turns out to be Krishna, one of the Gods. Krishna explains to Arjuna that the purpose of life is to know God and that each man must do his duty. Good deeds will bring good results and put man closer to God; bad deeds will bring bad results. Krishna points out that it is not bad for a person to kill within the line of duty or in self defense. It is Arjuna's duty to fight and win. The story ends with Arjuna's victory in battle. The moral of the story is that duty should be done without emotion or desire.

Over the years of Indian history, and today, scenes from the Mahabharata have been told by the village storyteller, dramatized on the Indian stage and repeated in many books. There are few Indians who are not familiar with the content and the teachings of it. The great Indian leader, Gandhi called the Gita, "a dictionary of conduct." This poem is also well known to other Asians in Thailand, Cambodia, Burma, Indonesia and elsewhere.

The Ramayana

The Ramayana was written about 400 B.C. It tells the story of Prince Rama and his wife Sita. Rama loses his throne to his step brother and for 14 years is forced to travel through India. During his travels he has many exciting adventures.

One day Sita is kidnapped by the evil demon Rawana, king of Sri Lanka (Ceylon). After many battles and setbacks Rama, with the help of his loyal brother, Lakshmana and the brave monkey general, Hanuman, finally traps Rawana on the island of Sri Lanka (Ceylon). The monkeys led by Hanuman build a bridge of stones to connect the mainland to the island. Rama kills Rawana in a fierce and bloody battle. Sita is then rescued. Without the help of the monkeys this victory would not have been possible. For this reason it is said monkeys are considered sacred by the Hindus.

Hanuman is looked on as the god of strength and loyalty. He is considered the special friend of athletes.

After 14 years of wandering Rama returns to his home to become king. Rama and Sita are welcomed with great happiness. And according to one of the more popular endings of the Ramayana, Rama and Sita live happily ever after.

However, another ending tells how the people felt that Sita had not remained true to Rama while living with Rawana. The people insist that Rama send Sita away and he does. The lesson is that Rama places the wishes of his people above his own wishes.

To generations of Hindus Rama, Sita and Lakshmana have shown how human beings should behave. Their loyalty, love, devotion, obedience and sense of duty have been a model held up to Indian children.

Early History

The Indus Valley Civilizations

The earliest civilizations on the Indian subcontinent arose about 2500 B.C. These civilizations were located in the Indus Valley of the north west in what is now Pakistan. The most important cities, Harappa and Mohenjo Daro, were among the most skillfully designed cities in the ancient world. Buildings were made of brick. Streets were wide and houses comfortable. There appears to have been plenty of water. Many of the families had their own wells. Drainpipes were used to carry waste water away from the city.

Craftsmen had learned to use copper and brass, as well as gold and silver. Cotton was used for clothing. A system of writing was developed in Mohenjo Daro, but no one has been able to find the meaning of what was written. Little is known about the government, society and religion of the cities, or the areas around them. These early civilizations began to crumble under the force of Aryan invaders from beyond the mountains.

The Aryans Invade India

The Aryans were wandering herdsmen. They left their homes in search of better land to graze their sheep. The fertile valley of the Indus attracted them. The Aryans conquered the Dravidians (the original people of India). They advanced eastward into the Ganges River Plain. The Dravidians fled southward.

The Aryan tribes decided to settle down in India. They became farmers, finding it pleasant to live in India after the hardships they had suffered on the dry plains of what is now southern Russia. In poetry and song they expressed their thanksgiving. They kept the memories of their conquests, their ideas about man and life, and their rituals and ceremonies in the *Vedas*.

Between 1500 B.C. and 500 B.C. the Aryans developed the main characteristics of what came to be the Hindu way of life. During this thousand year period many Aryan tribes moved into Northern India. Gradually, small kingdoms began to appear. Each kingdom was ruled by a prince called a *rajah*. While in India, the Aryans began to change their ways of living. They brought new ideas into India, but they also became more like those who already lived in India.

The Greeks Invade India

In 326 B.C. a Greek king, who had made up his mind to conquer the world, appeared in India on the banks of the Indus. His men, far from home, tired and afraid of the unknown that lay before them, refused to go on. Alexander the Great's invasion was brief, but it was important. The armies had brought with them ideas from the Greek and Persian civilizations. These different ways of thinking and doing things influenced India.

The Maurya Empire

Another important result of the invasion was its influence on a young Indian leader, Chandragupta Maurya. Alexander had destroyed the small kingdoms and republics in the northwest. When Alexander left, Chandragupta quickly included the area in his kingdom. In the next hundred and fifty years the Mauryas built a great empire in North India.

Ashoka Rules Wisely

Great as Chandragupta was, his grandson Ashoka was even greater. Ashoka is thought by many to have been the greatest king that India ever had, and one of the greatest rulers who has ever lived in any country at any time. He is remembered and respected most because, although he was a powerful and mighty warrior, he decided not to use force to rule or to extend his kingdom. He decided to rule following the principles of Buddhism. He commanded his officials and subjects to be just and considerate in their conduct. Punishments for many crimes were made less severe.

Buddhism

The people of India were ready to accept a new religion and a new set of ideals. The rule of the Brahmins (Priests of the Veda) was harsh and unfair. Many Indians were unhappy, and opposition grew. Buddhist priests called on the people to gain knowledge, be just, ethical and compassionate, as the best way to live. They spoke against the caste system and the complicated ceremonies and rites that the Brahmins followed.

The Fall of Buddhism

Ashoka sent people all over India to spread Buddhist ideas. Indians by the millions accepted the teachings of Buddha. After the death of Ashoka many changes crept into Buddhism. It survived and grew stronger in many parts of Asia, but in India it almost disappeared. Today there are only about a million Buddhists in India.

The fall of Buddhism had many causes. Hinduism was broad and tolerant, and it accepted many of the teachings of the Buddha. Buddhists in India were quite willing to compromise with the beliefs and customs of Hinduism. Indian Buddhism eventually became so much like Hinduism that it was regarded as a part of Hinduism. The final blow to Buddhism in India was delivered by the Muslims. Pushing into India from the eighth century on, they destroyed the great Buddhist monasteries, burned the libraries, and killed the monks. Most of the monks who survived left India. Buddhism could not stand these blows, and never again was Buddhism important in India.

The Guptas

Soon after the death of Ashoka, the Maurya Empire of North India began to fall apart. For the next six hundred years invaders swept over the Indian Plains. In time, the invaders were either driven out or became Hindus. Meanwhile, the Deccan and South India were entering the mainstream of Indian history. Peoples of these regions made important contributions to Hinduism. The southern area was called the Tamil country, after the main Dravidian language in use there. The peoples of the Tamil country began to combine the Hindu traditions of the Aryans with their own Dravidian folklore to produce some of India's finest poetry, epics and music.

The Importance of Trade

Trade was an important part of life in India during these six hundred years. Important trade routes were developed to link India with west Asia and the Mediterranean world. In the Deccan and South India trade increased, as traders from China and Arabia visited Indian ports. Sea trade flourished, and peninsular India, long overshadowed by the states of the north, began to gain in influence and power.

India's contacts with Southeast Asia developed as a direct result of her trade with the West. Southeast Asian lands were largely unsettled and undeveloped. However, they produced spices, much in demand in the West. Indian traders sailed to various parts of Southeast Asia, and many settled in Southeast Asian lands. The Indians brought their customs and their religions, Buddhism and Hinduism, to Southeast Asia.

In North India, the period of invasions came to an end when the Gupta family, led by another Chandragupta, united the kingdoms of the north. The Guptas ruled for over two hundred years (320-550 A.D.). It was a period of stable government and great accomplishment. Indian scholars, writers and artists distinguished themselves by advancing knowledge, and by producing masterpieces of art, literature and architecture.

Gupta Accomplishments

In the field of mathematics the Indians developed Arabic numerals, the idea of zero, and the idea of infinity. In medicine Gupta India was far advanced. They had learned to diagnose and treat many ailments. Surgery was well advanced. Surgeons set broken bones, performed Caesarian sections, and used plastic surgery to repair mutilations. Indian doctors were aware of an important fact not understood by Western doctors until modern times, that cleanliness can prevent infection.

Kalidasa was the greatest of the poets and playwrights of the period. Some of his plays are still performed in India and in other countries of the world. His drama *Sakuntala*, a love story about a king and his beautiful bride, can be read in English. The early Hindu story tellers delighted in fairy tales, folklore and animated fables. In Gupta times many of these tales were gathered into a collection. This passed, eventually, by way of the Arabs, into European literature. In this way, many modern European writers are indebted to the Hindus for the form or plot of their tales (*Arabian Nights*)

The Guptas encouraged the development of music and dance. They spent large sums of money on the building of temples. Painters and sculptors were well rewarded for their work. Gupta palaces were richly decorated, and were always showplaces.

Nearly all the art and architecture was of a religious nature. The peak of art and architecture was reached in the Deccan. The magnificent cave temples at Ajanta and Ellora took nearly a thousand years to build. All were cut out of solid rock. The outside walls were decorated with sculptured figures, columns and fresco paintings. South India has some of the finest free-standing temples in the world.

Self-Government in Gupta India

One of the features of Indian development was the reliance of Indians on local self-government. This was a direct result of the political confusion that existed for long periods of Indian history. With princes constantly at war, the villages were free to conduct their own affairs. Village councils, always an important part of Indian life, provided leadership for the peasants. The reliance on local government continued as each succeeding century saw the failure of the Indian people to unite into a truly national state.

The Muslims in India
The Delhi Sultanate

From the eighth century on, the course of Indian history was influenced by the expansion of Islam. The conflict between Islam and Hinduism made for tensions in Indian life. The followers of the two religions were far apart on matters of belief and custom. For centuries these differences caused great troubles between the two groups. Not long after the Gupta Empire fell apart, Muslims began to move on India. Their first expeditions against India were unsuccessful but, by 712, they had taken over the state of Sind. The Muslim kingdoms bordering India gained strength. Mahmud of Ghazni and Muhammed Ghori led armies into India. Their successors set up the Delhi Sultanate. A Sultanate is a Muslim kingdom ruled by a Sultan. For several centuries most of northern and much of central India was controlled by the Sultans.

However, the Sultans had a difficult time keeping order and resisting attacks from outside of India. The most notable attackers were the Mongols—Ghenghis Khan, Tamerlane and Babur.

The Mughal Dynasty

Babur brought an end to the Delhi Sultanate, and a new and powerful Indian Empire was started. The new Muslim rulers set up the Mughal (Mogul) Empire. Akbar the Great, Babur's grandson, established a firm basis for the Empire. He was a first-rate organizer and an exceptional administrator. He included capable Hindus in the government, and won their loyalty and cooperation. He eliminated the head or poll tax placed on Hindus, thus gaining the cooperation of most Hindus. He tried to combine the best teachings of Christianity, Islam and Hinduism in a new religion, the Divine Faith, but he failed.

His policies were followed by the next two rulers, but the last of the mighty Mughals, Aurangzeb, reversed some policies, which led to the distintegration of the Empire. His biggest error was trying to enforce Islamic law and customs. This drove the loyal Hindus away. Aurangzeb quarreled with traditional friends like the Sikhs and the Rajputs. He wasted much wealth and energy in trying to conquer the Marathas, and was never successful.

The Mughal Empire did not end with Aurangzeb's death. His descendants remained on the throne in Delhi until 1857. But their kingdom shrank until it included only the area around the capital.

The Mughal rulers took pride not only in their political and military achievements, but also in cultural advances. Having great wealth, the Mughal kings were patrons of the arts. The new Mughal school of art became known especially for its portraits, pictures of animals, and use of color. The Mughals were also interested in the construction of beautiful buildings. The most famous building of this period is the Taj Mahal, designed by Emperor Shah Jahan as a tomb for his wife. The Mughals encouraged the use of Persian for both writing and speaking. Little by little, Persian was fused with Hindi, the language of North India. The result was the creation of a new language, Urdu.

The Mughals were never in control of all of India. The Rajputs were a powerful force in Northwest India. The Rajputs were proud of their fighting ability, and deserve much credit for preserving Hinduism in the northwest. Another people of the northwest who caused trouble for the Mughals were the Sikhs. The founder of Sikhism was Nanak. He combined what he felt was the best of Islam and Hinduism. From Islam he borrowed the idea of one God, and a distaste for the caste system. From Hinduism he borrowed the idea of toleration of widely differing points of view. The Sikhs became a powerful, militant and hard working group. Men did not cut their hair or shave their faces. All Sikhs adopted the common name "Singh," meaning lion. The Sikhs fought hard to preserve their religion against the Mughals.

A third people who actively resisted the Mughals were the Marathas, who lived near the western Ghats. They fought well and resisted the Mughals, contributing to their downfall.

The Taj Mahal in Agra. Taj Mahal—crown of the palace—is an abbreviation of
Mumtaz Mahal, the title of the wife of the Emperor Shah Jahan (1627-1658). Before
Mumtaz Mahal died, she made her husband promise that he would raise over her
grave a mausoleum worthy of the love they shared for nineteen years of married life.
About 20,000 workers, masons, stonecutters and jewellers worked twelve years to
complete the central mausoleum. Marble, sandstone and semiprecious stones were
brought from all over India and other parts of Asia. Mumtaz Mahal's remains were
given final burial exactly below the central point of the dome. The central mausoleum
is surrounded by beautifully arranged gardens with water channels and fountains.
The surrounding buildings—mosques and tombs of other members of the royal family
and the ladies-in-waiting—took another ten years to complete.
Many years later, in 1666, Shah Jahan died. His body was buried alongside the body
of his beloved wife, from whom he had been separated for thirty-six years.
Credit: *Government of India Tourist Office*

The British in India

European Trading Companies in India

While Akbar ruled, European ships began to call at Indian ports in increasing numbers. Portugal was the first nation to claim land in India. Vasco Da Gama landed on the Malabar coast in 1498, and Portuguese settlements were made on India's west coast near Bombay almost immediately after. The Portuguese were followed by the Dutch, French and British. Trade was the main reason for their voyages. From India the Europeans hoped to get cotton goods, spices, silk and indigo, a plant from which a blue dye is made. The Europeans set up trading companies to handle the business at rented seaport areas off the mainland of India. It was in this way, for example, that the British East India Company founded the cities of Madras, Calcutta and Bombay.

The British East India Company

During the period of Mughal rule these European companies were becoming more and more involved in Indian affairs. This was especially true of the French and English East India Companies. Their involvement led to wars against each other in India. The rivalry between the French and the English in India was part of a larger clash of interests in Europe and America. Led by Robert Clive, the English East India Company was victorious. At the Battle of Plassey, in 1757, Clive defeated the ruler of the state of Bengal. This victory, coming after an earlier British defeat of French troops in South India, gave the British control of much of India. The rajahs were unable to unite, and were thus defeated one by one.

In the late 1700s the English Parliament decided that the East India Company was not doing its job well. The English government increased its role in India. The British began social, land and tax reforms. Some of the reforms were not liked by the Indians.

The Sepoy Rebellion

Indian dissatisfaction with British rule came to a head in the Sepoy Rebellion of 1857. The Indians did not have a single leader, and the attempt to break British power failed. Indians feel that this revolt was the first blow struck for independence, and call it "The Great Revolt." The rebels were crushed, but the East India Company was abolished. India was *annexed* (added) to the British Empire in 1876.

By the time India was annexed to the British Empire, it was obvious that the sub-continent was of great value to Britain. It supplied employment for thousands of British citizens, provided a market for goods manufactured in British factories, and was an excellent place to invest money. Indians, too, benefited from British rule, especially those who could afford to develop Indian industry. However, many Indians felt that the disadvantages of being under British rule far outweighed any advantages.

Development of Indian National Feeling

After the Sepoy Rebellion, a new type of leader emerged in India to oppose the

Mohandas K. Gandhi is regarded as the father of Indian independence. His belief in non-violence has influenced people all over the world. (*Top*)
Credit: *Information Service of India*

Jawaharlal Nehru was the first Prime Minister of India. He earned world recognition as a leader in the movement for Asian independence. (*Bottom*)
Credit: *Information Service of India*

British. This leader was often educated in English universities, and was familiar with the English tradition of political rights. He wanted to share in the governing of his own land. The Indian National Congress, which was founded in 1885, was set up to help achieve this goal. Within the group there were many different opinions about how to gain their goals. Most members did not call for independence, but for a share in ruling India. A small, but vocal minority, led by Bal Tilak, called for all means to drive out the British, even if this meant revolution. The Congress was also opposed by Muslims, who were suspicious of the motives of the Hindu-led Congress Party. The Muslim League was set up in 1906 under the leadership of Sayyid Ahmad Khan to protect Muslims from Hindu domination.

The Indian nationalist movement began to change from a passive, patient movement to an aggressive, demanding one during and after the First World War. The Nationalists were disappointed by British rejection of their wartime requests for more rights. The Indian people were angered by the Rowlatt Acts, which restricted the rights of Indians, and by the Amritsar Massacre. The British attempted to calm the Indians with the Montagu-Chelmsford Reforms. These Reforms gave Indians a larger share in their government, but the clamor for self-government never died.

Mohandas K. Gandhi and Jawaharlal Nehru

The upsurge of nationalist feeling brought the Indians a new and great leader. He was Mohandas K. Gandhi. He made the nationalist movement a struggle against British rule. His goal for India was *swaraj*, self rule free of all foreign control. To achieve this, Gandhi believed in *ahimsa*, the Indian idea of non-violence. His program called for a non-violent non-cooperation against the British. Gandhi is remembered in India both for his success in awakening the people to the need for self government and for his humanitarian efforts.

The late twenties and thirties were years of trouble in India. A new group of leaders, including Jawaharlal Nehru, began to ask for independence. Parliament passed the Government of India Act in 1935, which set up a partnership between Indians and the British government. However, this law was only partially successful in quieting the troubles.

Independence and Partition

The outbreak of war in Europe in 1939 brought about the final split between the British and the Indian Congress Party. Gandhi, Nehru and their followers refused to support the British war effort unless their demands for independence were met. The Muslim League, cooperating with the British, was now committed to the setting up of a separate Muslim state. At the end of the war the British government left its Indian Empire. The British had decided to partition the Indian subcontinent into two nations, Pakistan and India. On August 15, 1947, in the midst of violence involving millions of deaths (including the assassination of Gandhi) and great disorder, two new nations came into being. This division was based on the failure of Indian Hindu and Muslim leaders to solve their religious differences.

British Contribution to Indian Civilization

Great Britain ruled in India for almost two hundred years. During that long period of time the British brought many things to India. These institutions have had a great affect on India today.

1. The British set up an *educational system* in India which stressed Western culture, history, attitudes, and beliefs. It was through this system that India's leaders of today learned about the Western ideals of freedom and liberty.

2. The British gave India a *common language*. As we have learned, India is a nation of many languages. This fact explains why it was difficult for even educated Indians to communicate with one another. This lack of a common language was the most serious block to national unity. This problem still exists but the use of English as the common language has proved to be a partial solution.

3. The British example of *parliamentary government* has resulted in the setting up of a representative government in India. As does Great Britain, the Indians have a cabinet and a legislature (parliament). The parliament is elected by the people. The members of the cabinet must be members of parliament.

   Instead of a queen or king, as in England, India has a president who is the head of the state. The president of India, like the Queen of England, has little power. As in England, the Prime Minister is the real head of the government. As in England, the Prime Minister is head of the largest political party which holds a majority in the lower house of parliament. At present, Morarji Desai is the Prime Minister. The New Congress Party holds a large majority of the *lok sabha,* the lower house of the Indian Parliament.

4. The British brought to India the idea of the rule by law. This idea replaces the idea that the king is the only giver and interpreter of law. The constitution of India has many provisions which guarantee the freedom and rights of the individual.

India After Independence

Independent India committed itself to democracy. Under Nehru's leadership, a constitution was drafted and a new political structure set up. India's federal system provided the central government with broad political powers. The new state tried to improve the social and economic welfare of the people by passing laws to eliminate social abuses, including the caste system. The government also set up five-year plans for economic improvement, by industrializing and improving agriculture. However, after more than twenty-five years, India still faces staggering social and economic problems. In the field of foreign affairs India has sought friendship with China and cordial relations with both the United States and Russia. However, until its problems at home are solved, India cannot hope to become a leader on the international scene.

Like India, newly independent Pakistan faced difficult problems after partition. More than ten years passed before a government emerged which was capable of

An adult education class in Calcutta. The Indian government has tried to increase
educational opportunities for all Indians. (*Top*)
Credit: *Information Service of India*

Modern office building in Chandigarh. Unlike most Indian cities which grew without
plan, Chandigarh was designed by a group of architects from many countries.(*Bottom*)
Credit: *Information Service of India*

handling the many, nearly impossible tasks. State planning, backed up by large scale private investment, resulted in a great expansion of industry. In foreign affairs Pakistan was concerned with the containment of India, its unfriendly neighbor. Pakistan has been friendly with the United States, but a spilt between India and China has brought Pakistan and China closer together.

India Attempts to Modernize

India Follows a Mixed Economy

When India became independent its leaders recognized the urgency of strengthening the Indian economy. The leaders of the new India were determined to raise the standard of living, which was among the lowest of the major nations in the world. Indian leaders agreed to establish a "mixed economy," which combines the use of private capital and public funds in the development of industry, mining and farming. The government would prepare a master plan for developing the nation's resources. That master plan was set up in a series of five-year plans.

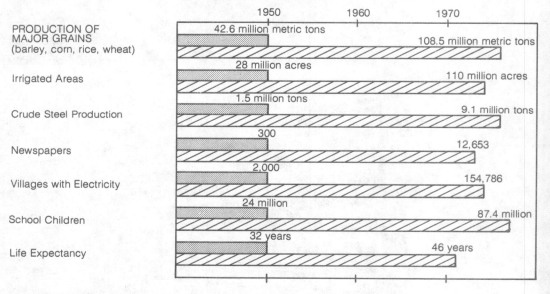

PROGRESS IN INDIA SINCE 1950

	1950	1960	1970
PRODUCTION OF MAJOR GRAINS (barley, corn, rice, wheat)	42.6 million metric tons		108.5 million metric tons
Irrigated Areas	28 million acres		110 million acres
Crude Steel Production	1.5 million tons		9.1 million tons
Newspapers	300		12,653
Villages with Electricity	2,000		154,786
School Children	24 million		87.4 million
Life Expectancy	32 years		46 years

SOURCES: *Encyclopaedia Britannica;* Department of Statistics, Ministry of Planning, India; Food and Agriculture Organization; *Worldmark Encyclopedia of the Nations.*

The Problem of Population Growth

Agricultural expansion was stressed in the first Five-Year Plan of 1951. (See section on Agriculture.) As a result, the output of food has been greatly increased. However, a serious complicating factor is India's great increase in population. The sharp rise is not due to a rise in birth rate. Rather it can be traced to the introduction of modern medicine, improved methods of fighting disease, and the development of an efficient system of famine relief. The seriousness of the population problem can be judged from the chart below:

1948—345 million
1957—392 million
1961—439 million
1967—501 million
1971—548 million (last census)
1977—615 million (estimated)   Growth rate: 2.1% a year

SOURCES: *Encyclopaedia Britannica;* United Nations *Statistical Yearbook.*

Even in a year free of droughts and floods, the population growth more than offset agricultural gains.

The Need for Capital

India has also attempted to increase industrialization, but this has not been easy, because India lacks capital. In 1961 the government launched its third Five-Year Plan. The purpose was to make an all-out effort to strengthen and build industry. Unfortunately, India soon found itself at war with China. Fearing the worst, Indian leaders hurried to strengthen military defenses. This could only be done by scrapping plans for industrial development.

In 1965 India experienced the worst drought of the century. Faced with the threat of famine, money had to be used to buy food. By the time the third Five-Year Plan ended in 1966, India appeared to be little better off than when the plan began.

Resources

India is among the world's leading producers of bauxite. Bauxite ore is used in the making of aluminum. Chromium and copper are also mined in great amounts. Much of the world's mica comes from India. Mica is used in making electrical equipment. Monazite, from which uranium and thorium come, is also mined. Uranium and thorium are valuable sources of atomic energy. Emeralds are mined in Pakistan and gold is mined near Mysore in South India. From India's forests come such valuable woods as cedar and teak. Its rivers can produce large amounts of water power to make electricity.

Although some oil has been found in India, it is far from enough to satisfy the needs of the country. India is almost completely dependent on the Middle East for its oil. India's other important mineral shortages are in lead, tin, zinc, nickel and tungsten. Land surveys are being made to learn what other minerals may be found in India.

Steel Production

India has very large amounts of some very important minerals such as coal, iron and manganese. These minerals are all needed in the making of steel. It is estimated that India may have as much as 25% of the world's supply of iron. India mines about 70 million tons of coal per year. Most of the coal is mined in the Deccan Plateau. India ranks third in the world in the mining of manganese which is used to harden steel. The Tata steel plant in Jamshedpur in northern India, west of Calcutta, is the largest in India. India is now producing more than 7 million tons a year, about one-twentieth that of the United States. India needs more steel than it produces and must increase its production. Recently, the U.S., West Germany, and the Soviet Union agreed to help build additional modern steel mills in India.

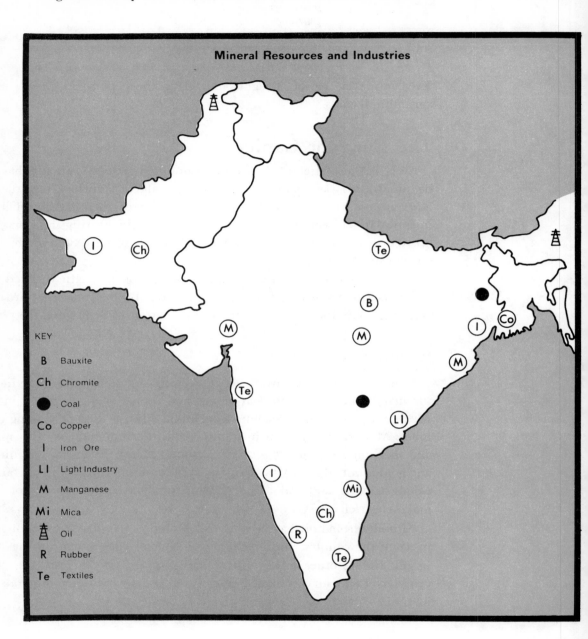

Mineral Resources and Industries

KEY

B	Bauxite
Ch	Chromite
●	Coal
Co	Copper
I	Iron Ore
Ll	Light Industry
M	Manganese
Mi	Mica
⚒	Oil
R	Rubber
Te	Textiles

Industry

At present, the manufacture of textiles is the single largest industry in India. India has contributed to the fashion world such well known materials as calico, muslin, cashmere and madras. India has the world's largest jute manufacturing industry. Jute is a plant which can be used in the making of rope, carpets, and burlap bags.

Other large scale industries include sugar processing, motion picture making, cement, leather, glass, rubber, and paper production.

Cottage industries are those in which goods are produced in the home. Hand looms are used in place of power driven machines. The Indian government believes these cottage industries offer a good use for Indian labor. At present handicrafts, the making of silk goods, and the making of *khadi* (homespun) are the major products of the cottage industry. In addition very skilled men work in brass, copper, silver, and gold to make artistic objects for export.

Indian Scientific Advancement

In May 1974, India's scientists set off an underground nuclear explosion in the Rajasthan Desert. This nuclear blast was widely criticized by many countries. Critics said that India was a poor nation that could barely feed its people; by developing an atomic bomb, the Indians had wasted valuable resources. Also, the blast had added to the arms race and opened the way for other nations to become nuclear powers.

The Indian government answered this by saying that India had a right to do as it saw fit with its resources. With this new source of energy available, India would be less dependent on oil. The Indian government felt that in the future the Indian people would benefit greatly from this advance.

The Indians have also launched a space satellite. This was accomplished with the assistance of the Soviet Union. The Russians supplied materials and the launch took place from Soviet soil. The purpose of this satellite shot was to look for X-rays in space and to detect ultraviolet radiation in the night sky. An unstated purpose was to show that India is a great nation and can do what the other great nations have done.

Problems

India's social needs are of tremendous proportions. Education is a prime problem which the government has not been able to solve. There are not enough facilities, books and other materials, and trained teachers. The dropout rate is very high. Competition for admission to university programs is fierce.

The housing situation becomes more and more serious as time goes by. With the growth of cities, this becomes a more pressing problem for which the government has not come up with solutions.

The promotion of health has become an important function of the Indian government. Campaigns have been launched to get villages to avoid polluting water supplies. The government has subsidized the education of doctors and nurses, built hospitals and clinics, and sponsored medical research. India recognizes the need for birth control, and has initiated educational programs to achieve this end.

The government has acted to improve the lives of Untouchables. Untouchability is now illegal. All professions and trades are now open to them. Seats in the national and state legislatures are reserved for representatives of their own choice. Penalties for discrimination were set up, and laws were passed giving Untouchables specific government jobs. Since their living conditions were even worse than those of Indians in general, the government furnished financial aid to raise their standard of living.

A COMPARISON: UNITED STATES AND INDIA

Income per Person

```
[=================================================] $3750 U.S.
[=] 104 - India
```

1969

	INDIA	U.S.
FOR EACH TEACHER	367 PEOPLE	85 PEOPLE
FOR EACH DOCTOR	5780 PEOPLE	700 PEOPLE
FOR EACH CAR	1305 PEOPLE	3 PEOPLE
FOR EACH PHONE	548 PEOPLE	2 PEOPLE
FOR EACH RADIO	97 PEOPLE	1 PERSON

1975

Value of gross domestic product per person:

U.S. $7,087
India $ 137

	INDIA	U.S.
FOR EACH TEACHER	236 PEOPLE	90 PEOPLE
FOR EACH DOCTOR	4,166 PEOPLE	621 PEOPLE
FOR EACH MOTOR VEHICLE	285 PEOPLE	1.6 PEOPLE
FOR EACH TELEPHONE	168 PEOPLE	1.4 PEOPLE
FOR EACH RADIO	41 PEOPLE	½ PERSON

SOURCES: *Encyclopaedia Britannica; Statesman's Yearbook;* United Nations *Statistical Yearbook;* U.S. Census.

The condition of India's millions of Untouchables has improved slightly since 1948. Legislation to help them is one thing; the acceptance of change by Hindus is another. Deep-rooted attitudes and customs have not been so easy to sweep away.

Indira Gandhi Rules India

On June 25 1975, the Prime Minister of India, Indira Gandhi, announced that secret groups were planning a revolution. She announced the temporary *suspension* (ending) of civil liberties. She also arrested the leaders of all the opposition parties. None of those put in jail would be allowed to appeal to the courts for release. In addition, for the first time since India won its independence from Britain in 1947, all Indian newspapers and all news articles written by foreign reporters were censored.

What brought about this historic act which ended democracy in India for at least the time being? Mrs. Gandhi, the daughter of the first Prime Minister Jawaharlal Nehru, became Prime Minister in 1966. She was not expected to be a strong leader.

However, she introduced a sweeping ten-point program for remaking India into a socialist democracy. After she ordered that 14 private Indian banks be *nationalized* (owned by the government) she was thrown out of the Congress Party. She then formed her own party—The New Congress Party (NCR). In 1971 she called for a national election. The NCP used the Hindi slogan *Garibi hatao* (Abolish poverty). The results of the election gave the NCP two-thirds of the seats in the lok sabha, the Indian parliament.

But "Garibi hatao" came back to cause problems for her government. Poor crops, poor management of the economy, and the rise of the world prices for fertilizers and oil created seemingly unsolvable economic problems. Corruption spread in the government and Mrs. Gandhi seemed not to care. She was charged by Jaya Prakash Narayan, a leader of the opposition and follower of Mohandas Gandhi, with wanting to become a dictator.

It was discovered by a judge in her home city of Allahabad that she had won election to the lok sabha illegally in 1971. The judge said she would have to leave parliament if a higher court upheld his decision. Since the Prime Minister of India must be a member of parliament, Mrs. Gandhi would be forced out of that office too.

Mr. Narayan and other leaders called for Mrs. Gandhi to resign. When she refused Narayan announced that a massive *civil-disobedience* (*satyagraha*) campaign would begin. Narayan and other leaders called for the army and police force to *mutiny* (disobey their officers). At this time Mrs. Gandhi decided to act. At her order the president of India "proclaimed a state of emergency." Civil liberties were suspended and the opposition leaders were arrested.

Mrs. Gandhi said that with this "limited democracy" she can attack poverty more forcefully. She promised that the peasants' great *burden* (weight of debt) will be lessened. She also promised that rural lands would be redivided more equally. Finally, she promised to attack the problem of India's massive inflation (over 30% in 1974).

In March 1977, Mrs. Gandhi eased the state of emergency that had existed for nineteen months. At the same time she called for national elections to be held in March 1977. She hoped that the people of India would show their approval for her program and the state of emergency.

Mrs. Gandhi had seemingly achieved much. Corruption and black market operations had been cut. The grain harvest had been good, and for the first time in many years grain surpluses existed. The economy was improving, and inflation had slowed. Attempts were made to control the growth of population through family planning, birth control and sterilization.

But all of this was achieved at a price. Mrs. Gandhi had said she was acting to protect India's democracy. But the facts showed that democracy had been greatly limited. Leaders of opposition groups were put in jail. Newspapers that criticized the government were censored or closed down. Charges of corruption and bribe taking were made against Mrs. Gandhi's son Sanjay and other members of the government.

The leader of the opposition was Morarji Desai. He told the Indian people that if Mrs. Gandhi were reelected she would again take all rights away from the people and set up a dictatorship.

Another important issue was the sterilization and birth control situation. Thousands of Moslems who opposed the government's forced sterilization of men voted against Mrs. Gandhi and her Congress party.

The results of the election were a great surprise. Mrs. Gandhi was defeated. For the first time since independence in 1947 India was not to be ruled by the leaders of the Congress party. The Indian people had spoken in the way a democratic people speak — by the vote. A peaceful revolution had taken place. The Indian people wanted changes and did not trust Mrs. Gandhi to make those changes.

India Under Morarji Desai

Morarji Desai was 81 years old when he became prime minister of India in March 1977. He told the Indian people, "You must not fear the government as you have feared it all these past months. We are your servants, not your masters."

With these words Desai began his rule of India. He released almost all the people who had been put in jail during the state of emergency. He removed most censorship rules and allowed many newspapers to reopen. All constitutional civil rights were returned to the Indian people.

Desai said the birth control and sterilization program would be entirely voluntary. However, he hoped that the program would be continued and that India's population growth could be controlled. Desai hoped that laws would be passed to give the untouchables greater civil rights and greater legal protection. Land reforms were to be continued to ensure the Indian people a greater share of the nation's wealth.

Full democracy has returned to India. Only time will indicate the success or failure of the new democracy in India.

India and World Politics

India's Policy of Nonalignment

In its foreign relations, India follows a policy of what is called nonalignment. This policy means that India prefers not to line up with any particular country or group of countries in military alliances or treaty agreements. India, however, always takes a side in international disputes. Indian leaders want to feel free to take whichever side of a question they feel will be best for their people and, in their opinion, for the other peoples in the world.

India and the U.S.

Between the United States and India the ties of friendship have been strong. These have been strengthened in recent years by visits to India by President Eisenhower, and by the many visits to the United States by former Prime Minister Nehru and the present Prime Minister, Mrs. Gandhi. India receives more aid from the United States than any other country. The largest part of this aid has been in the form of wheat shipments.

However as a result of a quarrel between India and Pakistan over the situation in East Pakistan (See: *The Problem of Bangla Desh*), relations between the U.S. and

India worsened. The U.S. angered India by continuing to send arms to the Pakistanis. The Indians felt these arms would be used to fight the Bangla Desh guerrillas and possibly against India itself. In November 1971, Indira Gandhi, the Indian Prime Minister, visited President Nixon in the U.S. in the hope of improving relations.

India and the Soviet Union

India also looks upon the Soviet Union as a friend. The leaders of both countries have exchanged many visits. The amount of Soviet aid is much less than that from the United States, but India is happy to have help of all kinds from all sources. Indians also feel they can get military help from Russia to help protect their borders from invasion by the Chinese.

The Russians have not disappointed their Indian friends. While India and Pakistan were quarreling over trouble in East Pakistan in the summer of 1971, the Russians signed an agreement with India. India and Russia agreed to help each other in case of a war. The Russians also sent modern arms and jet planes to India.

In December 1973, Leonid Brezhnev, leader of the Soviet Communist Party, visited India. The Russians and the Indians signed a 15-year economic agreement. The Russians promised to increase trade with India. In addition the Russians agreed to help with Indian plans for the building of new steel mills and to supply India with fertilizers, chemicals, and crude oil. The Russians wanted the right to dock their Indian Ocean warships in India's harbors but Mrs. Gandhi, the Indian Prime Minister, resisted the request.

India and China

India hoped to have friendly relations with her giant neighbor to the north, the People's Republic of China. India was one of the first countries to break off relations with the defeated Chinese Nationalist government, and to recognize the People's Republic. India consistently led the attempt to have China admitted to the United Nations. In 1954 Nehru and Chou En-lai, the Chinese Foreign Minister, agreed on the "Five Principles of Peaceful Coexistence," a pledge of peaceful, neighborly relations between India and China.

However, the Chinese were interested in other things than peaceful coexistence. The Chinese occupied Tibet in 1950. The presence of Chinese forces along the borders of India, Bhutan and Nepal disturbed Nehru. In 1960 the Chinese occupied Longju, an Indian frontier post. This led to fighting between Chinese and Indian soldiers. In 1962 Chinese troops made a deep advance into Indian territory, and then withdrew. Clearly, India, a nation dedicated to peaceful coexistence, was no match for the Chinese.

India and Pakistan

The most important and delicate problem in foreign affairs that faces India is her relation with Pakistan. A bitter dispute over Kashmir is a major factor in poisoning relations between India and Pakistan. Kashmir is important to each country as a "buffer zone" against the other and against China. Kashmir is also important because its rivers supply water to the Indus irrigation system, which is used by both India and Pakistan. Each country was afraid its neighbor might monopolize the water if it controlled the source.

The United Nations tried to solve the problem by working out an arrangement for sharing the water, and by setting up an election to decide which nation the people wanted to belong to. India at first agreed, but changed its mind because Muslims greatly outnumber Hindus in Kashmir. In 1956 India made the part of Kashmir its army controlled part of India. Tension between the two nations over Kashmir grew until, finally, in 1965 heavy fighting broke out. A truce was arranged, but relations have not improved.

India's Changing Role

During its early years of independence, India enjoyed great popularity among the new nations of Asia and Africa. India played an active role in the United Nations and was highly respected. Nehru was the idol of the developing countries and the hero of anti-colonialists. The whole world listened when he spoke. But time has not been kind to India. Failure to solve domestic problems, and the sacrifice of ideals to advance national interest have damaged India's image. Moreover, since Nehru's death, no Indian leader commands the respect among other nations which had been his. Today, with grim problems at home and an explosive situation on its borders with China and Pakistan, India cannot afford to assume a position of leadership in the world.

The Problem of Bangladesh

When India was partitioned in 1947 as many Muslims as possible were put into Pakistan and as many Hindus as possible in India. The main center of Indian Moslems was in the northwestern part of the Indian subcontinent. However another large center was in the northeast in a section known as Bengal. The people of this area—the Bengalis—had lived here for centuries. They are Hindus and Muslims in religion. To solve the problem Bengal was divided between India and Pakistan. Pakistan Bengal was called East Pakistan. Over 1000 miles of Indian territory separated East Pakistan from West Pakistan.

For the Bengalis this solution was not entirely satisfactory. Bengal is a hot, rainy, fertile, heavily populated area. West Pakistan is drier, less fertile and less densely populated. The Muslims of Bengal have developed a different culture from the people of West Pakistan. Their ideas, language and customs are much closer to the Hindu Bengalis, than to the Muslims of West Pakistan.

From the beginning the people of East Pakistan were unhappy and their leaders fought for better conditions. The leading export of Pakistan was jute. Jute was grown mainly in East Pakistan. Most of the money received from the sale of the jute was used to improve conditions in West Pakistan. The use of other resources and capital was also unequally shared. The pressure for greater freedom and even *autonomy* (self-rule) grew.

In early 1971 Pakistan held a general election. Almost all Bengalis voted for the Bengali candidates of the Awami Party led by Sheik Mujibur Rahman (known to his admirers as Mujib). As a result of this the Bengalis had elected enough delegates to gain control of the Pakistan National Assembly. This meant that the Bengalis would be able to elect Mujib, their leader, Prime Minister for all of Pakistan. The Bengalis felt they would then achieve their goals of more self-government and justice.

However, the West Pakistanis, led by President Mohammed Yahya Khan, looked at the problem differently. To give East Pakistan (Bengal) greater freedom might lead to the breakup and destruction of the state of Pakistan. He also felt that his government had given a fair deal to the Bengalis. Yahya decided to crush the Awami Party opposition and eliminate the threat to Pakistani unity. In a lightning, surprise attack the Pakistani army arrested most of the leaders of Bengali Muslims including Mujib. The army moved into East Pakistan in large numbers and occupied most of the main centers. Fighting soon broke out between Bengali guerrilla nationalists and the West Pakistan army.

Reports coming from East Pakistan claimed that hundreds of thousands of men, women and children—Muslim and Hindu, were killed by the army. Homes were destroyed. Millions left East Pakistan and moved into Indian Bengal. The threat of famine and disease epidemic existed. But worse yet, the threat of war between India and Pakistan grew.

The East Pakistan Bengali leaders who survived declared East Pakistan independent and set up a new nation called Bangladesh. Since the Pakistani army ruled most of the main centers of East Pakistan, the Bangladesh started guerrilla warfare in East Pakistan and used Indian territory for bases. The guerrillas attacked army out-posts and patrols. The army arrested thousands. More refugees fled into India. (It was estimated that there would be 10 million refugees in India from East Pakistan by the end of 1971.) Clashes broke out between units of the Indian Army and the army of Pakistan. In late 1971, the situation had become so serious that many observers felt that war between India and Pakistan might be inevitable.

In December 1971, fighting broke out between Bengalis and Pakistanis. Indian troops raced across the border to aid the Bengalis. In 14 days the Pakistanis were defeated and they surrendered. The state of Bangladesh was born.

In January 1972, the government of Pakistan, now led by Zulfikar Ali Bhutto released the Bengali leader, Sheik Mujibar Rahman, in an effort to improve relations with the new nation. Mujibar became the Prime Minister of the government of Bangladesh.

In September 1973, after 21 months of discussion, India and Pakistan agreed with Bangladesh approval to a peace settlement. The main points of the settlement were: 1. there was to be a prisoner of war exchange; 2. all Bengalis stranded in Pakistan at the end of the war would be allowed to return to Bangladesh; and 3. a "substantial" (large) number of Biharis (non-Bengali Moslems) in Bangladesh would be allowed to go to Pakistan.

With Prime Minister Mujibar in control, Bangladesh came under the influence of India and the Soviets, primarily because of U.S. support of Pakistan. Many of the country's industries were nationalized. In 1974, responding to riots and violence, the government instituted emergency powers. Mujibar was assassinated and the government suffered a series of coups.

In 1977, a new government was established with a central constitution. Bangladesh's relations with India deteriorated over water rights disputes.

The mutual hatred and suspicion cannot and will not disappear overnight, but it will be possible now to keep it from becoming greater. The countries can now pay more attention to the great problems of survival that they each face.

The sacred cow on the streets of New Delhi. *Credit: Photo Researchers/George Daniell*

Summary of Key Ideas

The Subcontinent of India and Pakistan

A. **India's varied geographic features** helped to shape its culture and history.
1. India is considered to be a subcontinent of Asia.
2. The Himalaya Mountains in the north, jungles in the northeast, and oceans and seas to the east and west have in part isolated India from the rest of Asia.
3. Geographic features have influenced the development of local cultures, and have aided the development of regionalism.
4. The monsoon plays a vital role in the life of the people of India.
5. River valleys and coastal regions are centers of population.
6. Climate has affected the development of culture and history.
7. Most of India has a subtropical climate.

B. **Outside forces have brought great changes to Indian society, culture, government and religion.**
1. The Dravidian civilizations at Mohenjo-Daro and Harrapa show the advanced state of the first Indian civilization.
2. Aryan invaders from the north brought many changes to the subcontinent.
3. The Islamic religion was brought to India by traders and invaders.
4. The Indian spice trade had a great effect on Indian history and the history of America, Africa and Southeast Asia.
5. *No* all-India empire existed throughout the history of the subcontinent. Political history was regional.
6. The British gained control after defeating an Indian-French army at Plassey. The British ruled through Indian leaders.
7. The subcontinent became the "brightest jewel in the British crown." Conflicts and challenges to traditional ways of life developed.
8. The Sepoy Rebellion stimulated the growth of nationalism.
9. The 20th century has been marked by struggles between Indian nationalists and Great Britain and between Hindu and Muslim nationalists.
10. The careers of Gandhi and Nehru show the struggle for Indian independence.

C. **Economic problems present great troubles for the leaders of India.**
1. The monsoons dominate economic life in most parts of India.
2. Over 80% of the people live in rural areas. There are over 500,000 villages, averaging about 100 families each.
3. Rice is the main food and is important as a money-raising crop.
4. Wheat, millet, tobacco and cotton are raised in drier areas.
5. Small-scale farming on a subsistence level is the rule for India.

6. Population pressure makes it difficult for people to survive in the face of poverty and hunger.
7. The Indian government has adopted programs to increase agricultural production and encourage birth control.
8. India has a mixed economy. Public and private funds are used to develop the land and industry.
9. India receives aid from both the U.S. and the Soviet Union.
10. India faces all of the problems of a developing nation.

D. **Religion is a way of life which influences the social structure, history, economic activity and political organization of India.**
1. Religion often regulates customs, diet, occupations and other aspects of life.
2. Knowledge of Hinduism is a must for an understanding of India's past and present.
3. Hindus believe in reincarnation (rebirth of the soul). This is part of the Hindu belief in the holiness of all living things.
4. Religious differences between Hindus and Muslims have historic roots and have greatly influenced the development of modern India.

E. **India has played an important role in world affairs since independence.**
1. India's size and differences in religion, language and ethnic background create political unrest within its borders.
2. The new state of Bangladesh creates a new set of problems for India.
3. Relations between India and Pakistan have been poor since independence.
4. India has tried to follow a policy of nonalignment and to maintain friendly relations with all, especially the U.S., USSR, and China.
5. Border disputes with China, rooted in past history, have caused war between the two, and a troublesome situation still remains.
6. Problems with Pakistan have led India to closer relations with the Soviet Union and distrust of the U.S.
7. India has been an active member of the United Nations.

UNIT VI

Exercises and Questions

Vocabulary

Directions: Match the words in Column *A* with the correct meaning in Column *B*.

Column A

1. migration
2. paddies
3. illiterate
4. caste
5. untouchables
6. annexed
7. ahimsa
8. dharma
9. reincarnation
10. swaraj

Column B

(a) added to something.
(b) self rule.
(c) movement of people or animals.
(d) the act of returning to some form of life after death.
(e) rice fields.
(f) Indian idea of non-violent action.
(g) the lack of ability to read or write.
(h) outcast people of India.
(i) social division of the Indian people by birth and according to occupation.
(j) Hindu rules of life, which control a person's actions.

Completion

Directions: Complete the following sentences using the terms below.

Vedas	Deccan	Himalayas	Moksha	Ghats
Dravidians	Hindi	Harrapa	Monsoons	Tamil

1. .... is the language and the name given to the people of South India.
2. .... was a city of early India.
3. .... is the book of ceremonies and rituals written by the Aryan people of India.
4. .... is the final resting place of the souls of Hindus.
5. .... are the original people of India.
6. .... are the low mountains found on both the east and west coasts of India.
7. .... is the name given to the central plateau of India.
8. .... are the mountains of Northern India.
9. .... is the language most spoken in India.
10. .... are the seasonal winds which affect India and much of Asia.

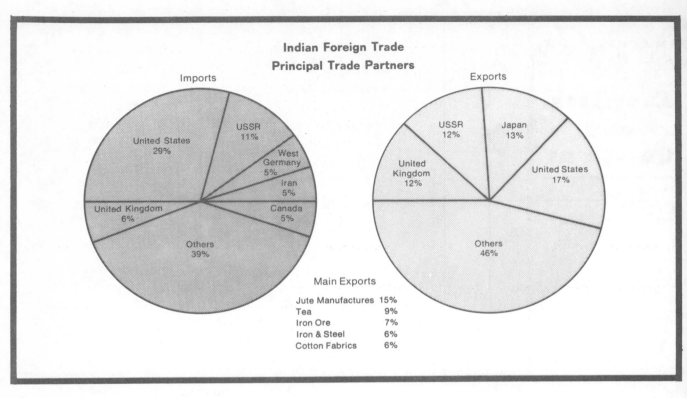

Indian Foreign Trade
Principal Trade Partners

Imports

United States 29%
USSR 11%
West Germany 5%
Iran 5%
Canada 5%
United Kingdom 6%
Others 39%

Exports

USSR 12%
Japan 13%
United Kingdom 12%
United States 17%
Others 46%

Main Exports

Jute Manufactures	15%
Tea	9%
Iron Ore	7%
Iron & Steel	6%
Cotton Fabrics	6%

Chart Analysis

Directions: Select the statement which best answers the question or completes the sentence. Use only the information given in the chart and graphs.

1. This graph is an example of a
   (a) pictograph
   (b) line graph
   (c) pie graph
   (d) bar graph

2. The leading trading partner of India is
   (a) the United Kingdom
   (b) the United States
   (c) the USSR
   (d) Canada

3. Which of the following groups of products are exported from India?
   (a) Jute, cotton goods, coffee
   (b) Jute, tea, wool
   (c) Jute, tea, iron and steel products
   (d) Jute, iron ore, coal

4. Which of the following statements can be proven by information given in the chart and graph?
   (a) India exports more than 70% of its products to Europe.
   (b) India exports more to the United Kingdom than any other nation.
   (c) India imports more than 70% of its products from Europe.
   (d) The United States and the USSR take about 40% of Indian's import trade.

5. Which of the following statements can be proven false by information from the chart?
   (a) Jute is India's most important export.
   (b) Japan takes more than 10% of India's exports.
   (c) The U.S. supplies almost 1/3 of India's imports.
   (d) India has very little trade with her Asian neighbors.

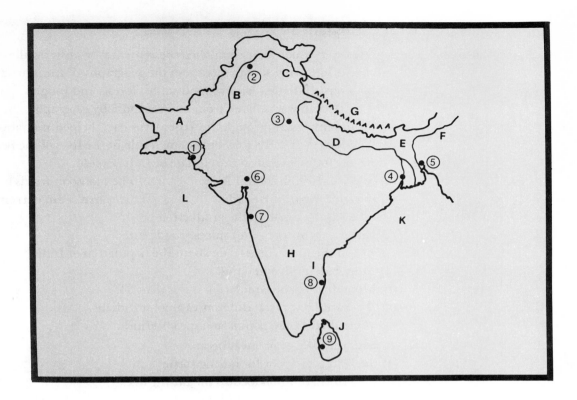

Map Exercise

Directions: Answer the following questions based on the map of India.

1. The Himalaya Mountains are shown by the letter
   (a) A (b) C (c) G (d) F

2. The capital city of India is shown by the number
   (a) 1 (b) 2 (c) 3 (d) 4

3. The letter "D" represents the
   (a) Indus River (b) Ganges River (c) Thar Desert (d) GHATS

4. Sri Lanka (Ceylon) is shown by the letter
   (a) J (b) K (c) L (d) H

5. The letter "H" is located on the
   (a) Thar Desert (b) Ganges Valley (c) Carnatic Coast (d) Deccan

6. The numbers 4 and 7 are important seaports. They are
   (a) Madras and Bombay (b) Madras and Calcutta (c) Bombay and Calcutta
   (d) Calcutta and Karachi

7. A delta is found near which of the following groups of cities
   (a) 1, 4, 5 (b) 2, 3, 4 (c) 3, 4, 5 (d) 1, 6, 7

8. Bangladesh is shown by the letter
   (a) A (b) B (c) E (d) K

9. The river "D" flows mainly
   (a) East to West (b) West to East (c) North to South (d) South to North

10. The number 8 shows the location of the city of
    (a) Dacca (b) Madras (c) Bombay (d) Calcutta

Multiple Choice

Directions: Select the answer which best completes the sentence or answers the question.

1. All of the following statements about the geography of India are true *except* which?
   (a) Southern India is a land of mountains, forests and jungles.
   (b) The Deccan was isolated from most of India by geography.
   (c) Mountain passes through the Himalayas have helped migrations into India.
   (d) The Rivers of India play only a small role in the lives of the people.

2. All of the following affect the climate of India *except*
   (a) cold winds from central Asia   (b) The monsoon winds from the south
   (c) the wide range of latitude   (d) the warm ocean currents along the coasts

3. India leads the world in the production of
   (a) wheat   (b) tea   (c) spices   (d) jute

4. Which of the following is *true* about the population of India?
   (a) Most Indians live in cities.
   (b) More than ½ the population is less than 34.
   (c) There are few racial differences among Indians.
   (d) More than ½ the population speaks Hindi.

5. Indians eat little or no meat because
   (a) the land is too poor for raising cattle
   (b) the Hindu religion forbids the raising of cattle
   (c) the Hindu religion forbids the eating of meat
   (d) all of these

6. The earliest writing system in India was developed in
   (a) Mohenjo Daro India   (b) Gupta India
   (c) Maurya India   (d) Mughal India

7. The earliest civilization in India was located in the valley of the
   (a) Ganges River   (b) Indus River   (c) Brahmaputra River   (d) Godavari River

8. All of the following were accomplishments of Harrapa and Mohenjo Daro *except*
   (a) use of gold and silver   (b) buildings made of brick
   (c) development of the Vedas   (d) drainpipes to carry water

9. The Aryans
   (a) came to India from the island of Ceylon
   (b) were farmers who settled in Mohenjo Daro
   (c) were conquered by the Dravidian herdsmen
   (d) conquered the Dravidians and settled in India

10. Alexander the Great's invasion of India was important because
    (a) it brought new ways of thinking and doing things to India
    (b) it destroyed the power of the Mauryas
    (c) it prevented the growth of a great Indian Empire
    (d) it led to the growth of many small kingdoms and republics

11. Ashoka is remembered as a great king because
    (a) he introduced the Hindu religion
    (b) he was a just and considerate ruler
    (c) he conquered new lands for his empire
    (d) he built up the power of the Brahmins

12. Buddhism did not succeed in India because
    (a) Hinduism accepted many of the ideas of Buddha
    (b) the Muslims destroyed the Buddhist monasteries
    (c) Buddhists were willing to compromise with the beliefs of Hinduism
    (d) all of the above three reasons

13. A great poet of India was
    (a) Chandragupta   (b) Kalidasa   (c) Aurangzeb   (d) Muhammed Ghori

14. The Mughals developed a new language called
    (a) Hindi   (b) Punjabi   (c) Urdu   (d) Marathi

15. The Rajputs were
    (a) religious leaders of North India
    (b) Muslims who came to India from Persia
    (c) Sikhs who fought against the Muslims
    (d) warriors who helped preserve Hinduism in North India

16. The Sikhs believed in all of the following *except*
    (a) one God   (b) the Caste System   (c) toleration   (d) hard work

17. The battle of Plassey was important because the
    (a) British were driven from India
    (b) Japanese were driven from India
    (c) English gained control of much of India
    (d) Rajahs of India united against the French

18. The Sepoy Rebellion was caused by
    (a) rivalry between the French and the English
    (b) the hatred of the Moslems for the Hindus
    (c) the rivalry between the East India Company and the British Parliament
    (d) Indian unhappiness with British rule

19. The Sepoy Rebellion was important because it
    (a) drove the British out of India
    (b) was thought of as the first blow struck for independence
    (c) strengthened the rule of the East India Company in India
    (d) destroyed Indian nationalism

20. An example of Indian nationalism was the
    (a) formation of the Congress Party
    (b) partition of India
    (c) formation of the East India Company
    (d) signing of the Rowlatt Acts

21. Which of the following events was the result of the other three
    (a) the passing of the Rowlatt Acts   (b) The Amritsar Massacre
    (c) Montague-Chelmsford Reforms   (d) World War I

22. The Government of India Act of 1935
    (a) gave India its independence   (b) was successful in quieting Indian protests
    (c) was an attempt to quiet Indian protests   (d) gave India independence

23. At the end of the World War in 1945 the British
    (a) still refused to leave India   (b) helped to set up a united India
    (c) agreed to partition India into two nations   (d) assassinated Gandhi

24. The best way to describe the economy of India is
    (a) capitalistic   (b) socialistic   (c) communistic   (d) mixed

25. All of the following are true about India's economic development *except* which?
    (a) Private capital is combined with public funds to aid development.
    (b) The government set up a master plan for the development of resources.
    (c) Agricultural production now meets the needs of the Indian people.
    (d) The War with China has caused economic development to slow down.

26. The leading industry of India today is
    (a) textiles   (b) steel   (c) automobiles   (d) electronics

27. Which of the following groups of minerals are used in steel production?
    (a) copper, iron, coal   (b) iron, coal, manganese
    (c) copper, nickel, bauxite   (d) coal, iron, bauxite

28. The Indian policy of *nonalignment* means India
    (a) does not get involved in international disputes
    (b) refuses to accept aid from the U.S. and Russia
    (c) wants to feel free to take any side that helps India
    (d) has not joined the United Nations or other international groups

29. All of the following statements are true about India's foreign relations *except* which?
    (a) India has followed a policy of friendship toward the U.S. and Russia.
    (b) India was one of the first nations to recognize the Chinese People's Republic.
    (c) India has consistently voted to have the People's Republic of China admitted to the United Nations.
    (d) China and India have developed strong ties of friendship.

30. The present Prime Minister of India is:
    (a) Morarji Desai   (b) Jawaharlal Nehru   (c) Mohandas Gandhi
    (d) Indira Gandhi

Thought Questions

1. How did geographic features affect the development of Indian civilization?
2. (a) Describe the climate of India.
   (b) How has the climate of India affected the lives of the people?
3. How have differences of race and language affected India?
4. Why might the North Indian Plain be called "The Bread Basket of India?"
5. Why has this area often been called a subcontinent?
6. Why are the river valleys of India so densely populated?
7. "The monsoons mean life and death to the people of India." Explain.
8. "The growth of population is India's greatest problem." Tell why you agree or disagree with this statement.
9. "Religion in India has served to unite and to drive the people apart." Explain what this statement means. Do you agree? Why?
10. Describe the achievements of the people of Mohenjo Daro, and Harrapa.
11. What contributions were made by each of the following groups to Indian civilization? (a) Aryans (b) Mauryas (c) Guptas (d) Mughals (e) British
12. How did the English gain control of India?

13. Why was the Sepoy Rebellion important in Indian history?
14. Why was India called "the most precious jewel in the Crown of the British Empire?"
15. "The British both helped and hurt the people of India." Give some evidence to show the truth of the statement.
16. Gandhi was called Mahatma, "The Great Soul." Do you think he deserved the name? Why?
17. (a) If you were a member of the Indian government what would you feel are most important problems of India?

    (b) What suggestions might you make to solve those problems?
18. Why is the village thought to be the heart of Indian life?
19. (a) Describe the caste system.

    (b) Why has the caste system been a block to progress in India?
20. (a) Describe the main ideas of the Hindu religion.

    (b) Why is "Hinduism more than a way of life?"
21. (a) Describe India's policy of nonalignment.

    (b) How has this policy affected India's relations with the U.S., Russia and China?
22. Why has Kashmir become a problem between Pakistan and India?
23. (a) Many of the people of India do not have as much food as they need. Why is this so?

    (b) How has the Indian government tried to solve this problem?
24. Why have historians called Gupta India the "Golden Age of Indian History?"
25. How has Islam affected life in India? Why has conflict developed between Hindus and Muslims?
26. What does the Ramayana and Mahabharata tell us about the way the people of India feel about life?
27. How did the British control of India affect the lives of the Indian people?
28. (a) Why did Indira Gandhi decide to suspend civil rights in India?

    (b) If you were a member of the opposition how would you feel? Why?

    (c) How does the suspension of civil rights affect the lives of the Indian people?
29. "India in the past two years has proved it is a modern scientific nation." Explain why you would agree or disagree with this statement.
30. "India has made great efforts and is succeeding in solving its food problem." Do you agree or disagree with this statement? Explain.

Which of the Following Does Not Belong in Each Group?

1. Rivers of the subcontinent of India: Indus, Ghats, Ganges, Brahmaputra
2. Cities of the Indian subcontinent: Calcutta, Bombay, New Delhi, Rangoon
3. Languages of India: Bengali, Telugu, Jain, Marathi
4. Leaders of Indian nationalism: Tilak, Gandhi, Nehru, Clive
5. Important ideas of Hinduism: Vedas, Moksha, Dharma, Karma
6. Geographic regions of the Indian subcontinent: Deccan, Malabar, Ghats, Malacca
7. Mughal rulers: Ashoka, Akbar, Babur, Shah Jahan
8. Indian developments in mathematics: Arabic numerals, the idea of zero, the idea of infinity, geometry
9. Literature of India: Upanishads, Ramayana, Mahabharata, Swaraj.

The emancipation of India's women is finally taking place. This is the daughter of a military attache who raised local eyebrows with her mini sari. *Credit: United Press International*

Puzzle

Directions:

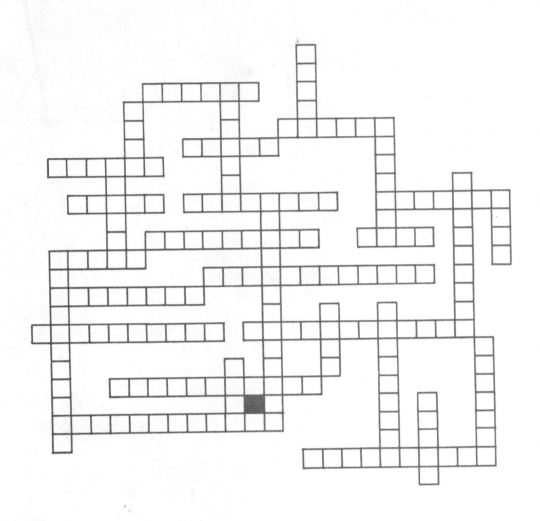

4 LETTERS
JUTE
RICE
SARI
SOUL
THUG

5 LETTERS
CASTE
CURRY
DELTA
HINDU
SEPOY

6 LETTERS
ARYANS
BUFFER
CALICO
DHARMA
SPICES

7 LETTERS
DYNASTY
MONSOON
RAJPUTS
REBIRTH

8 LETTERS
BRAHMINS
CONGRESS

9 LETTERS
BUDDHISTS
PAN CHAYAT
PARTITION

10 LETTERS
ILLITERACY
MIGRATIONS

11 LETTERS
NATIONALISM
SUBSISTENCE

12 LETTERS
CIVILIZATION
SUBCONTINENT
UNTOUCHABLES

13 LETTERS
REINCARNATION

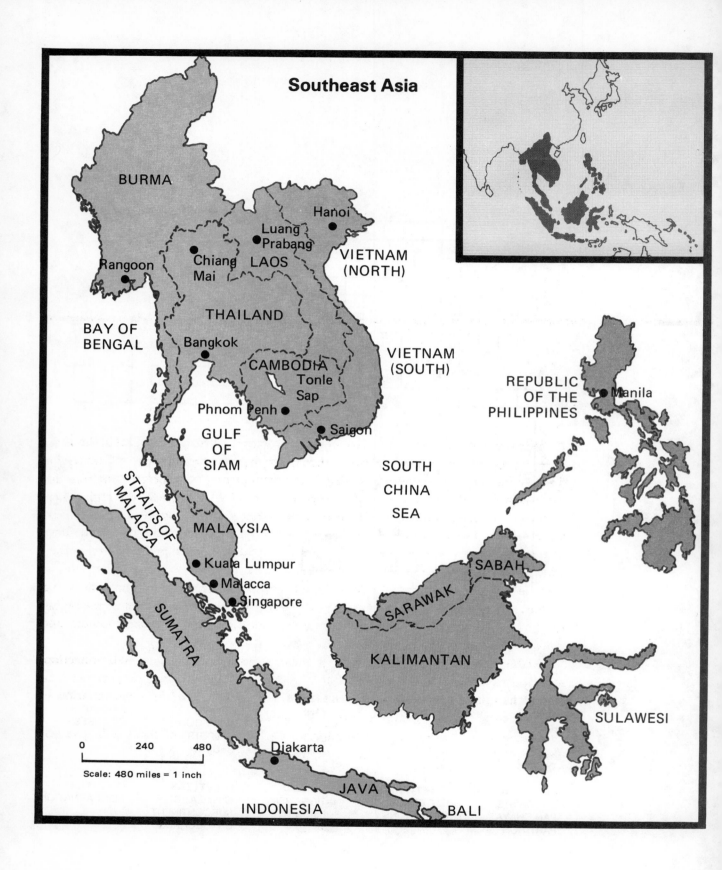

Southeast Asia

BURMA

Rangoon

Chiang Mai

Luang Prabang

Hanoi

VIETNAM (NORTH)

LAOS

BAY OF BENGAL

THAILAND

Bangkok

CAMBODIA

Tonle Sap

VIETNAM (SOUTH)

Phnom Penh

Saigon

GULF OF SIAM

SOUTH CHINA SEA

REPUBLIC OF THE PHILIPPINES

Manila

STRAITS OF MALACCA

MALAYSIA

Kuala Lumpur

Malacca

Singapore

SUMATRA

SARAWAK

SABAH

KALIMANTAN

SULAWESI

0   240   480

Scale: 480 miles = 1 inch

Djakarta

JAVA

BALI

INDONESIA

UNIT VII Southeast Asia

Introduction and Setting

"When a Thai or Vietnamese farmer is asked where his people *originated*, he is apt to reply that they have always lived in this village because he can, after all, remember his grandfather. Throughout Southeast Asia tradition may be supreme, but time has little meaning. Early Chinese and European travelers who roamed this region kept records, now important *sources* for Western scholars, but the Southeast Asians themselves were indifferent to history. What they knew or cared about the past came down to them not in any systematic account, but in myths and legends that were, to their ears, just awesome or charming or literary magic." [1]

"Southeast Asia is a green world of islands and peninsulas, so underpopulated and underdeveloped that there is a surplus of raw materials for export. Much of the region has recently emerged from colonialism, with resulting problems of economic and political development." [2]

"Reduced to their essentials the problems of Southeast Asia are: self-protection, self-support, and self-government. They arise out of the strategic importance and untold wealth of the area, which the Communists desire, and the determination of the peoples of Southeast Asia to govern themselves." [3]

These are just three views of Southeast Asia. A discussion of them will give you some insight into the people, their land and their problems.

---

[1] Stanley Karnow, *Southeast Asia* (New York: Time-Life Books, 1967).
[2] G. B. Cressey, *Asia's Land and People* (New York: McGraw-Hill Book Co., 1963).
[3] Carlos P. Romulo, "The Position of Southeast Asia in the World Community," *Southeast Asia in the Coming World*, P. W. Thayer, ed. (Baltimore: Johns Hopkins University Press, 1953).

Distances and Diversity

The term Southeast Asia was first used by American military commanders in World War II to give a geographical unity to a *region* noted for its *diversity* and for the distances which separate its peoples from one another.

Almost 300 million people live in Southeast Asia. The region has neither cultural nor political unity. The peoples of the independent nations which now exist in Southeast Asia are of many races and religions. Their present *cultures* and cultural differences are a result of these factors.

The nations themselves show great cultural diversities within their own national borders. This fact explains why it has been difficult to form modern nations with *stable* governments and stable economies.

Shared Experiences

Even though these differences exist we can study Southeast Asia as a region. This is so because of geographic reasons. In addition, the peoples of the region have shared historic and ethnic ties as well as common experiences.

Our study of the area will revolve around five major ideas.

1. Foremost is the idea that people are most important in the setting of Southeast Asia. In regard to this, a key point will be the part that geographic and physical features have played in influencing the lives of the people of the region.
2. Outside forces have greatly influenced historical developments in Southeast Asia. Trade and colonial control have changed the course of Southeast Asian cultural and historical development on several occasions.
3. The people of Southeast Asia include a variety of ethnic and religious groups, religious beliefs, social groups, customs and nationalities. This diversity has created many problems for the newly formed independent nations.
4. The nations of Southeast Asia are in the midst of dramatic change.
5. Southeast Asia's location and economic *potential* make it a key area in present and future world affairs.

We will begin our study of Southeast Asia by looking at the geography of the region to see how it affects the people living there.

Topography

Southeast Asia is a region of *islands* and *peninsulas*. In the northwest is the Indo-Chinese Peninsula, which extends off the continent of Asia. Stretching southward from this peninsula is a long, narrow body of land called the Malay Peninsula. The narrowest part of this peninsula is called the *Isthmus* of Kra. To the south and east are the islands of Indonesia and the Philippines. Together, the islands and peninsulas of Southeast Asia form a land area about half the size of the United States.

Mountain ranges and seas help to divide Southeast Asia into many *isolated* parts. Some of the seas are connected to the great Pacific Ocean. Others are arms of the Indian Ocean. Along some of the sea coasts are lowlands that are densely populated. Many of the river plains between the mountain ranges also have *dense* population.

The rivers of Southeast Asia are the scene of great activity. Here we see the
Singapore River with the city of Singapore in the background.
Credit: *Singapore Economic Development Board*

Mountain Barriers

If we were able to look down from an airplane on *mainland* Southeast Asia we would see many mountains. In the north are high ranges that separate most of Southeast Asia from the rest of Asia. Extending southward from these *barriers* are several other mountain ranges. They reach through the region like giant fingers, and stretch on into the sea.

The mountains are forested. These forests are very dense on the ranges that stretch along the edges of the peninsula, for the rainfall here is the heaviest. (Can you explain why?) On the central highlands that receive less rainfall the forests are less dense.

Rivers and River Valleys

Between the mountain ranges are several great rivers and river valleys. In the western section are the valleys of the Irrawaddy and Salween Rivers. These rivers begin in the mountains of Burma's northern border and flow southward to the sea. As we

Rivers of Southeast Asia

look to the southeast, we see the valley of the Chao Phraya (Menam) in Thailand. Farther east is the mightly Mekong River. It flows across Kampuchea (formerly Cambodia) and southern Vietnam. In the northeast part of Southeast Asia is the Red River of northern Vietnam.

Where the large rivers of the region flow into the sea, they form *deltas*. The deltas are formed mainly by sand and silt carried there by rivers from the land through which they flow. The delta of the Red River is one of the most densely populated areas of Southeast Asia. Some of the other deltas, such as that of the Irrawaddy, were large swamps until recent times. Now, however, many of these swamps have been drained for rice farms and, in Vietnam, the delta of the Mekong is used for rice and rubber plantations.

Several of the region's important cities are located on these deltas. Among them are Rangoon in Burma, Bangkok in Thailand, Saigon and Hanoi in Vietnam.

Coastline

Another feature is the long coastline of the Malay Peninsula, with the narrow strait between Malaya and Sumatra. As a result, Southeast Asian seaports have always been important stopping points on the trade route between China and India. Not only did all sea trade between China and India go through the strait, but the seasonal pattern of the monsoons also made it necessary for early traders from China and India to spend several months in a Southeast Asian port waiting for the winds to change so they could return or go on. With foreigners living in the ports for long periods of time, the people became thoroughly familiar with alien ways.

The Great Lake

Mainland Southeast Asia has only one large lake. This is the Great Lake (Tonle Sap) in the central lowland of Kampuchea. The Tonle Sap was once an inlet of the sea. Over the centuries, however, the mouth of the inlet has been filled in, and it forms a part of the delta of the Mekong River.

Climate

Temperature

As we have already noted, dense forests cover much of Southeast Asia. In most of the area the *climate* is *humid* and the rainfall is heavy. Temperatures do not change much from summer to winter.

If we look at our maps of the region we can see the reason for the constant high temperature. The equator passes through the area. In the summer months the temperature frequently rises to 100°F or more. It is cooler on the upland plateaus and in the mountains, where it may become quite cold at night. There is no part of Southeast Asia that is more than fifteen degrees from the equator.

Seasons, Monsoons and Rainfall

Though the temperature does not change much throughout the year, the amount of rainfall does. In many parts of Southeast Asia the year is divided into a rainy season and a dry season.

Summer is the rainy season in Southeast Asia. In some places the rains come every day. Warm ocean winds from the southwest help to bring the rains. These winds, which only blow from the southwest during the summer, are called the summer *monsoons*.

The winds that blow during the dry season come mainly from across the seas to the northeast. When they reach the mainland, they are forced to rise in order to cross the Annamese Highlands along the coast of Vietnam. This causes the winds to cool, which in turn causes some rainfall. Therefore, by the time they have crossed the mountains, the winds have become drier and warmer. Instead of giving off rain, they pick up *moisture* from the land. This is the main reason the land west of highlands is dry during the winter. These winds are called the winter monsoons.

The people of Southeast Asia cannot get along without the monsoons. Without this rainfall the rice fields would not be flooded. When the rains are late, or too little rain falls, the crops fail and millions of Asians face starvation.

Some parts of the region are drier than others. One of the drier regions is the central highlands of Burma. The dryness is caused by the location of the valley. (Can

Meo people who live in the mountains of Southeast Asia. (*Top*)
Credit: *Tourist Organization of Thailand*

Lowland Thais in modern Thai dress. (*Bottom*)
Credit: *Tourist Organization of Thailand*

you explain why?) When we examine this dry area we find farmers working in fields of millet, cotton and other crops that need less rainfall than rice.

Peoples and Languages

Peoples

Some of the people in Southeast Asia are descendants of those settlers who came to the area about 4,500 years ago. They were of average height, with black hair and brown skin. The ancestors of others came to the area from lands to the north and west, over the past 1000 to 2000 years. They spoke many languages, had different religions, and followed different ways of life. Even today many new immigrants are making their homes in Southeast Asia. Because of intermarriage and mixed backgrounds it is difficult to describe the typical Southeast Asian.

Indonesian peoples moved into the Malay Peninsula and islands of southeast Asia. On the mainland, the first people to settle down were the Mons in Southern Burma and the Khmers in Cambodia. North of them were the Burmese. To the east, in northern Vietnam, were the Vietnamese, who settled in the Tongkin area and the Red River Delta. South of them were the Chams, who were related to the Indonesians. A last group, the Shan, or Thai, began moving into Southeast Asia in the eleventh and twelfth centuries A.D. after a long time in southern China.

Languages

Many languages are spoken in Southeast Asia. In any one country you may find several different languages. Some of the languages, such as Burmese, Thai and Lao, are like Chinese. Others are quite different.

A number of European languages are also spoken. English is spoken in every Southeast Asian country, mainly in the cities. It is especially common in the Philippines, Malaysia, Singapore and Burma. Many people in Vietnam, Kampuchea and Laos know French. Dutch is widely spoken by Indonesians. In the Philippines some Spanish is spoken. In the large Chinese communities all over Southeast Asia the languages of South China are spoken. Immigrants from South India still use Tamil and other Dravidian languages of their homeland.

Population Distribution

Altogether, there are more than 230 million people in Southeast Asia. This means that there are more people living in Southeast Asia than in the United States. The number of people living in the area is becoming larger every year. More medical care, better food, and cleaner living habits have helped to bring this about. Fewer babies now become sick and die, and adults live longer than they used to. Today there are more than twenty times as many people living in Southeast Asia than there were in 1800. In many parts of Java and Thailand, and on the Red River Delta of northern Vietnam, there are more than 1,500 people living on each square mile of land.

Urban Centers of Population

In the densely populated areas of Southeast Asia there are some large cities. Several of these have a million or more people. All of the largest cities are sea ports or river ports to which the products of nearby mines, forests and fields are brought for *export*. Except for Bangkok, in Thailand, these cities were formerly colonial government centers or trade centers.

Some of the countries of Southeast Asia have more cities than others. Indonesia has a larger number of cities than the others. Most of these are located on the island of Java. The largest city of Southeast Asia is found on Java—Djakarta. In each country on the Indo-Chinese Peninsula, the capital city is also the largest city of the country (Rangoon in Burma, Bangkok in Thailand, Hanoi and Ho Chi Minh City in Vietnam). The Philippines have several important cities, but Manila is by far the most important. In the Malay Peninsula the most important cities are Singapore and Kuala Lumpur.

Mountain Tribesmen

However, most of the people of Southeast Asia are farmers and live in villages, which we will examine below. After we leave the cities and the lowland farm areas, we might travel for miles without seeing a house or a single person. Large parts of this area are covered with swamps, forested plains and mountains. In the *remote* highland areas are tribes who often live in a manner which would appear to be very backward and primitive to us. Two examples are the Meo and Moi tribes. Some of the tribesmen are small, dark skinned people who make their living as hunters and *food gatherers*. Others have light brown skins like the people of the lowlands. They usually clear small patches in the forests for farmland.

If we visited the village of some of the mountain tribesmen of Thailand, we might find that the people there spoke a different language from that of the lowland people. Most lowland villagers in Thailand belong to a group called the Thai. However, the mountain people are divided into different groups that do not dress alike or speak the same language. All the countries of Southeast Asia have different groups of people living within their borders. In Indonesia alone, a hundred or more different languages or *dialects* are spoken.

In all the countries of Southeast Asia the lowland people feel they are superior to the mountain peoples. This has resulted in a great deal of discrimination and prejudice against the mountain people. In Thailand trouble has increased and fighting has broken out in the mountains against the government.

Indians and Chinese in Southeast Asia

Some groups of people are newcomers from other countries. In recent years, many people from China have come to this region to work in the oil fields, mines and plantations. Today there are over twelve million Chinese in Southeast Asia. They now run many of the plantations, shops, businesses and banks. Most Chinese have kept their own language and customs, instead of learning to live as the people of their new homeland do. They are not always welcomed by the people of Southeast Asia.

Malay house on stilts. Why has this house been constructed on stilts? (*Top*)
Credit: *Mission of Malaysia to the United Nations*

Typical architecture of an Indonesian house. (*Bottom*)
Credit: *Consulate General of Indonesia*

In addition, there are people from India and Pakistan who are in a similar position to the Chinese and are also not very well liked.

Village Life

For over a thousand years the people of Southeast Asia have lived mainly on the countryside. They have earned their living mainly as farmers. The center of their lives has been the village. Each village usually has been small but almost always self-sufficient. The villagers have tried to provide for all of the needs of all of the people of the village.

Let us imagine we are able to walk through a village in Southeast Asia. We would come into the village along a *klong* (canal) or along a narrow dirt road. The village has about 50 small houses all built on stilts, close to the *klong*. The houses are made of bamboo and wood. The roofs are steep and pointed. They are thatched with nipa palm leaves. Around each house is a garden. In the garden we can see flowers, fruit trees, coconut palms, and a small vegetable section.

The work of the village centers around the growing of rice. In late June or July the farmer plants his seed beds. He sows the seeds by scattering a great many seeds by hand. In this method many seeds are wasted. Five weeks later the farmer transplants the seedlings by hand with the help of his neighbors. In late November or early December the crops are ready to be harvested. The harvest is also brought in by hand. The rice fields begin right at the back doors of the homes of the villagers. The *paddy* or rice field is flooded to aid the growth of rice.

As we continue our walk through the village there is much to see that is interesting. The well is always a busy place. A large crowd of women is at the well. They are talking in loud voices. The well is like an American supermarket—a place to meet friends and talk about town gossip. Nearby we see other buildings which are used as tool sheds. All the members of the village use the tools and the tool sheds in a cooperative way. In a grove of trees near the village we see a building called the *wat* or village temple.

The village headman knew we were coming and has prepared a meal for us. The house is built on stilts or high posts. This protects the floor from flood waters when the river overflows its banks in the rainy season. The open space under the house is used as a storage place for farm tools. The water buffalo, which is used for plowing and many other jobs, is also kept there.

The first room we enter is really a covered porch. It is shady and cool. The family spends a great deal of time here. The sleeping rooms are right next to the porch and are also cool. In these rooms there is a storage chest made of teakwood and sleeping mats rolled up against the wall. At night the mats are unrolled and are used as beds. In most houses in the village there are no water faucets or electric lights. The village water supply is the well. The members of the family bathe every day in the river. The houses are lit with kerosene or coconut oil lamps.

The dinner is ready. The stove on which the food was cooked is made of clay and looks like a flower pot. There is a low table in the center of the room. There are cushions placed around the table. Our host asks us to seat ourselves on the cushions. The meal begins with a coconut and shrimp soup. This is followed by small bits of

Terraced rice field in mountainous Java, Indonesia. Rice is the major food and is also an important export. (*Top*)
Credit: *Consulate General of Indonesia*

Thai farmer ploughing a rice field in central Thailand. The water buffalo is used throughout Southeast Asia as a beast of burden. (*Bottom*)
Credit: *Tourist Organization of Thailand*

Village Life   413

broiled meat served on thin bamboo skewers with a spicy peanut sauce. This is called *satay*. Next we are served a delicious spiced chicken curry. Along with the curry we can eat some squash, peas or beans. The salad seems to be a great favorite with our host and he eats it with great delight. For desert we have fried bananas and fruit served in a sweet syrup. Tea is served throughout the meal. We ask our host why the food is so spicy. He tells us that it is very hot during this time of the year. Therefore, most of the meals are light but spicy so that the appetite is stimulated.

To eat we use a spoon made of a coconut to dip the rice, vegetables and the curry from the serving bowls into our own bowls. Then we eat the food with our fingers.

Most of the people of Southeast Asia live in villages similar to the one described. The only differences will be caused by the type of village, in terms of its location in relation to a canal, river or road. The clothes the people wear and the customs they follow differ greatly from place to place. However, most of the people of Southeast Asia are farmers and therefore, their lives are similar in many ways.

Agriculture

The Soil

Southeast Asia is one of the world's important farming regions. In most parts the climate is always warm, so crops can be raised all year round. Most of Southeast Asia also has heavy rainfall. Some parts produce large amounts of rice, rubber and other products to sell to foreign countries. There is enough unused land here to raise even larger amounts of farm products.

Only about nine out of every hundred acres of land are planted in crops. In most of Southeast Asia, the main farmlands are on the river plains and coastal lowlands. The *silt* that the rivers wash down from the mountains helps make these lowlands fertile. On the island of Java, people have made level fields on the slopes of volcanoes by building stairlike *terraces*. Ashes and other materials from the volcanoes help to make the soil in these fields very rich. Some mountain slopes in Northern Luzon in the Philippines are terraced also.

Swampy lowlands and forested mountains cover much of the rest of Southeast Asia. The soil in many of these wilderness areas is poor. Heavy rains have washed out the minerals and other materials needed by plants. Mosquitoes carrying malaria and other diseases make some of these areas unhealthy places in which to live. If the mosquitoes were cleared out, the swamps drained, and the land cleared and fertilized Southeast Asia would have more farmland.

Products

Rice is Southeast Asia's most important crop. About six out of every ten acres of farmland are planted with rice. It is the most important food crop of the people of the area. It is also an important export crop. Burma, Thailand and Kampuchea (Cambodia) raise more rice than they need and so are the world's largest rice exporters.

People in Southeast Asia raise other food crops to eat. In the drier regions farmers grow corn, sweet potatoes and other crops that need less moisture than rice. Most farmers raise vegetables such as beans, which provide protein that people in the

United States get from meat. Mango, papaya and other fruit trees grow around most village houses. Sugar cane is also raised.

Southeast Asia exports other farm products besides rice. It provides nine-tenths of the world's natural rubber. Three-fourths of the world's copra comes from Southeast Asia. Copra is the dried meat of the coconut. Oil palms grown in the area also provide large quantities of vegetable oil.

Other tropical crops grown in Southeast Asia are coffee, tea and spices. Cinchona trees are grown in Indonesia. A medicine called quinine is obtained from the bark. Kapok, used in making pillows and life belts, abaca, a fiber used in making rope, pineapples and tobacco are other Southeast Asian products.

Agricultural Problems

About three-fourths of Southeast Asia's workers make a living by farming. Most of the farmers use *primitive* farming methods. They plant and harvest their crops by hand and use simple tools, such as hoes and sickles. Water buffalo or oxen pull their plows. Sometimes rats, grasshoppers or other pests destroy part of the crop. Most of Southeast Asia's farmers need to use more fertilizer. In the parts of Southeast Asia that have a dry season, irrigation is needed to help crops grow when there is no rain.

In the highlands and mountains the people clear away the trees and high grass on the hills in order to farm the land. After using the land for a few years the soil loses its fertility. The hill people leave. The heavy rains now wash the top soil from the bare hills and river banks into the river. This process is called *erosion*. Large amounts of rich soil have been washed down the rivers of Southeast Asia. The large river deltas at the mouths of the Red, Mekong, Choa Phraya and Irrawaddy Rivers are formed by the washing down of this rich top soil. The deltas become rich, fertile farmlands, but much of the upriver land is destroyed for farming.

Heavy rains have another effect on the soil. They wash minerals out of the soil. The process of washing minerals out of the soil is called *leaching*. Much soil is ruined for most types of vegetation, except for the trees that send down deep roots.

There are other serious problems that the farmers face. Better roads are needed so that farmers may transport their products to market more easily. In many countries of Southeast Asia, only one-third to one-half of the farmers own their own farms or are free from heavy *debts*. Landowners often charge high rents, and men who lend money to farmers or market their goods often ask unfair payment for these services.

Some work is being done to help Southeast Asia's farmers. In several countries *land reform* laws have been passed. These laws are aimed at providing more land and homes for farmers. *Cooperatives* are being started in some places to help farmers market their products and borrow money. In addition, farm experts from other parts of the world are working with the Southeast Asians to discover ways of raising better crops and livestock in the area.

Religion

Different Religions

Southeast Asia has been a meeting place of the religions of the world. Small groups have worshipped nature (animism) since early times. Later, the great religions of man were brought to Southeast Asia.

Buddhist temple in Bangkok
Credit: *Tourist Organization of Thailand*

Buddhism was brought from India. Today it is the main religion of Burma, Thailand, Vietnam, Kampuchea (Cambodia) and Laos. In these countries Buddhist temples and statues of Buddha may be seen everywhere.

Hinduism was also brought from India. It existed for many centuries in Southeast Asia, but has died out in most places. In modern times, it has been followed mainly on Bali, in Indonesia.

Islam, the religion based on the teachings of Mohammed, has many followers. Islam was brought to Southeast Asia about six hundred years ago by traders, merchants and sailors. Islam is the chief religion of Malaya, Indonesia and the southern Philippines.

Christianity was brought to the Philippines by the Spanish in the 16th century. Today, over 80% of the people of the Philippines are Catholic. The French later spread Christianity in Vietnam, and there is still a large minority of Christians living there.

Buddhism

Buddhism had its beginnings in the foothills of the Himalayas in India. Gautama, the great teacher of Buddhism and founder of the religion, was born about 567 B.C. He was the son of a king and a member of the Kashatriya (warrior) caste. He was a Hindu. As a young man, Gautama became upset over the differences between his own life of ease and comfort and the suffering of most people. He left the palace and went into the forest to look for wisdom. After six years of isolation from society, and strict, simple living, he had not found the wisdom he had looked for. He swore not to move from under a Bo tree until he found the key to free man from his suffering. Finally, after forty-nine days, Enlightenment was gained. Gautama became the Buddha, and Buddhism was born. The name Buddha means "Enlightened One."

Buddhism is very different from the religions of the Western world. As a result, it seems difficult for Westerners to understand. Buddhism is not so much a religion, but a way of life, like Hinduism. Buddhism has no gods, or even a supreme being, and no belief in a soul.

Buddha, after gaining Enlightenment, spent the rest of his life spreading his ideas. The main ideas of Buddha's teaching are:

1. The Four Noble Truths:

1. Existence is suffering.
2. Suffering comes from desire.
3. The cure for suffering is the extinction of desire.
4. To achieve the extinction of desire, there is an Eightfold Path of Conduct.

   a) Right views   e) Right speech
   b) Right effort   f) Right conduct
   c) Right mindfulness g) Right livelihood
   d) Right intentions   h) Right concentration

As a definition of Rightness, Buddha offered five moral rules:

1. Let not one kill any living being.
2. Let not one take what is not given to him.
3. Let not one speak falsely.
4. Let not one drink intoxicating drinks.
5. Let not one be unchaste.

<table>
<tr>
<td>

2. **Key ideas of Buddhism:**

</td>
<td>

1. Self-salvation is for any man his most immediate job.
2. Nirvana is the goal of all Buddhists. Nirvana is a state of extinction or the stopping of the Wheel of Rebirth (reincarnation). The idea of Nirvana cannot be put into words. It can only be felt.

</td>
</tr>
<tr>
<td>

3. **Terms associated with Buddhism:**

</td>
<td>

a — *Pagoda*: In almost every village of India and Southeast Asia, there is a wat or compound which is called a pagoda. The pagoda serves as the educational and social center of the community. The people voluntarily support the wat and the monks, for it is a way of merit to Nirvana.

b — *Merit*: good works

c — *Bonze*: Buddhist monk

d — *Stupa*: large mound of earth, usually covering a relic or relics of the Buddha.

e — *Sutra*: a thread on which the teachings of the Buddha were strung; also a sermon of the Buddha.

</td>
</tr>
</table>

Early History of Southeast Asia

Early Settlers

Long before civilization came to Europe and the West, tribesmen from the neighboring lands of Tibet, China and India traveled into the green valleys of the Indo-Chinese Peninsula. They decided to settle there and begin a new life. Some of their descendants journeyed and settled in the Malay Peninsula and the island *archipelagos* of Southeast Asia. Most of the newcomers had light brown skin and eyes that appeared to be somewhat slanted. They knew how to make better tools and weapons than the smaller, dark skinned people already living there. The newcomers had moved into the area because they had been forced to leave their own homelands by invading armies of the Chinese Emperors.

On the arrival of these "foreigners," the original dark skinned settlers were forced back into the *remote* mountains and jungles. Today their descendants can still be found living in these areas. Others stayed in the valleys and coastal plains, intermarried and lived with the newcomers. As time went on, more and more settlers arrived, and the same process happened again.

By the first century A.D. there were many different groups of people living in Southeast Asia. Some groups in the remote regions gathered roots and other foods, or they hunted. Other groups used the "slash and burn" method of farming. Trees would be burned down in order to clear the land for farming. The ashes were used for natural fertilizer. When the soil in the clearings was no longer fertile, they moved on and cleared new lands. This type of agriculture is still carried on in the hills of Southeast Asia.

The peoples in the coastal lowlands and river valleys grew rice in flooded fields. This is called "wet rice agriculture." It meant the beginning of settled villages. The irrigation system took a long time to build, lasted a long time, and did not use up the soil. It also meant that people would have to cooperate to make the system work. The irrigation system was used by all, and everyone had to agree on when and how it should be used. Rights important to Americans, such as the right to own private property, would have been disruptive there. The individual had to give up his individual rights for the sake of the community as a whole. For the individual, the village world gave security. No one had to work or be alone in facing problems, and no one starved while his neighbor had plenty.

Another result was that it was now possible to grow more rice than was needed by the community. Except during the planting and harvest seasons, the rice fields needed little attention. Many people were free to do other work, and extra rice was available to feed them. Some stopped growing rice and became priests, *artisans* (craftsmen), merchants and, later on, rulers.

The family became the main unit of society. However, it did not become as important an institution as it did in Chinese and Indian cultures. People felt trust for their relatives rather than strangers, but beyond this the extended family, with the many social relationships as known in China, did not develop in Southeast Asia. A fact that demonstrates this is that in most of the countries of Southeast Asia (before the coming of the Europeans) there was no tradition of using family names.

In contrast to the rest of Asia and to most early societies, some of the Southeast Asian cultures gave important roles to women. Throughout the area we find that much of the village marketing and trading is still handled by women.

Indian and Chinese Influence

In addition to these settlers who came overland, Southeast Asia had visitors who came by sea. Southeast Asia is located on the water route between India and China, so travelers and merchants journeying between these two lands stopped in Southeast Asia. Seamen from Southeast Asia also traveled to India and China.

Some of the Indian traders established trading settlements in the area. Later, religious leaders and other people from India also settled in these trading towns. From these Indians the peoples of Southeast Asia learned about the Hindu and Buddhist religions. The Southeast Asians borrowed Sanskrit as their written language. The Indians also brought with them new ideas about art, government and architecture. Southeast Asians did not copy their Indian teachers exactly. Southeast Asia did not, for example, take the Indian caste system. Instead, as in the case of the Africans and Islam, they *adapted* Indian ideas to their own needs and interests, and created something different and new of their own. It is important to note that different parts of Southeast Asia made different adaptations, and this resulted in differences among Southeast Asian nations which still exist today.

The only exceptions to the general pattern of Indianization were the Philippines, which were off the main India-China trade route, and Vietnam, which came under Chinese rule in 111 B.C., and remained Chinese for a thousand years.

Some of the Indian trading settlements grew into powerful cities that were able to gain control of neighboring cities. Kingdoms were established which fought against each other, often to gain more power and territory. Several kingdoms grew into great empires that at one time controlled large parts of Southeast Asia.

The Empires of Southeast Asia

Funan and Srivijaya

As a result of the trade with India and China, small ports at the mouths of rivers along the Malay Peninsula and the mainland coast came into existence. When the Roman Empire and the Han Dynasty of China reached greatness, there was a great increase in trade between the Mediterranean world and China. Southeast Asian ports grew in power and wealth because of their strategic location on this trade route.

Funan, at the southern tip of present-day Vietnam, became one of the largest empires in Southeast Asian history. Funan was powerful because the earliest route of the India-China trade went across the narrow Isthmus of Kra, connecting the Malay Peninsula to the mainland. Later, sailors learned how to cut straight across the China Sea to the tip of Malaya. Funan began to fall. Its place as the most important trading state was taken by the empire of Srivijaya, which centered on the strait of Malacca.

Khmer Empire

Both Srivijaya and Funan owed their wealth to trade, not to agriculture. However, many inland states arose, whose wealth was based on rich, fertile soil. The Cambodian, or Khmer Empire was one of the more important. From the ninth through the thirteenth centuries, the Khmer kings gained control of most of the fertile lowlands of the Southeast Asia mainland. The Khmer capital was located at Angkor, near the Tonle Sap (near Siemreap, in modern Kampuchea (Cambodia)). Ruins of the magnificent stone temples built in this city still stand today. One temple, the Angkor Wat, is among the largest religious buildings in the world. The temples and other art and writings that still remain show not only a pattern of Indian influence, but are also the best examples of how Indian ideas were adapted to local customs.

The Khmer Kingdom, having used its wealth and energy on temple building, was too weak by the thirteenth century to stop attacks from the Thai states to the west. One by one, Khmer border provinces were captured and, within two centuries, the Khmer State ceased to be of importance. All that remained was what is now modern Kampuchea (Cambodia). Today the Kampucheans and the Thais still recall the old wars and the destruction that resulted. They have not forgiven each other, and this fact prevents closer cooperation between these two countries that have similar problems.

Kingdoms of the Indo-Chinese Peninsula

From about the fourteenth century to the eighteenth century, mainland and island history took different paths. More or less continual warfare brought about the outlines of the present mainland countries. Vietnam, which had been under Chinese influence for a thousand years, gained its independence in the tenth century. Its leaders steadily expanded Vietnam's borders southward from the Red River. Vietnam reached its present borders by the eighteenth century.

Meanwhile, Cambodia (Khmer Empire) was shrinking under Vietnamese and Siamese (Thai) pressure. One of the many Thai states became the Kingdom of Laos in the fourteenth century. Siam expanded steadily and, by the eighteenth century, it was the strongest and most stable of the mainland countries. Burma was divided between the Mons in the south and the Shan-Thais in the north.

Islamic Kingdoms

On the Malay Peninsula and on the islands of Indonesia a new outside force brought many changes. This new force was Islam. It came by way of India. Moslem merchants from Northwest India were among the most active in the Indian Ocean trade. Following the commands of their religion, they preached their faith while carrying on trade.

Islam was accepted by many Southeast Asian states. It allowed them to trade and make money. With a world religion of this kind, the rulers could have a strong set of beliefs to oppose those of Hindu states. Islam provided a reason and a bond for opposing the European Christians who came to Southeast Asia to control trade.

For these reasons, Southeast Asia became Moslem quite rapidly. Where Indian influence was weak, Islam became strong. However, Islam merged with existing ways of life, and took on a Southeast Asian flavor.

Westerners Come to Southeast Asia

Portugal

Five hundred years ago spices such as pepper, cloves and nutmeg were far more important than they are today. Spices helped to preserve food and make it taste better. The main spice-producing areas of the world were in Southeast Asia. The eagerness of Europeans to obtain spices from this region helped shape its history.

In 1498, a Portuguese explorer named Vasco da Gama sailed into the harbor of Calcutta, India. From India, ships could sail on to the distant spice lands of Southeast Asia. Vasco da Gama's discovery of an all-water route to the spice lands was very important. The old routes between Europe and the spice lands crossed both land and water. Goods shipped along these routes had to be loaded and unloaded many times. This was expensive and inconvenient. Also, the old routes were controlled by the Moslems, who were unfriendly to the Europeans. With the new route, Portuguese traders were now able to transport goods more quickly and cheaply. In order to make as much money as possible, the Portuguese wanted to control the spice trade completely. They captured many important ports from the Moslems and established fortified posts in Southeast Asia. They patrolled the seas near the spice regions to keep out ships of other nations. Portugal also tried to spread Christianity in the spice lands. It had little success, however, for most of the Portuguese who came to Southeast Asia behaved like conquerors and were hated by the people of the area.

Spain

Portugal was not the only nation that wanted an all-water route to the spice lands. Spain was also eager to discover one. In 1519, Ferdinand Magellan set out to find a sea route to the Moluccas, the islands from which most of the spices came. Magellan sailed west, hoping to come to the East. On his voyage he came to the Philippines. Magellan and his crew were the first Europeans to visit these islands. Before long, much of the Philippines was under Spanish control.

Other Europeans

At the end of the sixteenth century, Dutch ships began coming to Southeast Asia. The Portuguese had made enemies with so many Southeast Asian people that the latter welcomed other traders. Before long, British, French, Swedish and Danish trading ships were also coming to the region.

The European traders who came to Southeast Asia did not want anyone to interfere with their trade. Warships and soldiers from Europe were sent to the region. Often, Europeans attacked each other's ships. Sometimes they used force to make the people of Southeast Asia trade with them.

The more powerful European countries gained control of large territories. What is now the country of Indonesia became a Dutch colony. Britain gained control of Burma, Malaya and northern Borneo. The territory now occupied by Vietnam, Laos and Kampuchea (Cambodia) was taken over by the French. The Philippines were owned by Spain until 1898, when they were taken over by the United States. Only Thailand, formerly known as Siam, remained independent.

Reasons for European Interest

At first, most Westerners who came to Southeast Asia wanted to obtain spices. Soon, however, it was discovered that this region could provide valuable goods. There were rich mineral deposits, and the climate was suitable for growing tropical plants such as sugar cane and rubber trees. Mines and plantations were established. Roads and railroads were built to carry products to port cities, from which they could be shipped overseas.

Europeans Brought Progress

The Europeans influenced the region in many important ways. The colonial governments that were set up by the Europeans gave the framework for the new national states that grew after 1945. The Westerners brought peace to a part of the world that had been torn by warfare. Colonialism gave to many peoples of Southeast Asia their first feeling of belonging to a national group.

A second result of Europeans in Southeast Asia was the development in each of the countries of a single major city. These cities became centers of modern life. For example, Rangoon was a small village when the British first came to Burma. It grew to be a city of half a million people by 1945. The Dutch set up their capital in Indonesia—Batavia, now called Djakarta—in what were then swamps. Today Djakarta is the largest city in Southeast Asia, with a population of over three million. Singapore, Bangkok, Ho Chi Minh City and Manila each became such a center in its respective country.

A third result which followed was that modern schools were established and

Western learning was introduced. Western education opened the minds of Southeast Asians to the possibilities of a better life. The spread of education gave the younger generation ideas and attitudes different from those of their parents. Although Southeast Asian women have generally had more freedom than most Asian women, their increased opportunities to attend school and find employment have given them a greater degree of freedom.

Another development caused by the Europeans was an important change in village economy. The self-sufficient village where the farmer produced only for himself and his neighbors slowly disappeared. In its place the Europeans encouraged the farmer to grow crops for either world markets or for larger urban markets.

Modern hospitals and improved health standards were also established by the Europeans. This resulted in a population explosion which put great pressure on the customs and traditions of Southeast Asia. The infant mortality rate decreased; the number of young people increased greatly. For the first time the importance of youth had to be accepted.

Western Rule Caused Hatred

However, Westerners are remembered more by the Southeast Asians for the ways they neglected the region. Most Westerners were mainly interested in making money. They thought of Southeast Asia as a source of raw materials for their own use. Since the Western nations wished to sell their industrial products in Southeast Asia, little modern manufacturing was established in the region. In addition, people from the Western nations held nearly all of the important jobs. For this reason, only a few of Southeast Asia's people were able to get the kind of experience they needed for self-government.

Many Southeast Asian people were dissatisfied with Western rule and wished for independence. Late in the nineteenth century, people in several Southeast Asian countries began a movement to end colonial rule. The leaders of the independence movements were often Southeast Asians who had learned about democracy and other political ideas while studying in the West.

Nationalism in Southeast Asia

Many Southeast Asians were unhappy under Western rule, and wished to be free to govern themselves. Late in the nineteenth century, nationalists in several countries in Southeast Asia began to work for independence. In each country under European rule, separate nationalist groups grew.

Indonesia

In Indonesia the Dutch used Javanese workers (Java is the main island of Indonesia) in the government service, but paid them lower salaries and gave them lower rank than that given to the Dutch. In addition, the Moslem peasants were disturbed by Dutch interference in trade, farming, and village customs. These situations led to the first signs of nationalism. Groups were formed to set up newspapers and schools, which expressed a desire for independence.

Thai dancers.
Credit: *Tourist Organization of Thailand*

When independence did not come by these peaceful means, a group of Indonesians led by Ahmed Sukarno set up a militant nationalist party in 1927, which used various methods to gain independence. Sukarno was later arrested and sent away from Java. The Dutch were afraid of this nationalist feeling, and did all they could to destroy it.

Vietnam

The French gained complete control of the Indo-Chinese Peninsula by 1890. The French used only a few Vietnamese in the colonial government. They did not offer Western education to many Vietnamese. As long as those educated Vietnamese tried to adapt to French culture, they were treated as Frenchmen. On the other hand, those who thought of independence for Vietnam had no way to express their ideas. Finally, in the 1920s, a number of small nationalist groups were formed, but achieved little. (700 members of the Nationalist Party were executed in 1929 for trying to throw out the French.) The Vietnamese Communist Party was formed under the leadership of Ho Chi Minh in 1930, but it also did little.

Thailand

Siam (Thailand), alone of the Southeast Asian countries, was never a colony of a Western power. Its history is evidence that progress can come without colonialism. The preservation of Siam's independence, and its modernization, were the work of two rulers, Mongkut (King Rama IV), and his son Chulalongkorn (King Rama V) Nationalism in Siam took the form of preserving independence, and borrowed from the West the means of preserving this independence.

Burma

Burma fell under the control of the British between 1852, when Lower Burma was conquered, and 1886, when Upper Burma was overcome. The British ended the *monarchy* (rule by the king). The monarchy was the center of Burmese national pride, and stood for Burmese culture and history. Indians were brought in as cheap labor, and were hated by the Burmese. Rice became a major export crop, but few of the profits went to the farmer who grew it. In the late 1920s and the 1930s, a series of riots took place. Burmese farmers attacked Indian laborers, the only enemies against whom they could express their anger.

A mild nationalist movement was tolerated. The British promised to give Burma its independence as soon as possible. In 1937, the British allowed a Burmese Prime Minister to hold office as a step toward independence. This change created a new situation. A new group of younger leaders began to demand immediate independence.

Philippines

The United States took the Philippines from the Spanish in 1898. The Filipinos wanted independence immediately. A revolt, led by Emilio Aguinaldo, lasted from 1899 to 1902. The Filipinos were defeated. The Americans promised self government and independence as soon as the United States felt the Filipinos were ready for it.

Within twenty years, a Filipino legislature was running the government. However, the legislature was under the control of *caciques* (chiefs), who were not nationalists, and really did not represent the people. Despite this situation, the United States kept its promise.

In 1935 the Commonwealth of the Philippines was set up. It had a Filipino president and national assembly (legislature). The United States kept control of foreign affairs and military defense. It was agreed that the Philippines would gain complete independence after ten years.

By 1941 nationalist movements existed in each nation of Southeast Asia. However, except in the Philippines and Burma, independence seemed to be a distant dream. But events of the next few years were to cause a complete change in the situation.

World War II and Japanese Control

In 1939 war broke out in Europe. France and Holland were defeated by Germany. Great Britain was fighting for its life. Their colonies in Southeast Asia were left on their own. Here the agent of independence entered the drama.

Japan — The Agent of Independence

Soon after World War II started in 1939, the Japanese realized that this was a good time to gain control of Southeast Asia. Japan needed more oil, iron and other raw materials than she had. She also needed markets for her manufactured goods. On December 8, 1941, Japanese bombers moved toward Clark Field in the Philippines. A few hours earlier, on December 7th, other Japanese planes had bombed Pearl Harbor in Hawaii.

By August 1942, almost all of East Asia was controlled by the Japanese. The Germans had overrun the Netherlands and France, and were attacking Great Britain. Of course, these three Western powers could not send soldiers to defend their distant colonies in Southeast Asia.

The Japanese claimed that they only wanted to drive the Western powers out and *restore* "Asia to the Asians." But the people of Southeast Asia very soon realized that this was just an excuse for Japanese *imperialism*. The Japanese wanted to *exploit* Southeast Asia for themselves. In many places the Japanese treated the people more harshly than the Westerners ever had. Bands of *guerrillas* were organized to oppose the Japanese, and the British and Americans gave these groups weapons whenever possible, even though some of these groups were led by Communists.

Although Japanese occupation lasted only about four years, its *impact* on the Southeast Asian struggle for independence was great. First, Europeans were eliminated from top jobs in government and business and replaced by native Southeast Asians. Second, Western *prestige* was also destroyed by anti-Western *propaganda* in the newspapers, on radios and over loudspeakers. Third, the Japanese granted "independence" to Burma and the Philippines. Finally, the Japanese trained native armies to help them maintain control. This trained military leadership was very important in the fight for independence that followed the defeat of Japan.

Japan's Defeat and Its Results

After the defeat of Japan in 1945, nationalist leaders seized control of their governments from local Japanese commanders. All of the countries of Southeast Asia declared their independence. The United States *recognized* Philippine independence in 1946, and the British granted Burma independence in 1947. The French and the Dutch, as weak as they were from the war, did not recognize the independence of Vietnam and Indonesia until after long years of fighting with the nationalists of those countries.

In the span of a few years, about 170 million people who had lived under Western colonial rule for decades or centuries had become independent.

Independence and Its Results

We have seen that the Second World War encouraged the people of Southeast Asia in their desire for independence. Now we will look into the situation that was created after the war, and how it led to today's events in Southeast Asia.

Burma and the Philippines

European rule in Southeast Asia was gone when World War II ended. The British recognized this fact. They recognized the independence of Burma at 4:20 A.M. on January 4, 1948 (time set by proper *astrological* calculations). The United States had long promised independence to the Philippines, and it was granted in 1946. In other areas, however, European powers refused to withdraw, and the years following World War II were bloody and bitter.

Indonesia

There was bloody and savage fighting in Java, where Indonesians, armed and trained by the Japanese, fought against the Dutch. In December, 1949, after four years of fighting, the Netherlands recognized the independence of the Indonesian Republic, with Ahmed Sukarno as President.

Vietnam

Even more bloody was the struggle in Indo-China. For a brief time in March, 1946, Ho Chi Minh and the French in Hanoi agreed to a Democratic Republic of Vietnam, which would keep its economic ties with the French. But Charles de Gaulle, who was president of France at this time, refused to give up any part of the old French Empire. War broke out in 1946 and, for almost the next eight years, the French unsuccessfully tried to defeat the *Viet Minh guerrillas*. At a conference held in 1954 France agreed to the independence of Vietnam. But the country was *partitioned* (divided) into two parts. One was controlled by Ho and was Communist, and the other was ruled by a series of weak, *unstable* leaders, who ruled through the army, and gave little to the people in the way of *reform* and freedom. Under the Geneva Agreements, the French holdings in Indo-China were divided still further by the setting up of the independent countries of Laos and Cambodia.

Malaya

Malaya was granted its independence after the British and the Malayans had successfully beaten off an attempt by the Communists to gain control of the rich Malay Peninsula. After the Malaysian *Federation* (Malaya, Brunei, Sarawak and Singapore) was set up, Singapore demanded its independence, and in 1965 this was granted. Singapore wished to be independent because most of the people of Malaysia were Malays and Moslems, while the people of Singapore were mainly Chinese and Buddhists.

Thailand

Thailand had never become a colony of any European nation. The rulers of Thailand during the period of Colonialism ruled without a constitution and without a limitation on its powers. In the 1930's a revolution took place. A constitution was written which took much power away from the king. This power was given to an elected leader and elected representatives of the people. However the experiment in democracy did not last long. The army, which was losing importance under the constitution, was unhappy. Army generals plotted to take over the government. They succeeded and for almost forty years have been the real rulers of Thailand.

Since the war years there have been successful attempts by rivals in the Thai army to take over the government. There have been many changes in leadership but usually the leader was an army officer. The army rulers did away with the last Thai constitution in 1971. Late in 1973 the army-controlled government was overthrown by a student revolution.

The revolution was successful because the King, Bhumibol, was in favor of it. Bhumibol has little power but he is looked on as the symbol of the Thai nation and is very popular with the people. He joined with student leaders, his civilian advisors, and with young army officers to force the Army generals to give up control of the government.

The new constitution of 1974 includes land reform, pensions for farmers, and direct election of local government officials. Bhumibol is in favor of reforms. He feels that the people should be given more economic security and a greater voice in the Thai government. With his support the new constitution will have a good chance to succeed.

Problems Following Independence

When independence was granted, few nations of Southeast Asia were ready for it. Most had high levels of illiteracy, low levels of political experience and unstable economies. Independence did not bring the people the new ease, riches and importance they dreamed it would. As a result, leaders lost faith in democracy, and *dictatorial* governments have grown up. Many Southeast Asians have become *disillusioned* and bitter.

Here we have the picture of more than thirty years since the end of World War II. Events in Southeast Asia today show the results of this period. Many American soldiers and Asian peasants died in the jungles of Vietnam because of these events. An understanding of them may help in some small way to prevent future Vietnams.

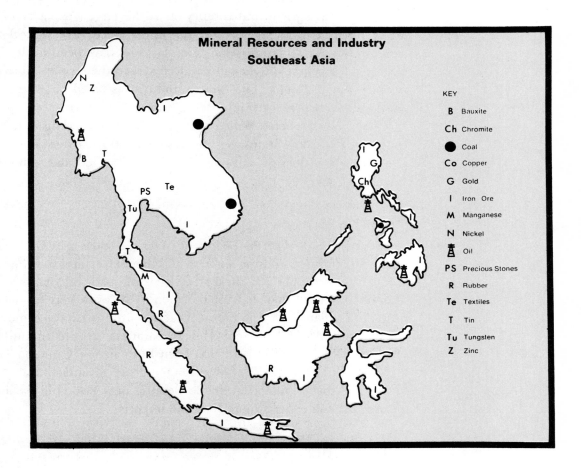

The Economy of Southeast Asia

Southeast Asia is a storehouse of natural resources. In times past, several Western nations wanted to make certain they could obtain the products of this region. They gradually gained control of all of Southeast Asia except Thailand. They hired many workers from China and India, for most Southeast Asians did not want to leave their farms to take jobs in mines or on plantations.

When the nations of Southeast Asia became independent they faced a number of problems. One of the most important was to build economies that would support their growing populations.

Southeast Asia sells large quantities of its raw materials to other parts of the world, for it does not have enough factories to use all these goods. In some years, foreign countries pay low prices for Southeast Asian exports. Then, many people who have jobs in tin mining or other industries earn less money.

Most nations of the region are working to establish more factories. This will help them to make better use of their raw materials. It will also help to provide new jobs for the people.

Burma

Burma is an agricultural country. It is the largest exporter of rice in the world. Many Burmese work in rice and saw mills. Since 1948, a steel mill, spinning and weaving factories, jute mills and brick factories have been built. The Lawpita hydro-electric power plant supplies cheap electricity to the people. More than half of Burma is covered with forests. The lumber industry is based on Burma's teak forest. Teak is a hard wood used in shipbuilding and making furniture.

All Burmese economic policies have been based on socialism; that is, the government controls certain key industries and resources. Burma does not look for foreign aid, and the help it does get is small. The lack of capital and technical skills holds back Burma's development.

Malaysia

About three-fifths of the people of Malaysia make a living by farming. Many are subsistence farmers, raising enough for themselves and a little more for sale. The production of rubber and tin for export is the basis of Malaysia's economy. Rubber accounts for more than half of the money Malaysia gets from exports. Malaysia is the largest producer of iron ore in Asia. The iron is exported mostly to Japan. There are timber mills and oil refineries on Sarawak. To aid in building up Malaysia's industry, a hydroelectric plant has been built in the Cameron Highlands. Malaysia must import rice to feed its people. One great advantage Malaysia has in building industry is that capital is available because of a favorable balance of trade, which means Malaysia exports more than she imports.

Philippines

The Philippines, since independence, have faced great economic problems. Despite billions in aid, the Philippines have made little progress. Most of the nation's industries are located in or near Manila. The average annual income has not risen in the past ten years, and remains between 150 and 200 dollars a year, per person. Corruption in the government has sapped the strength from reform, and most of the aid money has never been used to help the people. Under Ramon Magsaysay, President from 1954 to 1957, land reform was put into effect. He gave land and homes to the Filipino farmers. He started peasant credit projects, highway programs to help crop marketing, and civil service reforms. The biggest problem is the nation's population growth, which is among the highest in the world. Economic growth has not kept pace with population growth.

Thailand

Thailand has fertile soil, and most of the people work in agriculture, or in processing and transporting agricultural products. Rice is the chief crop and export. The prosperity of Thailand is due in part to this crop. Manufacturing, through growing, contributes only fifteen percent of Thailand's national income. Teak, rubber and tin are also exported. Thailand imports textiles, petroleum, chemicals, iron and steel, and machinery.

Indonesia

Indonesia has not developed as fast as might be expected from a country rich in natural resources (rubber, petroleum, tin and others). The most important industries —shipbuilding, textiles, cement making and paper production—are small. About three-quarters of Indonesia's exports come from outside of Java. These areas outside of Java, however, receive only about one-quarter of the imports. The mishandling of government money under President Sukarno also weakened the economy.

President Sukarno had used up all of Indonesia's assets in building his power and glorifying himself. By 1966 the country was on the edge of bankruptcy. Inflation spread throughout the islands making money almost worthless. Since 1966 when he was removed from power, Indonesia has made a recovery. The new government has cut inflation and increased exports. Now more is exported, especially oil, than is imported. Foreign governments have invested much money in industry and mining. As a result there has been improvement in agriculture, the expansion of industry, and the development of more of Indonesia's resources.

However there are still great problems. Unemployment is very high. Overcrowding of people on the island of Java is a very serious problem. (Density on Java is 1500 per sq. mile.) The riches from the oil industry go mainly to a few millionaires. Hardly any touches the lives of most of the people. Much of the industry and business is in the hands of Japanese, Chinese and other non-Indonesians.

Riots in early 1974 showed the feelings of the people for the Japanese and Chinese. To meet this problem President Suharto has issued an order that any foreigner who wants to do business in Indonesia must go into partnership with a *pribumi* (a native born Indonesia). At least half of the ownership must be in the hands of the *pribumi*.

In late 1977 riots again broke out. These riots were led by students who objected to rising food prices, restrictions on political activities and corruption among leading government officials. In order to stop the riots President Suharto ordered the closing of newspapers. Many students were thrown in jail. Protests continue, but President Suharto, using the loyal support of the army, has been able to remain in power.

Economic Problems

The nations of Southeast Asia face all of the problems that developing nations have. Most of the countries are too poor to construct enough dams and factories without outside help, but are too proud to ask for that help. There are not enough trained scientists, engineers and mechanics. Schools are needed to train them. There is a lack of railroads and other means of transportation to bring goods to and from the market. However, efforts are being made to tap the tremendous natural resources of Southeast Asia. The most notable of these is the Mekong River Plan. The four countries of Laos, Thailand, Vietnam, and Kampuchea are cooperating in the development of the river to provide for hydroelectric power, irrigation, and navigation. The Southeast Asians have made some progress, but only peace, stability and outside aid will create the economic miracle they desire.

U.S. TRADE WITH SOUTHEAST ASIA (Selected Countries)
(values in millions of dollars)

	Exports				Imports			
	1968	1975	1976	1977	1968	1975	1976	1977
INDONESIA	167	810	1,036	763	174	2,447	3,277	3,756
MALAYSIA	54	393	536	561	240	812	994	1,393
PHILIPPINES	436	832	819	876	436	834	994	1,230
SINGAPORE	102	994	965	1,172	29	564	728	916
THAILAND	186	357	347	510	81	240	307	384
VIETNAM	270	213	1	.....	2	7	1	.....

SOURCE: International Monetary Fund, *Direction of Trade.*

TRADE AND COMMERCE IN SOUTHEAST ASIA (Selected Countries)

Country	% of Trade To U.S.	% of Trade From U.S.	Leading Trade Partners Exports %	Leading Trade Partners Imports %	Major Exports Product %
BURMA (1976)		7	Indonesia (14) Singapore (13)	Japan (33) China (9)	Rice (58) Teak (23)
CAMBODIA (1973)		69	Hong Kong (23) Japan (22)	U.S. (69) Thailand (11)	Rubber (93)
INDONESIA (1976)	29	17	Japan (42) U.S. (29)	Japan (26) U.S. (17)	Oil (66) Timber (9)
LAOS (1974)		5	Thailand (73) Malaysia (11)	Thailand (49) Japan (19)	Timber (81) Tin (11)
MALAYSIA (1976)	16	13	Japan (21) Singapore (18)	Japan (21) U.S. (13)	Rubber (23) Tin (11)
PHILIPPINES (1976)	36	22	U.S. (36) Japan (24)	Japan (27) U.S. (22)	Sugar (18) Coconut oil (12)
SINGAPORE (1976)	15	13	Malaysia (15) U.S. (15)	Japan (16) Saudi Arabia (16)	Petroleum products (23) Machinery (19)
THAILAND (1976)	10	13	Japan (26) Netherlands (13)	Japan (32) U.S. (13)	Rice (14) Tapioca (12)
VIETNAM (1975)		19	USSR (15) China (11)	China (23) USSR (20)	Clothing (10) Fish (10)

SOURCE: *Encyclopaedia Britannica.*

ASEAN

In 1967 the nations of Southeast Asia set up the Association of Southeast Asian Nations (ASEAN). The purpose of ASEAN is to encourage the nations of Southeast Asia to cooperate with each other in trade, economic planning, and economic development. In the years that ASEAN has existed there has been very little cooperation and planning.

Why? It seems the nations of Southeast Asia are more interested in gaining immediate (now) and short-term advantages for themselves. They have not looked for the common good of all of the nations or toward the long-term advantages of cooperation.

As an example, in late 1973 Indonesia wanted to buy Thailand's rice. Thailand wanted to buy Indonesian oil. But Indonesia had already promised to sell her oil to other nations and Thailand in the same way had promised to sell her rice to others. If ASEAN was working as it should, problems like this could be solved even before they happened.

In 1973 the energy crisis made the situation in Southeast Asia very serious. Thailand, Singapore and the Philippines could not get enough oil from the Middle East. Malaysia and Indonesia produced oil but could not produce enough to help. (Indonesia sends 70% of her oil to Japan.)

The members of ASEAN were impressed with the way the oil producing countries united to set up an oil policy. The nations of Southeast Asia now have proof that with cooperation they can improve their nations' positions. There is now more hope that ASEAN will be able to achieve the purpose it was set up for.

In 1974 ASEAN acted to play "honest broker" between Malaysia and the Philippines. Malaysia was angry at the way in which the Philippines had handled a Muslim uprising (revolt) on the island of Mindinao in the Philippines. ASEAN members tried to keep things from getting worse by giving Malaysia and the Philippines a place to talk about their disagreement. While no agreement was worked out, both nations have agreed to continue discussions.

In the energy (oil) crisis ASEAN acted strongly. Discussions were held in early 1974. Indonesia, a large oil producer, said it would make every effort to supply oil to its ASEAN neighbors. The five ASEAN nations (Indonesia, Malaysia, Philippines, Thailand, and Singapore) agreed to cooperate to ease each others' shortages. They also agreed to joint industrial planning and development of Southeast Asia.

Agreements were made with the European Economic Community (the Common Market) and Japan. These nations have agreed to consider the needs and interests of the ASEAN nations when setting up their economic policies.

In 1976 the leaders of the member nations held their first summit meeting. They met on the island of Bali in Indonesia. Two major agreements came out of the Conference: a Declaration of *Concord* (agreement) and a Treaty of *Amity* (friendship).

The Declaration of Concord noted the members' desire to continue to expand economic cooperation. In addition, the members agreed to set up a trade agreement among the five nations. They also approved plans for setting up large industrial projects. These projects would use the resources of all the members in common. Special attention was paid to the problem of sharing food and energy resources in time of need.

The Treaty of Amity looked to setting up a High Council of Ministers to settle disputes among the members. The nations spoke of the need for greater mutual assistance in technical aid. Agreements were also reached on improving economic cooperation for the common benefit of the five nations.

Finally, those present agreed that the only real solution to the problem of rebellions in their own countries and in neighboring countries was economic progress and improvement of the lives of the people.

Foreign Relations

The struggle to survive is as important to the nations of Southeast Asia as it is to the rest of the world. The nations of Southeast Asia know that they are caught between two powerful forces at a time in history when the atomic bomb has changed the nature of warfare. The need for survival has led different nations to look for different solutions to the problem. The Philippines and Thailand have looked to the United States for protection against the Communist countries. Malaysia and Singapore had tied their futures to Great Britain. Since the British have decided to drop their role as protectors, both Malaysia and Singapore have shifted more toward neutral policies. Vietnam has aligned with the Soviet Union.

Burma

Burma was neutral at first, though it leaned toward the Communists. Burma has now become neutral and leans slightly toward the West because of the fear of Communist China.

Indonesia

Indonesia under President Sukarno was pro-Communist. When the Communists tried unsuccessfully to take over the government, Sukarno was replaced as President by an Army general (Suharto) and the Communists were wiped out. Indonesia now leans to the West. General Suharto was reelected in 1973 to another 5-year term, although the Moslem opposition made substantial gains in the elections held in 1977. The military, however, retains political control of the country.

Thailand

Thailand's foreign policy has traditionally leaned toward the strongest nation in the area. The Thais played off the British and the French in the late 19th and early 20th century. The Thais always favored the stronger of the two. This was the main reason Thailand was able to keep its independence. In the 1930s and early '40s the Thais supported the Japanese. When it became clear that Japan would lose the war, the Thais switched their support to the United States and its friends. After the war the Thais followed American policy. Now with the U.S. reducing its power in Southeast Asia the Thais will tend to look for better relations with the People's Republic of China.

Laos

Laos has tried to remain neutral. However, during the Vietnamese conflict, both the Pathet Lao, a Communist group, and the U.S. Central Intelligence Agency (CIA) made serious attempts to gain control of parts of Laos. In April 1974, a coalition government consisting of Communists and non-Communists was set up. Souvanna Phouma, a non-Communist, was premier and Phoumi Vongvichit, a Communist, became vice-premier and minister of foreign affairs. In July 1974, Premier Souvanna Phouma had a heart attack and Phoumi was named acting premier.

By the end of 1974, all foreign troops had withdrawn from Laos. The Laotians said they would be willing to accept economic aid from all nations, both Communist and non-Communist. A Lao People's Democratic Republic was proclaimed in December, 1975. Presently the head of state is President Souphanouvong. At this time it seems likely that Laos will have a Communist government.

Kampuchea (Formerly Cambodia)

Cambodia would also have liked to follow a neutral policy. Its location near Vietnam made it of importance to the North Vietnamese as a supply base. Prince Sihanouk, President of Cambodia, tried to remain on friendly terms with the Chinese and the Vietnamese. However, as the war continued in Vietnam and more and more Vietnamese entered Cambodia, Sihanouk tried to strengthen his ties with the U.S. in order to protect himself from the North Vietnamese. In 1970, while Sihanouk was out of the country, the army revolted and made one of its generals, Lon Nol, President. The North Vietnamese began to move their army toward the capital, Phnom-Penh. Lon Nol asked for American aid, which was given to him immediately. In late 1970 Lon Nol suffered a stroke and the government came under the control of a group of military leaders. However, by early 1972 Lon Nol had recovered sufficiently to regain control of the government.

Fighting continued in Cambodia throughout the period from 1973 to 1975. The United States sent war matériel in great quantities to the Cambodian army of Lon Nol. However, the aid did little to help control the Khmer Rouge (as the Communist forces were called). Communist pressure grew, coming closer and closer to the capital of Phnom-Penh. By April 1975, the situation was hopeless. Lon Nol left Cambodia for "health reasons." The Communists occupied Phnom-Penh, and it appeared that the civil war in Cambodia was over.

The new government was Communist-controlled (North Vietnamese Communists) and anti-American. In May 1975, Cambodian gunboats attacked the unarmed American merchant vessel *Mayaguez* well outside Cambodian territorial waters, capturing the ship and its crew of 39 American seamen. Within a few days American planes bombed Cambodian airfields. American marines attacked an island off the coast of Cambodia where the seamen were thought to be held as prisoners. The *Mayaguez* and its crew were released by the Cambodians.

In an effort to eliminate all opposition, the Communist government of Cambodia started a policy of repression in 1976. Reports coming from Cambodia stated that thousands of Cambodians had been executed. Many thousands of other Cambodians had been sent to re-education centers to be made into supporters of the government.

By early 1978 the Cambodian capital of Phnom-Penh had become a ghost city. In 1975 the population of Phnom-Penh had been over 2 million. In early 1978 the population reported to be about 20,000. The people had been forced to leave and live in the countryside. It is *estimated* (guessed) that about 1.2 million people have been executed by the government. Money has become worthless. Thousands of bills lay on the streets of the deserted capital. The government has stated that it has no plans to rebuild the capital. Lastly, the name of Cambodia has been changed to Kampuchea.

The Vietnam Conflict

When Vietnam was given its independence in 1954, it was divided at the seventeenth parallel. Under the terms of the Geneva Agreement, an election for the whole of Vietnam was to be held in 1956. These elections were never held. The South Vietnamese government, supported by the United States (neither of whom had signed the 1954 Geneva Agreement), refused to take part in any election for fear the Communist North would win.

When it became clear no elections would be held, the North Vietnamese helped organize the National Liberation Front (NLF) to reunite the country. The NLF set up a guerilla group, the Viet Cong, to fight in the South Vietnam countryside. By 1960 the NLF controlled more than 80% of the land. The government of South Vietnam asked the United States to send supplies and technicians to act as advisors.

The United States became involved because it hoped to prevent the Communists from gaining complete control of the country. At first, American involvement was restricted to the role of advising. But when the situation did not improve, the United States sent over five hundred thousand soldiers into Vietnam to fight.

American planes began to bomb North Vietnam. As American raids increased, and more and more Americans poured into Vietnam, the Chinese and Russians increased their aid to the Viet Cong, and North Vietnamese army units began operating in the South.

Why were the Americans in Vietnam? President Johnson, who ordered the soldiers into Vietnam, stated on April 7, 1965, "Our objective is the independence of South Vietnam and its freedom from attack. We want nothing for ourselves, only that the people of South Vietnam be allowed to guide their own country in their own way."

However, there were many Americans who did not agree that the U.S. became involved in Vietnam for these aims. They felt that President Johnson and President Nixon had not been entirely honest and truthful with the American people. In the summer of 1971, the publication of U.S. government documents, known as the *Pentagon Papers,* showed that the American government had not given all the facts to the people.

By 1968 Americans in great numbers had begun to speak out against the war, and the government began to look for ways to get out of it. In March 1968, President Johnson ended the bombing of most of North Vietnam. The North Vietnamese accepted this as an attempt to look for peace, and agreed to begin peace talks in Paris in May. The talks were enlarged in December 1968, to include both the Communist NLF and the anti-Communist government of South Vietnam.

In May 1969, President Richard Nixon proposed a peace plan for Vietnam, one feature of which was a mutual withdrawal of United States and North Vietnamese troops. Since then the United States had been withdrawing troops regularly. The fighting had also decreased in Vietnam. However, in early 1970 the United States launched an attack against the North Vietnamese in Cambodia. The purpose, as stated by President Nixon, was to destroy the North Vietnamese power to launch an attack on the Americans while they were leaving South Vietnam. American losses in Vietnam rose to over fifty-five thousand dead. Over a million Vietnamese were killed and the land in both the North and South was destroyed.

Peace in Vietnam

Finally on January 23, 1973, President Nixon announced to a war-weary America that "we today have concluded an agreement to end the war and bring peace with honor in Vietnam and Southeast Asia."

The terms of the agreement were divided into nine parts or "chapters." They were:

1. All parties will respect the independence and unity of Vietnam as recognized by the 1954 Geneva Agreements.

2. A cease-fire throughout Vietnam but not in Cambodia or Laos was to begin on January 27, 1973, with all military units remaining in place. All U.S. troops were to be withdrawn within 60 days and all U.S. military bases in South Vietnam were to be *dismantled* (taken apart).

3. All military prisoners were to be released within 60 days.

4. The right of the people of South Vietnam to determine their own political future was specifically included.

5. The Demilitarized Zone (DMZ) was recognized as a temporary military boundary between two parts of Vietnam that are expected to become reunited through peaceful negotiation between their two governments.

6. An International Control Commission and Supervision (ICCS) was set up to watch over (*supervise*) the truce.

7. Self-determination and neutrality for Laos and Cambodia were agreed to.

8. The U.S. pledged itself to aid in the reconstruction, specifically, of North Vietnam and also throughout the Indo-Chinese Peninsula.

9. All parties agreed to put the agreement into effect.

There still remained, however, the unsolved problem of the other wars in Southeast Asia—in Laos and Cambodia. Although attempts were made to set up cease-fires in both places, war continued into the summer of 1973, and the coming of peace did not seem to be near at hand.

In the first year of peace after the signing of the peace agreement in January 1973, nearly 13,000 South Vietnamese soldiers and over 2000 civilians were killed. According to reports, 45,000 North Vietnamese and Viet Cong also have died.

From the start of the cease-fire the four-nation International Commission of Control and Supervision (ICCS) was powerless to halt the fighting. The Canadian members of the ICCS were so unhappy with the Commission's lack of power that they quit in August 1973. The Canadians felt that they were sent to observe a peace and came to watch a war. The other ICCS members—Poland, Hungary, Indonesia and Iran—were not very active in trying to keep the peace.

The cease-fire agreement also called for the setting up of a council of South Vietnamese and Viet Cong. This was supposed to be the beginning of a new *coalition* (joining of both sides) government for South Vietnam. But the council was never set up because no one could decide who should be on it.

There were some economic problems in South Vietnam that became very serious. American aid had been cut. President Thieu was forced to cut exports and raise taxes. The people of South Vietnam were not happy at this. South Vietnam suffered from increasing inflation. Prices steadily went up. The price of rice doubled and the price of sugar tripled.

In the North the Communist government made some progress in repairing the damages of war. The government put strict controls on prices and tried to increase production of food and other goods. Aid from the outside was not great. Peace, however, allowed the North Vietnamese to turn toward efforts at improving the lives of the people.

The Troubled History of Vietnam in a Capsule

Year	*Event*
1-938 A.D.	Vietnam under Han China control. The Chinese had conquered Vietnam 200 years before. This conquest and control is much of the reason for Vietnamese fear and distrust of the Chinese even today.
939 A.D.	The independence of Vietnam was achieved under the leadership of Ngo Quyen.
1000-1800	Expansion of a Vietnamese state on the Indo-Chinese Peninsula. At the same time, different Vietnamese families fought each other for control of the government. Vietnam was not unified in this period.
1750	Beginning of French economic and trading interests and interference in Vietnam affairs.
1802	The unification of Vietnam's three areas (Annam, Tonkin, Cochin China) achieved by Emperor Ghia Long.
1881-1885	French actively colonized Vietnam and all of the Indo-Chinese Peninsula including Cambodia and Laos.
1930	Communist Party set up in Vietnam by Nguyen Ai Quoc (Ho Chi Minh).
1940	Vietnam invaded by Japanese.
1941	Viet Minh League (League for Independence of Vietnam) was set up under the leadership of Ho Chi Minh.
1941-1945	Ho Chi Minh leads a guerilla war against the Japanese with American advice and help.
1945	Japanese proclaim the independence of Vietnam. Vietnamese Republic set up with Hanoi as capital. Ho Chi Minh is leader of the new state.
1945-1954	French return. French try to destroy Viet Minh state and with American aid a 10-year war goes on.
1954	French surrender an important base at Dien Bien Phu in May. In July a cease-fire agreement is made.
1954	At Geneva an agreement is reached dividing Vietnam at the 17th parallel. The U.S. and the new government of South Vietnam refuse to sign.
1960	Viet Cong National Liberation Front is organized in South Vietnam.
1964	U.S. Defense Department reports U.S. destroyers were fired upon by North Vietnamese in the Gulf of Tonkin (later proved untrue). Beginning of U.S. intervention in Vietnam.
1964-1973	U.S. troops and planes actively fight Viet Cong and North Vietnamese in Vietnam.
1973	In January, Secretary of State Henry Kissinger and Le Duc Tho of North Vietnam sign agreement ending U.S. intervention.
1974	Fighting had never stopped in Vietnam but in May it became much heavier.
1975	Spectacular Communist military successes lead to the collapse of the South Vietnamese army and government. In April the Viet Cong set up a Provisional Revolutionary Government to rule South Vietnam.

The Situation in Vietnam after 1975

In late 1974 and early 1975 the situation in Vietnam began to change. Opposition to President Thieu of South Vietnam increased because of corruption in his government and because of Thieu's refusal to allow greater civil rights for the people. Inflation also grew worse. In addition, United States military and economic aid was greatly reduced. The Thieu government found it more and more difficult to maintain economic, social and military *stability* (balance).

Communist pressure by Viet Cong and North Vietnamese within South Vietnam grew. South Vietnamese generals were afraid to fight and made serious mistakes. By April 1975, the situation had become extremely serious. Hue, Danang and most of the important cities of South Vietnam, except for Saigon, were in Communist hands.

President Thieu felt he had been betrayed by the United States. He said promises had been made to him by Secretary of State Henry Kissinger and former President Nixon guaranteeing aid in case of trouble. Thieu felt that the United States was not a trustworthy ally.

With defeat facing him, Thieu resigned as president. A new government led by General Duong Van Minh (known as Big Minh) was set up. Its objective was to *negotiate* (work out) a peace with the Communists. On April 30, 1975, the South Vietnamese government surrendered unconditionally to the Viet Cong. Minh handed over all power to the Viet Cong Provisional Revolutionary Government, thus ending the conflict.

In the years since Vietnam has been united much has occurred. The Vietnamese have followed a strong policy in relation to their neighbors. The Vietnamese opposed the Bali Summit meeting of ASEAN (page 433). They looked at this meeting as if the nations of Southeast Asia were ganging up on Vietnam. They felt that ASEAN was being used to oppose the revolutionary and reform movements in Southeast Asia.

At the same time efforts were made to improve relations with their neighbors. Visits were made by high-ranking Vietnamese to Indonesia, Thailand, the Philippines, Singapore and Malaysia. Hints were sent out that Vietnam wanted peace and might join ASEAN sometime in the future.

War Between Vietnam and Kampuchea

In December 1977 and January 1978, Vietnamese troops moved into an area of Kampuchea called the Parrot's Beak that juts into Vietnamese territory. Heavy fighting resulted. Both sides admitted that many had died in the fighting. The Vietnamese took over most of the area and did not seem willing to leave.

The reason for the attack lies in past history. The Kampucheans and Vietnamese have hated each other for centuries. When the Khmer Rouge took over Cambodia in 1975 many thousands of Vietnamese living there were massacred. In 1976, the Vietnamese tried to assassinate Premier Pol Pot of Cambodia. In the spring of 1977, Cambodia began to make raids into Vietnam from the Parrot's Beak. By December the Vietnamese had had enough, and the invasion began.

The situation could become even more dangerous. Vietnam is interested in setting up a *confederation* (loose union of states) in which Vietnam, Laos and Kampuchea will be included. Vietnam, of course, would control the union, and Vietnam is supported by the Soviet Union in her plans. Kampuchea is opposed to any confederation ruled by Vietnam and Kampuchea is supported by the People's Republic of China.

In December, 1978, and early 1979, Cambodian rebels, aided by thousands of Vietnamese soldiers, defeated the Kampuchean army. A new government was set up. The new government was friendly to Vietnam. The Vietnamese army remained in control of large areas of Kampuchea (Cambodia). Then, in an announced attempt "to teach Vietnam a lesson," China attacked Vietnam along its northern border. The Soviet Union came to the rescue of its ally by supplying it with arms. The situation remains tense and the outcome is uncertain.

Stamps of Southeast Asia.

เดลินิวส์

ประจำวันพุธที่ 6 กันยายน พ.ศ. 2521

โรงงานผลิตอาวุธ

ตามที่นายกรัฐมนตรีในฐานะรัฐมนตรีว่าการกระทรวงกลาโหม ได้ให้สัมภาษณ์ผู้สื่อข่าว เมื่อวันเข้าบ้าน มอบหน้าที่ รัฐมนตรีว่าการกระทรวงกลาโหมว่า ในการเข้ารับหน้าที่รัฐมนตรีว่าการ กระทรวง กลาโหม ได้ วางนโยบายและเป้าหมายในอันที่จะเชื่อมโยงกันประเทศและช่วยเหลือประชาชนร่วมด้วย และระยะการพัฒนาอาวุธ ให้ก้าวหน้าต่อไป และอันนี้ที่จะให้ต่างประเทศเข้าร่วมลงทุน ในการผลิตอาวุธบางประเภทด้วย ซึ่งนับว่าเป็นนโยบายที่ชอบด้วยเหตุผล

ใต้ฝุ่นลูกใหม่

พรบ.เงินเดือนข้าราชการ ผลงานชิ้นเอกของสภาฯ

ตุลาการ
　　□　ต่อจากหน้า 2

[ตามด้วยเนื้อความบทความเรื่องตุลาการ ซึ่งเป็นข้อความภาษาไทยจำนวนมากในคอลัมน์กลาง]

□ อ่านต่อหน้า 20

ต่อยครั้งหมัด

กุล ตระภูลการ

ถ้าหากจะพูดกันตรง ๆ ก็กล่าวว่าจะถูกตอกหน้าว่า "ไอ้ร้า" จะเรียกว่า "เลว" ก็ไม่ใช่เลว เพราะเรื่องมันจะจริง...

...

กุล ตระภูลการ

ยอ.หอ...อย่าห่วง

มีข่าวตามยุคคมสมัยของการปรับเงินเดือนข้าราชการอยู่ข่าวหนึ่ง จะเป็นข่าวประเภทปลุกปลอบขวัญยกเว้าของแพงก็เห็นจะอนุโลมให้กันได้ แค่จะให้คนเชื่อถือว่าเป็นความจริงทันจะยากนัก

...

"ชาล หน"

War as seen through the eyes of these North Vietnamese children.
Credit: *Soviet Mission to the United Nations*

Summary of Key Ideas

Southeast Asia

A. **Geographic features have influenced the lives of the people of Southeast Asia.**

   1. Southeast Asia is the area to the south of China and to the east of India.

   2. It can be divided into two regions—the mainland and the islands.

   3. Southeast Asia lies on either side of the equator.

   4. The people of Southeast Asia live mainly in the river valleys.

   5. The area has similar temperatures and climate. Seasons are mainly wet or dry.

   6. Altitude has an important effect on both temperature and climate.

   7. The rhythm of the monsoon determines the patterns of economic activity.

   8. Because of its history and location, Southeast Asia has been a battleground.

   9. Geographic features restrict travel and communication among the various parts of Southeast Asia.

   10. Development of strong tribal and regional consciousness is a result in part of mountainous terrain and dense jungles.

   11. Rice agriculture has become the main economic activity because of the monsoons.

B. **Outside forces have influenced the history of Southeast Asia.**

   1. The history and culture of Southeast Asia has been greatly influenced by the cultures of India and China.

   2. Southeast Asia has been traditionally used for important trade routes between the Indian and Pacific Oceans.

   3. Rich resources have attracted foreign interest in the area.

   4. Great kingdoms developed and declined in different periods.

   5. With the exception of Thailand, all Southeast Asian countries have been under the control of European powers.

   6. The Europeans found Southeast Asia a culturally advanced area.

   7. The Europeans were responsible for certain achievements. Their negative accomplishments are also apparent.

   8. Nationalistic movements based on anti-colonialism and anti-European domination began soon after colonial rule was set up.

   9. World War II played an important role in the achievement of nationalist hopes for independence.

C. **Societies of Southeast Asia are made up of a variety of social classes, ethnic and racial groups, religious faiths, nationalities and languages.**

1. Many groups of people have moved from the interior of Asia to settle in Southeast Asia.

2. Muslims, Indians and Chinese have influenced cultural and social developments.

3. Buddhist and Muslim religious teachings provide systems of values and ways of life for most of Southeast Asia.

4. Art, music, architecture and the dance have been influenced by Indian and Chinese cultures.

5. Most people live in villages where society tends to change slowly.

6. The extended family structure is found in most of the area.

7. Serious problems of health, education and welfare exist.

8. Traditional values, thoughts and actions are often in contrast and conflict with Western culture.

D. **The independent countries of Southeast Asia have been concerned with political stability and economic development.**

1. After independence, some Southeast Asian goverments followed Western, liberal ideas. Following some disappointments, a swing away from democratic and liberal practices occurred.

2. Inexperience in national self-government, economic underdevelopment, and involvement in the Cold War complicate the search for stability.

3. Monarchy, military dictatorship and dictatorship by Communist groups dominate many Southeast Asian governments.

4. Many powerful nations are drawn into the affairs of Southeast Asia because of its instability, economic underdevelopment and location.

5. The area has had many political revolutions.

6. Most people live on a bare subsistence level.

7. Southeast Asia has many important natural resources. However, much of the mineral wealth has been used for the advantage of the colonial powers and little for the people of Southeast Asia.

8. Rice has a tremendous influence on the economic life of the people.

9. Regional cooperation on such projects as the Mekong River Plan offers possibilities for economic development.

10. The governments of Southeast Asia have used both capitalistic and socialistic methods of developing their nations.

UNIT VII

Exercises and Questions

Vocabulary

Directions: Match words in Column *A* with the correct meaning in Column *B*.

Column A

1. source
2. diversity
3. region
4. stable
5. ethnic
6. potential
7. isolated
8. adapt
9. remote
10. primitive
11. exploit

Column B

(a) characteristic of the earliest times; simple
(b) to charge something to meet one's needs
(c) distant; far off and hidden
(d) to be set apart from others
(e) what can, but has not yet, come into being
(f) area
(g) varied; different
(h) firm; steady
(i) place where something begins or comes from
(j) of a national or religious group
(k) make unfair use of other people's things

Completion

Directions: Complete the following sentences:

1. Goods which are sent in trade from your country to another are called ....

2. Southeast Asian religious temples are called ....

3. The dried meat of the coconut is called ....

4. A deposit of mud and loose soil that is washed down a river is called ....

5. The winds that greatly affect life in Southeast Asia are called the ....

6. The control of a weak nation by a strong is called ....

7. Soldiers who are not part of a regular army are called ....

8. A union of a group of states is called a ....

9. The method used to farm on the slope of a mountain or volcano is called
   ....

10. Good works in the Buddhist religion are called ....

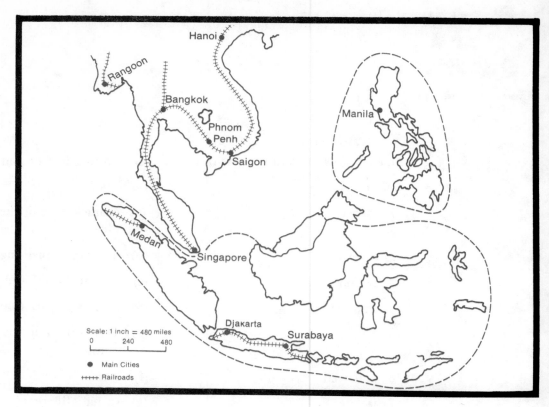

Map Exercise

Directions: In each of the following you have four choices. Choose the only correct answer.

1. Which of the following cities is located on a *gulf?*
   (a) Manila   (b) Phnom Penh   (c) Hanoi   (d) Bangkok

2. Which of the following cities is found on an *island?*
   (a) Manila   (b) Phnom Penh   (c) Hanoi   (d) Bangkok

3. Which of the following cities is found near a *lake?*
   (a) Manila   (b) Phnom Penh   (c) Hanoi   (d) Bangkok

4. Which of the following cities is found on a *peninsula?*
   (a) Manila   (b) Singapore   (c) Medan   (d) Djakarta

5. If you went from Hanoi to Saigon you would probably travel in which direction?
   (a) North   (b) South   (c) East   (d) West

6. Saigon is located to the *east* of
   (a) Hanoi   (b) Rangoon   (c) Manila   (d) Djakarta

7. The distance from Singapore to Djakarta is about
   (a) 250 miles   (b) 500 miles   (c) 1000 miles   (d) 1250 miles

8. Which of the following are over 1000 miles from each other?
    (a) Hanoi and Manila
    (b) Hanoi and Saigon
    (c) Bangkok and Singapore
    (d) Djakarta and Surabaya

9. Which of the following cities are *not* connected to each other by the railroad?
    (a) Hanoi and Saigon
    (b) Djakarta and Surabaya
    (c) Rangoon and Bangkok
    (d) Phnom Penh and Hanoi

10. Using information on the map *only* which of the following statements is *true*?
    (a) The distance from Medan to Djakarta is greater than the distance from Rangoon to Manila.
    (b) The railroad lines were built only in a west to east direction.
    (c) Most of this area is made up of islands and peninsulas.
    (d) Most of the islands are in the northern section of the area.

Chart Analysis

Directions: Using the chart on p. 432 answer the following questions. Of the four choices choose only the correct one.

1. To which of the following nations did the U.S. export more than it imported in 1968?
    (a) Indonesia   (b) Malaysia   (c) Philippines   (d) Thailand

2. Which of the following showed a decrease in both imports and exports in trade with the U.S. between 1968 and 1969?
    (a) Indonesia   (b) Malaysia   (c) Philippines   (d) Thailand

3. Which of the following nations showed the greatest growth of imports from the U.S. between 1968 and 1969?
    (a) Indonesia   (b) Malaysia   (c) Singapore   (d) Thailand

4. The word *export* means
    (a) to trade   (b) to bring goods into a country
    (c) to send goods to another country   (d) the value of goods bought and sold

5. One conclusion you might make from the information in this chart is
    (a) All nations included show a growth of trade with the U.S.
    (b) Vietnam has a very serious trade deficit with the U.S.
    (c) Malaysia has a very serious trade deficit with the U.S.
    (d) Thailand exports teak and tea to the U.S.

Multiple Choice

Directions: Select the letter of the correct answer.

1. The geographic position of Southeast Asia has influenced its development in that
    (a) it is set apart from the rest of the world
    (b) it is a natural area for the development of industry

(c) it has forced Southeast Asian countries to conquer neighboring lands

(d) it has made it an important trade center between the Indian and Pacific Oceans

2. Rivers are said to have the opposite effect of mountains because
   (a) rivers are great sources of mineral wealth, and mountains are not
   (b) mountains have kept people apart, while rivers have brought people together
   (c) mountains have good soil, while river valleys do not
   (d) mountains are great sources of natural resources, while rivers are not

3. Which of the following is *not* a major feature of Southeast Asian geography?
   (a) Southeast Asia has an extremely long coastline.
   (b) Southeast Asia is a region of islands and peninsulas.
   (c) Mountains and seas help to unite Southeast Asia.
   (d) Several important cities are located near the river deltas.

4. To get away from heat in the areas near the equator you would go to the
   (a) low coastal lands   (b) highlands   (c) river valleys   (d) interior flatlands

5. The mountain people of Southeast Asia are beginning to fight the governments of their countries because
   (a) they are Communists
   (b) they feel they are not given equal rights
   (c) they believe they are superior to the lowland peoples
   (d) they are not allowed to trade with the lowland peoples

6. Most of the people living in Southeast Asia today are probably descendants of people who
   (a) came from other places in Asia   (b) were the first settlers in Southeast Asia
   (c) came from the island archipelagos of Southeast Asia   (d) were not Asians

7. The people of the hills practice slash and burn farming because
   (a) Western advisors said it was the best method
   (b) the area is cleared, and the ashes provide fertilizer
   (c) the cleared land is used for building of cities
   (d) they produce too much to be used by their government

8. The peoples of the plains tend to regard the peoples of the hills as
   (a) interesting neighbors   (b) backward people   (c) dangerous enemies
   (d) crop destroyers

9. One of the major concepts of Southeast Asian history is which of the following?
   (a) All Southeast Asian nations have developed the same culture.
   (b) Southeast Asia has felt the impact of many cultures.
   (c) Chinese culture has dominated all of Southeast Asia.
   (d) Southeast Asia has been completely Europeanized.

10. The movement of people from the north to the south into Southeast Asia was caused by
    (a) the desire to move into a warmer climate
    (b) the desire to increase trade
    (c) the direction of the river valleys through the area
    (d) no apparent reason

11. The spread of Indian culture in Southeast Asia was accomplished through
    (a) the spread of Buddhism   (b) contacts with Indian merchants
    (c) the use of Sanskrit as the written language   (d) all of these

12. Which of the following groups were *not* most influenced by the Indians?
    (a) Khmers   (b) Thais   (c) Cambodians   (d) Vietnamese

13. The Khmer Empire is best remembered for its
    (a) development of mathematic and scientific knowledge   (b) conquest of
    Southeast Asia and Indonesia   (c) driving out the Chinese from Vietnam
    (d) great temple building

14. Which of the following is *not* an important part of Buddhism?
    (a) reincarnation   (b) caste system   (c) merit   (d) Nirvana

15. Europeans became interested in Southeast Asia for all of the following reasons
    except which?
    (a) The Europeans wanted help extend native dictatorships.
    (b) The Europeans were interested in spreading their religion.
    (c) The Europeans wanted to gain control of the spice trade.
    (d) The Europeans became interested in the rich minerals of the area.

16. The first Europeans to become involved in Southeast Asia were the
    (a) Portuguese   (b) Spanish   (c) English   (d) French

17. The French gained control of which of the following areas?
    (a) Burma, Malaya, Borneo   (b) Indonesia, Thailand, Vietnam
    (c) Laos, Cambodia, Vietnam   (d) Cambodia, Thailand, Burma

18. The only nation which kept its independence was
    (a) Burma   (b) Thailand   (c) Indonesia   (d) Laos

19. Nationalists are people who want
    (a) a Communist country   (b) to conquer other countries
    (c) to govern themselves   (d) petroleum and other natural resources

20. Sukarno was the leader of which of the following nationalists?
    (a) Burmese   (b) Thai   (c) Vietnamese   (d) Indonesians

21. The Japanese attacked Southeast Asia because they wanted
    (a) to conquer the U.S.   (b) raw materials and markets for goods
    (c) to test their military strength   (d) "Asia for the Asians"

22. Which of the following was *not* the result of the Japanese occupation of Southeast
    Asia?
    (a) Western prestige was destroyed.   (b) Nationalist armies were trained.
    (c) Communists took over the areas.   (d) Top positions in the government
    were filled by Southeast Asians.

23. Which pair of countries gained independence peacefully?
    (a) Burma & Philippines   (b) Indonesia & Vietnam   (c) Burma & Malaya
    (d) Philippines & Indonesia

24. The leader of the Vietnamese nationalist movement was
    (a) Lon Nol   (b) Ho Chi Minh   (c) Mongkut   (d) Sihanouk

25. The word *partitioned* means
    (a) divided   (b) added   (c) combined   (d) subtracted

26. Subsistence farming means
    (a) farmers produce more than enough for themselves and their families
    (b) farmers raise many kinds of crops
    (c) the soil is rich enough to raise many kinds of crops
    (d) farmers raise just enough for their own use

27. Most metal ores of Southeast Asia are exported rather than smelted down because
    (a) there is a higher price paid for the ores
    (b) Southeast Asians have never learned to smelt metals
    (c) there is a lack of large supplies of good quality coal
    (d) they are too lazy to build plants

28. Which of the following groups of products are important in Southeast Asia?
    (a) rice, copra and oil palms   (b) rice, wheat and copra
    (c) rice, mangoes and cotton   (d) wheat, kapok and tobacco

Thought Questions

1. How have differences that existed among the peoples of Southeast Asia affected the situation in the region today?

2. How does topography affect the climate of Southeast Asia?

3. How does climate affect the lives of the people of Southeast Asia?

4. How is life in a Southeast Asian village affected by the environment?

5. "Buddhism is more than a religion. It is a way of life." Explain.

6. How did geography affect the historical development of Southeast Asia?

7. How did spices change the history of Southeast Asia?

8. (a) How did the West aid the development of Southeast Asia?
   (b) Why do Southeast Asians dislike the West?

9. Why was the Japanese occupation (1941-1945) important in Southeast Asian history?

10. How have the governments of Southeast Asia tried to solve their problems of underdevelopment?

11. "Cultural diversity is an important factor in Southeast Asia." Explain.

12. (a) What is meant by "monsoons"?
    (b) How do the monsoons affect the lives of the people of Southeast Asia?

13. What were the factors that encouraged nationalism in each of the following areas?
    (a) Indonesia   (b) Vietnam   (c) Thailand   (d) Burma   (e) Philippines

14. "The road to survival in Southeast Asia follows many paths in foreign policy." Describe the paths followed by each of the nations below.
    (a) Laos   (b) Kampuchea   (c) Burma   (d) Indonesia

15. (a) Why did the U.S. become involved in Vietnam?
    (b) What were the terms of the peace settlement?

16. (a) How have the Chinese and Indians influenced life in Southeast Asia?
    (b) What differences exist among life-styles in Southeast Asia, China and India?

17. "Europeans made many contributions to improve life in Southeast Asia"—explain why you agree or disagree with this statement.

18. "ASEAN is important to the development of Southeast Asia." Explain.

19. Why were the North Vietnamese and Viet Cong able to take over the government of South Vietnam?

20. How would you describe the situation that now exists in Kampuchea and Laos?

Bankok Temple Guard. **Credit: *Murray D. Zak***

Puzzle

Directions: Place the words below in their proper place in the puzzle.

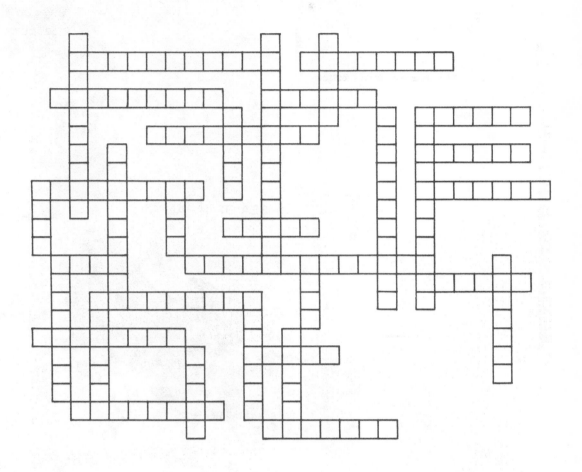

4 LETTERS	5 LETTERS	6 LETTERS	7 LETTERS	8 LETTERS
RICE	BONZE	ETHNIC	DIALECT	BARRIERS
SILT	HUMID	PAGODA	EROSION	BUDDHISM
TEAK	KLONG	REGION	ISLANDS	MAINLAND
THAI	MERIT	REMOTE	ISTHMUS	TERRACED
	SATAY	STUPAS	NIRVANA	

9 LETTERS	10 LETTERS	11 LETTERS	13 LETTERS
DIVERSITY	PENINSULAS	ELECTRICITY	HYDROELECTRIC
NEGOTIATE		NATIONALIST	REINCARNATION
PETROLEUM		PARTITIONED	
PRIMITIVE			
STABILITY			

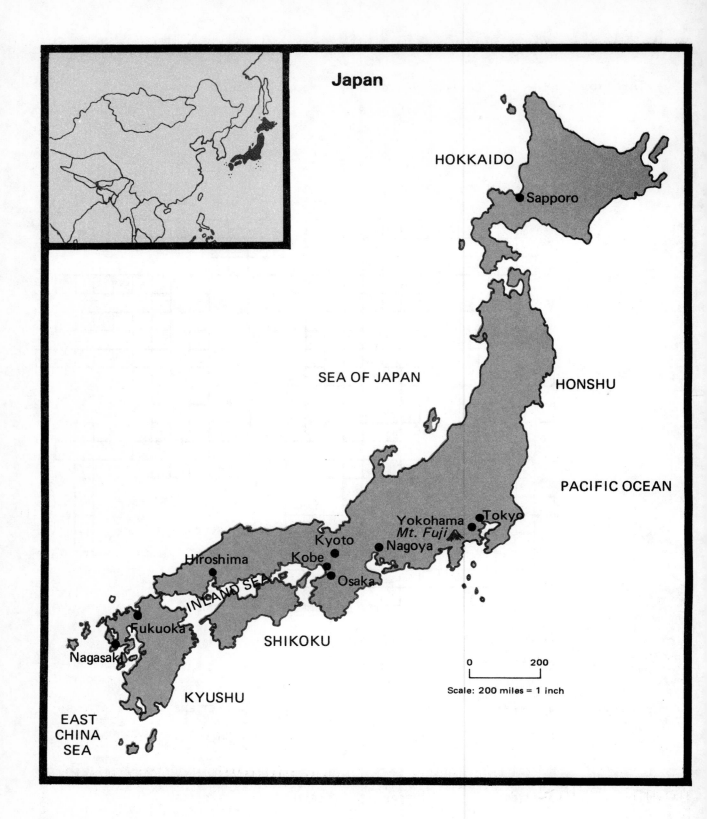

Japan

HOKKAIDO

Sapporo

SEA OF JAPAN

HONSHU

PACIFIC OCEAN

Yokohama
Mt. Fuji

Tokyo

Kyoto

Nagoya

Hiroshima

Kobe

Osaka

INLAND SEA

Fukuoka

SHIKOKU

Nagasaki

KYUSHU

EAST
CHINA
SEA

0   200

Scale: 200 miles = 1 inch

UNIT VIII Japan

Land and Climate

An Island Nation

The name Japan is not used by the Japanese. They call their country Nihon, or Nippon, meaning "Land of the Rising Sun." Their flag, a bright red ball or sun on a white background, is easily recognized.

The Japanese people believe that the god Izanagi stood on the floating bridge of heaven and looked down on the sea below. In his hand he held a jewel tipped spear. He dipped the sword into the ocean and began to stir the waters. When he removed the spear from the ocean, drops of salt water fell from its tip and formed a group of islands.

The Japanese island group is located off the east coast of Asia. It is part of the "Fire Rim of the Pacific," a great chain of volcanoes lying along the west coast of the Americas and then curving down the eastern shores of Asia. There are about 3,400 islands in all. These islands are scattered over a large area. Japan is shaped like a dragon. The head is the island of Hokkaido, the body Honshu and Shikoku, and the tail Kyushu. The outermost tips of the island chain are separated by almost 1,400 miles.

Most of the 3,400 islands are small and useless. There are four main islands. Hokkaido, in the north, has poor land and a hard winter climate. This island is still Japan's frontier, as the West was to the United States in the 1870s. Just south of Hokkaido is the main island of Honshu. Tokyo and the other great cities of modern Japan lie on its southeastern and southern coastal plains. Southwest of Honshu is the island of Kyushu, which is second in importance to Honshu. Shikoku, the southern island, is separated from Honshu by the calm waters of the Inland Sea.

View from Mt. Washu. A distant view of Shikoku Island. (*Top*)
Credit: *Japan National Tourist Organization*

In-no-shima Island. (*Bottom*)
Credit: *Japan National Tourist Organization*

Topography

Japan is a rugged, mountainous group of islands. Sometimes the islands are rocked by earthquakes. The mountains rise from the floor of the ocean, five or six miles deep (25,000-30,000 feet), to a height of over two miles in some places. Mt. Fuji (Fujiyama) reaches 12,500 feet into the sky. The distance from coast to coast is less than two hundred miles anywhere in the islands.

The islands, by their very shape, *ensured* (made it possible) that communication and transportation overland would always be a problem. Almost 80% of the land surface is mountainous. Nearly 600 mountains are 6,000 feet in altitude or more. The remaining 20% is very *arable* (good for farming) land divided into three main areas. These three great areas of fertile land lie along the eastern coast of the island of Honshu. The largest is the Kanto plain. The others are the Nobi and Kinai plains. The struggle for the control of these lands is the key to Japanese history. (Why do you think this is so?) Throughout Japan's existence these plains have attracted the Japanese people. Today the great cities of Tokyo, Nagoya and Osaka are in the center of these areas.

The Kinai plain, by its position in the center of Honshu, has tended to become the *hub* (center) of Japan. Until modern times the capital of Japan was found in the Kinai (Nara, Kyoto). To the Japanese the Kinai area has been known as the "Home Provinces."

Japan has many rivers. Hundreds of streams race from the highlands to the sea. The rivers are short and swift. The longest, Shinaino, is only 229 miles long. Because most of them are *navigable* (able to be sailed on) for only a few miles, these streams have little importance for transportation. They have been *barriers* (blocks) to travel and trade. However, throughout Japan's history the rivers have given water for irrigating the rice fields. Today the rivers are important for the production of electric power for homes and industry.

The Importance of the Sea

As an island nation, Japan has always relied heavily upon the sea. Its long, irregular coastline makes possible the growth of good harbors, such as Tokyo-Yokohama, Nagoya, Kobe and Osaka. Smaller harbors serve the needs of hundreds of fishing villages which dot the shores of the islands and which have made possible Japan's development into the leading fishing nation in the world. The main highway of Japan is the great Inland Sea. In addition to being the main avenue of trade within Japan, the Inland Sea serves as a trade route for foreign trade.

The sea has served Japan in another way—as an effective barrier between the nation and the rest of the world. Japan has been able to borrow what it wishes from other cultures and civilizations without being conquered by them.

The sea has served Japan in another way—as an effective *barrier* between the nation and the rest of the world. The Japanese islands are 100 miles across the sea from Asia at the southern tip of Korea. Therefore it has been easy for the Japanese to *adapt* from Asia what they wanted and to keep out what they did not want. In the entire history of Japan there was only one case of foreign invasion and, incidentally, only one case of a Japanese attempt to conquer an area outside of Japan before the modern period of Japanese history. Apparently barriers work both ways.

Climate

Like most parts of the United States, Japan has four seasons. In northern Japan the climate is a humid continental one. Summers are hot while winters are cold and long, with January temperatures well below freezing. In the rest of Japan the winters are usually mild, with many sunny days. Summers are usually mild to warm, with the average summer temperature 60°F in Hokkaido, 70°F around Tokyo, and in the 80s in Shikoku. In the sub-tropical south the heat can be unpleasant because it is very humid and there is much rainfall. This heavy rainfall is important for rice cultivation.

Japan is affected by the monsoons (winds). In the summer the monsoons blow from the ocean and cool the eastern side of Japan. In the winter the winds blow in the opposite direction, from the Asian mainland. These winter winds bring cold weather to northern Japan. The mountains prevent the cold weather and snow from reaching the eastern and southern parts of Japan.

Another factor that influences climate is ocean currents. The warm Japanese Current, or Black Stream, which moderates the winter climate and warms it in summer, flows as far north as Tokyo Bay. To the north of Tokyo, in Honshu and around Hokkaido, the cold Oyoshio, or Kurile Current chills the northern coasts.

Japan is often hit by typhoons. These storms, which arise far to the south, frequently strike the densely populated eastern coast of Japan with great force. Floods and landslides are often started as a result of the storm. Great tidal waves, which rush in from the ocean, also cause tremendous damage and loss of life.

The People and Their Language

The People

Organized human life emerged later in Japan than in other parts of Asia. The Japanese people are a mixture of racial stocks that came from mainland Asia. The descendants of the first group of settlers still live in Japan. They are the Ainu, who are Caucasian and live on Hokkaido.

The first inhabitants were hunters and fishermen. They were followed by peoples from mainland Asia who knew how to farm rice. These later arrivals are the ancestors of today's Japanese.

Most Japanese are classified as Mongoloids (like Mongolians) because of their physical characteristics. They have straight black hair and dark, almond-shaped eyes, and are shorter in height than present-day Westerners. Their skin color ranges from fair to yellowish to brown. The Japanese strongly resemble the Northern Chinese and Koreans.

Japanese calligraphy—The Japanese learned the art of calligraphy from the Chinese. (*Top*)
Credit: *Consulate General of Japan, N.Y.*

Japanese boy using an abacus, an ancient calculator for doing arithmetic. Japanese education makes use of both old and new methods. (*Bottom*)
Credit: *Japan National Tourist Organization*

The Japanese Language

The Japanese are united by a common spoken language. This has made it easier for the Japanese to achieve political and cultural unity more quickly than other Asian nations.

The Japanese language is mainly *polysyllabic* (most words are composed of several syllables). But Japanese is not difficult to speak and pronounce, and spelling is simpler than English or French. There is no accent on any syllable in a Japanese word; all syllables are stressed equally, with very few exceptions.

The Japanese borrowed their system of writing from the Chinese, adapting it to Japanese needs. For centuries the Japanese had no way to write down their language. The Japanese people memorized events and traditions and passed them on by word of mouth. After a time, through their contacts with China, they discovered the advantages of writing, and began to adopt the Chinese system. In this system, each character stands for an idea or object, rather than a sound, as in the Roman alphabet. However, the Japanese did not accept the Chinese spoken language. The result is that the spoken language of Japan differs greatly from Chinese. For example, "Japan" is written 日 本 , in Chinese characters. The Chinese pronunciation is "jih-pen," but the two characters are pronounced "ni-hon" (or Nippon) by the Japanese. (日 , meaning sun, 十 本 , meaning origin, = Where the sun has its origin, or "Land of the Rising Sun").

To the Chinese written system the Japanese later added their own written system, based on syllables or tables of syllables called Kana, rather than the English system of individual letters. Written Japanese is ordinarily formed by a combination of Chinese characters, Kanji, and Kana syllables.

The Japanese also use the Roman alphabet for certain limited purposes. Along the railways, for instance, the names of stations are often shown in three systems of writing—Chinese, Kana, and Roman letters. Since all Japanese school children study English from the seventh grade through high school, such signs are not at all confusing to most riders. It is also important to note that Japan has the highest rate of literacy in Asia and possesses the most well-developed educational system.

Life in Japan

The Blending of the Old and the New

The most important aspect of life in Japan is the blending of the old and the new. Although willing to adopt better ways of doing things from other cultures, the Japanese retain much that is traditional.

In the past, the Japanese people glorified the family and discouraged individual action. There were certain approved patterns of behavior, and women had a low position in Japanese society. The father was master of the house and demanded complete obedience. Many changes in Japanese family life appeared after 1945. The complete power of the Japanese male as head of the household was broken. Women have been given a large measure of equality. Japanese women now work in factories and offices, as in the West.

The Japanese Home

The "typical" Japanese home is very unlike our own. It is constructed mostly of wood, bamboo and straw. The rooms are separated from one another by *shoji*, light, sliding screens made of paper stretched over a wooden frame. The house has little furniture. The Japanese often use as a heater a small charcoal stove called a *hibachi*.

The floor, which is raised several feet above ground level, is covered by reed mats called *tatami*. Since few homes have chairs, family members and visitors sit cross-legged on pillows. The family sleeps on heavy quilts spread on the matted floor. Bathing is done in a huge wooden vat or tile tub filled with extremely hot water.

The Effect of Cultural Diffusion

Contact with the West has brought changes to Japan. Children use chairs and desks in classrooms, but they sit on the floor while they do their homework at home. The national sport of Japan is baseball. Western style clothing is worn to business, but the traditional kimono and robes are still worn at home. In time, the Japanese might abandon the traditional ways, but now and for many years to come the two styles will exist side by side.

Appreciation of Beauty

Appreciation of the beauty and greatness of nature has been a part of Japanese life since earliest times. This fondness for the world of nature is seen in many aspects of daily life. Holidays and festivals coincide with major changes in the cycles of the seasons. The objects of everyday use, such as clothing, umbrellas, fans and dishes are decorated with designs from nature, revealing the Japanese awareness of things around them.

Religion

Shrines and temples can be found everywhere in Japan. They are the places of worship of Shintoism and Buddhism, the principal religions of the Japanese people. In the last hundred years thousands of Japanese have become Christians. Freedom of religion is guaranteed by the Constitution of 1947, and no particular religion can receive preference over another. In addition, no one religion can be the state religion. This is an important change because before 1945 Shintoism was the state religion.

Shintoism

Shintoism was a religion developed only in Japan. Shinto means "the way of the gods" from two Chinese words—*Shin* meaning "good spirits" and *Tao* meaning "the way." Shintoism is based on the worship of nature and good spirits called *Kami*. This religion has no bible. Shintoism is based on man's feelings toward the world around him.

The *Kami* are powers or spirits loosely referred to as gods but are really "a superior or extraordinary force." The Kami live in shrines, animals, birds, plants, mountains, waterfalls, storms and in most natural things. There are thousands of them. The light and heat of the sun and the waves of the sea are caused by the power of the **Kami**. These spirits are never looked on with fear but with friendly closeness, love, and thankfulness.

Shinto has no formal prayer book. *Norito* (prayers), in poetic form, are presented by priests at the hundreds of shrines throughout Japan.

Shinto has three important symbols: a sword which represents the virtue of wisdom and correct action; a string of jewels which represents kindness, generosity, and obedience; and a mirror which stands for truthfulness and reflects all things good and bad. The Japanese believe that without these three basic virtues—wisdom, kindness, and truthfulness—peace, happiness, and a good life cannot exist either for individuals or for the nation.

Buddhism

Buddhism is the major religion of Japan today. More than half the people of Japan are Buddhists. Many Buddhists also follow Shinto custom and ceremony. Buddhism was founded in India 2,500 years ago. It was brought to Japan by the Chinese about 1,500 years ago, and spread rapidly among the nobles and the upper classes. The common people did not at first accept Buddhism because they found it hard to agree with a religion which prohibited marriage of priests, and which was not happy and gay. As Buddhism was adapted to the needs and feelings of the Japanese, more people became Buddhists. New sects, including Zen, made Buddhism Japanese. As a result, thousands became Buddhists.

Zen Buddhism

The Zen sect of Buddhism came to Japan from China in the Kamakura period (1192-1333). The main idea of Zen is to find self-understanding, called *satori* or enlightenment. Believers in Zen feel that prayer and religious worship are a waste of time. Personal character and discipline are important. *Meditation* (thinking) is the main form of worship.

The goal of Zen is to bring the person to satori—to help people go from thinking to knowing. Satori comes to a fortunate few—often in a sudden flash. To develop the proper frame of mind, one must use *koans* (Zen riddles). Here are some examples of koans: "What is the sound of one hand clapping?" "What happens to the fist when the hand is open?" When the Zen believer feels that reasonable analysis and logic do not help in finding the answer (for in reality there are no answers) progress toward satori has been made. Zen followers lead a simple life close to nature.

Zen has influenced Japanese education, literature, painting, foreign affairs, history, theatre, and many other parts of Japanese life.

Other Religions

Confucianism, the complicated moral code of China, has had much effect on Japanese thought and behavior. Christianity ranks behind Shintoism and Buddhism. Christianity first came to Japan in the 1500s, but was banned from 1637 to 1873. Since the ban was lifted, many Japanese have decided to become Christians. Today, about 800,000 Japanese claim to be Christians.

The great Kamakura Buddha was built in the 13th century and is made of copper and gold. Buddhism is the main religion of the Japanese people. (*Top*)
Credit: *Consulate General of Japan, N.Y.*

Three-storied pagoda of the Kiyomizu Temple in Kyoto was built in the 17th century. (*Top*)
Credit: *Consulate General of Japan, N.Y.*

Great Torii (gate) of Itsukushima Shrine. The torii (in the water) is found in front of all Shinto shrines. Before entering the shrine, one must pass through the torii to become purified. Note the stone lanterns in the foreground. (*Bottom*)
Credit: *Consulate General of Japan, N.Y.*

Japanese Arts

Tea Ceremony

Japanese art and skills have been influenced by their contact with China and Korea. However, they have been so developed and refined that they have become strictly Japanese. The tea ceremony (*Chanoyu*) is an example. It features the serving of *matcha,* powdered green tea. It is prepared for a few art lovers in a simple bare room close to the beauties of nature. The tea is prepared in slow, graceful motions and drunk slowly from a bowl. The bowl and other articles used are then admired and discussed. The ceremony is designed to make a person one with nature, to see beauty in simplicity and economy of movement. It is an art, not a means of offering refreshment. Every detail of participation is governed by tradition, and the ceremony is both a spiritual experience and a mental exercise.

Ikebana (Flower Arrangement)

Ikebana is the art of flower arrangement. In this art, as in *Chanoyu* (tea ceremony), Zen Buddhism has played an important role. Ikebana uses line, color, and rhythm to create floral designs; branches, stems, and flowers are the materials.

Ikebana tries to show the slow passage of time. This is shown both in materials and types of arrangement. Blossoms in full bloom or dried leaves are used to show the past. The present is shown by half-open blossoms or perfect leaves. Buds are used to show the future.

Curves are used to suggest spring; a full spread of blossoms and leaves to show summer; a thin, square grouping, autumn; and a dark, quiet arrangement, winter. The three stem lines symbolize: Heaven (the tallest stem), Man (the second stem), and Earth (the shortest stem).

The flower arrangements are usually placed in the *tokonoma* which is an alcove or corner in the most important room in the Japanese home. At first, many scholars believe, the tokonoma was the family altar, dedicated to Buddha. Today it is used for scrolls, floral arrangements and to display art work.

Bonsai

For centuries the Japanese have developed the art of *dwarfing* (making small) trees. This art is called *bonsai*. These dwarf trees are used for ornaments in rooms or to decorate a garden. They are planted in pots.

The growth of the plants is controlled by pruning (cutting) so that the trees are trained into the shapes of ancient big trees. The trunk of the tree, the spreading of the roots and the spacing of the branches are very important. It is important because they are used to give an old appearance to the tree. The empty spaces in the pot are used to suggest plains or distant mountains.

The pot in which the trees are planted plays an important part in the plan of bonsai. The shape and size of the pot is decided on by the kinds of plants it holds. The pots are usually plain but some are highly decorated. However, the pots should blend in with the natural surroundings.

Today many Japanese still learn the art of bonsai as a hobby. Here is another example of the Japanese desire to try to understand and remain close to nature.

Theatre

Nō Drama

Japanese theatre is unique. During the late 14th century the Japanese created a new form of drama, the *Nō play*. The Japanese drew upon older traditions of music and dance in the developing of the Nō drama. It was created to entertain the wealthy. The Nō makes use of simple stage settings. The backdrop is often a single pine tree. This simpleness shows the influence of Zen Buddhism on this form of drama.

In Nō plays there are usually three roles—an old man, a woman, and a samurai (warrior). Nō plays are usually short. They are presented as a group of plays and single performances may last up to six hours. The groups of plays are by subjects such as: God plays, warrior-ghost plays, women plays, and demon plays. Dancing and chanting accompany the action of the play. Masks and beautifully designed costumes are worn by the actor-dancers.

Bunraku

A later development in Japanese theatre was the puppet play, known as *Bunraku*. This form was developed in the 17th century in Osaka. The foremost writer of Bunraku was Chickamatsu, who is sometimes called the "Shakespeare of Japan."

The Bunraku puppets are nearly life-size and are very lifelike. They are controlled on the stage by a team of three puppeteers who are visible to the audience. The puppeteers' performances depend upon long years of practice and teamwork. The techniques of Bunraku have remained basically the same. Many of the techniques, plays, and music exist only through the memory of the puppeteers since there are no written texts. The art of constructing Bunraku puppets is dead since no living artist is now making puppets. The theatre is able to continue only through the use of the remaining puppets—some of which are more than 250 years old. Bunraku performances are given today and the Japanese regard it as a national cultural treasure.

Kabuki

The most popular type of drama for the Japanese is *Kabuki*. Kabuki was also developed in the 17th century. It had its beginnings in the puppet play and the Nō drama. Kabuki is made up of drama, dance, music, and singing. (The word *Kabuki* is made up of Chinese characters for music, dance, and singing.)

Kabuki was first presented in specially built theatres for the middle class and poorer people. The stage was very large. Many devices were used to give more action. Trap-doors allowed actors to disappear from sight and wires could move them through the air. Revolving platforms allowed rapid changing of sets. Fire, smoke, lighting, and ghosts were new innovations of Kabuki.

All roles in Kabuki, both male and female, were, until recently, played by men. In the 17th century a law banned women from the stage and all-male Kabuki became traditional. Actors taking feminine roles were trained from childhood to walk, talk, and behave like women. The actors wear brightly colored costumes, and wigs which dazzle the eye. Kabuki leaves nothing to the imagination; everything is exaggerated. Color, sound, speech, and dramatic action combine to excite the senses and the emotions.

Chickamatsu, who wrote many puppet plays, also wrote for Kabuki. The stories are somewhat like fairy tales. The favorite subject for both Bunraku and Kabuki was the conflict between duty and personal desires—duty usually won out in the end. Many of the plays are based on tales and legends of early Japan. Sometimes playwrights poked fun at government officials. The deeds of heroes and villains in Japan's many wars have been favorites year after year. There is little development of characters or the relationship of character to action. However, the skillful and magical combination of color, music, action, and words hypnotizes the audience. Truly one is carried away by the spectacle.

Kabuki is also popular outside of Japan; it has been performed with great success in both New York and Chicago. Kabuki today is Japan's most popular and grand theater.

Literature

Japanese literary history is rich. Poetry has been written for over a thousand years. Good poetry was collected in anthologies. The most famous collection was the *Manyoshu* (Collection of Ten Thousand Leaves). It was completed in 760 and contains more than forty-five hundred poems and songs. The *Manyoshu* is the most important literary achievement of early Japanese history; it marks the Nara period (710-794) as the Golden Age of Japanese poetry. The great majority of the poems in this collection are called "short poems" (tanka) of 31 syllables, divided into sections of 5-7-5-7-7 syllables. Normally a "short poem" suggests a natural scene and then changes into an emotional feeling. Most short poems are difficult to translate. The following, from the ninth century, is simple enough, though its simplicity may make it less typical of the style:

Haru tuteba	When spring comes
Kiyuru koori no	the melting ice
nokori naku	leaves no trace.
Kimi ga kokoro mo	Would that your heart too
ware ni tokenan	melted thus toward me.

Two hundred years later a second anthology of about eleven hundred poems was assembled by order of the emperor. It was called the *Kokinshu* (Ancient and Modern Collection). The preface to this anthology is one of the earliest examples of prose written in Japanese. The author of this preface also wrote a poetic travel diary called the *Tosa Diary*. Many other diaries were written at this time telling us much about Japan in early times.

The Pillow Book of Sei-Shonagon, the most famous diary, was written between 950 and 1000 by Sei-Shonagon, a lady-in-waiting to the empress. In it one can find a day-by-day description of court life with witty comments and deep insight into people and events. Japan's greatest novel was also written at this time. The *massive* (very

Kabuki is Japan's famous drama form. It developed in the 17th century. Many of its most famous plays have delighted audiences for more than two centuries with little change. (*Top*)
Credit: *Consulate General of Japan, N.Y.*

The Japanese have developed several unique sports.
Sumo wrestling. (*Bottom*)
Credit: *Japan National Tourist Organization*

large) *Genji Mongatari* (*The Tale of Genji*) was written by Lady Murasaki Shikibu. This novel revolves around the adventures and loves of the imaginary Prince Genji. It gives a vivid description of the people, ceremonies, and customs of the Japanese upper class. The *Tale of Genji* has had a great influence on Japanese literature and through Arthur Waley's translation it has become one of the great world classics.

In the late 11th and 12th centuries romantic accounts of the Fujiwara (837-1160) court were written. *Eiga Monogatari* (*The Tale of Splendor*) covers the period 889 to 1092 in chronological order and the *Okagami* (*Great Mirror*) the period from 850 to 1025 in biographic style.

A popular form of writing was about the many wars. These stirring war tales are historically accurate in broad outline, but they are also full of imagined and romantic detail. The greatest of these war tales is the *Tale of the House of Taira*.

In the 17th century, a time of peace, more and more Japanese learned to read. The art of printing, which had been known to the Japanese as early as the 8th century, became more developed. These two factors led to a great increase in the number of books published. Many of the early books of this time were on religion or history; some dealt with the amusement quarters of the fast-growing towns.

From this beginning, Ihara Saikaku (1642-1693) developed character portrayals of amusing townsmen. His important works were *An Amorous Man, An Amorous Woman,* and *Twenty Examples of Unfilial Conduct in This Land.* His writing was clear-cut and critical as well as humorous.

Haiku poetry was also developed in this period. One of the earliest and probably the greatest haiku poet was Matsuo Basho (1644-1694), a former samurai who became a poet and traveler. His most famous work, *The Narrow Road of Oku,* is a poetic account of a trip to northern Honshu.

The Japanese borrowed much from their neighbors; but they adapted and improved on the forms and skills making them uniquely Japanese.

Early Art and Architecture

The earliest known Japanese art forms are the *haniwa* figures of men, animals, and horses of the third century. Architectural examples are not that old. Since most buildings were built of wood they have not survived. However the Japanese, in rebuilding their many shrines, have always carefully copied the examples of the past. Today, examples of the early-style Japanese architecture can be seen in the holy shrines at Ise.

With the introduction of Buddhism into Japan, art flourished. The full-sized Buddhist images and realistic portrait statues of the Nara period are fine works. The artists used bronze, wood, clay and lacquer for their work.

The Japanese mastered Chinese architectural and bridge building techniques and many other skills. The Buddhist temples built in Japan during the seventh and eighth centuries are the best remaining examples of classic Chinese T'ang architecture. The Golden Hall and the *pagoda* (temple) of the Horyuji are probably the oldest wooden buildings in the world. The Golden Hall has many beautiful statues and its walls are covered by frescoes like the Buddhist cave temples in India.

Zen Art and Architecture

Zen Buddhism influenced the development of a style of landscape painting. The greatest of the Zen artists was probably Sesshu (1420-1506). The Zen artist wanted to show the main parts of nature by leaving out minor details and by showing with bold brush strokes what was important. In Zen paintings, people, temples, bridges, and boats usually appear as minor details blending into the great pattern of nature.

Large heavy-roofed Zen temples were common, but the smaller, lighter Silver (Gin Kakuji) and Golden (Kinkakuji) Pavilions near Kyoto are better examples of the spirit of the times. A more important development of this time was landscape architecture. The setting of the buildings and the surrounding garden became an important art form. The Zen spirit can best be seen in the "rock garden" of the Ryoanji in Kyoto.

Sumi-e and Ukiyo-e

Japanese ink or brush painting with black ink is called *Sumi-e*. This is a very delicate style. It began during the 13th century (Kamakura period). The painter hopes to come close to nature. Artists try to paint how they feel about a thing rather than to paint a living quality. During the Kamakura Period a monk painted *The Naichi Waterfall* which is one of the finest landscape paintings now existing. It shows the artist's love of nature. Scroll paintings which still exist from this period show many things about Japanese life and customs.

In the 15th century Japanese artists produced some of the finest black and white pictures ever printed. The most famous of these painters were Shuban and Sesshu. They were influenced by the Chinese of that century and by the Sumi-e painters. Most of their paintings are very simple, with only a few brush strokes. The object of the painters is to show the wonders of nature. The painter tries to leave the viewer with a sense of peace and the goodness of the surroundings.

Another art form is *Ukiyo-e*. Ukiyo-e is often translated as "floating world." The Ukiyo-e painters were influenced by the colorful theatre and the world of pleasure. Ukiyo-e is a kind of wood block-printing. The artist tries to create landscapes and other forms of nature in a realistic way.

Japanese artists before the 17th century painted only for temples, palaces, and castles. The Ukiyo-e painters had many more colorful subjects to paint. They also had many more people who were able to buy and who were interested in buying paintings. At first they painted this floating world of pleasure in bright colors. It was not realistic painting. Each artist painted according to his own imagination. Moronobu was one of the earliest artists of this group.

When the demand for Ukiyo-e paintings became greater, artists began to cut their drawings on blocks of wood. It was now possible to print large numbers of copies or prints. These prints could be sold very cheaply. The Japanese liked to have them as souvenirs of a favorite actor or beautiful woman or to enjoy a much dreamed about, pleasurable experience. It was from these penny prints that the country people learned about city life.

The earliest prints were done only in heavy black lines on white paper. Late in the 18th century the Edo (Tokyo) printmakers added rose-red and green. Still later the multi-colored print (*nishki-e*) was developed. The two greatest artists of the Ukiyo-e block-print school were Hiroshige and Hokusai.

The Ukiyo-e had a great influence on European art. In 1865 a Frenchman named Bracquemond who drew designs on French pottery happened to see some Hiroshige prints among the paper wrappings used on a package from Japan. He showed the prints to his friends and to some painters. Many of the French artists were impressed with the bright colors and the flowing lines of movement.

In 1867, Ukiyo-e works were shown at the Paris International Exhibition. These works were the most looked at at the exhibition. They were also inexpensive. Monet, Degas, and van Gogh—all French impressionist painters—became collectors. Many later works of these impressionists show the style of Ukiyo-e.

In early 1975 the Metropolitan Museum of Art in New York City set up an exhibition comparing the Ukiyo-e and impressionist painters. The Museum placed paintings of both groups side by side. Similiarities in subject (seascapes, field scene, people), use of color, and use of line were obvious. It is clear that the impressionists learned much and borrowed some from the Ukiyo-e artists.

Early History

The First Settlers

Archaeology tells us that man has existed in Japan for the past 100,000 years. Japan was once *linked* (joined) to the mainland mass of Asia. People traveled from the mainland to what is today the island nation of Japan over a land bridge. Then the oceans, *swelled* (the level raised) by the melting ice of the glacier, covered the land bridge. Japan was cut off from Asia by the new *straits* (narrow bodies of water between land masses) that have played such a great part in Japan's later history.

Japan was settled mainly by peoples from the mainland of northeast Asia. These people came to the islands over a long period of time. They came to Japan over the land bridge that had existed for thousands of years. These early settlers were probably hunters and food gatherers. They are the ancestors of the modern Ainu people of northern Japan. Farming was introduced about 2,900 years ago (9th century B.C.). Archaeological evidence, myths and legends, and the reports of Chinese visitors lead us to the conclusion that Japan's social and political organization remained simple until about 1,500 years ago.

The Gods Create Japan—Legend of Jimmu Tenno

As part of Japanese history, Japanese schools taught, that Izanagi, a god, and Izanami, a goddess, were ordered to create a land on earth. They were given a coral spear. They dipped the spear into the ocean. When they took the spear out of the water, they allowed drops of water to drip from the point of the spear. These drops formed islands. Japan was *created*.

Amateratsu, goddess of the sun and daughter of Izanagi and Izanami, inherited all of the earth. She sent her grandson, Ninigi, to rule the islands created by her parents. When Ninigi was about to leave heaven, Amateratsu gave him three things that would make life easier for him: an iron mirror, a necklace of precious jewels and the "Cloud Cluster Sword." Armed with these objects, which were to become the Japanese crown jewels, Prince Ninigi came to Japan. He married and passed the three objects to his grandson, Jimmu Tenno. Jimmu became the first earthly emperor of Japan on February 11, 660 B.C.

This is the legend of the founding of Japan, which many Japanese, even today, accept as fact.

The Yamoto Kingdom

In fact, many, many small kingdoms were set up in various parts of the islands. Some of them had contacts with the nearby and more culturally advanced states of China and Korea. The most powerful kingdom was that of Yamoto, whose control extended from southern Japan up to Tokyo. The Yamoto introduced Chinese civilization into Japan.

A great figure of the Yamoto was Prince Shotoku. He was mainly a statesman and teacher. The Prince realized that his people had much to learn from the Chinese. He built a Japanese state on the Chinese model, and helped to spread Buddhism. Prince Shotoku set up landholding, tax systems, law codes and a military organization based on the Chinese system.

After the death of Shotoku, a group of reformers revolted and set up a program of change. This was the Taika program of "Great Reforms." The aim of the program was to set up a unified kingdom under one ruler. The program was never fully carried out, but brought about lasting changes in Japanese government, society and life. Most important, it established for all time the claim of the Yamoto ruler to the throne of Japan.

To make his claim clear, the Emperor ordered an official history of Japan to be written. One book was called the *Kojiki* (Record of Ancient Matters), and a second was called the *Nihonji* (Chronicles of Japan). The *Kojiki* and the *Nihonji* are the "bibles" of Japan. They record the earliest history of the Japanese people. The main subject is the sun goddess and her descendants, the rulers of Yamoto. It said that the emperors were of divine origin (born of gods) and were superior to all other chiefs. No one since has challenged the right of the imperial family to "rule" Japan, if only as puppets.

As we have noted, the Great Reforms never were fully carried out. Among those ideas that were never put into effect was that of national military service. There was to be no national army ruled by the emperor. This fact created many problems for the emperors of Japan up until the Restoration in 1867.

Law and order and the defense of the kingdom was left to the large landowners. Supporters of these powerful landowners called themselves "Samurai." The word *Samurai* can be roughly translated as "those who serve." This original meaning, it seems, had little to do with warfare and the military. However, the definition changes a great deal through Japanese history. The Samurai as a living institution and as a group died out in the 19th century. However, it is impossible to understand Japanese society and culture today without understanding the Samurai and their values.

The Japanese still continue the Samurai ideal of personal loyalty and responsibility to an employer. This is found in Japanese industry and trade today. The paternal feeling that managers and owners of the great Japanese industries have toward their workers is based on the relationship of the great landlords to their Samurai followers. In recent years the Japanese have enthusiastically responded to television serials, movies and comic books telling of the heroic and swashbuckling exploits of the Samurai.

Kamakura Shogunate

Minamoto Yoritomo established a military government at Kamakura, which ruled most of Japan. He took for himself the title of Shogun (general, or leader), with the privilege of giving it to his sons. The Emperors of Japan, without control of the army, became helpless puppets. Japan was to be ruled under a Bakufu, or Shogunate, until 1868.

During the Kamakura period (1192-1333), feudalism, which existed in Europe also, spread through the land. Feudalism is a system of landholding and service to a lord. Allies of the Shogun, the highest lord, were appointed police officers, tax collectors, and commanders of the army, and were given grants of land. In return, they performed military service for the government.

In the 13th century the feudal Samurai met a real test. Japan was invaded twice by the undefeated and seemingly unbeatable Mongols, who had already conquered China. But these wild horsemen from Central Asia suffered defeat at the hands of the Samurai. Skilled with bow and sword, the Samurai were a match for the Mongols, and typhoons struck the invading fleet, crushing Mongol hopes of conquest. The Japanese called these winds *Kamikaze,* or "winds of the gods."

However, the battles with the Mongols weakened the government to such a great extent that a revolt led by a new military leader of the Ashikaga overthrew the Kamakuras.

Ashikaga Shogunate and Civil War in Japan

During the following two and a half centuries (1338-1567) feudalism was steadily extended in Japan. Since the Ashikaga Shoguns were unable to control the powerful military lords (daimyo), warfare was almost continuous. The fighting reached its climax in the 16th century. The achievements of three great military leaders, Nobunaga, Hideyoshi and Ieyasu, brought unity and peace to Japan.

Nabunaga is remembered for his ending of the Ashikaga Shogunate. Hideyoshi established a united Japan, and a single ruler dominated the entire country. However, it was Ieyasu, of the house of Tokugawa, who gained the richest rewards. He founded the third and last military Shogunate in Japan.

Tokugawa Shogunate

In order to establish himself as Shogun, Ieyasu was forced to fight and, at the battle of Sekigahara, near Kyoto, he won a great victory. This battle marked the end of the feudal warfare that had been part of Japanese life for several hundred years. Two hundred and fifty years of peace were to follow (1603-1868). The daimyo

A Japanese cheerleader at the National Intercity Baseball Championships at Tokyo's Korakuen Stadium. Colorful cheerleading teams accompany amateur baseball teams to the competitions. Credit: United Press International

夕刊 讀賣新聞

THE YOMIURI SHIMBUN
EVENING EDITION (旧甲) 第36673号

読売新聞社

9月6日 水曜日

平仮名でしゃべる

桃井 かおり

〈779〉

自衛隊憲法明記を

中曾根氏が改憲具体案

カーフェリー衝突

愛媛沖 船腹に大穴、浸水

244人脱出後に転覆

浅瀬で転覆したカーフェリー「さいとばる」 ——本社ヘリからけさ8時15分

衝突状況図

台風15号で航路変更

5日、ワシントンでストラウス米通商交渉特別代表（右）と握手する中川農相。後方（左）は牛場対米経済担当相（AP）

オレンジ、牛肉輸入漸増案

米が強い不満表明

農産品交渉

A Japanese newspaper. Credit: Consulate General of Japan

were controlled, and a new system of centralized feudalism was set up. In order to protect themselves, the Tokugawas introduced a policy of national isolation. This policy, which lasted for two hundred years, kept out foreign interference, but at the cost of almost all cultural and commercial contacts with foreign nations. New ideas were considered a threat to the established order.

Japanese society was frozen into four classes: Samurai, peasant, artisan, merchant. The responsibilities of members of each class were fixed by law. Despite the Tokugawa policy of preventing change, change did come. As a result of peace, trade within Japan grew. Towns became important and many cities arose. The city merchant grew rich from trading, and from lending money to the feudal Samurai. As the years passed, the position of the Samurai worsened. With no wars to fight, there was no booty to win.

In the 19th century the Tokugawa Shogunate began to crack. The unhappy Samurai began to plot against the Shogun. The Bakufu was criticized and blamed for the nation's problems. At the same time, foreign pressure to change the policy of isolation was intensified. In 1854, Commodore Matthew C. Perry of the United States forced the Shogun to sign a trade treaty. Treaties with other nations followed. Isolation was ended, and the weaknesses of the Tokugawas became obvious. Enemies of the Shogunate united under the slogan "Revere the Emperor; expel the barbarians," and struck for power. In 1868 the last military Shogunate came to an end, and the age of modern Japan began.

Japan Enters the Modern World

Meiji Restoration

As criticism of the Shogunate grew, Japanese began to question the whole idea of the rule of the Shogun. Japanese historians became aware that the imperial family, living in Edo (Tokyo), had once led Japan. The idea of an imperial restoration (bringing the emperor back into power) grew. On November 9, 1867, following the death of the Shogun, the young Emperor Mutsuhito Meiji (Meiji, meaning enlightened rule) was given full authority to rule Japan. On January 3, 1868, the Emperor abolished the Shogunate.

The new Meiji regime was led by a small group of young ex-Samurai and merchant-bankers. The old power group of Shogun and supporters was replaced with a new group of influential men with military and financial power, who chose to use the Emperor as a symbol of their authority. For the average Japanese it really did not make any immediate difference that the Emperor had replaced the Shogun. The real difference was in how the new leaders chose to direct the nation. The direction they picked happened to have a deep influence on Japan's future.

The Program of the Meiji

The new leaders wished to set up a modern, centralized state. To guide their policies, they looked to the great powers of the West. First, opposition within Japan was ended. A rebellion led by the Satsuma clan was ruthlessly put down. Rebellions would no longer trouble the Japanese. Next, the government set up a commission to draw up a constitution, which was issued as a gift in 1889. The new constitution borrowed much from the Prussian (German) Constitution. The state was greatly strengthened. Great power was given to the Emperor, whose position was justified under the Shinto religion and legends. A *bicameral* (two house) legislature, called the Diet, was set up with limited power. A prime minister and his cabinet were to be picked by the Emperor and, in theory, were responsible *only* to the Emperor. Actual power was concentrated in the hands of the Emperor's advisors. The constitution proclaimed the rights of the people, but with a major restriction: the interests of the state came first. The ministers of the army and navy were most powerful. The army and navy could destroy a cabinet they opposed by resigning from it or by refusing to serve in it. This power had tragic consequences for the Japanese people. It encouraged the growth of *militarism,* which plunged Japan into the fateful war with the United States.

Industrialization

Industrialization was viewed by the Meiji leaders as the key to modernization. With state support, tremendous energy and will, many economic innovations were introduced. Textile production became the chief industry. The government needed capital, but refused to borrow from foreign nations because Japan wanted to give no foreign power the slightest reason for getting involved in Japanese affairs. The land and tax system was changed to meet the needs of industry. The peasants were given legal possession of the land. Taxes were placed on the land based upon its value. Often unable to pay their taxes, farmers were forced to borrow money at high interest rates, or to sell their land. Once they lost the land, they became tenant farmers, renting the land they farmed. Rents were high and conditions were difficult, but tenant farming continued. By using cheap labor, and instilling national pride in the workers, the Japanese made slow but steady progress and, within a generation, Japan had succeeded in laying down the basis for a completely modern industrial system.

Nationalism and Imperialism Grow

Japan's desire to modernize was matched by a desire to keep its independence. A cautious policy was followed toward foreign nations, to further Japan's security. The Japanese were successful in removing the "unequal treaties" with Western nations which gave those nations special privileges in Japan. Nationalism was stirred, and the greatness and "divine mission" of the Japanese was proclaimed.

After cleaning their own house, the Japanese began to look outward. Korea, the peninsula that pointed like a knife at Japan's heart, was Japan's chief concern. In 1894, with the idea of gaining control of Korea, Japan attacked China. Within three months the Japanese had completely defeated the Chinese. This quick defeat disturbed Russia, France and Germany, who also wanted parts of China. The Europeans forced a peace on the two Asian nations. Japan was forced to give up its dream of controlling Korea. Russia now moved into the area; thus, Japan had a score to settle with Russia. In 1902 Japan signed a military alliance with Great Britain. This treaty assured Japan that France would not join Russia if the latter went to war with Japan.

The war between Japan and Russia came in 1904, and was a strain on both countries. The Japanese attacked the Russian fleet by surprise in Port Arthur, and badly damaged it. A second fleet was destroyed by the Japanese at the Tsushima Straits. On land, the Russians were driven out of Korea, and the Japanese captured Port Arthur and Mukden in Manchuria. Theodore Roosevelt, the President of the United States, brought the two sides together. Russia gave up some land to Japan, and left Korea to the Japanese. In 1910 Japan solved its Korean problem by *annexing* (adding) Korea to Japan.

Japan Becomes a Great Power

Japan's rise to a place among the great powers was speeded up during World War I (1914-1918). The Japanese declared war on Germany, and took over Germany's interests in China and the Pacific. The war also gave Japan the chance to build up its industry and trade. As a result of the war, Japan became the foremost power in Asia, and one of the five great powers in the world.

During the 1920s Japan went through a period of political, social and economic unrest. Government reforms were introduced. In 1925 all men were given the right to vote. New political parties, often of a radical nature, were founded, and factory workers and peasants were allowed to organize into unions. The conservatives, nevertheless, managed to remain in power.

In international affairs Japan tried to adjust to her new position and to the changing world. Siberia became a target for her ambitions. Worried about Japan's rising naval strength, the Western powers called together all the naval powers to meet in Washington. The purpose of the Washington Conference was to limit the number of warships. This and other issues led to tense relations between Japan and the West.

War with China

In the early 1930s angry military leaders and nationalist super-patriots decided to act. They blamed the government for the country's economic and social problems. They proposed that territorial expansion at China's expense would solve Japan's problems. Manchuria, a rich and sparsely settled area, interested them greatly. With fertile lands and rich deposits of coal and iron, the area would be of great value to the overpopulated and impoverished Japan. These officers provoked an incident at Mukden, and war began with China. Manchuria was quickly overrun and taken into the Japanese Empire. Within Japan, the opponents of expansionism and militarism were terrorized and assassinated.

In 1937 Japan went to war with China in an effort to assert its dominance in Asia. Inside Japan, the government moved toward stricter controls of all aspects of life. The war in China, and expansion into Indo-China led to trouble with the United States. The key to Japanese dreams was the rich area of Southeast Asia. The area had an abundant supply of raw materials, especially oil and rubber, and its conquest promised to solve many of Japan's economic and military problems. No great resistance was expected, since France, Great Britain and the Netherlands were deeply involved in war in Europe. Only the United States had the power to block Japan's plans.

War with the United States

On December 7, 1941, the Japanese launched a surprise attack on American bases in the Pacific. The Japanese had taken the supreme gamble. They were to lose.

The Japanese battle plan had been to strike lightning blows at the Europeans in the Pacific, i.e., to overrun Malaya, the Philippines, Burma and the Netherlands East Indies, and then offer peace. Victorious, at first, the Japanese soon found themselves in trouble. The United States rapidly recovered from early defeats and losses. What the Japanese feared most was a long war, and this was what they got. The Japanese navy suffered its first defeat at Midway. The Americans went on the offensive, and slowly moved closer to Japan itself. Its armed forces defeated in the Pacific, the home islands, blockaded and under attack, Japan prepared for an all-out defense of its homeland. On August 6 and August 9, 1945, the first atomic bombs were dropped on Hiroshima and Nagasaki. The Japanese government was now faced with a horrible fate and, on August 15, 1945, the Emperor announced over the radio that he had decided to surrender.

Japan, for the first time in its history, had been completely defeated, and faced occupation by a foreign army.

Japan After World War II

Occupation by the United States

Japan was defeated in the Second World War. The American army occupied Japan from 1945 to 1952. The Japanese government was put under the control of General Douglas MacArthur and the American army. As punishment for starting the war and invading various areas, Japan lost its empire and was forbidden to have an army or navy. The occupation government encouraged changes in all phases of Japanese life.

Reform in Government

The core of United States reforms in postwar Japan was a new Constitution to replace the old "gift" of 1889. The new Constitution went into force in May, 1947. It is one of the most democratic bodies of law in the world today.

For the first time, full political power was placed in the hands of the Japanese people. Emperor Hirohito still reigns, but he has little power. He announced to the people on January 1, 1946, that he was a mortal human being like themselves, and not godlike. All citizens over twenty, both men and women, may vote, and women may serve in the government. The top political body is the two-chamber National Diet. The House of Councilors serves for six years, and the lower, more powerful House of Representatives is elected for four years. The Prime Minister is usually the leader of the strongest party in the Diet. He appoints a cabinet to help him govern. If he is defeated on a bill, or if the Diet votes "no confidence" in the government's policy, the House of Representatives may be dissolved and a new election called.

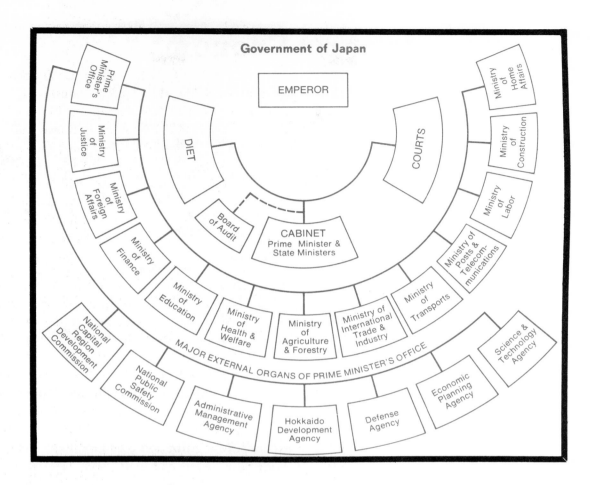

Government of Japan

EMPEROR

DIET

COURTS

CABINET
Prime Minister &
State Ministers

Board of Audit

Prime Minister's Office

Ministry of Justice

Ministry of Foreign Affairs

Ministry of Finance

Ministry of Education

Ministry of Health & Welfare

Ministry of Agriculture & Forestry

Ministry of International Trade & Industry

Ministry of Transports

Ministry of Posts & Telecommunications

Ministry of Labor

Ministry of Construction

Ministry of Home Affairs

MAJOR EXTERNAL ORGANS OF PRIME MINISTER'S OFFICE

National Capital Region Development Commission

National Public Safety Commission

Administrative Management Agency

Hokkaido Development Agency

Defense Agency

Economic Planning Agency

Science & Technology Agency

The Prime Minister and all his cabinet members must be civilians. Military officers may not hold cabinet posts. The Constitution prohibits Japan from waging aggressive war again. The Constitution also guarantees a long list of basic rights. Many of these are like the Bill of Rights of the United States Constitution.

The economic gains made by Japan since 1945 have been outstanding. The old industrial system of a few great industrialists has been changed as many new groups have been allowed to open businesses. Today Japan ranks among the three greatest manufacturing and trading nations in the world. Improved economic conditions have caused changes in traditional behavior. In general, the welfare of all the people has been greatly improved.

Japan has remained a democracy since the end of occupation in 1952. Several major political parties have competed for leadership, but the conservatives usually have managed to keep power.

For many years Japan did not wish to play a leading role in world affairs. The government was satisfied to improve economic conditions. For its national defense, Japan had the United States to defend it, and followed the American lead in international affairs. However, since the late sixties, the Japanese have decided to go it their own way. The Japanese people are split on what course to follow, but Japan is again playing the role of an important power in the world.

Japan's Economy

The Road to Economic Modernization

When Japan entered the modern world after the Meiji Restoration in 1868, it was recognized by the Japanese leaders that industrialization was the key to the future. Japan became a beehive of activity. However, the leaders of Japan saw many existing problems. The lack of trained technicians was critical. The government, therefore, set up technical schools and began the teaching of modern science. Promising students were also sent to Europe and the United States for higher education and special training. The government used foreign engineers as teachers and advisors in the new schools and factories.

Another problem, at the beginning, was a lack of capital. Private capital was in short supply, and the little that existed was invested in banking and domestic trade. The government itself showed the way by building and operating small factories. These factories produced military supplies, iron, textiles, cement and glass products. The government also set up the first railroad and telegraph, and built a merchant marine.

With this as a basis, and a continued favorable attitude on the part of the government toward industry, private businessmen began to invest and build. This was the beginning of the huge firms of Mitsui and Mitsubishi, which still exist today.

Except for the war years (1914-1919), Japan had an unfavorable balance of trade (more imports than exports). Modernization could not be achieved without a great expansion of foreign trade. But Japan had little to export, except for silk. Silk was in great demand in the West, and ranked for years at the top of Japan's export list. However, neither silk nor cotton textiles could earn enough to pay for Japan's growing import list. Japan's resources were never sufficient to meet the needs of a great industrial power, and Japan was forced to depend on foreign sources for raw materials. Its chief minerals are coal, gold, copper and sulfur. To keep its factories going, Japan must import oil, cotton, rubber, iron ore and a host of other materials.

The Economy at the End of the War

When Japan surrendered in 1945, its economic situation was desperate. Not only had Japan lost its Asian colonies and, therefore, its main sources of raw materials, but a quarter of its national wealth had been destroyed by the war. Yokohama and Tokyo, making up one of the most important economic complexes in the world, were in ruins. Close to two million Japanese had been killed, and ten million were homeless.

The Americans poured food, raw materials, industrial equipment and technical know-how into Japan, and the Japanese began to rebuild. By 1955 Japan was able to export more than it imported, leaving money for expansion of the economy.

Sensational Economic Growth

Since then, Japan's economic growth has been outstanding. Coal, iron and steel production zoomed to new highs. Machine tools, locomotives and automobiles

A village in Japan—Millions of Japanese live in villages such as this one. Note the
thatched roofs made of straw. (*Top*)
Credit: *Japan National Tourist Organization*

Japan old and new. A modern Western-style hotel and an ancient guardhouse for the
Imperial Palace moat meet together and fuse in a unique harmony in Tokyo. (*Bottom*)
Credit: *Consulate General of Japan, N.Y.*

streamed off brand new assembly lines. The Japanese created the second largest electronics industry in the world. Today the Japanese are the leading manufacturers of radios, transistors, television sets and computers, as well as optical goods such as cameras, microscopes.

Japan Must Import to Live

Wool	100%	Wheat	91.7%
Cotton	100%	Sugar	86%
Crude Oil	99.7%	Coal	65%
Iron Ore	99.3%	Lumber	47%
Soy Beans	96.4%		

Mining and Manufacturing Production in Japan (1938-1965)

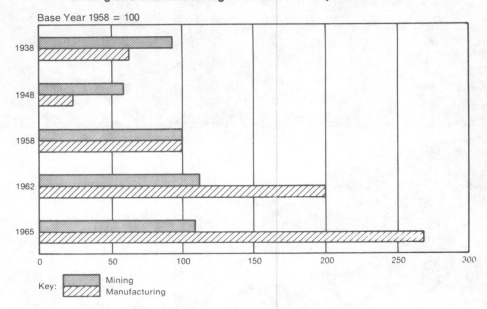

Myths About Japan's Economic Growth

A number of myths have grown up about Japanese industrial growth in the past 20 years. One common myth is that the growth is based mainly on the use of "cheap labor." It is not. Many parts of Asia have lower labor costs as well as more raw materials. These nations have not achieved what the Japanese have. To be sure, Japan's labor rates are generally lower than those in many Western countries, but in steel and machine production, direct labor rates are at European levels.

Another myth has it that Japanese growth is the result of exports. In fact, the success of Japanese companies in the export market grows out of high demand at home. In manufactures, from umbrella frames to motorcycles, the first growth took place to supply a growing home market with the export growth following 3 to 5 years later.

A third myth is the view that the Japanese were copiers who were unable to produce original products or technology. But every country has, in the opening stages of industrialization, begun by copying. Japan did its copying in the 1930s, and today, the Japanese invest as much in research and development as Germany does and more than Great Britain, France and Italy do.

A fourth myth is that this growth is just temporary and caused by good luck. The fact is that the rate of Japanese economic growth has been quite steady since the beginnings of industrialization in the late 19th century.

Reasons for Economic Growth

Instead of relying on myths to explain this growth let us look at some possible reasons. Three key factors in the Japanese system help us to understand the growth: unusual methods of raising capital, a *unique* (one of a kind) relation of government and business, and a special way of using labor.

To the Western business man the whole Japanese business structure seems to float on a sea of *IOUs* (loans). Most Japanese business depends on making loans from banks instead of raising capital by selling stocks and bonds. The banks which make the loans depend on the Bank of Japan (owned by the Japanese government) for their credit. In fact, the Japanese government is a watchful and skillful partner in everybody's business.

The Japanese factory worker, technician, clerk or manager is employed for life or at least as long as the company survives. The money he earns is set *not* by his job or how well he works *but* by his age, education and length of service. The workers identify themselves with their company and its interests. Since pay is related to age, a fast growing company or industry keeps labor costs low by hiring directly out of schools. As a result of this the skills level of workers remains high. Since status and salary do not depend on types of jobs or how well the jobs are done, rigid work rules and definition of jobs are almost unknown in Japan. This explains in part why the Japanese have been able to adopt the latest labor saving devices and production methods without the opposition of Japanese labor unions.

Agricultural Recovery

Japan's recovery in agriculture has been almost equally outstanding. The occupation government began a land reform program which was very successful. Land held by great landlords was distributed to all Japanese farmers. Two-and-a-half acre plots were sold to several million farm families at very low prices. Within a few years, almost all farmers owned their own land, many for the first time. The percentage of landless and tenant farmers is now lower in Japan than in almost any country in the world.

Inspired by the land reform and generous government *subsidies* (payment) Japanese farmers have rapidly increased their output. By using modern scientific methods, they have gotten some of the world's highest crop yields per acre, especially of rice. By the 1960s Japan was actually producing more rice than it could use.

Japan has been able to control its population growth to some extent. Realizing that a continuation of the rate of population growth that existed up to 1945 would hamper rather than help recovery, the Japanese government passed laws encouraging family planning. The number of births began to drop. The rate of increase of population fell from over two million during the occupation to less than a million, annually, during the sixties.

Problems That Japan's Economy Faces Today

There are some problems, however. Because of its rapid growth and expansion Japanese industry faces a shortage of skilled workers, and the drop in population growth shows that this shortage may get worse in the future. The delicate Japanese economy can be easily upset. In 1971 the Japanese agreed to set a *quota* (limit) on Japanese textiles that could be sold in America. As a result of lower exports many Japanese workers lost their jobs. Similar quotas could cause further economic upset.

Since World War II ended Japan has operated on a policy of stimulating industrial growth. At the same time the Japanese government has not spent money on public transportation and communications systems, roads, schools and housing. The movement of people from the farms to the city has created greater housing shortages. The average Japanese living in Tokyo lives in 4½ tatami mats of living space (81 sq. ft.), while fewer than half of Tokyo's families have a bathtub, and only 37% are served by sewers. (For all of Japan only 15% of all houses are served by sewers.)

With the third highest economic position in the world, Japan ranks 19th in per capita (per person) income. Little of Japan's wealth seems to have reached down to the average Japanese. For this reason Japanese have for the first time begun to protest their situation. Complaints about pollution and lawsuits against corporations have grown. Indeed communities have become so angered over the ill effects of *Kogai,* as the Japanese call environmental upset, that many industries find it impossible to overcome public resistance to the building of new plants.

The Japanese government recognizes the seriousness of the situation. Former Prime Minister Sato said, "During the 1960s we thought there was no welfare without economic growth. For the 1970s we must say there can be no economic growth without economic welfare."

Sapporo, on the Island of Hokkaido, is the main city on Japan's frontier. Note the
mountains. Hokkaido has very cold winters. Snow and ice sculptures are part of the
annual snow festival.
Credit: *Consulate General of Japan, N.Y.*

Kakuei Tanaka, who became prime minister in late 1972, made an attempt to direct Japan's energy toward problems at home. Tanaka suggested that $2 billion be spent on Japanese roads, railroads, communications and on social services. Included in Tanaka's goals were a national pension system, a five-day work week and an attempt to move people and industry from the crowded Pacific seaboard to the inland areas. These plans attempted to stimulate the *domestic* (home) economy while taking money from the promotion of exports. In addition, the plans aimed to improve the quality of life by limiting pollution and overcrowding.

But events in 1973 upset all of these plans. Inflation became a very serious problem. Prices went up. The Japanese were forced to devalue the yen (make the yen worth less). The energy crisis hit Japan very hard. Japan must import all of its oil. Most of it comes from the Middle East. The Arab nations prevented normal shipments of oil to Japan. This created shortages of oil for Japanese industry. There were also shortages of other vital raw materials such as iron ore and lumber. The result of these shortages was a fall in production and an increase in unemployment. The government had to forget its plans to redistribute population and industry throughout Japan.

Prime Minister Tanaka was forced to resign from office in early 1976. This was caused by a scandal. Many Japanese government officials, including Tanaka himself, had received money from the American company Lockheed Aircraft. The purpose of the "money gift" was to encourage the Japanese government to buy Lockheed planes for the Japanese Air Force and Japan Air Lines.

Tanaka was replaced by his deputy, Takeo Fukuda. The problems faced by Fukuda remained the same. The attempts to solve these problems were eased by greater Japanese exports and productivity. In addition, Japan found new fuel sources in China, while also improving its relations with the Arabs. The Japanese have also requested the help of the United States. They would like the United States to sell them the *technology* (know-how) for building a nuclear reprocessing plant. This plant would produce atomic power, thus lessening Japan's need for foreign oil.

The "miracle of Japanese production" seems to have slowed down—at least for the present—but the Japanese have the capacity and ability to extend it for a long time to come.

Japan's Place in the World Today

During the years of the occupation Japan had little to do with the outside world. Most Japanese were involved with the problems of daily survival. Japan's foreign affairs were the responsibility of the occupation government.

Japanese-American Relations

After the occupation Japan made a new start in the international community. In 1956 Japan joined the United Nations. The Japanese re-established diplomatic relations with most governments of the world. Fearing the threat of Chinese Communism, Japan remained dependent on the United States and its military strength for its security. In 1952 a United States-Japan Mutual Security Pact was signed, which gave the United States the major responsibility for defending Japan against aggression. From the beginning, many Japanese opposed this pact, but it is still in effect. Another sore spot between the United States and Japan was the continued occupation of Okinawa and the Bonin Islands by Americans. The Japanese felt that these islands were always a part of Japan, and saw no reason why they should be deprived of lands that were not acquired through imperialist expansion. In 1968 the United States returned the Bonins. In June, 1971 the U.S. promised to return Okinawa as quickly as possible to Japan and in May, 1972 the promise was kept. For the most part, the Japanese have followed a pro-American policy, while still holding on to independence of action.

American efforts to improve relations with the People's Republic of China have caused some uneasiness in Japan. The Japanese fear that a more friendly American policy with China will be at the expense of Japan. The Japanese have decided to protect their interests by following a more independent policy in relation to China and the Soviet Union. In addition, the Japanese have increased their defense budget so that their Self-Defense Forces would be more able to protect an independent policy.

In the summer of 1973 President Nixon and Prime Minister Tanaka met and agreed to continue the friendly cooperation that had existed. The U.S. agreed to support Japan's effort to become a permanent member of the Security Council of the United Nations. This would give Japan the veto power and make her the equal of the U.S., the USSR, France, China and Great Britain. The United States and Japan also agreed to build a uranium-enrichment plant in the U.S. that would give Japan a fuel supply for its new nuclear power plants.

Relations with the United States have remained good; however, some dark clouds have formed. The United States is worried about its trade deficit with Japan (over $5 billion in 1976) and feels that American products are kept out of Japan by government restrictions. The United States would like the Japanese to lower exports to the United States on a voluntary basis. In addition, the United States does not want the Japanese to "dump" goods (sell them below cost) in the United States (these goods include autos, color television sets and electrical products).

On the other hand, the fall of Vietnam has caused the Japanese to worry about American plans for Korea. At present, United States troops are stationed in South Korea. Large amounts of economic and military aid are also being sent to South Korea from the United States. The Japanese wonder if this will continue, because President Carter has said that United States troops will be out of Korea in the next few years. Since Korea "is a dagger pointing at Japan," the concern of the Japanese is very real. The Japanese look to the United States to help maintain the *stability* (balance) in the eastern part of Asia by remaining strong in that area.

Japanese Relations with the Soviet Union

Relations between Russia and Japan have been steadily improving. This has been caused, in part, by the split between China and the Soviet Union. Hoping to win Japan to its side, Russia began in the sixties to give Japan a larger share of its trade. Early in 1972 Soviet Foreign Minister Andrei Gromyko was invited to visit Japan. At that time the two governments announced plans to begin negotiations on a treaty formally ending the state of war that has existed between the two nations since 1945. There was also a hint that negotiations were in the works on the territorial dispute over the Russian-held Kurile Islands. In addition, economic discussions were held in Tokyo about further increases in trade between the two countries and a project to build a $2.5 billion Russo-Japanese Pipeline that would connect a vast Siberian oil field at Tyuman with the Soviet port of Nakhodka, more than 4000 miles away on the Sea of Japan.

In October 1973, Prime Minister Tanaka went to Moscow to continue discussions with the Russians over the five small islands north of Hokkaido still controlled by the Russians. These islands are very important to the Japanese fishing fleet. The Russians have controlled the islands since the end of World War II. The Japanese offered cash and technical aid to the Russians to help develop Siberian resources. The Russians would like this help but would also like greater cooperation between themselves and the Japanese toward the People's Republic of China. Japan is not ready at this time to move closer to the Russians.

By 1974, the Russians and the Japanese had six major development projects under study or negotiations. These projects involve crude oil development in Tyumen, Siberia; natural gas production in Yakutsk, Siberia; oil and natural gas development in Sakhalin; coking coal development programs south of Yakutsk; forestry development in the Soviet Far East Region; and paper and pulp production in Siberia. Here too, relations between the two nations are far from perfect. The Russians still resist returning Japanese islands which they control; and there are still disputes over fishing areas.

In February 1978, the Russians offered the Japanese a peace treaty and a good neighbor *pact* (agreement). Japan refused to sign the treaty and the pact because the Russians still refuse to return the small group of islands at the southern end of the Kurile island chain, just north of Hokkaido. In the pact the Soviets offered to settle all disputes by peaceful means. In addition, the pact stated that neither the Soviet Union nor Japan would allow the use of their territories "for any actions that could *prejudice* (affect badly) the security of the other." (This provision could apply to U.S. bases in Japan.)

The islands in dispute are the Haboman Islands—Shikoto, Kunashiro and Etoroforu. The Soviet Union says they are part of the Kurile Islands, which the Russians took from Japan at the end of World War II in 1945. The Japanese say the islands are not part of the Kuriles and that these islands are closely linked to Japan by history and by customs and traditions.

Japanese Relations with China

Japan's most pressing and difficult decisions in the seventies are related to relations with China. Japan has been suspicious and fearful of its powerful neighbor on the Asian mainland. When the Communists came into power in China in 1949, the Japanese were interested in keeping their friendship and establishing profitable trade relations. However, Communist policies and actions worried the Japanese.

When the Chinese exploded their first atomic bomb in 1954, the Japanese were thoroughly frightened. Many Japanese believed that Japan's safety could be maintained by merely proclaiming and believing in peace, but with China setting off

486 Japan

more nuclear devices yearly, the issues of national defense and Chinese-Japanese relations have become more vital to the Japanese.

In November 1971, the Japanese made direct appeals for discussions on trade to Chou En-lai, the Chinese Premier. These appeals were ignored by Chou. However, by improving relations with her neighbors, the Japanese succeeded in changing Chou's mind. In October 1972, Prime Minister Tanaka paid a visit to China. It was an historic meeting that ended almost a century of hostility between Asia's two great powers. An agreement was signed to end the "state of war" between the two countries and set up diplomatic relations immediately. Japan's trade with China, which had begun to grow in the sixties, was expected to grow to over a billion dollars as a result of better relations. The Japanese cut their official relations with the Nationalist Chinese on Taiwan, as a friendly act to the People's Republic of China. (However, the Japanese still hope to keep their trade and business ties with the Nationalists.)

In 1974, Japan and China made an agreement on civil aviation. For the first time in over 40 years scheduled air service between China and Japan now operates. Despite some improvement in relations, the Japanese were very concerned and unhappy over Chinese nuclear testing and have made strong protests to the Chinese in Peking.

In 1978, Japan and China signed a peace treaty ending more than 30 years of unfriendly relations. Along with the peace treaty, the Chinese and Japanese signed a long-term trade agreement. The Chinese will export oil and other raw materials to China.

Japan's Relations with Her Other Asian Neighbors

One of Japan's dreams in the sixties was to play an important economic role in Southeast Asia. Japan has tried to heal the wounds left by invading Japanese armies during World War II, by providing financial and technical aid for the countries of Southeast Asia. (Philippines, Indonesia). The Vietnam War presented a serious problem to the Japanese. They decided to support the American position. However, in March 1972, the Japanese sent an official trade delegation to Hanoi, North Vietnam. This was the first formal contact ever between the two governments. Relations with Thailand and Burma have been limited to relatively minor trade agreements.

As to Japan's other Asian neighbors, we must note a change taking place. The change seems to indicate a new independence of action and a weakening of U.S. influence on Japanese policy. We have already told of the Japanese meeting with the North Vietnamese while the Vietnam War was still in progress. At about the same time (March, 1972) the Japanese Government recognized the new nation of Bangla Desh—a country the U.S. had not recognized at that time.

Relations with both North and South Korea, have shown improvement. In 1965 Japan and South Korea signed a group of treaties which set up formal diplomatic relations between the two nations. Japan agreed to give long term economic aid to South Korea, and trade relations between the two nations have increased. The Japanese have made efforts to improve relations with North Korea. There have been some unofficial discussions, and plans for a trade agreement appear to be nearing completion.

The Japanese have made large investments in most Southeast Asian nations, especially Thailand and Indonesia. In Indonesia alone the Japanese plan to build a $700 million gas project on Kalimantan and Sumatra and a $500 million hydro-electric power and aluminum smelter development in Asahan. Despite these moves there is still great anti-Japanese feeling in the area. In late 1973 there were student riots in both Indonesia and Thailand directed against the Japanese. The people of Southeast Asia have still not forgotten the Japanese role in World War II and are afraid that Japan will try to gain control of their country through their business investments.

In 1976 the Chinese began to export oil to Japan. The Japanese in return increased their export of industrial machinery to China. Relations between the two nations have been improving steadily. Both have common goals in foreign policy and economics. As long as these aims are similar, relations remain good.

Japan in the Seventies

In the sixties, former Prime Minister Sato spoke for many of his countrymen when he announced that Japan wished to have an influence in world affairs equal to its economic power. In the seventies this may become a reality. The Japanese are fully aware of their power and just as aware of its responsibilities. We have seen that the Japanese are developing a more independent foreign policy. They are trying to improve relations with all their neighbors. Japan's great trade has had an important *impact* (effect) on countries all over the world. The Japanese realize they must set limits on export trade or lose the friendship of the U.S. and the countries of Western Europe. They are making attempts to limit exports by turning their attention to improving life at home. The policies of democratic Japan today stand in sharp contrast to those of the Japanese Empire of the thirties and forties.

The face of Jimmy Carter appears on a television program in Japan. *(Top) Credit: United Press International*

Four young women celebrate the summer festival which Japanese legend says brings about a rich crop and good health. *(Bottom) Credit: United Press International*

Tokyo's subway system offers excellent service as a way to get around the city. *(Top)*
Credit: Werner Stoy/Camera Hawaii

A Japanese shopping arcade. *(Bottom) Credit: P. McCutcheon*

490 Japan

Summary of Key Ideas

A. **Geographic factors have greatly influenced Japan's history and development.**

   1. Japan is part of a chain of volcanic islands which make up the "Fire rim of the Pacific."

   2. The islands are mountainous; only one-sixth of the land is usable for agriculture.

   3. There are many rivers, but all are short and not really navigable.

   4. Japan has a long, irregular coastline with many good harbors.

   5. Japan is lacking in all basic industrial raw materials except water power.

B. **Continuity and change are characteristics of Japan's political history.**

   1. Early Japan was greatly influenced by Chinese civilization.

   2. For 1000 years before 1868 Japan lived in an age of feudalism under the rule of a Shogunate and a Samurai Code.

   3. Japan entered the modern world with the Meiji Restoration.

   4. Rapid modernization and industrialization have been accompanied by social and cultural changes.

   5. Strong nationalism, rapid industrial expansion, and the need for raw materials led to a militaristic foreign policy and wars.

C. **The Japanese have adopted basic political ways of the West.**

   1. The first Japanese Constitution of 1889 gave great power to the Emperor and his advisors.

   2. The Japanese adopted many customs of representative government but power remained in the hands of a small group of military and nationalist leaders until 1945.

   3. The 1947 Constitution set up a democratic limited monarchy. The Emperor is "a symbol of the state and the unity of the people."

   4. A basic part of Japan's foreign policy is to participate actively in the U.N. and keep friendly relations with the great powers.

D. Major changes have taken place in Japanese society and culture since 1945.

   1. The Japanese are racially and ethnically united. (Exception: The Ainu are Caucasian)

   2. The major religions are Shintoism and Buddhism.

   3. The old family system has been greatly weakened.

   4. The farmer's new position as a landowner has given him more status.

   5. Japan has the highest rate of literacy and the most highly developed educational system in Asia.

   6. Japan has a long rich heritage of artistic creation and appreciation for beauty.

E. Japan has become a modern industrial nation despite its lack of natural resources.

   1. The main problem of Japan's economy is the lack of basic raw materials.

   2. An important asset is the development of Japan's labor force. They include skilled labor, scientists, managers and technicians.

   3. After the Second World War Japan made a spectacular recovery.

   4. Compared with the rest of Asia, Japanese agriculture has a large percentage of owner-farmers.

   5. Japan is the leading fishing nation in the world.

   6. The United States has become Japan's most important trading partner.

UNIT VIII

Exercises and Questions

Vocabulary

Directions: Match the words in Column *A* with the correct meaning in Column *B*.

Column A	*Column B*
1. Chanoyu	(a) Japanese art of flower arrangement
2. Matcha	(b) Japanese puppet plays
3. Ikebana	(c) Japanese form of poetry
4. Nō	(d) one part of the official written history of Japan
5. Bunraku	(e) Japanese tea ceremony
6. Nihon	(f) famous collection of Japanese poetry
7. Haiku	(g) storms which affect Japan
8. Manyoshu	(h) Japanese name for Japan
9. Kojiki	(i) a form of Japanese drama
10. typhoons	(j) powdered green tea.

Column A	*Column B*
1. Chickamatsu	(a) first Emperor of Japan
2. Basho	(b) established a united Japan in the 16th century
3. Lady Murasaki	(c) an American sailor who opened Japan to Western trade
4. Jimmu Tenno	(d) a famous playwright of Bunraku and Kabuki
5. Hideyoshi	(e) first Japanese Emperor not looked on as a god
6. Ieyasu	(f) Emperor who ended the Shogunate and led Japan into the modern world

7. Matthew Perry

8. Mutsuhito Meiji

9. Douglas MacArthur

10. Hirohito

(g) author of *The Tales of Genji*

(h) American military commander of Japan after World War II

(i) Shogun who ended the feudal war and established 250 years of peace

(j) a great Haiku poet of Japan

Population Pyramid

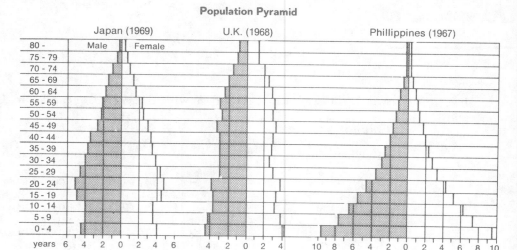

POPULATION OF JAPAN BY AGE AND SEX (Census of 1975)

(in thousands)

Age	Total	Male	Female	Age	Total	Male	Female
All ages	111,933	55,115	56,819	40-44	8,210	4,125	4,085
1	1,906	973	933	45-49	7,354	3,658	3,696
1-4	8,059	4,121	3,937	50-54	5,807	2,635	3,172
5-9	8,956	4,587	4,368	55-59	4,647	2,061	2,587
10-14	8,267	4,226	4,041	60-64	4,277	1,922	2,354
15-19	7,904	4,037	3,868	65-69	3,471	1,577	1,895
20-24	9,087	4,569	4,518	70-74	2,548	1,138	1,410
25-29	10,870	5,493	5,377	75-79	1,629	688	941
30-34	9,263	4,627	4,636	80-84	810	310	500
35-39	8,422	4,212	4,210	85+	400	124	276

SOURCE: United Nations *Demographic Yearbook*.

Graph Analysis

Directions: Select the statement which best answers the question or completes the sentence. Use only the information given in the graph and chart.

1. The above graph can best be decribed as:
   (a) pictograph   (b) line graph   (c) pie graph   (d) bar graph

2. Most Japanese fall into which of the following age groups?
   (a) 10-19   (b) 20-29   (c) 30-39   (d) 40-49

3. Which of the following conclusions is true?
   (a) The death rate among Japanese below the age of 20 is the greatest of the three countries.

(b) The birth rate in the Philippines is the greatest of the three countries.

(c) Women seem to live longer than men in these three nations.

(d) About 20% of all Japanese are over 70 years of age.

4. Which of the following conclusions is false?

(a) About 35% of all of the people of the Philippines are below the age of 10.

(b) There are more Japanese women than men.

(c) Most Japanese boys were born between 1965 and 1969.

(d) The Japanese seem to have the most even distribution of population.

5. The total population of Japan is about:

(a) 102,648   (b) 50,431   (c) 52,216   (d) 102,648,000

Completion

Directions: Complete the following sentences, using the words listed below:

Ainu	Samurai	Daimyo	Diet	Zen
Shogunate	Feudalism	Kabuki	Kami	Nihonji

1. .... is a system of landholding and service to a lord.

2. .... is a form of drama unique to Japan.

3. .... were the first people who lived in Japan.

4. .... is one of the official history books of early Japan.

5. .... are worshiped as parts of nature which arouse fear, awe or love.

6. .... is the Japanese lawmaking body.

7. .... is a new form of Japanese Buddhism.

8. .... were the warriors of feudal Japan.

9. .... were the military barons of Shogunate Japan.

10. .... was the military government that ruled Japan for over a thousand years.

Multiple Choice

Directions: Select the letter of the correct answer.

1. A nation like Japan, made up of many islands, is called

(a) an inlet   (b) an archipelago   (c) an isthmus   (d) a peninsula

2. Hokkaido is like the American frontier of the 1870s because

(a) only Indians are allowed to live on the island.

(b) it is a dry plain like the American West.

(c) the climate and poor soil do not attract many Japanese.

(d) the Japanese government has built many forts.

3. The most important of the main islands is

(a) Honshu   (b) Kyushu   (c) Shikoku   (d) Hokkaido

4. Which of the following Japanese cities is likely to receive large amounts of snow in winter?

   (a) Tokyo   (b) Yokohama   (c) Hiroshima   (d) Sapporo

5. All of the following statements about Japanese geography are true *except* which?
   - (a) The Japanese islands are part of a great chain of volcanoes.
   - (b) Japan has hundreds of short, swift rivers.
   - (c) Japan has a long, regular coastline and few good harbors.
   - (d) Japan is made up of thousands of islands scattered over a large area.

6. The mountainous topography of Japan
   - (a) prevents large density of population in any areas of Japan
   - (b) leaves little land for the raising of crops
   - (c) causes Japanese to live mainly on the plateaus of Shikoku
   - (d) gives Japan protection from the monsoon winds

7. The sea has been important to Japan for all of the following reasons *except* which?
   - (a) It is a source of food and work for the Japanese.
   - (b) It is the main route of transportation and communication.
   - (c) It has been an effective barrier between Japan and the rest of the world.
   - (d) It prevented the development of a unified Japanese nation until 1900.

8. Japan's climate is affected by all of the following factors *except*:
   - (a) the monsoon winds which blow from the ocean
   - (b) the winter winds from the mainland, which blow onto all of Japan
   - (c) the Japan Current, which moderates the winter climate and warms in summer
   - (d) the differences in latitude between Northern and Southern Japan

9. Which of the following statements is true about the Japanese language?
   - (a) Spoken Japanese is very much like Chinese.
   - (b) Most words in Japanese are made up of only one syllable.
   - (c) The language has served to unite the Japanese.
   - (d) Most words have many syllables, and the stress is very important.

10. The Japanese system of writing
    - (a) was borrowed entirely from the Chinese, and is unchanged today
    - (b) was borrowed from China and the West, and adapted to meet Japan's needs
    - (c) is not used today because most Japanese have learned English
    - (d) was a Japanese creation, with no outside influence important

11. Which of the following statements best describes Japanese life today?
    - (a) The Japanese have become completely modernized, and little is left of traditional life.
    - (b) The Japanese have rejected modernization, and almost all Japanese customs are traditional.
    - (c) The Japanese have blended traditional ways with the new, to meet the needs of modern life.
    - (d) The Japanese have rejected Western ideas, and accept Chinese customs.

12. All of the following are examples of cultural diffusion *except*:
    - (a) the development of the Japanese writing system

(b) the development of the Shinto religion

(c) the national sport of Japan is baseball

(d) the use of desks and chairs in schools

13. All of the following have been important religions of Japan *except*

(a) Shintoism   (b) Buddhism   (c) Islam   (d) Christianity

14. Which of the following religions is entirely based on the worship of nature?

(a) Shintoism   (b) Buddhism   (c) Islam   (d) Christianity

15. All of the following statements are true of the early history of Japan *except* which?

(a) The Yamotos used China as a model for forming a Japanese Kingdom.

(b) For more than a thousand years the Emperor had little or no power.

(c) The Tokugawas began their rule by encouraging contact with the West.

(d) Under the Tokugawas a policy of preventing change was followed.

16. Which of the following events occurred after the other three?

(a) Kamakura Period   (b) Fujiwara Period   (c) Ashikoga Period

(d) Tokugawa Period

17. The slogan, ''Revere the Emperor, expel the Barbarians,'' was directed against

(a) the Tokugawa Shogun and the Chinese

(b) the Emperor and the Westerners

(c) the Chinese and the Westerners

(d) the Tokugawa Shogun and the Westerners

18. The year 1868 is important in Japanese history because

(a) the age of modern Japan began

(b) Matthew Perry opened Japan to the West

(c) the Samurai defeated the Mongols

(d) a policy of national isolation was begun

19. Which of the following events was the result of the other three?

(a) The rebellion of the Satsumo Clan is put down.

(b) The Meiji Emperor abolishes the Shogunate.

(c) Matthew Perry opens Japan to the West.

(d) Japan becomes a modern world power.

20. The Meiji ruler did all of the following to modernize Japan *except*:

(a) put down a rebellion of those who opposed modernization

(b) give the Japanese a new Western style constitution

(c) establish agriculture as the key to modernization

(d) stir the nationalism and proclaim the glory of Japan

21. Japan's attack on China and Russia are examples of

(a) militarism   (b) cultural diffusion   (c) isolation   (d) industrialization

22. Which of the following events happened *before* the other three?

(a) Japanese invasion of Manchuria   (b) World War I

(c) Japanese attack on American bases   (d) Russo-Japanese War

23. Manchuria was important to Japan for all of the following reasons *except* which?

(a) It had fertile soil.   (b) It had rich deposits of coal.   (c) It was a good market because of its large population.   (d) It had rich deposits of iron.

24. The Washington Conference was called because the Western powers
    (a) wished to end the war between China and Japan
    (b) feared the growing naval strength of Japan
    (c) wished the Japanese to leave Manchuria
    (d) wanted Japan to attack Russia in Siberia

25. Which of the following was *not* a problem of Japanese economic development?
    (a) lack of trained technicians   (b) lack of hydroelectric power
    (c) lack of capital   (d) unfavorable balance of trade

26. Which of the following events led to the other three?
    (a) Land reform program gives more land to the Japanese farmers.
    (b) Japan is given a new, more democratic constitution.
    (c) Japan is defeated by the U.S. in the Second World War.
    (d) Japan creates the second largest electronics industry.

27. After World War II ended
    (a) the Emperor was removed from power
    (b) full political power was placed in the hands of the people
    (c) all industry was destroyed and Japan became an agricultural country
    (d) Japan was forced to become a colony of the United States

28. The Japanese
    (a) rejected Western technology and skills
    (b) accepted Western technology and skills
    (c) use only American raw materials
    (d) trade only with the United States

29. Today the Japanese form of government is
    (a) a republic   (b) an absolute monarchy   (c) a constitutional monarchy
    (d) a feudal kingdom

30. (a) The Washington Conference takes place.
    (b) Japan joins the United Nations.
    (c) Americans occupy Japan after the Japanese surrender

    In which order did these event take place?
    (a) abc   (b) bca   (c) cab   (d) acb

31. Which one of the following groups is correctly paired?
    (a) Zen-Satori   (b) Ikebana-Matcha   (c) Nō-Bonsai   (d) Kabuki-Suim-e

32. Which of the following men was an important Japanese painter?
    (a) Chickamatsu   (b) Basho   (c) Suikaku   (d) Hiroshige

33. Which of the following art forms influenced European art?
    (a) Ikebana   (b) Ukiyo-e   (c) Suim-e   (d) Nō

Thought Questions

1. How does the geography of Japan affect the lives of the people?

2. How has the fact that Japan is made up of many islands affected the lives of the Japanese people?

3. (a) Describe the factors that cause the climate of Japan?
   (b) How do these factors affect the lives of the Japanese people?

4. Why might we call Japan "The Land of the Gods"?

5. Why did feudalism grow in Japan?

6. Why were the Samurai important in Japanese history?

7. Nobunaga "harvested the rice"; Hideyoshi "cooked the rice"; Ieyasu "at the rice." Explain this statement.

8. How did the Meiji Restoration affect the Japanese people?

9. a. Why did the Japanese decide to expand their island kingdom?
   b. Describe the steps taken by the Japanese to reach their dream of expansion and control of Asia.

10. "Japan's recovery from defeat has been a miracle." Give examples to support this statement.

11. The Japanese have been called "copiers of ideas" and "borrowers of ideas." Explain which of the two is more accurate.

12. "An asset of the Japanese is their willingness to learn from others." Explain this statement.

13. Why has Japan been able to become a leading industrial nation despite its small area and few natural resources?

14. How has the life of the Japanese people changed since the end of the war?

15. Describe each of the following forms of Japanese art.
    (a) Nō Drama   (b) Kabuki   (c) Haiku   (d) Ikebana

16. Describe Japanese relations with each of the following since 1945:
    (a) United States   (b) Russia   (c) China

Explain why you agree or disagree with the following statements:

17. "Japan still has many economic problems to solve."

18. "The languages of the Chinese and the Japanese are the same, yet they are very different."

19. "Exports are the lifeblood of Japan."

20. "Japan's agricultural system has been through a revolution since 1945."

21. "The literature of early Japan gives us little or no information about life in Japan."

22. "Japanese theatre is unique."

23. "Japanese art and culture have had little affect on the West."

24. Using the rules of Haiku discussed in this unit compose a Haiku verse.

25. How have myths about Japan influenced what we believe about Japan and the Japanese people?

Puzzle

Directions: Place the words below in their proper place in the puzzle.

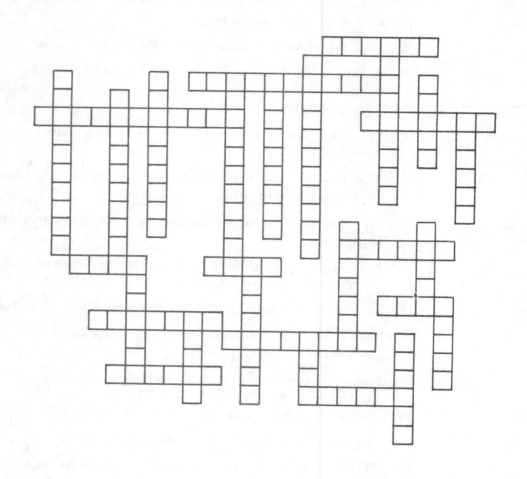

4 LETTERS	**5 LETTERS**	**6 LETTERS**	**7 LETTERS**
AINU	HAIKU	ABACUS	BUNRAKU
DIET	SUMI-E	BONSAI	HIBACHI
KAMI	TIDAL	LEGEND	IKEBANA
MYTH	TORII	KABUKI	SAMURAI
		KIMONO	
		UNIQUE	

8 LETTERS	**9 LETTERS**	**10 LETTERS**	**11 LETTERS**
TYPHOONS	IRREGULAR	EARTHQUAKE	ARCHIPELAGO
VOLCANIC	SHINTOISM	MILITARISM	CALLIGRAPHY
	SHOGUNATE		RESTORATION
			TRADITIONAL

Japan

Final Review

I Directions

The questions below are based on the map of an imaginary land. Select the number of the correct answer.

1. The letter on the map which is on a lake is: (1) D   (2) E   (3) I   (4) J

2. The letter on the map which is on an island is: (1) D   (2) E   (3) I   (4) J

3. The letter on the map which is on a peninsula is: (1) D   (2) E   (3) I   (4) J

4. The distance from point A to Point K is about:
   (1) 800 miles   (2) 1200 miles
   (3) 1600 miles   (4) 2000 miles

5. In what direction would you travel if you went from A to B?
   (1) North   (2) South
   (3) East   (4) West

6. Which of the following places will be highest in altitude?
   (1) D   (2) E   (3) I   (4) J

7. Which of the following cities would have the best harbor?
   (1) A   (2) B   (3) L   (4) M

8. In which direction does river N flow?
   (1) North   (2) South
   (3) East   (4) West

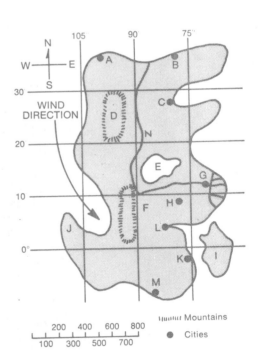

9. Which of the following cities is found on a Delta? (1) C (2) G (3) J (4) K

10. If the wind is blowing from the North-west you would probably find a desert at: (1) C (2) D (3) F (4) K

11. Which of the following places is cloest to 10° North Latitude and 75° West Longitude? (1) C (2) G (3) K (4) F

12. The climate of I is most probably:
    (1) cold and rainy   (2) warm and dry
    (3) cold and dry   (4) warm and rainy

13. 10° North Latitude and 90° West Longitude is the location of a:
    (1) Lake   (2) Mountain   (3) Peninsula   (4) Delta

14. A *Strait* is located near:
    (1) 75° West Longitude   (2) 105° West Longitude
    (3) 10° North Latitude   (4) 0° Latitude

II Matching

Match the definitions in Column B to the words in Column A.

Column A

1. culture
2. topography
3. diffusion
4. isolation
5. imperialism
6. underdeveloped
7. diversity
8. traditional
9. revolution
10. primitive

Column B

(a) customs that have been handed down from generation to generation

(b) characteristic of earliest times; simple; not advanced

(c) varied; different

(d) distant; far off; hidden

(e) the way of life of a group of people

(f) important change in government, economy or society

(g) ideas which are brought from one culture to another (customs too)

(h) an area where the resources have not been fully put to use

(i) an area where resources have not been fully used

(j) the surface of the land

III   Using the names below, complete the following.

Gandhi   Mao Tse-tung   Mansa Musa   Mutsuhito Mejii   Karl Marx

Buddha   Confucius   Lenin   Peter the Great   Stalin

1. .... was the leader of the Russian Revolution of November, 1917.

2. .... was the author of the *Communist Manifesto* and father of modern Communism.

3. .... was a Russian Tsar who tried to westernize Russia.

4. .... was a Japanese Emperor who began the modernization of Japan.

5. .... was an Indian nationalist who believed in passive resistance and non-violent action.

6. .... was the leader of the Communist Revolution in China.

7. .... was a philosopher who set up the rules of conduct under which most of the Chinese people lived for centuries.

8. .... was a ruler of a wealthy advanced West African Kingdom.

9. .... was a Russian dictator who made Russia a great industrial nation.

10. .... was the Prophet and founder of Islam, the main religion of the Middle East.

11. .... was the founder of a religion followed by most of the people of Southeast Asia and many people in China and Japan.

IV   Multiple Choice

Select the letter of the correct answer in each of the following:

1. All of the following are examples of cultural diffusion *except* the
   (a) Russian alphabet
   (b) Japanese Shinto religion
   (c) use of English in India
   (d) Russian Orthodox religion

2. Rivers are important to the development of a culture. Which of the following rivers is *incorrectly* paired with the area it is located in?
   (a) Volga River — Soviet Union   (b) Mekong River — Southeast Asia
   (c) Yangtze River — China   (d) Ganges River — Middle East

3. Civilization began in river valleys. Which of the following river valleys is *correctly* paired with the civilization founded there?
   (a) Hwang Ho — China   (b) Indus — Iraq
   (c) Nile River — Egypt   (d) Tigris — India

4. Which of the following nations was *never* a colony of a Western nation?
   (a) Ghana   (b) Thailand   (c) Vietnam   (d) Tanzania

5. Civilizations make many contributions to world civilization. Which of the following civilizations and its contribution is *incorrectly* paired?
   (a) the idea of zero — India   (b) Islam, Christianity, Judaism — Middle East
   (c) invention of paper — Japan   (d) block printing — China

6. China and Russia became Communist countries. Which of the following statements is *not true* of both countries?
   (a) At the time of the Revolution in each country most of the people were farmers.
   (b) Civil Wars had to be fought before each Communist group gained complete control of its country.
   (c) Rebellions had broken out in both countries many times before the Communist group gained control of its country.
   (d) Both countries set up systems of communes to improve agriculture.

7. All of the following are problems of developing nations *except* all
   (a) have a lack of capital for development.
   (b) lack natural resources for development.
   (c) lack trained workers for development.
   (d) have inadequate transportation systems.

8. Defeat in a great war; serious food shortages; failure to sign a peace treaty; a workers' council rebellion — these four (4) situations led to which of the following events:
   (a) the partition of India and Pakistan
   (b) the Russian Revolution of November, 1917
   (c) the Chinese Revolution of 1912
   (d) the Mejii Restoration in Japan

9. (a) Islam   (b) Buddhism   (c) Hinduism   (d) Judaism
   These are 4 great religions of man. In which of the following orders were they founded?
   (a) abcd   (b) bcda   (c) cbda   (d) bcad

10. Which of the following minerals is *not correctly* paired with the product it is used to make?
    (a) iron and coal to make steel
    (b) bauxite to make aluminum
    (c) uranium to make nuclear power
    (d) lead for materials used in pencils

V Essays

1. "Geography has played a part in the history of all nations. Show how geography has influenced the history of the following areas.
   (a) Russia (b) India (c) China (d) Japan

2. Man has always used the earth's resources for a living. In each of the following areas show how the people have tried to make use of the resources of that area.
   (a) Southeast Asia (b) Africa (c) The Middle East (d) Russia

3. Cultural diffusion has not played an important role in the development of culture in most nations or areas. Explain why you agree or disagree with this statement. Use examples from each of the following areas to support your opinion.
   (a) Russia (b) Japan (c) Southeast Asia (d) Africa (e) China

4. Civilizations and nations decline and fall apart as men fail to adapt to new situations and circumstances. Explain this statement. Give examples from the following areas to support your explanation.
   (a) Russia (b) China (c) Middle East (d) Southeast Asia

5. Problems of the developing nations are similar in many ways. These nations have tried various ways to solve these problems.
   (a) What common problems have the developing nations had?
   (b) Compare the methods used by India, China and Japan to solve their problems.

6. Cultural contributions are not the monopoly of any ethnic or racial group. Using examples from your study of Africa, China, Russia and India explain why you agree or disagree with the statement.

7. Though history never repeats itself exactly, similar events have repeated themselves in the history of a nation.
   Show by examples from your study of Russia, China, India and the Middle East that this statement is true.

8. Historians draw from every field of knowledge to improve their understanding of the past.
   (a) Explain in your own words the meaning of this statement.
   (b) What methods do historians use to recreate and interpret the past?

9. Within each of the areas studied there are ethnic, language and religious differences.
   (a) Give examples of these differences in Russia, Southeast Asia, India and Africa.
   (b) How have these differences affected the development of these nations?

10. Ideas have a great effect on people. What effect have the following ideas had on people?
   (a) anti-Semitism (b) Communism (c) racism (d) nationalism

Bibliography

UNIT I   SUGGESTED READING—GENERAL

Brown, Ina Corinne. *Understanding Other Cultures.* New York: Prentice Hall, 1963.
Ceram, Curt W. *Gods, Graves and Scholars.* New York: Knopf, 1967.
Dean, Vera M. *The Nature of the Non-Western World.* New York: New American Library.
Welty, Paul T. *The Asians, Their Heritage and Their Destiny.* New York: Lippincott, 1976.

MENTOR–UNESCO ART BOOK SERIES
(New York: New American Library)

Ettinghausen, Richard. *Turkish Miniatures from the 13th to the 18th Century.* 1965.
Fagg, William. *The Art of Central Africa, Sculpture and Tribal Masks.* 1967.
Kitzinger, Ernest. *Israeli Mosaics of the Byzantine Period.* 1965.
Lasareff, Victor. *Russian Icons From the 12th to the 15th Century.* 1962.
Rawson, Philip. *Japanese Paintings From Buddhist Shrines and Temples.* 1963.
Rowland, Benjamin. *The Ajanta Caves: Early Buddhist Paintings From India.* 1963.

UNESCO SERIES–THE RACE QUESTION IN MODERN SCIENCE
(New York: United Nations Press)

Comas, Juan. *Racial Myths.* 1976.
Jahoda, Marie. *Race Relations and Mental Health.* 1960.
Leiris, Michael. *Race and Culture.* 1958.

UNIT II   SUGGESTED READING—SOVIET UNION

Cowles, Virginia. *The Romanovs.* New York: Harper & Row, 1971.
Cressey, G. B. *Soviet Potentials: A Geographic Appraisal.* Syracuse, N.Y.: Syracuse U. Press, 1962.
Fainsod, Merle. *How Russia Is Ruled.* Cambridge, Mass.: Harvard U. Press, 1963.
Harcave, Sidney. *Russia, A History.* New York: Lippincott, 1968.
Kennan, George. *Russia and the West Under Lenin and Stalin.* New York: Little, Brown, 1961.
Klyuchevsky, Vasili. *Peter The Great.* New York: Random House, 1961.
Reed, John. *Ten Days That Shook the World.* New York: Random House, 1960.
Salisbury, Harrison. *Russia.* New York: Atheneum, 1965.
Teall, Kaye M. *From Tsars to Commissars: The Story of the Russian Revolution.*
     New York: Messner, 1966.

Vernadsky, George. *A History of Russia.* New Haven: Yale U. Press, 1961.

Von Laue, Theodore. *Why Lenin, Why Stalin: A Reappraisal of the Russian Revolution, 1900-1930.* New York: Lippincott, 1964.

Werth, Alexander. *Russia: The Post-War Years.* New York: Taplinger Pub. Co., 1972.

Wolfe, Bertram. *Three Who Made a Revolution.* New York: Dell, 1964.

Zagoria, Donald. *The Sino-Soviet Conflict, 1956-1961.* New York: Atheneum, 1964.

FICTION

Bunin, Ivan. *The Gentleman From San Francisco And Other Stories.* New York: Washington Square Press, 1963.

Carlisle, O. A. & Styron R. (Edit.). *Modern Russian Poetry.* New York: Viking Press, 1972.

Gogol, Nicolai. *Dead Souls.* New York: Norton, 1971.

Houghton, Norris. *Great Russian Plays.* New York: Dell, 1960.

Koestler, Arthur. *Darkness At Noon.* New York: Macmillan, 1941.

Pasternak, Boris. *Doctor Zhivago.* New York: Pantheon Books, 1958.

Sholokov, Mikhail. *And Quiet Flows the Don.* New York: Random House, 1965.

Solzhenitsyn, Alexander. *One Day in the Life of Ivan Denisovich.* New York: Dutton, 1963.

_____. *Cancer Ward.* New York: Farrar, Strauss, Giroux, 1969.

_____. *The First Circle.* New York: Bantam, 1976.

Tolstoy, Leo. *War and Peace.* (abridged). New York: Dell, 1955.

Turgenev, Ivan. *Fathers and Sons.* New York: Penguin, 1975.

Yevtushenko, Yevgeny. *Stolen Apples.* New York: Doubleday and Co., 1972.

UNIT III   SUGGESTED READING: THE MIDDLE EAST AND NORTH AFRICA

Avi-Yonah, Michael. *The Holy Land.* Michigan: Baker, 1976.

Casson, Lionel. *Ancient Egypt.* New York: Time-Life, 1965.

Cattan, Henry. *Palestine: The Road to Peace.* New York: International Publication Services, 1971.

Desmond, Stewart. *Early Islam.* New York: Time-Life, 1967.

Ellis, Harry B. *The Arabs.* New York: Collins-World, 1958.

Harkabi, Yehoshafat. *Arab Attitudes Toward Israel.* New Jersey: Transaction Books, 1974.

Kritzeck, James (ed.). *Anthology of Islamic Literature.* New York: New American Library, 1975.

Laqueur, Walter. *The Israel-Arab Reader.* New York: Bantam Book, 1976.

_____. *Struggle For the Middle East: The Soviet Union and the Middle East 1958-68.* New York: Macmillan, 1969.

_____. *The Road to Jerusalem.* New York: Macmillan, 1968.

Lewis, Bernard. *The Arabs in History.* New York: Harper & Row, 1966.

Peretz, Don. *The Middle East.* New York: Houghton Mifflin, 1973.

_____. *The Middle East: Selected Reading.* New York: Houghton Mifflin, 1973.

Sweet, Louise. *Peoples and Cultures of the Middle East.* New York: Doubleday, 1970.

Warren, Ruth. *The First Book of the Arab World.* New York: Watts, 1963.

UNIT IV   SUGGESTED READING—AFRICA SOUTH OF THE SAHARA

Brooks, Lester. *Great Civilizations of Ancient Africa.* New York: Scholastic Book Services, 1971.

Burke, Fred. *Africa: Regional Study.* New York: Houghton-Mifflin, 1974.

Chu, Daniel & Skinner, Elliot. *Glorious Age in Africa: The Story of Three Great African Empires.* Doubleday, 1965.

Clark, Leon (ed). *Through African Eyes: Culture in Change.* New York: Praeger, 1971.

Davidson, Basil. *The Lost Cities of Africa.* New York: Little, Brown, 1970.

————. *African Kingdoms.* New York: Time-Life, 1971.

Dobler, L. & Brown, W. A. *Great Rulers of the African Past.* New York: Doubleday, 1965.

Drachler, Jacob (ed). *African Heritage.* New York: Macmillan, 1964.

Fuller, Hoyt W. *Journey To Africa.* Chicago: Third World Press, 1971.

Glubok, Shirley. *The Art of Africa.* New York: Harper & Row, 1965.

Hoff, Rhoda. *Africa: Adventures in Eyewitness History.* New York: Walck, 1963.

Hughes, Langston. *First Book of Africa.* New York: Watts, 1965.

Kamm, Josephine. *Explorers Into Africa.* New York: Macmillan, 1970.

Kenyatta, Jomo. *Facing Mount Kenya.* New York: Random House, 1962.

Moore, Clark & Dunbar, Ann. *Africa Yesterday and Today.* New York: Bantam, 1969.

Morehead, Alan. *The Blue Nile.* New York: Harper & Row, 1972.

Nielsen, W. A. *Africa.* New York: Byline Books—New York Times, 1966.

Paton, Alan. *Land and People of South Africa.* New York: Lippincott, 1972.

Rotberg, R. I. (ed). *Rebellion In Black Africa.* New York: Oxford U. Press, 1971.

Shinnie, Margaret. *Ancient African Kingdoms.* New York: New American Library, 1970.

Vlahos, Olivia. *African Beginnings.* New York: Penguin, 1977.

Williams, John A. *Africa: Her History, Lands and People.* New York: Cooper Sq. Pub., 1967.

Wright, Rose. *Fun and Festival from Africa.* New York: Friendship, 1967.

FICTION

Abrahams, Peter. *Mine Boy.* New York: Macmillan, 1970.

Achebe, Chinua. *A Man of the People.* New York: Doubleday, 1966.

————. *Things Fall Apart.* New York: Fawcett, 1976.

Feldman, Susan (ed). *African Myths and Tales.* New York: Dell, 1970.

Kane, C. H. *Ambiguous Adventure.* New York: Collier Book, Macmillan, 1969.

Paton, Alan. *Cry, The Beloved Country.* New York: Scribner, 1961.

UNIT V SUGGESTED READING—CHINA

Barnett, A. Doak. *China After Mao.* Princeton, N.J.: Princeton U. Press, 1967.

Birch Cyril, ed. *Stories From a Ming Collection.* New York: Grove Press, 1968.

Buck, Pearl. *Man Who Changed China: Sun Yat-Sen.* New York: Random House, 1953.

Cahill, James F. *Chinese Painting.* New York: Rizzoli International, 1977.

Chatterji, B. R. *Modern China: A Short History.* New York: International, 1969.

Clubb, O. Edmund. *Communism in China.* New York: Columbia U. Press, 1968.

Fairbank, John. *The United States and China.* Cambridge: Harvard U. Press, 1971.

Fitzgerald, C. P. *Chinese View of Their Place in the World.*
   New York: Oxford University Press, 1969.

Fremantle, Anne. *Mao Tse-Tung: An Anthology of His Writings.*
   New York: New American Library, 1971.

Goldston, Robert. *The Rise of Red China.* New York: Bobbs Merrill, 1967.

Latourette, K. S. *China.* New York: Prentice Hall, 1964.

————. *The Chinese: Their History and Culture.* New York: Macmillan, 1964.

Levenson, J. R. *Modern China: An Interpretive Anthology*. New York: Macmillan, 1971.

Melby, John F. *The Mandate of Heaven: Record of a Civil War, China 1945-1949*. Toronto: University of Toronto Press, 1968.

Myrdal, Jan. *Report From A Chinese Village*. New York: Pantheon, 1965.

Robinson, Thomas. *Cultural Revolution in China*. Berkeley: Univ. of Calif. Press., 1971.

Rowe, David. *Modern China: A Brief History*. New York: Anvil-Van Nostrand, 1959.

Schafer, Edward H. *Ancient China*. New York: Time-Life, 1967.

Schwartz, Harry. *China*. New York: Byline Book-New York Times, 1965.

Scott, John. *China: The Hungry Dragon*. New York: Parent's Magazine Press, 1967.

Snow, Edgar. *Red Star Over China*. New York: Grove Press, 1968.

_____. *Red China Today: The Other Side of the River*. New York: Random House, 1971.

Yutang, Lin. *The Wisdom of China and India*. Modern Library, 1955.

UNIT VI SUGGESTED READING—INDIA AND PAKISTAN

Barth, A. *Religions of India*. Mystic: Verry, 1969.

Basham, A. L. *The Wonder That Was India*. New York: Grove Press, 1959.

_____. *Aspects of Ancient Indian Culture*. New York: Asia Publisher's House, 1970.

Butani, D. H. *India of the 1970's*. Mystic: Verry, 1972.

Chopra, M. K. *India: The Search For Power*. New York: International Publications Service, 1969.

Embree, Ainslee T. *The Hindu Tradition*. New York: Random House, 1972.

Fischer, Louis. *The Life of Mahatma Gandhi*. New York: Macmillan, 1962.

Gaer, Joseph. *Fables of India*. New York: Little, Brown & Co., 1955.

Goetz, Herman. *The Art of India*. New York: Crown, 1959.

Kalidasa. *Shakuntala and Other Writings*. New York: Dutton, 1959.

Kublin, Hyman. *India*. New York: Houghton Mifflin, 1973.

_____. *India: Selected Readings*. New York: Houghton Mifflin, 1973.

Lamb, Beatrice P. *India: A World in Transition*. New York: Praeger, 1975.

Nehru, Jawaharlal. *The Discovery of India*. New York: Anchor-Doubleday, 1960.

Pitt, Malcolm. *Introducing Hinduism*. New York: Friendship Press, 1955.

Spear, Percival. *A History of India, Vol. II*. Baltimore: Penguin Books, 1966.

Tagore, Rabindranath. *A Tagore Reader*. New York: Beacon Press, 1966.

Wiser, William & Charlotte. *Behind Mud Walls*. Berkeley: U. of California Press, 1972.

Yutang, Lin (ed). *The Wisdom of China and India*. New York: Modern Library, 1955.

FICTION

Narayan, R. K. *The Financial Expert*. Ann Arbor: Michigan U. Press, 1953.

Singh, Khushwant. *Train to Pakistan*. Greenwood Press, 1975.

UNIT VII SUGGESTED READING—SOUTHEAST ASIA

Allen, Richard. *Short Introduction to the History and Politics of Southeast Asia*. New York: Oxford U. Press, 1970.

Bloodworth, Dennis. *Eye For The Dragon: Southeast Asia Observed, 1954-1970*. New York: Farrar, Straus and Giroux, 1970.

Buell, H. *Main Streets of Southeast Asia*. New York: Dodd, 1962.

Burling, Robbins. *Hill Farms and Padi Fields: Life in Mainland Southeast Asia.* Englewood Cliffs: Prentice-Hall, 1965.

Buss, Claude A. *Southeast Asia and the World Today.* New York: Anvil-Van Nostrand, 1958.

Butwell, Richard. *Southeast Asia Today and Tomorrow: Problems of Political Development.* New York: Praeger, 1969.

Durden, Tillman. *Southeast Asia.* New York: Atheneum, 1966.

Fall, Bernard. *Street Without Joy.* New York: Schocken, 1972.

Harrison, Brian. *Southeast Asia: A Short History.* New York: St. Martin, 1966.

Honey, P. J. *Communism in North Vietnam.* Greenwood Press, 1963.

Myrdal, Gunnar. *Asian Drama: An Inquiry into the Poverty of Nations.* New York: Pantheon, 1972.

Landon, Kenneth P. *Southeast Asia: Crossroads of Religion.* Chicago: U. of Chicago Press, 1974.

Ripley, S. Dillon. *Land & Wildlife of Tropical Asia.* New York: Time-life, 1964.

Steinberg, David J., et al. *In Search of Southeast Asia: A Modern History.* New York: Praeger, 1970.

UNIT VIII   SUGGESTED READING—JAPAN

Benedict, Ruth. *The Chrysanthemum and the Sword.* New York: Houghton Mifflin, 1969.

Bergamini, David. *Japan's Imperial Conspiracy.* New York: Morrow, 1971.

Blyth, R. H. *A History of Haiku. 2 vols.* Japan Publications, 1964.

Earhart, H. Byron. *Japanese Religion: Unity and Diversity.* Belmont: Dickenson, 1974.

Feis, Herbert. *The Road to Pearl Harbor.* Princeton: Princeton U. Press, 1950.

Fitzsimmons, Thomas. *Japanese Poetry Now.* New York: Schocken, 1973.

Kublin, Hyman. *Japan.* New York: Houghton Mifflin, 1973.

Latourette, K. S. *The History of Japan.* New York: Macmillan, 1957.

Leonard, Jonathon. *Early Japan.* Time-Life, 1968.

Lord, Walter. *Day of Infamy.* New York: Holt, Rinehart, Winston, 1957.

Meyer, Milton. *Japan: A Concise History.* Littlefield, 1976.

Morton, William S. *Japan: Its History and Culture.* New York: Crowell, 1970.

Nakane, Chie. *Japanese Society.* Berkeley: U. of California Press, 1970.

Newman, Robert. *The Japanese: People of the Three Treasures.* New York: Atheneum, 1964.

Sansom, George B. *Japan: A Short Cultural History.* New York: Prentice-Hall, 1962.

Shively, D. H. *Tradition and Modernization in Japanese Culture.* New Jersey: Princeton U. Press, 1971.

Tiedemann, Arthur. *Modern Japan.* New York: Anvil-Van Nostrand, 1962.

Toland, John. *The Rising Sun. 2 vols.* New York: Random House, 1970.

FICTION—JAPAN

Akutagawa, Ryunosuke. *Rashomon and Other Stories.* Liveright, 1970.

Buck, Pearl. *The Big Wave.* New York: Day, 1973.

Keene, Donald. *Four Major Plays of Chikamatsu.* New York: Columbia U. Press, 1964.

Manyoshu. *The Manyoshu.* New York: Columbia U. Press, 1969.

Murasaki, Shikibu. *The Tale of Genji.* New York: Knoff, 1976.

Mishima, Yukio. *The Sound of Waves.* New York: Knopf, 1956.

Sei, Shonagon. *The Pillow Book of Sei Shonagon.* New York: Penguin, 1971.

Waley, Arthur. *The NŌ Plays of Japan.* New York: Grove Press, 1957.

Index

Abraham, 120
Abu Dhabi, 133, 135-136
Abu Rhudeis oil fields,
    161-163
acupuncture, 282, 284
Affonso I, 225
Africa, North. *See* Middle
    East
Africa, Sub-Sahara, 195-273
    agriculture in, 251-254
    and Arabs, 223-224
    arts of, 211, 213-215
    climate of, 201-202
    current problems, 236-250
    early history, 215-217
    East African cities, 220-221
    East African kingdoms,
        222-223
    economy of, 251-258
    European imperialism in,
        230-231, 233
    and Europeans, 224-230
    family life in, 207-208
    geography and isolation,
        195, 198
    industry in, 256-258
    nationalism and
        independence, 233-235
    people and languages, 203,
        205, 207
    religions of, 210-211
    resources of, 254-256
    and slave trade, 225-227
    topography of, 198-199,
        201
    tribalism in, 208-210
    and US, 227, 241, 249-250,
        258

and USSR, 245-250, 258
    West African kingdoms,
        217-220
Afrikaners, 237
Aguinaldo, Emilio, 425
Ainu, 458, 470
Akbar, 373, 375
Alexander I, 48-49
Alexander II, 50-53
Alexander III, 53
Alexander the Great, 370
Algeria, 17, 107, 130,
    137-138, 150, 153, 167,
    175, 230
Allah, 117, 119
Amin, Idi, 242-243
Amritsar massacre, 377
Angkor Wat, 420
Angola, 230, 235, 242,
    246-249
animism, 415
apartheid, 237-240
Arabian Nights, 126-127
Arab League, 132, 166
Arabs, 18, 109, 112-115, 117,
    126-127, 132-133, 143-145,
    205, 220, 223-225
Arafat, Yasir, 146-147,
    159-160, 162
archipelagos, 418
Armenians, 38
arms limitation talks, 75, 78,
    80-81, 85-86
Aryans, 369-370
ASEAN, 432-433, 439
Ashantis, 208, 226
Ashikaga period, 472
Ashoka, 370

Askia Mohammed, 220
Assad, Hafez el-, 157, 175
Assam, 359
Atherton, Alfred, 168
atomic bombs, 476
Aurangzeb, 373
Axum culture, 217
Azerbaijanis, 38

Babur, 373
Babylonians, 123
Baghdad, 126-128
Bahrein, 107
Baker, Samuel, 228
Balfour Declaration (1917),
    142
Bali, 417
Bangkok, 406, 410, 422
Bangladesh, 353-354,
    387-390, 487
Bantu Authorities Act, 238
Bantus, 205, 222-224,
    237-240
Basho, Matsuo, 468
bazaars, 115, 126
Bazargan, Mehdi, 132
bedouins, 112-113, 136
Begin, Menachem, 17,
    165-168, 170-171, 173,
    175-176
Belgian Congo. *See* Zaire
Bengal, 375, 388-389
Benin (Dahomey), 230, 235,
    242
Benin culture, 214
Bhagavad-Gita, 368
Bhumibol, 428
Bhutan, 387

Biafra, 236
Bible, 120, 123
Biharis, 389
Bolsheviks, 57-59
Bombay, 354
Bonin Islands, 485
bonsai, 464-465
Bophuthatswana, 239
Borneo. *See* Kalimantan
Botswana, 235-242
bourgeoisie, 57-58
Boxer rebellion, 304
Brahmins, 358, 365, 370
Brezhnev, Leonid, 79-80, 84,
    160, 387
Britain, 375, 377-378
Bruce, James, 227
Brunei, 428
Brzezinski, Zbigniew, 172
Buddha, 370, 417
Buddhism, 300-301, 370-371,
    417-418, 462, 468, 471
Bunraku, 465-466
Burma, 234, 406-407,
    409-410, 414, 417,
    421-422, 425-427, 430,
    434, 476, 487
Burton, Richard, 228
Burundi, 235-237, 242
Bushmen, 205, 213, 216
Byelorussians, 38

Calcutta, 354, 359
caliphs, 126-127
Callié, René, 227
calligraphy, 288

Cambodia (Kampuchea), 328, 333, 406-407, 409, 414, 417, 420, 422, 428, 432, 434, 437-441
Cameroon, 235, 253
Camp David summit conference (1978), 175-176
Canaan, 119-120
Canton, 302
capital, 11-12, 57, 82, 139-140
capital goods, 63
caravans, 201
Carter, Jimmy, 14, 74-75, 86, 166, 168, 170, 172-176, 249, 485
castes, 363, 365-366, 378
Castro, Fidel, 249
Catherine the Great, 47-48
Caucasoid, 6-7, 458
Central African Empire, 235, 253
Ceylon. See Sri Lanka
Chad, 18, 235, 253-254
Chaldeans, 125
Chams, 409
Chandragupta Maurya, 370
Changamire empire, 222-223
Chanoyu, 464
Chao Phraya River, 406, 415
Cheka, 59
Chiang Kai-shek, 305-307, 326
Chickamatsu, 464-466
Ch'in dynasty, 277, 298
China, Nationalist. See Taiwan
China, People's Republic of, 12, 19, 216-217, 277-351
  agriculture in, 317-318, 320
  ancient, 296-298
  Chinese Revolution, 303-307
  climate of, 280-281
  Communists in, 305-307, 309. 311-312
  economy of, 317-318, 320-324
  education in, 316-317
  family life in, 291-294
  foreign policy of, 333-335
  geography and isolation, 277
  and India, 378, 380-381 387, 389-390
  and Japan, 303-304, 306, 320, 324, 326, 333, 460, 471, 474-475, 486-488
  language of, 294-295
  life and society in, 284-288, 312-317
  Manchus, 301-303
  Nationalists in, 305-307
  people of, 281-282, 284
  resources of, 320-321
  social classes in, 288-291
  and Southeast Asia, 407, 409-410, 412, 418-420, 435, 441
  and Taiwan, 326-327, 330, 334
  topography of, 277, 279-280
  and US, 324, 326-331, 334
  and USSR, 305, 307, 309, 322, 331-333
  women in, 315-316
  writing of, 295-296
Ch'ing dynasty, 301
Chirau, Jeremiah, 241
Chou dynasty, 297-298
Chou En-lai, 311-312, 320, 330, 333-334, 387, 487
Christianity, 109, 126-128, 132, 164-165, 175, 228-229, 231, 373, 417, 421, 461-462
Chuang Tzu, 287
Chulalongkorn, 425
clans, 294
class struggles, 57-58
Click languages, 205
climate, 5-6, 18
Clive, Robert, 375
collective farms, 60, 64, 322-323
colonialism, 422
Comintern, 77
Communism, 52, 57-59, 71-72, 75, 77, 149, 309, 314, 316-317, 331-332, 434-435
Confucianism, 284-287, 291, 462
Confucius, 285
Congo, Democratic Republic of. See Zaire
Congo (kingdom), 225
Congo (republic), 235, 247
Congo River. See Zaire River
Constantinople, 41
consumer goods, 63, 67, 82
Crusades, 127
Cuba, 244-250
cultural diffusion, 3, 8-9, 461
Cultural Revolution, 311, 317
culture, 1-4, 6-7
cuneiform, 123
Cyrillic alphabet, 38, 41-42

da Gama, Vasco, 224, 375, 421
Dahomey (kingdom), 226
Dahomey (republic). See Benin
Daniel, Yuli, 73
David, 119-120
Dayan, Moshe, 167
de Gaulle, Charles, 427
Deccan Plateau, 354, 371-372, 381
Delhi, 372-373
deltas, 406
Deng Xiaoping, 296. See Teng Hsiao-ping
Desai, Morarji, 378, 385-386
détente, 75, 81, 85-86
Dharma, 365-366
Diaz, Bartholomew, 224
Diet (Japanese), 476-477
dissent, 73-75
Djakarta, 410, 422
Djibouti, 235, 244-245
Dravidians, 369
droughts, 18, 253-254, 312-313, 360
Duma, 54, 56

Eastern Orthodoxy, 41
Edo. See Tokyo
Egypt, 19, 81, 107, 121-123, 130-132, 137-140, 143-145, 149-176, 216-217, 230
Eiga Monogatari, 468
Eisenhower, Dwight, 81, 386
embargoes (oil), 137, 154, 162, 171, 484
energy, 18-19, 66, 154, 484
environment, 3, 80
Equatorial Guinea, 235, 247
Eritrea province, 230, 244-245
Estonians, 38, 85
Ethiopia, 174, 230, 244-247 253-254
European Security Conference (1975), 73, 84-86
Everest, Mount, 353
exclusive economic zone, 22

Faisal (Iraqi king), 132
Faisal (Saudi king), 154, 160-162
Fantis, 208
fellahin, 113-114
fetishes, 214
fishing, 20-22
five-year plans, 60, 322
food, 17-22

Ford, Gerald, 81, 84-85, 161, 163
Formosa. See Taiwan
Fuji, Mount, 457
Fujiwara period, 468
Fukuda, Takeo, 484
Fulani, 236
Funan, 420

Gabon, 235, 246
Gambia, 230, 235, 251
Gandhi, Indira, 378, 384-387
Gandhi, Mohandas K., 234, 377
Ganges River, 354, 356, 359, 369
Gao, 219-220
Gautama. See Buddha; Buddhism
Gaza Strip, 143-144, 152, 169-172, 175
Genghis Khan, 44, 373
Genji Mongatori, 468
Georgians, 38
Ghana (kingdom), 218-219
Ghana (republic), 230, 233, 235, 242, 251, 253-254, 257-258
Ghats, 354, 356
Ghazni, Mahmud of, 372
ghettos, 142
Ghori, Muhammed, 372
Ginzburg, Aleksandr, 74
Gobi Desert, 279
Golan Heights, 144, 150, 152-153, 156-157, 163, 169, 171
Gold Coast. See Ghana (republic)
Great Leap Forward, 323
Great Russians, 38, 40-41
Great Wall of China, 298, 301
Greeks (ancient), 41, 126, 370
"Green Revolution," 17, 19
Gromyko, Andrei, 160, 485
Guinea, 234-235, 242, 255
Guinea-Bissau, 246-247
Guptas, 371-372

habitat, 3-4
haikus, 468
Hammurabi, 123
Han dynasty, 300, 420
Han people, 281
haniwa art, 468
Hanoi, 406, 410, 487
Hausas, 205, 207-208, 223, 236
Hebrews, 119-121, 123, 125, 142

Hegira, 117
Helsinki agreement (1975), 73, 84-86
Herzl, Theodore, 142
Hideyoshi, 472
hieroglyphics, 122
Himalaya Mountains, 279, 353, 356
Hindi, 357-358, 373
Hindu Kush, 353
Hinduism, 356, 363, 365-366, 368, 371-373, 377, 388-389, 417
Hirohito, 476
Hiroshige, 470
Hiroshima, 476
Hittites, 125
Ho Chi Minh, 425, 427
Ho Chi Minh City (Saigon), 406, 410, 422
Hokkaido, 455, 458
Hokusai, 470
homelands (Bantu), 238-239
Hong Kong, 282, 293, 320
Honshu, 455, 457
Horn of Africa, 244-246
Hottentots, 205
Hsia family, 297
Hua Kuo-feng, 312
Huang-ho River. See Yellow River
human rights, 73-75, 85-86
Hundred Schools, 298
Hussein (Jordanian king), 132, 146, 152, 159, 162, 175
Hussein, Sharif, 131
Hutus, 236-237

Ibos, 208, 236
Ieyasu, 472
Ife culture, 213-214
Ikebana, 464
imperialism, 230-231, 233, 303-304, 333, 426, 474-475
India, 10, 17, 217, 234, 328, 352-400
  agriculture in, 358-360
  ancient literature of, 366, 368-369
  British in, 375, 377-378
  and China, 378, 380-381, 387, 389-390
  climate of, 356-357
  early history, 369-371
  economy of, 380-381
  Guptas, 371-372
  after independence, 378, 380
  industry in, 381-383
  land, 353-354, 356
  modernization attempts, 380-386
  Moslems in, 372-373. See also Bangladesh; Pakistan
  people and languages, 357-358
  religions of, 363, 365-366
  resources of, 381
  and Southeast Asia, 407, 409, 412, 417-421
  and US, 359-360, 378, 380, 382, 384, 386-387
  and USSR, 360, 378, 382-383, 387
  village life in, 360, 362-363
  and world politics, 386-388
Indonesia, 216, 409-410, 415, 417, 421-423, 425, 427, 431, 433-434, 439, 476, 487
Indus River, 354, 369
Inland Sea, 455, 457
Inner Mongolia, 279
International Monetary Fund, 13
International Women's Year (1975), 23
Iran, 107, 132, 133, 135-137, 150
Iraq, 107, 131-133, 135, 137-138, 149-150, 164, 167, 174, 244
Irrawaddy River, 406, 415
Isaac, 120
Islam, 107, 109, 115, 117, 119, 125-128, 132, 174, 223-224, 371-373, 377, 388-389, 417, 421
Israel, 17, 40, 81, 107, 109, 114, 133, 136-176
Ivan the Terrible, 45
Ivory Coast, 230, 235

Jackson, Henry, 83
Jahan, Shah, 373
Japan, 17, 154-155, 454-505
  arts in, 464-466, 468-470
  and China, 303-304, 306, 320, 324, 326, 333, 460, 471, 474-475, 486-488
  early history, 470-473
  economy of, 478, 480-482, 484
  land and climate of, 455, 457-458
  life in, 460-461
  modern history, 473-476
  people and language, 458, 460
religions of, 461-462
and Southeast Asia, 426-427, 433, 475-476, 487-488
and US, 474-478, 484-485
and USSR, 53, 474-475, 485-486
after World War II, 476-477
Jarring, Gunnar, 144
Java, 409-410, 414, 423, 431
jen, 285
Jerusalem, 142, 167
Jews:
  in Israel, 109, 142, 144, 146
  in USSR, 40, 73-75, 83
Jimmu Tenno, 470-471
Johnson, Lyndon, 81, 437
Jordan, 107, 131-132, 135, 137, 143-147, 152-153, 159, 162, 167, 169, 173, 175
Judaism, 109, 119-121

Kabuki, 465-466
Kalahari Desert, 201
Kalidasa, 372
Kalimantan (Borneo), 422, 487
Kamakura period, 462, 472
kamikaze, 472
Kampuchea. See Cambodia
Karma, 365-366
Kashmir, 387-388
Katanga province. See Shaba region
Kazakhs, 38, 281
Kenya, 17, 215, 230-231, 233, 235, 242-243, 251
Kenyatta, Jomo, 17, 233, 242
KGB, 74
Khalid, 161
Khayyám, Omar, 127
Khmer kingdom, 420
Khmer Rouge, 333, 440
Khmers, 409
Khomeini, Ayatollah, 132
Khrushchev, Nikita, 81
Khyber Pass, 353
kibbutzim, 114
Kiev, 41-42
Kikuyus, 208, 235
Kilimanjaro, Mount, 199, 227
Kilwa, 220-221, 225
Kinai plain, 457
Kirghiz, 38
Kirkuk oil fields, 135
Kissinger, Henry, 81, 83, 85, 138, 152-153, 155-157, 159, 161-163, 331
klongs, 412
koans, 462
Kobe, 457
Kokinshu, 466
kolkhoz, 64
Komsomol, 71
Koran, 117, 119
Korea, 474-475
Korea, North, 320, 327-328, 487
Korea, South, 327-328, 485, 487
Korean war, 77, 326-327
Kosygin, Aleksei, 80-81, 153, 330
Krishna, 368
Kuala Lumpur, 410
Kublai Khan, 301
Kung Fu-tzu, 285
Kuo-yu, 294
Kuomintang, 305-306
Kurile Islands, 486
Kush culture, 217
Kuwait, 107, 133, 135-137, 152, 154
Kyoto, 469
Kyushu, 455

Lao Tzu, 287
Laos, 328, 333, 409, 417, 420, 422, 428, 432, 434, 438-440
Latvians, 38, 85
Leakey, Louis, 215
Lebanon, 107, 131-132, 135-136, 146-148, 152-153, 164-165, 167, 175
Lenin, Nikolai, 52, 58-59, 71, 314
Leningrad (St. Petersburg), 46, 56, 59
Leo Africanus, 224
Lesotho, 235
Li people, 281
Li T'ai-po, 301
Liberia, 230, 255
Libya, 107, 130, 133, 135, 138, 164, 166-167, 174-175, 230, 243, 247
Lin Piao, 311
Lithuanians, 38, 85
Liu Shao-ch'i, 311
Livingstone, David, 228
Lon Nol, 434, 440
Long March, 306, 316
Luthuli, Albert, 239
Lydians, 125

MacArthur, Douglas, 476
Madagascar, 216, 235
Madras, 354

Magellan, Ferdinand,
421-422
Magsaysay, Ramon, 430
Mahabharata, 368
Malagasy Republic. *See*
Madagascar
Malawi, 235, 254
Malay Peninsula, 404, 406,
409, 418, 420-421
Malaya. *See* Malaysia
Malaysia, 356, 406, 409-410,
417, 421-422, 428, 430,
433, 439, 476
Mali (kingdom), 219-220, 223
Mali (republic), 230, 235, 253
Malin, Daniel F., 237
Manchuria, 280, 301, 306,
318, 320, 475
Manchus, 301-304
Mandarin Chinese, 294
Mandate of Heaven, 298,
301, 304
Mangope, Lucas, 239
Manila, 422, 430
Manyoshu, 466
Mao Tse-tung, 296, 305-307,
309, 311-314, 316-317,
321-323, 326, 328-330, 335
Maoism, 314
Marathas, 373
Marco Polo, 301
Marshall, George, 306
Marx, Karl, 53, 57-58, 62,
314
Masai tribe, 208
Matanzima, Daliwonga, 239
Matope, 222
Mau Mau, 235
Mauritania, 235, 253
Maurya empire, 370
Mayaguez, 440
Mbumba, Nathaniel, 249
Mecca, 117, 119
Meiji, Mutsuhito, 473
Meiji period, 473-474
Meir, Golda, 152, 156
Mekong River, 406-407, 415,
432
Menam River, 406, 415
Meroë, 217
Mesopotamia, 121-123, 125
Middle East, 107-194, 484
Arab-Israeli conflict,
142-145
and big powers, 148-150
cities of, 114-115, 117
economic development of,
139-140, 142
education in, 140

European imperialism in,
129-131
farming in, 113-114
industry in, 140
instability of, 140
land and climate of,
109-110, 112, 139
Moslem civilization,
125-128
nationalism and Arab
unity, 131-133
nomads in, 112-113
and oil, 133-139
Ottoman empire, 128-129
Palestine problem, 145-148
people of, 112-115, 117
religions of, 117, 119-121
since 1973, 150-159
terrorism in, 147-148
and US, 109, 135-137, 145,
148-150, 152-157,
162-163, 167-168,
171-176
and USSR, 109, 145,
148-150, 152-154,
156-157, 159-160, 167,
171, 173-174
wars:
1948, 133, 143-145
1956, 143, 145
1967, 137, 143-145, 147,
149, 155
1973, 137-138, 150-155
minerals, 20, 22
Ming dynasty, 301
Minh, Duong Van, 439
missionaries, 228-229
Mobutu Sese Seko, 247,
249-250
Mohammed, 117, 119,
126-127
Moksha, 366
Mondale, Walter, 75
Mongkut, 425
Mongoloid, 6-7, 281, 458
Mon₀'s, 42, 44-45, 128, 301,
373, 472
Monomotapa empire, 222
monotheism, 119-120
Mons, 409, 421
monsoons, 280, 356, 407
Montagu-Chelmsford
reforms, 377
Morocco, 107, 130, 144, 146,
159, 166, 230, 257
Moscow, 45, 59
Moses, 120, 142
Moslem religion. *See* Islam
mosques, 115, 119, 127-128

Mozambique, 230, 235,
241-242, 246-248
Mugabe, Robert, 241
Mughal (Mogul) empire, 373,
375
mullahs, 129
Mumtaz Mahal, 373
Murasaki Shikibu, 468
Musa, Mansa, 219
Mutota, 222
Muzorewa, Abel, 241

Nagasaki, 476
Nagoya, 457
Namib Deserb, 201
Namibia (South-West Africa),
230, 240, 254
Nanking, 305
Napoleon Bonaparte, 48-49
Nara period, 468
Narayan, Jaya Prakash, 385
Nasser, Gamal Abdel, 132
nationalism, 14-17, 131,
233-235, 304-305, 423,
425-426, 474-475
nationalization, 135, 321
Nazis, 143
Negroid, 6-7, 203
Nehru, Jawaharlal, 377-378,
384, 386-387
Nepal, 387
Neto, Agostinho, 247-249
New Delhi, 354
Nicholas I, 50
Nicholas II, 54, 56, 59
Niger, 235, 253-254
Niger River, 199, 227
Nigeria, 207, 209, 213, 217,
230, 235-236, 242, 246,
255, 257
Nile River, 110, 121-123, 199,
216, 227-228
Nirvana, 418
Nixon, Richard, 80-81, 85,
139, 157, 159, 329-331,
387, 437-439, 485
Nkomo, Joshua, 241
Nkrumah, Kwame, 233
NKVD, 60
Nō drama, 465
Nobunga, 472
Nok culture, 213, 217
nomads, 112-113, 128, 136,
253
nonalignment, 386
North Africa. *See* Middle East
Nzinga, 225

oasis, 112

Obote, Milton, 242
oceans, 19-22
Octobrists, 71
Ogaden region, 245
oil, 13, 18, 20-21, 66, 10?
113, 133-139, 149, 154
162, 171, 320, 324, 48?
486
Okagami, 468
Okinawa, 485
Oman, 107
Opium War, 302-303
Oprichniki, 45
Organization of African
Unity, 249
Organization of Petroleu?
Exporting Countries
(OPEC), 18, 137-139, 1?
174
Orlov, Yuri, 74
Osaka, 457
Ottoman empire, 128-129
142

paddies, 412
pagodas, 418
Pakistan, 234, 353-354, 3?
377-378, 380-381, 386-3?
412
Palestine:
ancient, 119-121, 142
British mandate, 131,
142-143
modern Arab state,
144-148, 159-160, 16?
167, 170-171, 173, 17?
Palestine Liberation
Organization (PLO), 17?
146-148, 159-162, 164-1?
171, 173-175, 333
Pan-Arabism, 132
Pan-Islamism, 132
panchayats, 360
Park, Mungo, 227-228
Pasternak, Boris, 72
Pathet Lao, 333, 434, 440
"peaceful co-existence," 7?
387
peasants, 51-54, 56, 60, 2?
290-291, 303, 313
Peiping, 305
Peking, 301, 305, 307
Penglungs, 281
Perry, Matthew C., 473
Persia. *See* Iran
Persian Gulf, 110, 135
Persians (ancient), 125
Peter the Great, 46-47
petrodollars, 137-138, 161
172

pharaohs, 122
Philippines, 320, 409, 414, 417, 419, 422, 425-427, 430, 433, 439, 476, 487
Phnom Penh, 434, 440
Phoenecians, 125
Phoumi Vongvichit, 440
pictographs, 295
Pillow Book of Sei-Shonagon, 466
Pioneers, 71, 309
Plassey, battle of, 375
Po Chu-i, 301
pogroms, 142
Pol Pot, 441
pollution, 20, 80
polygyny, 207
population, 4-6, 18-19
Populists, 53
Portugal, 224-225, 246, 375, 421
proletariat, 57-58
Provisional Government, 56-59
Pugachev, 48
Punjab, 354
purges, 60, 62, 311
Pygmies, 205
pyramids, 123

Qaddafi, Muammar el-, 167
Qatar, 107, 133, 135
Quotations from Chairman Mao, 314, 335

rabbis, 121
race, 6-7
Rahman, Mujibur, 389
rain forests, 201-202
rajahs, 370, 375
Rajputs, 373
Ramadan, 119
Ramayana, 368-369
Rangoon, 406, 409
Rasputin, 56
Rebmann, Johann, 227
Red Army (Japanese terrorists), 17
Red Army (USSR military), 60
Red Guards, 311
Red River, 406, 409, 415
refugees, 146, 164
reincarnation, 363, 365-366
religion, 7
resources, 11, 19-22
revolutionaries, 52-53
Rhodesia, 230-231, 235, 237, 240-242, 246, 254, 333
Rift Valley, 201

Riurik, 41
Roberts, Holden, 247-248
Roosevelt, Theodore, 475
Rowlatt Acts, 377
Rozwis, 222
Russia. *See* Union of Soviet Socialist Republics
Russo-Japanese War, 54, 474-475
Rwanda, 235-237

Sadat, Anwar el-, 153, 156-157, 160-168, 170-171, 174-176
Sahara Desert, 195, 198, 201, 216
Sahel, 253-254
Saigon. *See* Ho Chi Minh City
Saikaku, Ihara, 468
Saladin (Salah-al-Din), 127
SALT negotiations, 75, 80
Salween River, 406
samizdat, 73
Samurai, 471-473
San Min Chu-I, 304-305
Sanskrit, 419
Sarawak, 428, 430
Sato, Eisaku, 482, 488
satori, 462
Satsuma family, 473
Saud, 136
Saudi Arabia, 107, 117, 131, 133, 135-138, 154, 159-162, 166, 173-175, 243
savannas, 201-202
security police, 45, 50, 59-60, 74
Sei-Shonagon, 466
Selassie, Haile, 244, 254
Senegal, 235, 253
Sepoy rebellion, 375
serfs, 48, 51-52
Sesshu, 469
Shaba region, 249, 254-255
Shang dynasty, 297
Shans, 409, 421
Sharon, Ariel, 171
Shcharansky, Anatoly, 74-75
sheiks, 113
Shih Huang-ti, 298
Shikoku, 455
Shintoism, 461-462, 474
Shoguns, 472-473
Sholokhov, Mikhail, 72-73
Shotoku, 471
Shuban, 469
"shuttle diplomacy," 155
Siam. *See* Thailand
Siberia, 34, 40, 50, 59-60, 475, 486

Sierra Leone, 230, 235, 242, 255
Sihanouk, Norodim, 434
Sikhs, 373
Sinai Peninsula, 143-144, 152-153, 155, 160-163, 167, 169, 171, 175
Sind, 372
Singapore, 282, 356, 409-410, 422, 428, 433, 439
Sinkiang, 279, 281, 320, 333
Sinyavsky, Andrei, 73
Sithole, Ndabaningi, 241
slave trade, 225-227
Slavs, 38, 41
Smith, Ian, 240-241, 246
Sobukwe, Robert, 239
socialism, 304-305
Solomon, 120
Solzhenitsyn Alexander, 73, 85-86
Somalia, 230, 235, 244-245
Songhai, 220, 223
South Africa, 230, 235, 237-240, 246-248, 251, 254-255, 257, 333
South-West Africa. *See* Namibia
Southeast Asia, 293, 300, 302, 320, 371, 402-452
agriculture in, 414-415
and China, 407, 409-410, 412, 418-420, 435, 441
climate of, 407, 409
early history, 418-420
economy of, 429-433
empires of, 420-421
Europeans in, 421-423
foreign relations of, 434-435
independence of, 427-429
and India, 407, 409, 412, 417-421
and Japan, 426-427, 433, 475-476, 487-488
nationalism in, 423, 425-426
people and languages, 409-410, 412
religions of, 415, 417-418
topography of, 404, 406-407
and US, 422, 425-426, 434-440
and USSR, 441
village life in, 412, 414
World War II, 426-427
Souvanna Phouma, 440
Soviet Union. *See* Union of Soviet Socialist Republics

soviets, 56
space exploration, 67, 80, 87
Speke, John, 228
Sri Lanka (Ceylon), 353, 356
Srivijaya, 420
Stalin, Joseph, 17, 59-60, 62, 77
Stanley, Henry, 228
steppes, 36, 202
Sudan, 152, 166, 228, 230, 235
Sudanic languages, 205
Suez Canal, 109, 130-131, 136, 143-144, 150, 153, 155, 157, 162
Suharto, 431, 434
Sui dynasty, 300
Sumi-e, 469
Sukarno, Ahmed, 425, 427, 431, 434
Suleiman, 128-129
sultans, 129, 372-373
Sumatra, 406, 487
Sumerians, 123
Sun Yat-sen, 304-305
Sundiata, 219
Sung dynasty, 301
survival, 1-2
Swahili, 207, 224
Swaziland, 235
Syria, 81, 107, 131-132, 135, 137, 143-146, 149-150, 152-153, 156-157, 159, 162, 165-167, 169, 175, 246

Tadzhiks, 38
taiga, 36, 45
Taipei, 326
Taiping rebellion, 303
Taiwan, 19, 293, 307, 326-328, 330, 334, 387, 487
Taj Mahal, 373
Talmud, 121
Tamerlane (Timur Leng), 128, 373
Tamils, 371, 409
Tanaka, Kakuei, 484-487
Tang Chu, 287
T'ang dynasty, 300-301, 468
Tanganyika. *See* Tanzania
Tanzania, 215, 230, 235, 242-243, 247, 251, 254
Taoism, 284-285, 287-288
tea ceremony (Chanoyu), 46?
Ten Commandments, 120
Teng Hsiao-ping, 296, 312, 331, 335
terrorism, 15-17, 147-148, 159
Thailand, 320, 406, 409

414, 417, 420-422, 425, 428-429, 431-433, 435, 439, 487
Thais, 409-410, 421
Thar Desert, 353
Thieu, Nguyen Van, 439
Third World, 12-14, 23, 137, 254, 333
Tibet, 279, 281, 328, 387, 418
Tigris and Euphrates Rivers, 110, 121, 123
Tilak, Bal, 377
Timbuctu, 219-220, 227
Tiran Straits, 143
Togo, 235, 242
tokonoma, 464
Tokugawa period, 472-473
Tokyo, 455, 457, 470, 473, 478
Tonle Sap, 407
Touré, Sekou, 234, 242
Transjordan. See Jordan
Transkei, 238-240
tribal mark, 209
tribalism, 208-210, 231, 236, 257
Trotsky, Leon, 59
Truman, Harry, 306
tsars, 45
Tshombe, Moise, 248-249
Tu Fu, 301
Tunisia, 107, 130, 137, 152, 166, 230
Turkey, 107, 128-132, 136, 149
Turkmen, 38
Tutsis, 236-237

Uganda, 230, 235, 242-243, 251
Uighurs, 281
Ukiyo-e, 469-470
Ukrainians, 38
underdevelopment, 9-14, 137
Union of Soviet Socialist Republics (USSR), 11-12, 17, 32-105
  in Africa, 245-250, 258
  and China, 305, 307, 309,
322, 331-333
  climate of, 35-36
  cultural life in, 70-75, 77
  early history, 41-45
  economy of, 62-64, 66
  education in, 70-71
  foreign policy of, 77-78
  history, 41-62
  and India, 360, 378, 382-383, 387
  and Japan, 53, 474-475, 485-486
  literature and the arts, 71-73
  location of, 33-34
  and Middle East, 109, 145, 148-150, 152-154, 156-157, 159-160, 167, 171, 173-174
  in nineteenth century, 48-53
  peasants in, 51-52
  people of, 38, 40-41
  religion in, 75, 77
  revolutionary movements in, 52-59
  size of, 33-34
  and Southeast Asia, 441
  under Stalin, 59-60, 62
  standard of living, health, and welfare, 67-69
  topography of, 33-35
  and US, 59, 66, 74-75, 78, 80-86
United Arab Emirates, 107, 133, 135-136
United Nations (UN), 13, 17-18, 21, 23, 143, 147, 153-155, 159-160, 164, 169, 175, 234-235, 240, 327, 329, 334, 387-388, 484-485
UN Conference on Trade and Development (1964), 13
UN Emergency Force (UNEF), 143, 155
UN World Food Conference (1974), 17

United States (US), 11-12, 19, 21
  and Africa, 227, 241, 249-250, 258
  and China, 324, 326-331, 334
  and India, 359-360, 378, 380, 382, 384, 386-387
  and Japan, 474-478, 484-485
  and Middle East, 109, 135-137, 145, 148-150, 152-157, 162-163, 167-168, 171-176
  and Southeast Asia, 422, 425-426, 434-440
  and Third World, 13-14
  and USSR, 59, 66, 74-75, 78, 80-86
  and Vietnam. See Vietnam war
Untouchables, 383-384
Upanishads, 368
Upper Volta, 235, 242, 253
Urdu, 373
Ussuri River, 333
Uzbeks, 38

values, 3
Vance, Cyrus, 168, 176
Vedas, 366, 369
veld, 202
Viet Cong, 333, 437-439
Viet Minh, 427
Vietnam, 16, 78, 320, 328, 333, 406-407, 409-410, 417, 419-420, 422, 425, 427-429, 432, 434, 436-441, 487
Vietnam war, 78, 80-81, 330, 436-439, 485, 487
Vikings, 41
Vladimir of Kiev, 41
Vorster, Johannes, 246-247
Vozhnesensky, Andrei, 73

wadis, 110

Washington Conference, 4
Watergate affair, 81, 157
Watusis, 205, 208
Weizman, Ezer, 168, 171
West Bank, 144, 146, 152, 159, 163, 167, 169-173
West (Si) River, 279
women, 22-23, 71, 293, 315-316
World War I, 56-57, 130-1 142, 230, 377, 475
World War II, 77, 81, 83, 131, 143, 149, 233-234, 306, 321, 327, 426-427, 476, 487
Wuhan, 320

Yahweh, 120-121
Yahya Khan, Mohammed, 389
Yamoto kingdom, 471-47
Yangtze River, 279, 318
Yellow (Huang-ho) River, 277, 279, 297, 317
Yemen, Northern, 107
Yemen, Southern, 107, 1 167, 174-175, 246
Yen Chien-ying, 312
Yevtushenko, Yevgeny, 7
Yokohama, 457, 478
Yoritomo, Minamoto, 47
Yorubas, 208, 236
Yuan dynasty, 301
Yuan Shih-kai, 305

Zaire, 210, 230-231, 235, 2 246-250, 254-255
Zaire (Congo) River, 199, 210, 224-225, 228
Zambezi River, 199, 222, 1
Zambia, 235, 242, 254-25
Zanzibar. See Tanzania
Zen Buddhism, 462, 464-4 469
Zimbabwe. See Rhodesia
Zimbabwe, Great, 222-22
Zionism, 142, 164
Zoroastrianism, 125
Zulus, 208